WITHDRAWN

International Communication

This comprehensive *Reader* brings together seminal texts in media and communication studies from both traditional as well as more recent scholarship. It is organized to reflect the growing internationalization of the field, with clearly defined sections covering key aspects of global communication – from historical literature to policy documents – as well as regional perspectives and cultural and political writings on communication from across the globe.

The main purpose of the *Reader* is to provide a critical overview of the dynamics of the internationalization of communication – both on the theoretical terrain and in a more empirically grounded analysis – to encompass the landscape of global communication. Designed for use with university courses, *International Communication: A Reader* is divided into six parts and includes, in addition to core academic readings, key policy documents that demonstrate the development of the political, economic and technological infrastructure underpinning the global system of media and communication.

Additional features include:

- A timeline showing the chronology of main events in global communication.
- Relevant websites for further research.

The *Reader* will be an invaluable teaching resource across the world, as international perspectives become an integral part of the teaching methodology, content, structure and organization of courses.

Daya Kishan Thussu is Professor of International Communication at the University of Westminster in London. The founder and managing editor of the journal *Global Media and Communication*, his key publications include *Internationalizing Media Studies*; *News as Entertainment*; *Media on the Move*; *International Communication*, and *Electronic Empires*.

International Communication

A Reader

Edited by

Daya Kishan Thussu

Routledge
Taylor & Francis Group

LONDON AND NEW YORK

First published 2010
by Routledge
2 Park Square, Milton Park, Abingdon, Oxon OX14 4RN

Simultaneously published in the USA and Canada
by Routledge
270 Madison Avenue, New York, NY 10016

Routledge is an imprint of the Taylor & Francis Group, an informa business

Typeset in Perpetua and Bell Gothic by
RefineCatch Limited, Bungay, Suffolk
Printed and bound in Great Britain by
CPI Antony Rowe, Chippenham, Wiltshire

British Library Cataloguing in Publication Data
A catalogue record for this book is available from the British Library

Library of Congress Cataloging-in-Publication Data
International communication : a reader / edited by Daya K. Thussu.
    p. cm.
    Includes bibliographical references and text.
    1. Communication, International.   2. Mass media and technology.   3. Communication and
culture.   4. Mass media policy.   5. Globalization.   I. Thussu, Daya Kishan.
P96.I514848 2009
302.2—dc22   2009002072

ISBN 10: 0–415–44455–1 (hbk)
ISBN 10: 0–415–44456–X (pbk)

ISBN 13: 978–0–415–44455–2 (hbk)
ISBN 13: 978–0–415–44456–9 (pbk)

Contents

About the editor

DAYA KISHAN THUSSU is Professor of International Communication at the University of Westminster in London where he leads a Masters Programme in Global Media. A former Associate Editor of Gemini News Service, a London-based international news agency, he has a PhD in International Relations from Jawaharlal Nehru University, New Delhi. Among his key publications are: *Internationalizing Media Studies* (2009); *News as Entertainment: The Rise of Global Infotainment* (2007); *Media on the Move: Global Flow and Contra-Flow* (2007); *International Communication – Continuity and Change*, second edition (2006); *War and the Media: Reporting Conflict 24/7* (2003) and *Electronic Empires – Global Media and Local Resistance* (1998). He is the founder and Managing Editor of the Sage journal *Global Media and Communication*.

Acknowledgements

I SHOULD LIKE TO express my gratitude to the authors and publishers as well as organizations for giving permission to include their work in this collection. I am very grateful to my research student Janne Halttu for his help in procuring and organizing material for this project. My biggest thanks are reserved for my editor at Routledge, Natalie Foster, for her patience, support and understanding, without which this *Reader* would not have been possible.

The following were reproduced with kind permission. While every effort has been made to trace copyright holders and obtain permission, this has not been possible in all cases. Any omissions brought to our attention will be remedied in future editions.

1) Satellites and global communication – Joseph Pelton
Excerpt from Pelton, J. (2004) Satellites as Worldwide Change Agent, Chapter 1, pp. 3–32 from: Joseph Pelton, Jack Oslund and Peter Marshall (2004) (eds.) *Satellite Communications: Global Change Agents,* Mahwah (NJ): Lawrence Erlbaum. Copyright 2004 by Taylor & Francis Group LLC – Books. Reproduced with permission of the author and Taylor & Francis Group LLC – Books in the format Textbook via Copyright Clearance Center.

2) The global network society – Manuel Castells
Castells, M. (2008) The New Public Sphere: Global Civil Society, Communication Networks and Global Governance. *The ANNALS of the American Academy of Political and Social Science,* pp 616: 78–93. © 2008, American Academy of Political & Social Science. Reproduced by kind permission of the author and SAGE Publications.

3) Impact of WTO on global communication – Eli Noam
Chapter 15, Noam, E. 'Overcoming the three digital divides' pp. 423–434 in:

Geradin, D. and Luff, D. (eds.) (2004) *The WTO and global convergence in tele-communications and audio-visual services*. Cambridge: Cambridge University Press. © Cambridge University Press 2004, reprinted with permission.

4) Global media policy – Marc Raboy
Excerpt from: Raboy, M. (2004) The WSIS as a political space in global media governance. *Continuum: Journal of Media and Cultural Studies* 18(3): 347–361. Taylor & Francis Ltd, http://www.informaworld.com, reprinted by permission of the author and publisher.

5) Media and modernization – Daniel Lerner
Lerner, Daniel (1963) Toward a Communication Theory of Modernization, in PYE, LUCIAN W.; *POLITICAL CULTURE AND POLITICAL DEVELOP-MENT*. © 1965 Princeton University Press, 1993 renewed PUP Reprinted by permission of Princeton University Press.

6) Communication and post-colonialism – Raka Shome and Radha Hegde
Excerpt from Shome, R. and Hegde, R. (2002) Postcolonial Approaches to Communication: Charting the Terrain, Engaging the Intersections. *Communication Theory*, 12(3): 249–270. Reproduced by permission of Blackwell Publishing Ltd.

7) Development communication – Srinivas Melkote
Chapter 8, Melkote, S. 'Theories of Development Communication', pp. 129–146, in Mody, B. (2003) (ed.) *International and Development Communication: A 21st Century Perspective*. Thousand Oaks: Sage. Copyright 2003 by Sage Publications Inc Books. Reproduced with permission of the author and Sage Publications Inc Books in the format Textbook via Copyright Clearance Center.

8) Communication and digital capitalism – Dan Schiller
Schiller, D. (2001) World Communications in Today's Age of Capital, *Emergences: Journal for the Study of Media and Composite Cultures* 11(1): 51–68. Taylor & Francis Ltd, http://www.informaworld.com, reprinted by permission of the author and publisher.

9) Media imperialism – Oliver Boyd-Barrett
Boyd-Barrett, O. (1998) Media imperialism reformulated. Chapter 9, pp. 157–176, in Thussu, D. K. (ed.) *Electronic empires: Global media and local resistance* London: Arnold. © 1998 Selection and editorial material Daya Kisham Thussu. Reproduced by permission of Edward Arnold (Publishers) Ltd.

10) Homogenizing media cultures? - Daniel Hallin and Poulo Mancini
Excerpt from chapter 8, The Forces and Limits of Homogenization, pp. 251–295, in Hallin, D. and Mancini, P. (2004) *Comparing Media Systems*. Cambridge: Cambridge University Press. © Daniel C. Hallin and Paolo Mancinci 2004, published by Cambridge University Press, reprinted with permission.

11) The global media system - Robert McChesney
Excerpt from Chapter 2, The Media System Goes Global, pp. 78–118, from McChesney, R. (1999) *Rich media, poor democracy: communication politics in dubious times*. Copyright 1999 by the Board of Trustees of the Unversity of Illinois. Used with permission of the author and the University of Illinois Press.

12) Contra-flow in global media – Daya Thussu
Thussu, D. K. (2006) Mapping global media flow and contra-flow, chapter 1
pp. 11–32, in Thussu, D. K. (ed.) *Media on the Move: Global flow and Contra-flow*, London: Routledge. Reproduced by permission of the publisher.

13) Anglo-American Media in decline? – Jeremy Tunstall
Chapter 1, Anglo-American, Global, and Euro-American Media Versus Media
Nationalism, pp. 3–10, in Tunstall, J. (2008) *The Media were American*. Oxford:
Oxford University Press. By permission of Oxford University Press, Inc.

14) Cultural imperialism – Herbert Schiller
Schiller. H. (1991) Not yet the post-imperialist era. *Critical Studies in Mass
Communication*. 8 (1) 13–28. Taylor & Francis Ltd, http://www.informaworld.com, reprinted by permission of the author and publisher.

15) Communication and cultural proximity - Joseph Straubhaar
Straubhaar, J. (1991) Beyond Media Imperialism: Asymmetrical Interdependence and Cultural Proximity, *Critical Studies in Mass Communication*, 8: 1–11.
Taylor & Francis Ltd, http://www.informaworld.com, reprinted by permission of
the author and publisher.

16) The Islamic Internet – Lina Khatib
Khatib, Lina (2003) Communicating Islamic Fundamentalism as Global Citizenship. *Journal of Communication Inquiry*. 27(4): 389–409. © 2003, SAGE Publications. Reproduced by kind permission of the author and SAGE Publications.

17) Alternative media – John Downing
Downing, J. (2003) Audiences and readers of alternative media: the absent lure
of the virtually unknown. Reproduced with permission from *Media, Culture &
Society*. 25: 625–645. By permission of the author and Sage Publications Ltd.

18) Global communication as ideology – Armand Mattelart
Mattelart, A. (2002) An Archaeology of the Global Era: Constructing a
Belief, reproduced with permission from *Media, Culture & Society,* 24: 591–
612. By permission of the author and Sage Publications Ltd.

19) Communication as propaganda – Harold Lasswell
Lasswell, H. (1927) The Theory of Political Propaganda, *The American Political Science Review*. 21 (3): 627–631. © The American Political Science
Association, published by Cambridge University Press, reproduced with
permission.

20) Soft Power – Joseph Nye
Nye, J. (2008) Public Diplomacy and Soft Power, *The ANNALS of the American
Academy of Political and Social Science,* 616: 94–109. © 2008, American
Academy of Political & Social Science. Reproduced by kind permission of the
author and SAGE Publications.

21) Media and sovereignty – Monroe Price
Price, Monroe E., Media and Sovereignty: The Global Information Revolution
and Its Challenge to State Power, pp. 171–198, © 2002 Massachusetts Institute
of Technology, by permission of The MIT Press.

22) Global media consumption – Elahu Katz and Tamar Leibes
Excerpt from Chapter 2, Reading Television: Television as Text and Readers as Decoders pp. 8–19 in Katz, E. and Liebes, T. (1993) *The Export of Meaning: Cross-cultural Readings of Dallas*. Second edition, Cambridge: Polity Press. Reproduced by permission of Polity Press Ltd.

23) Arjun Appadurai, 'Disjuncture and difference in the global cultural economy'. In *Public Culture*, Volume 2, no. 2, pp. 1–24. Copyright, 1990, Duke University Press. All rights reserved. Used by permission of the publisher.

24) Cultures of diasporic media – Karim H. Karim
Karim, K. H. (2004) Re-Viewing the 'National' in 'International Communication': Through the Lens of Diaspora, *The Journal of International Communication* 10(2): 90–109. Reproduced with permission.

25) Decentred globalization – Kochi Iwabuchi
Koichi Iwabuchi, 'Taking "Japanization" Seriously: Cultural Globalization Reconsidered (Chap.1)', in *Recentering globalization: popular culture and Japanese transnationalism*, pp. 23–50. Copyright, 2002, Duke University Press. All rights reserved. Used by permission of the publisher.

26) Hybridity and globalization – Marwan Kraidy
Kraidy, M. (2002) Hybridity in Cultural Globalization, *Communication Theory*, 12 (3): 316–339. Reproduced with permission of Blackwell Publishing Ltd.

27) Global creative convergence - Mark Deuze
Deuze, M. (2007) Convergence culture in the creative industries, reproduced with permission from *International Journal of Cultural Studies*, 10(2): 243–263. By permission of the author and Sage Publications Ltd.

KEY DOCUMENTS AND REPORTS

Excerpt from: UNESCO The new world information and communication order. Resolution 4/19 in *Records of the General Conference*, 21st Session, Belgrade, 23 September to 28 October 1980, pp. 68–71. © UNESCO 1980

Excerpt from: MacBride Report
Many Voices, One World. Communication and Society Today and Tomorrow. Report by the International Commission for the Study of Communication Problems (MacBride Report), Conclusions and Recommendations, pp. 253–258. © UNESCO 1980

Excerpt from: Annex on Telecommunications of General Agreement on Trade in Services (GATS), 1995. Reproduced by kind permission of the World Trade Organization (see http://www.wto.org/english/res_e/booksp_e/pub_catalogue_e.pdf and http://www.wto.org/english/res_e/booksp_e/nonwtopub_e.pdf for more WTO publications).

The World Intellectual Property Organization (WIPO) Phonograms and Performances Treaty (WPPT), 1996 and WIPO Copyright Treaty (WCT) 1996 Source: World Intellectual Property Organization.

Excerpt from: UNESCO Universal Declaration on Cultural Diversity.
Universal Declaration on Cultural Diversity, adopted by the 31st Session of the General Conference of UNESCO, Paris, 2 November 2001. © UNESCO 2001

Google software principles, 2006. Reproduced by kind permission of Google.

Excerpt from: UNESCO Convention on the Protection and Promotion of the Diversity of Cultural Expressions
Convention on the Protection and Promotion of the Diversity of Cultural Expressions, adopted by the 33rd Session of the General Conference of UNESCO, Paris, 20 October 2005. © UNESCO 2005

Excerpt from: Second Phase of the WSIS (16–18 November 2005, Tunis) Tunis Agenda for the Information Society WSIS-05/TUNIS/DOC/6

Excerpt from: Second Phase of the WSIS (16–18 November 2005, Tunis) Tunis Commitment WSIS-05/TUNIS/DOC/7. Reproduced with kind permission of ITU.

Directive of the European Parliament and of the Council Amending Council Directive 2007/65/EC which amends the Television without Frontiers Directive, renaming it 'Audiovisual Media Services Directive' (AVMSD), December 2007, Author: European Communities
Source: http://ec.europa.eu/avpolicy/reg/tvwf/index_en.htm (Only European Community legislation printed in the paper edition of the Official Journal of the European Union is deemed authentic.)

Excerpt from: US Government: Transformational Diplomacy: Office of the Spokesman, US Department of State, Washington, DC, January 18, 2006. Source: U.S. State Department.

Excerpt from: Joint Project Agreement between the U.S. Department of Commerce and the Internet Corporation for Assigned Names and Numbers: September 29 2006
Source: Internet Corporation for Assigned Names and Numbers ww.icann.org/en/general/JPA-29sep06.pdf

Bridging the pretxtization gap. Resolution 123, ITU, 2006. Reproduced with kind permission of ITU.

Excerpt from: US Government: Digital Freedom Initiative: A joint program of the US Department of Commerce, US Agency for International Development, US Department of State, Peace Corps, US Small Business Administration, and USA Freedom Corps.
Source: U.S. Agency for International Development www.usaid.gov

Chronology

Source: Revised and updated from Thussu, 2006.

4000 BC	Sumerian writing on clay tablets.
3000 BC	Early Egyptian hieroglyphics.
2500 BC	Papyrus replaces clay tablets in Egypt.
1500 BC	Phonetic alphabet in use in West Asia.
300 BC	Phoenicians bring Phonetic alphabet to Greece.
100 BC	Roman alphabet developed from Greek model.
AD 100	Papermaking invented in China.
150	Parchment in use, books begin to replace scrolls.
600	Book printing invented in China.
618	China's T'ang Dynasty (618–907) creates a formal handwritten publication, the *ti pao* or 'official newspaper' to disseminate information to the elite.
676	Paper and ink used by Arabs and Persians.
868	Chinese translation of the Sanskrit text *Vajracchedikā-prajñāpāramitā-sūtra* (*Diamond Sutra*), the world's earliest dated book printed on paper in China.
1000	Movable type made of clay in China.
1150	Arabs bring paper from China to Europe.
1170	Arabic numericals introduced in Europe.
1453	Gutenberg Bible printed.
1476	First print shop in England.
1511	First printing press in the Ottoman Empire.
1535	First press in the Americas set up in Mexico.
1578	First printing press set up in India.
1644	Private bureaux which compose and circulate official news in the printed form known as the *Ch'ing pao* start in China.
1650	*Einkommende Zeitung* ('incoming news'), the world's first daily publication, starts in Leipzig.

1665   Newspapers first published in England.

1704   First newspaper advertisement published in the *Boston News Letter*.

1742   *General Magazine* prints first American magazine advertisement.

1777   First regular newspapers in France.

1780   *Bengal Gazette* founded in India.

1783   *Pennsylvania Evening Post* is America's first daily newspaper.

1785   First issue of *The Times* newspaper in London.

1789   Article XIX of Rights of Man declares 'free communication of thought and opinion'. First Arabic newspaper *Al-Hawadith al-Yawmiyah* (The Daily Events) in Egypt.

1791   First Amendment of the US Constitution provides model for freedom of press. The *Observer*, Britain's oldest surviving Sunday newspaper, established.

1793   Inauguration of the optical telegraph in France.

1821   *Manchester Guardian* founded.

1822   The beginnings of the modern Catholic missionary press in France.

1826   *Le Figaro* founded in France.

1827   Photography invented.

1828   *Freedom's Journal*, first African-American newspaper in the US, launched.

1831   *The Sydney Morning Herald* founded. First Turkish newspaper in the Ottoman Empire, the 'Almanac of Events', published.

1833   The first issue of the *New York Sun* – the beginning of the penny press.

1835   Creation of the Havas news agency, the world's first wire service.

1837   Invention of electric telegraph by Samuel Morse.

1838   *The Times of India* founded. First commercial telegraph link in England.

1843   Creation of the first modern US advertising agency. *The Economist* founded.

1844   First commercial telegraph – between Washington and Baltimore.

1845   First issue of *Scientific American*.

1848   Creation of Associated Press.

1849   Creation of the German news agency Wolff.

1851   France–England underwater cable link. Creation of Reuters.

1854   Telegraph used by military in Crimean War. First overseas Chinese newspaper founded in San Francisco.

1856   British decree regulating the relations between the press and military during the Crimean War.

1860   Telegraph is widely used to distribute news accounts of US Civil War. England and India linked by telegraph.

1861   *New York Times* founded.

1865   Founding of the International Telegraph Union – first telegraph regulations. Creation of the US advertising agency J. Walter Thompson. International Morse code adopted.

1866   First transatlantic cable becomes operational. Typewriter invented.

1869   Creation of the US news agency APA, later UPI.

1870   News agency cartel (Havas/Reuters/Wolff) divides up world market.

1871   Underwater cables laid down in China and Japanese seas.

1874   Cable network laid down in the South Atlantic.

1875   Universal Postal Union Founded. *Al-Ahram* established in Cairo.

1876   Alexander Graham Bell patents telephone. *Buenos Aires Herald* founded in Argentina. *Corriere della Sera* founded in Italy.

1878	Invention of the phonograph. First telephone lines in the US.
1880	*New York Graphic* prints first halftone photographs.
1881	French law passed establishing freedom of the press.
1884	Adoption of Greenwich Mean Time as world standard time.
1885	Berlin Telegraph Conference: first provisions for international telephone service.
1886	Invention of the linotype. Berne International Convention on Copyright.
1888	Founding of the *Financial Times*.
1889	Founding of the *Wall Street Journal*.
1890	French popular daily *Le Petit Journal* reaches a circulation of a million copies. *Asahi Shimbun* (morning sun) founded in Japan.
1891	*Jornal do Brasil* founded.
1893	United International Bureaux for the Protection of Intellectual Property (best known by its French acronym BIRPI) created in Berne. First international press congress in Chicago.
1894	*Rossiiskoe Telegrafnoe Agentstvo* (RTA), first Russian news agency, founded. First comics appear in US newspapers.
1896	Colour printing for comics. Lumière Brothers develop motion picture camera. Britain's first popular newspaper, *Daily Mail*, founded. Adolph Ochs adopts an 'information' style of journalism at the *New York Times*.
1897	Marconi patents wireless telegraph.
1899	J. Walter Thompson establishes 'sales bureau' in London. Sun Yat Sen founded *Chung-kuo Jih-pao* (Chinese daily paper).
1901	First wireless transatlantic telegraph transmission – from England to Canada.
1902	First radio transmissions of the human voice.
1906	Berlin Conference on Wireless Telegraphy: creation of the International Radiotelegraph Union. Electromagnetic spectrum divided into bands for different services.
1907	Founding of the French newsreel, *Pathé*.
1909	Creation of the first syndicate for the distribution of comic strips, crossword puzzles and other features.
1911	First film studio built in Hollywood.
1912	First editions of *Pravda* (Truth).
1913	First Indian feature-length film, *Raja Harishchandra*, released.
1914	Audit Bureau of Circulation formed in the US, standardizing auditing procedures and tightening up definitions of paid circulation.
1915	First foreign advertising agency established in Shanghai. Creation of the King Feature Syndicate and beginning of the internationalization of comics.
1917	Petrograd Telegraph Agency declared central information organ of Soviet Government. Radio used to announce victory of communist revolution.
1918	Kodak develops portable camera. Establishment in France of a special committee for 'aesthetic propaganda abroad'.
1919	Soviet Russia begins international broadcasting. US links with Japan via wireless. General Electric creates Radio Corporation of America to take over monopoly of American Marconi Company and create first transnational US communications conglomerate.
1920	IBM produces first electric typewriter. International Telephone and Telegraph founded. First radio station in Africa set up in Johannesburg. Turkish news agency Anadolu Ajaansi founded.
1921	The Komintern becomes an instrument of international communication.

1922   First regular radio broadcasts and first radio commercial in New York. First issue of *Reader's Digest*.

1923   *Time*, first 'news magazine', founded.

1924   Creation of CCIF (International Telephone Consultative Committee) in Paris. Disney creates first filmed cartoon.

1925   The Telegraph Agency of the Soviet Union (TASS) founded. Creation of CCIT (International Telegraph Consultative Committee) in Paris. Brazil's *O Globo* newspaper founded.

1926   Beginning of sound cinema. NBC begins network broadcasting, linking 25 stations in 21 US cities. First commercial telephone service between the US and the UK by long-wave radio.

1927   Radiotelegraph Conference in Washington: creation of the CCIR (International Radio Consultative Committee). BBC founded. *One Man's Family*, popular radio soap opera, begins in the US, lasts until 1959. Establishment of the first two international advertising networks (J. Walter Thompson and McCann Erickson). First radio broadcasts in China. AP begins newsphoto distribution. CBS formed.

1928   First 'all-talking picture' – *Lights of N.Y.* First public display of Disney's *Mickey Mouse* cartoon, with sound.

1929   First regular Soviet radio broadcasts destined for abroad, in German, French and later in English. *Business Week* launched. Cable & Wireless founded, merging all British international communications interests.

1931   International religious radio starts with creation of Radio Vatican. Chinese news agency, Xinhua, founded.

1932   Empire Service of the BBC set up. Telegraph Union changes name to International Telecommunication Union (ITU). Gallup poll established.

1933   Hitler creates the Ministry of Propaganda and Enlightenment of the People under Goebbels. First 'Fireside Chats' by US President Roosevelt utilizes radio medium. Radio Luxembourg, Europe's first major commercial broadcaster, goes on air. *Newsweek* starts publication.

1934   Creation of the Federal Communications Commission in the US. Regular TV transmission in Soviet Union. First news agency in Iran, Pars Agency, founded. The documentary *Triumph of the Will* celebrates Nazi power.

1935   Italy begins Arabic broadcasting to the Middle East. France starts shortwave radio transmission for overseas listeners.

1936   First issue of *Life*. First Gallup polls in a political campaign. Inauguration of BBC television studio.

1937   *West African Pilot*, first nationalist newspaper, founded in Nigeria. *Guiding Light*, first radio soap opera, aired in the US. Disney's first feature-length film, *Snow White and the Seven Dwarfs*, premièred. *Institut Français de Presse*, oldest centre for the study of media in France, created.

1938   The International Convention Concerning the Use of Broadcasting in the Cause of Peace comes into force. The International Advertising Association founded in New York. Radio surpasses magazines as source of advertising revenue in the US. Arabic Service becomes the first foreign-language section of the BBC Empire Service. First international edition of *Reader's Digest* published in London.

1939   First TV broadcasts in the US. Paperback books start publishing revolution.

1941   First TV advertisement broadcast – in the US. China Radio International founded.

1942   Creation of Voice of America. The US organizes the War Advertising Council to help voluntary advertising for war effort. *Why We Fight* series of effective documentary propaganda.

1944   Agence France Presse founded. First issue of *Le Monde.*

1945   UNESCO established. France creates commercial international station Radio Monte Carlo.

1946   First large-scale electronic digital computer founded in the US. First TV sponsorship for a sporting event in the US.

1947   Transistor developed. International photo agency, Magnum, founded in the US. International Organization for Standardization founded.

1948   UN Conference on Freedom of Information. *People's Daily* (*Renmin Ribao*) launched in China. First drive-through McDonald's restaurant – the term 'fast food' coined.

1949   Network TV begins in the US. *Stop the Music,* first TV quiz show in the US.

1950   First broadcast by Radio Free Europe. First international credit card, Diner's Club, launched. International Communication Association (ICA) founded.

1951   NBC's *Today* programme begins, mixing news and features. International Press Institute founded.

1952   Universal Copyright Convention adopted. Sony develops stereo broadcasting in Japan. International Federation of Journalists, the world's largest organization of journalists, founded.

1953   United States Information Agency (USIA) created. Deutsche Welle starts broadcasting. First broadcast by Radio Liberty.

1954   First transistor radio produced in the US. McCarthy hearings on television. CBS becomes the largest advertising medium in the world. Trans World Radio, US-based global evangelical radio, starts broadcasts from Morocco. Colour TV broadcasting begins in the US.

1955   'The Marlboro Man' advertisement for Marlboro, the world's best-selling cigarette, launched – it becomes top advertising icon of twentieth century. First Disneyland opens. Independent Television (ITV) starts transmission in Britain.

1956   First transatlantic underwater telephone cable.

1957   The Soviet Union launches the first space satellite – Sputnik ('travelling companion'), sending first radio signals from space. The International Association for Media and Communication Research (IAMCR) established.

1958   UN establishes Committee on the Peaceful Uses of Outer Space.

1959   ITU Geneva conference makes first radio-frequency allocations for space communications.

1960   Nixon–Kennedy debates televised. NASA launches ECHO-1, first telecommunications satellite. In-flight movies introduced on airlines.

1962   AT&T launches Telstar-1, first privately owned active communications satellite, linking the US with Europe. First telephone communication and TV broadcast via satellite – ECHO-1.

1963   ITU organizes First World Space Radiocommunication Conference in Geneva. Hughes designs and launches the world's first geosynchronous communications satellite, SYNCOM-II.

1964   Creation of Intelsat (International Telecommunications Satellite Organization). The USSR launches its first communication satellite (Molnya). Inter Press Service founded. First electronic mail – in the US.

1965   Launching of the first geostationary communications satellite, Early Bird, of the Intelsat system.

1966   Xerox introduces facsimile machines.

1967   The US and the Soviet Union sign Treaty on Peaceful Uses of Outer Space.

1968   Portable video recorders introduced. Reuters starts the world's first computerized news distribution service.

1969   The Internet born as a US Defense-backed experimental network called ARPANET (Advanced Research Projects Agency Network). Brazilian television company Globo established. Intelsat provides global TV coverage of Apollo lunar landing to 500 million people.

1970   International direct dialling between London and New York first introduced.

1971   ITU conference on space communications adopts Regulation 428A to prevent spillover of satellite broadcast signals into countries without their prior consent. Soviet Union organizes Intersputnik, a satellite telecommunications network linking socialist countries. Intel introduces first microprocessor – 'the computer chip'.

1972   Debate in UNESCO and UN General Assembly on an agreement to regulate direct-broadcast satellites. UNESCO adopts declaration of principles for satellite broadcasting, including requirement that for direct satellite broadcasting there be prior agreement between the sending country and the receiving countries.

1973   First steps towards New World Information and Communication Order (NWICO) debate.

1974   First direct broadcasting satellite, ATS 6, launched. Opinion polls show that TV overtakes newspapers as prime source of news for most Americans.

1975   Non-aligned news agencies pool created. European Space Agency formed. Fibre-optic transmission developed. Cable brings multi-channel TV to the US. Radio France Internationale created. Microsoft founded.

1976   India launches SITE project for use of satellites for education. UNESCO conference in Nairobi endorses call for NWICO. Apple computer launched.

1977   Creation of the International Commission for the study of communications problems (UNESCO) under Sean McBride. Eutelsat (European Telecommunications Satellite Organization) founded.

1978   Videotext developed. Japan launches first Yuri satellite. Intelsat provides coverage of World Cup Football matches to 1 billion people in 42 countries.

1979   World Administrative Radio Conference (WARC) in Geneva (ITU) revises radio regulations. Inmarsat formed. First consumer advertisements on Chinese television. Sony invents Walkman.

1980   Publication of the McBride Commission report. Ted Turner launches CNN, world's first all-news network.

1981   IBM brings out its first personal computer. The all-music channel MTV goes on air.

1982   The Falklands War: first appearance of the practice of organizing pools of journalists. INSAT (Indian National Satellite) communication satellite launched. Compact Disc (CD) player launched in Japan.

1983   World Communication Year. First Eutelsat satellite launched. Worldnet, USIA's global public affairs, information and cultural TV network, launched. US starts anti-Cuban Radio Marti. Cellular (mobile) telephones available in the US.

1984   Green Paper by the EC on 'Television without Frontiers'. US giant Hughes launches Leasat to create a global military communications network. Indonesia launches its first satellite Palapa. Federal Communications Commission grants PanAmSat (Pan American Satellite) rights to launch and exploit a private satellite system. China develops first Chinese-language computer operation system. Canal Plus, first pay

TV channel in France, launched. Michael Jackson's *Thriller* album sells more copies than any other to date.

1985   The US withdraws from UNESCO. PeaceNet – the first alternative national computer network in the US – established. Arabsat launches its first communication satellite. Brazil becomes first South American country to launch its own satellite – Brazilsat. CNN International launched. Reuters starts a news picture service and takes control of TV news agency Visnews. Capital Cities buys ABC, creating the world's largest entertainment company. Reporters Sans Frontières founded in Paris. America Online (AOL) founded.

1986   Uruguay Round of GATT negotiations begin. The UK withdraws from UNESCO. First alternative satellite network Deep Dish TV Satellite Network established in the US. China's national satellite telecommunications network operational.

1987   EC Green Paper on telecommunications. USSR ends jamming of VOA.

1988   First ASTRA satellite launched by a private European organization. Pan-Arabic newspaper, *Al-Hayat*, launched in London. USSR ends jamming Russian service of Deutsche Welle.

1989   Merger of Time and Warner Bros. Sony buys Columbia pictures. First private satellite launched in the US. Sky, first satellite TV, launched in Britain. Interfax agency started in Soviet Union to supply news, mainly to foreigners. UNESCO publishes first *World Communication Report*. British researcher Tim Berners-Lee creates World Wide Web.

1990   ASIASAT, first commercial Asian satellite, launched. The US starts TV Marti. CNN becomes a global news network with Gulf crisis. Microsoft launches Microsoft Windows 3.0.

1991   BBC World television launched as a commercial venture. STAR TV, the first pan-Asian television network, launched. France launches Telecom 2A satellite. Russian edition of *Reader's Digest*.

1992   Turkey's TRT Avrasya channel beams programmes via satellite to Turkic republics in Central Asia. The browser Mosaic brings the Internet to non-technical computer users. Spain launches Hispasat satellite. The Bible becomes the first book available on CD-Rom.

1993   World Radio Network launched on ASTRA in Europe. OIRT, the former union of eastern European broadcasters, merges with European Broadcasting Union. First World Telecommunication Standardization Conference by ITU. China's first international optical cable system, linking it with Japan, becomes operational. May 3 proclaimed by the UN General Assembly as the yearly observance of the World Press Freedom Day.

1994   CD-ROM becomes a standard feature on personal computers. Turkish-owned satellite Turksat launched. World Trade Organization (WTO) created. APTV, a global video newsgathering agency, launched. BBC Worldwide, commercial arm of BBC, created. DirecTV launches first digital DBS service in the US. Yahoo! launched.

1995   PanAmSat becomes the world's first private company to provide global satellite services with the launch of its third satellite – PAS-4. Trade-Related Aspects of Intellectual Property Rights (TRIPS) agreement, comes into force. Bloomberg television launched. First computer-animated feature film, *Toy Story*, released.

1996   CNN becomes part of Time Warner, making it the world's biggest media corporation. The US passes Telecommunications Act. Radio France Internationale takes over Radio Monte Carlo. WIPO enters into a cooperation agreement with WTO to implement TRIPS Agreement. The US launches Radio Free Asia. Information Technology Agreement signed within WTO to liberalize global trade in IT. The French Canal Satellite becomes Europe's first digital platform. MSNBC, a cable and on-line news service, launched by Microsoft and NBC. Cybermag *Slate* started. Japan launches Digital Versatile Disc (DVD) video players.

1997   EU revises its directive on 'Television without Frontiers'. Lockheed Martin Inter-sputnik, a joint venture of Lockheed Martin and Intersputnik, comes into force. WTO's telecommunication accord.

1998   ITU's World Telecommunication Development Conference launches project on e-commerce for developing countries. RFE/RL launches Radio Free Iraq. AP takes over Worldwide Television News. Internet breaks Monica Lewinsky story. British consortium On-Digital launches world's first terrestrial digital TV service. Google founded.

1999   World Wide Web used for propaganda during NATO's war in Kosovo. Internet advertising heads towards $3 billion. Global mobile satellite communications pro-vider, Inmarsat, becomes first inter-governmental organization to be transformed into a commercial company. Viacom merges with CBS.

2000   Billions watch the Millennium celebrations on global TV. AOL merges with Time Warner. CCTV-9, the English-language channel, launched from Beijing. Internet becomes accessible over mobile phones.

2001   Terrorist attacks in New York and Washington media spectacle. Intelsat privatized. Al-Jazeera becomes internationally known for its coverage from Afghanistan. Videophones used. Shanghai Media Group, China's first media conglomerate, formed. Wikipedia launched

2002   Fox News in US redefines broadcast journalism. *Fahrenheit 9/11* becomes most successful documentary film. Social networking site MySpace launched.

2003   Texting makes the SARS epidemic internationally known. US launches *Al-Hurra,* a propaganda channel in the wake of Iraq invasion.

2004   Web-logs become important during US presidential election. China emerges as the world's largest exporter of information technology products. South Korea has highest broadband penetration in the world.

2005   Mobile phones exceed fixed lines in the world. Pod-casting introduced. Television companies start providing content for mobile telephones. *Telesur,* first public news network reaching across Latin America, launched. Intelsat takes over Panamsat. Internet governance dominates UN World Summit on Information Society. Russia TV, a global English-language channel, launched from Moscow. UNESCO adopts the Convention on the Protection and Promotion of the Diversity of Cultural Expressions. EU launches first satellite of its Galileo global navigation project. Mobile telephone subscribers cross 2 billion mark, 31 per cent mobile penetration worldwide. Video-sharing site YouTube is created. News Corporation acquires MySpace.

2006   Al-Jazeera starts international service in English. Inmarsat launches Broadband Global Area Network. Google buys YouTube.

2007   BBC Arabic, its first publicly funded international television channel, goes on air. Al-Jazeera starts a documentary channel. Iran's English-language international network Press TV launched. EU amends its 'Television without Frontiers' directive to further liberalize television industry. iPhone released. Sony Pictures become first major US studio to produce a Hindi-language movie: *Saawariya.*

2008 News Corporation acquires *Wall Street Journal*. China surpasses the US as
      country with the world's largest blogger population. Web becomes major contribu-
      tor to US election campaign. 1.5 billion people in the world on-line (21 per cent
      of global population). Google agrees deal with major US publishers to digitize
      books. Disney's first Indian-made animated feature film in Hindi *Roadside Romeo*
      released. BBC introduces iPlayer service, allowing access to its TV and radio
      programmes via PC.

Daya Kishan Thussu

INTRODUCTION

AS MEDIA AND COMMUNICATION studies has grown worldwide as a field of academic inquiry – a reflection of the huge impact of globalization on media and communication – its research approaches and agendas are being increasingly internationalized. This change has been influenced in no small part by the rapid globalization of media and cultural industries and consumption of their products across continents in real time. The internationalization of higher education, with the changing profile of students and researchers, as well as a much greater mobility and interaction among the academic community, has further strengthened the international dimension of the study of media, culture and communication.

This comprehensive *Reader* aims to bring together some of seminal texts in media and communication studies from both traditional as well as more recent scholarship. It is planned and organized in a manner that reflects the growing internationalization of the field, with clearly defined sections covering key aspects of global communication – from historical literature to policy documents – as well as cultural and political writings on communication, representing a range of perspectives. The readings have been reproduced in their original form, unabridged.

The main purpose of the *Reader* is to provide a critical overview of the dynamics of the internationalization of communication – both on the theoretical terrain and in a more empirically grounded analysis – to encompass the landscape of global communication. Designed for use with university courses, the *Reader* is divided into six parts and includes, in addition to core academic readings, key policy documents that demonstrate the development of the political, economic and technological infrastructure underpinning the global system of media and communication.

Part 1 Infrastructure for international communication

This first part of the *Reader* deals with the infrastructure of global communication. Particularly significant is the growth of communication satellites, which provide the cheap, dependable and fast communication services essential for transnational corporations and governments to operate in the global electronic marketplace. Aptly described as 'trade routes in the sky' (Price, 1999), the extraordinary growth of communications via satellites in the 1990s and the first decade of the twenty-first century can be compared to the technological leap forward of cabling the world for telegraph in the nineteenth century. As Joseph Pelton's contribution shows, satellites have played a crucial role in bringing about political and economic change in the world. Pelton, who knows more than most academics about satellites, having worked for Intelsat (the world's largest satellite company) and NASA, has written extensively on the impact – technological, political and cultural – of satellites on global communication. The reading included here provides an excellent overview of how satellites have acted as a 'worldwide change agent', transforming our lives.

The creation of a global network society is in some ways a natural progression of technological advancement. Manuel Castells, who is credited with conceptualizing the idea of 'a network society', argues, in his contribution, that global networks are helping to create a new public sphere in which global civil society, communication networks and global governance intersect, creating transnational connections outside the control of the governments. Eli Noam, representing the digital dreamers, suggests that the liberalization of global telecommunication infrastructure has contributed to overcoming digital divides. Noam, a distinguished exponent of liberalization of technology, and currently Director of the Columbia Institute for Tele-Information, has consistently argued for democratization and globalization of new information and communication technologies, suggesting that they can be agents for development.

Marc Raboy, who has written widely on global media policy, examines how the United Nations World Summit on the Information Society (WSIS) – held in 2003 and 2005 – created a new political space in global media policy-making processes. It was the first UN summit, Raboy reminds us, where representatives from the civil society were officially invited to participate in deliberations. Though civil society groups disproportionately represented the Western world, Raboy suggests that their presence was symbolically significant – creating 'a precedent in international relations'.

Part 2 Theoretical terrains

Readings in the second part tackle some theoretical terrains. Media and modernization was and is a major area of debate within international communication. At the heart of modernization theories was the notion that communication could be used to spread the message of modernity and transfer Western economic and political models to the newly independent countries of the global South. One of its earliest exponents was Daniel Lerner, a political science professor at the Massachusetts Institute of Technology, and the author of the classic work in the field, *The Passing of Traditional Society* (Lerner, 1958). Here we include Lerner's seminal essay, first published in 1963, which attempts to provide a 'Communication Theory of Modernization'.

An alternative perspective is provided by theorists operating within the post-colonial intellectual tradition. Raka Shome and Radha Hegde embark on 'Postcolonial Approaches to Communication: Charting the Terrain, Engaging the Intersections', providing an overview of post-colonial theorizing (emanating mostly within literary studies), and argue that these perspectives can be deployed effectively to communication studies. Their essay, published in 2002 in the special themed issue of the ICA journal *Communication Theory* – the first time a US national journal in the field of communication devoted an entire issue to post-colonial theorizing – makes a strong case for alternative perspectives on conceptualizing international communication. Development communication is both part of the modernization discourse and a post-colonial communication discourse. 'Development theory' was based on the belief that the mass media would help transform traditional societies. This pro-media bias was very influential and received support from UNESCO and many governments in developing countries. Srinivas Melkote's contribution provides a succinct overview of the key 'theories of development communication'. With digitization communication theories have received a new fillip and Dan Schiller makes this connection in his 2001 article 'World Communications in Today's Age of Capital'. Schiller argues that in the era of globalized electronic communication 'on a unified and ubiquitous capitalist basis' the demands of transnational capital dominate in 'redefining the social purposes and institutional functions of world communications'. Examining this reorganization of global communication in the context of telecommunications, audiovisual and on-line services, he suggests that 'the hallmark of our age of capital is that, perhaps above all by revolutionizing the means of communication, large corporations have acquired massive new freedom of manoeuvre in their attempts to reintegrate markets for labour power, goods and services, and thus to pursue accumulation on a global scale'.

Part 3 Global media systems

The third part of the *Reader* provides material on different types of media systems in a global context. Readings in this part focus on the tension between media power of mainly, though not exclusively, US-based media and communication conglomerates and the growing trend towards media contra-flow from peripheries of the media globe to the metropolitan centres of global production and distribution.

Oliver Boyd-Barrett, credited with the theory of media imperialism, presents a reformulated version of his theory – first promulgated in a famous essay published in the late 1970s (Boyd-Barrett, 1977). In an article written for a collection of essays on globalization of media which I edited (Thussu, 1998) and included here, Boyd-Barrett conceded that his original formulation did not sufficiently take into account intra-national media relations as well as different types of audiences, but maintained that it was still a useful analytical tool to make sense of the media world. The growing tendency towards homogenization of media cultures is at the heart of the reading taken from the much-cited survey of comparative media systems by Daniel Hallin and Paolo Mancini, who discuss 'The Forces and Limits of Homogenization'. The commercial nature of the global media system is explained in detail by Robert McChesney in a chapter from his 1999 and aptly titled book *Rich Media, Poor Democracy: Communication Politics in Dubious Times*. McChesney's concerns about what he calls 'hyper-commercialism' of the media and the hegemonic power of mainly US-dominated international media, have found echoes among scholars working within the critical tradition of media and communication research as well as outside it. One indication of this is the fact that despite being published by a university press and largely focusing on the media in the US, *Rich Media, Poor Democracy* has had a global impact. The globalization of telecommunication and media systems has transformed the media landscape globally. The media world today is characterized by multi-vocal, multi-media, multi-directional flows of cultural products in both public and private domains. I have been particularly keen on this phenomenon of a *contra*-flow in media products from the peripheries to the centre of global media production as well as movements within the South itself. The growth of non-Western media is discussed in the reading which maps out the terrain dividing the media flows into two categories: the dominant flows – such as the US-dominated products – from news and current affairs (CNN, Discovery) through youth programming (MTV), children's television (Disney), feature films (Hollywood), sport (ESPN) to the Internet (Google) – as well as what I have described as subaltern flows. These latter *contra*-flows are further divided into transnational and geo-cultural flows – the former includes the Indian film industry, popularly referred to as Bollywood; the Latin American telenovelas and al-Jazeera news network, and the latter is represented by media outlets like the Chinese network Phoenix; the pan-Arabic newspaper *Al-Hayat* and such web-based media as islamon-line.net. The excerpt from Jeremy Tunstall's book *The Media Were American*, sets out a radically different position on the presence of American media in the contemporary world from his well-known study *The Media are American*, published in 1977. Tunstall's change of perspective is based on the study of high-population media markets – such as India, China, Indonesia – where American products are not to be seen on prime-time television and much of the media output is domestically produced or, even if it is foreign in origin, it is skilfully indigenized to suit local cultural and cognitive preferences.

Part 4 Dominant and alternative discourses

In the fourth part of the *Reader*, contributors deal with dominance and alternative discourses on international communication. The notion of cultural imperialism is most closely associated with the work of Herbert Schiller who, for most of his professional life, was interested in examining the capacity of the US government and big corporations to promote the values of consumer capitalism to people across the Third World. The *Reader* includes a much-cited article of Schiller, 'Not Yet the Post-imperialist Era', published in 1991 in the journal *Critical Studies in Mass Communication*. At the heart of Schiller's argument was the analysis of how, in pursuit of commercial interests, huge US-based transnational corporations, often in consort with Western (predominantly US) military and political interests, were undermining the cultural autonomy of the countries of the South and creating a dependency on both the hardware and software of communication and media in the developing countries. Schiller defined cultural imperialism as: 'the sum of the processes by which a society is brought into the modern world system and how its dominating stratum is attracted, pressured, forced, and sometimes bribed into shaping social institutions to correspond to, or even to promote, the values and structures of the dominant centre of the system' (Schiller, 1976: 9).

The cultural imperialism thesis came under a good deal of criticism, not least for the reasons that it tended to take too deterministic a role of media and communication, ignoring other aspects such as culture, history, gender and ethnicity, and also collapsing the very real and distinct differences between and among Third World countries – Singapore (a city state) and India (a country of continental size and complexity) were sometimes discussed in the same vein and were both seen as part of the developing world. It also generally ignored the question of media form and content. One important contribution against this 'totalistic' thesis was Joseph Straubhaar's work which examined why cultural proximity may influence media use. In his well-known article 'Beyond Media Imperialism: Asymmetrical Interdependence and Cultural Proximity', published in the same year and in the same journal as Schiller's article, he argued for a more nuanced approach in analysing global-local cultural interaction.

An example of such alternative readings of the dominant political-economy-inspired discourses is the article on the Islamic Internet by Lina Khatib 'Communicating Islamic Fundamentalism as Global Citizenship' which examines how on-line communities are creating new transnational communication. Suggesting that the Internet is used by Islamic groups as a 'portable homeland', she argues that cyberspace has become an enabling tool through which these groups protect, strengthen and communicate their multiple identities.

One key criticism of the cultural imperialism thesis was that it avoided studying media reception. It was an extremely useful discourse to understand the production and distribution of media products within a transnational circuit. However, often influenced by geo-political and commercial heavyweights, it ignored the audience, how people receive the media messages and how these influence their thinking. Such absences were not just in the study of mainstream media, but also among alternative media, as John Downing's article demonstrates. Downing notes that, despite alternative media users representing the most 'active' aspects of media consumption and interpretation, the study of audiences for alternative media remains a hugely under-researched area. He urges the need for the exploration of the user dimension of alternative media by media and communication scholars in conjunction with innovative anthropologists, sociologists, historians and political scientists.

Part 5 Communication and power

The relationship between communication and power is the theme of the fifth part of the *Reader*. The ideological role of the mass media is one key theme running through the readings included in this part. Armand Mattelart, one of the world's leading scholars of media ideology, argues in his article 'An Archaeology of the Global Era: Constructing a Belief,' published in English in 2002, that ideology remains a central configuration in communication at a global level.

The role of mass media as an instrument for political propaganda is the theme of the short piece by the American political scientist Harold Lasswell, one of the world's best-known exponents of the theory of political propaganda. Lasswell did pioneering work on the systematic analysis of propaganda activities during wartime and wrote perceptively about the power of the media, especially radio, in shaping the worldview of citizens, an issue which became particularly pronounced during the First World War. Writing in the 1920s Lasswell proposed a theory of political propaganda in a short but influential article that appeared in *The American Political Science Review* and is reproduced here.

A softer version of propaganda is the use of 'soft power' to promote national interest. Joseph Nye, who coined the phrase, argues in a piece published in 2008 in a special themed issue on public diplomacy of the prestigious journal *The ANNALS of the American Academy of Political and Social Science*, that soft power is a central component of public diplomacy in the era of globalized communication. Nye defines 'soft power' as simply 'getting others to want the outcomes that you want — [it] co-opts people rather than coerces them'. In a global information age, he suggests, power 'will include a soft dimension of attraction as well as the hard dimensions of coercion and inducement. The ability to combine hard and soft power effectively is "smart power" '. Media and foreign policy figure prominently in the excerpt in the *Reader* from another distinguished American scholar, Monroe Price, 'Toward a Foreign Policy of Information Space', taken from his 2002 book *Media and Sovereignty: The Global Information Revolution and its Challenge to State Power*. Price argues that transnational media have forced a refiguring of state sovereignty, particularly in the case of weaker states and states in the process of political and economic transition.

Part 6 Cultures of global communication

Contributors to the final part of the *Reader* examine the relationship between culture(s) and international communication – an area which has been largely ignored in literature informed mainly by the political economy approach to communication and media studies. In the post-Cold War, post-modern world, culture, ethnicity, gender and identity are becoming increasingly important in academic discourses on globalization. One area which the political economists generally neglected was patterns of global media consumption. The excerpt from the widely cited book *The Export of Meaning: Cross-cultural Readings of Dallas* by Elihu Katz and Tamar Liebes, shows that consumption of television programmes can vary in specific cultural contexts, indicating that media texts could be polysemic and therefore amenable to different interpretations by audiences, who may not merely be passive consumers but 'active' participants in the process of negotiating meaning. Their study was based on readings of the 1980s US drama *Dallas* which had led to the discourse about 'Dallasization' of global television.

A biographical note may be relevant here: when the editor of this *Reader* visited Britain for the first time in 1988 on a Commonwealth Scholarship, his colleagues were surprised to find that the words 'who killed JR?' did not mean anything to him and that he had not been exposed to the ubiquitous Hollywood-generated television culture. In India where the editor was raised and educated, we were protected from such cultural influences and instead were steeped in a locally produced popular entertainment – no less dramatic. This local element and its growing interaction with the global (read Western) popular culture has engaged a good many sociologists, anthropologists and scholars working within the media and cultural studies field. One leading voice pointing out the dynamic and the dilemmas between heterogenization and homogenization of globalizing cultural forces and the resultant 'heterogeneous dialogues' is the US-based Indian anthropologist Arjun Appadurai. His 1990 article 'Disjuncture and Difference in the Global Cultural Economy', first published in the journal *Public Culture*, a version of which we reproduce in the *Reader*, is a seminal text, and the concept of the 'scapes' – 'ethnoscape', 'technoscape', 'finanscape', 'mediascape' and 'ideoscape' – to describe the dynamics of contemporary global diversity has become a useful trope for analysing cultural globalization. Appadurai argues that these 'scapes' influence culture not by their hegemonic interaction, global diffusion and uniform effects, but by their 'disjunctures' – their differences, contradictions and counter-tendencies.

One of the scapes that Appadurai discusses concerns ethnoscapes, the movement of populations across countries, whether voluntary – via globalization of professional services; of higher education; international labour for transnational corporations; international non-governmental sector or multilateral bureaucracies – or forced – as a result of fleeing poverty, prosecution or war. These have made the global ethnoscape a rich area for international communication research. The growth of diasporic media, with Chinese, Indian, Arabic, Nigerian and Mexican being the largest, has spurred a new sub-field of communication and media research. How the diasporic audiences distinguish the national from the international is the theme of the article from Karim H. Karim, himself a member of the South Asian diaspora, who has written about and researched transnational diasporic cultures for many years.

The growth and circulation of diasporic media also indicate that there is more than just one centre of globalization. The dominant discourses on globalization have tended to ignore the role of the regional and national narratives, in some cases more significant in the study of cultural aspects of globalization. The excerpt from Japanese scholar Koichi Iwabuchi's 2002 book *Recentering Globalization: Popular Culture and Japanese Transnationalism* makes a convincing case for the primacy of the national and the regional over the global. Iwabuchi discusses this in the context of the widespread popularity of Japanese cultural products – from Sony to Manga – in the global cultural market. The cultural *mélange* that the global/regional/national/local generates can lead to a hybridized media and cultural product. Marwan Kraidy, whose 2002 article 'Hybridity in Cultural Globalization' is included here, provides a sophisticated case for going beyond the binaries of the local and the global and examining the processes behind this interaction. As a case study Kraidy examines a series of articles on 'American Popular Culture Abroad' published during 1998 by the *Washington Post*. Hybridity, Kraidy argues, is 'a conceptual inevitability' in a globalized world where hybridity and hegemony intersect, and helps us better understand what he terms 'critical cultural transnationalism'. Kraidy developed this argument further in his book *Hybridity, or, the Cultural Logic of Globalization*, published in 2005.

The role of communication and information technologies in creating a new hybridized and glocalized, as well as a more participatory media culture is the theme of the final reading in this part. In his article, Mark Deuze maps the convergence of culture within the creative industries, looking at examples from journalism, advertising, marketing communications and public relations. Deuze notes that the increasing use of 'interactive advertising' or 'citizen journalism' offers possibilities of going beyond the opposing models of corporate co-optation and audience resistance and instead focusing on cultural convergence between professionals and amateurs and how such practices affect the new digital media ecology.

Key documents and reports

As a point of departure from other existing *Readers* in the field of media, cultural and communication studies, we have included a section with key documents and reports from multilateral organizations, as well as governments, which have had a global impact on communication policies and practices.

The first of these is Resolution 4/19 passed by the UNESCO General Conference in October 1980. The resolution endorsed the demand mainly from Non-Aligned countries to establish a New World Information and Communication Order (NWICO). The NWICO protagonists argued, as most clearly articulated by Tunisian Information Minister Mustapha Masmoudi, that the international information system reinforced and perpetuated inequality, with harmful effects for the countries of the South, which were heavily dependent on the North for both software and hardware in the information sector (Masmoudi, 1979). The demands for a NWICO emerged from a series of meetings of the Non-Aligned Movement, notably Algiers in 1973 and Tunis in 1976. A landmark was reached with the Mass Media Declaration by the UNESCO General Conference in 1978, which recognized the role the mass media played in development, and in December of that year, the 33rd session of the United Nations General Assembly adopted a resolution on the New World Information and Communication Order.

The excerpt from the MacBride Commission report, a document that, for the first time, brought information- and communication-related issues onto the global agenda, follows the key arguments put forward by NWICO supporters. The International Commission for the Study of Communication Problems, to give it its formal name, was set up in 1979 under the chairmanship of Sean MacBride and submitted its final report to UNESCO in 1980. Its 82 recommendations covered the entire gamut of international communication issues.

The world of international communication has arguably been most profoundly affected by the General Agreement on Trade in Services (GATS), the first multilateral, legally enforceable agreement covering trade and investment in the services sector, which came into force in 1995.

Particularly relevant for international communication is its Annex on Telecommunications, reproduced here, which stated that foreign and national suppliers of telecom facilities should be treated equally, thereby exposing domestic telecommunications industries to international competition. As a premium multilateral institution in the arena of culture and communication, UNESCO has taken many steps to sustain cultural and creative diversity in the world. One of its most important documents was the Universal Declaration on Cultural Diversity, adopted by its General Conference in 2001. The Declaration discusses cultural diversity in the context of pluralism, human rights, creativity and international solidarity and suggests an action plan to implement it effectively. Four years later, the UNESCO Convention on the Protection and Promotion of the Diversity of Cultural Expressions was adopted at its General Conference, reproduced in the *Reader* along with the document on Universal Declaration on Cultural Diversity. 'Cultural diversity refers to', according to the UNESCO, 'the manifold ways in which the cultures of groups and societies find expression. These expressions are passed on within and among groups and societies. Cultural diversity is made manifest not only through the varied ways in which the cultural heritage of humanity is expressed, augmented and trans-mitted through the variety of cultural expressions, but also through diverse modes of artistic creation, production, dissemination, distribution and enjoyment, whatever the means and tech-nologies used'. It states in particular that 'cultural activities, goods and services have both an economic and a cultural nature, because they convey identities, values and meanings, and must therefore not be treated as solely having commercial value'. Among the guiding principles of the convention were the principle of respect for human rights and fundamental freedoms, sovereignty, equal dignity of and respect for cultures, international solidarity and cooperation, complementarity of economic and cultural aspects of development, sustainable development, equitable access and openness and balance.

With the globalization of cultural industries, the protection of intellectual property rights has become increasingly prominent. We reproduce the summaries of two key international treaties in this field. The 1996 Performances and Phonograms Treaty (WPPT) administered by the World Intellectual Property Organization (WIPO), and which came into force in 2002, deals with intellectual property rights of performers (actors, singers, musicians), as well as producers of phonograms, and covers the right of reproduction, distribution, rental and the right of making available. WIPO's Copyright Treaty (WCT), which also came into force in 2002, updated the 1886 Act of the Berne Convention for the Protection of Literary and Artistic Works, and gave the authors rights of distribution, rental and communication to the public and adding computer programs and databases as new subjects to be protected by copyright.

Information and communication-related issues have also become progressively important for the United Nations, as evidenced by its World Summit on the Information Society (WSIS) which was conceived and launched in 1998 and organized in two phases. The first phase was concluded in Geneva in 2003 where the Geneva Declaration of Principles and Plan of Action was adopted. The second phase was convened two years later in Tunis, where the importance of information and communication technologies for economic and social development was emphasized. The Tunis Commitment, reproduced here along with the Tunis Agenda for the Information Society, are important documents which might influence policy on information societies.

Another key organization in relation to international communication, the International Telecommunication Union (ITU), historically considered telecommunications as a public utility, following a policy of cooperation, not competition, a position that it abandoned in the post-Cold War era. Since the mid-1990s, the ITU has become a champion of a liberalized, deregulated and privatized global communication environment, as indicated by its resolution on bridging the standardization gap between developing and developed countries, passed at its 2006 Plenipotentiary Conference. One of its goals is: 'disseminating information and know-how to provide the membership and the wider community, particularly developing countries, with capabilities to leverage the benefits of, *inter alia*, private-sector participation, competition, globalization, network security and efficiency and technological change in their ICT [information and communications technology] sector, and enhancing the capacity of ITU Member States, in particular developing countries, for innovation in ICTs'.

Promoting ICTs for development and linking it to the idea of freedom has been a salient part of the US government's foreign policy, as shown by the 2003 Digital Freedom Initiative, a joint programme of the Department of State, Department of Commerce, US Agency for International Development, Peace Corps, US Small Business Administration and USA Freedom Corps, to help 'meet the challenge by promoting free market based regulatory and legal structures and placing volunteers in businesses and community centers to provide small businesses and entrepreneurs with the information and communications technology skills and knowledge to operate more efficiently while competing in the global economy'. The importance of ICTs to promote foreign policy interests also features in the 2006 US government 'Transformational Diplomacy'. This new diplomacy will make 'creative use of the Internet' noting that '21st century technology will be used to engage foreign publics more directly via the media and Internet, and to better connect diplomats in real time'. In the same year, the US Department of Commerce entered into the Joint Project Agreement with the ICANN (Internet Corporation for Assigned Names and Numbers) 'for the purpose of the joint development of the mechanisms, methods, and procedures necessary to effect the transition of Internet domain name and addressing system (DNS) to the private sector'. Given the growing importance of Google in global communication, we also include the company's Software Principles, first presented in 2004 and updated in 2006.

The liberalization of media and communication has also affected media regulation, even in Europe – home to public-service broadcasting – as the revised version of the 'Television without Frontiers' directive of the European Union indicates. The directive was adopted in 1989 and revised in 1997 to coordinate pan-European audio-visual space within which a set of common regulations of television broadcasting can operate. With the expansion of digital broadcasting, the European audio-visual media have mushroomed and competition has grown. The revised TwF directive, introduced in 2007, allows 'legitimate product placement', 'where the viewer is adequately informed of the existence of product placement. This can be done by signalling the fact that product placement is taking place in a given programme, for example by means of a neutral logo'.

The *Reader* also includes a chronology of international communication, URLs of relevant websites as well as a list of suggested further reading. The collection of such rich and relevant information and analysis under one cover provides much-needed material, both historical and contemporary, on the dynamics of global communication in its political, economic, cultural and technological contexts. It is hoped that this *Reader* will contribute to the understanding of the impact of the globalization of media and communication on research and teaching in the field and therefore be a valuable guide for students and teachers of communication and media, especially those interested in the international aspects of media, culture and communication.

References

Boyd-Barrett, O. (1977) Media imperialism: towards an international framework for the analysis of media systems. In Curran, J., Gurevitch, M. and Woollacott, J. (eds) *Mass communication and society*. London: Edward Arnold.

Kraidy, M. (2005) *Hybridity, or, the cultural logic of globalization*. Philadelphia: Temple University Press.

Lerner, D. (1958) *The passing of traditional society: modernizing the Middle East*. New York: Free Press.

Masmoudi, M. (1979) The new world information order. *Journal of Communication*, 29(2): 172–85.

Price, M. (1999) Satellite broadcasting as trade routes in the sky. *Public Culture*, 11(2): 69–85.

Thussu, D. K. (ed.) (1998) *Electronic empires: global media and local resistance*. London: Arnold.

Tunstall, J. (1977) *The media are American: Anglo-American media in the world*. London: Constable.

Schiller. H. (1976) *Communication and cultural domination*. New York: International Arts and Sciences Press.

PART 1

Infrastructure for international communication

Joseph N. Pelton

SATELLITES AS WORLDWIDE CHANGE AGENTS

The medium is the message means . . . that a totally new environment has been created. We have extended our central nervous system itself in a global embrace, abolishing both space and time as far as our planet is concerned.

—Marshall McLuhan (1966, pp. ix, 19)

COMMUNICATIONS SATELLITES HAVE REDEFINED our world. Satellites and other modern telecommunications networks, together with TV, have now altered the patterns and even many of the goals of modern society. Satellites, for better or worse, have made our world global, interconnected, and interdependent. Worldwide access to rapid telecommunications networks via satellites and cables now creates widespread Internet links, enables instantaneous news coverage, facilitates global culture and conflict, and stimulates the formation of true planetary markets. Satellites change our world and affect our lives. This book [the original publication] is an exploration of how satellites are a global agent of change in an incredible range of ways. These include the spanning and spread of new technology, news, culture, sports, entertainment, economic markets, global politics, and much more.

The editors' prior introduction is intended to be a roadmap guide to our efforts to explain the many sides of the satellite world—past, present, and future. This chapter seeks to introduce in a general way the wide dimensions of that world and how it impacts our planetary society in a myriad of ways. Some of these are now so familiar that they are almost hidden from public view. For instance, most people know that direct broadcast TV comes from satellites, but are unaware that cable TV (from HBO to CNN) needs satellites to obtain most of its programming. A U.S. congressman is purported to have said: "Why do we need weather satellites when I can turn on my television and see the latest report on my local channel?"

Satellite technology and systems have evolved tremendously in the past 40 years, but as is seen in the technology sections of this book, this development continues apace.

Satellites and the nation state

Ever since the Treaty of Westphalia in 1648, the *world* has been defined by what is called the *nation state*. Prior to that time, conflicts and wars often revolved around the borders of city states and communities of interest, not nations. Prior to the modern national state, wars were fought over disputed territory, stolen property, kidnapped damsels, religious conflicts, and ethnicity, not on the basis of the national interests of independent countries. For the last 300 years, however, national sovereignty has been king. Under the Westphalian system, as it has become known, the established authority of a state was responsible for internal laws, national subjects, national punishment, and even defined national religious beliefs. "No man is an island," but under international law countries were supposed to be. The international system, as it evolved based on the sovereignty of the nation state, had weaknesses, but it did create an international law of minimum order. As Fernand Braudel has explained in his massive trilogy on life up through the 18th century, institutional structure is key to the advance of civilization (Braudel, 1979a, 1979b, 1979c).

Until the 1950s, nations or national empires such as those of Britain and France were amazingly self-contained. Admiral Perry may have opened up Japan, and Europe may be becoming a community of nations, but prior to 1965—the date when Early Bird, or Intelsat I, became operational—overseas communications were incredibly limited and expensive. Most communications (over 99%) were within national boundaries. Likewise international commerce was quite sparse, and multinational corporations were only just beginning to emerge. In the age of satellites and fiber optic cables, it is now possible to operate global corporations, carry out free trade on a worldwide basis, and instantaneously control systems from halfway around the planet. Millions of telecommuters, what might be called *electronic immigrants*, now work daily in another country via modern telecommunications connections. In many ways, satellites have made such an international world possible. It has enabled a world that operates beyond the nation state technically and economically viable.

Analysts such as Robert B. Reich (1991), author of *The Work of Nations: Preparing Ourselves for 21st Century Capitalism*, believe that the nation state is becoming passé or only marginally relevant. Such analysts, often associated with a group known as the Tri-Lateralists, perceive the growing influence of international corporations, global financial transactions, and science and technology, and suggest that the nation state is losing influence and control in our modern world. Each year those who make their way to the Global Economic Conference in Davos, Switzerland, seem to increasingly define those individuals and entities with true power in a 21st-century world. At the opposite end of the spectrum, religious mullahs are also attacking the nation state on the basis of cultural and ethnic grounds.

The world has certainly experienced more change in its economic, cultural, social, scientific, and political systems in the last 40 years than at any time in history. Further, the rate of global change due to satellites, telecommunications, information technology, electronic funds exchange, and other forms of advanced science and technology will, if anything, continue to accelerate ever more rapidly in the years ahead. When one considers that the value of global electronic fund transfers in 2002 were about $300 trillion and ran at over $1 trillion per day for 2003, it is hard to deny that the world today is dramatically different than only two generations ago.

In short, this is not an easy time for a world shrunk by technology and yet fractured by fundamental religious beliefs and terrorism. One part of our modern world believes that the structure of our world can be defined in dollars, patents, and gigabytes of information, but another part, steeped in radical beliefs and concepts such as Jihad, define our world much differently. The question is whether the 300-year-old concept of the nation state can cope effectively with this ever-speeding swirl of change and conflict. As satellites have made our world smaller and smaller, the elements of conflict and cultural difference have begun to emerge as increasingly important, and the nation state appears to be in need of redefinition. Some would say that the terrorists' attacks on September 11, 2001, and the U.S. response in terms of a war against terrorism mark the start of the end of the Westphalian concept of the world politic. Yet the rise of the world corporation, the emergence of global entertainment and news, and the pervasive reach of modern telecommunications and information networks gave rise to fundamental shifts in the world community decades before the A1 Qaida attacks on the World Trade Center buildings and the Pentagon.

Thus, we seem to have advanced technology in conflict with the traditional nation state as well as with traditional religious beliefs and cultural values. At the start of the 21st century, a third axis of technological conflict with yet another value has increasingly emerged. There is increasing concern about technology and development and its potential conflict with our environment, global warming, and the need for sustainable patterns of living over the longer term. Some fear that population explosion, unchecked consumption of petrochemical fuels, and other destructive environmental practices threaten our future. Runaway development, consumption, and unchecked technology are seen by many as a challenge to the sustainability of the human race on Earth.

Recent projections showing that the population growth could ebb by the mid-21st century and the world population could actually shrink in coming decades are seen as hopeful signs. Other new environmental, remote sensing, and meteorological technologies also give new hope for a "new greening" of the planet another generation or so hence. Yet environmentalists from the Club of Rome, the Sierra Club, and other groups are not equally optimistic about the future. On both sides of the environmental debate, satellites are peculiarly positioned to play a powerful role. As one reads further into this book, one can find satellites represent a powerful technology whose force can be channeled in many directions.

For better or worse, satellite systems will continue to play a key part in redefining the political, scientific, cultural, and economic systems of the 21st century. Here are some of the ways that satellites will define our future. These themes are replayed and amplified in the chapters that follow.

Satellites and globalism

Over the past decade, space activities have contributed nearly $1 trillion to the global economy. Satellite communications represent about a third of that figure. During 2003, satellite communications directly represented $40 billion in worldwide revenues and nearly $75 billion in directly related economic activities. If one looks beyond the role of satellites (in narrow terms of telecommunications) and begins exploring the multiplier impact on the global economy, the overall impact is vastly more important on our planet as a whole. For instance, a good percentage of the world's hundreds of trillions of dollars in electronic funds transfer (EFT), as reported by the World Bank for 2003, went via satellite. This stunning amount represents a figure that is more than four times the global Gross National Product (GNP) for all countries of the world—nearly a $100 trillion. Money in a service economy circulates faster and faster and must do so to create an actual payoff that can be measured as national economic productivity.

Satellites now beam down to us 24 hours a day, 7 days a week—a Niagara of information, entertainment, and business transactions. This massive dump of data is now accomplished by means of over 12,000 satellite video channels, produced not only in Hollywood, but in Bollywood, India; Cairo, Egypt; and other film production centers as well. Connectivity and electronic access around the world have reshaped just about everything that defines business, cultural, and even religious life in the Third Millennium. An evangelist or a pornographer can reach a billion people "live via satellite."

The operation of communications satellites in today's society is now so pervasive that they have become invisible like electric motors or indoor plumbing, but occasionally an event occurs that signals both their presence and importance. A few years ago, a Panamsat Galaxy satellite (then owned by the Hughes Communications Company) covering much of the United States failed. That satellite was carrying the video distribution for CNN News and the CNN Airport channel, and thus many people were aware of the failure. Far more important, this satellite was also providing the paging service for a large percentage of the U.S. public, including a high percentage of doctors. This disrupted the medical system of the entire United States, and thousands of operations and the provision of emergency care at hospitals all over America were thrown into a great tangle. On the Evening News Hour with Jim Lehrer, the executive director of the Satellite Industry Association and I were invited to explain how not only the United States but the entire world was now dependent on hundreds of communications satellites that provide communications for business, education, health care, and news. We made clear that improved restoration planning was critical to avoid a repeat of the "satellite paging crisis" of the day.

On a more positive note, Japan has turned to satellites in the wake of the great Kobe earthquake of the early 1990s. When the earthquake hit, all terrestrial communications via fiber optics and coax cable were instantly destroyed. Only the wireless satellite circuits for national and international connectivity survived. Today, throughout Japan, there is a Local Government Wide Area Network (LGWAN) that consists of over 5,000 satellite terminals that have been installed against the possibility of another major earthquake disaster, and soon this network will include 10,000 very small aperture antennas (VSATs). Around the globe, satellites are increasingly seen as a way to maintain communications in case of a natural or man-made disaster or terrorist attack. No other technology interconnects the world so incredibly well and reaches so many remote locations. Some 220 countries and territories are linked together via satellite. Fiber optic systems connect less than half that number of countries. The smallest, most isolated, and most land-locked countries and territories in the world are linked via satellite. As you see later, this has changed things forever.

One can argue that the impact of satellite communications around the world on business and the citizenry has been good, bad, and occasionally even indifferent. In the chapters that follow, we see evidence of all three results.

Satellites have changed the world as much as TV or the telephone

Change spawned by electronic connectivity is everywhere—from news to terrorism, from education and health care to warfare. Marshall McLuhan, the Father of the "Global Village," was wrong—or at least only partially right—when he said that the new "cool" and "mentally involving" media of TV was the message! As we explore our electronic world, we find it is actually much more complex than even McLuhan sought to describe.

However, the futurist James Naisbitt (1980) was probably right when he suggested that global connectivity was perhaps of equal or greater importance to media content in shaping today's world. Naisbitt thus challenged McLuhan when he suggested that instantaneous distribution of information globally was the key to the future. In his book *Megatrends*, he suggested that satellite communications, by making modern electronic media "omnipresent" and "instantaneously accessible," was creating the "ultimate force of change" in modern times. In short, Naisbitt argued that satellite systems were creating the global village—not TV by itself.

Instantaneous information also has other unintended consequences:

1.   An abundance of rapid information overloads our sensory systems and competes for attention. Thus, information in the modern context must be as contemporary as possible. As a result, information today is less enduring.
2.   New constraints on decision makers emerge as news is contemporaneous with policymaking.
3.   Policymakers try to avoid this amplification of news by ever-increasing forms and processes of secrecy and intelligence.
4.   The media can also be fed false and misleading information, and the pace with which it flows is so short and fast that facts cannot be checked adequately—the major problem is to determine what is really real.

Indeed, it was satellites that brought TV and global telecommunications rather quickly and dramatically to an increasingly small planet in the 1960s. The 1968 Olympics in Mexico City was the first true international electronic media event, but satellite TV service was still limited at that time. The countries of the Indian Ocean region were not yet included in the world of instant messaging in 1968. That was to change forever 1 year later.

The Apollo Moon Landing in the middle of 1969 became the world's first truly global event. Satellite service to the Indian Ocean region via an Intelsat III satellite was achieved just a little over 1 week before this huge media and scientific event changed our view of our small planet in a significant way. Over a half-billion people watched "live" what had seemed pure science fiction only a decade before. By the time of the Montreal Summer Olympics in 1972, satellite technology had made possible a global audience of over 1 billion. In less than a decade, the earth had been "dramatically shrunk" by satellite networking and broadcasting. Global TV programs evolved rapidly over the decade that followed. At the start of the decade, they were revolutionary events. By the end of the 1970s, they were commonplace occurrences, and the phrase "live via satellite," which once inspired a sense of awe, began to disappear from TV screens as irrelevant information.

Satellites, as much as any other technology, thus served to create what can legitimately be called *globalism*. Communications satellites reshaped our vision of humanity when we first saw "Earth Rise" from the moon in the last gasp of the 1960s.

The 21st-century world is different in many ways, but global interconnectivity is certainly one of the most fundamental shifts that now separate us from our past history. Just as mass access to books and newspapers created a new world for us centuries earlier, global media separates us from the near-term past.

Before satellites (i.e., as recently as 1964) there were only a few hundred poor-quality telephone circuits to interconnect the entire world. These submarine cable voice links often resulted in "clipped-off" conversations due to an antiquated technology called Time Assigned Speech Interpolation (TASI). This was a poorly chosen acronym, but perhaps well suited to an even poorer technology. Today, Sri Lanka, Kenya, and Uruguay each operate more overseas voice circuits than were in worldwide use 40 years ago. Well over 200 countries have ready access to international radio and TV broadcasts via satellite, and this is viewed as routine.

Before the end of the 21st century, we will be linked via space communications not only to everywhere on our planet, but to the moon and maybe other parts of our solar system. The national, regional, and global linkages that satellites provide are comparable in impact on our planet to that of telephones, TV, the jet airplane, or nearly any other modern technology.

The global information revolution and information overload

Communication satellites, more than any other of the advanced electronic media during the short period since the 1960s, have stimulated a true global information revolution. Submarine cables and fiber optic networks have served to integrate the most economically advanced countries together, but they have not been at the core of creating true global interconnectivity. As described in more detail in a later chapter, in the 1980s and early 1990s, Sidney Pike of CNN almost single handedly brought satellite TV to scores of countries that had never seen international news transmissions before.

Today, satellite systems such as Intelsat, Panamsat, SES Astra, Eutelsat, Asiasat, and nearly 100 other space networks provide literally thousands of international connecting links between the countries of the world, in comparison with fiber systems that are typically providing only a few score of point-to-point link-ups. Global TV is still largely a satellite-based phenomenon and will remain so for some time to come.

Global society—at least as measured in simple quantitative terms such as human population, information available to global society, cultural linkages, medical science, and longevity—has changed more since the 1960s than the patterns of human life changed during 1 million years of cave man civilization.

This startling rate of change in the state and nature of human society is not hyperbole, but simple fact. Nor should it necessarily be considered a positive accomplishment. Actually such "superspeed" change should be comprehended as both a source of wonder and even more so of concern. The last 35 to 40 years—and not coincidentally also the era of satellite communications—represents a sea change for world society. We have witnessed much more change (at least in tangible things that we can measure) than ever occurred in vast spans of time in the early days of human history.

World population has expanded by over 3 billion people in the last 40 years. Further, according to UN projections, the people to be educated in the next 40 years outnumber all those people educated since the dawn of human society. Satellites, in terms of expanding international business, broadening international scientific interchange, increasing media distribution, and extending Internet to the world community, have often driven this curve of change.

In fact if we look at the 5-million-year history of humankind and proto-humans as being represented by a 10,000-story building that is 20 miles high, we find that the last 40 years (the time that we have had broadband global communications capability via satellite) represent only a matter of some inches of space on the top floor of this imaginary megastructure (see Fig. 1.1).

Yet if we were to envision a building representing not human history, but the accumulation of global information (Fig. 1.2), we see a dramatically different building from this perspective. The top 8,500 stories of the building of global information would have been built since the launch of the first operational satellite, and some 6,000 floors would have been added since the advent of the Internet. In the next 15 years, if we maintain the same index scale of "progress," the currently projected amount of information in our building of global information would soar outward at an even more astonishing rate. In fact the information in our global database is now doubling perhaps every 3 years (and some would argue it is doubling in only 9 months time). Thus, the "building of global information" could mushroom to 160,000 stories (320 miles into space) before we reach 2020, and of this information only 2,500 stories would predate the age of satellites. This building, which represents our global database, would represent the ultimate Tower of Babel and truly reach into outer space.

This is to say that in about 15 years the totality of global information systems could

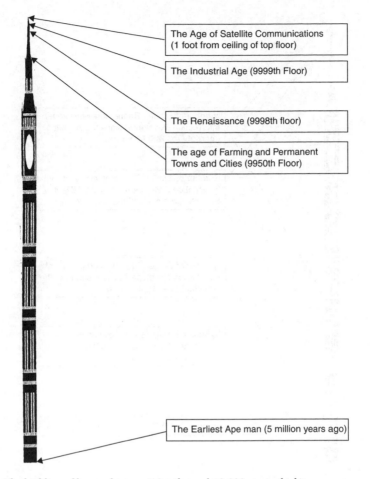

The Age of Satellite Communications
(1 foot from ceiling of top floor)

The Industrial Age (9999th Floor)

The Renaissance (9998th floor)

The age of Farming and Permanent
Towns and Cities (9950th Floor)

The Earliest Ape man (5 million years ago)

Figure 1.1 The building of human history (20 miles and 10,000 stories high).

increase some 16 times in size. Just the information represented by environmental data captured by NASA's Mission to Planet Earth, called the Earth Observation System, will have increased to nearly 3,000 terabytes of information or the equivalent of 1,000 Libraries of Congress. If we sought to organize, store, and retrieve this remote sensing information on a fully interactive basis on a national and international scale, this would create problems of communications almost unimaginable a few years ago. (Some people even fear that without some new standards of information management, the Internet as presently organized could reel out of control due to simple "information overload.")

Beyond the global village into the age of the worldwide mind

The satellite, other wireless systems, and fiber communications networks will not only assist in creating the oft-quoted "Global Village," but will soon start to fashion what might be called a "Worldwide Mind." By the end of the 21st century, broadband systems will link humanity together in almost unimaginable ways (see Pelton, 1999). In another century, this "intellectual network" can be expected to reach not only to the most remote reaches of our earth and ocean, but also out across the broad reaches of our solar system. Some day we will

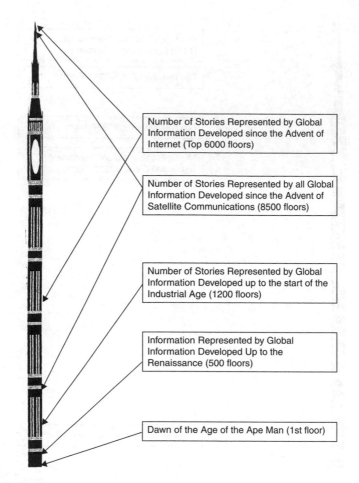

Number of Stories Represented by Global Information Developed since the Advent of Internet (Top 6000 floors)

Number of Stories Represented by all Global Information Developed since the Advent of Satellite Communications (8500 floors)

Number of Stories Represented by Global Information Developed up to the start of the Industrial Age (1200 floors)

Information Represented by Global Information Developed Up to the Renaissance (500 floors)

Dawn of the Age of the Ape Man (1st floor)

Figure 1.2 The building of global human information (20 miles and 10,000 stories high).

turn on our TV and check the weather for the day not only on our planet, but others as well. Since the events of 9/11, however, we understand that quite different scenarios are possible. Technology does not always promise progress and better horizons.

Technological innovation and broader band instantaneous communications can no longer be seen as "guaranteed progress" for the human species. There are clearly problems ahead. Serious issues arise from the fact that some so-called *developing* economies and societies live virtually completely outside this rapidly expanding "E-Sphere" of accelerating scientific knowledge and electronic data systems. These problems will be heightened if the G-8 and other economically advanced countries continue to be thoroughly integrated into this global web of information while other nations and societies, for technical, economic, or cultural reasons, are excluded.

In only a few decades, the most developed countries of the Organization of Economic Cooperation and Development (OECD) can extend their knowledge base and economic wealth well beyond limits that we can now only imagine. Yet what does this portend for our increasingly small planet if the process leaves the poorest and least educated societies behind? Today we talk of the issue of the "Digital Divide," but the potential scale of the problem is not well understood. The prospects of staggering gaps of information on one small planet are fundamental and sobering to contemplate.

This issue of the Digital Divide could easily escalate rapidly in only 20 years. The

United Nations, national aid agencies, and nongovernmental organizations that provide international aid and relief services have now identified the Digital Divide as one of the world's most important issues and problems. Satellite networks can serve to extend this problem by providing advanced electronic systems to promote the growth and expansion of multinational business enterprises or minimize this problem by the provision of tele-education and telehealth services. It is likely that advanced satellite networks will serve both causes.

Yet another way to consider the issue of satellites and their role in the future life of our evolving "E-Sphere" or "Worldwide Mind" is that global information is being collected and stored at an astonishing rate. In mathematical terms, the growth of information globally is not just accelerating, but growing in accord with a third-order exponential. This is to say that global information systems are not merely accelerating—the rate of acceleration is increasing. This is what physicists call *jerk* for obvious reasons.

More simply we can say that the generation of global information is growing at least some 200,000 times faster than our global population. (This, in mathematical terms, is a swift turtle trying to catch the Space Shuttle.) The problems of surviving and adapting to such a "Super Speed" world are not small. In fact we are now looking to future satellites and computers that can operate hundreds of times (if not thousands of times) faster than today's impressive machines. These machines of tomorrow, most likely powered by concepts known as quantum communications and quantum computing, may possibly allow us to keep up with the flow of new information that will flow across our increasingly small "intellectual telecity," which I call the "E-Sphere" or the "Worldwide Mind."

Intel has already indicated that by 2005 or so it will have desktop computers that process at speeds of 10 GHz from a single chip. This means that easily accessible computers for the mass consumer market can process the equivalent of a human lifetime of reading and speaking in a single second. Satellite links in another decade could be operating at the hundreds of Gigabit level and fiber optic connections providing connections at the terabit/second level. (This means moving the equivalent of several Libraries of Congress per minute.)

The continued expansion of digital services in the areas of video, multimedia, broadband Internet, and IP services—barring some catastrophic disaster—will thus only continue to mushroom in the coming years. This increased speed of processing and broadband communications will give rise to a staggering array of new services.

The speed with which this is projected to occur over the decade ahead is shown in Fig. 1.3, with the different shadings identifying existing, new, and projected services to occur within the next 10 years. The driving force will be cheap processing power. The challenge will be for fiber optic and satellite networks to keep pace—not only by providing faster and faster transmission speed, but by furnishing them at low cost and with high reliability and security, especially in wireless and mobile systems. The biggest challenge of all may be filtering out unwanted information.

New patterns of global trade, political process, and social change

Although a good case might be made for other instruments of change, this book presents the case for satellites and how they will represent the prime key to globalization. The rise of globalism will undoubtedly bring changes to education, health care, entertainment, and business. Low-cost services and user terminals that support easy communications by satellite are likely to complicate international trade in products, but especially so in relation to services. This will seem particularly true as more and more electronic immigrants work

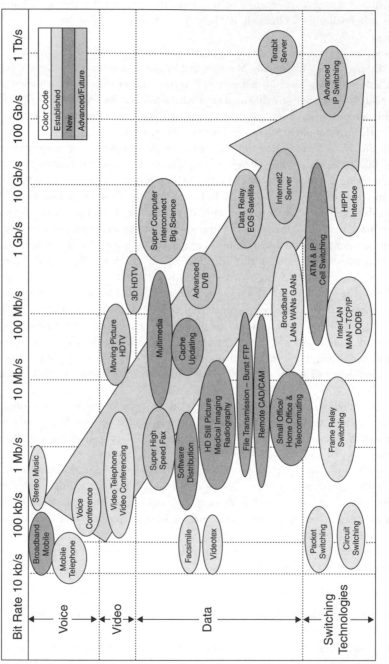

Figure 1.3 The continued growth of broadband services 2002–2015.

across international boundaries. Today more than 1 million people are what I call *electronic immigrants* or *international teleworkers*. This special class of workers might live in Barbados, Jamaica, India, Pakistan, or Russia, but work in the United States, Japan, or Europe. These international teleworkers actually have been around for decades, and many now accept such a way of life as normal.

Within a decade, it could well be 10 or even 20 million people who are professional business nomads and who will find their way to work on electronic beams of digital information, sometimes halfway around the world. Such trends, and the parallel efforts to facilitate global communications, will make national and international satellite links just as common and convenient as cell phones or global TV shows are today. In 20 years, the cost of communicating across town, across a country, or around the world could well be much the same—just as Arthur C. Clarke predicted decades ago. What is not known is whether this will generate supranational relationships and institutions that could well confound the working of today's national states or of regional, ethnic, or religious cultures.

The nation state, a modern invention, is only a few centuries old. Countries are actually the manifestation of what is fundamentally a 16th-century technology (i.e., low-cost printed materials in mass distribution) and then of the 18th-, 19th-, and 20th-century industrial revolutions that followed. The role of the nation state in a global service economy has yet to be clearly defined.

Marshall McLuhan, Fernand Braudel, and others taught us to analyze the relationship among communications, technology, and political history. They and others such as Georg Hegel, Jacques Ellul, Lewis Mumford, Victor Ferkiss, and Norbert Weiner, from widely different perspectives, examined how technology has reshaped modern life. We certainly know that the rise of mass printing and the dissemination of knowledge on a broad scale in the 16th century (a lag time of about 100 years after Guttenberg's famous press appeared on the scene in Europe) changed the world of the Renaissance. The free exchange of ideas and the resulting intellectual intercourse gave rise to the concepts of both individualism and political systems, which were the precursor to the modern nation state. Political and technological philosophers as diverse as Siegfried Gideon in *Mechanization Takes Command* and Jacques Ellul in *Technological Man*, on the liberal side of the argument, and Marshall McLuhan, Norbert Weiner, and Buckminster Fuller, on the "scientific side" of the spectrum, have all suggested that these intellectual changes reshaped human society in fundamental ways.

Essentially philosophers such as Henry David Thoreau, Jacques Ellul, and Lewis Mumford have seen technology as adversely affecting and "dehumanizing" society, whereas others such as Norbert Weiner and Buckminster Fuller have seen technology not only as positive, but almost as an inevitable outcome of humanity's intellectual development. Thus, the technological positivists see technology as the ineluctable quest of human civilization.

Regardless of which interpretation we choose, the nation state is showing its age as we start the 21st century. All of these writers and more suggest that political institutions may need to be reinvented. Exactly how national political systems adapt to an electronic world whose business and economic systems work on the basis of split-second communications across the world is clearly a challenge. Political systems work within relatively small, intimate, and low-moving communities and cultures, and thus are often ill equipped to cope with their faster (and other more wealthy) protagonists. This is just one of the more interesting puzzles of our technological age. Certainly the institutions that provide global communications, including satellites, are currently in a hubbub of change and transformation. One thing we know: "Faster is not necessarily better."

Today with the rise of global information systems, worldwide e-commerce and media, and planetary science and engineering, the dawning of a new age seems to be occurring. Yet we see another landscape: We see fundamentalist and closed cultures with absolutist political systems. These societies are many centuries old, and in many cases the political and religious leadership of these entities actually despises the results of global connectivity and modernity. In many cases, they despise Western culture, human and political freedoms, and civil rights, and they have contempt for the "loose morals" and "materialism" of what seems to them a depraved society.

We are certainly living in a time of turmoil and cultural striving. These "gaps" in philosophy and culture impact not only the "West's relationship" with Afghanistan, Iraq, Pakistan, Borneo, or the rain forests of the Congo. These gaps also stretch across the hopes and values that divide urban and rural America and separate suburban communities and the inner city. Similar conflicts are present throughout other advanced nations as well.

The point to note here is that satellite communications is neither the cause nor the focus of change. Yet it is these systems, along with fiber optics, cybernetics, and computer networks, that speed up the process of conflicting knowledge and values both within countries and across the broad reaches of our globe. In some ways, we have been warped by a new kind of electronic reality. This has been called *telegeography*. Within this concept, distance (at least in the modern commercial world) no longer has much meaning, and it is culture, intellect, and speed of electronic connection that now create dysfunctional gaps in our plantary system, not physical separation.

In the age of broadband networking, New York, Tokyo, Paris, Singapore, Berlin, Moscow, and London are closer together than Okmulgee, Oklahoma is to Arkadelphia, Arkansas or Zamengoe, Cameroon is to Gaborone, Gabon.

Digital communications machines, for better or worse, now integrate our global business systems and many national and ethnic societies. Our versatile space communications systems link together our TV sets, telephones, GPS receivers, computers, terabyte databases, and portable Internet phones. This process has made our world smaller and more intimate in new and different ways. We have now seen the advent of new and more powerful satellite systems. Truly anybody can stay in touch anytime and anywhere—if they want to do so. Via the Worldspace satellite system, it is possible to receive hundreds of radio channels in the world's most remote rain forest or arid desert. Via mobile satellite systems such as Inmarsat, Thuraya, New ICO, or New Iridium (to name only a few), one can use a specially equipped cell phone or lap top transceiver to communicate to the world or link to Internet from ships at sea, from aircraft in the stratosphere, or from the most remote island—and for an increasingly low cost.

Furthermore, billions of people can choose what they wish to watch on any one of hundreds of satellite TV channels. They can do this by direct satellite, satellite-fed cable TV, or simply by going to the Internet to watch their favorite show via "video streaming" or listen to their favorite music by CD downloading. Ultimately one will be able to watch virtually any movie ever made via the right connection on the Web. Today, people in developed countries and a growing number of those in developing countries can quickly connect to tens of thousands of "information networks" to learn about virtually any conceivable subject or watch any form of entertainment or amusement. Censorship will have become obsolete.

Soon we may be paying more for screening out unwanted information than for connecting to the global network. Yet those without access to the networks or those unable to pay to access information may be pushed further away from modernity. These isolated communities may not rue being isolated from global entertainment. (Many would say it is a plus.) Yet these individuals are also being limited in their access to education, health care, and unfiltered news. At the most fundamental level, there is also a question that goes beyond how to access global networks and whether it will be affordable. This is whether one wishes to have access to and intercourse with Western technological society at all. Is such access good or bad? Right or wrong? Beneficial or destructive?

An increasingly complex and interdisciplinary world

This book [the original publication] is focused on satellites. The information here is thus largely based on how satellite technology came to be, what is or is not available from satellite systems, and what impact they have made on our world—past, present, or future. That is not to say that satellites are the source of all modern telecommunications or networking systems. Clearly they are part of a "telecommunications gestalt" that now enables planetary communications to work with great efficiency at an increasingly low cost.

Satellites have made an enormous impact, as the following chapters clearly explain. Nevertheless, companion systems and technologies are also a key part of the digital revolution that is bringing us such change at a constantly increasing pace. If we look around, there are other candidates that might be labeled the "prime movers" of modern change. Thus, we now find an array of "kissing cousin" technologies that create electronic intimacy and information formation and exchange. The list of prime change agents for Western technological society could certainly include computers, biotechnology, artificial intelligence, space exploration, telecommunications devices, the Internet, missiles, atomic weapons, lasers, fiber optics, or TV.

We do not dispute that these other technologies have also had a profound effect on the world and have also reshaped our lives. In fact we try to show in this inter-disciplinary investigation of the field of satellite communications just how communications and information technologies fit together. It takes a good deal of engineering and standards making to create seamless networks that enable global media, global business, global science, global education, global health care, and global news to all work together. That having been said, the impact on satellite technology and modern planetary systems simply cannot be denied.

The following chapters [in the original publication] describe how satellites can and will fundamentally alter the state and nature of human existence. Satellite news and entertainment have made us more globally aware and interconnected. Today, telephone connections and satellite-based Internet penetrate to the core of urban ghettoes, the battlegrounds of the Middle East and Afghanistan, and the remote reaches of schools and clinics in the midst of jungles and deserts. Satellites reach from university laboratories and mountain top telescopes to the living rooms of houses—all the way from the United States to Borneo.

By a combination of history, political analysis, business, and trade information, a diverse mix of people who have lived through the satellite revolution will attempt to explain, probe, and analyze how satellite communications have swept forward the wild fire of change, innovation, and globalism.

Today the six sextillion-ton mass of dirt, stone, water, and air that orbits the sun as the third planet in the solar system is much the same in its chemical and physical composition as it was thousands or even millions of years ago. Yet in terms of the organization of the human bio and political systems, life is fundamentally different today than it was at the dawn of the space age less than a half century ago.

Satellites and new patterns of world living

Human civilization has changed in significant ways from the days when we attempted to launch the first tiny artificial communications satellites in the early 1960s. The first steps came quickly with the launch of Score (1958), Courier (1960), Telstar (1962), Relay (1962), Syncom (1963), and the world's first commercial communications satellite (spring 1965). Today's largest and most powerful satellites are some 10,000 times more capable than the first small satellites of the mid-1960s in terms of performance and lifetime. The first operational satellite resembled a largish 80-pound coffee can with a pipe sticking out the top. It showed little commonality with today's monster satellites, with a wingspan of some 100 feet (about 30 meters). Contemporary satellites include huge, high-gain antennas that are some 40 feet in diameter (i.e., 12 meters across). The history of this technology and how it happened is told in greater detail in chapter 2.

The most important thing to know is that the story of communications satellites and the development of new and exciting technology is far from over. The Japanese experimental satellite—the ETS VIII—will soon deploy a huge antenna that is 17 meters by 19 meters in size. The next three decades will likely produce satellite designs that are radically different from the golden boxes from which protrude solar panel wings, considered the latest in technology today. In later chapters, we discuss and show concepts of the possible designs of the future. The most impressive designs for the future, however, may not be the satellites in the skies, but the tiny broadband communications, computing, and navigational devices that we can wear on the wrist or perhaps even implant in our bodies.

When it comes to identifying global change agents, satellites and other related media have much to brag about. Yet satellite system designers and operators from DirecTV to Astra and from Intelsat to Panamsat have a good deal to be concerned about as well. The technology that brought us the potential for worldwide education and health care, as well as electronic diplomacy and unprecedented economic growth, also spawned global MTV, Cinemax, the "Gong Show," "Baywatch," and nonstop game shows and commercials. Communications and navigational satellites can also be powerful instruments of war that ensure that "smart bombs" are delivered to their targets with deadly accuracy. In short, the communications satellite can be seen as a mixed blessing; satellite systems can instantaneously bring us the ravages of war as easily as nudity and violence. These capabilities, the result of a free and open society, are a concern to an astonished and often outraged global audience. Satellites have certainly forced us to view our expanding space capability with everything from glee to horror.

Television first occurred within national boundaries. Programming was sent out over localized radio waves within neighborhoods, cities, and sometimes across a nation. However, this was extremely difficult to accomplish in the 1950s with the terrestrial transmitters and coaxial cable systems that existed then. The early days of TV spearheaded change, but not global revolution. It was actually only when satellites came on the scene in the mid-1960s that worldwide change began to occur.

In the 40 years that have followed, satellites have brought us change in every possible way—in terms of culture, business, and even warfare. It is satellite systems that have made Internet a truly global experience. Without satellites, the Internet would not be a force in countries as diverse as Mongolia, Bolivia, Zaire, and Vanuatu. Today, fiber optic networks are a key part of the global network, but fiber only interconnects about half of the world's nations. If one wants to reach the more than 200 countries of the world—places like Lesotho, Truk, or Tuvalu—satellites are the medium of choice.

In his book of essays entitled *Utopia or Oblivion?*, Fuller (1971) singled out the unique aspects of satellite technology. Fuller explained nearly three decades ago why geosynchronous satellite systems represented a "breakthrough technology" that allowed us to accomplished much more with much less. He called this phenomenon *ephemeralization*; Buckminster suggested that this breakthrough in intelligence is critical to human evolution and to achieve his ultimate dream—that "intelligence in the universe" might ultimately overcome entropy.

He argued that the satellite created a virtual sea change in human existence (akin in its force and range of impact to the printed word or electrical power). In 1973, at the White House World Communications Year observance that I luckily got to attend, Fuller, 2 weeks prior to his death, argued that the uniqueness of human intelligence is in the ability to do things in totally new ways. He suggested that ephemeralization is not only essential, but forms an ineluctable part of human development. Thus, ephemeralization is the ability to achieve tasks or activities of the past in ways that are orders of magnitude more efficient in terms of time, energy, consumption of resources, and reduced cost. In "Bucky's" view, it represents the best long-term hope for human survival.

The amazing new satellite technologies yet to come

Advances such as books, electricity and electric motors, artificial intelligence, solar energy, the telephone, TV, the Internet, computers, and satellites have unlocked a new future for humanity. Fuller's view of the need for humans to search for new pathways to the future takes on almost religious implications in his writings. These breakthroughs or fundamental discoveries are needed to divert us from conventional pathways to profound societal and physical change. To Fuller, the satellite, electronic computers, the transistor, and parallel inventions are destiny.

Such basic knowledge, he argued, can unlock capabilities and possibilities that are a basic departure from simple extrapolations that represent the trajectories of past civilizations. Figure 1.4 shows how satellite systems are continuously able to do more with proportionately fewer resources. As noted earlier, the satellites of the near-term future, although they require only 10 to 20 times more resources to deploy, are as much as 10,000 times more capable than the earliest satellites. The marvel of these new satellites is that they can work with user terminals that are ever smaller in size and cheaper in cost. Thus, these new microterminals can soon become almost universally available anywhere at anytime. This type of dramatic technical innovation helps to generate and sustain a global revolution in worldwide TV, communications services, and expanded access to the Internet.

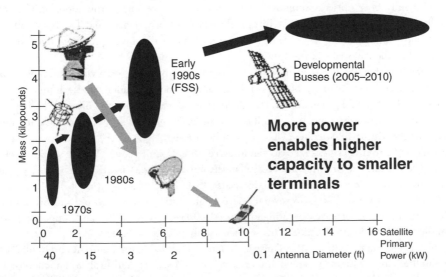

Figure 1.4 Changing nature of Satcoms.

The new satellite applications on the horizon

What do Buckminster Fuller, James Naisbitt, and others mean when they refer to satellites and other telecommunications technologies as giving rise to a global revolution? Ultimately they are referring to a change that impacts us all and can be seen in just about everything. The implications reverberate everywhere—to business, education, health care, entertainment, public safety, and even armed conflict. There is today global trade at the level of tens of trillions of dollars (U.S.) that only 30 years ago was measured in billions of dollars. Even discounting inflation, this is a huge increase.

Furthermore, this international trade of the past involved a much greater element of colonial or neocolonial exploitation than it does today. When satellite communications came to the island nation of Samoa well over two decades ago, the prices of exports increased on the order of 30%, and the price of imports dropped by about 30%. This is because prices could be negotiated via satellite rather than set by the last freighter to steam into port.

We now have a court of world public opinion that stems from worldwide and instantaneous electronic news coverage. We now have worldwide banking, stock trading, and electronic funds transfer at a level that exceeds $100 trillion a year. Global satellite communications, fiber optic networks, and terrestrial wireless have over the past decade begun to create not a "global village," but what might be called the earliest manifestations of a "global brain" or an "E-Sphere" (Pelton, 1999, p. 1).

Part of this new worldwide mind has created an omnipresent Hollywood and MTV culture around the world. Other parts have created global, political, and cultural observatories that span our planet. Yet others have enabled research networks that interlink Nobel scientists in a nonstop quest for new knowledge. America, the land of the Internet and nonstop satellite TV and video streaming, is now at once the primary envy as well as the primary source of perceived evil of the world. Like Janus, our nonstop electronically fed society faces both ways. It marches forward and backward at the same time.

TV broadcasters like Ted Turner, John Malone, Rupert Murdoch, and Kerry Packer of Australia would never have risen to prominence without the satellite. The same is true about MTV, HBO, and a host of other media organizations. Clearly not all change is good nor is it evil. What satellites are today, however, are virtually omnipresent.

Certainly fiber optic systems now transport a huge portion of this global traffic, but satellites started the revolution. Satellites still carry most of international TV. They still link North and South together as global networks interconnect the developing countries to each other and to the countries of the OECD.

Some see this satellite-driven revolution as a way to bring new services and new forms of care and comfort to many of the 6 billion people on our planet. These human beings survive without potable drinking water, electricity, education, health care, or the hope of prosperity. From this perspective, satellites are an instrument of knowledge and enlightenment. In the words of Socrates: "There is only one evil, ignorance, and only one good, knowledge." From this perspective, satellites represent knowledge. When we at Intelsat began Project Share (Satellites for Health and Rural Education) in the mid-1980s, we did not know what to expect. Little did we realize that the Chinese National TV University experiment that we started with several dozen small earth terminals would mushroom into a vast educational enterprise operating in over 90,000 remote locations and supporting over 5 million students in rural China. This seemed satellites at their best.

Others see things differently. These critics look at global entertainment and media "live via satellite" as decadent Western imperialism or at least as "cultural and technological imperialism." They see only a "dark" technology. International satellite transmissions certainly bring to unreceptive audiences such things as scantily clad bodies, "loose morals," and sophomoric "Baywatch" programming. Such "Western" TV and movies disturb societies that follow traditional religions and values. Many perceive this blatant and undiscriminating spread of Western technology as undermining the family and religious authority. Certainly this overpowering satellite and media power were clearly seen by the former Taliban rulers of Afghanistan and the Al Qaida as the "devil" that must be attacked.

In short, there are many—even beyond Osama bin Ladin and his band of terrorists—that see satellites, electronic media, computers, TV, and the Internet as Western forces of evil. Yet they embrace the same technology to fight those who violate their belief systems. They see the danger of open and uncontrolled communications.

Satellites at the intersection of Eastern and Western cultures

Arthur Clarke likes to tell the story of the elite and "hip" society attending soirees in New Delhi who say that Hollywood programming is okay for them—the educated elite—to see, but such fare is inappropriate for the rural population of remote India. They insist the rural poor should not "see things that they do not understand and would misinterpret." *Noblesse Oblige* is a natural trait for humans the world over.

Religious and other critics see "Western technology" and "Western cultural values" based on scientific rather than religious principles as being increasingly at odds with traditional systems of belief. This is not new. Yet now in the wake of the national U.S. calamity of September 11, 2001, the magnitude of the rift has been exposed. The concerns about the stresses of modernity have been present for some time, but no one in the West has willingly conceded that advanced technology and traditional societal and religious beliefs are indeed in "fundamental conflict" in both senses of the word.

In the 19th century, Ralph Waldo Emerson said: "Technology is in the saddle and rides mankind." However, he was warning about the economic and social stresses of lost jobs and regimentation in the face of automation and the depersonalization of society—not about a cultural invasion of a hostile philosophic, religious, and cultural thought system. Lewis Mumford and Jacques Ellul (noted earlier) wrote their own warnings in the 1950s and 1960s, albeit in more contemporary language and concepts. These warnings and concerns, however, were in terms that could be sorted out in Western thought and even in liberal versus conservative political terms.

Today, however, we face something entirely new. We have received some interesting academic insights in recent years about the scope and nature of the problem. We have been able to read about the perspectives provided by Professor Benjamin R. Barber in *McWorld vs. Jihad*, by Samuel P. Huntington in the *The Clash of Civilizations*, and, most recently, by Bernard Lewis in *What Went Wrong: Western Impact and Middle East Response*. These scholars help us understand the wide gap between instant electronic linkage and empathetic understanding across religious and cultural gaps.

We are constantly being shown that instant electronic contact does not eliminate cultural barriers or distrust across religious, social, and economic barriers. However, we are only beginning to recognize that the super-speed change in our technology is leading us not only to new heights of intellectual and scientific understanding, but also to disconnects between cultures that have different values and cultural objectives.

Technology provides a powerful duality. Its positive impacts could be called *telepower*, on the one hand, and the negative impacts might be called *teleshock*, on the other hand. The divisions and emotional rifts that separate our worlds are no longer just economic, but also cultural, religious, educational, and even scientific and technological. Technology can no longer be considered a tool with neutral value until applied. From the perspective of religious fundamentalists, it can be a threat or even a demon.

There are ironies and discontinuities at work here. The Al Qaida and other fundamental extremists actively use the tools of modernity and communications to organize and fight "Western Influence." Nevertheless one should not assume that their anger is directed just at the wealth or religious belief of infidels. They want separation from outside influence at all levels. A Western technology and capitalist marketing system as a "system of influence" is certainly considered a hostile force.

The choice of the World Trade Center and the Pentagon as the focus of the Al Qaida attack was not accidental. These targets were chosen as symbolic "homes" of the enemies. These sites represented the very source of capitalist technology and the U.S. military-industrial complex. Had the capability been there, they also might have tried to flood Silicon Valley and send a missile into the Hollywood Oscar awards.

The events that led to the living horror of passenger aircraft being turned into missiles of destruction on September 11, 2001, undoubtedly have their roots in electronic technology's relentless assault on change. This is a clear and violent backlash against the Western change wrought by communications satellites and outside technology.

There are indisputable clashes afoot in the 21st century. We can no longer dispute the "frightened" and "frightening" reactions by fundamentalists. They have inspired a cadre of followers who resist the miasma of change that modern technology enables and global satellite networks render global and universal throughout our planet. There is fear as well as hostility expressed by those who resist the inevitable changes that modern science and technology make possible and constantly accelerate. This book must address such issues because it is focused on the change, innovation, and progress that satellites have brought to the world. Here is but one example.

Algeria was the first developing country to establish a domestic satellite system. For the Algerian desert people, change came quickly. Algerian government officials leased space segment capacity from the Intelsat global satellite system and then bought earth stations from GTE to link its major regional cities together in 1974 and 1975. The thought was to bring telephone and some evening TV news to remote locations for the first time. For centuries, the bazaars in these desert towns had opened at sunrise and closed at sundown, but in only a few days the markets closed at 5:00 p.m. because that was when the satellite TV shows began. Satellites (as well as VCRs) brought "forbidden fruit" to many traditional cultures, and the religious leaders were the first to feel the attack on their society, culture, and religion. It is no accident that the most rapid growth of VCR ownership in the 1970s and 1980s came in the Middle East. It was such devices that allowed forbidden programming to be seen at last.

Satellite technology has been a "hand maiden" of change and innovation to global society and culture now for four decades. It has enabled not only new technology to evolve, but for it to be broadly shared. It has also been a source of cultural invasion and change more powerful than Alexander the Great and Genghis Khan could have ever dreamed of having at their command. The satellite revolution is thus only a part of a global torrent of change that robotics, biotechnology, artificial technology, fiber optics, computers, the Internet, TV, VCRs, DVDs, and Spandex have brought to an unsuspecting world. During the age of satellites, the world population has expanded by many billions. Fundamentalists from the most traditional of societies are fearful of this change—and for good reason.

The need to cope with "telepower" and "teleshock"

The shape and form of this E-Sphere will change to reflect the stark realities of a global culture in conflict. For years satellites and fiber have created super-speed information networks. These powerful tools have created more and more centralization in the nodes of global civilization located in New York, Los Angeles, Washington, DC, Paris, London, Berlin, Tokyo, Moscow, Beijing, Shanghai, Singapore, and other centers of power.

New concerns about terrorism, urban pollution, energy consumption, traffic congestion, and soaring real estate values could alter the shape of change and modernization. One of the key lessons that should have been learned from 9/11—namely, avoid overcentralization and employ telecommuting more—were largely lost.

Unbridled technological change, instantaneous free-market globalism, and e-commerce on the Internet may very well contain doses of "teleshock" that cancel out the positive gains of "telepower." This book tries to explain not only the scope and type of satellite-driven change, but also where restraint and prudent limits to electronic technology may well be needed. The future of satellites and their opportunity for aiding future generations are thus likely to be conditional. The challenge is to devise "smarter and wiser" systems rather than simply "faster and broader-reaching" networks.

Recent demonstrations at the meetings of the World Economic Forum, the World Bank, the World Trade Organization, and other forums where technology, free trade, and capitalism are promoted have shown that the circle of concern goes beyond fundamentalist religious zealots. There is a wide range of critics who would like to see satellites and information networks in the 21st century being marshaled to create new and more enlightened forms of modern society, but not promote unbridled technological growth as envisioned by pro-technology gurus (Fuller, 1971, chap. 1). Labor unions, environmentalists, social reformers, and others fear "teleshock" tremors still to come.

We can indeed still use satellites, fiber, and innovative wireless technology to create a new type of future that transcends the goals of 19th-century capitalist-led democratic liberalism as defined by Adam Smith and John Locke. As bright and intelligent as those political economists were in their day, their ideas are now out of date.

We could indeed use some innovative thoughts about the interrelationship between democracy and technology. We may well need to invent some new institutions and political philosophies to cope with the 21st century. We probably need to sort out ways to use our most modern of information technologies in a better way. We may need to use our technology to fuel societal and environmental preservation rather than faster growth. We should move toward "electronic decentralization" so that we can move ideas rather than people and avoid the folly of putting all of our people and resources in huge and environmentally unsound megastructures like the World Trade Center.

Changing education, health, demographics, and patterns of work

We may need to use our technology to re-instill intellectual freedom in education. Likewise we may wish to use technology to create "smart market" systems that reconnect supply and demand to meet longer term social and economic goals rather than short-term profits. There are many lessons that the Enron collapse, 9/11, and the widening ozone hole in our atmosphere can teach us if we would only listen. Better use of our communications systems is just one of these lessons.

We could use 21st-century satellite and fiber networks to restructure and improve the nature of our cities, reinvent our institutions, and reinvent the fabric of our work and daily lives. The war on terrorism and the problems associated with efficient education and health care systems could help us devise more humane patterns of global growth and sustainable development. We could learn that the most advanced of our satellite and fiber technologies are tools that extend beyond the narrow realm of business. We can use the satellite systems of the future to create interesting and rewarding telecities. These same technologies can help liberate workers via telecommuting systems and make more effective use of electronic immigrants.

We may also invent new forms of electronic and cultural educational and health care systems that replace conventional physical integration with intellectual freedom. These new models of 21st-century development based on electronic and optical technologies could give new meaning to our understanding of words like *neighborhood*, *city*, or *country*. The power of satellites to redefine our world has actually only begun to be tapped in their first 40 years of existence. Out of adversity and questions about the goal of information and media technology in society, new answers and new solutions may well be found.

In the 21st century, we will find workers going to their offices electronically, whether across towns or villages or across the globe. The same electronic restlessness and seeking of security via decentralization, plus the desire to reduce costs, will reinforce patterns of distance education and health care. We will find ways to use satellite and other information technologies to reduce air and water pollution, reduce energy consumption, and even transfer property values. It is here that satellites may create new win-win strategies for workers, capitalists, and environmentalists. New development and economic growth in the 21st century may thus be accomplished by means of satellite and fiber-based electronic propinquity rather than by physical adjacencies.

Constantly evolving technology versus the striving by many for stability and traditional values will be a key part of the story of the 21st century. This book is thus a series of stories and historical facts that are intertwined with some future speculations about the rise of new global systems. Satellites and other new media are slowly but surely revealing a new worldwide environment.

We particularly explore what globalism means in this new age—in this amazing, startling, and frightening new millennium. It seems that both technology and global consciousness are a one-way gate. Once you go through, you cannot easily return to the past. In this regard, satellites have proved—for better or worse—to be one of the most powerful gateways to the future.

In the next few chapters, we relate an interesting, rich, and often untold history, and we also seek some insights into the future. It is the story of scientists and engineers who developed new technologies, sometimes against the odds and other times in the face of fierce competition. It is also the story of international conflict and institutional change and innovation.

Part of the story relates to the cold war and U.S. reactions to postwar conditions and the needs of an increasingly global market place, which puts much more stress on trade in services than in goods and products. It is also the story of Europe and its desire to become a space power and to use satellites to meet its social and economic needs. It is a story of how Japan and Australia have often been the voice of reason, compromise, and plain old good common sense when issues of global satellite power politics have emerged.

It is a story of how the USSR used satellites as a key element of cold war power and influence, sometimes with great effect and sometimes with less than the desired results. All the economically developed countries of the OECD—from Japan, to Canada, to Australia and New Zealand, to Europe—have played roles in satellite system development. Also the developing countries have effectively used satellites to reach isolated populations and escape from the neocolonialist impact that traditional lines of communications imposed throughout the first half of the 20th century and beyond. There are few technologies that have had such a pervasive impact around the world. When CNN produced the satellite-delivered program called the "Day of Five Billion" a little over a decade ago, there was virtually no political entity across the planet that did not play a role, and over 150 countries aired the program. Nearly 80 countries produced some segment of this remarkable program that recognized the significance of the continuing rapid growth of humanity globally. It also demonstrated that more than 200 countries and territories around the world have a vested interest in satellite networks.

Conclusions

This book [the original publication] is an interrelated and integrated group of chapters that address satellite systems and their impact on the world. These chapters address satellite technology, satellite business and economics, satellites and global politics and regulation, satellites and social services, and even satellites and the future. The attempt is thus to tell the story of satellites from different perspectives and via different disciplines. Too often the world of satellite technology is severed from its social, economic, cultural, and political impacts.

We hope that the reader will first see the satellite story in terms of technology development—past, present, and future. Then it moves to satellite history and regulation. Next, the book morphs into other stories about global business, global TV news, entertainment, and sports—about the many ways satellites have altered our world.

The 12,000 satellite video channels around the world today bring us news, entertainment, the Olympics, and even wars "live via satellite." The Iraq "regime change" of 2003 was the most televised war in history—it was truly "live via satellite."

One of the many stories in this book is that of satellites, the Internet, and the electronic systems we call *cyberspace*. In truth, without satellites, the Internet would not yet have become the global phenomena that it is today. Finally, this book addresses major problems of global concerns about what might be considered negative applications of satellite systems. It provides perspective on a new hope for tomorrow. Satellite systems, by shaping world opinion and allowing teleeducation and telehealth to become available on a global scale, offer new hope for world peace and knowledge. Satellites represent one of the keys to a successful global economy. Satellites offer dual use of networks for commercial and military purposes, for education as well as propaganda and misinformation, for targeted bombs or targeted information.

The forces that shape the world of telecommunications and satellites are more than just technology, business, entertainment, social applications such as health, or education. It is the gestalt of these forces and interests all at once. An attempt to depict the interdisciplinary model that defines the scope and shape of the analysis of this book is shown in Fig. 1.5.

Some believe that, because communication satellites are largely high-tech tools (almost literally supercomputers with specialized software that are deployed in the skies), the stories of these space systems might be dry, straightforward, and devoid of emotion. The truth is that the stories surrounding the development and implementation of satellite communications are filled with elements of intrigue and joy. Just like all forms of human enterprise, the story of satellites sometimes involves conflict, criminal activity, and deception and at other times it offers new hope for the human condition by providing new forms of education, health care, or mitigation of disasters. Change often comes at a considerable price. In today's world of technological innovation, progress can often blend with a sense of loss. The story of communications satellites, in this sense, is certainly no different.

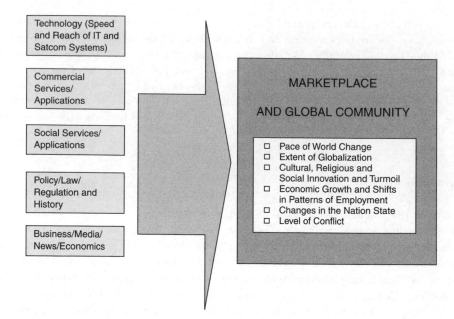

Figure 1.5 Model for global satellite communications systems and interaction with the global marketplace and political history.

References

Barber, Benjamin R., (1996), *McWorld vs. Jihad*, New York: Ballantine.

Braudel, Fernand, (1979a), *The Perspective of the World: Civilization and Capitalism—15th–18th Century (Volume 3)*, New York: Harper & Row.

Braudel, Fernand, (1979b), *The Structures of Everyday Life: Civilization and Capitalism—15th–18th Century (Volume 1)*, New York: Harper & Row.

Braudel, Fernand, (1979c), *The Wheels of Commerce: Civilization and Capitalism—15th–18th Century (Volume 2)*, New York: Harper & Row.

Fuller, R. Buckminster, (1971), *Utopia or Oblivion: The Prospects for Humanity*, New York: Bantam Books.

Huntington, Samuel P., (1996), *The Clash of Civilizations and the Reckoning of World Orders*, New York: Simon & Schuster.

Lewis, Bernard, (2002), *What Went Wrong: Western Impact and Middle East Response*, London: Oxford Books.

McLuhan, Marshall, (1966), *Understanding Media: The Extensions of Man*, New York: Signet Books.

Naisbitt, James, (1980), *Megatrends*, New York: Alfred Knopf.

Pelton, Joseph N., (1999), *E-Sphere: The Rise of the World Wide Mind*, Bridgeport, CT: Quorum Books.

Reich, Robert B., (1991), *The Work of Nations*, New York: Alfred A. Knopf.

Background readings

The Economist, "A Connected World: A Survey of Telecommunications," September 13, 1997.

Ellul, Jacques, (1969), *The Technological Society*, New York: Knopf.

Ferkiss, Victor C., (1969), *Technological Man: The Myth and the Reality*, New York: Mentor Books.

ITU, (1997), *World Telecommunications Development Report*, Geneva, Switzerland: International Telecommunication Union.

Logsdon, John *et al.*, (Editors), (1998), *Exploring the Unknown: Selected Documents in the History of the U.S. Civil Space Program, Volume III, Using Space*, Washington, DC: NASA.

Roszak, Theodore, (1985), *The Cult of Information*, New York: Pantheon Books.

Wattenberg, Ben J., (2002), *The Birth Dearth*, Washington, DC: The American Enterprise Institute.

Whalen, David J., (2002), *The Origins of Satellite Communications 1945–1965*, Washington, DC: The Smithsonian Institution Press.

Chapter 2

Manuel Castells

THE NEW PUBLIC SPHERE: GLOBAL CIVIL SOCIETY, COMMUNICATION NETWORKS, AND GLOBAL GOVERNANCE

The public sphere and the constitution of society

BETWEEN THE STATE AND society lies the public sphere, "a network for communicating information and points of view" (Habermas 1996, 360). The public sphere is an essential component of sociopolitical organization because it is the space where people come together as citizens and articulate their autonomous views to influence the political institutions of society. Civil society is the organized expression of these views; and the relationship between the state and civil society is the cornerstone of democracy. Without an effective civil society capable of structuring and channeling citizen debates over diverse ideas and conflicting interests, the state drifts away from its subjects. The state's interaction with its citizenry is reduced to election periods largely shaped by political marketing and special interest groups and characterized by choice within a narrow spectrum of political option.

The material expression of the public sphere varies with context, history, and technology, but in its current practice, it is certainly different from the ideal type of eighteenth-century bourgeois public sphere around which Habermas (1989) formulated his theory. Physical space—particularly public space in cities as well as universities—cultural institutions, and informal networks of public opinion formation have always been important elements in shaping the development of the public sphere (Low and Smith 2006). And of course, as John Thompson (2000) has argued, media have become the major component of the public sphere in the industrial society. Furthermore, if communication networks of any kind form the public sphere, then our society, the network society (Castells 1996, 2004a), organizes its public sphere, more than any other historical form of organization, on the basis of media communication networks (Lull 2007; Cardoso 2006; Chester 2007). In the digital era, this includes the diversity of both the mass media and Internet and wireless communication networks (McChesney 2007).

However, if the concept of the public sphere has heuristic value, it is because it is inseparable from two other key dimensions of the institutional construction of modern societies: civil society and the state. The public sphere is not just the media or the sociospatial sites of public interaction. It is the cultural/informational repository of the ideas and projects that feed public debate. It is through the public sphere that diverse forms of civil society enact this public debate, ultimately influencing the decisions of the state (Stewart 2001). On the other hand, the political institutions of society set the constitutional rules by which the debate is kept orderly and organizationally productive. It is the interaction between citizens, civil society, and the state, communicating through the public sphere, that ensures that the balance between stability and social change is maintained in the conduct of public affairs. If citizens, civil society, or the state fail to fulfill the demands of this inter-action, or if the channels of communication between two or more of the key components of the process are blocked, the whole system of representation and decision making comes to a stalemate. A crisis of legitimacy follows (Habermas 1976) because citizens do not recognize themselves in the institutions of society. This leads to a crisis of authority, which ultimately leads to a redefinition of power relationships embodied in the state (Sassen 2006).

As Habermas (1976) himself acknowledged, his theorization of democracy was in fact an idealized situation that never survived capitalism's penetration of the state. But the terms of the political equation he proposed remain a useful intellectual construct—a way of representing the contradictory relationships between the conflictive interests of social actors, the social construction of cultural meaning, and the institutions of the state. The notion of the public sphere as a neutral space for the production of meaning runs against all historical evidence (Mann 1986, 1993). But we can still emphasize the critical role of the cultural arena in which representations and opinions of society are formed, de-formed, and re-formed to provide the ideational materials that construct the basis upon which politics and policies operate (Giddens 1979).

Therefore, the issue that I would like to bring to the forefront of this analysis is that sociopolitical forms and processes are built upon cultural materials and that these materials are either unilaterally produced by political institutions as an expression of domination or, alternatively, are coproduced within the public sphere by individuals, interest groups, civic associations of various kinds (the civil society), and the state. How this public sphere is constituted and how it operates largely defines the structure and dynamics of any given polity.

Furthermore, it can be argued that there is a public sphere in the international arena (Volkmer 2003). It exists within the political/institutional space that is not subject to any particular sovereign power but, instead, is shaped by the variable geometry of relationships between states and global nonstate actors (Guidry, Kennedy, and Zald 2000). It is widely recognized that a variety of social interests express themselves in this international arena: multinational business, world religions, cultural creators, public intellectuals, and self-defined global cosmopolitans (Beck 2006). There is also a global civil society (Kaldor 2003), as I will try to argue below, and ad hoc forms of global governance enacted by international, cona-tional, and supranational political institutions (Nye and Donahue 2000; Keohane 2002). For all these actors and institutions to interact in a nondisruptive manner, the same kind of common ideational ground that developed in the national public sphere should emerge. Other-wise, codestruction substitutes for cooperation, and sheer domination takes precedence over governance. However, the forms and processes of construction of the international public sphere are far from clear. This is because a number of simultaneous crises have blurred the relationships between national public spheres and the state, between states and civil society, between states and their citizens, and between the states themselves (Bauman 1999; Caputo 2004; Arsenault 2007). The crisis of the national public sphere makes the emergence of an international public sphere particularly relevant. Without a flourishing international public sphere, the global sociopolitical order becomes defined by the realpolitik of nation-states that cling to the illusion of sovereignty despite the realities wrought by globalization (Held 2004).

Globalization and the nation-state

We live in a world marked by globalization (Held et al. 1999; Giddens and Hutton 2000; Held and McGrew 2007). Globalization is the process that constitutes a social system with the capacity to work as a unit on a planetary scale in real or chosen time. *Capacity* refers to technological capacity, institutional capacity, and organizational capacity. New information and communication technologies, including rapid long-distance transportation and computer networks, allow global networks to selectively connect anyone and anything throughout the world. *Institutional capacity* refers to deregulation, liberalization, and privatization of the rules and procedures used by a nation-state to keep control over the activities within its territory. *Organizational capacity* refers to the ability to use networking as the flexible, interactive, borderless form of structuration of whatever activity in whatever domain. Not everything or everyone is globalized, but the global networks that structure the planet affect everything and everyone. This is because all the core economic, communicative, and cultural activities are globalized. That is, they are dependent on strategic nodes connected around the world. These include global financial markets; global production and distribution of goods and services; international trade; global networks of science and technology; a global skilled labor force; selective global integration of labor markets by migration of labor and direct foreign investment; global media; global interactive networks of communication, primarily the Internet, but also dedicated computer networks; and global cultures associated with the growth of diverse global cultural industries. Not everyone is globalized: networks connect and disconnect at the same time. They connect everything that is valuable, or that which could become valuable, according to the values programmed in the networks. They bypass and exclude anything or anyone that does not add value to the network and/or disorganizes the efficient processing of the network's programs. The social, economic, and cultural geography of our world follows the variable geometry of the global networks that embody the logic of multidimensional globalization (Beck 2000; Price 2002).

Furthermore, a number of issues faced by humankind are global in their manifestations and in their treatment (Jacquet, Pisani-Ferry, and Tubiana 2002). Among these issues are the management of the environment as a planetary issue characterized by the damage caused by unsustainable development (e.g., global warming) and the need to counter this deterioration with a global, long-term conservation strategy (Grundmann 2001); the globalization of human rights and the emergence of the issue of social justice for the planet at large (Forsythe 2000); and global security as a shared problem, including the proliferation of weapons of mass destruction, global terrorism, and the practice of the politics of fear under the pretext of fighting terrorism (Nye 2002).

Overall, as Ulrich Beck (2006) has analyzed in his book *Power in the Global Age*, the critical issues conditioning everyday life for people and their governments in every country are largely produced and shaped by globally interdependent processes that move beyond the realm of ostensibly sovereign state territories. In Beck's formulation, the meta-power of global business challenges the power of the state in the global age, and "accordingly, the state can no longer be seen as a pre-given political unit" (p. 51). State power is also undermined by the counterpower strategies of the global civil society that seek a redefinition of the global system. Thus,

> What we are witnessing in the global age is not the end of politics but rather its migration elsewhere. . . . The structure of opportunities for political action is no longer defined by the national/international dualism but is now located in the "global" arena. Global politics have turned into global domestic politics, which rob national politics of their boundaries and foundations. (p. 249)

The growing gap between the space where the issues arise (global) and the space where the issues are managed (the nation-state) is at the source of four distinct, but interrelated, political crises that affect the institutions of governance:

1. *Crisis of efficiency:* Problems cannot be adequately managed (e.g., major environmental issues, such as global warming, regulation of financial markets, or counterterrorism intelligence; Nye and Donahue 2000; Soros 2006).

2. *Crisis of legitimacy:* Political representation based on democracy in the nation-state becomes simply a vote of confidence on the ability of the nation-state to manage the interests of the nation in the global web of policy making. Election to office no longer denotes a specific mandate, given the variable geometry of policy making and the unpredictability of the issues that must be dealt with. Thus, increasing distance and opacity between citizens and their representatives follows (Dalton 2005, 2006). This crisis of legitimacy is deepened by the practice of media politics and the politics of scandal, while image-making substitutes for issue deliberation as the privileged mechanism to access power (Thompson 2000). In the past decade, surveys of political attitudes around the world have revealed widespread and growing distrust of citizens vis-à-vis political parties, politicians, and the institutions of representative democracy (Caputo 2004; Catterberg and Moreno 2005; Arsenault 2007; Gallup International 2006).

3. *Crisis of identity:* As people see their nation and their culture increasingly disjointed from the mechanisms of political decision making in a global, multinational network, their claim of autonomy takes the form of resistance identity and cultural identity politics as opposed to their political identity as citizens (Barber 1995; Castells 2004b; Lull 2007).

4. *Crisis of equity:* The process of globalization led by market forces in the framework of deregulation often increases inequality between countries and between social groups within countries (Held and Kaya 2006). In the absence of a global regulatory environment that compensates for growing inequality, the demands of economic competition undermine existing welfare states. The shrinking of welfare states makes it increasingly difficult for national governments to compensate for structurally induced inequality because of the decreased capacity of national institutions to act as corrective mechanisms (Gilbert 2002).

As a result of these crises and the decreased ability of governments to mitigate them, nongovernmental actors become the advocates of the needs, interests, and values of people at large, thus further undermining the role of governments in response to challenges posed by globalization and structural transformation.

The global civil society

The decreased ability of nationally based political systems to manage the world's problems on a global scale has induced the rise of a global civil society. However, the term *civil society* is a generic label that lumps together several disparate and often contradictory and competitive forms of organization and action. A distinction must be made between different types of organizations.

In every country, there are *local civil society actors* who defend local or sectoral interests, as well as specific values against or beyond the formal political process. Examples of this subset of civil society include grassroots organizations, community groups, labor unions, interest groups, religious groups, and civic associations. This is a very old social practice in all societies, and some analysts, particularly Putnam (2000), even argue that this form of civic engagement is on the decline, as individualism becomes the predominant culture of our societies. In fact, the health of these groups varies widely according to country and region. For instance, in almost every country of Latin America, community organizations have become a very important part of the social landscape (Calderón 2003). The difference between these groups in varying nations is that the sources of social organization are increasingly diversified: religion, for instance, plays a major role in Latin America, particularly non-Catholic Christian religious groups. Student movements remain an influential source of social change in East Asia, particularly in South Korea. In some cases, criminal organizations build their networks of support in the poor communities in exchange for patronage and forced protection. Elsewhere, people in the community, women's groups, ecologists, or ethnic groups, organize themselves to make their voices heard and to assert their identity. However, traditional forms of politics and ideological sources of voluntary associations seem to be on the decline almost everywhere, although the patronage system continues to exist around each major political party. Overall, this variegated process amounts to a shift from the institutional political system to informal and formal associations of interests and values as the source of collective action and sociopolitical influence. This empowers local civil society to face the social problems resulting from unfettered globalization. Properly speaking, this is not the global civil society, although it constitutes a milieu of organization, projects, and practices that nurtures the growth of the global civil society.

A second trend is represented by *the rise of nongovernmental organizations (NGOs) with a global or international frame of reference in their action and goals*. This is what most analysts refer to as "global civil society" (Kaldor 2003). These are private organizations (albeit often supported or partly financed by public institutions) that act outside government channels to address global problems. Often they affirm values that are universally recognized but politically manipulated in their own interest by political agencies, including governments. In other words, international NGOs claim to be the enforcers of unenforced human rights. A case in point is Amnesty International, whose influence comes from the fact that it is an equal-opportunity critic of all cases of political, ideological, or religious repression, regardless of the political interests at stake. These organizations typically espouse basic principles and/or uncompromising values. For instance, torture is universally decried even as a means of combating greater "evils." The affirmation of human rights on a comprehensive, global scale gives birth to tens of thousands of NGOs that cover the entire span of the human experience, from poverty to illnesses, from hunger to epidemics, from women's rights to the defense of children, and from banning land mines to saving the whales. Examples of global civil society groups include Medecins Sans Frontieres, Oxfam, Greenpeace, and thousands of others. *The Global Civil Society Yearbook* series, an annual report produced by the London School of Economics Centre for Global Governance and under the direction of Mary Kaldor, provides ample evidence of the quantitative importance and qualitative relevance of these global civil society actors and illustrates how they have already altered the social and political management of global and local issues around the world (e.g., Anheier, Glasius, and Kaldor 2004; Glasius, Kaldor, and Anheier 2005; Kaldor, Anheier, and Glasius 2006).

To understand the characteristics of the international NGOS, three features must be emphasized: In contrast to political parties, these NGOs have considerable popularity and legitimacy, and this translates into substantial funding both via donations and volunteerism. Their activity focuses on practical matters, specific cases, and concrete expressions of human solidarity: saving children from famine, freeing political prisoners, stopping the lapidation of women, and ameliorating the impact of unsustainable development on indigenous cultures. What is fundamental here is that the classical political argument of rationalizing decisions in terms of the overall context of politics is denied. Goals do not justify the means. The purpose is to undo evil or to do good in one specific instance. The positive output must be considered in itself, not as a way of moving in a positive direction. Because people have come to distrust the logic of instrumental politics, the method of direct action on direct outputs finds increasing support. Finally, the key tactics of NGOs to achieve results and build support for their causes is media politics (Dean, Anderson, and Lovink 2006; Gillmor 2004). It is through the media that these organizations reach the public and mobilize people in support of these causes. In so doing, they eventually put pressure on governments threatened by the voters or on corporations fearful of consumers' reactions. Thus, the media become the battleground for an NGO's campaign. Since these are global campaigns, global media are the key target. The globalization of communication leads to the globalization of media politics (Costanza-Chock 2006).

Social movements that aim to control the process of globalization constitute a third type of civil society actor. In attempting to shape the forces of globalization, these social movements build networks of action and organization to induce a global social movement for global justice (what the media labeled, incorrectly, as the antiglobalization movement) (Keck and Sikkink 1998; Juris forthcoming). The Zapatistas, for instance, formed a social movement opposed to the economic, social, and cultural effects of globalization (represented by NAFTA) on the Mexican Indians and on the Mexican people at large (Castells, Yawaza, and Kiselyova 1996). To survive and assert their rights, they called for global solidarity, and they ended up being one of the harbingers of the global network of indigenous movements, itself a component of the much broader global movement. The connection between many of these movements in a global network of debate and coordination of action and the formalization of some of these movements in a permanent network of social initiatives aimed at altering the processes of globalization, are processes that are redefining the sociopolitical landscape of the world. Yet the movement for global justice, inspired by the motto that "another world is possible," is not the sum of nationally bound struggles. It is a global network of opposition to the values and interests that are currently dominant in the globalization process (Juris 2004). Its nodes grow and shrink alternately, depending on the conditions under which each society relates to globalization and its political manifestations. This is a movement that, in spite of the attempts by some leaders to build a program for a new world order, is better described by what it opposes than by a unified ideology. It is essentially a democratic movement, a movement that calls for new forms of political representation of people's will and interests in the process of global governance. In spite of its extreme internal diversity, there is indeed a shared critique of the management of the world by international institutions made up exclusively of national governments. It is an expression of the crisis of legitimacy, transformed into oppositional political action.

There is a fourth type of expression of global civil society. This is *the movement of public opinion*, made up of turbulences of information in a diversified media system, and of the emergence of spontaneous, ad hoc mobilizations using horizontal, autonomous networks of communication. The implications of this phenomenon at the global level—that were first exemplified by the simultaneous peace demonstrations around the world on February 15, 2003, against the imminent Iraq war—are full of political meaning. Internet and wireless communication, by enacting a global, horizontal network of communication, provide both an organizing tool and a means for debate, dialogue, and collective decision making. Case studies of local sociopolitical mobilizations organized by means of the Internet and mobile communication in South Korea, the Philippines, Spain, Ukraine, Ecuador, Nepal, and Thailand, among many other countries, illustrate the new capacity of movements to organize and mobilize citizens in their country while calling for solidarity in the world at large (Castells et al. 2006). The mobilization against the military junta in Myanmar in October

2007 is a case in point (Mydans 2007). The first demonstrations, mainly led by students, were relatively small, but they were filmed with video cell phones and immediately uploaded on YouTube. The vision of the determination of the demonstrators and of the brutality of the military regime amplified the movement. It became a movement of the majority of society when the Buddhist monks took to the streets to express their moral outrage. The violent repression that followed was also filmed and distributed over the Internet because the ability to record and connect through wireless communication by simple devices in the hands of hundreds of people made it possible to record everything. Burmese people connected among themselves and to the world relentlessly, using short message service (SMS) and e-mails, posting daily blogs, notices on Facebook, and videos on YouTube. The mainstream media rebroadcast and repackaged these citizen journalists' reports, made from the front line, around the world. By the time the dictatorship closed down all Internet providers, cut off mobile phone operators, and confiscated video-recording devices found on the streets, the brutality of the Myanmar regime had been globally exposed. This exposure embarrassed their Chinese sponsors and induced the United States and the European Union to increase diplomatic pressure on the junta (although they refrained from suspending the lucrative oil and gas deals between the junta and European and American companies). In sum, the global civil society now has the technological means to exist independently from political institutions and from the mass media. However, the capacity of social movements to change the public mind still depends, to a large extent, on their ability to shape the debate in the public sphere. In this context, at this instance of human history, how is governance articulated in social practice and institutions?

Global governance and the network state

The increasing inability of nation-states to confront and manage the processes of globalization of the issues that are the object of their governance leads to ad hoc forms of global governance and, ultimately, to a new form of state. Nation-states, in spite of their multidimensional crisis, do not disappear; they transform themselves to adapt to the new context. Their pragmatic transformation is what really changes the contemporary landscape of politics and policy making. By *nation-states*, I mean the institutional set comprising the whole state (i.e., national governments, the parliament, the political party system, the judiciary, and the state bureaucracy). As a nation-state experiences crises wrought by globalization, this system transforms itself by three main mechanisms:

1. Nation-states associate with each other, forming networks of states. Some of these networks are multipurpose and constitutionally defined, such as the European Union; others focus on a set of issues, generally related to trade (e.g., Mercosur or NAFTA); while still others are spaces of coordination and debate (e.g., the Asia-Pacific Economic Cooperation or APEC and the Association of Southern Asian Nations known as ASEAN). In the strongest networks, participating states explicitly share sovereignty. In weaker networks, states cooperate via implicit or de facto sovereignty-sharing mechanisms.
2. States may build an increasingly dense network of international institutions and supranational organizations to deal with global issues—from general-purpose institutions (e.g., the United Nations), to specialized ones (e.g., the International Monetary Fund, World Bank, NATO, the European Security Conference, and the International Atomic Energy Agency). There are also ad hoc international agencies defined around a specific set of issues (e.g., environmental treaties).

3. States may also decentralize power and resources in an effort to increase legitimacy and/or attempt to tap other forms of cultural or political allegiance through the devolution of power to local or regional governments and to NGOs that extend the decision-making process in civil society.

From this multipronged process emerges a new form of state, the network state, which is characterized by shared sovereignty and responsibility, flexibility of procedures of governance, and greater diversity in the relationship between governments and citizens in terms of time and space. The whole system develops pragmatically via ad hoc decisions, ushering in sometimes contradictory rules and institutions and obscuring and removing the system of political representation from political control. In the network state, efficiency improves, but the ensuing gains in legitimacy by the nation-state deepen its crisis, although overall political legitimacy may improve if local and regional institutions play their role. Yet the growing autonomy of the local and regional state may bring the different levels of the state into competition against one another.

The practice of global goverance through ad hoc networks confronts a number of major problems that evolve out of the contradiction between the historically constructed nature of the institutions that come into the network and the new functions and mechanisms they have to assume to perform in the network while still relating to their nation-bound societies. The network state faces a *coordination problem* with three aspects: organizational, technical, and political. The state faces organizational problems because agencies that previously flourished via territoriality and authority vis-à-vis their societies cannot have the same structure, reward systems, and operational principles as agencies whose fundamental role is to find synergy with other agencies. Technical coordination problems take place because protocols of communication do not work. The introduction of the Internet and computer networks often disorganizes agencies rather than facilitating synergies. Agencies often resist networking technology. Political coordination problems evolve not only horizontally between agencies but also vertically because networking between agencies and supervisory bodies necessitates a loss of bureaucratic autonomy. Moreover, agencies must also network with their citizen constituencies, thus bringing pressure on the bureaucracies to be more responsive to the citizen-clients.

The development of the network state also needs to confront an ideological problem: coordinating a common policy means a common language and a set of shared values. Examples include opposition to market fundamentalism in the regulation of markets, acceptance of sustainable development in environmental policy, or the prioritization of human rights over the *raison d'etat* in security policy. More often than not, governments do not share the same principles or the same interpretation of common principles.

There is also a lingering geopolitical problem. Nation-states still see the networks of governance as a negotiating table upon which to impose their specific interests. There is a stalemate in the intergovernmental decision-making processes because the culture of cooperation is lacking. The overarching principles are the interests of the nation-state and the domination of the personal/political/social interests in service of each nation-state. Governments see the global state as an opportunity to maximize their own interests, rather than a new context in which political institutions have to govern together. In fact, the more the globalization process proceeds, the more contradictions it generates (e.g., identity crises, economic crises, and security crises), leading to a revival of nationalism and to the primacy of sovereignty. These tensions underlie the attempts by various governments to pursue unilateralism in their policies in spite of the objective multilateralism that results from global interdependence in our world (Nye 2002).

As long as these contradictions persist, it is difficult, if not impossible, for the world's geopolitical actors to shift from the practice of a pragmatic, ad hoc networking form of negotiated decision making to a system of constitutionally accepted networked global governance (Habermas 1998).

The new public sphere

The new political system in a globalized world emerges from the processes of the formation of a global civil society and a global network state that supersedes and integrates the preexisting nation-states without dissolving them into a global government. There is a process of the emergence of de facto global governance without a global government. The transition from these pragmatic forms of sociopolitical organization and decision making to a more elaborate global institutional system requires the coproduction of meaning and the sharing of values between global civil society and the global network state. This transform-ation is influenced and fought over by cultural/ideational materials through which the political and social interests work to enact the transformation of the state. In the last analysis, the will of the people emerges from people's minds. And people make up their minds on the issues that affect their lives, as well as the future of humankind, from the messages and debates that take place in the public sphere. The contemporary global public sphere is largely dependent on the global/local communication media system. This media system includes television, radio, and the print press, as well as a variety of multimedia and communications systems, among which the Internet and horizontal networks of communication now play a decisive role (Bennett 2004; Dahlgren 2005; Tremayne 2007). There is a shift from a public sphere anchored around the national institutions of territorially bound societies to a public sphere constituted around the media system (Volkmer 1999; El-Nawawy and Iskander 2002; Paterson and Sreberny 2004). This media system includes what I have conceptualized as mass self-communication, that is, networks of communication that relate many-to-many in the sending and receiving of messages in a multimodal form of communication that bypasses mass media and often escapes government control (Castells 2007).

The current media system is local and global at the same time. It is organized around a core formed by media business groups with global reach and their networks (Arsenault and Castells forthcoming). But at the same time, it is dependent on state regulations and focused on narrowcasting to specific audiences (Price 2002). By acting on the media system, particu-larly by creating events that send powerful images and messages, transnational activists induce a debate on the hows, whys, and whats of globalization and on related societal choices (Juris forthcoming). It is through the media, both mass media and horizontal networks of communication, that nonstate actors influence people's minds and foster social change. Ultimately, the transformation of consciousness does have consequences on political behavior, on voting patterns, and on the decisions of governments. It is at the level of media politics where it appears that societies can be moved in a direction that diverges from the values and interests institutionalized in the political system.

Thus, it is essential for state actors, and for intergovernmental institutions, such as the United Nations, to relate to civil society not only around institutional mechanisms and procedures of political representation but in public debates in the global public sphere. That global public sphere is built around the media communication system and Internet networks, particularly in the social spaces of the Web 2.0, as exemplified by YouTube, MySpace, Facebook, and the growing blogosphere that by mid-2007 counted 70 million blogs and was doubling in size every six months (Tremayne 2007). A series of major conferences was organized by the UN during the 1990s on issues pertinent to humankind (from the condition of women to environmental conservation). While not very effective in terms of designing policy, these conferences were essential in fostering a global dialogue, in raising public awareness, and in providing the platform on which the global civil society could move to the forefront of the policy debate. Therefore, stimulating the consolidation of this communication-based public sphere is one key mechanism with which states and international institutions can engage with the demands and projects of the global civil society. This can take place by stimulating dialogue regarding specific initiatives and recording, on an ongoing basis, the contributions of this dialogue so that it can inform policy making in the international arena. To harness the power of the world's public opinion through global media and Internet networks is the most effective form of broadening political participation on a global scale, by inducing a fruitful, synergistic connection between the government-based international institutions and the global civil society. This multimodal communication space is what constitutes the new global public sphere.

Conclusion: public diplomacy and the global public sphere

Public diplomacy is not propaganda. And it is not government diplomacy. We do not need to use a new concept to designate the traditional practices of diplomacy. Public diplomacy is the diplomacy of the public, that is, the projection in the international arena of the values and ideas of the public. The public is not the government because it is not formalized in the institutions of the state. By *the public*, we usually mean what is common to a given social organization that transcends the private. The private is the domain of self-defined interests and values, while the public is the domain of the shared interests and values (Dewey 1954). The implicit project behind the idea of public diplomacy is not to assert the power of a state or of a social actor in the form of "soft power." It is, instead, to harness the dialogue between different social collectives and their cultures in the hope of sharing meaning and understanding. The aim of the practice of public diplomacy is not to convince but to communicate, not to declare but to listen. Public diplomacy seeks to build a public sphere in which diverse voices can be heard in spite of their various origins, distinct values, and often contradictory interests. The goal of public diplomacy, in contrast to government diplomacy, is not to assert power or to negotiate a rearrangement of power relationships. It is to induce a communication space in which a new, common language could emerge as a precondition for diplomacy, so that when the time for diplomacy comes, it reflects not only interests and power making but also meaning and sharing. In this sense, public diplomacy intervenes in the global space equivalent to what has been traditionally conceived as the public sphere in the national system. It is a terrain of cultural engagement in which ideational materials are produced and confronted by various social actors, creating the conditions under which different projects can be channeled by the global civil society and the political institutions of global governance toward an informed process of decision making that respects the differences and weighs policy alternatives.

Because we live in a globalized, interdependent world, the space of political codecision is necessarily global. And the choice that we face is either to construct the global political system as an expression of power relationships without cultural mediation or else to develop a global public sphere around the global networks of communication, from which the public debate could inform the emergence of a new form of consensual global governance. If the choice is the latter, public diplomacy, understood as networked communication and shared meaning, becomes a decisive tool for the attainment of a sustainable world order.

References

Anheier, Helmut, Marlies Glasius, and Mary Kaldor, eds. 2004. *Global civil society 2004/5*. London: Sage.

Arsenault, Amelia, 2007. The international crisis of legitimacy. Unpublished working paper.

Arsenault, Amelia, and Manuel Castells. Forthcoming. Structure and dynamics of global multimedia business networks. *International Journal of Communication*.

Barber, Benjamin R. 1995. *Jihad vs. McWorld*. New York: Times Books.

Bauman, Zygmunt. 1999. *In search of politics*. Stanford, CA: Stanford University Press.

Beck, Ulrich. 2000. *What is globalization?* Malden, MA: Polity.

——— . 2006. *Power in the global age*. Cambridge, UK: Polity.

Bennett, W. Lance. 2004. Global media and politics: Transnational communication regimes and civic cultures. *Annual Review of Political Science* 7 (1): 125–48.

Calderón, G., Fernando, ed. 2003. *Es sostenible la globalización en América Latina?* Santiago, Chile: Fondo de Cultura Económica PNUD-Bolivia.

Caputo, Dante, ed. 2004. *La democracia en America Latina*. Pograma de Naciones Unidas para el Desarrollo. Buenos Aires, Argentina: Aguilar, Altea, Alfaguara.

Cardoso, Gustavo. 2006. *The media in the network society*. Lisbon, Portugal: Center for Research and Studies in Sociology.

Castells, Manuel. 1996. *The rise of the network society*. Oxford, UK: Blackwell.

——— , ed. 2004a. *The network society: A cross-cultural perspective*. Northampton, MA: Edward Elgar.

——— . 2004b. *The power of identity*. Malden, MA: Blackwell.

——— . 2007. Communication, power and counter-power in the network society. *International Journal of Communication* 1:238–66.

Castells, Manuel, Mireia Fernandez-Ardevol, Jack Linchuan Qui, and Araba Sey. 2006. *Mobile communication and society: A global perspective*. Cambridge, MA: MIT Press.

Castells, Manuel, Shujiro Yazawa, and Emma Kiselyova. 1996. Insurgents against the new global order: A comparative analysis of Mexico's Zapatistas, the American militia, and Japan's Aum Shinrikyo. *Berkeley Journal of Sociology* 40:21–59.

Catterberg, Gabriela, and Alejandro Moreno. 2005. The individual bases of political trust: Trends in new and established democracies. *International Journal of Public Opinion Research* 18 (1): 31–48.

Chester, Jeff. 2007. *Digital destiny. New media and the future of democracy*. New York: New Press.

Costanza-Chock, Sasha. 2006. *Analytical note: Horizontal communication and social movements*. Los Angeles: Annenberg School of Communication.

Dahlgren, Peter. 2005. The Internet, public spheres, and political communication: Dispersion and deliberation. *Political Communication* 22:147–62.

Dalton, Russell J. 2005. The social transformation of trust in government. *International Review of Sociology* 15 (1): 133–54.

——— . 2006. *Citizen politics: Public opinion and political parties in advanced industrial democracies*. Washington, DC: CQ Press.

Dean, Jodi, Jon W. Anderson, and Geert Lovink, eds. 2006. *Reformatting politics: Information technology and global civil society*. New York: Routledge.

Dewey, John. 1954. *The public and its problems*. Chicago: Swallow Press.

El-Nawawy, Mohammed, and Adel Iskander. 2002. *Al-jazeera: How the free Arab news network scooped the world and changed the Middle East*. Cambridge, MA: Westview.

Forsythe, David P. 2000. *Human rights in international relations*. Cambridge: Cambridge University Press.

Gallup International. 2006. The voice of the people. International survey conducted for the World Economic Forum. http://www.gallup-international.com/.

Giddens, Anthony. 1979. *Central problems in social theory: Action, structure, and contradiction in social analysis*. Berkeley: University of California Press.

Giddens, Anthony, and Will Hutton. 2000. *On the edge: Living with global capitalism*. London: Jonathan Cape.

Gilbert, Neil. 2002. *Transformation of the welfare state: The silent surrender of public responsibility*. Oxford: Oxford University Press.

Gillmor, Dan. 2004. *We the media. Grassroots journalism by the people for the people*. Sebastopol, CA: O'Reilly.

Glasius, Marlies, Mary Kaldor, and Helmut Anheier, eds. 2005. *Global civil society 2005/6*. London: Sage.

Grundmann, Reiner. 2001. *Transnational environmental policy: Reconstructing ozone*. London: Routledge.

Guidry, John A., Michael D. Kennedy, and Mayer N. Zald. 2000. *Globalizations and social movements: Culture, power, and the transnational public sphere*. Ann Arbor: University of Michigan Press.

Habermas, Jürgen. 1976. *Legitimation crisis*. London: Heinemann Educational Books.

———. 1989. *The structural transformation of the public sphere*. Cambridge, UK: Polity.

———. 1996. *Between facts and norms: Contributions to a discourse theory of law and democracy*. Cambridge, MA: MIT Press.

———. 1998. *Die postnationale konstellation: Politische essays*. Frankfurt am Main, Germany: Suhrkamp.

Held, David. 2004. *Global covenant: The social democratic alternative to the Washington consensus*. Malden, MA: Polity.

Held, David, and Ayse Kaya. 2006. *Global inequality: Patterns and explanations*. Cambridge, UK: Polity.

Held, David, and Anthony G. McGrew, eds. 2007. *Globalization theory: Approaches and controversies*. London: Polity.

Held, David, Anthony G. McGrew, David Goldblatt, and Jonathan Perraton, eds. 1999. *Global transformations: Politics, economics and culture*. Cambridge, UK: Polity.

Jacquet, Pierre, Jean Pisani-Ferry, and Laurence Tubiana, eds. 2002. *Gouvernance mondiale*. Paris: Documentation Française.

Juris, Jeffrey. 2004. Networked social movements: The movement against corporate globalization. In *The network society: A cross-cultural perspective*, ed. Manuel Castells, 341–62. Cheltenham, UK: Edward Elgar.

———. Forthcoming. *Networking futures: The movements against corporate globalization*. Durham, NC: Duke University Press.

Kaldor, Mary. 2003. *Global civil society: An answer to war*. Malden, MA: Polity.

Kaldor, Mary, Helmut Anheier, and Marlies Glasius, eds. 2006. *Global civil society 2006/7*. London: Sage.

Keck, Margaret E., and Kathryn Sikkink. 1998. *Activists beyond borders: Advocacy networks in international politics*. Ithaca, NY: Cornell University Press.

Keohane, Robert O. 2002. *Power and governance in a partially globalized world*. London: Routledge.

Low, Setha M., and Neil Smith, eds. 2006. *The politics of public space*. New York: Routledge.

Lull, James. 2007. *Culture-on-demand: Communication in a crisis world*. Malden, MA: Blackwell.

Mann, Michael. 1986. *The sources of social power*, vol. I, *A history of power from the beginning to A.D. 1760*. Cambridge: Cambridge University Press.

———. 1993. *The sources of social power*, vol. II, *The rise of classes and nation-states, 1760–1914*. Cambridge: Cambridge University Press.

McChesney, Robert Waterman. 2007. *Communication revolution: Critical junctures and the future of media*. New York: New Press.

Mydans, Seth. 2007. Myanmar comes face to face with a technology revolution. *International Herald Tribune*, October 3.

Nye, Joseph S. 2002. *The paradox of American power: Why the world's only superpower can't go it alone*. New York: Oxford University Press.

Nye, Joseph S., and John D. Donahue, eds. 2000. *Governance in a globalizing world*. Washington, DC: Brookings Institution Press.

Paterson, Chris A., and Annabelle Sreberny, eds. 2004. *International news in the 21st Century*. Eastleigh, UK: University of Luton Press.

Price, Monroe E. 2002. *Media and sovereignty: The global information revolution and its challenge to state power*. Cambridge, MA: MIT Press.

Putnam, Robert D. 2000. *Bowling alone: The collapse and revival of American community*. New York: Simon & Schuster.

Sassen, Saskia. 2006. *Territory, authority, rights: From medieval to global assemblages*. Princeton, NJ: Princeton University Press.

Soros, George. 2006. *The age of fallibility: The consequences of the war on terror*. New York: Public Affairs.

Stewart, Angus. 2001. *Theories of power and domination: The politics of empowerment in late modernity*. London: Sage.

Thompson, John B. 2000. *Political scandal: Power and visibility in the media age*. Cambridge, UK: Polity.

Tremayne, Mark, ed. 2007. *Blogging, citizenship, and the future of media*. London: Routledge.

Volkmer, Ingrid. 1999. *News in the global sphere: A study of CNN and its impact on global communication*. Eastleigh, UK: University of Luton Press.

———. 2003. The global network society and the global public sphere. *Journal of Development* 46 (4): 9–16.

Chapter 3

Eli Noam

OVERCOMING THE THREE DIGITAL DIVIDES

Introduction

WE FIND OURSELVES TODAY at one of those great divides of economic history, where we can either go forward into the unknown, or go back, with a sigh of relief, to familiar territory. The new economy – dot-coms, newstyle telecom entrants, new media companies, e-commerce sites etc. – has become an old-style bust. The adults are back in charge. Legacy is in. Balance sheets are in. Blue chips are in. We need not listen anymore to the purveyors of hype, about how bits play by different business rules than atoms, how the silicon economy is different from the carbon one, and how a P/E ratio need not have any E that stands for earnings, as long as that e- stands instead for electronic.

Yet, it would be tragic if we let the pendulum swing too far, or use this breathing space for smug self-satisfaction rather than regrouping, retooling and re-planning. The black ships challenging the old economy may have retreated over the horizon, but they will be back. No temporary slow-down should obscure the fact that we have just gone through something very fundamental.

With Internet connectivity progressing at a dizzying rate, the focus of attention has shifted to those left behind. The short-hand word for this concern is the 'digital divide'. Underlying virtually every discussion about this digital divide in Internet connectivity is the implicit assumption that such a divide is a bad thing, requiring us to 'do something'. But maybe we should first pause for a moment and understand the implications of ending this divide. If we do that, we might end up changing our perspective on Internet policy in an important way: away from a focus on *Internet connectivity*, and towards the creation of *e-commerce*.

For a number of years US administrations have been talking prominently about the digital divide. However, if one looks at the US government's own numbers, one can reach a more hopeful conclusion. With present trends continuing, in a few years Internet connectivity will be near universal in rich countries, like electricity or television. A major reason is that the access mechanisms to the Internet will have changed and become user-friendly or user-independent. The Internet will soon be liberated from the complex gateway bottleneck of the personal computer, arguably the least friendly consumer mass product ever made.

There will be many other gateways to the Internet, such as regular phones or TV sets. Therefore, for the rich world the universality of narrowband Internet connectivity will not be an issue.

It is most likely that an Internet differentiation will emerge along dimensions of *quality*. High-speed broadband Internet access requires an upgrade of the infrastructure – whether telecom, cable or wireless – which must be recovered through higher prices. Income, location and demand will be factors for bandwidth consumption. Broadband will therefore be the digital divide issue for wealthy countries. Yet, one cannot expect that high-speed Internet access (most likely used by consumers primarily for video applications) would command the same societal priority as the basic type of Internet service.

But the transformation in rich countries of the divide into a gentle slope does not mean that the issue will not last and persist for the poor countries of the developing world. And in an interdependent world this becomes a problem not just for the South, but also for the North, because such a gap will inevitably lead to international conflict.

In talking about the Internet for poor countries, it is easy to feel like a modern-day Marie Antoinette. Let them eat laptops. Of course the Internet is important. But is it really a priority? The answer is yes, because tomorrow's problems originate in today's actions and omissions. There is no luxury to solve other problems first. The world does not stand still and wait.

Spain and Portugal, the first European colonisers of the New World, were the world's leaders in shipping, which was the primary communications technology in the sixteenth and seventeenth centuries. They had the best vessels, navigation equipment, maps, seafaring skills and weapons. This combination catapulted the Iberian region to prosperity. And yet, by the eighteenth century, these countries had fallen behind England in industrial hardware and scientific software. They missed the next revolution, and centuries later have yet to catch up.

Today we are at the beginning of another revolution, driven by the Internet, and the question is: what is the cost of falling behind this time?

It is important to distinguish between three kinds of gap. The first gap is that of *telecommunications connectivity*. This gap is being closed by investment in infrastructure and by liberalising policy reform. In consequence, the telephone penetration of the developing countries has been improving. Governments have been making telecom connectivity a priority. Overcoming this gap is therefore something that engineers, investors and governments now know how to do. But progress in telecom connectivity, difficult as it may be, will prove to be the easy part.

The second type of gap is that of *Internet access*. In 2000, only 3% of Internet computer hosts were domiciled in non-OECD countries. Telecom and Internet are related, of course. Internet usage is much more expensive in developing countries, both relative to income and in absolute terms. For an ISP in Argentina, to lease a T-1 equivalent capacity ($\sim$ 1.5 Mbps) line from a phone company cost, in 1999, fifty times as much as it did in the US. Of course, progress is being made in Internet connectivity, too. For Latin America, growth exceeds 50% annually. But closing this gap, too, will prove to be, relatively speaking, an easy task. In fact, it is easier to overcome this gap than the one in telecom infrastructure. Once telephone lines exist, it is not very difficult to connect a computer or a simple Internet device to them. Specific policies to encourage Internet usage include to establish flat-rate telecom pricing on local calls; to accept widespread use of IP telephony; to create public Internet access points such as kiosks at public places, government departments or post office; and to use e-mail for some government business with citizens.

Internet connectivity does not take care of the third and critical gap, which is that of *e-commerce*. In fact, progress in overcoming the first and second gaps may exacerbate the third gap. Today, developing countries account for only 5% of world commercial websites and receive only 2.4% of world Internet commerce revenues. In contrast, twelve countries will account for almost 85 percent of e-commerce and eight countries will account for 80% of e-content.

To understand why this is so, let us make three observations about the global dynamics of e-transactions:

1.   the price of international transmission is dropping rapidly;
2.   domestic internet penetration is increasing rapidly; and
3.   most e-commerce applications have strong economies of scale.

Low-cost global transmission leads to a large rise in electronic transactions with consequences for business. Of course, traditional ways of doing business will not disappear, just as the mom-and-pop store did not vanish when supermarkets emerged. But the energy and dynamism will be in electronic modes of commerce. And here, US firms will be the most successful. They will be technologically at the leading edge, with risk capital at their disposal, with the advantage of being an early entrant and having a large home market. Once a firm establishes a successful model for the US market, invests the fixed costs, and secures nearly non-existent transmission prices, there is no reason to stop at the border.

The implications are that e-commerce will be dominated by firms from the US and other electronically advanced countries. Closing the first two gaps therefore exacerbates the third gap by creating the highways and instrumentalities for rich countries to sell in poor countries.

Of course, it is not purely a one-way street. The Internet also provides poor countries with opportunities to participate and share information. We have all heard stories about how a local craftsman in a remote village can now access the world market for his woodcarvings. True, for certain types of product marketing becomes easier. But for most mass products, the complexities of sophisticated e-commerce sites are great. These complexities are greater still for information products and services and will be even greater in a broadband internet environment where the production costs of attractive e-sites are high.

What counts is not absolute but relative cost reductions, relative advantage of e-commerce go to advanced countries. One lesson we have learned the hard way is that it is expensive to do e-commerce well. E-commerce operations are difficult. They are vastly more involved than running a website and a shopping cart. Many systems need to be in place and integrated. Some elements needed are supply chain EDI (electronic data interchange), payment systems, integration with financial institutions, fulfilment systems, customer data mining, production, customisation, community creation and the creation of consumer lock-in by additional features. Intermediaries need to be reshaped. Processes are accelerated domestically and internationally, at lightning speed, great reliability, easy scalability, and flexibility of configuration.

What are some of the implications?

Instead of being that frictionless competitive capitalism rhapsodised about by many people, many parts of the new economy will actually be a fortress of market power. Economies of scale are returning. On the supply side, the fixed costs of e-commerce operations tend to be high, but the variable cost of spreading the service to the entire world is relatively low – the classic attributes of a 'natural' monopoly. On the demand side, there are 'positive network externalities' of having large user communities. Put these three things together – high fixed costs, low marginal costs and network externalities – and there are real advantages to being large.

All of this is still true for the emerging broadband Internet. The costs for consumer e-commerce sites will rise considerably. Text and still images will not be sufficient in a competitive environment and expensive video and multimedia will be required.

This low share has been disturbing. For several centuries, culture flowed largely in one direction: out of Europe, and to the colonies and the rest of the world. Then, after World War I, the flow reversed direction for the young medium of film. Around the world, audiences flocked to Hollywood movies. European cultural elites, shocked at the loss of control over their publics, led a counter-charge. They promoted protectionism to support centuries-old national cultures against a few vaudeville theatre promoters who had pitched their tents in Hollywood. But, despite seven decades of effort, this challenge remains.

And now, a new medium is knocking – television over the internet – and the question is what will enter when the door is opened. Will it be a multicultural richness of many national sources or will it be more Hollywood?

The knee-jerk response to this question is to invoke Internet platitudes. Anybody can enter, you can't tell a dog on the Internet, a bit is a bit, silicon economics are different from carbon economics, Internet penetration is higher in Finland than in the US, etc. It is as if the Internet community, staunchly internationalist and multicultural by outlook and background, does not want to face the very question of whether it contributes to the further ascendancy of US mass culture.

For electronic media, transmission technology is destiny: it affects format, content and economics. It used to be expensive to move information; now it is cheap. We can do old things in new ways, new things in old ways, and new things in new ways.

So now we are in the midst of an historic move: from the *kilobit* stages of individualised communications to the *megabit* stage, and within the foreseeable future, to the *gigabit* stage. The implications of this transition are as great as the change from a horse-and-cart system and railroads to automobiles and airplanes had been in the twentieth century.

Let us analyse the relative costs of audio-visual media. Each form of delivery has its specific cost characteristics, which have implications. These calculations will be order-of-magnitude only.

Internet TV

The cost of Internet TV content is hard to estimate. It includes a lot of low-budget, experimental, volunteer TV programmes. There is a significant need to keep costs down, especially in the early stages. At the same time, the whole point of Internet TV is to be more than standard, linear TV. The whole point is interactivity, multimedia and new creation. The interactivity and multimedia aspects of the medium require additional features beyond straight video. And, after an initial amateur period, competition will soon be fierce for audiences, and commercial providers of Internet TV will have to offer quality content. Therefore, once broadband Internet is available to most households and once people will consider it nightly among their entertainment options, it cannot possibly be produced cheaply.

Hence, the programme cost of original content that is not merely the replay or retransmission of traditional video will be no lower than that of linear cable TV, and will more likely be higher. Distribution costs are 1.85 m¢ per second and user.[1] This is forty times higher than the distribution cost per cable channel. The reason is that individualisation requires significantly larger transmission resources. A similar disadvantage exists in another synchronous mass-audience medium, broadcast TV, where the ratio is 1:27. Hence, Internet TV can function economically only as a premium medium or a specialised medium. This defines several types of application.

The use of the Internet purely as a distribution medium

Internet TV for video-on-demand (VOD)

Delivery of films, at the very top of the distribution chain, occurs immediately after cinema distribution and maybe even ahead of it (there is probably no better way to generate a worldwide buzz for a movie than distribution of it through the Internet). It is more expensive to distribute than cable and TV, but viewers can be charged more, in a more differentiated way.

Specialised programmes

Thin and specialised audiences that would not be served by synchronous TV would be amenable to specialised programmes. For example, those desiring to watch TV programmes in Hungarian, or soccer matches of their home team in Stockholm while they are vacationing in Spain, or on specialised topics would be well served by Internet TV.

Office viewing

Perhaps the most popular use of Internet TV might be by office workers who cannot watch broadcast or cable TV. The economics of all three types of such content delivery depends on the size and willingness-to-pay of such audiences. Content would often be already produced – e.g. Hungarian soccer on TV – and would reach wider audiences. Only if such audiences become a significant factor are they likely to affect the content itself and its production budget.

The use of the Internet as a storage medium: archived programmes

Old video and film become accessible by viewers as they link to servers that store them. The content costs for such programmes have already been incurred. Archive access would benefit, in particular, documentaries, because they tend to depreciate more slowly than most entertainment programmes.

Use of the Internet as an interactive medium

Interactive content supplementary to one-way distribution

Here, a two-way channel is added to a one-way broadcast programme, enabling the viewer to obtain additional information about the main programme, or, more likely, to engage in commercial transactions.

Interactivity and multimedia applications

This includes using the medium in ways that cannot be done over regular, one-way TV. This content type is the main innovative aspect of Internet TV, and should be our main focus. It enables new genres of programmes rather than merely a more flexible access to traditional programmes. It is, however, also by far the most expensive content to produce, both because it cannot fall back on existing content, and because it requires complex designs and software programming.

Furthermore, it is the major form of content that can prevail economically due to its uniqueness, against established and upgraded channels such as those of cable TV. This will be developed further now.

Basic economics drives applications

Our previous analysis showed that the cost advantages of cable-style distribution over Internet-style distribution are significant, by a factor of about forty. The increased efficiency and declining cost of fibre does not mean that all pipes will become individualised. This is a common mistake made by people who argue that transmission is becoming cheap. It drops just as much for cable TV distribution. The relative cost of shared (synchronous) transmission is still much lower than that of non-shared, asynchronous transmission. At best, the two will coexist, with the individualised Internet channels providing the premium offerings. At worst, Internet TV will never become competitive enough to be a mass medium and will remain a niche offering.

What the drop in cost means, however, is that the impact of distance becomes much less and that both synchronous and asynchronous networks can be designed for national and global distribution rather than for local distribution. This means that terrestrial TV loses the protection of distance, and that satellite and cable TV lose the protection of limited spectrum on licensing.

From the numbers it is quite clear that one would not want to use Internet TV for regular video content distribution. For that purpose, cable TV and its fibre digital variants will be much cheaper. Internet TV's market is for applications that go beyond regular TV: distant, specialised, archived, interactive, asynchronous, linked, multimedia.

To produce such interactive content is expensive. It requires creativity, lots of programmers, and significant alpha and beta testing, and many new versions. It might be a bit like *Dungeons and Dragons* meets *Baywatch* meets *Survivor*. It also exhibits strong economies of scale on the content production side, and network externalities on the demand side. Both favour content providers that can come up with big budgets, diversify risk, distribute also over other multiple platforms, create product tie-ins, and establish global user communities.

Even for non-premium programme, such as creative small productions, or sex-shows and games – where the absolute production costs are lower, the economic advantages of a large user base still apply.

And these requirements will favour US companies when Internet TV emerges as a serious offering. The US has a large Internet community, significant hardware and software entrepreneurial energy barely contained by the recent economic downturn, a financial system that provides risk capital, big content-producing companies with worldwide distribution and with experience in reaching popular audiences, talent in content creativity and technology from all over the world, efficient geographic clusters in production and technology, the cultural prowess of the world's superpower, language, a diverse culture, and a university system that generates technology and entrepreneurship. These factors are also available elsewhere, but probably nowhere else in such a combination. On the other hand, the US lacks the supportive mechanism of public TV that exists in Europe and Japan.

Thus, the medium of Internet TV combines the strengths of the US economy and society in entertainment content, Internet, and e-transactions. Add to that economies of scale, and there is nothing on the horizon that can match it. And, therefore, Internet TV will be strongly American. Participants from other countries will also be players, but most likely either domestically without much global reach, or global players who will offer basically American-style content to the world, like sitcoms and the Italian 'spaghetti westerns' of the past.

The Internet is a revolution, and it is a characteristic of revolutions that they create many losers – banks will be threatened by electronic global financial institutions; universities will find their students migrating to distance education; TV broadcasters will be bypassed by global Hollywood video servers; etc. Most institutions will be losing the protection of distance, and will be exposed to world markets.

It is characteristic of losers, especially if they are domestically still large and powerful, to seek protection through the political sphere. And, therefore, there will be an inevitable global political backlash against e-commerce. This is likely to take the form of restrictions, by countries on the wrong side of the e-commerce gap. And there will be a strong likelihood for international cyber-trade wars.

Centuries ago, in Spain, the powers resisting the industrial revolution and its reshaping of domestic power were the Church, the State, and agricultural economic interests. They won out, and Spain was slowed on the road to industrialisation. A similar scenario will play itself out as we enter the digital economy, and as the losers begin to organise themselves.

The main alternative to future conflicts over cyber-trade and the best remedy for the gap in e-commerce is for developing countries to create progress in e-commerce that makes the electronic highways into two-way routes. But what can a developing country do, concretely? This is much more difficult than catching up with telecom densities, because it is a question of general societal modernisation, not just of an infrastructure construction programme.

There is no single strategy, no silver bullet. But here are several suggested elements.

1. Telecom policy of entry and investment based on market forces and competition.
2. Use the government as the lead user, to help create domestic critical mass and experts. The US military had been successful in getting the Internet started initially. Government operations such as procurement should move to the web. This would create transparency, reduce procurement costs, and force domestic suppliers to move to electronic marketing. Governments could also provide some services electronic-ally, such as the filing of forms and applications, or information on subjects such as health, education, taxes and agriculture.
3. Be prepared to ignore domestic consumer markets. It takes too much time to develop them. The focus should instead be on the global market, mostly business-to-business. The domestic consumer market is relatively small, but the global internet market is huge and open. The creation of free trade zones for e-commerce is one concrete step in that direction.
4. Develop niche markets. Leverage cultural proximity. Examples could include:

    - regional hub: Tunisia for North Africa;
    - language: Brazil for Portuguese speakers;
    - religion: Saudi Arabia for Moslems; and
    - economics: Bahrain for the oil industry.

5. Reform the legal system to make e-transactions possible. The recognition of digital signatures is an example. Adapt commercial codes to online environments and update rules applying to liability, contract, privacy and security issues. Examples include the UNCITRAL Model Law (1996), and the ITU EC-DC project. It is also essential to combat the fraud, illegal operations and piracy that undercut the emergence of a domestic industry.
6. Strengthen the physical delivery infrastructure and investments in it. One cannot sell abroad if one cannot ship quickly. This is one of the secrets of Singapore's success. This includes the physical delivery infrastructure of harbours, airports and export facilities.

7. Strengthen the investment climate. Provide tax incentives for e-commerce and e-exports, offer low international telecom rates, support micro-credit institutions, encourage local entrepreneurship and cooperatives, and support the venture capital industry and incubators.
8. Support technological education. Investments are important, but not as important as IT skills and a new economy mindset. There are 3.8 R&D scientists and technicians per 1,000 people in developed countries and only 0.4% per 1,000 in developing countries.
9. Create wealth incentives. Permit e-commerce entrepreneurs to become rich through the Internet, thereby fuelling the emergence of local start-ups.
10. Encourage foreign investments.
11. Provide back-office functions to major e-commerce sites as a way to establish experience. India and Jamaica are examples.

Most well-informed people understand the importance of e-commerce. But they often do not have a sense of urgency. Right now, the foundations are being laid for a great new economic system and for a new generation of business empires. Even if less developed countries cannot be expected to be among the leaders, there are enough emerging countries and striving firms that could be suppliers and not only buyers. India, for example, may be a poor country by most measures, yet it could become an e-commerce participant beyond its growing Internet technology role.

Success in e-commerce means participation in modernisation, but also participation in the disruptions brought about by modernisation. The Internet will lead to less stability, more fragmentation and less consensus. But the alternative is much less palatable. Failure to participate in global e-commerce means fundamental long-term economic stagnation.

Different countries are affected differently, depending on, among other things, their economic mix. The US had a troubled industrial sector, and the new economy was one way to resume growth. US society is also capable of change, being perhaps strongest in situations of accelerating change – 'second derivative' situations. In contrast, Europe and Japan had stronger old economies, and are stronger in managing steady growth – 'first derivative' economies. And less developed countries had, for a multitude of reasons, the greatest difficulties in changing to new economy activities, primarily because these require substantial societal modernisation and infrastructure investments.

This is then the challenge to developing countries. To get moving, to move beyond the first gap, that of telecommunications, by overcoming the traditional policy squabbles about the rights of entrants and the privileges of incumbents – issues that will seem in a few years quite trivial – and to close the second gap, that of the Internet. They should also deal aggressively with the closing of the e-commerce gap, because it is the real, critical and fundamental threat – as well as a major opportunity – to them and a way to improve economic relations around the world.

Note

1   Based on US $40/mo for a 1 Mbps internet channel.

Chapter 4

Marc Raboy

THE WSIS AS A POLITICAL SPACE IN GLOBAL MEDIA GOVERNANCE

We are firmly convinced that we are collectively entering a new era of enormous potential, that of the Information Society and expanded human communication. In this emerging society, information and knowledge can be produced, exchanged, shared and communicated through all the networks of the world. All individuals can soon, if we take the necessary actions, together build a new Information Society based on shared knowledge and founded on global solidarity and a better mutual understanding between peoples and nations. We trust that these measures will open the way to the future development of a true knowledge society. (WSIS, 2003a, art. 67)

WELL, MAYBE NOT QUITE, but this extract from the final declaration of the World Summit on the Information Society (WSIS) does indicate something about the flights of rhetoric that have accompanied that event.

The first phase of the WSIS, which concluded in Geneva in December 2003, highlighted a range of questions about issues and process that will characterize communication governance well into the twenty-first century. Without having resolved them, it indicates a new paradigm for global governance, in which information and communication issues are central, and in which new actors, particularly those that can be characterized under a general rubric of global civil society, will be increasingly involved.[1] This is good news for democracy even if it must be taken with a large pinch of salt.

The WSIS has opened a new phase in global communication governance and global governance generally. Through a particular mix of official and parallel activities, the process identified the problematic issues in global communication, indicated the range of views on how to deal with them, provided various blueprints of what should and could be possible in the way of solutions, and gingerly explored ways of dealing with these questions in the future. This is typical of the emerging new paradigm in communication governance.

What authorizes such an upbeat assessment? Basically this: the global governance environment in communication (as in much everything else) is based on the interaction and interdependence of a wide array of actors and policy venues. Needless to say, power is not equally distributed among actors, and some sites of decision making are more important than others. National governments still wield tremendous leverage both on the territories they govern and as the only legally authorized participants in international deliberations. Here again, the disparities are enormous but in all cases national sovereignty is no longer absolute. Multilateral bodies, transnational corporations, and international treaties powerfully constrain the role of every nation-state. Global governance is increasingly referred to as a multi-stakeholder process. The WSIS experience has transformed this framework most notably by sanctifying the place of global civil society as an organized force in this process.

The WSIS is the third attempt within the UN system to deal with information and communication issues on a global scale. In the optimistic climate of the post-war era, the Universal Declaration on Human Rights spelled out, in 1948, what the great democratic revolutions of the eighteenth century had struggled to achieve: that the capacity to seek, receive and impart information is a basic human right. In the 1970s, in the post-colonial climate of the Cold War, the non-aligned nations sparked a debate on a 'new world information and communication order' (NWICO), drawing attention to such questions as the inequalities in North–South information flow, the cultural and economic bias of technology and the lack of communication infrastructure in the so-called Third World. The year 1948 was a moment of consensus, but the debates of the 1970s were fraught with conflict. Both had in common, however, an exclusive reliance on states and governments as the only legitimate political actors.

The WSIS promised to be different. Conceived and launched in 1998, the WSIS arrived in a context marked by buzzwords such as technological convergence and globalization. The politics of the WSIS was marked not only by consensus and conflict among the world's governments but also by a larger politics of definition, pitting governments against non-governmental actors, namely NGOs and other civil society associations. In the immediate wake of the Geneva phase of the WSIS, it is a commonplace among most observers that it was civil society that kept the debate on track, re-introduced the crucial elements left unresolved or unrealized in 1948 and the 1970s, and organized itself responsibly to put forward a vision truly reflective of the interests of the world community. If civil society had not reared its difficult head at the WSIS, it would have had to be invented.

The end of the first phase of the WSIS in Geneva on 12 December 2003 marked the end of a long process that began five years earlier, at a plenipotentiary conference of the International Telecommunication Union (ITU). Huge efforts were invested in this undertaking. The different parties—civil society, private sector, governments and intergovernmental organizations—all battled to influence the results according to their own respective visions and, especially, interests.

With more than 11,000 registered participants, the WSIS fit into the mould of recent UN summits. But this was the first world summit to tackle issues of communication policy and governance. The spread of digital technologies—which summit organizers characterized as a 'revolution'[2]—and its social, political, economic and cultural impacts, were sufficiently important for the ITU to plunge into organizing the summit on a grand scale.

Certain governments found themselves in the midst of controversies. Hostile to the participation of civil society, countries such as Pakistan, Iran, Russia and China found themselves at odds with the liberal democracies. China notably struggled (ultimately in vain) to exclude any reference to media and human rights from the official texts. Attempts were made to subordinate the accepted universal right to freedom of expression to that of national governments to exercise sovereignty in this area. The United States insisted on making information security a central point.

Intellectual property rights pitted certain developing countries such as Brazil and India against the leading industrial economies. So did the question of funding the bridging of the digital divide. Senegalese President Abdoulaye Wade vigorously promoted the idea of a 'Digital Solidarity Fund' which captured the imagination of participants (aided by a slick television advertising campaign on CNN Europe during the week of the summit) but did not convince the governments that would be called upon to pay. The Senegalese plan for a fund based on an automatic check-off on sales of ICT products rebuffed the governments of the United States, the European Union, Canada and Japan. A compromise emerged in favour of a voluntary plan, and the issue was referred to the second phase of the summit slated for Tunis in 2005.[3]

In general, then, there is no clear funding mechanism provided for the proposals contained in the WSIS Declaration of Principles and Plan of Action. This is clearly a failure and evidence of a flagrant lack of political will on the part of governments to take the necessary steps towards a genuine implantation of the principles adopted by the summit. With the president of the summit Preparatory Committee, Adama Samassékou, having himself declared that 'the funding of concrete actions will be the first measure of success of the Summit' (ATS, 2003), this reversal is even more significant with respect to the expectations raised by the WSIS agenda.

The current regime of Internet governance was another issue seriously challenged by countries concerned about the US government's role as overseer of the Internet Corporation for Assigned Names and Numbers (ICANN). This complex question was also referred to Tunis. The summit mandated UN Secretary General Kofi Annan

> to set up a working group on Internet governance, in an open and inclusive process that ensures a mechanism for the full and active participation of governments, the private sector and civil society from both developing and developed countries, involving relevant intergovernmental and international organizations and forums, to investigate and make proposals for action, as appropriate, on the governance of Internet by 2005. (WSIS, 2003b, art. C6)

The first point of the task force's mandate is to come up with a working definition of Internet governance . . .[4]

Considering that the two issues considered critical by governments—Internet governance and the funding of the information society—were pushed off to Tunis, then clearly little was accomplished from a governmental point of view. But the summit seems nonetheless to have provided international diplomacy with a lexicon for speaking about the information society and a shopping list of issues it encompasses.

Beyond general principles and a minimalist Plan of Action, the official documents produced by the WSIS reflect a highly contested worldview. According to authors Marita Moll and Leslie Regan Shade (2004):

> The Draft Principles and Agenda for Action are extraordinarily ICT focused thus 'resuscitating a ruse reminiscent of the heights of the "dot com" folly: addition of prefix "e-" to any given area of human activity to cast it as an "ICT issue" (e-administration, e-learning and so on)'. This technocratic discourse, although not unusual given its predominance in other policy discussions on ICTs for development, lends itself to top-down decision making rather than collaborative processes. And, the focus on the digital divide supports industry imperatives that market forces are the only way to provide technological resources. This emphasis obscures important issues related to the social infrastructure, such as increasing educational resources in support of literacy, and even to providing viable physical resources in communities.
>
> Absent from the WSIS discourse are debates about whether or not ICTs are appropriate tools for development, a contemporary debate that has been

rehashed with the activities surrounding the DOT Force (Digital Opportunities Task Force), the G8 initiative to 'ameliorate the digital divide' in developing countries. As with the DOT Force, official WSIS discourse is relatively uncritical; as in previous debates on strengthening communication systems for developing countries, current discussions are concerned with the 'how and when to "connect" communities in the South instead of with the why, who, under what conditions, and with what implications'. And, similar to the DOT Force pronouncements, WSIS reveals its allegiance to the modernization paradigm, wherein technology is equated with development.

Steve Buckley (2003), president of the World Association of Community Radio Broadcasters (AMARC), picks up this critique of a technocentric utopia that is at the core of WSIS official discourse:

> It should be obvious to anyone living outside a fictional Internet utopia that the poor people need clean water more than they need fast connectivity even though access to good information can help make water clean.
>
> Others have argued compellingly that giving universal access to the Internet will cost a lot and accomplish little. Bill Gates, speaking in October 2000 at a Seattle conference on the 'digital dividend', famously argued that investment in health and literacy is more important for poor people than providing access to PCs and the Internet.
>
> Charles Kenny, an economist with the World Bank, has estimated that the worldwide subsidy needed for everyone living on $1 a day to get one hour of access a week might reach $75 billion—considerably more than the global total aid flows each year.

At this rate, the bridging of the digital divide seems unlikely, to say the least, in a world where global aid flow is dropping dramatically.[5]

Thus the WSIS does not provide the means for its ambitions; its principal official output is a text (composed of two documents, actually) destined to remain essentially unapplied. The second phase of the WSIS, in Tunis in November 2005, will be the occasion for noting the progress made since Geneva. Tunis will likely be for the WSIS what Johannesburg 2002 was for the Rio Summit on the environment: a moment to underscore the lack of concrete measures taken to move towards agreed-upon goals.

The real interest in the summit from a governance perspective lies in the result of civil society participation:

> Participation in WSIS has meant an enormous effort for civil society organizations, both in terms of human and financial resources, and many have not been able to participate, especially those from less developed countries. Despite these difficulties, we have produced numerous contributions, we have come up with concrete and diverse proposals. (Marzouki, 2003)[6]

The WSIS is the first UN summit where civil society was officially invited to be a participating partner—although understanding of what such 'partnership' might mean was highly contentious. Many saw this as a fabulous opportunity, and they were disappointed. But the rules and parameters of global governance have shifted as a result of the WSIS. Obviously, official decisions continue to be negotiated in intergovernmental structures, but the gains made by civil society will resonate. For the first time since the creation of the United

Nations, a formal structure was created for inclusion of civil society; the establishment of an official 'Civil Society Bureau' made up of representatives of civil society organizations participating in the summit creates a precedent in international relations. Table 4.1 shows the organizational structure of the WSIS.

The autonomous structures created by civil society participants themselves, meanwhile, form the basis of a new model of representation and legitimation of non-governmental input to global affairs. Importantly, civil society maintained a high degree of cohesiveness throughout the preparatory process and was able to mobilize and gather together disparate resources in order to produce strong and high-quality input reflecting a wide consensus. Culminating in the Civil Society Declaration entitled *Shaping Information Societies for Human Needs* (WSIS, 2003), the collaboration of dozens of disparate groups in this process remains one of the key successes of the WSIS. Table 4.2 shows the organization of civil society participation in the WSIS.

Civil society had to struggle hard to maintain a minimally acceptable degree of participation. Official meetings were open or closed according to the unilateral decision of government delegates, and the real impact of the numerous contributions of civil society

Table 4.1 The organizational structure of the WSIS

Official bodies

"High Level Summit Organizing Committee"
Chaired by the secretary-general of the International Telecommunication Union (ITU), coordinates UN input into the Summit.

Government Division	UN Agencies' Division	Private Sector Division	Civil Society Division
Secretariats for the respective partner groups taking part in the Summit, in charge of communication, facilitating participation, circulating position papers and ensuring that each partner's input is reflected in the Summit's official documents.			

Bureaus	
Intergovernment Bureau (created at Prepcom1)	Civil Society Bureau (created at Prepcom2)
Look after the logistics of participation and communication for the parties concerned.	

Unofficial bodies
(Entry points for non-government actors)

Coordinating Committee of Business Interlocutors (created prior to WSIS)	Civil Society Plenary (created at Prepcom1)
Gather input from members and produce common positions: spaces for discussion and exchange.	

Table 4.2 Organization of civil society participation in the WSIS

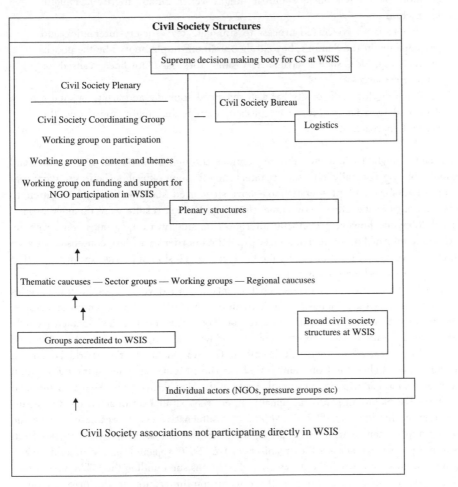

remained weak. An informal study undertaken in September 2003 by a volunteer group of researchers showed that 60 per cent of the proposals of civil society up to that time had been completely rejected, 15 per cent were sort of taken into account, and 25 per cent had made it in to the then-current working documents.[7]

As the summit approached, Bruce Girard and Seán Ó Siochrú (2003), of the Communication Rights in the Information Society (CRIS) campaign, made a rather severe assessment of the relative success of civil society participation. The promise of inclusion, loudly proclaimed by the event's organizers, was for the most part not realized:

> So while promises of a new type of summit were undoubtedly sincerely meant, the reality falls far short of these. Most of the hopes expressed at the Paris meetings were unfilled.

There is little or nothing in the way of new modalities for participation for civil society, and indeed existing modalities have not been optimised. The future holds, at best, further uncertainty.

No protocol has ever been issued outlining and confirming the transparency of the entire WSIS process, from Bureau to accreditation procedures.

Civil society has been offered no representation on the Bureau, though the creation of a Civil Society Bureau might yet facilitate more meaningful interaction.

There is no concerted process to stimulate civil society interaction and participation in the Summit, beyond the minimum implemented by the poorly funded CSD; ideas such as civil society 'animators' have not been realised for want of resources.

Funding for civil society has also remained sporadic and arbitrary, and a dedicated fund has yet to be established, though this might improve as the Summit approaches.

Civil society sought to influence the negotiations through both official intervention and informal lobbying. Formally, civil society intervened through official declarations, participation in roundtables and presentation of short structured statements upon invitation to official meetings of the official government plenary. Its best results were obtained around informal lobbying, however. Thematic intergovernmental working groups, for example, relied on the informal input of civil society expertise in order to achieve consensus between conflicting government positions—despite the formal exclusion of non-government participants from these working groups.

In order to achieve such results, civil society had to develop a sophisticated series of networking activities. Alongside the activities within its own autonomous structures, necessary for establishing positions and achieving consensus, civil society lobbied friendly government delegations and was thus able to influence the outcome in certain targeted areas. It also organized its own side events in Geneva, including the World Forum on Communication Rights, the Community Media Forum, Media Liberties in the Information Society, as well as participating in several events of the World Electronic Media Forum[8] and the ICT for Development platform.[9] Finally, an entirely parallel set of activities was organized under the heading of *WSIS? WE SEIZE!*,[10] an alternative event organized outside the summit complex, thus marking not only a geographic but also an ideological distance from the summit proper. Put simply, the organizers of *WE SEIZE!* rejected the social, political and economic premises on which the debates and discussions surrounding the WSIS were based. They proposed instead to re-imagine the role of communication in the organization of society.

All told, civil society maintained a high degree of presence within, alongside and outside the WSIS, through a series of structured and unstructured activities which led to a credible body of output as well as inclusion of many of its key ideas in the official texts.[11]

Nonetheless, through its critical engagement in the process, civil society actors maintained a critical distance from the official outcomes. As a collective entity, it ultimately ceased contributing to the official texts and concentrated instead on producing its own declaration.

Sally Burch (2004), who co-chaired the civil society working group on Content and Themes, summed up the view of an active participant observer in an article in *Media Development*, the journal of the World Association for Christian Communication, shortly following the summit:

LIVERPOOL JOHN MOORES UNIVERSITY

Routing	*3	

Ship To: UK 1858900

LIVERPOOL JOHN MOORES UNI
GROUND FLOOR,RM RF07, ACQ
MARYLAND STREET
LIVERPOOL
MERSEYSIDE
L1 9DE

Volume:
Edition:
Year: 2010
Pagination: xxiii, 590 p.
Size: 25 cm.

RUSH

ISBN	Qty	Sales Order
9780415444569	1	F 11602433 1
Customer P/O No		Cust P/O List
245654		24.99 GBP

Title: International communication :

Format: P (Paperback)
Author: Daya, Thussu
Publisher: Routledge
Fund: SCR1–2009
Location: NONE
Loan Type: NONE
Coutts CN: 7493009

Order Specific Instructions
R.LI, 1X7D, 2X21D,

COUTTS INFORMATION SERVICES LTD.:

Most CSOs (Civil society organizations) concur, nonetheless, that overall the official Declaration and Action Plan express tepid commitments and show feeble political will of governments to address the fundamental issues . . .

It took over a year for governments to agree to mention even the Universal Declaration of Human Rights (UDHR) as a basis for the Information Society. The full quote of Article 19, on freedom of expression, was also hotly debated, and only accepted by some countries when accompanied by a qualifying clause that could open the door to national exceptions.

The reference to 'the right to communicate', included in initial drafts of the Declaration, was subsequently eliminated from the official documents, as there was no consensus on its interpretation. For some, it implies universal access to telecommunications (and as such, interestingly, was supported by both ITU Secretary-General Yoshiu Utsumi and by Kofi Annan, UN Secretary-General). For others, such as the CRIS Campaign, it embraces the full range of existing rights associated with communication, but also implies the need to consecrate new rights, that are becoming necessary in the present communications context.

Some small advances were achieved by civil society at the WSIS in relation to a number of such issues, although many of them might be more accurately described as 'damage control', that is, avoiding inclusion of the most unacceptable language, which even so could not always be averted.

[. . .]

In summary, most actors in the WSIS process will be able to find language in the final documents that they can use as support for their agendas, and to leverage support from governments and international institutions. But many other issues are absent or inadequately dealt with and overall there is little coherence. The Civil Society Declaration is a much more coherent document that—while there is room for further development and refinement of the proposals—will be a reference point, not only for the next phase of the WSIS but also for many organizations concerned with these issues in other spheres.

So, despite its disappointment in the tangible outcomes—to be expected—civil society has already moved towards a new paradigm and has begun to articulate a new conception of society based on communication between human beings. It is not a question of building a more equitable information society, but of developing a communication society, reviewing structures of power and domination that are expressed and sustained through information and media structures.

Independently of the official outcome of the summit, the great achievement of civil society remains the great degree of coordination between the entities making it up, the development of networks, expertise and common projects, exchange of ideas and particular ways of doing things, as well as articulation of an alternative discourse within the respectable and visible framework of a high-level UN meeting.

The Civil Society Declaration adopted unanimously at the plenary session on 8 December 2003 is thus more than a political document outlining a set of principles; it is the concrete manifestation of a long process that could lead to a profound change in the ways in which non-government actors can influence international relations. It is an accomplishment that can reassure civil society in its quest for a more effective role in the sea changes currently taking place in global governance.

Governance is a polysemic concept which its users tend to adapt to the context in which they are speaking. There is no wholesale agreement on what the term might mean (and this article is not the place to go into that discussion). That said, international institutions tend to invent definitions of governance that suit them. For the World Bank (1992), for example: 'Governance is the manner in which power is exercised in the management of a country's economic and social resources for development.' The World Bank thus sees three fundamental aspects to governance: (1) the form of political regime; (2) the process through which authority is exercised over social and economic resources for national development; and (3) the capacity of governments to design, formulate and implant policies and carry out their functions.

As described, this process is unquestionably vertical and hierarchical. Governance, in this view, belongs to governments. There is no room for interaction or interrelations between structures and different levels of application. The governed are not included in the process. Such a definition actually makes it difficult to capture the many facets of the reality that it purports to describe. The United Nations Development Programme (UNDP, n.d., p. 33), on the other hand, proposes a substantially different definition of governance:

> Governance—the exercise of political, economic and administrative authority in the management of a country's affairs at all levels. Governance is a neutral concept comprising the complex mechanisms, processes, relationships and institutions through which citizens and groups articulate their interests, exercise their rights and obligations and mediate their differences.

Far more dynamic, this definition takes account of the broad political, economic and administrative aspects of governance. It takes account of the plurality of actors involved in the process of governance and of the complex nature of the multi-layered environment in which they are involved. All are expected to articulate their interests and exercise their rights and obligations while negotiating their differences.

These two definitions present an interesting contrast between a traditional, hierarchical vision of global governance and a process of dynamic integration that is open to new actors participating at different levels.

Many authors see the WSIS as exemplifying the deep changes taking place in global governance. For Padovani and Tuzzi (2003):

> We assume that new forms of politics are possibly emerging, with new actors being more and more recognized as legitimate on the global scene; international intergovernmental organizations, private entities and civil society organizations.
>
> We think of the Summit as a 'shift in the location of authority' both for the fact that there is a recognized need to face challenges posed by and to societal transformation at the highest political level and for the fact that a number of supra-national political instances [. . .] involved in the attempt to regulate such changes converge in this process; (2) we see the 'emerging transnational civil society' mastering its capacity to become part of a high level political process building on former experiences, not only acting as an observer or submitting contributions, but also influencing in different ways the development of the process and suggesting ways for a better involvement of non-governmental actors; (3) we can see the WSIS as an opportunity for the 'intellectual, political, and economics elites' to debate respective orientations relating to the transformation of information economies and knowledge societies; (4) finally we witness a gathering around such process, precisely of members of that epistemic elite defined by Roseau as the 'technicians, experts in knowledge', trying

to bring their perspectives and contribution of a 'common vision of the Information Society'.

For Padovani and Tuzzi, the concept of governance can no longer be applied exclusively to the intergovernmental sphere; we are witnessing the emergence of an embryonic global public sphere, in which new actors and new modes of decision making are being put in place.

The inclusion of non-traditional actors in the WSIS, foreseen by the organizers from the start, is an illustration of the changes taking place in the sphere of global politics. That said, while it is important not to be too hasty to idealize the role of civil society in the WSIS, there can be no question that the creation of an autonomous, open and inclusive structure, the WSIS Civil Society Plenary, and its production of the Civil Society Declaration—despite their shortcomings—provide a model for the blending of issues and process which should inspire all those who are thinking about possibilities for a new global politics, not only in communication but in global affairs (Raboy, 2004).

The WSIS can thus be seen as a meeting place of various tendencies currently jockeying with one another to influence the changing structures of global communication. The general decision-making models in international relations, as well as policy-making mechanisms, procedures and modes of participation, are all in the process of being reshaped. The WSIS is seen by many observers as an arena where the transformations affecting global governance are being played out. It is a kind of laboratory where the initial steps of a new form of governance are being tested. A number of factors support this thesis: the UN precedent of a summit with a multi-stakeholder executive secretariat, the insistence on private-sector and civil society inclusion in the official process, the creation of a Civil Society Bureau, the credibility and legitimacy achieved by civil society through its own self-governing collective action—all of these require serious consideration post-WSIS. This consideration goes beyond whatever one might think about the issues raised by the summit and how they have been dealt with. The WSIS process has shaken the status quo of global governance. It should be seen as a laboratory experimenting with a new distribution of power involving emerging as well as established social forces.

The WSIS is also interesting as an encounter between diverse analytical frameworks in global communication; between opposing views of how to define the information society, and what that might mean. The stakes of the WSIS were conceptual, philosophical and discursive as well as political in the narrow sense. The WSIS reconstructed positions that had already been debated in other international fora; it also deconstructed definitions and framed new struggles over meaning. Among other things—and not the least—it brought back to the table many of the key points of the NWICO debate left unresolved a quarter of a century earlier.

Thirty years ago, in the NWICO debate, the governments of developing countries challenged the premises on which international information flow was based, contesting the then-dominant paradigm of global communication (Najar, 2001). The NWICO vision eventually pulled back and left its place to an essentially Western, capitalist model of an international communication order. The explosion of globalization, deregulation and the rise of neo-liberalism have all contributed to a utopian mercantile vision of information and communication, in which ICTs pave the way for a grand and generous information society, generating wealth and good things for all to consume, distributing its benefits across all sectors of society.

This ideology was generally assumed by the ITU—which typically sees no need for access to civil society in its structures, preferring to build 'public–private' partnerships with the private sector. Many civil society actors were thus dismayed to see the lead role for the

WSIS accorded to the ITU rather than, say, UNESCO. These fears were for the most part justified. Questions of hardware dominated over questions of culture, education, equity and knowledge. The summit itself contravened established ECOSOC procedures in accrediting, for the first time in a UN meeting, individual commercial entities as well as their collective associations. Civil society had to back-pedal quickly to include issues of copyright, concentration of media ownership and cultural diversity in the WSIS agenda.

Nonetheless, these and other themes left behind in the wake of the NWICO debate surfaced in the position defended by civil society. The Civil Society Declaration *Shaping Information Societies for Human Needs* addresses these issues and revitalized a conception of information and communication that had seemed buried for good in the rarefied atmosphere of international diplomacy. As noted by Seán Ó Siochrú (2004), international spokesperson for the CRIS campaign:

> First, its [the Civil Society Declaration's] use of language was markedly different: it does not refer to the 'information society' but to 'information and communication societies'. The plural form is used to indicate that there are many possible such societies, not just one; and the term 'communication' is there to ensure that the wider agenda is to the fore, encompassing media more broadly, issues around knowledge ownership and public domain, cultural diversity, concentration and commercialization of media—indeed almost all the issues that were debated so hotly two decades before in UNESCO.
>
> Initiated and forcibly terminated between governments in the compromised setting of the Cold War, followed by a decade or more in the wilderness, it has now shaken off its Cold War cobwebs and taken a decisive move towards rejuvenation in the hands of civil society. If this process continues, the broader issues of the 'communication society' may now begin to generate the alternative paradigms needed, not simply to address the 'digital divide' but to take on the wider issues of the growing role of communication and knowledge in our society.

The notion of 'information and communication societies', a key conceptual feature for civil society, signals the semantic divide with the official Declaration of Principles; it crystallizes the rejection of the intergovernmental vision, its limits and biases, and proposes to go further and break down barriers, address fundamental issues, and put forward a new order:

> There is no single information, communication or knowledge society: there are, at the local, national and global levels, possible future societies; moreover, considering communication is a critical aspect of any information society, we use in this document the phrase 'information and communication societies.' For consistency with previous WSIS language, we retain the use of the phrase 'Information Society' when directly referencing WSIS. (WSIS Civil Society Plenary, 2003)

In thus opposing the approach articulated in the official documents (all buried under a single notion of an information society) this simple footnote to the Civil Society Declaration expresses and consecrates the split between two visions of social life and human relations. The WSIS Civil Society Declaration proposes above all a plural vision of information and communication societies.

Contrary to the NWICO debate, sustained essentially by a number of governments in the total absence of civil society, the WSIS presented a thoroughly different quality precisely because of civil society's presence. But the NWICO spectre haunted the WSIS and particularly civil society within it, to a certain extent. Once promoted by the MacBride Commission, the idea of a 'right to communicate' provoked a controversy separating the CRIS campaign and its supporters such as (ALAI, ALER, APC, AMARC, CAMECO, IPS, PANOS, etc.) from the partisans of 'freedom of expression' (such as Reporters sans frontières, the International Federation of Journalists and the World Press Freedom Committee). The right to communicate and freedom of information appeared to represent alternative social choices when they were indeed discursive positions.

To the extent that 'communication rights' develop and encompass new issues (such as intellectual property rights and Internet governance), the WSIS has updated old debates, situated them in new arenas of action, and provided a platform for new players.

The WSIS is therefore above all a space of confrontation between opposing communicational paradigms. The opposition to the current dominant model has been reorganized in a new political space where civil society is called upon to be increasingly present. The WSIS exemplifies, therefore, the important trends emerging in global governance, encouraging civil society to participate more actively in defining a new global public sphere and to integrate more deeply to developing transnational public policy.

Websites

Heinrich Böll Foundation, http://www.worldsummit2003.de/en/nav/14.htm
ICT 4 Development Platform, http://www.ict-4d.org/Marketplace/en/default.htm?languageId=en
World Electronic Media Forum, http://www.wemfmedia.org/
World Summit on the Information Society, official Website, http://www.itu.int/wsis/
WSIS? WE SEIZE!, http://www/geneva03.org/

Notes

1   There is no simple definition of 'civil society'. For the purposes of this article, we shall use that of the United Nations Development Program: 'individuals and groups, organized or unorganized, who interact in the social, political and economic domains and who are regulated by formal and informal rules and laws'. The UNDP also provides a useful definition of 'civil society organizations': 'the multitude of associations around which society voluntarily organizes itself and which can represent a wide range of interests and ties, from ethnicity and religion, through shared professional, developmental and leisure pursuits, to issues such as environmental protection or human rights' (UNDP, n.d., p. 32).

2   'We are indeed in the midst of a revolution, perhaps the greatest that humanity has ever experienced' (Official WSIS Website, http://www.itu.int/wsis/); reference deleted in February 2004.

3   The Senegalese president did not leave empty-handed, however. Following up on the generally more progressive tone set at the Summit on Cities in the Information Society (World Summit of Cities and Local Authorities on the Information Society, 2003), the municipalities of Lyon and Geneva pledged a total of €600,000 to launch the fund, and numerous NGOs also committed themselves to support the plan.

4   The full mandate of the working group is to: 'develop a working definition of Internet governance; identify the public policy issues that are relevant to Internet governance; develop a common understanding of the respective roles and responsibilities of governments, existing intergovernmental and international organisations and other forums as well as the private sector and civil society from both developing and developed countries; [and] prepare a report on the results of this activity to be presented for consideration and appropriate action for the second phase of WSIS in Tunis in 2005' (WSIS, 2003b, art. C6).

5   'OECD countries spent a miserly 0.23% of GDP on aid in 1998, compared to 0.37% in 1980 and 0.48% in 1965. There was a drop of $4 billion in aid to the poorest 48 countries between 1998 and 1992' (Martin, 2002).
6   Author's translation from the original French.
7   'Does input lead to impact? How governments treated civil society proposals in drafting the 19 September 2003 Draft Plan of Action', 24 Sep. 2003, Available at: http://www.worldsummit2003.de/en/web/467.htm
8   See http://www.wemfmedia.org/
9   See http://www.ict-4d.org/Marketplace/en/default.htm?languageId=en
10   See http://www.geneva03.org/
11   All major documents produced by civil society during the first phase of the WSIS are available on the Heinrich Böll Foundation Website at: http://www.worldsummit2003.de/en/nav/14.htm

References

Anonymous (2003) 'Does input lead to impact? How governments treated civil society proposals in drafting the 19 September 2003 Draft Plan of Action', 24 Sep., Available at: http://www.worldsummit2003.de/en/web/467.htm

ATS (2003) 'Sommet de l'information, la mésentente s'installe', *La Tribune de Genève*, 28 Sep., Available at: http://www.geneva2003.org/wsis/index_c02_1_06.htm

Buckley, S. (2003) 'Community media and the information society', *International Freedom of Expression eXchange*, Available at: http://www.ifex.org/en/content/view/full/55412/

Burch, S. (2004) 'Global media governance: reflections from the WSIS experience', *Media Development*, vol. 1, Available at: http://www.wacc.org.uk/modules.php?name–ews&file=article&sid=1485

Girard, B. & Ó Siochrú, S. (2003) 'Civil society embroiled in the system', in *Société de l'information et coopération internationale: development.com*, Institut universitaire d'études du développement, IUÉD, Geneva, Available at: http://www.unige.ch/iued/wsis/DEVDOT/ 01906.htm

Martin, J. (2002) 'Ergebnisse und Perspektiven globaler Entwicklungszusammenarbeit nach der Monterrey-Konferenz', *Financing for Development*, Available at: http://www2.weed-online.org/ffd/index.htm

Marzouki, M. (2003) 'Caucus des droits de l'homme au nom de la Plénière de la société civile', 18 Jul., Available at: http://www.iris.sgdg.org/actions/smsi/hr-wsis/dhsi-sc-180703.html

Moll, M. & Shade, L. R. (2004) 'Vision impossible? The World Summit on the Information Society', in *Seeking Convergence in Policy and Practice*, Canadian Centre for Policy Alternatives, Ottawa, Available at: http://www.globalcn.org/en/article.ntd?id=1983&sort=1.10

Najar, R. (2001) 'Pour un nouvel ordre mondial de l'information', *Le Courrier de l'UNESCO*, Dec., Available at: http://www.unesco.org/courier/2001_12/fr/medias.htm

Ó Siochrú, S. (2004) 'Will the real WSIS please stand-up? The historic encounter of the "information society" and the "communication society"', *Gazette: The International Journal of Communication*, vol. 66, nos 3–4, pp. 203–224, Available at: http://www.worldsummit2003.de/download_en/Gazette-paper-final.rtf

Padovani, C. & Tuzzi, A. (2003) 'Changing modes of participation and communication in an international political environment. Looking at the World Summit on the Information Society', Conference paper, *IPSA Congress*, Durban, South Africa, Available at: http://www.ssrc.org/programs/itic/publications/civsocandgov/Padovani.pdf

Raboy, M. (2004) 'The World Summit on the Information Society and its legacy for global governance', *Gazette: The International Journal of Communication*, vol. 66, nos 3–4, pp. 225–232, Available at: http://www.lrpc.umontreal.ca/wsis-raboy-gazette.pdf

United Nations Development Programme (UNDP) (n.d.) *Glossary of Key Terms*, Available at: http://magnet.undp.org/Docs/!UN98-21.PDF/!GOVERNA.NCE/!GSHDENG.LIS/Glossary.pdf

World Bank (1992) *Governance and Development*, World Bank, Washington, DC.

World Summit of Cities and Local Authorities on the Information Society (2003) *Draft Declaration of Lyon*, Available at: http://www.wsis2005.org/wsis/documents/pc3/declaration/dec_lyon_eng.pdf

World Summit on the Information Society (WSIS) (2003a) *Declaration of Principles. Building the Informa-*

tion Society: a Global Challenge in the New Millennium, Available at: http://www.itu.int/dms_pub/itu-s/md/03/wsis/doc/S03-WSIS-DOC-0004!!MSW-E.doc

World Summit on the Information Society (WSIS) (2003b) *Plan of Action*, Available at: http://www.itu.int/dms_pub/itu-s/md/03/wsis/doc/S03-WSIS-DOC-0005!!MSW-E.doc

WSIS Civil Society Plenary (2003) *Shaping Information Societies for Human Needs*, Civil Society Declaration to the World Summit on the Information Society, Available at: http://www.itu.int/wsis/docs/geneva/civil-society-declaration.pdf

PART 2

Theoretical terrains

Chapter 5

Daniel Lerner

TOWARD A COMMUNICATION THEORY OF MODERNIZATION: A SET OF CONSIDERATIONS

IN THE CITY of Teheran, in 1954, there were 36 registered "film companies." Only one of these companies had actually produced, distributed, and exhibited any films; the other 35 had yet to complete production of their first film.

How did this odd situation come about? The sequence of events begins at Teheran University, where the old traditions of Iranian learning and the new demands of Iranian modernization are locked in a deadly struggle, from which there issues annually a horde of distorted and disfigured progeny called "graduates." These are the young men who, under the compulsion to maintain or attain an elevated social status, attended or evaded four years of magistral lectures and passed a final examination. They have acquired certain standard adornments—i.e., acquaintance with Persian history and Shariya law, familiarity with the glories of Persian art and poetry, certified by the ability to quote yards of Firdausi and appropriate stanzas of Saadi.

These young men are all dressed up—but they have no place to go. They are much too numerous to be absorbed into the traditional social orders represented by government, army, priesthood. Already the Iranian government periodically discovers itself unable to meet the payroll of its swollen bureaucracy. Nor is Iran developing an adequate supply of new occupations deemed fitting for college graduates. These graduates face only the bleak prospect of unemployment and underemployment. Accordingly they seek to occupy themselves in ways that will be amusing if not rewarding. A half-dozen such graduates organize themselves around a 35 millimeter camera and form a "film company." But their outlook is dismal. Most of them will never produce a film; those who do will never be able to market it. It is unlikely that, even if they wish to show it free of charge, their film will ever be seen beyond their circle of friends. There are few cinemas in Teheran, and they are for commercial hire. Frustration and failure thus await most young Iranians who seek to make a career in the mass media.

The key factor in this unhappy situation is the uncertain and inadequate tempo of Iranian modernization. The supply of new life-opportunities does not keep pace with—is indeed steadily outpaced by—the burgeoning demands of the new literates. In 1958 I summarized the Iranian situation in the following terms, which remain cogent in 1962:

"Incorporation of new men is no easy task in a non-growth economy. Iran develops few of those constantly growing and changing occupational holes which embody young men in the elite structure. The clergy, the military, the bureaucracy—all these are charges on the public treasury, already overburdened and scarcely capable of expansion. The teaching corps is pitifully inadequate, but unlikely to multiply opportunities until Iran develops a modernizing economy in which literacy is an essential skill. Without an expanding business sector, there is little room for the lawyer and accountant, for the specialist in industrial management or labor relations, for the insurance broker or the investment manager, for the account executive or the public relations counsel. Advertising is stillborn and the mass media abortive. Where in Iran is 'the man in the gray flannel suit'? Whatever his unpopularity among Westerners wearied by opinion brokers, in Iran he would be a more useful stimulus to modernization than the agitational intellectual in a hairshirt of vivid hue.

"Given its limited absorptive capacity, Iran suffers from an over-production of intellectuals. In a society about 90% illiterate, several thousand young persons go through the classical routines of higher education each year. Learning no skills that can be productively employed, these collegians seek outlets in the symbol-manipulating arts toward which their humanistic studies have oriented them. Their effort supplies a poignant instance of usable training rendered useless by its social environment—newspapers without readers that last a week or a month, film companies that never produce a film. The mass media, as distinctive index of the Participant Society, flourish only where the mass has sufficient skill in literacy, sufficient motivation to share 'borrowed experience,' sufficient cash to consume the mediated product. In Iran the mass media are anemic and with them, annually, die a thousand hopes."[1]

The thousand hopes that die in Iran each year are multiplied into millions throughout the underdeveloped countries around the world that exhibit communication malfunctioning in their efforts to modernize. What is the common mechanism underlying these numerous cases where the communication gears fail to mesh with the motor of modernization? Various formulations have been offered us in the excellent chapters in this book. Each points to essential factors in a comprehensive theoretical understanding of the interaction between communications and political development. No paper achieves such a comprehensive theoretical understanding—a statement of such force as to suffuse us with the beautiful feeling of perfect illumination—as does a Newtonian account of the solar system as a *gravitational* system or a Wienerian account of all systems as *entropic* systems. It may be prudent at this stage of our knowledge about communication systems and social systems to aim at something less than this. The present effort is only a set of considerations drawn from an incomplete theoretical base.

The theoretical base of this paper is the proposition that modernity is an interactive behavioral system. It is a "style of life" whose components are *interactive* in the sense that the efficient functioning of any one of them requires the efficient functioning of all the others. The components are *behavioral* in the sense that they operate only through the activity of individual human beings. They form a *system* in the sense that significant variation in the activity of one component will be associated with significant variation in the activity of all other components.

The terseness of these definitions should not obscure the amplitude of the proposition, which is coterminous with the basic theorem of behavioral science—namely, that the operation of a social system, or sub-system, can be accounted for by the statistical distribution of behavioral components among its members. Thus a society operates its polity as a representative democracy if a large fraction of its members are qualified to vote, and regularly do vote, in elections that actually decide which of several competing candidates shall occupy the offices authorized to make decisions on specified issues of public policy. Thus a society operates its economy under capitalism in the measure that its members are free to decide how they shall use their own savings in order to maximize their own wealth. The statistical distribution of items that form the index—i.e., components of the system— determines how we characterize a society.

There is much that remains to be clarified in the behavioral conception of society. But it does, even in its present condition, authorize systematic efforts to locate linkages between personal and aggregative behavior, to establish reciprocity between individuals and institutions, to associate samples with systems. Operating on this authorization, this paper will seek to clarify how and why it comes about that the mass media function effectively only in modern and rapidly modernizing societies. We know empirically that this is so. Here we wish to develop further the idea that media systems and social systems have "gone together so regularly because, in some historical sense, they *had to* go together."[2]

I. The new revolution of rising frustrations

These considerations arise from reflection on the course of the developing areas over the past decade. It has not been a smooth course nor a consistent one. It has falsified the predictions and belied the assumptions of those who foresaw the coming of the good society to the backward areas. Among its casualties has been the assumption that if some particular input was made—i.e., investment capital, industrial plant, agricultural methods, entrepreneurial training, or any other "key factor" preferred by the analyst—then a modernization process would be generated more or less spontaneously. This is a serious casualty. As the editor of this volume has aptly written in his introduction: "Faith in spontaneity died soon after the first ex-colonial people began to experience frustrations and disappointment at becoming a modern nation."

This bitter experience is new to us and requires careful evaluation—particularly by those among us who want the defeats of the past decade to help prepare the modest victories that may still be hoped for in the next. The decade of the 1950s witnessed the spread of economic development projects around much of the world. This process of reviving cultures, emerging nations, and new states was widely characterized as a "revolution of rising expectations." People throughout the backward and impoverished areas of the world suddenly acquired the sense that a better life was possible for them. Now leaders arose who encouraged their people to believe in the immanence of progress and the fulfillment of their new, often millennial, hopes. A great forward surge of expectancy and aspiration, of desire and demand, was awakened during the past decade among peoples who for centuries had remained hopeless and inert. This forward feeling was shared by those of us whose unchanging task is to understand.

A significantly different mood characterizes our thinking about the decade before us. While rising expectations continue to spread around the underdeveloped world, those of us who retain our interest in comprehending or programming rapid growth have learned that the ways of progress are hard to find, that aspirations are more easily aroused than satisfied. There is a new concern that the 1960s may witness a radical counter-formation: a revolution of rising frustrations. Observers have had to temper hope with prudence, for the limits on rapid growth have become more clearly visible through our recent experience. There is a seasoned concern with maintenance of equilibrium in societies undergoing rapid change. Soberly, responsible persons now tend to look for guidance less to ideology than to theory, less to dogma than to data. A new era of systematic research into the mysteries of modernization has opened.

Any restless area presents social research with an excellent opportunity to meet the need for a theoretically sound, empirically based exposition of the process called modernization. To be sure, there are particularities in each situation. Particularities can be wedded to generalizations, however, if we focus social research in any area upon those aspects of the process which it shares with other regions of the world that are seeking to accompany rapid economic growth with rapid social change. The political function in this process is to maintain stable controls over these rapid changes—i.e., to preside over a dynamic equilibrium.

In these terms there are two main sets of problems that confront the development process everywhere: mobility and stability. By mobility we mean the problems of societal dynamism; by stability we mean the problems of societal equilibrium. Mobility is the agent of social change. Only insofar as individual persons can change their place in the world, their position in society, their own self-image does social change occur. Social change is in this sense the sum of mobilities acquired by individual persons. (In a more precise sense, as we shall see, societal equilibrium can be expressed as a ratio between individual mobility and institutional stability.)

It is fairly well established that a systemic relationship between the major forms of mobility—physical, social, and psychic—is required for a modern participant society. As to sequence and phasing, we have only the Western experience to serve as full-scale model. Historically, in the Western world mobility evolved in successive phases over many centuries. The first phase was *geographic* mobility. Man was unbound from his native soil. The age of exploration opened new worlds, the age of migration peopled them with men transplanted from their native heath. The second phase was *social* mobility. Once liberated from his native soil, man sought liberation from his native status. The transplanted man was no longer obliged to be his father's shadow, routinized in a social role conferred upon him by his birth. Instead, as he had changed his place on the earth, so he sought to change his place in society.

The third phase was *psychic* mobility. The man who had changed his native soil and native status felt obliged, finally, to change his native self. If he was no longer his father's shadow, then he had to work out for himself a personality that fitted his actual life situation. Once he had changed his ancestral home and inherited status, thereby transforming his place and his role, he had to transform himself in ways suitable to his new situation. The acquisition and diffusion of psychic mobility may well be the greatest characterological transformation in modern history, indeed since the rise and spread of the great world religions. It is in any case the most fundamental human factor that must be comprehended by all who plan rapid economic growth by means of rapid social change. For psychic mobility— what we have elsewhere called empathy—is the mechanism by which individual men transform themselves in sufficient breadth and depth to make social change self-sustaining.[3]

This Western experience is what gave us that faith in spontaneity which Professor Pye assures us died a little while ago. We assumed that in any country that was given the right amount of investment or training or whatnot empathy would rise and mobility would be accelerated—and the good society would be attained sooner or later. But the good society can only be attained later in the measure that advances are made to attain it at each stage, for in development terms the long run can only be a sequence of short runs. Hence stability is essential. The past decade has taught us that mobility, while indispensable to rapid social change, is not enough. It is a necessary but not sufficient condition of growth. Since mobility is a seeking for something better, it must be balanced by a finding—as, in equilibrium, a demand must be balanced by a supply. It is the continuing failure of many transitional societies to maintain the balance of psychic supply-and-demand that underlies the new revolution of rising frustrations.

II. The want:get ratio

The spread of frustration in areas developing less rapidly than their people wish can be seen as the outcome of a deep imbalance between achievement and aspiration. In simple terms, this situation arises when many people in a society want far more than they can hope to get. This disparity in the want:get ratio has been studied intensively in the social science literature in terms of achievement and aspiration. The relationship we here propose for study can be expressed by the following equation (adapted from an ingenious formula of William James[4]):

$$\text{Satisfaction} = \frac{\text{Achievement}}{\text{Aspiration}}$$

This formula alerts us to the proposition that an individual's level of satisfaction is always, at any moment of his life, a ratio between what he wants and what he gets, i.e., between his aspirations and his achievements. A person with low achievement may be satisfied if his aspirations are equally low. A person with high achievement may still be dissatisfied if his aspirations far exceed his accomplishments. Relative deprivation, as has been shown, is the effective measure of satisfaction among individuals and groups.

It is a serious imbalance in this ratio that characterizes areas beset by rising frustrations. Typically in these situations the denominator increases faster than the numerator—i.e., aspiration outruns achievement so far that many people, even if they are making some progress toward their goal, are dissatisfied because they get so much less than they want. Indeed, in some developing countries aspirations have risen so high as to annul significant achievements in the society as a whole.

How does such an imbalance in the want:get ratio occur? How can it be prevented or cured? What, in short, are the social institutions that affect the level of aspiration, the level of achievement, and the ratio between them? There are six institutions which function as the principal agencies of social change (or its inhibition): the economy, the police, the family, the community, the school, the media.

About the first five we can be very brief. If the economy can be made to supply all the opportunities needed to maintain reasonable equilibrium between achievements and aspirations—if the want:get ratio can be balanced by simply supplying all that people want—then there is no problem of frustration. Everyone is happy. Similarly, if the frustrations that arise are settled simply by police methods, then also there is no problem—at least, not for social research. Social research has little to contribute in situations of over-achievement or under-aspiration. Where riches outrun wants, where coercion inhibits desires, there social research is not needed. In most transitional societies that concern us, however, neither of these conditions obtains.

A more complex agency of social change is the family. Typically in developing areas the family acts as an instrument of conservatism and the retardation of change. It acts also, however, as an instrument of balance. To the degree that mobility involves the breaking of traditional family ties (and I believe the degree is high), this is a built-in destabilizer of the modernization process. How to replace the stability of traditional family ties by other methods is a deep problem of social equilibrium under conditions of rapid change.

Similarly, the community may act as a powerful force to promote or impede balanced growth. Here the force hinges upon the individuals who function as activators and enthusiasts of modernization. Where these people emerge and prevail, communities tend to become positive agents of the purpose that modernization seeks to accomplish. Otherwise, in the absence of effective activators and enthusiasts, the coalition of adversaries and indifferents that forms within every transitional community will impede growth and disrupt equilibrium.

The schools, under conditions of modernization, are necessarily instruments of social change. They must teach what is new and modern, what is desirable and obtainable, because they have no other curriculum worth supporting. There are of course important variations in the effectiveness with which different schools produce modernizers and their products serve modernization. We shall not discuss schools further here, despite their importance, because their institutional role and behavioral function—in our model of modernization— can be handled as a variant of the mass media in the communication process.

The mass media, finally, are a major instrument of social change. They make indispensable inputs to the psycho-political life of a transitional society via the minds and hearts of its people. Theirs is the critical input to satisfaction in emerging nations and to citizenship in new states. To perceive the communication crux of modernization, we must consider deeply three propositions: (1) that the mass media bring new aspirations to people—and then, since the empathic individual imagination quickly (logarithmically it appears)[5] outruns societal achievement, it brings dissatisfaction conceived as frustration of aspiration; (2) that, despite the now-evident risks of frustration, the mass media continue to spread around the world— inexorably and unilaterally; (3) that modernization—conceived as the maximization of satisfaction—can succeed (achieve more at less cost) if, and only if, a clarifying communication theory and practice are activated.

On the first proposition I have already written so much that I shall simply incorporate in this paper conclusions which any interested reader can pursue further in my (and other) published work.[6] On the second point I have published descriptive studies of the inexorable and unilateral spread of mass media around the world, showing that no society, once it acquires a media system, does go back to an oral system of communication.[7] In the next section of this chapter I want to explore *why* this is so. Then we shall turn to the third—and crucial—proposition about communication theory and practice.

III. How and why the mass media spread

If the mass media are to have some significant effect on modernization and democratic development—whether to facilitate or impede these desiderata—the first condition is that the mass media must spread. For, if the mass media do not spread, then we have no problem to discuss. We thus consider the question: what conditions determine whether the mass media spread?

One major condition is economic: the level of economic development in a country determines whether the mass media spread. All industrially developed countries produce mass media systems. No pre-industrial country produces mass media systems. Between these extremes lie the range of cases that interest us here, i.e., the developing nations. Here the general rule is that mass media spread in a direct and monotonic relationship with a rising level of industrial capacity. Where this rule applies, in general the spread of the mass media facilitates modernization. Where the rule does not apply, one may expect to find that the spreading mass media impede (or, perhaps more accurately, "deviate") modernization. Why does this simple rule have such general force as is here claimed?

The reasoning is clear if we consider information as a commodity. It is produced, distributed, and consumed like all other commodities. This brings information within the rule of the market. Notably, the supply-demand reciprocal comes into operation. This means that, to evaluate the functioning of a communication sub-system within a societal system, it is essential to consider—it may even be wise to begin with—the conditions that determine the efficient functioning of all economic processes: the capacity to produce and the capacity to consume.

We shall consider each of these briefly. Our discussion will draw its substance from the market economy model of the modern Western nations. It is in these countries, where the mass media developed in the private sector, that the mass media spread first historically, and where they remain today the most widespread in quantity of both production and consumption. Any account of this process that wishes to be relevant to happenings in the mass media around the world today must provide some reasonable explanation for the variant economic evolution of the mass media in the Communist countries and the developing countries. The Soviet system provides some especially interesting deviations from the rule of supply and demand, e.g., the political rule of enforced supply and acquiescent demand for a social commodity taken out of the economic market place. Events in the developing countries, such as India and Egypt, do not yet form a "system," but they do alert us to the possibility of new ways of handling information that differ significantly from the historic evolution in the modern West. We shall therefore try to frame our discussion in categories that *must* apply to the operation of mass media whether a country be capitalist, Communist, or neutralist.

Capacity to produce

There must be a capacity to produce. No country—whether its ideology be Hamiltonian, Stalinist, or Gandhian—can produce in formation via mass media until it has an economic capacity to construct and maintain the physical plant of the mass media. I have made a simple checklist of the items needed to produce mass media products. This checklist is neither precise nor comprehensive. It is simply a reminder of what it has taken historically and what it takes today to produce information via the mass media. A glance will indicate how much more complex this list would become if one were considering the most efficient means of producing information according to strict considerations of economic optima. But such considerations lie far outside the present purview of developing countries. For these countries the simple checklist will do [Table 5.1].

The items required to produce information via the mass media are grouped under the three categories of plant, equipment, personnel. The three categories, as well as the items

Table 5.1 Capacity to produce: a checklist

1. PLANT:	Buildings
	Utilities (power, light, water)
	Facilities (studios, workshops, offices)
2. EQUIPMENT:	Books (linotype)
	Newspapers (rotary)
	Magazines (rotogravure)
	Movies (film, camera)
	Radio (amplifier, transmitter)
	Television ("picture tube")
	[Future standard equipment: satellites]
3. PERSONNEL:	Copy producers (reporters, scripters, features)
	Copy presenters (actors, printers, "layout")
	Managerial corps (editor, publisher, producer, director)

listed within them, are arranged in ascending order of complexity. They may even be construed as a scale upon which rising levels of economic capacity could be calibrated. Thus, if one thinks of the contemporary United States, it may seem too rudimentary to list the "plant." Yet efforts to spread the mass media in the developing countries have foundered, and continue to founder today, on just the three items listed in this category.

Even the item of buildings is a large hurdle and frequent stumbling-block. For one thing, buildings of adequate shape and size do not exist in most of the villages and towns and small cities of the developing countries. The mass media are perforce restricted to the capital cities for just this reason. But even such a capital city as Teheran, as we have seen, does not have enough buildings of the right shape and size to permit production or consumption of many full-length movies. The buildings in which the mass media operate must be provided with efficient utilities, such as power, light, water. How could a proper newspaper operate in Teheran without efficient telephonic communication, without regular telephone links to the great oil refineries at Abadan, to the summer and winter residences of the Shah, to other capitals of the world—not to mention the electronic equipment needed for receiving the huge volume of daily news files coming from the international press services? Yet which of us does not remember some amusing or frustrating incident connected with his use of the telephone in a rapidly developing country? Which of us has not witnessed the inhibiting, and sometimes paralyzing, restrictions placed upon the mass media in these countries by the inadequacy of their facilities? Of the thirty-six film companies in Teheran, only one had studios. This was the only company that had managed to produce a full-length feature film.

The varieties of equipment required by the mass media are manifold, complicated, and expensive. I have listed the principal media in the historic order of their evolution, which corresponds also to the complexity of the equipment they required at the time their major development occurred. Thus the book publishing industry was able to develop on the basis of the simple linotype machine. A further technological advance made possible the spread of the mass circulation daily newspaper, namely the rotary press. Illustrated magazines were a medium of elite communication because of their cost until the development of rotogravure machines made possible the cheap production of millions of copies of illustrated monthlies and weeklies. Similarly, the rapid development in our century of movies, radio, and television as industries hinged upon the capacity of American industry to produce at acceptable prices the mechanical and electronic equipment which are indispensable to the functioning of these mass media. The communication revolution of our time was technological before it became anything else. It is not implausible that in our century communication satellites will become standard equipment for the efficient functioning of mass media systems in many countries throughout the world.

The economic level of any country hinges also upon the quantity and quality of its skilled personnel. Particularly in the mass communication industries the capacity to produce hinges upon the availability of a corps of communicators, i.e., a substantial body of personnel trained in the array of special skills required for immediate production. Needed first of all are the skills that produce copy—whether it be for the news columns of a daily paper, a feature article in a weekly magazine, the script of a radio program, or the scenario of a movie or television show. Consider in passing the variety of features that fill the pages of every major daily newspaper. What a great variety of tastes, skills, and interests are needed to produce all this copy! Reflect for a moment that the man who has written a novel rarely turns out to be the man best equipped to adapt his own work for production as a movie. The man who does this may well be a person of much less creative talent but with superior specialized skill in "scripting." Consider the further array of skills needed to present copy, after it has been produced, to the consuming public. Actors do this for the spoken word, printers for the written word. But consider the extremely specialized skill required for that essential presentation function performed by the so-called "layout man." To make such large enterprises as a daily newspaper, a radio station, or a film company operate efficiently, a skilled managerial corps is also necessary. These are the editors and publishers, the producers and directors who are the kingpins of the mass communications industries. Without these many and varied persons the mass media have no capacity to produce.

If we simply reflect on the developing countries we know best in these terms, we promptly perceive that these conditions may well determine whether the mass media will spread. In reflecting further on the central question—whether the spread of the mass media will facilitate or impede modernization—we must take account of another condition: the capacity to consume.

Capacity to consume

Three factors determine whether the capacity to consume media products spreads—and how fast—in any country: cash, literacy, motivation. There is a simple side to this matter. A person needs cash to buy a radio, a cinema ticket, a newspaper. If a newspaper costs as much as a loaf of bread, and if his ready cash is in a chronic state of short supply, then there is a diminishing probability that a person will consume newspapers. On the same simple level: only a literate person *can* read a book, paper, or magazine, and only a motivated person *wants* to read. The media flourish therefore in the measure that their society equips the individuals with cash, literacy, and motivation to consume their products.

There is a more complex sociology, however, that underlies each of these factors and their reciprocal interaction. It is no accident that the mass media developed in the monetized sector of every economy. The barter of country newspapers against farmers' produce or artisans' products was a brief and transitory phase—occasionally magnified in the senti-mental memoirs of superannuated country editors. The media grew in the monetized sector because this is the distinctively modern sector of every economy. The media, as index and agent of modernization, *had* to grow in the sector where every other modern pattern of production and consumption was growing or else remain stunted.

The efficient operation of a money economy was made possible only by a great trans-formation in the thoughtways and life-ways of millions of people. Historically, in any society the "sense of cash" is an acquired trait. It has to be learned, often painfully, by a great many people before their society can negotiate the perilous passage from barter to exchange. Consider, for example, this sentence on the traditional Anatolian peasantry by Professor H. A. R. Gibb: "We may suppose the *re'aya* to have been animated hardly at all by any idea of gain, and to have worked their land with a minimum of effort and very little knowledge."[8]

Gain, effort, knowledge—these are huge categories of discourse. For any adequate comprehension of the personality transformation which accompanied the shift from barter to cash in contemporary Turkey we are obliged to take these large terms in their historical sense. What has been acquired in one generation among a population that had always been ignorant and indifferent is precisely the sense of gain, effort, knowledge which came over centuries to guide personal behavior in the modern participant society of the West.

Cash is an essential solvent in modern life, and the achievement of rising per capita income distribution is a major objective of modern societies. Here the political and socio-logical problems of the developing countries become intertwined with their economic problems. Economies long caught in the vicious circle of poverty cannot easily break through into the modern industrial system of expanding production of goods and services. This fact reflects no inherent and inevitable distaste for the good things of life among developing peoples. It reflects rather the difficult communication process—which in the West occurred over several centuries—of stimulating desires and providing means for satisfying them where neither desires nor facilities have previously existed. Westerners engaged in economic development problems have only recently recognized that, once a start is made, the reciprocity between desires and facilities tends to operate in the new nations as elsewhere.

Consumption of media products is thus an economic function, but it performs simultaneously several other functions that are sociological, psychological, and political. Literacy is a technical requirement for media consumption. But literacy, once acquired, becomes a prime mover in the modernization of every aspect of life. Literacy is indeed the basic personal skill that underlies the whole modernizing sequence. With literacy people acquire more than the simple skill of reading. Professor Becker concludes that the written word first equipped men with a "transpersonal memory";[9] Professor Innis writes that historically "man's activities and powers were roughly extended in proportion to the increased use of written records."[10] The very act of achieving distance and control over a formal language gives people access to the world of vicarious experience and trains them to use the complicated mechanism of empathy which is needed to cope with this world. It supplies media consumers, who stimulate media production, thereby activating the reciprocal relationship whose consequences for modernization we have noted. This is why media participation, in every country we have studied, exhibits a centripetal tendency. Those who read newspapers also tend to be the heaviest consumers of movies, broadcasts, and all other media products. Throughout the Middle East illiterate respondents said of their literate compatriots: "They live in another world." Thus literacy becomes the sociological pivot in the activation of psychic mobility, the publicly shared skill which binds modern man's varied daily round into a consistent participant life-style.

Literacy is in this sense also a precondition for motivation. People who can read usually do read—as, indeed, they consume more of all the audio-visual products of the media (the well-known "centripetal effect") and participate more fully in all the modernizing activities of their society. What is required to motivate the isolated and illiterate peasants and tribesmen who compose the bulk of the world's population is to provide them with clues as to what the better things of life might be. Needed there is a massive growth of imaginativeness about alternatives to their present life-ways, and a simultaneous growth of institutional means for handling these alternative life-ways. There is no suggestion here that all people should learn to admire precisely the same things as people in the Western society. It is suggested, much more simply, that before any enduring transformation of the vicious circle of poverty can be started, people will have to learn about the life-ways evolved in other societies. What they subsequently accept, adapt, or reject is a matter which each man will in due course decide for himself. Whether he will have the capacity to reach a rational decision hinges, in turn, upon the fullness of his participation in the modernizing process as it works through every sector of his personal and social life. The final test comes in the arena of political participation.

Mass media and political democracy

Democratic governance comes late historically and typically appears as a crowning institution of the participant society. In countries which have achieved stable growth at a high level of modernity the literate individual tends to be the newspaper reader, the cash customer, and the voter.

The media teach people participation of this sort by depicting for them new and strange situations and by familiarizing them with a range of opinions among which they can choose. Some people learn better than others, the variation reflecting their differential skill in empathy. For empathy, in the several aspects it exhibits, is the basic communication skill required of modern men. Empathy endows a person with the capacity to imagine himself as proprietor of a bigger grocery store in a city, to wear nice clothes and live in a nice house, to be interested in "what is going on in the world" and to "get out of his hole." With the spread of curiosity and imagination among a previously quietistic population come the human skills needed for social growth and economic development.

The connection between mass media and political democracy is especially close. Both audiences and constituencies are composed of participant individuals. People participate in the public life of their country mainly by having opinions about many matters which in the isolation of traditional society did not concern them. Participant persons have opinions on a variety of issues and situations which they may never have experienced directly—such as what the government should do about irrigation, how the Algerian revolt could be settled, whether money should be sent to Jordan or armies to Israel, and so on. By having and expressing opinions on such matters a person participates in the network of public communication as well as in political decision.

The mechanism which links public opinion so intimately with political democracy is reciprocal expectation. The governed develop the habit of having opinions, and expressing them, because they expect to be heeded by their governors. The governors, who had been shaped by this expectation and share it, in turn expect the expression of *vox populi* on current issues of public policy. In this idealized formulation of the relationship, then, the spread of mass media cannot impede but can only facilitate democratic development.

But ideal types do not always match perfectly with their empirical instances. In the developed democracy of the United States, for example, the capacity to produce information via mass media is virtually unlimited. The capacity to consume media products—thanks to an abundant supply and widespread distribution of cash, literacy, motivation—is unparalleled anywhere in human history. The production-consumption reciprocal has operated efficiently on a very high level over many decades. Yet as American society presented the world with its most developed model of modernity, certain flaws in the operation of the system became apparent. I do not speak of the Great Crash of 1929—which exhibited a merely technical flaw in management of the economic sub-system. I speak of a much deeper flaw in the participant system as a whole, i.e., the emergence of non-voting as a political phenomenon. A generation ago Harold Gosnell called our attention to this danger. In recent years an alarmed David Riesman has generalized this phenomenon to the larger menace of political apathy. If Americans were really suffering from widespread apathy about their public life, then a cornerstone of our media-opinion system would be crumbling—namely, in our terms, the cornerstone of motivation. (We note in passing that in the developed democracy of France only a short while ago leading thinkers and scholars convened for solemn discussion of political apathy in France—of all places!)

If one danger to developed democracies comes from literate non-voters, the parallel danger to developing democracies comes from the reverse configuration, i.e., *non-literate voters!* Can universal suffrage operate efficiently in a country like India or Egypt which is 90 per cent illiterate? Can the wise Jeffersonian concept of a literacy test for voters be completely ignored nowadays because we have radio? President Nasser has proffered a counter-doctrine for the developing countries, to wit: "It is true that most of our people are still illiterate. But politically that counts far less than it did twenty years ago. . . . Radio has changed everything. . . . Today people in the most remote villages hear of what is happening everywhere and form their opinions. Leaders cannot govern as they once did. We live in a new world."[11]

But has radio really changed everything? When illiterate "people in the most remote villages hear of what is happening everywhere," what do they really hear? They hear, usually via the communal receiver at the village square in the presence of the local elite, the news and views selected for their ears by Egyptian State Broadcasting (ESB). Their receivers bring no alternative news from other radio stations. Being illiterate, they can receive no alternative news and views from newspapers and magazines and books published anywhere.

In terms of personal achievement almost nothing happens to these "people in the most remote villages" by way of Radio Cairo: broadcasting now supplies them with the kind of rote learning each acquired by memorizing the Koran (which he could not read) in childhood. But in terms of personal aspiration nearly everything happened to these people when radio came to their remote villages. For the first time in their experience—both the experience of centuries inherited through their parents and their own lives—these isolated villagers were invited (and by none less than their rulers!) to participate in the public affairs of their nation.

The invitation carried with it, however, none of the enabling legislation needed to make radio-listening an integrative agent of modernization. In a modern society the radio listener is also the cash customer and the voter. In the remote villages of Egypt, when the government inserted radio into the community, nothing else changed in the daily round of life—except the structure of expectations. This is the typical situation that over the past decade has been producing the revolution of rising frustrations. The mass media have been used to stimulate people in some sense. It does so by raising their levels of aspiration—for the good things of the world, for a better life. No adequate provision is made, however, for raising the levels of achievement. Thus people are encouraged to want more than they can possibly get, aspirations rapidly outrun achievements, and frustrations spread. This is how the vicious circle of poverty operates in the psychological dimension.

The impact of this psychic disequilibrium—its force as a positive impediment to modernization—has been disclosed by Major Salah Salem, the youthful Minister of National Guidance who tried to run the Egyptian mass media during the contest for power between Naguib and Nasser. Major Salem, finding his problems of national guidance insoluble, finally solved them by voluntarily locking himself in jail. There he prepared a memoir of his own frustration in the impossible task of converting an inert and isolated peasantry into an informed and participant citizenry by the mass media alone. Major Salem concludes: "Personally I am convinced that the public was wrong."[12]

In similar vein, Nasser has written retrospectively: "Before July 23rd I had imagined that the whole nation was ready and prepared, waiting for nothing but a vanguard to lead the charge. . . . I thought this role would never take more than a few hours . . .—but how different is the reality from the dream! The masses that came were disunited, divided groups of stragglers. . . . There was a confirmed individual egotism. The word 'I' was on every tongue. It was the solution to every difficulty, the cure for every ill."[13]

These judgments by leaders who were frustrated in their aspiration for quick and easy modernization reveal why transitional Egypt—in the dozen years since its liberation—has been so deeply frustrated. Can "the people," in Salem's sense, ever really be "wrong"? Can a social revolution ever really be accomplished in "a few hours"—or its failure attributed, in Nasser's sense, to "egotism"? Or is it, rather, that these young enthusiasts had never learned Lasswell's lesson—that political life is largely a question of "who gets what"? When people get involved in politics, it is natural that they should expect to get more of whatever it is they want. Instead of rebuffing such aspirations as egotism, the statesman of an enlarging polity and modernizing society will rather seek to expand opportunities for people to get what they want. He will seek above all to maintain a tolerable balance between levels of aspiration and achievement. In guiding the society out of the vicious circle toward a growth cycle his conception of the role of public communication is likely to be crucial.

IV. From vicious circle to growth cycle

"The vicious circle of poverty" is a phrase used to characterize the situation in which no sustained economic growth is possible because each specific advance is rapidly checked by some counter-tendency in the social system. The most important of such counter-tendencies is excessive population growth. Any significant economic progress tends to prolong life by reducing famine and pestilence. When death rates decrease more rapidly than birth rates—often, indeed, while birth rates are increasing—then rapid population growth occurs. In poor countries population growth tends to "lead" economic growth by setting rates of increase that must be attained so that the society can stay at its existing levels of poverty. No surpluses can be generated, hence no "leap forward" is possible. Singer has succinctly summarized "the dominant vicious circle of low production—no surpluses for economic investment—no tools and equipment—low standards of production. An under-developed country is poor because it has no industry; and it has no industry because it is poor."[14]

The picture looks quite different in a society which has broken out of the vicious circle and set its course toward the achievement of a growth cycle. The new situation is vividly illustrated by the following diagram [Figure 5.1].[15]

The story told by this diagram reaches its climax with the achievement of a significant rise in real income. Such a rise becomes significant when it enables the society simul-taneously to raise both demand and saving. We have seen that otherwise, in a poor society, small increases of income tend to be consumed promptly—with nothing left over for saving, hence investment. But when income rises rapidly enough to permit higher consumption and also higher saving, then the growth cycle is initiated. Higher investment leads to capital improvement and rising productivity, which in turn raise real income enough to encourage both higher saving and demand. Thereby higher investment is again stimulated—and the growth cycle becomes self-sustaining.

Specialists on economic development appear to be generally agreed on some version of this picture of the break-out from the vicious circle. There is less consensus, however, on the economic policies that will lead most efficiently from the break-out to the self-sustaining growth cycle. Contemporary economic thinking has tended to emphasize two quite different sets of theoretical analyses—which we may characterize as "disequilibria" and "balanced growth" theories—leading to different policies and programs.

It is difficult to resolve the issues between disequilibria and balanced growth on a

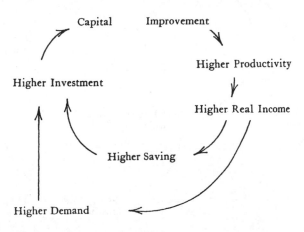

Figure 5.1 Economist's model of the growth cycle.

theoretical level. The arguments rest in both cases on factors extraneous to the economy—i.e., on the values, beliefs, and institutions of a country and, especially, on its capacity to change these psychosocial factors as may be required for sustained economic growth. For example: higher income, even if rapid and substantial, will not necessarily lead to commensurate increases of saving and investment. There are numerous cases where higher income has led only to conspicuous consumption of imported products or to savings that were invested only abroad—hence with no effect on production and growth at home.

The growth cycle, which stipulates that higher income must be coupled with both higher consumption and investment, is likely to occur only in a society where effort is associated with reward—where saving is likely to compound interest, where investment at home is likely to conjoin personal with patriotic satisfactions (rather than exploit the latter and deny the former). The association of effort with reward comes from the matrix of social institutions, psychological beliefs, political efficiency (in managing public adaptation to innovation) within which economic programs are obliged to operate.

The association of effort with reward, of aspiration with achievement, is a communication process. People must learn to make this association in their own daily lives—linking what they see with what they hear, what they want with what they do, what they do with what they get. Communication is, in this sense, the main instrument of socialization, as socialization is, in turn, the main agency of social change. To parallel the economist's model of the growth cycle, we may represent the conditions for an expanding polity and modernizing society as follows [Figure 5.2] (adapting the input functions proposed by Gabriel Almond).[16]

The modernization process begins with new public communication—the diffusion of new ideas and new information which stimulate people to want to behave in new ways. It stimulates the peasant to want to be a freeholding farmer, the farmer's son to want to learn reading so that he can work in the town, the farmer's wife to want to stop bearing children, the farmer's daughter to want to wear a dress and do her hair. In this way new public communication leads directly to new articulation of private interests.

Simultaneously—by analogy with the significant increase of real income that enables both saving and demand to rise simultaneously—new public communication activates new modes of socialization. If new interest-articulation parallels demand, then new socialization

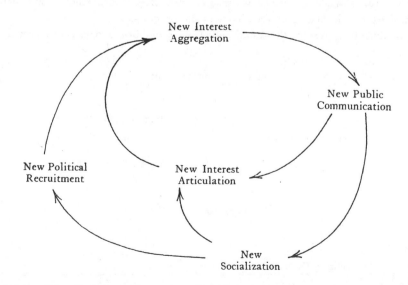

Figure 5.2 Conditions for an expanding polity and modernizing society.

parallels saving—the factor that will make possible new investment and, ultimately, the supply of new satisfactions for the new demands. So, while new communication is promoting new articulation of interests among the existing generation, it is also preparing a new generation who will incorporate these interests and go beyond them. The farmer's daughter who wants to show her face is likely to raise a daughter who wants to speak her mind. The farmer's son who wants literacy and a town job is likely to raise a son who wants a diploma and a white collar. Socialization thus produces, ideally, the new man with new ideas in sufficient quality and quantity to stablize innovation over time.

In order to incorporate innovation efficiently, a society must translate it from private interests into public institutions. An essential step forward must be made from the articulation to the aggregation of private interests—which, when aggregated and accepted in the polity, become the public institutions of a society. It is also necessary that a new process of political recruitment come into operation. Among the newly socialized generation some must be recruited into political life so that the new aggregation of interests into institutions may be accomplished and sustained. So it is that, starting from a breakthrough in communication, reinforced by new ways of socialization (ideas of what one's children may be and practices designed to achieve these aspirations), a new political class is recruited that aggregates the new interests articulated within the society in such fashion as to create its new institutions—its version of modernity.

V. Looking ahead

Our set of considerations has been presented tersely. We have merely raised and related considerations that need to be explored in depth. This is a task for social scientists in the decade ahead—a task that will be the better performed in the measure that we improve our understanding of the communication crux of the modernizing process.

Our understanding begins with recognition that the revolution of rising expectations has been a major casualty of the past decade. In its place has risen a potential revolution of rising frustrations. This represents a deep danger to the growth of democratic polity in the world. People who do not aspire do not achieve; people who do not achieve do not prosper. Frustration produces aggression or regression.

Aggression in today's transitional societies expresses itself through violence based on moralistic but often inhumane ideologies. Such doctrines, albeit in prettier euphemisms, authorize fear, greed, and hate to operate as racism, xenophobia, vengeance. Regression in these societies signals the return to apathy and the narcosis of resignation. Aggression among transitional peoples victimizes others; regression victimizes themselves. Neither process is compatible with the dynamic equilibrium that promotes modernization. Hence the global spread of frustration must be checked and a tolerable ratio of aspirations to achievements must be instigated.

Communication is the crux. In the introduction of this volume it was observed that "the state of politics is a function of the communication process." The communication catastrophe in transitional societies has been their failure to discourage—often, indeed, their effort to encourage—the "insatiable expectations of politics" that lead ultimately only to frustration. Short-sighted politicians have been sowing a storm they may not be able to harvest. The policy of whipping up enthusiasm on short-run issues by creating insatiable expectations has never produced long-run payoffs.

What is needed in the years ahead is a new conception of public communication as the crucial instrument which can promote psychic mobility, political stability under conditions of societal equilibrium. The mass media can be used to mobilize the energies of living persons (without creating insatiable expectations) by the rational articulation of new interests. Flanked by the schools and community leaders, the mass media can simultaneously induce a new process of socialization among the rising generation that will, among other effects, recruit new participants into political life. These two processes—short-run mobilization and long-run socialization—can then converge, a generation later, in new aggregations of private interests which are the stuff of a democratic polity.

What we have sketched here is of course an idealized model. In the measure that it corresponds to reality the model provides clarification and guidance for those who must think and act in the transitional lands. The task for future research is to determine under what conditions the model does or does not work, so that a better model may be developed to shape a more effective communication process where it is most needed. This calls for close and continuous cooperation between men of knowledge and men of action on the most challenging social problem of our time—the modernizing of most of the world.

Notes

1   Daniel Lerner, *The Passing of Traditional Society*, Glencoe, Ill., The Free Press, 1958, p. 362.
2   *Ibid.*, p. 438. See also Daniel Lerner, "Communication Systems and Social Systems," *Behavioral Science*, Vol. 2, No. 4, October 1957; Gabriel A. Almond and James S. Coleman, *The Politics of the Developing Areas*, Princeton, Princeton University Press, 1960, p. 536; Lucian W. Pye, *Politics, Personality, and Nation Building*, New Haven, Yale University Press, 1962, p. 15.
3   Daniel Lerner, *The Passing of Traditional Society*, p. 43. Also K. Gompertz, "The Relation of Empathy to Effective Communication," *Journalism Quarterly*, xxxvii, Autumn 1960, pp. 533–546.
4   William James, *Psychology: Briefer Course*, New York, Holt, 1923, p. 187.
5   This refinement of my basic theory I owe to my student Howard Rosenthal. See his "A Statistical Approach to Comparative Politics" (M.I.T. CENIS document number C/62–9, 1962), to be published shortly.
6   See note 2.
7   See Daniel Lerner, "Communication Systems and Social Systems."
8   Hamilton A. R. Gibb and H. Bowen, *Islamic Society and the West*, London, Oxford University Press, 1950, Vol. 1, Part 1, p. 244.
9   Carl L. Becker, *Progress and Power*, Stanford, Stanford University Press, 1936.
10   Harold Adams Innis, *Empire and Communications*, Oxford, Clarendon Press, 1950, p. 11.
11   Gamal Abdul Nasser, *Egypt's Liberation*, Washington, D.C., Public Affairs Press, 1955.
12   This memoir is quoted in D. Lerner, *The Passing of Traditional Society*, pp. 244–245.
13   Gamal Abdul Nasser, *op.cit.*, pp. 244–245.
14   Hans W. Singer "Economic Progress in Underdeveloped Countries," *Social Research*, xvi, 1, March 1949, p. 5.
15   Gerald M. Meier and Robert E. Baldwin, *Economic Development: Theory, History, Policy*, New York, Wiley, 1957, pp. 319–320.
16   Gabriel A. Almond and James S. Coleman, *op. cit.*, p. 17.

Chapter 6

Raka Shome and Radha S. Hegde

POSTCOLONIAL APPROACHES TO COMMUNICATION: CHARTING THE TERRAIN, ENGAGING THE INTERSECTIONS

THIS SPECIAL ISSUE WAS born out of a vision and a conviction that postcolonial and communication studies had something to offer each other. Instead of starting with the assumption that only communication scholarship had something to gain from postcolonial studies, we conceived this issue, rather, with the idea that the politics of postcoloniality is centrally imbricated in the politics of communication. Yet, the communication dimension (except media) has hardly received any attention in postcolonial studies, just as postcolonial issues, for the most part, have been elided in communication studies. We consequently recognized that bringing these two areas together could invite a productive reconceptualization of communication, as well as a thinking through of the politics of postcoloniality from the perspective of communication. Thus, we do not see postcolonial scholarship or communication scholarship in an "othering" relationship with each other. Rather, what we see are the ways in which various cultural phenomena of postcoloniality and communication are intertwined in each other, and how recognizing the postcolonial politics of communication opens up new vistas for communication scholarship.

In what follows, we introduce the field of postcolonial scholarship by providing a discussion of the questions and problematics it is concerned with. We then explore why postcolonial politics should be of concern to communication scholars. Our hope is that our audience will recognize the relevance of this interdisciplinary area for communication studies, and why engaging the "postcolonial"—both as an intellectual project and as a cultural phenomenon—enables us to rethink communication through new visions and revisions, through new histories and geographies.

Postcolonial studies: an overview

Postcolonial studies, broadly described, is an interdisciplinary field of inquiry committed to theorizing the problematics of colonization and decolonization. As a field it is positioned within the broader critical project of cultural studies that has had so much influence in communication scholarship. While postcolonial scholarship is committed to theorizing the problematics and contexts of de/colonization, its focus however is not merely the study of colonialism(s). That is, it is concerned not merely with chronicling the facts of colonialism. Its commitment and its critical goals, first and foremost, are interventionist and highly political. In its best work, it theorizes not just colonial conditions but *why* those conditions are what they are, and how they can be undone and redone (although more work is needed on this latter aspect). This is important to keep in mind for it emphasizes that not every study of colonialism would necessarily qualify as a postcolonial study. Merely describing or chronicling the facts of colonialism, without taking an emancipatory political stance, and without offering interventionist theoretical perspectives through which to examine the violent actions and erasures of colonialism, does not make a study postcolonial in its critical impulse.

To say this is not to guard boundaries (although we feel that it is desirable to guard some boundaries, less they become so open that we forget what it is we are opposing in the first place), rather, it is to posit that the best form of postcolonial scholarship, at the end as at the beginning, is always, to borrow Stuart Hall's (1992) words, a detour towards something more important. And that something more important is its transformative stance. Postcolonial scholarship, because of the politics of its emergence and the nature of the problems it is concerned with, exists in tension with established institutionalized knowledge. It attempts to undo (and redo) the historical structures of knowledge production that are rooted in various histories and geographies of modernity. This means that the questions and problematics of colonialism that postcolonial scholarship concerns itself with emerge from larger social contexts—contemporary or past—of modernity. In engaging with questions of colonialism and modernity, postcolonial scholarship often finds itself colliding with the limits of knowledge structures—in terms of scope and method—derived from, and enabled by, various imperial and national modernities within which Anglo-Euro academy was produced and is esconced. In the process it tries to redo such epistemic structures by writing against them, over them, and from below them by inviting reconnections to obliterated pasts and forgotten presents that never made their way into the history of knowledge. Thus, as Henry Schwarz (2000) notes of postcolonial studies, "it is not merely a theory of knowledge but a 'theoretical practice,' *a transformation of knowledge from static disciplinary competence to activist intervention*. Postcolonial studies would be pointless as a mere intellectual enterprise, since Western intellectual enterprise itself is fundamentally dependent on Europe's conquest and exploitation of the colonial world" (p. 4).

This was certainly the case with Edward Said's *Orientalism* (1978), Gayatri Spivak's *In Other Worlds* (1988b), the South Asian Subaltern Studies Collective writing nationalist "history from below" or, more recently, works such as Lata Mani's *Contentious Traditions* (1999) and Dipesh Chakraborty's *Provincializing Europe* (2000). These are projects that embody some of the most provocative intellectual offerings of the late twentieth century. These are works that methodologically and theoretically provide examples of what a rigorous interrogation of the linkages between colonialism and knowledge should look like. These studies confront us with the recognition that institutionalized knowledge is always subject to forces of colonialism, nation, geopolitics, and history. Postcolonial scholarship, then, by the very nature of its commitment and content exists as an interruption to established disciplinary content that was, and continues to be, forged through structures of modernity and histories of imperialism. This last point has particular relevance to communication scholarship, especially when we begin to historicize the field and link its emergence with a particular historical moment in the United States—the capitalism of post World War II America when the United States' position as a new world power was on the rise.

To a large extent, the critical impulses informing postcolonial studies are reflected in much of left leaning scholarship, including cultural studies, marxist theory, feminist theory, postmodern theory, queer theory, and more. So what makes postcolonial studies different? What is it about postcolonial scholarship that enabled it to perform such significant interruptions not just in mainstream knowledge, but also in its allied theoretical areas, such as the ones mentioned above? While our essay, in various ways, is an attempt to answer this question, suffice it to say for now that the inherent tense relationship between postcolonial studies and traditional institutionalized knowledge emerges from the fact that no other critical discourse has collided against the structures of colonial modernities in such a head-on fashion as postcolonial theory has. No other academic discourse has forced upon us, to this extent, a recognition of the mutual operations (and erasures) of history, geography, geopolitics, and international division of labor, through which institutionalized knowledge in the West (but not only) has been performed—even when that knowledge has tried to write against the grain of established ways of thinking, as in different versions of critical scholarship.

Thus, for example, when Anglo-Euro academy, riding on the radical waves of poststructuralism and postmodernism in the 1980s was celebrating or despairing the death of the subject, postcolonial scholarship forcefully historicized this subject as the subject of imperial Europe. It asked for whom the subject had died, if in fact it had, and what international histories may have gone into the production of this subject in the first place. So when Michel Foucault was overhauling and exposing the power/knowledge function through which institutionalized epistemes in the West had been performed, and the sovereign rational subject of Enlightenment had been constituted, by refocusing attention on the subjugated knowledges of madness, prisons, (homo)sexuality, Gayatri Spivak (1988a) came along and asked, but what if these subjugated knowledges were themselves a part of a larger history of imperialism whose connections spill over to the other side of the international division of labor? What if Foucault's ascribing of a normative stance to these particular types knowledge as "subjugated knowledge" once again normalized the subject of Europe, while on the other side of European capitalism languished forms of knowledge so far removed and so violated by the machinery of imperialism that they cannot even be accessed, let alone subjugated?

Similarly, when postmodern and poststructuralist feminist thought dominated paradigms in women's studies in the late 1970s and 1980s, by showing how the subject of modernity was a male bourgeioisie subject whose dominance needed to be theorized, or when it argued against essences by emphasizing the performativity of gender, postcolonial feminist scholars such as Rey Chow (1991, 1992), Chandra Mohanty (1991, 1996), Trinh Minh-ha (1986, 1989), and Gayatri Spivak (1985, 1988a, 1988b, 1990, 1992, 1993, 2000), among several others, insisted that the sexual difference through which the masculine subject of modernity had been privileged, or the performativity of gender through which essences were de/naturalized, must be connected to larger international histories, geopolitics, and colonial modernities. They argued that such connections complicate and interrupt postmodern and poststructuralist feminist theorizing by locating the reductive politics of sexual difference in the excesses of colonial modernity, and by forcing a recognition of race, nation, and imperialism, that had been elided in much of postmodern and poststructuralist feminist scholarship.

To sum up the distinctiveness of postcolonial studies from other forms of critical scholarship, then, it could be said that postcolonial scholarship provides a historical and international depth to the understanding of cultural power. It studies issues of race, class, gender, sexuality, and nationality, that are of concern to contemporary critical scholarship by situating these phenomena within geopolitical arrangements, and relations of nations and their inter/national histories. Further, many forms of critical scholarship tend to be nation centered. By this we mean that the scope of their engagement tends to be bound within national boundaries. The scope of postcolonial scholarship, on the other hand, because of the problematics it is concerned with, extends beyond the nation. This going beyond the nation however does not entail a static and apolitical engagement with inter/national relations. Rather, it entails geopoliticizing the nation and locating it in larger (and unequal) histories and geographies of global power and culture.

Finally, we think that postcolonial scholarship constitutes one of the most central critical lenses through which to name and theorize cultural conditions of contemporary society. This is because postcolonial scholarship theorizes the geographical, geopolitical, and historical specificities of modernities *within* which other forms of power—such as race, sexuality, culture, class, and gender—are located. This means that any engagement with these other forms of power is, at some level, always an engagement with geographical, historical, and geopolitical relations of modernities, whether these relations are explicitly recognized or not. This further means that the problematics that other forms of critical scholarship are concerned with are imbricated in relations of colonial modernities and in the various postcolonial politics that form the underside of such relations. This is not to say that the value of other forms of critical scholarship pales in comparison to that of postcolonial scholarship. Rather, it is to recognize that postcolonial scholarship, because of its focus on the various relations and effects of modernities, functions as an important, and perhaps even necessary, point of theoretical departure through which to engage and comprehend the complexities of these other forms of power.

So far, we have provided a brief sense of the impulses informing postcolonial scholarship. However this sense remains incomplete unless we connect it to the history of the emergence of postcolonial scholarship in the academy. The emergence of postcolonial studies in the Anglo-Euro scene can be traced to several sociological and intellectual conditions. The most obvious are the various decolonization movements that occurred in the wake of World War II. This was a time when various national liberation movements began to shake off, or challenge, territorial European colonial domination. A key event here was the Indian independence from British rule in 1947. New nation-states emerged in developing worlds that were gathered under the political entity of the "third world" (a term now contested) crystallized in the famous 1955 Non-Aligned Summit, now known as the Bandung Conference.

These decolonization attempts resulted in some predictable migratory situations. As a result of the depletion of raw materials and resources by former colonial powers, as well as previous suppression of any attempts by the colonized to produce a self-governing political structure, many of the emerging nation-states lacked, and consequently had to build, the infrastructure necessary to sustain a "civil society" (for example, stable economic and political relations). This complex historical moment resulted in a huge wave of "third world" migration to metropolitan centers of former and current colonial powers—powers whose presence had been constituted in the first place by this history of violence. The 1950s, 1960s, and 1970s, consequently witnessed an unprecedented wave of migrations of colonized peoples into the United Kingdom, and later the United States.

This wave of im/migration constituted, in many ways, a re/turn of the repressed, the "midnight's children" who arrived at the doors of neo/colonial power. Through this arrival they reminded the world, against the West's self-sanctioned forgetting, that "western metropole must [now] confront its postcolonial history, told by its influx of postwar migrants and refugees, as an indigenous or native narrative *internal to its national identity*" (italics added; Bhabha, 1994, p. 6). As a sociological condition, postcoloniality thus is the "always already" the underside of Anglo-Euro history, casting a long shadow on its self-proclaimed enlightenment and teleology of progress. The postcolonial condition is the supplement that haunts and taunts Euro modernities, speaks its tragedies and ironies. It is the violent name of the colossal failure of the project of European modernity and its master tropes such as democracy, self-determination, civil society, state, equality, the individual, free thought, and democratic justice—tropes that showed their limit and betrayed their own logic in the moment of colonialism. The postcolonial condition, following Dipesh Chakraborty (2000), can thus be described as one that emerged out of a refusal of the "waiting room" version of dominant histories by the colonized. These were histories that had performed themselves by ascribing to the colonized (and the subaltern) a status of "not yet" against which the colonized clamored "now" (p. 9).

This wave of migrations unleashed by the insistent "now" of decolonizations saw, among other things, an influx of intelligentsia into institutions of higher knowledge in the United States and Britain, among other countries. The English speaking culture of these nations played a major role in drawing English speaking ex-colonized peoples, and it was here that we roughly saw the institutionalized birth of postcolonial scholarship in the academy. Postcolonial intellectuals found themselves drawn into teaching areas such as comparative literature, international relations, development studies, and anthropology—in short, academic areas that maintained a focus on international cultural perspectives.

While this is one of the most central social conditions that resulted in the establishment of the academic area of postcolonialism, there are other social histories too that should not be ignored. An important one is America's neocolonial relation with several national sites after World War II. For instance, United States' relations with the Philippines, Vietnam, Mexico, and Korea, as well as its relations with internal colonies such as Hawaii, resulted in the emergence of Vietnamese, Philippine, Mexican, Korean, and Hawaiian diasporas within the United States. The politics of these diasporas are, of course, historically and geographically different, in terms of their postcolonial relations with the United States. Nonetheless, they confront us with the postcolonial histories and geographies that underwrite the production of North America. The postcolonial histories of these and other diasporas, however have unfortunately not gained the kind of legitimacy they should receive in postcolonial scholarship. This is partly because postcolonial scholarship has to strongly become associated with the South Asian diaspora—at least in its early phase of development. These other histories remind us that there are colonial contexts beyond the British commonwealth that must be accounted for in understanding the politics of postcoloniality. In addition, these other histories are also important to confront because they disrupt the myth of American exceptionalism, in which historical colonialism too often remains associated with Britain and Europe while post civil rights America positions itself as the new world of democracy, and the space for the production of new and liberatory forms of selfhood.

It is certainly not an accident, we think, that in the United States' academy, only those forms of postcolonial scholarship that have taken as their topic European or British colonialism have gained currency. America, as a site of colonialism whose history runs back several years, has only recently become a focus in postcolonial scholarship. This growing focus is evidenced in some sophisticated (but scant) work being done on Anglo America's various neocolonial relations with other national sites. For example, Walter Mignolo's (1995a, 1995b, 2000) work on Latin America and its historical connections with Anglo America, as well as San Juan Jr. (1995, 1996, 1999) and Vicente Rafael's (2000) work on Philippines' neocolonial relations with the United States, are important in this context. To bring up these other postcolonial histories, often eclipsed in our theorization of postcoloniality, is to recognize the heterogeneity and diverse potential of this area of work. At the same time, it is to acknowledge that the geographical scope of postcolonial studies is not a given.

Our discussion of postcolonial studies, so far, has been (deliberately) Anglo/Euro centered. That is, we have focused, for the main part, on the emergence of this intellectual area in relation to the time frame of European and Anglo colonialisms. This is, of course, necessary because European/Anglo modernities continue to remain one of the dominant forms of colonial modernities and hence their legacy and responsibility must be confronted.

But there is more to the story of postcolonial studies and there is more to the scope of this intellectual area. For instance, the historical relation between Japan and Korea, and Japan's economic stronghold in several parts of Asia, constitute important examples of colonial dominance produced by modernities outside of Euro/Anglo modernity. Recent scholarship within postcolonial studies has thus rightly begun insisting on the need to examine such other modernities that are not framed by the historical time of Europe. Scholars such as Tani Barlow (1997), San Juan Jr. (1999) and Timothy Mitchell (2000) have emphasized the importance of forging other lexicon through which to understand modernities that are not modeled on the European framework. For instance, Barlow (1997) argues that "if colonialism is said, in a categorical sense, to be best exemplified by the British Raj, and all other forms of colonialism are understood in reference to that historical model, then not only are all other formations derivative but conditions fundamentally unlike that originary design might indeed by inconceivable or unseeable" (p. 5). Clearly there is a danger in normalizing one historical time or one narrative of modernity as being constitutive of colonialism. Clearly there is a risk, at some level, of recentering the very narrative of European modernity that postcolonial studies aim to unsettle.

In recent times, postcolonial studies has shown a growing engagement with other forms of colonial and national modernities that were forged through other histories and other geographies. Such work is desirable and necessary. This diversity that needs to occur in postcolonial studies cannot, however, eclipse the story of European modernity or deny its geopolitical and global dominance. For at the end, as Dilip Gaonkar (1999, p. 13) has suggested, no discourse or interrogation of "alternative modernities" or "other modernities" can escape acknowledging the dominance of Western modernity given that Western modernity has traveled through cultural and economic relations, practices, and institutional arrangements to the rest of the world. Thus, even to think about, and resurrect, stories of other modernities is, at some level, to think through and against Western modernities (pp. 13–14).

The need for exploring other modernities, the need for embracing diverse perspectives on colonialisms that can remain sensitive to different contexts and times of colonialism, means that rigorous postcolonial scholarship must remain attentive to the context of colonialism. Taking postcolonial theories that emerged out of a study of a particular context of modernity or a particular historical time and mechanically applying them to other contexts and times can be problematic. It can be problematic because this can reproduce a dangerous acontextualism that is sometimes seen in postcolonial studies (especially, scholarship that comes out of literary studies where the "text" and "narrative" of colonialism become everything while the historical context disappears in the background). Additionally, such acontextualism can flatten the story of modernities by implicitly denying any change in its relations from one time to another, from one context to another.

So, for example, the theoretical perspective that Edward Said (1978) described as "Orientalism" works well to understand colonial formations in earlier times when the West-East, North-South, divide was still clear. But it does not work as well in contemporary times, in which the lines separating the East from the West, and the North from the South, are increasingly becoming porous under conditions of globalization. Similarly, the diasporic politics of "third space" or "border lives" produced by migratory waves of decolonization, that was cogently theorized by Homi Bhabha (1990, 1994), has more relevance to understanding postcolonial formations that emerged out of British colonialism, which saw massive territorial displacements of migrants into metropolitan centers. But the theory of "third space" does not work as well in regards to understanding the various diasporic politics of contemporary times which are not always predicated on the migrations of colonized people.

Today, because of the globalization of capital, complex forms of deterritorializations and reterritorializations are occurring in the lifestyles and everyday practices of inhabitants in many countries, which are producing new relations of displacements and diaspora *within* the nation itself. One thinks here of the cosmopolitical landscapes and lifestyles in cities such as Mumbai, New Delhi, Bangalore, Dubai, Muscat, and Hong Kong post-1997, where complex diasporas are being produced that often exist in stark contrast to the otherwise nationalist rhetorics of such nations. For example, the city of Bangalore in India is now one of Asia's biggest "tech cities"—the Silicon valley of South Asia. The changing and yuppified cultural and physical landscape of this city produces varied forms of cosmopolitanisms and varied re/placements of certain sectors of the population—mainly "thirty something" middle and upper-middle class professionals—that are not a result of any kind of colonial migration. Rather, they are indicative of how we need to rethink issues such as third space, diaspora, and nomadism—concepts that have become entrenched in the vocabulary of postcolonial studies. For example, we need to disassociate these concepts from their natural-ized association with resistance and international mobility. We need to understand how these categories—contrary to always being an "other" of the nation or an "other" of colonialism—are being rearticulated to the nation and through the nation, through new logics under transnational relations of capital and culture. If Homi Bhabha's (1990, 1994) "third space" of hybridity implicitly implied a "first" (the colonizer) and the "second" (the colonized), then today the temporal logic underlying the "third space" does not hold, for the "third space" could very well be a "fourth," a "fifth," a "sixth," and a "seventh space," and so on, with no clear sense as to what came before and what comes after. We live in a time of constant re/placement and reterritorialization as global capital connects, disconnects, and reconnects spaces in new ways and through constantly shifting lines of power. Thus the temporal, linear, and binary logic underlying the notion of "third space" fails in such a condition. The concept of the diaspora call[s] out for a situated-ness in a logic of space instead of only a logic of time, without offering any guarantees about its moral and political positioning.

Postcolonial thematics

The topic of modernity, as suggested above, constitutes the central investigative impulse of postcolonial studies. Situating modernity within the frame(s) of colonialism, postcolonial studies remains concerned with its various attendant topics such as nation and national identity, subalternity, diaspora, transnationalisms, cosmopolitanisms, de/territorializations of colonial and national power, the gendered and sexual politics of these relations, globaliza-tion, politics of im/migration, et cetera. In other words, postcolonial scholarship is con-cerned with phenomena, and effects and affects, of colonialism that accompanied, or formed the underside of, the logic of the modern, and its varied manifestations in historical and contemporary times. Postcolonial scholarship studies these relations not only from the framework of dominance but also from that of resistance. Thus, for example, studies of diaspora attempt to understand diasporic formations not merely as a phenomenon that is an effect of colonial occupations but also as a site of resistance to colonialism.

Postcolonial scholarship is not driven by any particular method. Because its questions emerge from larger social contexts, its method is therefore shaped by the questions posed by the contexts. Thus diverse methodological perspectives from ethnography to textual criticism can fall under its rubric. In this sense, postcolonial theory is committed to rigorous interdisciplinarity. Further, postcolonial scholarship is not shaped by any one philosophical tradition. Perspectives in Marxism, feminism, deconstruction, and psychoanalysis have all been used to understand the varied dimensions of historical and contemporary colonial conditions. There is however a need for more postcolonial work that focuses on the material dimensions of colonialism. A postcolonial Marxist approach is an obvious and powerful tool through which to examine the varied material relations of colonialism. In recent times, the works of scholars such as Aijaz Ahmad (1992), Arif Dirlik (1997, 2000), Akhil Gupta (1998), San Juan Jr. (1999), Aihwa Ong (1999), and Gayatri Spivak (1988a, 2000), among others, argue for an attention to, or have moved towards examining, the material relations of colonialism through the utilization of Marxist oriented approaches.

Postcolonial studies do not privilege any one methodology over another. Different philosophical traditions have been deployed to examine various changing contexts of colonialism. It is important to emphasize however that whatever method(s) may be used in postcolonial scholarship, there is one issue to which practitioners of postcolonial studies remain committed—methodological reflexivity. While working within a certain philosophical or methodological tradition (be it deconstruction or ethnography), postcolonial scholars remain acutely aware of the history, heritage, and legacies of such methods, and the dilemma that consequently confronts the researcher.

For example, in the field of ethnography (an area of significant relevance to communication scholars), Kamla Visweswaran's foundational work *Fictions of Feminist Ethnography* (1994) pushes and problematizes not only the boundaries of traditional ethnography predicated on the objectivity of the ethnographer, but even the boundaries of postmodern ethnography. This work is an examination of the narratives of a handful of elderly South Indian women who had participated in the Indian nationalist movement against British colonialism. In interviewing these women, and examining their narratives about their participation in the nationalist movement, Visweswaran shows how the subjects of her examination—the women—frequently refused or deflected the subject position of nationalists. They did this either in some sort of silent coalition whereby the old secrets or pain of the nationalist movement were being concealed, or through acts of betrayal whereby one woman would reveal some "secret" about another woman to the ethnographer. The women at times refused the very narrative, the very "fiction," of nationalism through which Visweswaran—the ethnographer—engaged them. Such "failures" of her ethnography were moments in which complex relations between the ethnographer, her methodology, and the subjects of ethnography came into the foreground. These were moments in which the history and memories of nationalism and colonialism shaped, constrained, and interrupted the project of her ethnography. This study foregrounds how nationalism and colonialism become the very context against which the methodology of ethnography, and the assumptions informing it, collide and struggle.

Thus, traditional methods and perspectives themselves become a part of the context of examination of colonialism that the postcolonial researcher forcefully becomes engaged in. They become a reminder, as it were, of the betrayals of the researcher by her method. But these betrayals, these "failures," simultaneously constitute the points at which the method becomes redone, reworked, and rearticulated. This has perhaps remained one of the most significant theoretical contributions of postcolonial scholarship—the way in which traditional methods and perspectives (including those in left oriented theory) inevitably undergo a makeover in which categories of history, geography, nation, and colonialism all play a part.

Communication and postcolonial theorizing

Given the richness and scope of postcolonial studies, how do we begin to form productive intellectual alliances between this theoretical body of work and the communication discipline? The connections, we believe, can be mutually informing and contribute to a more nuanced understanding of the contemporary scene of social transformation. There is a growing awareness of the limitations and parochialism of theory so steeped in Eurocentrism that it either ignores completely or oversimplifies the complexity of the "rest" of the world. This inadequacy is becoming increasingly transparent in the context of transnational connections and the unfolding drama of globalization.

The complexity of everyday life and cultural practices worldwide are changing with the proliferation of new technologies and an ever expanding world market. The ripple effect of these changes—felt across multiple areas of economic, social, and political life—make it very clear that globalization is, as Jameson (1999) reminds us, a "multileveled and relational phenomenon" (p. xi). This suggests that both materially and conceptually, we need to grapple with intersections at different levels. Whether it is high-speed communication systems, global migration, or the circulation of images, we are faced with the coming together of contradictory forces and incommensurable differences. The critical vein of postcolonial theory enables a complicating of these overlapping and interstitial spaces. It also powerfully reminds us that these global issues are not born fully formed, Minerva style, but rather have to be situated within the larger historical sweep of colonialism and its imperial centers as well as within both the present and the historical. The issues of intersection and historicity are significant to communication scholars in responding to this changing terrain of globality and its emerging sites of inquiry.

With this renewed interest across the academy in the area of culture and communication, the communication discipline has to respond and rise to the challenge of the times. If theory in communication is to reflect the exigencies of the global moment then we need to rethink the ways in which our intellectual quest relates to the cultural and social formations around us. The discipline at large valorizes a view of communication that is rooted in the West and is largely influenced by modernist intellectual and institutional structures. We need to revisit Grossberg's (1982) question: "What are the particular involvements and investments of communication in real historical social formations?" (p. 84). The politics of communication are of central importance in the understanding of the contradictions and ambivalence in our deeply divided world. To overlook this is to be not only reductive in our research endeavors but also intellectually misleading. Preserving and retrieving "innocent" knowledge (see Flax, 1992; Grossberg, 1997) does little to further a critical understanding of the intersecting lines of reality in today's seemingly connected yet divided world. Taking into account the historical genealogy of the field, a postcolonial intervention pushes for more socially responsible problematizations of communication. It is these critiques that will lead eventually to the production of a more just and equitable knowledge base about the third world, the other, and the "rest" of the world.

The terms communication and culture are often used synonymously, thereby collapsing concerns about issues of domination and geopolitical configurations affecting gender, sexuality, race, or ethnicity. In addition, critical scholars have been writing about the lack of attention paid to the historical in communication research (see Hardt & Brennen, 1993). The postcolonial connection is a powerful way of restoring the macro structures and the historical trajectories that frame contemporary social relations within the global/local nexus. Denaturalizing communication (to use Grossberg's words) and problematizing culture from a postcolonial perspective allows us to go beyond the descriptive and account for the ways in which the Western realities have spread across the world as the universal condition. Radhakrishnan (2000) argues that "it is the ability of the developed world to conceptualize and theorize its particular-organic empirical reality into a cognitive-epistemic formula on behalf of the entire world that poses a dire threat to other knowledges" (p. 40). The other is caught between the sweeping gesture of this universalizing mode and, at the other extreme, going nativist and subsuming everything under a culturalist argument. Both types of epistemic orientation within communication studies have to be subjected to critique in the context of transnationalism. The current preoccupation with globalization and multi-culturalism both in and outside the academy betray an ahistorical, benign articulation of culture and difference. Let us first examine the concept of globalization. The term inevitably heralds a connected world of utopian possibilities—the ultimate dream of corporate slogans. Behind the veneer of a seamless globe are the realities of deep divisions and inequities of exchange. The various flows of objects, persons, images, and discourse are as Appadurai (2000) emphasizes not "coeval, convergent, isomorphic, or spatially consistent" (p. 5). Appadurai also writes that although these disjunctive flows assume local forms, they have contexts that are anything but local. It is this simultaneity of production that demands our theoretical attention especially in terms of conceptualizing context within global/local configurations. Take for example the recent events in the UK involving a series of racially motivated attacks and confrontations between South Asian immigrants and white youths. The aggression has to be situated historically in order to understand the deep-seated resent-ments on both sides. The racism has to be understood as an extension of the colonial refusal to acknowledge the admittance of the periphery into the metropolitan centers. Meanwhile, the immigrants' deep-seated resentment of the colonizer is (re)enacted in the transplanted cultural space with memories of past and present ruptures. The immigrant, being outside of the nation, is only ambiguously admitted to the realm of citizenship. The encounters of the everyday are framed by the larger narration of political, economic, and cultural processes. The driving force of postcolonial work is to interrogate the universalizing discourse of Western modernity. As Radhakrishnan (2000) points out, the fact that "every local-native-indigenous reality has been touched by the morphology of modernism and the dominance of nationalism and the nation-state, makes it imperative for postcoloniality to participate on more than one level and in more than one location" (p. 37).

The Elian Gonzalez case in the United States is another instance of this simultaneity of multiple productions. The mythically recreated saga of the little Cuban boy, saved at sea off the coast of Florida, is evidence of how history, citizenship, politics, the global, local, and communication come together in complex ways which impact life in postcolonial globality. Charting the epistemic travel of the West and its influence on the rhythm of the everyday in different contexts, it becomes apparent that the past and present are produced and repro-duced simultaneously (see Harootunian, 2000). Struggles over race, ethnicity, and national belonging, need to be seen as the unfolding constitution of multiple realities collapsing over time and space dimensions.

Postcolonial engagements strive to provide theoretical frameworks to understand ways in which cultures are constituted and contested. As Spivak says in her interview in this issue, "The theoretical base of postcolonial studies also allows for multiplicity to be thought of in a way that is different from just simply the Rainbow Coalition." The rhetoric of multicultural-ism celebrates the diverse assemblage of cultures in their pristine flavors—colorful yet standing separate in their authenticity. The commodification of cultures and the production of the native is related to the production of postcolonial modernity (Chow, 1993). The native gets resurrected in essentialist trappings and fixed in static categories of ethnic culture. The discrete positioning of cultures without any sense of their interconnected histories reproduces the violence of colonial modernities and fixes difference in a spectacle of other-ness. The packaging of otherness promotes the interests of transnational corporatism and serves also as a politically correct gesture. Such multiculturalism, which often serves as a stand-in for progressive politics, completely misses the point about diversity as struggle and contestation. Complex issues of race and difference are domesticated according to Mohanty (1994) by formulating the problem in narrow, interpersonal terms and by rewriting historical contexts as manageable psychological ones (p. 157).

The logic underwriting these multicultural endeavors is that difference can be managed and used, if it is located at the level of the individual. As communication scholars, we are familiar with this long-standing association of the field with the autonomous subject of modernity—the independent agent who chooses and acts intentionally. The narrative of the individual subject is firmly entrenched in the dominant discourses on multiculturalism and often appears in the rhetoric of corporate multiculturalism. The goal of these metropolitan or corporate multicultural programs is not to get into the messy terrain of racial politics but rather to create a savvy and cosmopolitan work force who can "skillfully" navigate cultural difference (see Rouse, 1995). The liberal approach to multiculturalism is couched in a sanitized version of difference where the unspoken centers of power, and the normativity of whiteness, remain unquestioned. This cosmetic approach to multiculturalism does not question the systemic structures of power nor does it touch the contradictions and tensions written into the realities of everyday life. This is the colonial legacy that postcolonial criticism marks, unpacks, and questions.

Postcolonial theorists provide us with the intellectual fervor and language with which to deconstruct privilege and account for the complex interconnections between power, experience, and culture. The postcolonial is more than a mere description of the past and present. Its theoretical value, as Hall (1996) notes, lies precisely in its refusal of this here and there, then and now, home and abroad, perspective (p. 247). Both the liberal model of multiculturalism and the rhetoric of globalization still stay squarely within the provenance of an Euro-American metropolitan agenda. Postcolonial theorizations enable a rescripting of the encounter between cultures by firmly rejecting the "world-as-emporia" model. As long as we retain uncritical one-world narratives of the global scene, our accounts will remain at the level of marveling cappuccino drinking in Calcutta—along the lines of Iyer's (1989) popular travelogue *Video Nights in Kathmandu*. Postcoloniality has complicated the very meaning of interconnections between cultures.

The problems of our globalized world are challenging to articulate because we cannot view them as "secure, stable objects whose meaning and nature is established before hand by disciplinary convention" (Nelson & Gaonkar, 1996, p. 18). The postcolonial approach to question, reframe, and rethink epistemic assumptions is inspired by the spirit of resistant enquiry, the drive to return the colonialist gaze. A postcolonial critique does not work to once again set up cultures in polarities, but rather the discourse points to how the West and the "other" are constitutive of one another in ways that are both complicitous and resistant (see Giroux, 1992). Communication inquiry can contribute to theorizing this space of mutual constitution.

In the next section, we address how postcolonial theory allows communication scholars points of analytical entry for a more democratic rereading of the contemporary world from new, more self-reflexive locations.

Communication and postcolonial possibilities

Postcolonial scholarship has raised some very volatile questions and stirred debate across disciplines. In spite of its transdisciplinary successes, the influence of postcolonial scholarship has been very limited within the communication discipline. However, it might be worthwhile to situate this within the context of recent criticisms of postcolonial scholarship from various disciplinary sites. A major and recurrent attack is that postcolonial work is overly preoccupied with theory, resulting in scholarship that is obtuse and inaccessible (see Christian, 1990; Seshadri-Crooks, 2000; Shohat, 1992).

As Hall (1996) states eloquently, the postcolonial has become "the bearer of such powerful unconscious investments—a sign of desire for some, and equally for others, a signifier of danger" (p. 242). The charge of inaccessibility arises mainly because of the interdisciplinary thrust of postcolonial studies. The study of complex areas that cross the spectrum of time and space need specific vocabularies that are unlikely to be reader-friendly and understandable to spellchecker software! Arguing whether the use of words are jargon or overly complicated, Butler (1999) asserts, is not merely debating good and bad writing, but instead presents claims about the kind of world in which we should want to live. Simplifying concepts such as alterity, worlding, or subaltern might represent the very blunting of the political edge and intellectual thrust of postcolonial scholarship. As Grossberg (1997) writes, "I do not know of any correlation between accessibility and significance, which is not to claim that inaccessibility is a measure of significance" (p. 31). We do not claim that postcolonial scholarship is a series of easy-to-understand axioms. It is rather, a rich and complex emerging body of work that moves us to question and map the histories and geographies of our interconnections in more responsible ways.

There is a need within the communication discipline to develop intellectual resources to begin to talk about culture as a multiplicity of trajectories. The articles presented in this issue speak to some major areas of mutual interest and overlap between postcolonial theory and communication inquiry—representation, identity, hydridity, and agency.

Theorizing the politics of representation had its beginnings in poststructuralist thought and has been developed with great intellectual sophistication in postcolonial scholarship. Following the monumental work of Said (1978), the connections between the description of the other, circulation of that knowledge, and the politics of power were firmly established. Drawing on the work of Foucault and Gramsci, Said showed that the discourse of Orientalism works in the service of the West by consistently producing the East as inferior. Though this work has met its share of criticism (such as producing the East and West as static entities and as producing a monolithic view of Orientalism) Said's work has been inspirational in the field of postcolonial research and continued theorizations of representation (e.g. Sharpe, 1993; McClintock, 1995). Of particular interest is Mohanty's (1991) work on the monolithic construction of the third world woman in feminist literature. Arguing for cultural and historical differentiation in the representation of third world women, Mohanty argues against the collapsing of subaltern lives into one essentialized saga of oppression.

The circulation of images in popular culture is an area of considerable debate within the communication discipline. What is the cumulative effect and power of these images? How is knowledge about "other" cultures reproduced without affecting the global hegemonic order? How are different national groups represented in depictions of globalization? These last two questions are investigated in Parameswaran's essay in this issue, through analysis of images from a special issue of *National Geographic*. When refracted through the lens of postcolonial theory, the author argues that benevolent images of globalization begin to narrate another story.

Identity is the next important site where the interconnections of race, class, sexuality, and gender are played out in the larger field of geopolitical structures. The transnational context provides a scenario against which we can deconstruct and move away from essentialist and universalist understanding of identities. The key term that needs to [be] addressed in this context is the postcolonial notion of hybridity. Postcolonial theory has been historically interested in the questions of liminality, inbetweeness, and mestiza. At a time when the connections between space, place, and culture have been unsettled, new forms of cultural practices are being defined globally. Hybrid practices are flooding metropolitan centers such as New York and London—ranging from fusion music, cuisine, and fashion—and these vigorously express the meeting of margin and center in new locations. Hybridity is a powerful concept by which to theorize the conflicted and multiple affiliations of diasporic groups. Postcolonial scholars have worked with these realities in innovative ways and contributed to the understanding of identities in postcolonial globality (e.g. Bhabha, 1994; Hall, 1990; Gilroy, 1993; Mercer, 1994).

Hybridity is configured at the conjunction of the local, global, social, political, and legal to name some dimensions. It is above all a performative expression of transnational change, an area of imminent concern to communication scholars. In this issue, Kraidy argues that hybridity needs to be understood as a communicative practice constitutive of and constituted by, sociopolitical and economic arrangements. Examining a series of articles in the *Washington Post* on cultural globalization, he proposes a conceptual platform for a critical, cultural transnationalism problematizing issues of context, process, and representation central to intercultural and international communication.

Agency is also of mutual interest and concern to both postcolonial and communication scholarship. Once again there has been minimal engagement with the concept of agency in communication theory. In the modernist arrangement of things, agency is taken for granted. It was Spivak's landmark (1988a) piece that problematized the whole issue of agency and voice for the colonized. Examining colonial debates on widow immolation, Spivak demonstrates the predicament of the subaltern woman caught between forces of imperialism and patriarchy—there is no space from where the subaltern (sexed) subject can speak. It is this piece that also brought to center stage the issue of representing the subaltern, those denied access to the centers of hegemonic power. Problematizing location, voice, and agency have become a central concern of postcolonial scholarship. Who can speak? Who can represent? Do we position the colonized as incapable of speech? On the other hand, do we romanticize the speech of the colonized as resistant and thereby deflect the violence of the colonial encounter? Our challenge lies in theorizing exactly this interstitial space between agency and the lack thereof, between being constructed within structures of domination and finding spaces of exerting agency (see O'Hanlon & Washbrook, 1992). The bottom line is that agency is deeply bound to the politics of identity couched within the structures of gender, nation, class, race and diaspora.

In an examination of Polish and Hawaiian diaspora, Drzewiecka and Halualani's essay shows how communicative practices are used by diasporic groups to invent, reinvent and position themselves in relation to changing national, political, and economic contexts. The authors argue that focusing on the dialectical relationship between cultural practices and structural forces enables a complex understanding of diasporic politics, subjectivity, and communication. The essays presented in this issue collectively attempt to deconstruct the colonial disposition in our intellectual work and initiate a more democratic reconceptualization of communication forms and practices.

A final posting

There is a telling dramatic twist in Kureshi's (1996) short story, *My Son the Fanatic*. Parvez, an immigrant from Pakistan who drives a cab in England is caught off guard by his son who was raised all his life in the West. "The problem is this," the son tells his father, "You are too implicated in Western civilization." Immigrant father and son are pitted against each other in a strange reconfiguration of West and East in an unexpected order. In contradiction to all the linear models of immigrant lives, the scene captures the alienation that comes from unexpected quarters, the emergence of the political in everyday immigrant lives. While the son speaks of his religious faith, Parvez looks out the window to check that they are still in London. With that gaze of shock and disbelief, Kureshi poignantly captures the realities of cultural production and ruptures.

The contradictions and ambiguities written into postcolonial and diasporic lives under the conditions of globalization are complex subjects of study. Navigating these tensions requires both creativity and theoretical flexibility. The postcolonial move, we believe, enables the bridging of between multiple questions, issues, places, histories, and even disciplines. The reason is related, as we have argued throughout, to the very complexity of the postcolonial condition. Identities blur, overlap, and are contested within spaces that are neither coterminous nor coeval. People's lives and realities are situated within these trans-national forces where power asserts itself in what Grewal and Kaplan (1994) term "scattered hegemonies." It is this conjuncture or rather disjuncture that we are attempting to understand by engaging in postcolonial intellectual practice, that will result in a more democratic intervention in the global-local dialectic.

The project of postcolonial scholarship, as stated earlier, is concerned with more than just the historical explanation of colonialism. With the philosophic and political impulse in place, the research possibilities and connections within the discipline are many. We interviewed Spivak for this issue because we felt it was important to have her speak, as it were, to scholars in the communication discipline. As a preeminent postcolonial and feminist scholar, Spivak talks about the new directions that postcolonial work can and has branched into. "I myself find that it is not necessary to see anything innately critical or radical to remain postcolonial," says Spivak. What is important, she asserts, is that postcolonial work should be done with "complete academic responsibility."

It is the spirit of producing collaborative, academic work and furthering the dialogue on postcolonial theory and globalization within the communication discipline that led us and Lawrence Grossberg to launch this special issue devoted to postcolonial theorizing. We are grateful to the editor of *Communication Theory* for allowing us the space for putting together scholarship with a provocative edge. This is the first national issue of a communication journal devoted to postcolonial theorizing. By no means are we attempting to codify postcolonial scholarship. By definition, postcolonial theory has to maintain its flexibility and to use Spivak's term 'elasticity'. The conversation has started; we hope it yields in multiple directions and continues.

References

Ahmad, A. (1992). *In theory: Classes, nation, literatures.* New York: Verso.

Appadurai, A. (2000). Grassroots globalization and the research imagination. *Public Culture, 12,* 1–19.

Barlow, T. (1997). Introduction: On colonial modernity. In T. Barlow (Ed.), *Formations of colonial modernity* (pp. 1–20). Durham, NC: Duke University Press.

Bhabha, H. (1990). The third space. In J. Rutherford (Ed.), *Identity: Community, culture, difference* (pp. 90–118). London: Lawrence & Wishart.

Bhabha, H. (1994). *The location of culture.* New York: Routledge.

Butler, J. (1999, March 20). A "bad writer" bites back. *The New York Times,* p. A15.

Chakraborty, D. (2000). *Provincializing Europe: Postcolonial thought and difference.* Princeton, NJ: Princeton University Press.

Chow, R. (1991). Violence in the other country: China as crisis, spectacle, and woman. In C. Mohanty, A. Russo, & L. Torres (Eds.), *Third world women and the politics of feminism* (pp. 81–100). Bloomington: Indiana University Press.

Chow, R. (1992). Postmodern automatons. In J. Butler & J. Scott (Eds.), *Feminists theorize the political* (pp. 101–120). New York: Routledge.

Chow, R. (1993). *Writing diaspora: Tactics of intervention in contemporary cultural studies.* Bloomington: Indiana University Press.

Christian, B. (1990). The race for theory. In A. JanMohamed & D. Lloyd (Eds.), *The nature and context of minority discourse* (pp. 37–49). Oxford, UK: Oxford University Press.

Dirlik, A. (1997). *The postcolonial aura: Third world criticism in the age of multinational capital*. Boulder, CO: Westview Press.

Dirlik, A. (2000). *Postmodernity's histories: The past as legacy and project*. Lanham, UK: Rowman & Littlefield.

Flax, J. (1992). The end of innocence. In J. Scott & J. Butler (Eds.), *Feminists theorize the political* (pp. 445–463). New York: Routledge.

Gaonkar, D. (1999). On alternative modernities. In D. Gaonkar (Ed.), *Alter/native modernities* (pp. 1–18). Durham, NC: Duke University Press.

Gilroy, P. (1993). *The Black Atlantic: Modernity and double consciousness*. Cambridge, MA: Harvard University Press.

Giroux, H.A. (1992). Post-colonial ruptures and democratic possibilities: Multiculturalism as antiracist pedagogy. *Cultural critique, 21*, 5–39.

Grewal, I., & Kaplan, C. (Eds.). (1994). *Scattered hegemonies: Postmodernity and transnational feminist practices*. Minneapolis: University of Minnesota Press.

Grossberg, L. (1982). The ideology of communication: Post-structuralism and the limits of communication. *Man and World, 15*, 83–101.

Grossberg, L. (1997). *Bringing it all back home*. Durham, NC: Duke University Press.

Gupta, A. (1998). *Postcolonial developments: Agriculture in the making of modern India*. Durham, NC: Duke University Press.

Hall, S. (1990). Cultural identity and diaspora. In J. Rutherford (Ed.), *Identity: Community, culture, difference* (pp. 222–237). London: Lawrence & Wishart.

Hall, S. (1992). Cultural studies and its theoretical legacies. In L. Grossberg, C. Nelson, & P. Treichler (Eds.), *Cultural studies* (pp. 277–286). New York: Routledge.

Hall, S. (1996). When was the post-colonial? Thinking at the limit. In I. Chambers & L. Curti (Eds.), *The post-colonial question: Common skies, divided horizons* (pp. 242–260). New York: Routledge.

Hardt, H., & Brennen, B. (1993). Communication and the question of history. *Communication Theory, 3*, 130–136.

Harootunian, H. (2000). *History's disquiet: Modernity, cultural practice, and the question of everyday life*. New York: Columbia University Press.

Iyer, P. (1989). *Video nights in Kathmandu*. London: Black Swan.

Jameson, F. (1999). Preface. In F. Jameson & M. Miyoshi (Eds.), *The cultures of globalization* (pp. xi–xvii). Durham, NC: Duke University Press.

Kureshi, H. (1996). My son the fanatic. In I. Chambers & L. Curti (Eds.), *The post-colonial question: Common skies, divided horizons* (pp. 228–241). New York: Routledge.

Mani, L. (1999). *Contentious traditions*. Berkeley: University of California Press.

McClintock, A. (1995). *Imperial leather: Race, gender and sexuality in the colonial context*. New York: Routledge.

Mercer, K. (1994). *Welcome to the jungle: New positions in black cultural studies*. New York: Routledge.

Mignolo, W. (1995a). *The darker side of resistance: Literacy, territoriality and colonization*. Ann Arbor: University of Michigan Press.

Mignolo, W. (1995b). Afterword, human understanding, and Latin American interests. *Poetics Today, 16*, 171–214.

Mignolo, W. (2000). *Local histories/global designs: Coloniality, subaltern knowledges, and border thinking*. Durham, NC: Duke University Press.

Minh-ha, T. (1986). Difference: A special third world women's issue. *Discourse, 8*, 11–37.

Minh-ha, T. (1989). *Woman, native, other: Writing postcoloniality and feminism*. Bloomington: Indiana University Press.

Mitchell, T. (2000). Introduction. In T. Mitchell (Ed.), *Questions of modernity* (pp. 1–18). Minneapolis: University of Minnesota Press.

Mohanty, C. T. (1991). Cartographies of struggle: Third world women and the politics of feminism. In C. T. Mohanty, A. Russo, & L. Torres (Eds.), *Third world women and the politics of feminism* (pp. 1–47). Bloomington: University of Indiana Press.

Mohanty, C. T. (1994). On race and voice: Challenges for liberal education in the 1990s. In H. A. Giroux & P. McLaren (Eds.), *Between borders: Pedagogy and the politics of cultural studies* (pp. 145–166). New York: Routledge.

Mohanty, C. T. (1996). Women workers and capitalist scripts. In J. Alexander & C. Mohanty (Eds.), *Feminist genealogies, colonial legacies, and democratic futures* (pp. 3–30). New York: Routledge.

Nelson, C., & Gaonkar, D. (Eds.). (1996). *Disciplinarity and dissent in cultural studies*. New York: Routledge.

O'Hanlon, R., & Washbrook, D. (1992) After Orientalism: Culture, criticism and politics in the Third World. *Comparative studies in history and society, 34*, 141–167.

Ong, A. (1999). *Flexible citizenship*. Berkeley: University of California Press.

Radhakrishnan, R. (2000). Postmodernism and the rest of the world. In F. Afzal-Khan & K. Seshadri-Crooks (Eds.), *The pre-occupation of postcolonial studies* (pp. 37–70). Durham, NC: Duke University Press.

Rafael, V. (2000). *White love*. Durham, NC: Duke University Press.

Rouse, R. (1995). Thinking through transnationalism: Notes on the cultural politics of class relations in the contemporary United States. *Public Culture, 7*, 353–402.

Said, E. W. (1978). *Orientalism*. New York: Random House.

San Juan, E. (1995). On the limits of postcolonial theory: Trespassing letters from the third world. *Ariel, 26*, 89–116.

San Juan, E. (1996). *The Philippine temptation: Dialectics of Philippines-United States literary relations*. Philadelphia: Temple University Press.

San Juan, E. (1999). *Beyond postcolonial theory*. New York: St. Martin's Press.

Schwarz, H. (2000). Mission impossible: Introducing postcolonial studies in the U.S. academy. In H. Schwarz & S. Ray (Eds.), *A companion to postcolonial studies* (pp. 1–20). Oxford, UK: Blackwell Publishers.

Seshadri-Crooks, K. (2000). At the margins of postcolonial studies: Part I. In F. Afzal-Khan & K. Seshadri-Crooks (Eds.), *The pre-occupation of postcolonial studies* (pp. 3–23). Durham, NC: Duke University Press.

Sharpe, J. (1993). *Allegories of empire: The figure of woman in the colonial text*. Minneapolis: University of Minnesota Press.

Shohat, E. (1992). Notes on the post-colonial. *Social Text, 31/32*, 99–113.

Spivak, G. C. (1985). Three women's texts and a critique of imperialism. In H. L. Gates (Ed.), *Race, writing and difference* (pp. 262–280). Chicago, IL: University of Chicago Press.

Spivak, G. C. (1988a). Can the subaltern speak? In L. Grossberg & C. Nelson (Eds.), *Marxism and the interpretation of culture* (pp. 271–313). Urbana: University of Illinois Press.

Spivak, G. C. (1988b). *In other worlds*. New York: Routledge.

Spivak, G. C. (1990). *The postcolonial critic*. New York: Routledge.

Spivak, G. C. (1992). French feminism revisited: Ethics and politics. In J. Butler & J. Scott (Eds.), *Feminists theorize the political* (pp. 54–85). New York: Routledge.

Spivak, G. C. (1993). *Outside in the teaching machine*. New York: Routledge.

Spivak, G. C. (2000). *A critique of postcolonial reason*. Boston: Harvard University Press.

Visweswaran, K. (1994). *Fictions of feminist ethnography*. Minneapolis: University of Minnesota Press.

Chapter 7

Srinivas R. Melkote

THEORIES OF DEVELOPMENT COMMUNICATION

THIS CHAPTER EXPLORES THE scholarship and practice of communication for development and empowerment in the Third World. The exercise of explicating theories, concepts, and methodologies in development communication presents unique challenges. This exploration requires an understanding of key concepts and how these meanings compare and contrast with how they have been used and defined by others during different historical settings. The overarching concepts in this field are *communication*, *modernization*, *development*, *participation*, and *empowerment*. Combinations of these terms have yielded additional concepts and accompanying controversies. Thus, terminology has been problematic within the rubric of development communication and related areas and has varied significantly from text to text and one context to another. The distinction made between *development communication* and *development support communication* constitutes one such example. Development means different things to different scholars and practitioners. Therefore, the theory and practice of development communication cannot be meaningfully discussed without defining development as well as communication. Though the importance of defining development is obvious, relatively few studies of development communication bother to do so. In a recent meta-analysis, Fair and Shah (1997) looked at nearly 140 studies of communication and development and found that only about a third conceptualized development. Where definitions are provided, understandings about it vary. Though most would agree that development means improving the living conditions of society, there has been much debate on just what constitute improved living conditions and how they should be achieved.

The definition and boundaries of all these overlapping interdisciplinary areas have become even more fluid and nebulous in the past decade. The end of the Cold War in the early 1990s, alongside greater polarization along ethnic, religious, and nationalistic lines, increased transnationalization, increased information flow and influence, and a growing consciousness of marginalized groups and diminished resources have challenged and changed the issues and questions.

Over the years, there have been at least four perspectives or ways of thinking about and practicing development. The first is *modernization* that is based on neoclassical economic theory and promoting and supporting capitalistic economic development. This perspective assumes that the Western model of economic growth is applicable elsewhere and that the introduction of modern technologies is important in development. *Critical* perspectives constitute a second way of thinking about development. These perspectives challenge the economic and cultural expansionism and imperialism of modernization; they argue for a political and economic restructuring to produce a more even distribution of rewards and resources between and within societies. *Liberation* or *monastic* perspectives constitute the third area of scholarship and practice. These perspectives derive largely from liberation theology (Freire, 1970), which prioritize personal and communal liberation from oppression as the keys to self-reliance, which is seen as the goal of development. The fourth concept is *empowerment*. This construct is mentioned frequently in the communication and development literature of the 1990s, but terms, exemplars, levels of analysis, and outcomes have not been fully explicated. In addition, empowerment cannot be understood without first defining *power*. As such, this concept introduces the concepts of power and control in development theory and practice.

The theory and practice of development communication as described and analyzed in this chapter reflect varied underlying views about communication, development, and empowerment. Development communication scholars and practitioners still tend to be split between those who view communication as an organizational delivery system and those who view communication more broadly, as inseparable from culture and from all facets of social change. This orientation rests on certain assumptions consistent with divisions in views on development, empowerment, and development communication.

In this chapter, I attempt to provide an analysis of the theories used in communication for development (see Melkote & Steeves, 2001). First, I describe the discourse on modernization and the historical and conceptual biases introduced and reinforced by this discourse. The earlier communication theories inherited from the modernization paradigm and their institutional and context-related biases will be discussed in this section. Second, I describe and critique the theories in communication for development. I conclude by looking at the contemporary social and political situations in the developing countries that are characterized by unequal power relationships and structural inequities. I suggest communication approaches that better fit the contemporary challenges in Third World societies.

The paradigm of modernization

Among the most powerful paradigms to originate after World War II, with enormous social, cultural, and economic consequences for the Third World, was that of modernization. Modernization, an operational artifact of the concept "development," was based on liberal political theory and was therefore grounded in the grand project of the Enlightenment, namely, reasoning, rationality, objectivity, and other philosophical principles of Western science. In modernization theories, the definition of a modern nation resembled Western industrialized nations in all areas of society, including political and economic behavior and institutions, attitudes toward technology and science, and cultural mores. The economic model that grounded modernization theories was the *neoclassical* approach that had served as the basis for Western economies. The dominant paradigm was mainly concerned with economic growth as measured by gross national product (GNP) rates and encouragement of all factors and institutions that accelerated and maintained high growth in areas such as capital-intensive industrialization and technology with private ownership of factors of production, free trade, and the principle of laissez-faire.

The modernization paradigm emerged not only from economic theory but also from social evolutionary theory. At the macro level, theories applied Darwin's ideas to the process of modernization of human societies. The theories of social evolution influenced and gave rise to important concepts in the sociology of development such as, for example, the various bipolar theories of modernization. In these theories, the universal stages in the earlier theories of social evolution were reduced to ideal-typical extremes: gemeinschaft versus gesellschaft, traditional versus modern societies, and so forth. The Third World nations were usually described as traditional, whereas the industrialized nations of the West signified the modern counterpart. The advanced Western nations had a wide range of systemic autonomy, that is, their capacity to cope with a range of social, cultural, techno-logical, and economic issues in the process of social change. The Third World nations, on the other hand, lacking the higher differentiation of roles and institutions, the evolutionary universals, and other qualitative sociological characteristics of industrial societies, were limited in their capacity to cope with problems or crises or even master their environment. At the micro level, theories on individual psychological attributes stressed that attitudinal and value changes among individuals were prerequisites to the creation of a modern society. Scholars such as McClelland (1967), Lerner (1958), Inkeles (1966), and Rogers (1969) described certain value-normative complexes that were responsible for the modern-ization of individuals in the West and that the individuals in the Third World were lacking. These scholars posited that modernization of the Third World was dependent on changing the character of individuals living there to resemble more closely the attitudinal and value characteristics of people in Western Europe and North America.

Modernization theories provided the epistemological foundation for the initial theories in communication for development. This led to the inheritance of historical and institutional biases emanating from propaganda research conducted in the United States between the two world wars. During this period, the mass communication media were viewed as powerful instruments that could be successfully used to manipulate people's opinions and attitudes, and thereby their behaviors, in a relatively short period of time. The institutional bias involved in this research has been carefully analyzed and revealed by scholars (Glander, 2000; Simpson, 1994). Simpson (1994) reveals the social, political, and economic context to the powerful effects research. In particular, he points out the support and funding that this research received from powerful sponsors such as the U.S. government, Army, Air Force, and the CIA; the active professional links that academicians maintained with the above groups; and importantly, the one dominant view of media effects that was propagated to the exclusion of other, nonmainstream, views—a dominant view that was also very supportive of the then U.S. foreign policy. This bias of powerful effects of the media was incorporated in development communication theories during the 1950s and 1960s. Thus, the initial biases set the norm for the field that was not necessarily appropriate for the socioeconomic and cultural conditions that existed in Asia, Africa, the Caribbean, or Latin America. To compli-cate matters, young researchers from developing countries were being taken to the United States under the PL 480 Program (a food aid program) to be trained in the American mold.

Starting in the 1970s, there were serious criticisms leveled at the propositions of the modernization paradigm, especially by scholars from Latin America and Asia. They contended that the development process in the Third World countries did not fit the assumptions implicit in the modernization paradigm. The paradigm worked better as a description of social change in Western Europe and North America than as a predictor of change in developing countries. The neoclassical economic model that suggested a *trickle-down* approach to development benefits started losing credibility in the 1970s. The worldwide recession of the 1980s and the neoliberal economic reforms in the Third World countries left them even further behind. The criticisms of the sociology of development models were directed at the abstractness of the social theories, the ahistorical nature of the propositions, and incorrect nature of development indicators that constituted the "evolutionary univer-sals" proposed by scholars such as Parsons (1964). In addition, the value-enactment models of McClelland (1967), Hagen (1962), Inkeles and Smith (1974), Lerner (1958), Rogers (1969), and others were criticized for their ethnocentrism and for neglecting to account for the influence of structural constraints on individual action and enterprise. The modernization paradigm was further criticized for its negative view of culture, especially religious culture, for its patriarchal biases, and for its androcentrism. In the mainstream view, cultural traditions had to be destroyed if the Third World nations and peoples wanted to modernize. This notion no longer had overt supporters, though modernization processes still function to destroy, appropriate, or absorb indigenous traditions. Neo-Marxist scholars criticized many of the tenets of the modernization paradigm. To them, underdevelopment was not a process distinctly different from development. In fact, they constituted two facets of the same process. The *development of underdevelopment* (Frank, 1969) in Third World nations was and is related to the economic development of Western Europe and North America.

Below, I summarize some of the overt and covert biases of the dominant paradigm and its discourse. The list is not exhaustive, but rather should be seen as a start in the deconstruction of the dominant paradigm:

- Rationality and progress are synonymous with economic rationality and growth as articulated by the economic and political elite in the North, by multilateral organizations controlled by such elite, state bureaucrats, and by vested interests in the South (Braidotti, Charkiewicz, Hausler, & Wierninga, 1994).
- A higher and higher standard of living as quantified by indicators such as per capita income, per capita consumption of resources, and GNP constitutes a key goal. The bias is not necessarily the "well-being" of an individual or community that would include the material and nonmaterial aspects of life, but "well-having" that denotes maximum material consumption (Latouche, 1992).
- The dominant discourse aided by the positivistic scientific method has claimed to speak the "truth" about development. Thus, assumptions and images of modernity and progress as exported from the industrialized West have been uncritically accepted by the leaders of many recipient countries (Foucault, 1980). These assumptions frequently have overruled other analyses, such as folk-scientific descriptions of nature (Alvares, 1992).
- The prior histories of developing countries have been considered irrelevant to the enterprise of modernization. Communities have been stripped of their histories and cultures and a technocratic plan has been constructed for their future (Crush, 1995). Thus, objects of development are treated in a historical vacuum that precludes any analysis of previous initiatives and their harmful effects (Mitchell, 1995).
- Development concepts, initiatives, and their presumed benefits have been guided by master geographies constructed by the dominant states and institutions. Thus, notions such as the Third World, Oriental, African, and North-South have become stereotypes. Third World countries or poorer enclaves within them are incorrectly viewed as net receivers of development assistance (Hewitt, 1995).
- There is a strong biological metaphor in development discourse. *Entwicklung* or the process of social evolution was considered similar to the phylogenic changes in a biological organism. Over time, ontogeny imitated the irreversible and linear stages of phylogeny.
- The irrelevance of history leads to social problems that are interpreted as occurring naturally rather than as outcomes of politics, mismanagement, corruption, greed, or the exercise of power (Escobar, 1995; Wilkins, 1999). "Natural" hazards such as famine and drought, for example, are not regarded as possible outcomes of policy

failure, failures of research paradigms, or the crises of capitalist modernization ventures (Crush, 1995; Hewitt, 1995).

In essence, positivistic science has claimed to be the final arbiter of truth. As the Enlightenment values that undergird science are consistent with those of modern political-economic systems, science and scientific discourse, economics, and politics constitute mutually reinforcing systems. Thus, modern states, bureaucrats, elite in positions of power, and scientist-technocrats using science have taken over the responsibility of deciding what is truth and what is not. Post-structuralists such as Foucault (1980) have posited that as a servant of the state, science has been used not just to explain reality but to produce, control, and normalize. The process of normalization reduces heterogeneity by homogenizing individual feelings, desires, and actions.

Theories in communication for development

The theories in communication for development may be categorized under two heads: those that fall within the dominant paradigm of modernization that I have discussed above and an alternative paradigm that has been put forward as a desirable alternative to the overly prescriptive and top-down model of modernization (see Rifkin, 1996). The first family of theories comprises communication and modernization theory, the diffusion of innovations theory, social marketing approach, and entertainment-education strategies. Within the second family, approaches such as the participatory action research model and empowerment are included.

Theories and interventions within the dominant paradigm of modernization

Communication and modernization theory. In communication and modernization theory, communication was more than just an interplay between the source and receiver. It served as a complex system fulfilling certain social functions. Thus, the mass media came to serve as agents and indices of modernization in the Third World countries. Besides this macro-level analysis of the role of mass media, researchers also drew on communication effects research and on models describing social-psychological characteristics of individuals that were considered necessary for a successful transition from a traditional to a modern society.

Daniel Lerner's *The Passing of Traditional Society* (1958) illustrates the major ideas of the early mass media and modernization approach. Lerner identified and explained a psychological pattern in individuals that was both required and reinforced by the modern society: a mobile personality. This person was equipped with a high capacity for identification with new aspects of his or her environment and internalized the new demands made by the larger society. In other words, this person had a high degree of empathy, the capacity to see oneself in the other person's situation. Lerner stated that empathy fulfilled two important tasks. First, it enabled the person to operate efficiently in the modern society, which was constantly changing. Second, it was an indispensable skill for individuals wanting to move out of their traditional settings. The second element in Lerner's model was the mass media. They performed a special function: By exposing individuals to new people, ideas, and attitudes, they accelerated the process of modernization. Thus, the mass media were important agents of modernization. People in the Third World could expand their empathy by exposure to the mass media, which showed them new places, behavior, and cultures. In short, the mass media had the potential of blowing the winds of modernization into isolated traditional communities and replacing the structure of life, values, and behavior with ones seen in modern Western society.

The powerful role of the mass media in modernization was clearly implied in Lerner's (1958) and Schramm's (1964) research and many other studies in the 1950s and the 1960s. These studies complemented the postulates of the dominant paradigm of development. Mass media were the vehicles for transferring new ideas and models from the West to the Third World and from urban areas to rural countryside. Importantly, they were entrusted with the task of preparing individuals in developing nations for a rapid social change by establishing a "climate of modernization." The mass media were thought to have a powerful and direct influence on individuals. Thus, the bullet theory model of mass media effects seemed to hold in the Third World countries in the 1950s and 1960s, even though this model had been discarded earlier in North America (Mody, 2000). The strength of the mass media lay in their one-way, top-down, simultaneous and wide dissemination. They were considered as "magic multipliers" of development benefits in Third World nations. Administrators, researchers, and field workers sincerely believed in the great power of mass media as harbingers of modernizing influences. Therefore, information was considered the missing link in the development chain.

Diffusion of innovations theory. While scholars and policymakers were making macro-level arguments and funding experiments on the role of the media in supporting modernization, diffusion of innovations theory gradually evolved as the local-level framework to guide communications planning for modernization. Diffusion of innovations also had important theoretical links with communication effects research. The emphasis was on particular communication effects: the ability of media messages and opinion leaders to create knowledge of new practices and ideas and persuade the target to adopt the exogenously introduced innovations.

The diffusion of innovations approach is rooted in the postulates and implicit assumptions of exogenous change theory. The notion of exogenously induced change permeates assumptions of fundamental concepts in diffusion research. The earliest definition of development was "a type of social change in which new ideas are introduced into a social system in order to produce higher per capita incomes and levels of living through more modern production methods and improved social organization" (Rogers, 1969, p. 18). The necessary route for the change from a traditional to a modern person was understood as the communication and acceptance of new ideas from sources external to the social system (Fjes, 1976).

Everett M. Rogers, whose work has been central in this area, identified the following main elements in any analysis of diffusion of an idea or innovation: (1) the *innovation*, (2) its *communication* through certain *channels*, (3) among members of a *social system*, (4) over *time* (Rogers, 1971). Adoption was defined as the process through which the individual arrived at the decision to adopt or reject the innovation from the time he or she first became aware of it. The five stages were awareness, interest, evaluation, trial, and adoption. Diffusion studies indicated a great difference among the adopter groups in terms of their personal characteristics, media behavior, and position in the social structure. The relatively early adopters were usually younger, had a higher social status, had more favorable financial status, engaged in more specialized operations, and were equipped with greater mental abilities than later adopters. In terms of communication behavior, earlier adopters used more mass media and cosmopolite information sources. Also, the social relations of earlier adopters were more cosmopolite than for later categories, and the earlier adopters had more opinion leadership characteristics.

In sum, the diffusion of innovations research established the importance of communication in the modernization process at the local level. In the dominant paradigm, communication was visualized as the link through which exogenous ideas entered the local communities. Diffusion of innovations then emphasized the nature and role of communication in facilitating further dissemination within local communities. Thus, diffusion of innovations studies documented the impact of communication (interpersonal and mass media) on the change from a traditional to a modern way of life.

Social marketing approach. Over time, diffusion theory alone proved inadequate as a guide to communications planning in development campaigns. The diffusion concepts are imprecise, and the diffusion model does not sufficiently account for recipient feedback, which is crucial to campaign success. Communication efforts both in First World and Third World contexts have increasingly turned to science-based commercial marketing strategies to disseminate ideas to promote social causes, a process called *social marketing*. Examples in the First World include campaigns to discourage tobacco smoking, encourage use of auto seat belts, stop drinking and driving, promote healthful diets, discourage teen sex (or encourage safe sex), and prevent HIV/AIDS and other sexually transmitted diseases. In the Third World context, the major themes have included family planning, equal status for women, responsible sexual relationships, adult literacy, responsible parenthood, and HIV/AIDS prevention and control.

Until the early 1970s, communication models in family planning or other health-related areas reinforced the active source and passive receiver stereotypes. Communication campaigns used one-way, top-down, source-to-receiver transmission models with the belief that effects would occur autonomously once the target received the message (Rogers, 1973). Opinion leaders, change agents, and mass media outlets such as the radio were used to transmit persuasive messages. The assumption in these strategies was that knowledge was the missing link in the adoption and use of the service or product. The incorporation of social marketing techniques in the 1970s emphasized the challenges of changing the values and knowledge as well as behavior patterns of the receivers. Social marketing has introduced several new concepts in the dissemination of ideas and services: *audience segmentation, market research, product development, incentives*, and *facilitation* to maximize the target group's response (Kotler, 1984). Social marketers take a holistic view of the process by emphasizing the four Ps in the marketing chain: product, pricing, placement, and promotion.

Since the 1990s, the Population Communication Services (PCS), aided by the U.S. Agency for International Development (USAID), has adopted a strategic communication framework to overcome past weaknesses in family planning communication. Strategic communication describes an operational framework that incorporates the concepts of social marketing and behavior change models in the design, execution, and evaluation of communication strategies intended to influence behavior change. The concepts of audience research, market segmentation, product development, incentives, and promotion are contributions from social marketing research applied to strategic family planning communication. In addition, the communication process itself has evolved into a convergence model where participants create and share information in order to reach a mutual understanding. This orientation, then, pulls in formative research procedures such as focus groups, audience surveys, and pretesting of messages into communication research in family planning (Piotrow, Kincaid, Rimon, & Rinehart, 1997). Stage models in several disciplines such as social psychology, marketing, rural sociology, and psychotherapy identified a series of steps that an individual would pass through from first awareness to adoption. This hierarchy of effects in behavior change indicated a similar step process in family planning communication. Some of the most frequently used stage models of behavior change used in family planning are listed in Table 7.1.

Table 7.1 Stage theories in behavior change

Stage models	Hierarchy of effects	Source
Social psychology	cognition-attitude-behavior change	Hovland, Lumsdaine, and Sheffield (1949)
Diffusion of innovations	awareness-interest-evaluation-trial-adoption	Rogers (1962)
	knowledge-persuasion-decision-implementation-confirmation	Rogers (1995)
Marketing and advertising	attention-interest-comprehension-impact-attitude-sales	Palda (1966)
Social marketing	cognition-action-behavior-values	Kotler (1984)
Psychotherapy	precontemplation-contemplation-preparation-action-maintenance	Prochaska, DiClemente, and Norcross (1992)

The stage theories represent behavior change as a sequence of steps with intermediate goals. These dictate that the communication process should also be a stage process needing different messages and approaches at each step of the behavior change process.

Entertainment-education strategies. In mass communication theory, the minimal effects hypothesis was gradually losing its appeal by the early 1970s (Lowery & DeFleur, 1995). Since the early 1940s, research testing this hypothesis had showed that mass media were not particularly effective in changing opinions and attitudes of the audience members. However, new research in the area of agenda setting showed that the mass media were very effective in increasing the cognition levels of audiences of salient events and thus serving as important agents of surveillance (Shaw & McCombs, 1974). Another area of research labeled as the uses and gratifications perspective (Blumer & Katz, 1974) put the focus on an active audience member as opposed to the passive receiver stereotype depicted in the minimal effects theories. In the uses and gratifications model, audience members actively selected media products to satisfy a range of needs: new information, entertainment, news, relaxation, and more. This research showed that audiences were actively selecting radio and television programs to gratify their perceived needs. A parallel development in the Third World has been the trend toward increasing commercialization and privatization of television and radio channels. These concomitant developments have provided a fertile ground for the growth and popularity of entertainment-education programs. In this approach, educational content is embedded in entertainment programs in media such as the radio, television, records, videos, and folk theater.

Singhal and Rogers (1999) point out that entertainment-education programs either directly or indirectly facilitate social change. At the individual level, they influence awareness, attention, and behavior toward a socially desirable objective, and at the larger, community level, they serve as an agenda setter or influence public and policy initiatives in a socially desirable direction. Entertainment-education programs represent a unique kind of social marketing where pro-social ideas are marketed within media products. Results show primarily cognitive changes, though some changes have been recorded that require behavior and value shifts. Modeling theory, self-efficacy, and para-social interaction models have been used to predict and explain the hierarchy of effects produced by these media programs.

Approaches within an alternative paradigm for social change

This is an appropriate juncture to examine the changes in the notion of development and directed social change. The earliest descriptions of development were technologically deterministic and centered on quantifiable indicators such as the GNP. They stressed industrialization and economic growth while ignoring other human and nontechnological factors. The ferment in the field of development communication in the 1970s broadened the definitions to include growth with equity, provision of basic needs, meaningful employment, and rich and varied interpersonal relationships. Descriptions of directed change also incorporated the protection of the environment and native cultures. At present, the definitions tend to be qualitative and pluralistic. In this chapter, I see development as a process that should provide people with access to appropriate and sustainable opportunities to improve their lives and lives of others in their communities. This definition provides a segue to a comprehensive discussion of concepts and approaches that have attempted to provide people with credible opportunities to define their idea of development and construct approaches to achieving them.

An approach that has found wide support in the past 20 years has been the participatory approach to communication and development. Attempts at operationalization of the term *participation* range from those that reflect the dominant paradigm—the participation-as-a-means approach—to those that genuinely represent the case for a context-based paradigm —the participation-as-an-end approach (Ascroft & Masilela, 1989). The participation-as-an-end approach has received support from many scholars and administrators (Díaz Bordenave, 1989; Kothari, 1984). They argue that participation must be recognized as a basic human right. It should be accepted and supported as an end in itself and not for its results. The need to think, express oneself, belong to a group, be recognized as a person, be appreciated and respected, and have some say in crucial decisions affecting one's life are as essential to the development of an individual as eating, drinking, and sleeping (Díaz Bordenave, 1989). And participation in meaningful activities is the vehicle through which the needs described above are fulfilled.

Many scholars and practitioners over the past two decades have favored active participation of the people at the grassroots. On the surface, these signaled a positive departure from the earlier overly top-down and prescriptive approaches. However, the structure of elite domination was not disturbed as the participation that was expected was often directed by the sources and change agents. Although the people were induced to participate in self-help activities, the basic solutions to local problems had already been selected by the external development agencies. Critics argued that true participation should encourage social and political action by the people at all levels. The goal of participation efforts should be to facilitate *conscientization* of marginalized people globally of unequal social, political, and spatial structures in their societies. It is through conscientization and collective action that they perceive their needs, identify constraints to addressing these needs, and plan to overcome problems (Freire, 1970).

The term *participatory communication* has been frequently misunderstood and misused. Participation has been defined and operationalized in many ways: from pseudo participation to genuine efforts at generating participatory decision making (Ascroft & Masilela, 1989; Díaz Bordenave, 1989; Freire, 1970; White, 1994). There is a great deal of confusion about the outcomes desired and a contradiction between exemplars (or best practices) and phenomena of interest (or outcomes). Although the practice of participatory communication has stressed collaboration between the people and experts, a co-equal knowledge-sharing between the people and experts, and a local context and cultural proximity, the outcome in most cases has not been true empowerment of the people, but the attainment of some indicator of development as articulated in the modernization paradigm. Thus, participatory approaches have been encouraged, though the design and control of messages and develop-ment agendas usually have remained with the experts. Also, issues of power and control by the authorities, structures of dependency, and power inequities have not been addressed adequately within Third World settings (Wilkins, 1999). Thus, most of the participatory approaches have been essentially old wine in new bottles.

This postmodernist deconstruction of the participatory development paradigm puts the focus squarely on the contemporary power relations in society and the structures of inequi-ties that they create and strengthen. For "real" social change for individuals and groups trapped in the margins, the search is for development communication models and analytical tools that can address and overcome these systemic barriers. Two areas/concepts that look fruitful in this endeavor are participatory action research (PAR) and empowerment strategies.

Participatory action research. PAR encompasses an experiential methodology. In this process, the people on their own develop methods of consciousness-raising of their existential situ-ation; the knowledge that is generated or resuscitated is by collective and democratic means; and this is followed by reflection and critical self-evaluation, leading to endogenous participatory social action (see Figure 7.1). This in essence forms the praxis.

PAR has emerged as a forceful methodology-cum-action approach, principally as a reaction to the degradation of the economic and social conditions of poor and marginalized groups. PAR is dedicated to resuscitating both the power of marginalized people and their popular knowledge. The knowledge that PAR attempts to generate is specific, local, non-Western, and nonpositivist. Importantly, it is used to initiate collaborative social action to empower local knowledge and wrest social power inherent in knowledge away from the privileged (Friesen, 1999).

Domination of the poor and marginalized comes about in at least three ways: (1) control over the means of material production, (2) control over the means of knowledge production, and (3) control over power that legitimizes the relative worth and utility of different espistemologies/knowledges (Rahman, 1991). Those who have social power will legitimize their knowledge and techniques of knowledge generation as superior. Critical scholars have shown how local narratives, popular knowledge, cultural meanings, and social arrangements have been devalued in the dominant development discourse. Nearly all of the knowledge of the oppressed and the marginalized has been disqualified as inadequate and unscientific by the dominant forces (Foucault, 1980). As long as there are inequalities in knowledge relations between different sections of a society, there will be inequities in the relations of material production. Therefore, in PAR an important objective to achieve the liberation of the poor and the oppressed is to recapture their knowledge and narratives. Thus, the basic ideology of PAR is that endogenous efforts and local leaders will play the leading role in social transformation using their own praxis. The PAR approach, then, by resuscitating and elevating popular knowledge, attempts to create a counterdiscourse,

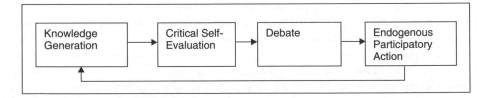

Figure 7.1 Praxis in participatory action research.

disrupts the position of development as articulated by the dominant discourse as problematic, causes a crisis in authority, and creates a space for marginalized groups to influence social change (White, 1999).

Empowerment. Much work has been done on empowerment in fields such as community organization, education, and community psychology, and we may do well by borrowing and adapting these concepts to development support communication. Although empowerment as a construct has a set of core ideas, it may be defined at different levels—individual, organization, and community—and operationalized in different contexts (Rowlands, 1998). Several working definitions of empowerment are available. However, given the nature of our work, which can be described as directed social change, and given the power inequities in societies that are posited as the major impediments to achieving meaningful change, it is important that the working definitions be linked directly to the building and exercise of social power (Speer & Hughey, 1995).

The following definitions and descriptions of the term *empowerment* are useful. According to Fawcett et al. (1984), "Community empowerment is the process of increasing control by groups over consequences that are important to their members and to others in the broader community" (p. 679). Rappaport (1987) describes empowerment as "a psychological sense of personal control or influence and a concern with actual social influence, political power, and legal rights. It is a multi-level construct applicable to individual citizens as well as to organizations and neighborhoods; it suggests the study of people in context" (p. 121). Another definition describes empowerment as "an intentional, ongoing process centered in the local community, involving mutual respect, critical reflection, caring and group participation, through which people lacking an equal share of valued resources gain greater access to and control over those resources" (Cornell Empowerment Group, 1989, p. 2). In summary, empowerment is the "manifestation of social power at individual, organizational, and community levels of analysis" (Speer & Hughey, 1995, p. 730).

The construct of empowerment has been mentioned quite often in the communication for development literature, but the terms, exemplars, levels of analysis, and outcomes have not been thoroughly explicated. Table 7.2 attempts to articulate elements for a conceptual framework of development support communication that is informed by the goals of the empowerment model. The concept of empowerment is heuristic in understanding the complex constraints in directed social change. It clarifies the empowerment-oriented outcomes and provides a useful niche for development communication.

Comparison of development communication theories and approaches

Table 7.2 provides a framework to compare the theories under the modernization paradigm with approaches under the empowerment model on several criteria. The phenomena of interest in the two approaches are vastly different and so are the underlying beliefs. The bias in the diffusion of innovations and social marketing approaches has been to favor exogenous ideas and innovations over the local. In the absence of active local people participation, such exogenously introduced changes most often result in social engineering by the government or the elite. In addition, the diffusion and social marketing approaches have been criticized for their pro-innovation bias and victim blame hypotheses. Although social marketing theoretically begins with a through analysis of local needs, campaigns have often been largely top-down with individual receivers treated as objects or targets for persuasion and change.

The differences are stark when it comes to the communication models used. The empowerment model puts the focus on a symmetrical relationship between relevant actors with all communication participants treated as subject-subject rather than the subject-object

Table 7.2 Comparison of development communication theories and approaches in the modernization and empowerment frameworks

	Development communication in the modernization framework[a]	*Development communication in the empowerment framework*[b]
Phenomenon of interest/goal	National and regional development, people development, community improvement	Empowerment of people, social justice, building capacity and equity
Belief	Underdevelopment due to economic, political, cultural, geographic, and individual inadequacies; due to lack of power and control on the part of the existence of a single standard (as articulated by diversity of standards)	Underdevelopment due to lack of access to economic, political, and cultural resources; underdevelopment people; experts)
Bias	Cultural insensitivity, environmentally unsustainable, standardization; change directed by external sources and ideas; deterministic process toward a predetermined end dictated by an external agency; pro-innovation bias; individual as locus of change and blame; victim blame hypotheses	Cultural proximity; ecological, diversity of standards; change directed and controlled by endogenous sources and ideas; open-ended and ongoing process of change; system blame hypotheses; group or community is paramount
Context	Macro and micro settings; very little interest in local cultures or power relationships and structural impediments in host society	Local and community settings; cognizant of formidable power inequities and systemic constraints
Level of analysis	Nation, region, individual	Individual, group or organization, community
Role of change agent	Expert, benefactor, nonparticipant	Collaborator, facilitator, participant, advocate for individuals and communities, risk taker, activist
Communication model	Linear, top-down, transmission of information using big mass media; media treated as independent variables with direct and powerful effects; pro-source bias; asymmetrical relationship (subject-object)	Nonlinear, participatory; used to convey information as well as build organizations; increased use of small media, traditional media, group as well as interpersonal communication; media treated as dependent variables; communication used for transaction, negotiation, understanding and not for powerful effects of a source; symmetrical relationship (subject-subject); horizontal flows

Type of research	Usually quantitative (surveys); some use of focus groups; contextual or evaluation research	Quantitative and qualitative; longitudinal studies; labor-intensive participatory action research
Exemplars mutual	Prevention of underdevelopment; remedy through/by experts; blame the victim; individual adjustment to a dominant norm; use of mass media to spread standardized messages and entertainment; messages that are preachy, prescriptive, and/or persuasive	Activate social support systems, social networks, help, and self-help activities; participation of all actors; empower community narratives; facilitate critical awareness; facilitate community and organizational power; communication used to strengthen interpersonal relationships
Outcomes desired	Modernization; economic growth; political development; infrastructure development; change in people's attitudes and behavior toward modernization objectives	Increased access of all citizens to material, psychological, cultural, and informational resources; honing of individual and group competence, leadership skills, useful life, and communication skills at the local level; honing of critical awareness skills; empowered local organizations and communities

a. Diffusion of innovations, social marketing, entertainment-education

b. Participatory action research, empowerment strategies

---

relationship found in the diffusion and social marketing approaches. Also, given its focus on the unequal power dynamics in societies, empowerment requires more than just information delivery and diffusion of technical innovations. The objective of development communication professionals is to work with the individuals and communities at the grassroots so that they eventually may enter and participate meaningfully in the political and economic processes in their communities/societies. This calls for grassroots organizing (Kaye, 1990) and communicative social action on the part of the poor, women, minorities, and others who have been consistently and increasingly marginalized in the process of social change. The implication for development communication, then, is a reconceptualization of its role. Greater importance will need to be placed on the organizational value of communication and the role of communicative efforts in empowering citizens.

It became increasingly clear in Asia and in Latin America that socioeconomic structural constraints greatly diminished the power of the mass media in overcoming problems of development. Far from being independent variables in the change process, the mass media were themselves affected by extraneous factors such as power imbalances and other structural and systemic barriers within societies. The dominant paradigm, with its exaggerated emphasis on the individual blame causal hypotheses regarding underdevelopment, obfuscated the social structural, political, and institutional constraints acting against individuals' efforts to change. Furthermore, what sets empowerment apart from the models informed by the modernization paradigm is that the locus of control in this process rests with the individuals or groups involved and not with the experts, the development communication professionals, or the sponsoring organizations. Although the professionals may have a role to play in designing intervention strategies, they are not the key actors. The key players are the people handling their problems in local settings and learning and honing their competencies in the concrete experiences of their existential realities.

Conclusion

Today, the poststructuralism and postmodernism embraced by leading theorists challenge universal truths and our notions of objective social reality. Epistemological plurality is the favored outcome in these approaches, which also assume that language actively constructs (vs. merely conveys) meaning and that it is more valuable to discover representational meaning than to find explanations. At the same time, political economists, socialist feminists, and others with Marxist leanings have cautioned against going too far in rejecting theories and methods of the social sciences to the neglect of real material structures that also—along with ideological factors—contribute to social inequalities, as well as to progressive change (e.g., Barrett, 1999). For development communication, the combined effect of all these trends has been to encourage the acceptance of multiple meanings, symbolic rationality (or irrationality), cultural specificity, change through human agency, communicative action and structuration, deconstruction of dominant ideology of power, and the strengthening of critical consciousness among the people in a community (Jacobson & Kolluri, 1999; Servaes, 1999; Tehranian, 1994).

In general, the intellectual ferment in the humanities and social sciences (with ethical, practical, and philosophical implications) has increasingly favored participatory approaches in development communication, as appropriate for each unique context. Some of the assumptions that undergird the ferment include the following:

1. The scientific method and the knowledge that it has generated are value laden reflecting the economic-political-cultural contexts involved. In general, there is a suspicion of logocentric views. One major area of criticism relates to notions of objectivity and causality.
2. As all knowledge systems and the scientific method are value biased, the accumulation of "objective" knowledge by such methods is a futile exercise. Universally valid explanations are nothing more than probabilistic explanations that have finite range and scope limitations (Jacobson, 1993).
3. Given the oppression of large groups of people—women; the poor; ethnic, racial, and linguistic minorities; refugees; and other marginalized people—ethical and practical concerns should take precedence in social science over principles of objectivity and detachment.
4. Therefore, the goal of research should be the liberation of the oppressed rather than the generation of objective generalizations (Servaes & Arnst, 1999) or the search for the ultimate truth, which is only a mirage.
5. Research, then, should be problem solving, "involved, relevant and activist, not afraid to tackle problems, take positions, or intercede on behalf of certain interests and intrude on the state of nature" (Rosenau, 1992, p. 173).

The basic premise guiding theory and practice in development communication (as articulated in the modernization paradigm) has been the notion that human societies are just and fair in their distribution of resources to individuals and groups within them and that all people, with some effort and help, can achieve the benefits that societies have to offer. Thus, as articulated in the dominant paradigm of development, if an individual or group does not possess "desirable" attitudes, opinions, behaviors, or other attributes, or does not participate effectively in a society's affairs, it is the individual who is deficient and thus needs to be taught skills and provided help. The earlier development communication models have accepted such a victim blame hypothesis. However, large sections of the population in the Third World continue to be impoverished and lack access to necessities that would make a qualitative improvement in their lives. The reality of the social and political situation in most developing countries is such that the urban and rural poor, women, and other people at the grassroots are entrapped in a dependency situation in highly stratified and unequal social and economic structures.

It is usually futile and may be unethical for communications and human service professionals to help solve minor and/or immediate problems while ignoring the systemic barriers erected by societies that permit or perpetuate inequalities among citizens. Certainly, sustainable change is not possible unless crucial problems in human societies such as the lack of economic and social power among individuals at the grassroots are addressed. More than 25 years ago, Latin American communication scholars such as Beltran (1976) and Díaz Bordenave (1976), among others, observed the oppressive social, political, and economic structures that exist in developing countries and that constitute barriers to progressive social change. Yet most of the models and strategies that followed have failed to address directly these constraints. Individuals are impoverished or sick or often are slow to adopt useful practices, not because they lack knowledge or reason, but because they do not have access to appropriate or sustainable opportunities to improve their lives. This is an issue of power. Unless scholars and practitioners are willing to recognize this and act on it, our work will be either ineffective or superficial, functioning as temporary band-aids for far larger problems. If development support communication (DSC) is to continue to play an effective role in social change processes, researchers and practitioners must address fundamental problems of unequal power relations.

The choice, then, for development communicators is to increasingly use the empowering theories and models discussed in this chapter and to devise even more appropriate communication models and analytical tools that can address and overcome these systemic barriers.

References

Alvares, C. (1992). Science. In W. Sachs (Ed.), *Development dictionary* (pp. 219–232). London: Zed.

Ascroft, J., & Masilela, S. (1989, February). *From top-down to co-equal communication.* Paper presented at the seminar Participation: A Key Concept in Communication for Change and Development, Pune, India.

Barrett, M. (1999). *Imagination in theory: Essays on writing and culture.* Cambridge, UK: Polity.

Beltran, L. R. S. (1976). Alien premises, objects, and methods in Latin American communication research. In E. M. Rogers (Ed.), *Communication and development: Critical perspectives* (pp. 15–42). Beverly Hills, CA: Sage.

Blumer, J., & Katz, E. (1974). *The uses of mass communication: Current perspectives on gratifications research.* Beverly Hills, CA: Sage.

Braidotti, R., Charkiewicz, E., Hausler, S., & Wieringa, S. (1994). *Women, the environment and sustainable development.* London: Zed.

Cornell Empowerment Group. (1989). Empowerment and family support. *Networking Bulletin, 1*(2), 1–23.

Crush, J. (1995). Introduction: Imagining development. In J. Crush (Ed.), *Power of development* (pp. 1–23). London: Routledge.

Díaz Bordenave, J. (1976). Communication of agricultural innovations in Latin America: The need for new models. In E. M. Rogers (Ed.), *Communication and development: Critical perspectives* (pp. 43–62). Beverly Hills, CA: Sage.

Díaz Bordenave, J. (1989, February). *Participative communication as a part of the building of a participative society*. Paper presented at the seminar Participation: A Key Concept in Communication for Change and Development, Pune, India.

Escobar, A. (1995). *Encountering development: The making and unmaking of the Third World*. Princeton, NJ: Princeton University Press.

Fair, J. E., & Shah, H. (1997). Continuities and discontinuities in communication and development research since 1958. *Journal of International Communication, 46*(2), 3–23.

Fawcett, S. B., Paine-Andrews, A., Francisco, V. T., Schultz, J. A., Richter, K. P., Lewis, R. K., Williams, E. L., Harris, K. J., Berkley, J. Y., Fisher, J. L., & Lopez, C. M. (1995). Using empowerment theory in collaborative partnerships for community health and development. *American Journal of Community Psychology, 23*(5), 677–697.

Fjes, F. (1976). *Communications and development*. Unpublished paper, University of Illinois, Urbana-Champaign, College of Communications.

Foucault, M. (1980). *Power/knowledge*. New York: Pantheon.

Frank, A. G. (1969). *Latin America: Underdevelopment or revolution*. New York: Monthly Review Press.

Freire, P. (1970). *Pedagogy of the oppressed*. New York: Seabury.

Friesen, E. (1999). Exploring the links between structuration theory and participatory action research. In T. Jacobson & J. Servaes (Eds.), *Theoretical approaches to participatory communication* (pp. 281–308). Cresskill, NJ: Hampton.

Glander, T. (2000). *Origins of mass communications research during the American Cold War*. Mahwah, NJ: Lawrence Erlbaum.

Hagen, E. E. (1962). *On the theory of social change*. Homewood, IL: Dorsey.

Hewitt, K. (1995). Sustainable disasters? In J. Crush (Ed.), *Power of development* (pp. 115–128). London: Routledge.

Hovland, C. I., Lumsdaine, A. A., & Sheffield, F. D. (1949). *Experiments in mass communication*. New York: John Wiley.

Inkeles, A. (1966). The modernization of man. In M. Weiner (Ed.), *Modernization: The dynamics of growth* (pp. 138–150). New York: Basic Books.

Inkeles, A., & Smith, D. H. (1974). *Becoming modern: Individual change in six developing countries*. Cambridge, MA: Harvard University Press.

Jacobson, T. L. (1993). A pragmatist account of participatory communication research for national development. *Communication Theory, 3*(3), 214–230.

Jacobson, T. L., & Kolluri, S. (1999). Participatory communication as communicative action. In T. Jacobson & J. Servaes (Eds.), *Theoretical approaches to participatory communication* (pp. 265–280). Cresskill, NJ: Hampton.

Kaye, G. (1990). A community organizer's perspective on citizen participation research and the researcher-practitioner partnership. *American Journal of Community Psychology, 18*(1), 151–157.

Kothari, R. (1984). Communications for alternative development: Towards a paradigm. *Development Dialogue*, pp. 1–2.

Kotler, P. (1984). Social marketing of health behavior. In L. W. Frederiksen, L. J. Solomon, & K. A. Brehony (Eds.), *Marketing health behavior* (pp. 23–39). New York: Plenum.

Latouche, S. (1992). Standard of living. In W. Sachs (Ed.), *Development dictionary* (pp. 250–263). London: Zed.

Lerner, D. (1958). *The passing of traditional society: Modernizing the Middle East*. Glencoe, IL: Free Press.

Lowery, S., & DeFleur, M. L. (1995). *Milestones in mass communication research* (3rd ed.). New York: Longman.

McClelland, D. C. (1967). *The achieving society*. New York: Free Press.

Melkote, S., & Steeves, H. L. (2001). *Communication for development in the Third World: Theory and practice for empowerment* (2nd ed.). New Delhi: Sage.

Mitchell, T. (1995). The object of development. In J. Crush (Ed.), *Power of development* (pp. 129–157). London: Routledge.

Mody, B. (2000). The contexts of power and the power of the media. In K. Wilkins (Ed.), *Redeveloping communication for social change* (pp. 185–196). New York: Rowman & Littlefield.

Palda, K. S. (1966). The hypothesis of a hierarchy of effects: A partial evaluation. *Journal of Marketing Research*, *3*, 13–24.

Parsons, T. (1964). Evolutionary universals in society. *American Sociological Review*, *29*(3), 339–357.

Piotrow, P. T., Kincaid, D. L., Rimon, J. G., II, & Rinehart, W. (1997). *Health communication: Lessons from family planning and reproductive health*. Westport, CT: Praeger.

Prochaska, J. O., DiClemente, C. C., & Norcross, J. C. (1992). In search of how people change: Applications to addictive behaviors. *American Psychologist*, *47*(9), 1102–1114.

Rahman, M. A. (1991). The theoretical standpoint of PAR. In O. Fals-Borda & M. A. Rahman (Eds.), *Action and knowledge: Breaking the monopoly with participatory action research* (pp. 13–23). New York: Apex.

Rappaport, J. (1987). Terms of empowerment/exemplars of prevention: Toward a theory for community psychology. *American Journal of Community Psychology*, *15*(2), 121–144.

Rifkin, S. B. (1996). Paradigms lost: Toward a new understanding of community participation in health programmes. *Acta Tropica*, *61*, 79–92.

Rogers, E. M. (1962). *Diffusion of innovations*. New York: Free Press.

Rogers, E. M. (1969). *Modernization among peasants*. New York: Holt, Rinehart & Winston.

Rogers, E. M. (1973). *Communication strategies for family planning*. New York: Free Press.

Rogers, E. M. (1995). *Diffusion of innovations* (4th ed.). New York: Free Press.

Rogers, E. M. (with Shoemaker, F. F.) (1971). *Communication of innovations: A cross-cultural approach*. New York: Free Press.

Rosenau, P. V. (1992). *Post-modernism and the social sciences*. Princeton, NJ: Princeton University Press.

Rowlands, J. (1998). *Questioning empowerment, working with women in Honduras*. London: Oxfam.

Schramm, W. L. (1964). *Mass media and national development: The role of information in the developing countries*. Stanford, CA: Standford University Press.

Servaes, J. (1999). *Communication for development: One world, multiple cultures*. Cresskill, NJ: Hampton.

Servaes, J., & Arnst, R. (1999). Principles of participatory communication research: Its strengths (!) and weaknesses (?). In T. Jacobson & J. Servaes (Eds.), *Theoretical approaches to participatory communication* (pp. 107–130). Cresskill, NJ: Hampton.

Shaw, D. L., & McCombs, M. E. (1974). *The emergence of American political issues: The agenda-setting function of the press*. St Paul, MN: West.

Simpson, C. (1994). *Science of coercion: Communication research and psychological warfare 1945–1960*. New York: Oxford University Press.

Singhal, A., & Rogers, E. M. (1999). *Entertainment-education: A communication strategy for social change*. Mahwah, NJ: Lawrence Erlbaum.

Speer, P. W., & Hughey, J. (1995). Community organizing: An ecological route to empowerment and power. *American Journal of Community Psychology*, *23*(5), 729–748.

Tehranian, M. (1994). Communication and development. In D. Crowley & D. Mitchell (Eds.), *Communication theory today* (pp. 274–306). Stanford, CA: Stanford University Press.

White, K. (1999). The importance of sensitivity to culture in development work. In T. Jacobson & J. Servaes (Eds.), *Theoretical approaches to participatory communication* (pp. 17–50). Cresskill, NJ: Hampton.

White, S. A. (1994). Introduction: The concept of participation. In S. A. White, K. S. Nair, & J. Ascroft (Eds.), *Participatory communication: Working for change and development* (pp. 15–32). New Delhi: Sage.

Wilkins, K. G. (1999). Development discourse on gender and communication in strategies for social change. *Journal of Communication*, *49*(1), 46–68.

Chapter 8

Dan Schiller

WORLD COMMUNICATIONS IN TODAY'S AGE OF CAPITAL

Introduction

MY TITLE INTENDS TO underline the decisive social fact of our epoch, which remains today as it has been for several hundred years an age of capital. More specifically, it recalls Eric Hobsbawm's[1] dissection of the period from the late 1840s to the mid-1870s, when capital was expanding self-confidently across the social field. 'In this era,' writes Hobsbawm, 'industrial capitalism became a genuine world economy and the globe was therefore transformed from a geographical expression into a constant operational reality.'[2]

Capital's dominion over a newly unified world market depended, as Hobsbawm shows, on the concurrent establishment of sprawling infrastructures for rail and water transport, and for electrical communication. This does not mean, simply, that the emerging industrial capitalism of the nineteenth century could build on a new, globe-encircling telegraph grid which was equally available for other purposes. Rather, it signifies that telegraph networks incorporated capital's objectives into their own political-economic identity. Thus, the telegraph functioned as what historian Daniel Headrick calls a 'tool of empire'[3] and, within the United States, its rates were pegged high enough to exclude all but businesses and perhaps 5% of the residential population from regular use.

But the paradoxical fact is that capital did not yet generally acquire direct, comprehensive, and enduring control of electronic communications – even in the United States, though the United States did go far and away the farthest in this direction. For disparate reasons, not yet adequately explicated by scholars, both telecommunications and broadcasting, as it later developed, became subject throughout most of the world to substantial state control and operation. The role of capital in electronic communications remained correspondingly restricted.

I want to argue that the current reorganization of world communications is historically significant, because and insofar as it is placing the field of electronic communications on a unified and ubiquitous capitalist basis. In our era, in turn, capital's demands predominate in redefining the social purposes and institutional functions of world communications.

To pursue these claims, we may usefully distinguish three aspects of the current reorganization of world communications, pertaining to telecommunications services; conventional audiovisual services; and emerging Internet and broadband services.

I can only devote a few words to each category, beginning with telecommunications.

Telecommunications today

Telecommunications system buildouts, at every scale from local loop to global grid, are occurring on an unparalleled scale throughout the world. In 1960, of nearly 142 million telephone lines worldwide, 86% were located in the United States and 17 Western European nations. By 1996, in contrast, the United States, Western Europe and Japan together controlled just 57% of a much larger total of world telephone lines, 744 million all told.[4] That number has since increased further – there are probably at least 900 million lines today, in addition to several hundred million wireless phones.

Surging capital investment in the sector is the critical prerequisite for this massive expansion of network access. Such investment has been drawn by multiple networking technologies. Cable operators in the United States, for example, are estimated to have spent $30bn to upgrade their systems for advanced telecommunications services.[5] Wireless telephony has taken an additional $67bn in domestic investment; worldwide, the figure is much higher.[6] A single US-based carrier – MCIWorldCom – has enlarged its proprietary network to link city centers throughout wealthy portions of the world; during 1999 alone, it paid out $7.9bn to expand its system, and it is not unique.[7] Satellite providers have spent additional billions to establish global systems and services, though the fate of some of these systems has been inauspicious. Overall world telecommunications investment in 1996 was $166.4bn.[8] Globally, said the chairman of the FCC in 1999, 'The private sector has invested over $600 billion to build . . . networks since 1994.'[9]

How are we to evaluate this massive upsurge? Have we transited from stagnation and underdevelopment in communications, to what UNESCO characterizes as 'abundant supply'?[10]

Household telephone access is diffusing quite rapidly throughout the global middle class. By historical standards, this constitutes a very significant – indeed, an unprecedented – achievement. So, too, per-call costs for long-distance transmission are approaching zero. And, finally, network capacity is growing by great leaps and bounds, making possible and, indeed, promoting, all manner of new services and applications. Taken together, these facts signify that the telecommunications industry, as it has been taken over by capital, has undergone a huge sectoral boom. The critical issue comprises the qualitative terms on which this revolution in the forces of production has proceeded.

To begin with, it needs to be stressed that extrapolations from present-day expansion to a 'wired world,' in which everyone is electronically enfranchised, are not credible. It behooves us to remember that, to this day, a quarter of all countries, mostly in Africa, are not able to guarantee one telephone for every 100 people.[11] Present policies are unlikely to make basic telephone access generally available to less-favored social strata.[12] To be sure, by historical standards, the current extension of network access is breathtaking. But it has limits, and these limits are set mainly by capital's quest for maximum profitability.

Vital though it is, moreover, consumer access to basic telecommunications is not – or at least should not be – the sole desideratum of the current expansion. Equally critical are issues pertaining to the production side of the equation: the dominant social purposes and institutional character of the new networks.

It is starkly evident that, to date, the needs and demands of transnational business and finance have claimed overarching priority throughout the entire process of telecommunications market expansion.[13] System building has gone forward, that is, only on the basis of radical changes in underlying policy; indeed, the very foundations of global telecommunications have been recast. By elevating the precepts of privatization, liberalization of market entry, and specialized services aimed at privileged groups, policy changes have resulted in enriching and empowering a few thousand giant companies and their affiliated strata.

The United States began the process by liberalizing conditions of entry and participation within the world's single largest domestic market. Ultimately, however, the neoliberal US model metamorphosized into a new global standard. Hundreds of billions of dollars worth of telecommunications stocks were floated on global capital markets during the 1980s and 1990s, as dozens of huge telecommunications privatizations – generally shepherded by US banks, lawyers, advertising agencies and management consultants – conferred corporate ownership and control over this strategic sector. Investment decisions in telecommunications now are made according to the same profit-and-loss calculus that governs the rest of the corporate economy; as one banker at Morgan Stanley explained, in regard to a less-than-successful stock offering for a private telecom company in Russia: 'Utilities [in Russia] are still seen as a public service rather than as a business that should generate profits for shareholders.'[14]

As the United States successfully exported its model to the rest of the world, in turn, an increasingly harmonized multilateral operating framework, affording predictable market access to equipment and services worldwide, was ratified through the WTO Basic Telecom Agreement in 1997.[15] This accord conferred a new measure of extraterritorial power on a body – the WTO – that enjoys no democratic remit.

The chief effects of this policy shift were to undermine the long-established principle of national integration of telecommunications, in favor of supranational systems and services catering to transnational corporate users. Herein there also can be seen a significant industrial shift. In contrast to earlier periods, when – often at the expense of major business users of telecommunications service – monopoly carriers cartelized the global telecommunications market, for the past couple of decades changed policies have benefited transnational business users.

Perhaps the most telling sign of this change in the terms of trade has been the build-up of overcapacity among rival long-distance networks, a condition that in late 2000 truly threatened the strategy and structure of blue-chip US companies such as AT&T and World-Com.[16] Relatedly, successful efforts to lower international rates privileged corporations and elite social strata, sometimes at the expense of local ratepayers and often at the expense of employees. In addition, for many less-developed market economies, telephone 'settlement' fees comprised the most- or second most-important source of hard currency overall; as these fees were unilaterally reduced at the behest of US authorities, an important source of general domestic finance was eroded.[17]

Above all, however, corporate carriers and business users have gained license to cooperate 'from above' in reintegrating telecommunications into their own workaday operations. This they are presently doing, on a colossal scale. This pan-corporate project of constructing transnational production chains around telecommunications systems aims to drive down the cost of telecommunications bandwidth to the point that a host of services, some such as education and training newly tradable as network-based offerings, can be developed and marketed globally.

To actualize this agenda will continue to require dramatic policy changes. The US Trade Representative thus has recently announced a major 'networked world' initiative 'to move our trading partners toward the flexible, sophisticated New Economy principles of America's network of telecommunications, information technologies and services industries':[18] '[W]e will seek the broadest possible cross-border market access in services . . . to realize the potential for firms to offer a full range of services over the telecommunications network,' she declares.[19] In other words, liberalized access to networks worldwide remains an ongoing project.

Audiovisual services

In 1965, 176 million TV sets existed worldwide, preponderantly in the wealthy nations. Thirty years later (1995) there were 1.16 billion sets in use; between 1980 and 1996, moreover, the number of sets per 1000 inhabitants in the developing countries increased sixfold, from 26 to 153; and in the mid-1990s, a milestone of sorts was passed when more television sets were located in LDCs (692 million in 1996) than in developed nations (669 million in 1996).[20] China, with over 300 million sets, today boasts the largest domestic prime-time viewing audience in the world.[21] TV system and channel proliferation have also been rapid and extensive; between 1990 and 1998, for example, the number of European cable, satellite and digital terrestrial television channels increased more than fivefold, from 103 to 594.[22] Despite continuing extreme inequalities in provision, again most severe throughout Africa, there can be no doubt that television has grown to comprise a global cultural infrastructure.

Again, however, a massive change in direction has concurrently reoriented the institutional structures of global television. As in the field of telecommunications, television system development has been largely handed over to capital. Corporately run systems have sprung up in dozens of countries; elsewhere, existing private systems have been expanded and enlarged. By 1995, some 50 countries, mainly in Western Europe and Latin America, possessed dual public–private systems,[23] with corporate systems enjoying growing power and momentum, and public-service broadcast systems facing funding cuts and other attacks. Transnational corporate distribution networks, moreover, comprise an operative reality; by 1998, non-national channels claimed significant audience shares in at least nine (mainly small) West European countries.[24] Across much of Asia and Latin America, satellite television systems like Galaxy and Star likewise have purchased a local presence in dozens of nations. Individual network services, such as CNN or BBC World, routinely reach across multiple borders.[25] Viacom actively tests its ability to use its MTV networks around the world as 'a global promotional platform,' for example, by striking an alliance with MGM to market the James Bond film ('The World Is Not Enough') to a teenage audience in the 300 million households the network reaches throughout Asia, Europe, Latin America and the United States.[26] Displaying its new global reach to sponsors, meanwhile, Discovery Channel made advertising history in 1999 by airing a special about Cleopatra at 9 pm across every time zone around the world.[27]

As these examples underscore, world television expansion has occurred not through the consolidation of public-service systems – which themselves rarely delivered as much as promised – but as a service catering to commercial advertisers (roughly encompassing the same group of transnational companies that demanded and benefited from concurrent changes in telecommunications). Television system restructuring, that is, has occurred principally as a business service, inasmuch as commercial broadcasting's *sine qua non* is to deliver most-needed audiences with maximum efficiency to the consumer product marketers that supply its major economic support.

The growth of these corporate commercial television systems, both domestic and transnational, has engendered considerable industrial (and cultural) volatility. Alliances and counteralliances are being forged on a daily basis. Nevertheless, some basic patterns are already apparent – and, absent a fundamental reorientation, these are unlikely to lose salience in succeeding months and years.

First, the television industry is undergoing a concurrent and intertwined process of vertical integration and transnationalization. Content producers and distributors are coming under unified (corporate) roofs, even as these newly diversified behemoths concurrently transnationalize. It is often observed that several of the largest 'US' media companies are today owned and controlled by non-US corporations such as Sony, Seagram, or News Corporation. But the significance of this fact is not well appreciated.

I am not aware of another instance where the world's leading power has voluntarily (for this change cannot be considered inadvertent) opened up such a strategic industry to substantial foreign ownership. Indeed, in the aftermath of World War I, the United States itself made a strenuous and successful effort to prevent an earlier generation of US broadcast technology from being integrated into a system dominated by Great Britain. There are significant limits on the current relaxation of US ownership restrictions, but the extent of the change is remarkable. In subsector after subsector, critical 'US' media companies have been acquired by foreign businesses; even Nielsen Media Research is owned by the Dutch media firm VNU, which already owns the *Hollywood Reporter, Adweek*, and *Billboard*.[28]

The transnationalization of the 'US' media industry in turn unleashed a decisive force for change within the *global* audiovisual sector. Sony, AOL-Time Warner and News Corporation have sunk billions of dollars into distribution systems for delivering entertainment to households around the world. 'US' entertainment companies have both partnered with newly authorized units of media industry capital abroad, and established their own distribution systems for delivering entertainment to households. As McChesney generalizes: 'What distinguishes the emerging global media system is not transnational control over exported media content . . . so much as increasing TNC control over media distribution and content within nations.'[29] Despite their vital structural significance for today's audiovisual sector, however, we are only beginning to analyze these emerging structures, and their political-economic and cultural effects – on either corporate or regional bases.[30]

In explicating this idea, it is worth noting the sometime assertion that US content hegemony is in decline – for such claims tend to misrepresent as much as they reveal. In the first place, 'US' corporate media content is less a national culture, than a highly selective and filtered expression of conflicted historical processes, in which the roles of capital and class, as well as foreign cultures, have persistently bulked large. For those of us who *live* in the United States, the problem is not that our media culture is 'American,' but that it incarnates antidemocratic practices that do repeated and protracted disservice to the popular majority. Second, as noted, 'US' media is no longer an adequate formulation even in economic terms, because around half of the top 'US' media companies themselves have become units within non-US-based parent conglomerates. In turn, as McChesney suggests, 'the impetus behind the global media system is far more corporate and commercial expansion than national geopolitics. . . . The global media system is better understood, then, as one that advances corporate and commercial interests and values, and denigrates or ignores that which cannot be incorporated into its mission.'[31] Third, and finally, the grounds for declaring that 'US' media content is threatened by changes in the structure of global media markets need to be specified with greater care than is customary.

The material bases of audiovisual production and distribution *are* changing. TV system development and channel proliferation worldwide are fueling an unrelenting explosion in demand for audiovisual product. The consequences of this demand growth have been two-fold. On one hand, exports by US-based megamedia companies have surged powerfully; Europe's negative trade balance with the US in films, television programs and video shot up to $5.6bn in 1996, and 'US' films have increased their share of the European market from

56% to 78% in a decade.[32] In 1997, to take still another example, 'US'-based media produced 88 of the 100 highest grossing movies in the world.[33]

On the other hand, however, equally apparent are escalating quantities of non-US-based local audiovisual production. The global television market annually held at Cannes (Mipcom), for example, has seen sales of US TV series giving pride of place to local productions. Big European media companies, in particular, can afford to bankroll more local programming, and thus Europe-based program producers 'look set to account for a larger share of the revenue in this rapidly expanding market.'[34] In 1998, there were no 'American' series and just two 'American' feature films among the 10 most popular programs in Britain, France, Germany and Italy.[35] In Mexico, the dominant TV operator, Grupo Televisa, expected to maintain its output of about 1,400 hours of telenovela programming through 2000; and these telenovelas permeated prime-time on its flagship channel 2.[36]

This change, I shall emphasize again, has not been comprehensive. Program exports from the United States continue to claim a vastly disproportionate share of the world's cultural attention. Still, the movement to local content production can hardly be denied.

The dynamics of this shift are fluid and complex. Large countries enjoy opportunities that are usually denied to poorer states and regions. Cultural work performed in dominant languages enjoys better commercial prospects, while secondary language status may also offer a measure of protection against the commercial takeover of cultural practice. Development of additional television systems and of new technological platforms (of which more below) continue to add volatility. The current political conjuncture in, say, Mexico, is quite different from that in China or Argentina, finally, and the character of local audiovisual production may well be marked by such differences. Yet two claims seem warranted.

First, once more, audiovisual system development has been rapidly and forcefully assimilated to the overarching logic of capitalist accumulation. In any given case, this need not automatically signify the paramountcy of particular transnational megamedia companies. In China, domestic media business interests have grown newly significant[37] and, in India, Zee Telefilms, owned by the Bombay-based Subhash Chandra, has become a power.[38] In Mexico, Venezuela and Brazil, likewise, national media businesses enjoy a significant dominance over their domestic media markets.[39] Such companies, sometimes worth billions of dollars, are also tending increasingly to target audiences on a transnational scale. 'Networks from capitalist Taiwan and communist China are chasing ethnic Chinese as far afield as South America, trying to earn a buck while waging a battle for the loyalties of 55 million overseas Chinese,' says one account of the 'explosion of ethnic channels that is changing the look of television around the globe.' Another signal: Arab Radio & Television is exporting its Arabic language channels outside the Middle East to reach as many as 30 million nonresident ethnic Arabs.[40] Even so, as Thussu concludes, these companies' global impact – unlike that of the US-based titans – is restricted mainly to their national markets and to diasporic communities.[41]

Withal, in the newly complex and dynamic worldwide media market, the interests of national media capital thus are increasingly aligned with those of transnational media groups. In Brazil where 34 million TV sets were sold in the five years beginning 1994, extending TV ownership by nearly one-third, to almost 87% of the nation's households, both Globo, a $5bn company which produces 2000 hours of entertainment programming a year, and its arch rival SBT (Sistema Brasiliero de Televisao) agree that foreign investment in Brazilian broadcasting should be authorized (on a minority basis). Why? Because the top tier of transnational media combines, with its vast program libraries and its preferred access to bank capital, is needed by *both* Brazilian media groups.[42] If Globo thinks it needs to deepen its involvement with the US-based behemoths, what are the options for smaller units of national capital?

A growing fraction of 'local' programming production, by extension, testifies not to the vibrancy of local culture, but to successful innovations in transnational corporate structure and function, involving a series of often-intricate co-production and other partnerships with national capital. Indeed a significant portion of 'local' cultural expression can be traced back to TNCs themselves. Some of the vibrancy of European television production, for example, stems from endeavors made by media capitalist Harry Evans Sloan, an American entertainment executive whose SBS Broadcasting progressed via a series of shrewd investments in new privatized European media during the late 1980s and 1990s, eventually amassing 18 channels in 13 markets. SBS planned to spend $1bn on European productions over the five years beginning 1999 – and another billion on Hollywood product.[43] On a larger scale, in 1999, Sony planned to create no less than 4000 hours of TV programming in foreign languages – more than twice its output of English-language programming – both for its own foreign channels and for sale to other groups.[44] US-based media combines, writes a business insider, 'may well maintain their leadership roles, but they will have to adapt to local audiences and include local content. Moreover, foreign content will begin to nudge its way onto the global hit parade.'[45]

The model for this development is the recording industry subsector of the entertainment business. In some nations today, as much as 70% of CD sales come from local performers – yet, as *Fortune* magazine explains, 'five global companies – Sony, Warner, Universal, Bertelsmann, and EMI – dominate the local scene as effectively as they deliver the international hits. That gives them two revenue streams – exports and local artists. "Twenty years from now, that model is going to proliferate across the spectrum of things we do," says Time Warner President Richard Parsons. Doing it right, he adds, "is probably the biggest challenge facing the company."[46] Thus Sony produces 33 hours a week of Hindi-language programming, and transmits it not only to India but also to Africa, Britain, North America and the Middle East; it also produces or co-produces 35 weekly hours of Mandarin-language programming, mostly for its Super TV channel that reaches most Taiwanese households – but with an eye on mainland China's 300 million TV households.[47] Viacom's MTV, a third of whose 300 million household viewers live in Asia, expects to see international revenues surpass US domestic receipts (currently around $1bn annually) within six or seven years.[48]

Where does the seat of power lie in these new arrangements?

It may safely be said that transnational corporate power over the audiovisual sector is not dispersing. An account of the abrupt resignation in 1999 of Rupert Murdoch's News Corporation's top European executive, Letizia Moratti – previously chairperson of the Italian state-owned national broadcasting channel RAI Television – illuminates this point. 'It was clear,' observed a reporter, 'that Mr. Murdoch thought of her as more of a door-opener and a lobbyist than a hands-on manager.' Murdoch himself had earlier stressed that Moratti was valuable chiefly for her connections, essential in furthering his designs on the European audiovisual market: 'She's a very distinguished citizen here, a popular one, and known throughout the broadcasting establishment in Europe. When things were difficult, she was able to pick up the phone and talk to any CEO or cabinet minister.' But even this distinguished citizen was apparently unable to wrest the power over merely regional strategy from her corporate parent. In Ms. Moratti's own words, 'It was necessary to give News Corp. Europe a central role within the European strategies of the group, in order to consolidate the results achieved to date and to face challenges ahead. This belief is not shared by News Corp.'[49]

'What we're seeing,' concludes one observer in regard to the international film industry, 'is the emergence of a two-tiered global system. English is the language of the international blockbuster, but lower-budget pictures can be made in almost any language for the home market, and a few . . . will even become international hits. Hollywood, with its vast corporate resources, can call the shots in both tiers.'[50]

But perhaps there will be those among us who declare that all this is simply evidence of the failings of an antiquated media structure, which is morphing into a system that will prove more conducive to democratic cultural expression – via the Internet.

Internet and broadband services

The Internet lies at the forefront of current struggles to reclaim the media system for democracy: not all the battles have been waged, let alone won, either by corporate capital or by those who oppose its reign. This said, the ongoing redevelopment of the Internet confirms that capitalist domination of world communications is deepening.

First and foremost, this is because Internet business, as a *New York Times* headline puts it, transpires mainly '.com to.com.' By far the largest share of Internet e-commerce flows – and is expected to keep flowing – between businesses, rather than between businesses and consumers.[51] Indeed, perhaps two-thirds of total Internet investment is being undertaken by businesses, to erect walled-off private systems known as intranets, while only one-third of such investment goes to the enlargement of the public Internet; and this imbalance has widened over the last five years.[52] Even these figures are deceptive because the lion's share of investment in the 'public Internet' does not intend to establish a liberated zone beyond the market, but precisely to create more effective sales channels through which to target upscale consumers.

'Devising a sustainable business model that works in the tempest known as the Internet seems as yet an impossibility,' suggests one management consultant, 'but I am sure that we are seeing the emergence of such a model.'[53] He can be confident because, while Web volatility remains very high (something like 44% of Web addresses in 1998 did not identify a site in 1999), big capital is poised to become the dominant force within the new medium's still-open segment.

The first sign of big capital's designs on the open Internet came with the privatization of what had been a quasi-public backbone facility in 1995; control over the Internet backbone then passed rapidly into the hands of a handful of major corporations such as WorldCom. The second sign arrived in the form of the deluge of advertising that almost concurrently began to inundate the World Wide Web. Every consumer product rolled out by Procter & Gamble or Unilever must now possess an Internet strategy as a plank in its overall marketing plan: 'integrated marketing' is the catchphrase employed by the advertising 'community.' The third sign of capital's unfolding efforts to seize and reorient the Net is the attempt to establish vertically integrated corporate control over Internet access and services. Actually, it's more accurate to say 'consolidate' vertically integrated corporate control over Internet access, because the leading Internet company – AOL, whose 18 million subscribers in early 1999 gave it around two-fifths of all US home accounts – already combines access with proprietary content and services.[54] AOL, where a captive user base indulges in cyberfrolics that revolve around different kinds of shopping, constitutes a preferred model of capitalist development in this sector.

To date, household Internet access has relied chiefly on dial-up modems, accessed via ordinary telephone lines. Several thousand 'narrowband' Internet service providers, in addition to AOL, cater to the U.S. residential market; in return for ten or twenty dollars a month (for free, if you accept yet more advertising) anyone with a PC and a telephone line can access the Web. Although Internet access costs substantially more in many other parts of the world, thousands of other ISPs have sprung up to serve the burgeoning market for access to the open Web – 169 in Mexico, for example, up from 23 in 1995.[55]

The current attempt by big capital is to take over the exploding market pioneered by these narrowband ISPs, most of which are small-scale outfits with only a few thousand subscribers, and some of which originated as noncommercial organizations with oppositional goals and principles. The corporate preemption of domestic Internet access has already translated into growing concentration within the ISP market. Although there remain thousands of small providers, mergers and network buildouts by big companies had allowed national service providers such as AOL, EarthLink, MSN, AT&T WorldNet and GTE Internet to capture 69% of the market by 1999. Local phone companies ranked second with 14% of the market, followed by long-distance companies, with 4%. Thousands of local ISPs shared the remaining market segment among themselves.[56] 'All the ISPs have to get a lot bigger or they're going to die,' declared Rob Norcross, a telecommunications management consultant, if only to increase their ability to bankroll investment in expensive broadband services.[57] In the era of broadband access, that is, concentrated corporate control seems destined to increase.

A few points about the political economy of this rolling technological frontier are warranted.

To begin with, the favored model seeks to integrate corporate control over underlying network facilities with control over the specialized software and services that govern Internet access and, in some measure, also navigation and content provision. The business goal is to develop multiple revenues streams: not just subscription fees, but also advertising and e-commerce revenues. To diversify revenue streams in this way, it will be necessary for big capital to wrest power over residential users' attention and itinerary in cyberspace, and not simply to charge for access. This is why leading ISPs have tried to develop or buy customized electronic guides and/or directory/portals to maximize the amounts of time consumers spend at their own and commercially associated sites.

In the wealthy countries, and to some extent elsewhere, this emerging proprietary model is additionally tied to the establishment of 'broadband' (high-speed) services over cable television systems, telephone networks, and other new media. Dial-up modem-based Internet access limits the speed and constancy of service, and thus it also constrains the development of what Microsoft and other top corporate executives hail as the Web lifestyle – where high-speed PC access within the home is on tap 24 hours a day, and can be tied in to a range of lucrative services, including communication, entertainment, shopping and, not least, education. Parallel extensions to mission-critical sites outside the home, including cars and shopping malls, and to mobile Web-access devices, are likewise unfolding.

If the carrot before them is a vision of using new services to pry loose dollars from well-heeled consumers and advertisers, then the stick behind is a ubiquitous fear among communication industry corporations that someone else will get there first, possibly stealing their current customers in the process. Local telephone companies have moved into broadband service provision on a prospectively vast scale (and satellite and local wireless systems are rolling out as well) – but cable operators face fewer public responsibilities under law within the giant and strategically critical US domestic market, and so it may turn out to be more widely significant that cable-based broadband systems moved forward first.[58] In the United States, the paragon example is AT&T, which spent $100bn to buy two of the top five cable MSOs, and bet the future of the company on the outcome. But other cable MSOs are also committed to a proprietary vision of broadband service provision. Broadband cable service was available, as of March 2000, to about 95% of the US population although, overall, there were just 4.3 million high-speed service subscribers.[59] On the other hand, a significant political fight developed over their efforts to develop proprietary control over both underlying network circuitry and Internet service provision.[60]

The process is, however, again transnational in scope, and merges local and regional pools of capital into projects led by a handful of transnational companies. During 1999, for example, AOL entered Hong Kong, looking toward the Chinese mainland, with a local Internet provider – China.com – as partner; Lycos had a joint venture with Singapore Telecom to provide local access and directory services throughout Asia.[61] Such partnerships also developed in Japan, where Softbank, a transnational player with large financial stakes in 100 US-based Internet companies, including Yahoo!, E*trade and (now Yahoo! owned-) Geocities, as well as 20 Japanese Internet companies,[62] allied with Microsoft and other companies to build an advanced fiber-optic network capable of supporting great streams of Internet traffic throughout Asia.[63] Yahoo! acquired Taiwan's largest portal site, Kimo.com, in late 2000, and competes in that market with a rival linked to Microsoft and Bertelsmann.[64] Meanwhile, AT&T partnered with Microsoft to invest in Japan's fragmented cable television market; paired with British Telecom, AT&T previously had acquired a 30% stake in Japan Telecom. Excite At Home, also aligned at least momentarily with AT&T, also formed joint ventures in Japan and Australia.[65]

Throughout Europe, even as privatized telecommunications operators like Deutsche Telekom and Telefonica tried to leverage their dominant positions within their home markets into broadband service dominance, roughly the same core group of transnational Internet companies again sought out local partners. Microsoft made significant cable infrastructure investments in England, France, Portugal and The Netherlands.[66] Microsoft and Liberty Media (which is likely to be spun off from AT&T, its nominal parent) developed broadband over cable services through a Dutch subsidiary of UnitedGlobalCom, a Denver-based provider of cable services to 7.7 million subscribers in 10 European countries.[67]

Latin America plays host to the same trend, although private investment groups and banks, and to some extent domestic capital, have claimed larger roles there thus far.[68] In Argentina, consultants suggest, about 1.6 million people had the economic power to connect to the Internet in 1999 – a figure that might double if terms of interconnection were relaxed via PC leasing schemes and flat telephone rates (compared with 3.8 million Brazilians and 2.1 million Mexicans).[69] At the end of 1999, Latin America as a whole had an estimated 7 million Internet users, and the figure was expected to climb rapidly – to 19 million by 2003.[70] Even if other Web platforms beyond PCs broaden usage beyond this, it behooves us to remember that several hundred million people live in Latin America.

But again, simple access is not the only issue. Market-led development in telecommunications, absent countervailing social pressure, attaches scant priority to anything beyond profitability. What is most significant about the overall process of broadband and Internet deployment, in turn, is that it has been cut free of all but nominal reference to the planetary majority. Improved sales channels to privileged strata all too obviously comprise the only vision motivating today's top planners. Thus 29 of the world's most powerful technology and media executives, including Steve Case of AOL, Thomas Middelhoff of Bertelsmann, Louis Gerstner of IBM, Michael Eisner of Disney, and Gerald Levin of Time Warner, met behind closed doors in Paris in September 1999 'to debate how to turn the wild Web into a family-friendly place to do business.'[71] That objective requires, perversely, that the Net be kept free of true social accountability. In turn, attempts to 'impose regulation' on the Internet continued to be attacked as pernicious infringements on free enterprise.

Two final points. First: it is becoming clear that, despite the existence of tens of millions of Web sites, the most popular Web sites are gaining an increasing advantage over their rivals. That is, basing this judgement on a study of large samples of Web traffic, a comparatively small number of sites 'command the traffic of a large portion of the entire Web population.' The top 5% of all sites in one sample of 120,000 — around 6000 sites — garnered three-quarters of all Web traffic; and just 119 sites received 32% of all visits.[72] Relentless promotion of blockbuster sites controlled by a scattering of companies may help to corral many — perhaps most — Web users into *de facto* adoption of a proprietary-service model.

Second: Analysts expect that more than half of the content on the Web will be offered in a language other than English by 2003, up from 20% in 1999.[73] A year later, about 80% of corporate Web sites in Europe offered users a choice of at least one language in addition to English, according to one survey.[74] But the use of local languages hardly ensures local — let alone democratic — control of cultural expression. Indeed, it actually may be a sign of corporate capitalism's increasing ability to parasitize cultural difference by marketing to it — just as ethnically segmented and targeted media marketing works toward that result within the United States. There is little room in the brave new world of cyberspace for those outside the privileged social strata, whether they live in New York City, Calcutta, or Rio de Janeiro.

Conclusion

Let us return to Hobsbawm, and to the mid-nineteenth century: 'The period from the late 1840s to the mid-1870s proved to be not so much, as the conventional wisdom of the time held, the model of economic growth, political development, intellectual progress and cultural achievement, which would persist, no doubt with suitable improvements, into the indefinite future, but rather a special kind of interlude.'[75]

Today's age of capital germinated during the decade or two leading up to 1989–92,[76] when the collapse of socialism enabled political-economic change to be expedited and intensified. The hallmark of our age of capital is that, perhaps above all by revolutionizing the means of communication, large corporations have acquired massive new freedom of maneuver in their attempts to reintegrate markets for labor power, goods and services, and thus to pursue accumulation on a global scale. How then will our own interlude of capitalist globalization end?

For the bombastic poets of neoliberalism, the question of course does not arise.[77] The ideological assertion of market dominance 'is so peremptory' (as the editor of *Le Monde Diplomatique* aptly remarks), that capitalist globalization 'has become, with its dogma and high priests, a kind of new totalitarianism.'[78]

But an end will come, just the same. Will the trigger be a protracted run against the dollar, or perhaps a stock market collapse, reflecting the prodigious US balance-of-payments imbalance? Will the abiding tendency to overproduction and episodic economic stagnation again spiral out of control? Or, might popular dissatisfaction with capitalist globalization attain political momentum sufficient to halt or at least fundamentally qualify the process? Who can say? But we may be confident that the current moment of triumphal expansionism, like its ancestors, will prove fleeting.

Notes

1   E.J. Hobsbawm, *The Age of Capital 1848–1875*, New York: Charles Scribner's Sons, 1975.
2   Hobsbawm, *Age of Capital*, pp. 46–47.
3   Daniel Headrick, *The Tools of Empire: Technology and European Imperialism in the Nineteenth Century*, New York: Oxford University Press, 1981.
4   Calculated from *UN Statistical Yearbook 1961*, pp. 398–400; and *ITU, WTDR 1998*, p. 14. See Dan Schiller, 'Deep Impact: The Web and the Changing Media Economy,' *Info* 1(1): 39.

5   Diane Mermigas, 'Budgeting for an Uncertain Cable Future,' *Electronic Media*, July 26, 1999: 23.

6   Council of Economic Advisors, 'Progress Report: Growth and Competition in U.S. Telecommunications 1993–1998,' February 8, 1999: 12 [available from http://www.ntia.doc.gov].

7   The same company has been fashioned through a succession of some 60 corporate mergers and acquisitions, most recently including a failed bid for Sprint, which collectively embody (conservatively estimated, including Sprint) around $180bn in investment in existing companies over the last several years. 'MCI Plans to Spend $6.5 Billion to Expand Overseas Operations,' *The New York Times*, March 2, 1999: C4; Richard Waters, 'MCI WorldCom Signals Spending Boost of $1.4 billion,' *Financial Times*, June 3, 1999: 15.

8   *ITU, WTDR 1998*, table 17, A-71.

9   William E. Kennard, chairman, FCC, 'Vision to Mission: A Blueprint for Architects of the Global Information Infrastructure,' Remarks Before the World Economic Development Congress, Washington, DC, September 23, 1999: 3. It is not clear whether this sum includes capital investments via mergers and acquisitions of existing telecommunications companies, or only new investment in networks – in which case it would signify a far more formidable change.

10   UNESCO, *World Communication Report: The Media and the Challenge of the New Technologies*, Paris: United Nations Educational, Scientific and Cultural Organisation, 1997, p. 11, quoted in Daya Kishan Thussu, *International Communication: Continuity and Change*, London: Arnold, 2000, p. 4.

11   UNDP, *Human Development Report 1999*, p. 62.

12   See J. Habib Sy, 'Global Communications for a More Equitable World,' in Inge Kaul, Isabelle Grunberg and Marc A. Stern (eds) *Global Public Goods*, New York: UNDP and Oxford University Press, 1999, p. 335.

13   Of the $454.5bn in US spending on information technology in 1997, significantly, business accounted for 88%. Sales to corporate and institutional customers constitute the lion's share of total revenues and profits for leading communications vendors. Seth Schiesel, 'The No. 1 Customer: Sorry, It Isn't You,' *The New York Times*, November 23, 1997, Section 3: 1, 10.

14   Paul Psaila, porftolio manager, in Suzanne McGee, 'Russia's Golden Telecom Launches IPO, But the Issue Fails to Score Big Success,' *Wall Street Journal*, October 1, 1999: A4.

15   Ambassador Charlene Barshefsky, US Trade Representative, 'Electronic Commerce: Trade Policy in a Borderless World,' The Woodrow Wilson Center, Washington, DC, July 29, 1999, p. 6.

16   Seth Schiesel, 'Phone Mergers That May Help Competition,' *The New York Times*, November 27, 2000: C1, C4.

17   Andy Reinhardt, Irene Kunii, Bruce Einhorn and Elizabeth Malkin, 'Dialing for Pennies,' *Business Week*, October 11, 1999: 103–106.

18   Ambassador Charlene Barshefsky, 'Trade Policy 1992–2000: The Clinton Record and the Road Ahead,' World Affairs Council, Los Angeles, September 25, 2000, p. 6.

19   Ambassador Charlene Barshefsky, 'The Networked World Initiative: Trade Policy Enters a New Era,' Federal Communications Bar Association, Washington, DC, October 23, 2000, p. 7.

20   *Unesco Statistical Yearbook 1998*, 6.5.

21   *World Radio TV Handbook*, Volume 52, New York: Billboard Books, 1998, pp. 410, 412, 414, 426.

22   Daya Kishan Thussu, *International Communication: Continuity and Change*, London: Arnold, 2000, p. 139.

23   Richard Parker, *Mixed Signals: The Prospects of Global Television News*, New York: Twentieth Century Fund Press, 1995, p. 8; and Richard Somerset-Ward, 'Public Interest Obligations in Broadcasting: International Comparisons,' *The Digital Beat* 1(5), April 16, 1999 (Benton Foundation listserve).

24   European Commission, *Report from the High Level Group on Audiovisual Policy, The Digital Age: European Audiovisual Policy*, Brussels, 1998, p. 13.

25   Charles Goldsmith, 'BBC World Overhauls its Programming with Newscasts That Will Take on CNN,' *Wall Street Journal*, September 21, 1999: B7.

26   Bruce Orwall, 'MGM Sets Accord With MTV Network for New Bond Film,' *Wall Street Journal*, September 29, 1999: B8; Bill Carter, 'How MTV Came to Be James Bond's Latest Ally,' *The New York Times*, November 2, 1999: C1, C6.

27   Leslie Cauley, 'Discovery is Tailoring 'Cleopatra' as a One-Stop Global Media Buy,' *Wall Street Journal*, March 10, 1999: B17.

28   Kyle Pope, 'VNU to Buy Nielsen Media for $2.5 Billion,' *Wall Street Journal*, August 17, 1999: A2.

29   Robert W. McChesney, *Rich Media, Poor Democracy*, Urbana: University of Illinois, 1999, p. 80. The European television industry, for example, is consolidating into a handful of dominant supranational conglomerates able to foot the bill for the migration to digital and pay-per-view TV, and to

integrated bundles of TV, telephone and Internet services. John Tagliube, 'A Media World to Conquer,' *The New York Times*, July 7, 1999: C1, C5.

30   The pioneering work is Edward S. Herman and Robert W. McChesney, *The Global Media*, London: Cassell, 1997.

31   McChesney, *Rich Media, Poor Democracy*, p. 103.

32   European Commission, *The Digital Age European Audiovisual Policy*, p. 15.

33   'Can Europe Go Hollywood?,' *Wall Street Journal*, November 30, 1998: A28 (editorial).

34   Frank Rose, 'Think Globally, Script Locally,' *Fortune*, November 8, 1999: 157; European Commission, *The Digital Age European Audiovisual Policy*, pp. 11, 17.

35   Tagliube, 'A Media World to Conquer.'

36   David I. Oyama, 'Televisa to Maintain Output of Soaps,' *Wall Street Journal*, October 4, 1999: A25.

37   Yuezhi Zhao, *Media, Market, and Democracy in China: Between the Party Line and the Bottom Line*, Urbana: University of Illinois Press, 1998.

38   David I. Oyama, 'News Corp. to Sell Indian TV Stakes,' *Wall Street Journal*, September 27, 1999: A27; 'Rupert Goes to Bollywood,' *The Economist*, October 2, 1999: 68, 72; Miriam Jordan, 'India's Stormy Politics Spawn a Television Titan,' *Wall Street Journal*, October 4, 1999: B1, B6.

39   John Sinclair, *Latin American Television: A Global View*, Oxford: Oxford University Press, 1999.

40   Michael Flagg, 'Broadcaster Seeks Arab TV Audience Beyond the Mideast,' *Wall Street Journal*, November 27, 2000: A34.

41   Thussu, *International Communication*, p. 222.

42   Matt Moffett, 'As "The Other World" Turns, TV in Brazil Gets Downright Odd,' *Wall Street Journal*, September 29, 1999: A1, A10.

43   Marlene Edmunds, 'Tube Triumph,' *Variety*, May 24–30, 1999: S1.

44   Elizabeth Guider, 'Sony Ups its Local Payoff,' *Variety*, July 26–August 1, 1999: 23. Also see Chuck Philips, 'Sony Chief Tuned in to World Beat,' *Los Angeles Times*, September 7, 1999: C1, C7.

45   Michael J. Wolf, *The Entertainment Economy*, New York: Times Books, 1999, p. 114. See also McChesney, *Rich Media*, pp. 105–106.

46   Rose, 'Think Globally, Script Locally,': 158.

47   Rose, 'Think Globally, Script Locally': 158.

48   Craig S. Smith, 'MTV Success Gives Viacom a Foothold in Huge, Fast-Growing China Market,' *Wall Street Journal*, October 25, 1999: A49E.

49   Martin Peers, 'News Corp.'s European Chief Executive Resigns After Dispute Over Her Role,' *Wall Street Journal*, September 29, 1999: B15.

50   Rose, 'Think Globally, Script Locally': 160.

51   Kim Cross, 'B-to-B, By the Numbers,' *Business 2.0*, September 1999: 109. An estimated 80% of e-commerce transactions in Mexico are business-to-business deals between big companies such as Microsoft and Citibank, which use Mexico as a launch point in Latin America for administrative and financial software programs. Andrea Mandel-Campbell, 'Mexico Raises Online Hat to the Middle Man,' *Financial Times*, September 29, 1999: 24.

52   Vinton Cerf, 'Transforming Impact of Internet,' Internet and the Global Political Economy Conference, University of Washington Center for Internet Studies, September 23, 1999.

53   Wolf, *The Entertainment Economy*, p. 194.

54   Tina Kelley, 'A World of Choices to Plug in to the Net,' *The New York Times*, May 20, 1999: D1, D7.

55   Vinton Cerf, 'Transforming Impact of Internet,' Internet and the Global Political Economy Conference, University of Washington Center for Internet Studies, September 23, 1999; Andrea Mandel-Campbell, 'Mexico Raises Online Hat to the Middle Man,' *Financial Times*, September 29, 1999: 24.

56   US Dept of Commerce, NTIA, 'Falling Through the Net: Defining the Digital Divide,' July 1999, p. 38, and Chart II-24b, p. 55.

57   In Karen Kaplan, 'EarthLink, MindSpring Agree to Merge,' *Los Angeles Times*, September 24, 1999: C1, C10.

58   Francois Bar, Stephen Cohen, Peter Cowhey, Brad DeLong, Michael Kleeman and John Zysman, 'Defending the Internet Revolution in the Broadband Era: When Doing Nothing is Doing Harm,' E-conomy Working Paper 12, August 1999: esp. 14–15.

59   US FCC, Common Carrier Bureau, Industry Analysis Division, 'High-Speed Services for Internet Access: Subscribership as of June 30, 2000,' October 2000: 2, 4. Also see Deborah A. Lathen, Bureau Chief, Cable Services Bureau, 'Broadband Today,' A Staff Report to William E. Kennard, Chairman, FCC, October 1999: 25.

60   Consumer Federation of America, 'Principles of Nondiscriminatory Access to Broadband Internet Communications Services,' August 16, 2000.

61   Intel had already invested in Pacific Century CyberWorks, another Hong Kong company, which plans to offer a high-speed broadband Internet service over cable systems to 110 million Asian households. Cable & Wireless likewise already provides broadband services in the region through a subsidiary. Yahoo! has a partnership with still another Hong Kong company, SmartOne telecoms, as well as eight of its own localized Asian sites. Jonathan Birchall, 'SingTel and Lycos to Extend Net Access in Asia,' *Financial Times*, September 15, 1999: 19.

62   Sheryl WuDunn, 'An Entrepreneurial Exception Rides the Internet in Japan,' *The New York Times*, July 26, 1999: C10; Norihiko Shirouzo and Jathan Sapsford, 'Japan's Softbank Unveils New Internet Deals,' *Wall Street Journal*, June 25, 1999: A15, A17.

63   Stephanie N. Mehta and Steven Lipin, 'Global Crossing to Unveil Asia Venture,' *Wall Street Journal*, September 8, 1999: A3.

64   Connie Ling, 'Yahoo! to Buy Largest Web Site in Taiwan for $146 Million in Stock,' *Wall Street Journal*, November 10, 2000: B5.

65   Steve Donohue, 'Excite@Home, Chello Vie for Overseas Modem Markets,' *Electronic Media*, June 28, 1999: 20, 30; Robert A. Guth, 'Juicing Up Japan's Web and Cable World,' *Wall Street Journal*, November 9, 2000: A21.

66   Geoffrey Nairn, 'Surfing the Net on a Broadband,' *Financial Times*, June 9, 1999: FT Telecoms, XV.

67   Leslie Cauley, 'Liberty Media, Microsoft Plan Europe Venture,' *Wall Street Journal*, 8 Sept 1999: B6; Donohue, 'Excite@Home, Chello . . .'; John Tagliube, 'A Media World to Conquer,' *The New York Times*, July 7, 1999: C1, 5.

68   In Argentina, data networker Diginet Argentina is partly owned by Goldman Sachs Group and the Rothschild family; its rival MetroRed is controlled by Fidelity Investments; and the privatized local telephone organizations with which they compete, Telefonica de Argentina and Telecom Argentina Stet-France Telecom, themselves are partly owned by foreign investors (Citibank, Hicks, Muse, Tate & Furst, and Telefonica; and Olivetti and France Telecom, respectively). Craig Torres, 'Data-Network Firms Find Fertile Ground in Argentina,' *Wall Street Journal*, October 5, 1999: A16.; Peter Hudson, 'Plug and Pay,' *Latin Trade*, May 1999: 60–63.

69   Ken Warn, 'Quickstep Raises Pace After Slow Tango,' *Financial Times*, September 1, 1999: 10.

70   James Ryan, 'In Spanish and Portuguese, Web Growth Spurt,' *The New York Times*, June 3, 1999: D1, D8.

71   Stephanie Gruner, 'Executives Meet to "Tame" the Internet, But Critics Fear a Loss of Innovation,' *Wall Street Journal*, September 13, 1999: A39J.

72   John Markoff, 'Not a Great Equalizer After All?,' *The New York Times*, June 21, 1999: C4.

73   Leslie Helm, 'The "World" in World Wide Web Becomes More Visible,' *Los Angeles Times*, March 22, 1999: C4.

74   Ben Vickers, 'Firms Push to Get Multilingual on the Web,' *Wall Street Journal*, November 22, 2000: B11A.

75   Hobsbawm, *Age of Capital*, p. 29.

76   Hobsbawm himself elsewhere calls this period 'the landslide.' Eric Hobsbawm, *The Age of Extremes*, New York: Pantheon, 1994, p. 401.

77   A point made well by Thomas Frank, 'It's Globalicious!,' *Harper's Magazine*, October 1999: 72–74.

78   Ignacio Ramonet, 'A New Totalitarianism,' *Foreign Policy*, Fall 1999 (116): 121.

PART 3

Global media systems

Chapter 9

Oliver Boyd-Barrett

MEDIA IMPERIALISM REFORMULATED

DURING THE 1990S THERE has been growing consensus in the literature (e.g. Tomlinson, 1991; Sreberny-Mohammadi, 1996) that previous models of international communication may be abandoned in a process of linear intellectual development that has moved through theories of international communication as propaganda, through to modernization and free flow, to dependency and cultural or media imperialism, supplanted in turn by theories of the 'autonomous reader' and culminating in discourses of globalization that play upon an infinite variety of combinations of 'global' and 'local'.

I want to argue that the narrative of linearity is suspect and that the concept of 'globalization' is a flawed conceptual tool which presumes to tell us that 'agency' no longer matters; intellectual development in the field of international communication appears not to proceed on the basis of exhaustive testing but lurches from one theory, preoccupation, dimension to another with inadequate attention to accumulative construction.

In particular I am interested in the concept of 'media imperialism'. Far from this being a now dead concept, I want to argue that (i) it has never seriously been tested; (ii) it still has much to offer as an analytical tool, and (iii) by incorporating some of the key concerns of 'globalization' theory, including hybridity and the weakening of nation-states, the concept can easily be modified for application to the present time. Even if we accept that the significance of (geographical) territory as a domain for communications control is declining, this would be a poor reason for relaxing the critique of what I call the 'colonization of communications space'.

Two models of media imperialism

The concept of media imperialism was developed within a broader analysis of cultural imperialism and dependency. Much of the basic analysis is heavily indebted to the works of Marx, Lenin and Rosa Luxemburg (see Boyd-Barrett, 1977a). Marxist analysis of imperialism was revisited by scholars in the 1960s and 1970s wanting to investigate the continuing dependence of post-colonial states on previous imperial powers within a context of post-Second World War US dominance. Political independence had to be judged within a context of continuing economic and cultural dependence (e.g. through education, ideas, media, language), not simply on specific ex-imperial powers, but on a capitalist world order which was dominated by the prevailing US industrial–military–political coalition (Baran and Sweezy, 1970). The strength of the capitalist world order has since been consolidated by the defeat of the Soviet Union and communist bloc. The USA is still the dominant economic and political power in the 1990s, but its share of global economic activity has nonetheless been in decline. Despite set-backs to the so-called 'tiger economies' of Southeast Asia in 1997–8, this part of the world, including Japan, India and China, is expected to continue its contribution to a major redistribution of economic power in the early part of the third millennium (although we should pause to note the part played by the USA, IMF and World Bank in bailing out some of these 'tigers' including, within a few months of 1997, Indonesia, South Korea and Thailand).

In this process of redistribution there is much evidence of alliances and interpenetration between erstwhile 'first-world' corporations and those of other parts of the world, and stronger evidence of two-way cultural flows. This process of redistribution can be viewed as a process of democratic, pluralistic levelling between nations; alternatively it may be seen as evidence of the reformation of a global economic power elite, now more broadly based, ethnically, but otherwise intensifying processes of corporate concentration without regard for national division and geography, as corporate giants battle it out on a global field of commercial war.

This changing configuration has implications for two principal models of media imperialism which were generated by scholars in the 1970s. The first was closely associated with Herbert Schiller (e.g. Schiller, 1976) and a group of Latin American scholars (e.g. Mattelart, 1979). Schiller's model understood US media imperialism in terms of its functions of selling media-related US hardware and software, promoting an image of the USA and of the world that was favourable to American interests, and of advertising American goods and services – directly through the provision of more channels for advertising, and indirectly through the display of consumer lifestyles.

More forceful than European models of political economy of that period, this view was a radical departure from the hitherto effects-dominated literature. It did not deal well with issues of meaning, audience and reception, which were to be the province of European cultural studies, but in its confident and comprehensive grasp of political economy and its relevance to media, it was unrivalled. It can be seen within the context of domestic and international opposition to the Vietnam War, which created a receptive environment for critiques of all forms of US expansionism. The thesis was simultaneously enriched and diluted by Tunstall's book, *The Media are American* (Tunstall, 1977), which explored a broader Anglo-American ambit of influence uniting old and new imperialisms, while also identifying significant centres of independent production. Latin American scholars (e.g. Mattelart, 1979) helped to locate media imperialism within a debate about how requirements of first-world economies, led by the United States, stunted the development of third-world economies. Just as Schiller's political economy undermined the effects paradigm in media research generally, so the Latin Americans undermined the 'modernization' paradigm, whose premise was that Western-style media expansion has a benign influence for national development.

The 'Schiller' model was based on powerful cases, particularly that of the USA, and also the influence of Great Britain and France. It can be critiqued for its restrictions of time and space (history and geography). In calling Schiller's model 'totalistic' (Boyd-Barrett, 1981/2) I drew attention to its presumption of continuing US dominance across time and space, a model so circular that it left no room for change or meaningful resistance. I also noted the uncompromising negativity of the analysis. An alternative approach would have been open to relative benefits and losses. There are many examples where US media influence arguably has had a liberating effect: for example, in countries where media systems are subject to authoritarian controls or to the cultural preferences of class elites (e.g. Schou, 1992).

An alternative model – I will call it the 'generic' model – developed in Europe. It also attributed great influence to the media expansion of major powers. It was rooted in Marxist theory and the media history of colonialism. It foregrounded the diversity of different dimensions of media expansion. It was committed to empirical demonstration above political rhetoric. Generic media imperialism is associated with my 1977 publications (Boyd-Barrett, 1977a, 1977b) and is also addressed in a 1980 publication by Chin-Chuan Lee. In my view it is widely applicable, across space and time, so that it can apply to UK–Ireland media relations or to those of Germany–Austria, Australia–New Zealand, China–Hong Kong–Taiwan, Egypt–Sudan, South Africa–Lesotho, Thailand–Laos, Russia and other republics of the Russian federation, etc.

This empirical model acknowledges the multidimensionality of media forms (see below) and degrees of dependence/imperialism. Therefore it allows for both high and low dependence – in this model, it does not really matter if there is a lot of it, or not much of it (it can be used to demonstrate the sometimes *weak* charges of media imperialism) nor need it be especially important whether the focus is the so-called 'third world' or the developed world. My starting point in 1977 was the preponderance of Hollywood products in UK cinema and the popularity of US soaps in British television. We can also apply this approach to media practices within nation-states, expressed territorially, or in such terms as inter-ethnic, inter-cultural, inter-class relations.

Both models are still useful

Both these models of media imperialism are still useful. Although I want to push the argument beyond nation-to-nation relations, there is considerable evidence still of unequal international media activity, coupling strong media exporters to heavy media importers, and the USA still figures, unquestionably, amongst the former. I will give some examples:

(i) The British film industry, which in the late 1990s is stronger than it has been for many years, is still overshadowed by the success of Hollywood products, not least because the main distribution chains are linked with Hollywood. Although 103 UK films were produced in 1997 (of which 17 were US backed), the 193 US films on release in the UK in 1997 commanded 73.5 per cent of box-office revenue (an improvement at least on the 91–3 per cent typical of the early 1990s) (*Financial Times Screen Finance*, 1998). Control of distribution and exhibition fosters the success of other US commercial activities, including film-related branding of toys, clothes and other goods (Wasko, 1994), and fast-food franchises, often located side-by-side with exhibition outlets. Hollywood film dominance inevitably carries over to video sales and television replays. In cinema, video, pay television, interactive television and multimedia markets, dominated largely by North American products, the best expectation of the European Commission is that European products could see an increase in their market share rise from only 13 per cent in 1995 to a still very modest 21 per cent in 2005; programme-makers expect to see their share of the industry's total revenue rise from 28 per cent in 1995 to 30 per cent in 2005 (private communication from Tony Robinson, 4 November 1997). Puttnam (1997) notes that in 1995 the European Community ran an audio-visual trade deficit with the USA of $6.3 billion, possibly growing to $10 billion by 2000. What this deficit means, argues Puttnam, is 'a fundamental dislocation between the world of the imagination, created by the moving image, and the everyday lives of people around the globe' (Puttnam, 1997: 8), one that is supported by an alliance between Hollywood (the Motion Picture Exporters' Association of America) and Washington.

(ii) Major 'wholesale' suppliers of international television and print news to television and radio stations and daily newspapers throughout the world are news agencies (AP and APTV, Reuters and Reuters Television, WTN), whose headquarters are in New York, London and Paris, which directly or indirectly represent a lineage of global hegemony that reaches back to the middle of the nineteenth century. In addition to these are a few international satellite broadcasters, including BBC World, CNN, MSNBC, Fox Television and BSkyB, which are clients of the wholesalers but Bloomburg have significant news-gathering staffs of their own whose services are sometimes redistributed by local television channels (Boyd-Barrett, 1997).

(iii) Global manufacture of personal-computer operating systems is almost entirely in the hands of one US corporation, Microsoft, whose annual revenues in 1997 were $11.4 billion. Microsoft was the world's fourth largest corporation in 1998, worth $99 billion (Farrelly and Ryle, 1998). Production of chips for such machines is largely controlled by another American corporation, Intel, which in 1998 was the world's seventh largest corporation valued at $93 billion. Gateway services to the Internet are mainly controlled by two US software products, Microsoft Internet Explorer and Netscape, and 96 per cent of all Internet sites are located within the rich twenty-seven-nation OECD area (with English its lingua franca), dominated by the USA (Keegan, 1997).

In a critique of Microsoft, Newman (1997) argues that it threatens to control the standards of the Internet. Web-page designers tend to support software standards that are compatible with the dominant browser, and Microsoft has been paying Internet service providers to bundle Explorer with their services. It has signed exclusive deals with companies like Time Warner and Disney where Microsoft's Explorer will be required for access to parts of the web sites which those companies are establishing. Through control of desktop operating systems and Internet browsers, Microsoft seeks to control the business computers managing web sites at the other end. It also represents a threat to the computing standards of the Internet-oriented Java language – an open standard for running software over the Internet created by Sun Microsystems and supported by hundreds of other companies. Java was designed to be platform-independent. Microsoft's goal, argues Newman, is to undermine this multi-platform function, using its combination of browsers, operating systems and developer tools to divert Java into a new Microsoft-controlled proprietary system that runs best only on Windows-based machines.

When Microsoft invested in Apple Computer in 1997 it agreed that in exchange Apple would bundle Explorer with every Apple computer and support Microsoft's Java standards. (Further battle for the Internet waged between Internet giants Microsoft and Netscape in 1998 with Netscape's development of a flexible software platform which would give users access to the programming in order to develop customized versions.) Over 65 per cent of new intranet sites are deployed on Microsoft Windows NT servers (Newman, 1997). Microsoft control extends beyond operating systems and software applications to development tools used by a majority of programmers and has strong dominance of the training programmes of IT professionals. It is increasingly involved in other media delivery systems, including Dreamworks SKG (Hollywood movies), WebTV Networks, low-orbit satellite (Teledesic), Comcast Corp – these last three will extend Internet access to non-PC consumers – and many others, even including Black Entertainment Television.

(iv) Principal global media companies identified by Herman and McChesney (1997) are News Corporation ($10 billion in 1996 sales); Time Warner ($25 billion in 1996 sales, of which two-thirds are from the USA); Disney (with $24 billion in 1997 sales, of which some three-quarters are from the US market); Viacom ($13 billion in 1997 income, four-fifths of which comes from the US market); Bertelsmann, the one European firm among the 'first tier' of media giants, with sales of approximately $15 billion in 1996, of which 66 per cent derives from Europe and 24 per cent from the USA; TCI (1996 income of $7 billion) – the leading US cable provider; Universal, bought from Seagram for $5.7 billion in 1995; General Electric, with total sales of $80 billion in 1996, of which 62 per cent were from the USA, and included by Herman and McChesney because it owns NBC, which had $5 billion in sales in 1996.

These sales figures are modest if hardware, computing and telephony are included, as they must be if we are to establish the extent of current colonization activities in the communications industries. In the case of telephony, for example, US–SBC Communications, the Texas-based telecoms company, offered $4.4 billion early in 1998 simply for the purchase of Southern New England Telecommunications, in a move into the long-distance telephony market. SBC had just previously made a $16.5-billion acquisition of PacificTelesis Group, giving it California, Nevada and undersea access to Asia and land access to Mexican and South American markets. In early 1998, US telecoms group GTE was set to raise its $28-billion cash offer for long-distance telecoms specialist MCI, in the event that rival group WorldCom's $37 billion agreed bid failed to proceed. We are talking here about sums of money that range between two to four times the entire size of News Corporation's annual revenues, bigger than the size of many individual national economies, such as those of Malawi, Angola, Bangladesh, Bolivia, Bulgaria, Ireland, Kenya, Malaysia, New Zealand or Pakistan.

Herman and McChesney identify three tiers of global media players. In the second tier, nearly half of the listed companies are from North America. The success of companies in the second and third tiers partly depends on strategic alliances among themselves and with companies in the top tier. Herman and McChesney argue that the global media market is still dominated by US interests and by the US domestic market, although its proportionate importance is bound to decline as other nations grow more prosperous and more media-active. Yet the world media system will continue to have a strong US flavour well into the next century. US companies can generally recoup costs from their domestic market and can then manipulate prices in overseas markets according to what each market is prepared to pay and the intensity of local competition. What these authors do not tell us, however, is the overall, global size of the media market and what proportion of this is commanded by each of their three tiers.

Even if such phenomena are historically specific, the concept of media imperialism is appropriate for the investigation of any periods in which access to or control of any dimension of media activity is controlled by any one nation or group at the expense at others. What I am indicating here is a reconceptualization of imperialism as a process having to do with the colonization of communications space. This may have an international character, as in the above examples, or may be represented by instances such as the dominance of television markets by single, home-grown corporations which dominate production and transmission within national markets, as in the cases of Brazil and Mexico (cf. Cole, 1996; Fox, 1997).

In this framework, communications space has no necessary relationship with territory nor with technology, but it does necessarily have to do with the resources and fora for human expression. In its analysis of those who gain control over such resources and fora, it is proposed that we can identify structural consistencies which do often relate to territory and other markers of identity, but more importantly have to do with political and economic power. It is in the relationship between communications space and power that we find justification for retaining the vocabulary of imperialism, especially upon investigation of the giant, intensifying and global concentrations of capital that have driven the development of media industries in recent decades. The model also insists on multidimensionality and on empirical measures: it can reveal the extent to which specific activities within particular sectors of the communications industries are controlled by identifiable agents or interests; final judgement as to whether the findings amount to 'colonization' of communications space is a relative judgement, one that takes account of the overall context and the values of different affected interests.

Territorial imperialism has as its object the conquest of a finite territory; the ambitions of conquerors may lead them to annex yet more territory; eventually they are stopped – by oceans, impassable or impregnable mountains, overwhelming adverse military power, etc. The object of ambition in the case of communications space does from some perspectives seem deceptively finite: a limited range of national newspapers, for example, can be said to be financially viable. One may add a further title, define a new audience or seduce one from existing publications, often at great cost and risk. Yet communications space demonstrates astonishing elasticity. Technical innovation, especially, often generates more space, and there have been many periods in which such space is radically extended – as in the case of the introduction of radio, for instance, or of the Internet – and temporarily there may seem to be enough space for every claimant.

But the value of communications space is enhanced relative to the size and quality of audiences which can be attracted to any given message for which the space is used. Those interests which have the resources and skills to attract large audiences and the revenues which attend such success typically gain great influence over regulatory structures governing producer and audience access. They achieve the power to define what the space is and how it should be used. We are beginning to see this happen with the Internet.

A feature of this model, therefore, is the symbiotic tension between the physical potential for communication, on the one hand, and technology, control and skills, on the other. That is to say, the physical potential for communication is itself extended or limited by particular choices as to the technologies that are employed for its exploitation, the regulatory structures which govern communication space and its uses, and the skills that users bring to the processes of communication. Technologies, regulatory structures and skills are resources of control, each of which has discriminatory tendencies: technologies may be more or less expensive, more or less suitable for certain forms of communication, even for certain languages of communication; regulations tend to favour certain categories of use and user over others; skills are the product of experience and training which are often in restricted supply.

Such inequalities are a common feature of trade relationships and have sometimes been attributed to the economics of competitive advantage, where success is often self-reinforcing. Such explanations do not render the phenomenon politically and culturally neutral in the way that some economists seem to imagine. In the case of media there are unique reasons for concern, having to do with relativities of power in access to mass audiences and to the infrastructures of any communications which are independent of physical proximity. Access to mass audiences is related to opportunities for the construction of dominating symbolic imagery, cognitive persuasion and affect, for political, economic and cultural purposes. Access to infrastructures has implications for the kinds of communication that are possible, and for the economic conditions under which use of such communications is permissible.

We can distinguish between media imperialism as an objective, empirical phenomenon and as a *discourse*. Worries about the import of popular US soaps may sometimes seem out of proportion when consideration is given to the decreasing proportion of audience attention – in some regions – that is spent in viewing them (see Goonasekera, 1996), the greater popularity of local productions, and strong evidence of local production and control of other areas of media activity, such as in radio or the press. Nonetheless, the discourse of concern about the presence of North American popular culture (or of any culture considered as 'other'), the dangers attributed to the values that this is said to represent, and the measures taken to reduce or off-set it, is worthy of serious study in itself, and especially for what insight it affords into the struggle for power over communications space, its resources, uses and audiences, or into the way in which such issues are incorporated within wider struggles.

The concept of 'imperialism', burdened by a weight of ideological baggage, sometimes unhelpful to this investigation (notably in its predisposition always to assume negative implications) helps us to (i) concentrate on *agency*; (ii) have regard for inequalities; (iii) be alert to communications regulation as conquest, never less so than when it is expressed as part of a natural or inevitable state of affairs (e.g. the 'scarcity of airwaves' justification for pre-1980s broadcasting monopolies; 'guarantee of universal service' for telecommunications monopolies; 'free market' for deregulation and privatization, etc.); (iv) and to be conscious of communications space as the site for struggle and resistance.

Definitions

My provisional definition of media imperialism (Boyd-Barrett, 1977b) was a sentence somewhat out of context of the main body of my work on this subject at that time, and does not well represent the overall argument. For example, the definition makes no explicit reference to authors or readers. This omission was not an endorsement of a 'hypodermic-needle' model of media effect; indeed, the article itself called for much more sophisticated treatment than was then common of the encounter between audiences and international media texts.

In choosing to talk of 'media imperialism' as opposed to 'cultural imperialism' I was not suggesting that we should consider media without full reference to their broader social, cultural, economic and political contexts, which would indeed have been a regressive step. Instead, I was concerned about the necessity for a focus on the media industries: only by taking into account the full complexity of this economic sector, by getting inside the 'black box' of meaningful production, could we generate theory that was adequate to the task and take us beyond the fairly crude political rhetoric that was part of the NWICO debate then at its height. Cultural studies was beginning to embark on a line of enquiry that led towards notions of the autonomous reader and polysemy of texts. Important and necessary though that development was, it diverted attention away from the political economy of communications production at a crucial moment of history in which the entire infrastructure and superstructure of communications industries, whose value ultimately rests on their audiences, were subject to egregious assault by gigantic concentrations of national and international capital.

Benefits of the concept

For all its limitations, there is a certain heuristic value in revisiting my original definition of media imperialism: 'The process whereby the ownership, structure, distribution or content of the media in any one country are singly or together subject to substantial external pressures from the media interests of any other country or countries without proportionate reciprocation of influence by the country so affected' (Boyd-Barrett, 1977b: 117).

One of its main strengths, I believe, is that it recognized that imperialism could vary between different media, and between different levels, dimensions or spheres of activity within any one sector of the media industries. The definition in itself refers to ownership, structure, distribution or content. It was quite possible, indeed common, for example, to find national ownership coexisting with high dependence on imports.

My 1977b article further differentiated between: the shape of the communication vehicle, a set of industrial arrangements, a body of values about ideal practice, and specific media contents. Placing the most manifest element of media activity, content, at the end of the list, this breakdown highlighted the relativity of media technologies: technologies as the products of commercial and other interests, not independent, inevitable or unalterable variables. It called attention to the structure and organization of media industries as matters of cultural, commercial and political convention (this could apply to the relationship between advertising and content, the contracting-out of production, etc.) which could and have been exported to other contexts. It also highlighted the relativity of professional and occupational ideologies and definitions of best practice: for example, Anglo-American construction of news-as-fact (selected according to values of eliteness, negativity, and so on) in opposition to French journalism of opinion, socialist journalism of agit-prop, or third-world journalism of development news.

In 1980, Chin-Chuan Lee differentiated between television-programme exportation, foreign ownership and control of media outlets, transfer of dominant broadcasting norms, media commercialism, the invasion of capitalist world views and infringement upon indigenous ways of life in adopting societies (Lee, 1980). This work demonstrates a general tendency in the literature to deal with only one medium at a time, whereas from the point of view of the whole culture, and of the audience, what matters is balance across available communications space. Internet and media convergence have extended the boundaries of traditional academic discourse about media. For example, we now need to allow for such concepts as gateway provider and telecommunications carrier. One model (KPMG, 1996) suggests a 'convergence value chain' that differentiates between: content, production, packaging, service provision, conveyance and consumer interface. There is scope for considerably more complexity, if we wish: content can be broken down into various stages of production, component supply (for example, animation, graphics, news-film, library services, still photographs) and programme formatting. We should also include factors to do with 'production' and 'readership' competency (for instance, IT skills) and consider who is involved in defining these, in relation to whose technologies, for what purposes or functions, and the distribution of such skills across relevant populations.

My 1977 model (Boyd-Barrett 1977a, 1977b) combined the elements of 'cultural invasion' and 'imbalance of power resources' between countries; imperialism could result through either deliberate export or through unintentional influence. There was nothing in the definition itself that proposed positive or negative values associated with the concept, except possibly in the choice of the term 'imperialism' to describe it.

Problems with the concept

There were some significant problems with the definition. It talked about inter-*media* relations, and excluded non-media interests. So in itself it did not invite consideration of the extra-media powers or interests (political, or related to non-media commercial activities of media owners and their business and propaganda goals) that had invested in media companies. The definition also talked about reciprocity of cultural trade-relationships between named countries. This privileges international relations, and ignores other relevant dimensions, including the range of choice available on domestic markets between sources of local origin. It assumes that nation-states are the basic building blocks within the field of global media activities, and that it is possible simply to associate particular media with particular countries. The globalization debate certainly raises questions about the sovereignty of nation-states, challenged as they are by both centrifugal forces from within (such as secessionist movements) and centripetal forces from without (through regional trade associations such as the EC, ASEAN, NAFTA, WTO, etc.), although I believe it exaggerates the extent to which this is a new problem.

However, too often there is a blurring of the distinction between global activity of corporations which have no strong domestic base, and corporations which do have strong domestic bases – generally in first-world countries – and have extensive (but rarely spread evenly) global activity. This raises the possibility to my mind that in this period to which we refer as globalization, the sovereignty of some nation-states is undermined to support that of others, another manifestation of neo-imperialism. But substantial powers are still invested in issues of sovereignty, whether in domains of trade, culture or politics, and the mapping of the place of media with respect to such issues is a live and legitimate topic for investigation. Because media systems are often complex hybrids of different agencies and actors, it is not advisable to make simple identification of whole corporations with particular national identities – this is precisely why we need to take account of the multidimensionality of media activity. At the same time, the media-imperialism thesis needs to encompass neo-colonialisms of inter-ethnic, inter-cultural, inter-gender, inter-generational and inter-class relations.

My 1977b definition ignored the question of audience; this is a significant but not irreparable omission. The model needs to take account of audiences, audience preferences; audience consumption of specified cultural products as a proportion of total media and non-media consumption. Yet we must not assume any simple correlation between colonization of communication space and the attitudes, beliefs and behaviours of audiences. We might expect in some circumstances to find precisely the reverse – it is in the nature of imperialism to provoke violent resistance. It is not in the area of effects that we need to look for justification of an enquiry into colonization of communications space, but in relation to the question: whose voices get to be heard, and which voices are excluded? That is all. Whether the voices that do get to be heard are popular with audiences, try to manipulate them, are honest or dishonest, intelligent and entertaining or otherwise, etc., is of great interest and importance, but within an overriding concern for the democratization of communication it is the obstacles in the way of access to mass audiences that should have research priority. Regardless of the sophistication of technologies, the degree of development and democratization, only a tiny fraction of the world's population possess the resources, opportunity and skills that permit such access. In an age of democracy we have media tyranny.

Not even the Internet is a response: access to the Internet requires equipment, gateway subscriptions and skills, but no amount of access to the Internet guarantees mass audiences: that requires the kind of technical and production skills that we associate with the large media corporations.

Applications

In recent years the global–local mix looks more complex than in the 1970s. In the 1990s as in the 1970s there are significant centres of media production which enjoy international influence in what used to be called the developing world: for example, Bombay for Hindi film, Cairo for Arabic television, radio and print production, Mexico and Brazil for *telenovelas*. Some new centres have appeared, as in the case of Hong Kong as supplier of television programming for mainland China, Taiwan and the Chinese diaspora; also, Australia, which in addition to state-subsidized film export trade has generated several soap operas which have proved successful in various other countries, generally English-speaking (but not the USA), notably Britain (Cunningham and Jacka, 1996). Major domestic broadcasters which used to be heavily dependent on imports now produce more of their own, or their spread of dependence on imports has extended to include sources that are alternative to traditional first-world offerings.

Many parts of the world enjoy an extended choice of programme and media products that would have been inconceivable in the 1970s, at least in terms of quantity. Cities such as Buenos Aires, where most households are served by multi-channel (fifty to sixty channels) cable television, or India, where local cable network clients have a choice of several international and domestic satellite-delivered television services in a variety of local languages, as well as in English and Hindi, are actually now more 'advanced' in this respect than the UK, where most of the population still receives only a range of four or five (depending on area) terrestrial networks, despite increasing availability of direct satellite broadcasting and cable. In Europe generally the number of television stations doubled in the period 1990–6 from approximately 125 to 250. Digital services increased from 10 in 1996 to 330 in 1997 (Agence Europe, 24 October 1997). Such increases in quantity are accompanied by increasing capacity and falling costs. For example, the cost to transmit one analogue channel on Astra in 1997 was roughly £4m p.a.; this falls to £500,000 with digital 8 to 1 compression, falling to £250,000 by 1998 (Singer, 1997). In some parts of the world, such as India, television-set ownership is now ahead of radio ownership (although half of all adults in India still possessed neither in 1993–5, cf. Mytton, 1996).

For the Middle East there are now several satellite television stations, catering mainly for Arabic populations, of which the most successful are based in Beirut, Cairo, London and Rome; many others are planned. In 1996 almost every Arab state operated at least one satellite television channel, and by 1997 there were over forty Arab commercial satellite channels (Ayish, 1997). In the United Arab Emirates, the bulk of the population is made up of immigrants from India and Pakistan. Locally available Arabic programming takes little account of their presence. Instead, this worker force has a choice of ten satellite channels beamed from the Indian subcontinent. In the USA, Canada, Australia and Great Britain, on the other hand, major ethnic groups are comparatively well catered for through ethnic broadcast, video and print media, and opportunities for specialist communication needs are increasing with the development of Internet websites.

The identity of major players, while still heavily represented by corporations with close links to the USA and other first-world countries including Japan, has also become more complex. Nowhere is this more evident than in the changing panorama of telecommunications growth, where privatized ex-PTTs such as those of Spain, Italy, Malaysia and others are increasingly involved in complex alliances (often with the giants, such as AT&T, British Telecom, Sprint or MTI) for the capture of overseas markets in local and long-distance telephony and related services, which increasingly include such activities as cable, subscription TV and mobile telephony.

The phenomenon of international journalism is still associated mainly with prestige titles (e.g. *Wall Street Journal*, *Financial Times*, *Time*, *Newsweek*, *International Herald Tribune*) selling to elite business audiences (Sparks, 1997), and most national press systems are still strongly 'local' in terms of ownership and structure; but the influence of international press corporations such as Murdoch's News Corporation (especially in the USA, Britain and Australia), or O'Reilly's Independent group (with strong interests in South African press and radio, for example) and Conrad Black's domination of the Canadian press through the Southam newspaper group, testifies to the continuing importance of corporatism in press journalism.

Growth of local production in, say, television content, may coexist with dependence on the purchase of programme-formats developed in the West and managed by first-world franchise agents and consultants. Centres that were once strong in local production may now be threatened and overtaken by international satellite distribution (Fox, 1997), which, because it reaches larger markets, attracts more advertising revenue and can sell more cheaply. This may now be a threat to hitherto Latin American giants. Availability of cable television, international satellite and video in India is weakening the influence of the Bombay film industry. Overall growth in capacity increases dependence on imports to fill available time, especially formulaic imports which guarantee the interest of large, international advertisers. Television today is increasingly a high-technology, low-personnel business run from modest offices and even private villas, where many of the essential operations, including programming, advertising sales, news provision and transmission, are contracted out to other companies, greatly complicating the issue of identities of origin.

Charting this growing complexity is a major task for scholars of international communication and may be the just cause for at least some element of celebration (Sreberny-Mohammadi, 1991). Persisting through this complexity, however, are the highly visible, imposing brand-names of transnational media power with indisputable first-world associations, incorporating such household names as Microsoft, News Corporation, Twentieth Century Fox, US Fox, HarperCollins, Asian Star Television, BSkyB, Times Warner, Viacom, HBO, Atari, Sony, Bertelsmann, NBC, EMI, Disney, ABC, Dreamworks, Bell South, America Online, ESPN, MTV, TCI, Polygram, DirecTV, New York Times, Reader's Digest, McGraw-Hill, Dow Jones, Reuters, British Broadcasting Corporation, Axel Springer, Canal-Plus, Reed-Elsevier, Pearson, and many, many others.

It is precisely to help make sense of this complexity that application of the framework of media imperialism continues to be relevant. In applying this conceptual framework, we are likely to find evidence of (i) considerable disparity between different areas of media activity, and (ii) considerable internal variations within any single area of media activity.

In the case of news agencies, for example, I concluded (Boyd-Barrett and Thussu, 1992; Boyd-Barrett, 1997) that this sector of the communications industry mapped better than many to patterns of 'imperialism', both in the past (in the nineteenth-century cartel operated by Reuters, the French Havas and German Wolff), and, in effect, though under much more open market conditions, still today, and I noted that:

i   The total number of global print agencies has diminished rather than increased.

ii   There has been a growth of television and Internet news providers but these are either closely tied to existing major media players in the USA and UK, principally, or represent new formations of capital, principally representing the USA.

iii   There is little evidence to suggest that major imbalances with respect to distribution of resources or attention, or arising from the application of Western news values, have grown weaker; indeed, they may have grown stronger.

iv   There is little encouraging evidence that alternative media (for example, DepthNews, Gemini, Inter Press Service) have had a significant impact on mainstream media.

The maintenance or even the intensification of evidence of media imperialism with respect to news agencies may coexist with an increase in, say, overall domestication of television content (although content is only one variable in the multivariable phenomenon of television production, text and supply). We would still have to take account of the fact that television is host to many different sources of material, and that national news programmes may contain much material taken from international news agencies; or that domestically produced television may be based on specific formats that have been 'bought in' from international players who hold copyright claims to those formats.

Even within the relatively strong-case context of news agencies, on further enquiry I have found that issues of media imperialism are enormously complicated and multivariable, and if this is the case with news agencies then it is almost certainly the case with other spheres of media activity. In a previous article (Boyd-Barrett, 1981/2) I identified three core dimensions in news-agency activity, and their component variables, with a view to demonstrating how different variables may move in different directions with respect to their significance for media imperialism. The core dimensions were:

i   the extent to which the media in a country are dependent upon services imported from and provided by the major news services (*dependency* dimension)

ii   the extent to which the nondomestic activities of the major agencies are affected by factors brought to bear on them by the national government or other indigenous powers within any specific client area (client countries or individual clients should not be regarded as wholly passive) (*production/processing* dimension)

iii the extent to which the content of major news services is culturally, politically, morally, or in any other way 'alien' to their clienteles (content or *cultural* dimension).

Illustrating the complexity, I will briefly summarize the findings relating to one of these three dimensions, namely dependency variables, where I concluded that in relation to how far developing countries are dependent, we can say that there is likely to be a high degree of cultural dependency by news-media clients on the service of the major Western news agencies under the following conditions:

i   when a high consumption of agency material exists, this consumption representing a high proportion of all news provided by retail news media, both across the various categories of news and across most news media

ii   when agency material represents a high proportion of all news made available to domestic client media from exogenous sources and a high proportion of all such news actually consumed for retail purposes

iii when alternative news sources also depend heavily in various ways on the activities of the major agencies and share important similarities with these (NB: this would affect much of the news available through available sources on Internet)

iv   in terms of news contents, dependence in general is reinforced by dependence in the identification of which stories are to be considered 'really important', and with respect to the general priorities ascribed to different categories of news, and if stories are not appreciably altered, shortened or augmented from other sources

v   retail media are unable to achieve alternative patterns of supply and consumption, and local political forces are not engaged in, or do not succeed in, establishing alternative supply patterns that also meet the legitimate requirements of news media and the general public.

We can also identify the following dependency variables:

vi   whether the services of all four major Western agencies are or are not equally available, and in practice whether dependence is intensified to reliance on only one or two of the major agencies

vii whether dependence upon the agencies as sources of *in situ* 'wholesale' news is or is not extended to their other services, such as those provided to foreign correspondents, consultancy, training, equipment assistance, the effective sub-leasing of agency communications to retail media, translation and so forth.

Conclusion

In arguing for the reformulation of the theory of media imperialism I am not saying that we should or need fail to take into account some of the flimsier elements of the cultural-imperialism theory generally or of the media-imperialism theory in particular. It should be said, nonetheless, that some of the arguments that have been rehearsed against both cultural and media imperialism (cf. Sreberny-Mohammadi, 1991) were only typical of cruder mani-festations of such theories. For example, generally speaking, it is not true that the media-imperialism theory assumed a hypodermic-needle model of media effects, nor does the theory require such a model to justify its importance. Nor is it true that those who argued about cultural and media imperialism held a simplistic view of non-Western cultures, assuming them to be pure and unsullied from previous cultural influences. This charge is a red herring.

The significance of media-imperialism theory is in part premised on the necessity to understand the nature of the relationship between national economies and the global capital-ist economy, and the role of culture and media in helping to sustain and reinvigorate that relationship. It is not true that media imperialism focused only on relations between first and third worlds and ignored relations of cultural inequality and imposition within the first world, as I have already indicated with reference to concerns about the influence of North American media in countries such as Canada and Britain and the rest of Western Europe. Nor is it true that the media-imperialism theory typically ignored sources of local production: such awareness was very much part of Tunstall's work, for example, at the very beginning of the debate.

There were two principal defects of the media-imperialism theory, in addition to those that I have already discussed. The first is that in the early days it was too much embedded in a radical political discourse against the USA. Less restrictively, it was embedded in a radical dependency discourse that grew from the work of Latin American scholars. This had value, as we have seen, in that it took account of the integration of the work of media as agents of political, cultural and commercial ideology and propaganda, and their value as hardware and software commercial products.

To this could be added the place of media within a discourse of national political and economic 'development': this is a controversial discourse, but we can certainly conclude from recent literature that media do have a role to play in constructions of nation and national identity (e.g. Scannell and Cardiff, 1991; Das and Harindranath, 1996), and that in a wide variety of ways, from fostering a demand for electricity through to facilitating business communications across modern telephony and computer networks, the media contribute to economic development and, at the very least, to the integration of business elites with the global economy. It is also important to take serious account of media contributions to education and information across a wide range of 'pro-social' contexts.

The media-imperialism theory was concerned initially with media inequalities between nations, and with how such inequalities reflected broader problems of dependency, but the metaphor of imperialism and colonialism was not sufficiently extended to include intra-national media relations (although the co-option of local elites into transnational business enterprise in opposition to the interests of non-elites was dealt with), or media fostering of inequalities between men and women, different ethnicities and between capital and labour. Arguably, the theory did not stress sufficiently the systematic patterns of ownership, industrial and technical structure, and ideology of practice that help to explain the extraordinarily limited opportunities for access to the means of production and transmission for addressing mass audiences – a scarcity of voices, a lack of diversity, that is characteristic of *all countries* of the world, and it is to this concern that the present chapter is mostly committed. The phenomenon of imperialism therefore is geographically all-pervasive.

The second major defect of the media-imperialism theory is that it has never been empirically applied to a sufficiently comprehensive degree. True, the field has benefited from a relatively modest number of individual case studies, generally focusing on single media in single countries, and sometimes focusing solely on one dimension of media activity, usually content.

In company with political economy and radical theory generally, the media-imperialism theory was set back by developments in the 1980s, including the reinvention of capitalist rhetoric by Reagan and Thatcher, the short-lived boom of the late 1980s, the growth of the 'tiger economies' in Southeast Asia and the decline of the communist East, all of which fed a growing scepticism about the validity and relevance of dependence and imperialism theories, scepticism which infected academe. In a changing climate of deregulation and enhanced communications capacity, there were significant increases in media production within some developing countries, alongside high population mobility and intensification of trade – promoting an increasing hybridity of global culture, ever more complex and more commodified, but everywhere more complex and commodified in the same sort of way. For a time these processes threw investigators off the scent, disguising the inevitability of global concentration behind a smokescreen of local proliferation. Cultural studies and postmodernism inspired facile counsel on the basis of notions of textual polysemy that there is nothing to fear from oligopolization, commodification and, too often, the moronization (or worse) of global communication space. The media-imperialism theory is a first step towards the measurement and evaluation of such trends with a view to holding responsible agencies accountable for what they do.

References

Ayish, M. (1997) Arab television goes commercial: a case study of the Middle East Broadcasting Centre, *Gazette*, 59.6, Dec., pp. 473–94.

Baran, P. and Sweezy, P. M. (1970) *Monopoly Capital*, Penguin, Harmondsworth.

Boyd-Barrett, O. (1977a) Mass communications in cross-cultural contexts, Unit 5 of *Mass Communication and Society*, Open University Press, Milton Keynes.

Boyd-Barrett, O. (1977b) Media imperialism: towards an international framework for the analysis of media systems, pp. 116–35 in Curran, J. and Gurevitch, M. (eds) *Mass Communication and Society*, Edward Arnold, London.

Boyd-Barrett, O. (1981/2) Western news agencies and the 'media imperialism' debate: what kind of data-base, *Journal of International Affairs*, 35.2, pp. 247–60.

Boyd-Barrett, O. (1997) Global news wholesalers as agents of globalization, pp. 131–44, in Sreberny-Mohammadi, A. et al. (eds) *Media in Global Context*, Arnold, London.

Boyd-Barrett, O. and Thussu, D. K. (1992) *Contra-flow in Global News*, John Libbey, London.

Cole, R. (1996) *Communication in Latin America: Journalism, Mass Media and Society*, Jaguar Books, Wilmington.

Cunningham, S. and Jacka, E. (1996) *Australian Television and International Mediascapes*, Cambridge University Press, Cambridge.

Das, S. and Harindranath, R. (1996) Nation-state, national identity and the media, Unit 22 of the MA in Mass Communications (by distance learning), Centre for Mass Communication Research, University of Leicester, Leicester.

Farrelly, P. and Ryle, S. (1998) Drug giants merger puts 10,000 UK jobs at risk, *Observer*, 1 Feb.

Financial Times Screen Finance, 8 Jan. 1998.

Fox, E. (1997) *Latin American Broadcasting: From Tango to Telenovela*, University of Luton Press, London.

Goonasekera, A. (1996) Asian audiences for Western media, Unit 44b in the MA in Mass

Communications (by distance learning), Centre for Mass Communications Research, University of Leicester, Leicester.

Herman, E. and McChesney, R. (1997) *The Global Media: The New Missionaries of Corporate Capitalism*, Cassell, London.

Keegan, V. (1997) What a Web we weave, *Guardian*, 13 May, pp. 2–3.

KPMG (1996) *Public Policy Issues Arising from Telecommunications and Audiovisual Convergence*, European Commission.

Lee, C. C. (1980) *Media Imperialism Reconsidered: The Homogenizing of Television Culture*, Sage, London.

Mattelart, A. (1979) *Multinational Corporations and the Control of Culture*, Harvester Press, Brighton.

Mytton, G. (1996) Audience research, Unit 25 in the MA in Mass Communications (by distance learning), Centre for Mass Communication Research, University of Leicester, Leicester.

Newman, N. (1997) *From Microsoft Word to Microsoft World: How Microsoft is Building a Global Monopoly*, A NetAction White Paper, Nathan@netaction.org.

Puttnam, D. (1997) Terminated, too, *Guardian*, 9 May, pp. 8–9.

Scannell, P. and Cardiff, D. (1991) *A Social History of British Broadcasting: Volume One 1922–1939: Serving the Nation*, Basil Blackwell, Oxford.

Schiller, H. (1976) *Communications and Cultural Domination*, M. E. Sharpe, New York.

Schou, S. (1992), Postwar Americanization and the revitalization of European Culture, pp. 142–58 in Schroder, C. and Skovmand, M. (eds) *Media Cultures*, Sage, London.

Singer, A. (1997) Speech to Royal Television Society, Cambridge Convention, 18–21 Sept.

Sparks, C. (1997) Towards a global public sphere? Paper presented to course conference, MA in Mass Communications (by distance learning), University of Leicester, 22 Nov.

Sreberny-Mohammadi, A. (1991) The global and the local in international communications, pp. 118–38 in Curran, J. and Gurevitch, M. (eds) *Mass Media and Society*, Edward Arnold, London.

Sreberny-Mohammadi, A. (1996) From globalization to imperialism and back again, Unit 19 in the MA in Mass Communications (by distance learning), Centre for Mass Communications Research, University of Leicester, Leicester.

Tomlinson, J. (1991) *Cultural Imperialism: A Critical Introduction*, John Hopkins University Press, Baltimore.

Tunstall, J. (1977) *The Media are American*, Constable, London.

Wasko, J. (1994) *Hollywood and the Information Age*, Polity Press, Cambridge.

Chapter 10

Daniel Hallin and Paolo Mancini

THE FORCES AND LIMITS OF HOMOGENIZATION

THE PRECEDING CHAPTERS [of the original publication] have described three distinct media system models, and many variations among individual countries. It is clear, however, that the differences among these models, and in general the degree of variation among nation states, has diminished substantially over time. In 1970 the differences among the three groups of countries characterized by our three models were quite dramatic; a generation later, by the beginning of the twenty-first century, the differences have eroded to the point that it is reasonable to ask whether a single, global media model is displacing the national variation of the past, at least among the advanced capitalist democracies discussed in this book. Increasingly, as McQuail (1994) put it, an "international media culture" has become common to all the countries we studied. In this chapter we will focus on this process of convergence or homogenization, first summarizing the changes in European media systems that tend in this direction, then moving on to the questions of how the change can be explained, its limits and countertrends, and its implications for media theory, particularly focusing on the debate about "differentiation" raised in Chapter 4 [of the original publication].

The triumph of the Liberal Model

The Liberal Model has clearly become increasingly dominant across Europe as well as North America – as it has, no doubt, across much of the world – its structures, practices, and values displacing, to a substantial degree, those of the other media systems we have explored in the previous chapters. Important qualifications need to be added to this claim; as we shall see later on, there are significant countertendencies that limit the spread of the Liberal Model in many countries or even transform that model itself. But in general, it is reasonable to summarize the changes in European media systems as a shift toward the Liberal Model that prevails in its purest form in North America.

Party newspapers and other media connected to organized social groups – media whose primary purposes were to mobilize collective action and to intervene in the public sphere and that once played a central role in both the Democratic Corporatist and Polarized

Pluralist systems – have declined in favor of commercial papers whose purpose is to make a profit by delivering information and entertainment to individual consumers and the attention of consumers to advertisers. In Finland, to take one typical example from the Democratic Corporatist system, the market share of politically aligned papers declined from 70 percent in 1950 to a bit more than 50 percent in 1970, and less than 15 percent in 1995 (Salokangas 1999: 98). Polemical styles of writing have declined in favor of "Anglo-Saxon" practices of separation of news and commentary and emphasis on information, narrative, sensation, and entertainment, rather than ideas. A model of journalistic professionalism based on the principles of "objectivity" and political neutrality is increasingly dominant.

In the field of broadcasting, the "commercial deluge" of the 1980s–90s has displaced the public service monopolies of an earlier era in favor of mixed systems in which commercial media are increasingly dominant. Broadcasting has been transformed from a political and cultural institution in which market forces played a minimal role into an industry in which they are central, even for the remaining public broadcasters who must fight to maintain audience share. Styles of broadcast journalism have shifted from informational forms centered around the political party system toward the dramatized, personalized, and popularized style pioneered in the United States (Brants 1985, 1998). Telecommunications industries have similarly been liberalized.

Patterns of political communication have also been transformed, away from party-centered patterns rooted in the same organized social groups as the old newspaper system, toward media-centered patterns that involve marketing parties and their leaders to a mass of individual consumers. Political parties, like newspapers, tend to blur their ideological identities and connections to particular social groups and interests in order to appeal to as broad an electorate as possible – they tend to become "catchall" parties. Politics is increasingly "personalized" or "presidentialized," as individual party leaders become more central to a party's image and appeal. Politics is also "professionalized," as parties and campaigns are increasingly run not by rank-and-file party members and activists – who are decreasing in number – but by specialists in political marketing often drawn from the media world. Berlusconi's Forza Italia is the purest example of this pattern – a party originally built without members, in which political and media professionals play a key managing role, and that exists solely as a marketing vehicle for the individual leader; but the tendency is general, also illustrated by Tony Blair's New Labour, for example, or Gerhard Schröeder's Social Democrats. Politics, finally, is more media centered, as the mass media become more independent as agenda setters, and as the "retail" politics of rallies, activist campaigning, and, in some countries, patronage give way, above all, to television-centered campaigning directed at a mass audience. What is true of elections is also generally true of the communication involved in the governing process.

These changes could be summarized by saying that European media systems, which in both the Democratic Corporatist and Polarized Pluralist Models are closely connected with the political system, have become increasingly separated from political institutions. This "differentiation" of the media system from the political system – to use the language of structural-functionalist theory – is one of the principal characteristics of the Liberal Model and generally occurred in the North Atlantic countries much earlier than in continental Europe. "Differentiation" of the media from the political system does not mean that media lose all relationship with the political world. Indeed it is commonly argued that media have come to play an increasingly central role in the political process, as they have become more independent of parties and other political actors, and as the latter have lost much of their ability to shape the formation of culture and opinion. Differentiation means, instead, that the media system increasingly operates according to a distinctive logic of its own, displacing to a significant extent the logic of party politics and bargaining among organized social interests, to which it was once connected. As Mazzoleni (1987) has put it, a distinctive "media logic" has increasingly come to prevail over the "political logic" subordinated to the needs of parties and political leaders, that once strongly dominated the communication process in Europe.

There are important difficulties with the concept of differentiation as a means of understanding change in European media systems. These have to do, first of all, with an important ambiguity about the notion of a distinctive "media logic," an ambiguity about whether this is essentially a *professional* or a *commercial* logic. And, as we shall see at the end of this chapter, there are difficulties — endemic to the structural-functionalist perspective from which the notion of differentiation is taken — about how to account for social and political *power*. Nevertheless, the idea that media systems in Europe have become increasingly differentiated from the political system, and in this respect have come to resemble the Liberal Model, is a good way to begin the discussion of the process of convergence.

What forces propel the homogenization of media systems, or their convergence toward the Liberal Model? Most accounts focus on "Americanization" and modernization, which in turn are closely connected with globalization and commercialization (Negrine and Papathanassopoulos 1996; Swanson and Mancini 1996; Blumler and Gurevitch 2001). We will attempt to clarify how these four processes — along with a fifth related process we will call secularization — have affected European media systems and how they are related to one another. We will begin with Americanization, and, more generally, with an examination of exogenous forces of homogenization, that is, forces outside of European societies that have pushed in the direction of convergence with the Liberal Model. We will then turn to endogenous factors, including the "secularization" of European society and politics and the commercialization of European media. The last two sections of this chapter will focus on limits and countertendencies to the process of homogenization and on the concepts of modernization and differentiation.

Exogenous forces of homogenization: Americanization and the development of a global culture of journalism

The notion of "Americanization" has been a popular starting point for analysis of media system change in Europe since the end of the 1960s, when the cultural imperialism perspective focused attention on the cultural power of the United States and its impact on media systems around the world (Schiller 1969, 1973, 1976; Boyd-Barrett 1977; Tunstall 1977). It clearly captures an important part of the process. Not only have European media and communication processes come to resemble American patterns in important ways, but there is clear evidence of direct American influence, starting at least from the late nineteenth century, when American forms of journalism were widely imitated. This pattern continued in the interwar period with the growing strength of Hollywood and of U.S. news agencies, accelerated after World War II as the United States became the world's political, economic, and cultural hegemon (Schou 1992), and in some ways accelerated further still with the global shift to neoliberalism in the 1980s. We generally associate Americanization today with the conservative influence of neoliberalism, but as a number of scholars have pointed out (e.g., Gundle 2000) leftist culture in Europe was also strongly affected by the "American dream."

The process described by the theory of cultural imperialism is essentially one of *outside* influence, involving the displacement of one culture by another imported culture. We will argue that, in fact, the changes in European media systems are driven above all by processes of change *internal* to European society, though certainly connected with the integration of

European countries into a global economy. Outside influences are clearly an important part of the story, however, and we will begin with a fuller discussion of American influence and the wider process by which a global culture of journalism has developed – including the influence of technology – before going on to the internal processes of change that are commonly referred to as "modernization."

As we have seen in the preceding chapters, international influences have been a part of media history from the beginning: Southern European media were deeply influenced by the French, and intense interaction among Northern European countries was central to the formation of their media culture. The influence has moved in many directions. German journalism, for example, has had significant influences on the American media. Josef Pulitzer worked in the large German-language press in the United States before starting his English-language newspaper industry, and German photojournalists moving to the United States during the 1930s had important influences on American photojournalism (as did European filmmakers in Hollywood at the same time). American influence on European media, as we have noted, goes back at least to the late nineteenth century. We saw in Chapter 5, for example, that the emerging French mass press was clearly influenced by the American, with one of the most important papers, Le Matin, owned by an American who said it would be a "unique newspaper . . . that will not have any political opinions . . . a paper of worldwide and accurate telegraphic news" (Thogmartin 1998: 93–4). Schudson (1995) shows that the practice of interviewing was spread to Europe by American reporters.

American influence clearly intensified following World War II, as the United States became the dominant political and economic power. It was not something that simply happened. As Blanchard (1986) has shown it was in part the result of an organized effort led by the American Society of Newspaper Editors (ASNE) and the U.S. Department of State to promote the U.S. conception of press freedom and journalistic professionalism around the world. The principal aim of the "free press crusade" was to reestablish democracy in European countries that had experienced fascism and to further the policy of containment against the political model of the Soviet bloc. One important manifestation was the influence exercised by the allies on the media systems of Germany, Austria, and Italy during the occupation. At the same time, the crusade reinforced the sphere of influence and market of American news agencies and mass media generally. The crusade Blanchard describes largely focused on international agencies – the United Nations and UNESCO – and in formal terms enjoyed limited success, in the sense that American proposals were often rejected. Nevertheless it contributed to the dissemination of liberal media principles that were indeed becoming increasingly hegemonic.

If the "free press crusade" of the 1940s and 1950s was connected with the political goals of the struggle against fascism and then the Cold War, other initiatives and associations were the result of the growing globalization of media industries. Markets had to be penetrated and expanded and there was a need for information on those markets, coordination of initiatives to develop them, and promotion of the conditions, including political and cultural conditions, suitable for their development. One association that pursued these ends was the World Association of Newspapers (WAN), which was founded in 1948 and now includes seventy-one national newspaper associations as members, and describes its goals as:

1. Defending and promoting press freedom and the economic independence of newspapers as an essential condition for that freedom.
2. Contributing to the development of newspaper publishing by fostering communications and contacts between newspaper executives from different regions and cultures.
3. Promoting cooperation between its member organizations, whether national, regional, or worldwide.

WAN pursues these objectives through training programs, conferences, publications, and lobbying with international organizations and governments. Its "Code of Newspaper Practices" approved in 1981 clearly reflects the influence of the Liberal conception of press freedom and professionalism, Point 1 reaffirming the basic principle of press freedom; Point 2 the need for impartiality; Point 3 the separation of news from commentary; down to Point 11 that reaffirms independence of the press from every outside pressure "whether by government, political parties, commercial interests or private individuals." The symbiosis between politics and journalism, which at one time represented constitutive characteristics of the Democratic Corporatist and Polarized Pluralist Models, is thus clearly rejected by the global commercial newspaper industry, in favor of an emerging liberal "common sense" of media freedom; to a large extent this is the "international media culture" described by McQuail (1994).

The role of WAN is a good illustration of Tunstall's (1977) argument that American influence on world media cultures resulted in part from the key role the United States played in the "production of knowledge." Formal journalism education and the academic study of communication were relatively strongly developed in the United States by the end of World War II. These institutions generated a coherent, readily exportable body of doctrine focusing around the liberal conception of press freedom and the idea of neutral professionalism that eventually had profound influence on media cultures in Europe and around the world.[1] The influence of *Four Theories of the Press* on media scholarship and education worldwide – an influence that, as we argue in Chapter 1, hindered even the theoretical conceptualization of other media systems – is a good illustration of Tunstall's point. Barnhurst and Nerone (2001: 276) in an analysis of the Americanization of newspaper design, similarly found that "U.S. consultants spread their design sensibility by touting modernist form as an efficient conveyor of local journalism and advertising. To bolster their argument, they could claim the ostensibly neutral support of legibility research and psychological principles." (Barnhurst and Nerone further argue that U.S. design techniques embodied a particular, liberal ideology about the role of the newspaper as an institution of the market more than of the political world.)

There is not a lot of systematic research, particularly of a comparative nature, on journalism education. But it does seem likely that American models of journalistic education have played an important role in changing cultures of journalism worldwide. There is a significant trend in the direction of a greater role for formal training in journalism. This is significant in itself – even apart from the content of that education – in the sense that the development of a distinct education track for journalists almost inevitably would seem to promote the development of a culture of journalism distinct from, among other things, party politics. We think it is likely, moreover, that the content of journalism education stresses exactly the conception of the media's role emphasized by WAN.[2] Splichal and Sparks (1994) seem to share this opinion, concluding their research on journalism education in twenty-two countries by stressing that, with some qualifications, journalism is moving from craft to profession thanks to the diffusion of common educational practices. Weaver (1998), in another work based on surveys of journalists, also stresses the importance of formal education in creating a global journalistic culture.

The example of WAN – which was heavily influenced by American newspaper publishers in its early years, but became very much an international institution – also illustrates another significant force in the development of a global media culture, one that by now has become much broader than "Americanization," namely the intensity of interaction among journalists worldwide. This takes place in many contexts. WAN, which is based in Paris, organizes international gatherings of journalists and other media personnel, and many other organizations play a similar role, including the European Journalism Training Association established by many European schools and institutes of journalism. Journalists also interact intensively in covering world events or international institutions (Hallin and Mancini 1994). This kind of interaction does not produce homogenization automatically; research on journalists covering EU institutions in Brussels has stressed the extent to which their reporting remains dominated by national political agendas.[3] But it does lead to diffusion of techniques, practices, and values, in the same way that national journalistic cultures began to develop as journalists assembled to cover emerging national political institutions. This interaction also takes place in a more mediated way through the global flow of information. Journalists are heavy consumers of global media, many of them based in the United States and Britain, both because these represent large powerful media organizations and because they are in English – the international *Herald-Tribune*,[4] the *Financial Times* and other representatives of the global business press,[5] CNN, and the BBC World Service, both radio and TV. Journalists also make heavy use of international news agencies, including wire services and global TV agencies such as Reuters TV and Worldwide Television News. The global sharing of news tends to increase both with technology, as new information technology makes it increasingly easy for journalists to access information from across the world at the touch of a button, and with commercialization, as priority is placed on low-cost news gathering. All of this tends to promote common conceptions of the journalist's role – the influence of Watergate mythology on journalism worldwide is a perfect example – and common styles of news presentation.

We have focused here on journalism, but similar processes have been at work in other areas of media and communication practice. Blumler and Gurevitch (2001: 400; see also Plasser 2000), for example, note that in the 1996 and 1997 election campaigns "experts of the British Labour Party and the Clinton team observed each other in action and shared their tactical expertise. . . ."

The role of technology

Technology can be said to be another "outside" force toward homogenization. In one of the most interesting chapters of *The Printing Revolution in Early Modern Europe*, Elizabeth Eisenstein (1983), building on an idea originally stressed by McLuhan, points out how the invention of the printing press produced a process of standardization, which over the next few centuries affected many aspects of culture and society. Writing styles and typefaces, as well as many social practices that were addressed in the content of books (Eisenstein uses fashion as an example) tended to spread to every country where the printing industry was diffused. Eisenstein's analysis reminds us that every technological innovation eventually leads to wide-ranging adaptations by individuals and social institutions. People tend to assume the behavior, forms, structures, and, in this case, communication procedures that are associated with the new technology, and this influence often produces common cultures of practice across different social contexts. Golding (1977: 304), in an analysis of the spread of western practices of journalistic professionalism to the developing world, made a similar point: "the transfer of professionalism runs parallel to the transfer of technology which can be alternatively understood as the problem of technological dependence."

The influence of technology cannot be separated from the social context in which technologies are adopted and implemented, of course, and we should not exaggerate the standardizing effects of technologies of mass communication. The printing press, for example, certainly diffused many communication practices. But as we have seen, quite different forms of print media developed in the different political contexts we have studied here, and their disappearance clearly owes much more to economic and sociopolitical forces than to any change in print media technology. Nevertheless, there is no doubt that the process of homogenization is also connected with technological innovation. Changes in television technology, for one thing, clearly played an important role in disrupting the existing media structure by facilitating cross-national broadcasting and the multiplication of channels, developments whose significance we will explore further in subsequent pages. In many ways technology has increased the ease by which media content can be shared across national boundaries, with journalists around the world having access on their computer screens to the same sets of words and images. News agencies, of course, have played this role for some time, providing news written in a single style, produced to a single set of news-gathering practices. The dominant news agencies of the twentieth century have been the British ones, and they have played an extremely important role in spreading the Liberal Model of journalism. Another more recent example would be a service similar to Evelina produced by European Broadcasting Union (EBU) that provides images, filmed according to a common standard and supplied to every European user. CNN is obviously another powerful instrument for the spreading of common procedures and skills, as is the Internet.

It is likely that the growth of professional education in journalism also is connected with technological change. As the written word is increasingly displaced by multimedia forms of presentation, the boundaries between production and journalistic labor become blurred, and technology comes to play an increasingly central role in journalistic practice. In this context it matters less what a journalist has to say about politics than whether she or he can create a compelling television narrative or an appealing visual display on a computer screen. This creates a need for specialized training of journalists, and probably tends to create a global culture of technical expertise that is relatively separate from national political cultures. Similar processes also take place in other areas of political communication, as, for example, the use of computers in political campaigning similarly produces a need for standardized technical expertise. The homogenization produced by technological innovation mainly involves younger professionals who are more exposed to innovations and more likely to have received specialized training focused on their use. This may be one reason generation gaps often exist between older journalists whose professional concerns revolve more around the political lines of their news organizations, and younger ones more concerned with "strictly professional" characteristics of their jobs (e.g., Ortega and Humanos 2000: 158).

Endogenous forces of change: "modernization," secularization, and commercialization

External influences on European media systems clearly have played an important role. As we have tried to show in the preceding chapters, however, the media systems that evolved in Europe – quite different in many ways from North American media systems – were deeply rooted in particular political histories, structures, and cultures. It is not plausible that they would have been transformed without significant changes in politics and society. European media professionals did not immediately or directly adopt American forms. To some extent, in fact, the *ideology* of the Liberal media system spread without actually changing journalistic or other media *practices*. We have always been struck by how common it is, in Southern Europe particularly, for journalists to express allegiance to the global notion of "objectivity," while they practice journalism in a way that is very much at odds with U.S. or British notions of political neutrality. Papathanassopoulos's (2001) analysis of the transformation of Greek journalism is consistent with this observation. The deeper penetration of liberal media practices has only occurred as structural transformation of European media and political systems has made these practices increasingly relevant and appropriate, and must be understood in the context of these deeper changes. We turn now, therefore, to the fundamental processes of internal change at work in European media systems.

One of the most common ways to understand these deeper processes of change is in terms of "modernization." In the 1963 classic *Communications and Political Development*, Pye wrote:

> in any society only a small fraction of political communication originates from the political actors themselves, and this proportion tends to decrease with modernization as increasing numbers of participants without power join the communications process. In a fundamental sense modernization involves the emergence of a professional class of communicators. . . . The emergence of professionalized communicators is . . . related to the development of an objective, analytical and non-partisan view of politics (78; see also Fagen 1966).

Pye's view is connected with structural-functionalism, which argues that societies tend to evolve toward greater functional specialization among social institutions, and greater differentiation of those institutions from one another, in terms of their norms, practices, and symbolic identities. For Parsons and other structural-functionalists, professionalization is central to this process. The notion of differentiation clearly does capture an important part of the change in European media systems. And if modernity involves, as Giddens (1990: 21) puts it, the "disembedding" or " 'lifting out' of social relations from local contexts of interaction and their restructuring across indefinite spans of time-space," it makes some sense to say that media systems in Europe have become increasingly "modernized." At the same time, the concept of modernization as it is commonly understood is problematic in many ways: not only does it carry dubious normative assumptions about the universal superiority of a particular model, there are also real problems with describing change in media systems in the countries covered here in terms of a unilinear shift toward greater differentiation, problems that we will explore in detail in the final sections of this chapter. We propose therefore to start with the more neutral and specific concepts of secularization and commercialization.

Mass media and secularization

The notion of secularization has been fundamental to understanding modernity since Marx, Weber, and Durkheim. What we mean by it here is the separation of citizens from attachments to religious and ideological "faiths," and the decline of institutions based on these faiths that once structured wide parts of European social life. Just as the Church is no longer able to control the socialization or behavior of populations now attracted to values and institutions outside the field of faith, so parties, trade unions, and other institutions that structured the political order Lipset and Rokkan (1967) once described as essentially "frozen," can no longer hegemonize the citizen's community life. The European political order was once organized around social institutions rooted in ideological commitments based on broad social divisions, especially those of social class and religion. The ties of individuals to these groups was central both to their identity and to their material well-being. These institutions also had broad functions in structuring the public sphere, creating and circulating cultural and political symbols, and organizing the participation of citizens in the life of the community. By secularization we mean the decline of a political and social order based on these institutions, and its replacement by a more fragmented and individualized society. With the general decline of parties, trade unions, churches, and similar institutions, the mass media, along with many other socialization agencies, become more autonomous of them, and begin to take over many of the functions they once performed.

The "depillarization" of Dutch society is perhaps the classic example of this change. Pillarization, as we saw in Chapter 6, was the separation of the population into organized subcommunities based on religious or political persuasion. The Dutch pillars maintained a wide variety of institutions – schools, hospitals, social clubs, welfare organizations, and mass media – and carried out a wide range of social functions, including the production of symbolic meaning, the "aggregation of interests" and organization of political decision making, the organization of leisure time, the provision of social welfare, and more (Lijphart 1968, 1977, 1999; Lorwin 1971; Nieuwenhuis 1992). In the field of communication, an individual could spend his or her entire life within a flow of representations structured by the institutions of a single pillar. By the 1970s, this structure had broken down, and "the average Dutch citizen had become primarily an individual consumer rather than a follower of a particular religious or political sector" (Nieuwenhuis 1992: 207).

A similar process has taken place in Italy, where two main political subcultures, the Catholic and the Communist, based on deeply rooted religious and political faiths, simultaneously represented the main instruments of political power and the most important socialization agencies in the country. The Catholic subculture was essentially, though not exclusively, linked to the structures of the Catholic Church, its charity organizations, and interpersonal networks. The Christian Democratic party was its political arm. The Communist subculture was built out of the first trade unions and workers' solidarity organizations. Associated with the Communist Party were many other organizations active in different fields: social solidarity, sport, culture, leisure, education, media, and so on (Galli 1968; Sani 1980; Trigilia 1981; Mannheimer and Sani 1987). In Italy as in the Netherlands – though more recently – these two subcultures and their organizations have declined in importance. The birth and the victory of Berlusconi's Forza Italia, relying almost completely on mass media for its connections with the electorate, is an excellent illustration of this decline – and of the tendency for media correspondingly to expand their social role.

In Scandinavia agrarian, conservative, liberal, and socialist parties, together with trade unions, once pervaded many fields of society, but have substantially declined. One interesting illustration of the shift "from a collectivist to an individualist political culture," and its effect on journalism, can be found in a content analysis of Swedish news media from 1925 to 1987 (Ekecrantz 1997: 408), which found the use of the term *we* was more frequent than the use of the term *I* in news discourse in earlier decades, with the relationship reversed by the 1980s. Similar stories can be told, with many local variations, about most of the countries covered in this book.

The decline of political parties is closely related to this process of "secularization," and is particularly important to understanding change in media systems. There is a large literature on the "decline of party," and some debate about whether, or in what sense, it has actually taken place. Some argue that parties have not so much declined as "modernized" and narrowed in their functions, that they are actually more effective in mobilizing voters at election time now that they have been professionalized and separated from their connections with institutions such as trade unions. Some argue that rather than speaking of "party decline" in general we need to look specifically at the decline of the traditional "mass parties" that were powerful in Europe through much of the twentieth century, as well as in the United States in an earlier form and an earlier period (Panebianco 1988; Mair 1990; Katz and Mair 1994). Mass parties served as central instruments for the representation and defense of social and economic interests, for "aggregating interests" and forming consensus, and served as important structures of communication through the interpersonal networks on which their organizations were built. Mass parties, among their other functions, were responsible for the production of social representations and imagery. In the service of this function they owned and controlled newspapers, and journalists working within these newspapers had the duty of spreading and defending the ideas of the party. Journalists' practices of information gathering, writing, and interacting with readers were rooted to a significant degree in the ideological framework and party-centered social network to which they belonged. Being at the same time both journalists and political figures, they acted according to models of practice shaped by specific political cultures that varied from country to country – hence the substantial differences we have found among national media systems.

The decline of the mass party, ideologically identified and rooted in distinct social groups, and its replacement by the "catchall" or "electoral-professional party" oriented not primarily toward the representation of groups or ideologies but toward the conquest of electoral market share, has been widely documented in political science (Kirchheimer 1966; Panebianco 1988). The stable psychological and sociological bonds that once existed between parties and citizens have been weakened in this transformation. Party membership has declined (as have church and trade union membership). So has party loyalty, measured either by identification with political parties or by partisan consistency in electoral behavior, at least in many cases. Voting turnout has declined in many countries. "When partisanship was closely tied to class and religion, the conjoint of social and political identifications provided a very strong incentive for party identifiers to turn out. These linkages, however, have withered in recent years . . ." (Dalton and Wattenberg 2000: 66). The "grassroots" political organizations that once tied parties to citizens have atrophied, while professional staffs concerned with media and marketing have grown. Individual leaders have become increasingly important to the appeal of parties, while ideology and group loyalties have become less so.

The weakening of mass political parties is in turn connected with a wider process of social change, which involves the weakening or fragmentation of the social and economic cleavages on which mass parties were built (Panebianco 1988). The clear lines of social division stressed originally in Marxist theory and later in the comparative politics literature of the post-World War II period have declined, some argue, to the vanishing point, with the result that mass parties have lost their social basis. A proliferation of social groups with specific economic needs has grown in importance, making the distinctions between owners and workers, landowners and peasants, less relevant. One important factor in this change is the fact that the manufacturing industries in which traditional working-class organizations were rooted have declined, displaced by the growing service sector. Perhaps most fundamentally, European economies have expanded and it seems likely that increased affluence and the growth of the consumer society resulted in an increasing emphasis on individual economic success rather than political defense of group interests. A different, though not necessarily incompatible interpretation of the effect of economic growth is Ingelhart's (1977) argument that affluence and the stabilization of liberal democracy led to the rise of "post-materialist values." This change in political culture is seen as undercutting the ideological divisions on which the old party system was based and making individuals increasingly unwilling to defer to the leadership of traditional organizations. It may in turn be related to the rise of new social movements raising issues that cut across traditional party lines.

These same factors cited by Ingelhart – affluence and the consolidation of parliamentary democracy within the context of a capitalist economy – may also be responsible for a marked decline in ideological polarization. There is evidence that the ideological differences between political parties has decreased (Mair 1997), though we will see later that there also may be countertrends, and it cannot necessarily be assumed that such differences will continue decreasing indefinitely. This is connected with the acceptance of the broad outlines of the welfare state by conservative parties and of capitalism and liberal democracy by the parties of the left. An important symbol of the shift would be the "historic compromise" that incorporated the Communist Party into the division of political power in Italy in the 1970s. The literature on "plural" societies such as the Netherlands, where the various subcultures had separate institutions at the grassroots level, often notes that the leaderships of these communities became accustomed to cooperation and compromise at the level of national state institutions.

Some accounts of change in European political systems also point to increased education, which might result in voters seeking information independently rather than relying on the leadership of political parties. In some accounts this is connected with a shift from voting based on party and group loyalty to issue-based voting. Some also mention that patronage systems have declined, in part because of economic integration, particularly with the formation of the European Monetary Union, and the pressures it puts on government budgets, undercutting the ability of parties to provide material incentives to their active supporters (Kitschelt 2000; Papathanassopoulos 2000). The rise of new demographic groups as a result of immigration may also have weakened the old order, both because the new populations are not integrated into traditional group-based structures and because tensions over immigration lead to the defection of traditional adherents.

Finally, many have argued that globalization and economic integration have weakened political parties by shifting the locus of decision making away from the national political spheres that the parties dominated. As Beck (2000) puts it, the nation state was the "container" for policy decisions as well as other social processes that affected citizens across most areas of life. The nation state has progressively lost this role of "container," and many of the decisions affecting its citizens are now taken at a supranational level, removing power from the state and therefore from political parties, organizations, and interest groups that represent the interests of the citizens. The constraints of the emerging global economic regime tend to force parties to abandon distinct policy positions that once defined their identities, and also hinders their ability to deliver benefits to their constituents. These constraints also specifically force the harmonization of media policy in many cases, often disrupting the previously existing relations between the state, political parties, and the media. Thus Canada feels pressure to abandon protection of national cultural industries and Scandinavia feels pressure to liberalize regulations on advertising. Clientelist patterns of political alliance in Spain, meanwhile, are disrupted by the fact that companies can appeal to Brussels to overturn regulatory decisions made in Madrid.

Media system change: cause or effect

The changes in European media systems outlined at the beginning of this chapter – particularly the shift toward catchall media, models of journalistic professionalism based on political neutrality, and a shift toward media-oriented forms of political communication – are surely related to this process of secularization. But which is the tail and which is the dog? Is media system change simply one result of these changes in society and politics, or might it play some independent role? To a large extent, media system change is certainly a result of the deeply rooted processes summarized previously, which have undercut the social basis of mass parties and of group solidarity and of a media system connected with them. It is clearly also true, however, that processes of change internal to the media system have been at work and it is quite plausible that changes in European media systems have contributed to the process of secularization. It is common in the literature on decline of political parties in Europe to point to the media system as one key source of change:

. . . [N]ew technologies and . . . changes in the mass media . . . have enabled party leaders to appeal directly to voters and thereby undermined the need for organizational networks . . . (Mair 1997: 39).

Increasingly . . . media have taken over [information and oversight functions] because they are considered unbiased providers of information and because electronic media have created more convenient and pervasive delivery systems. . . . The growing availability of political information through the media has reduced the costs of making informed decisions (Flanagan and Dalton 1990: 240–2).

The mass media are assuming many of the information functions that political parties once controlled. Instead of learning about an election at a campaign rally or from party canvassers, the mass media have become the primary source of campaign information. Furthermore, the political parties have apparently changed their behavior in response to the expansion of mass media. There has been a tendency for political parties to decrease their investments in neighborhood canvassing, rallies, and other direct contact activities, and devote more attention to campaigning through the media (Dalton and Wattenberg 2000: 11–12).

The element that emerges most strongly in these accounts is the rise of electronic media, which is considered to have undercut the role of political parties, and presumably also would have undercut the role of churches, trade unions, and other institutions of socialization. As we have seen in the preceding chapters, however, the electronic media were organized originally in Europe under political authority, and in most systems political parties had considerable influence on broadcasting, as did "socially relevant groups" in some systems, most notably the German. One might, therefore, have expected electronic media to *reinforce* rather than to undercut the traditional role of political parties and organized social groups. Why did this not occur?

One account of the impact of television is provided by Wigbold (1979), focusing on the particularly interesting Dutch case. Broadcasting was organized in the Netherlands following the pillarized model that applied to the press, education, and other cultural institutions. Each of the different communities of Dutch society had a separate broadcasting organization, just as they had traditionally had separate schools and newspapers. One might have thought that by extending their reach to a powerful new medium, the pillars would have become even more entrenched in Dutch society. Nevertheless, depillarization clearly did coincide historically with the rise of television. Wigbold makes the argument that Dutch television "destroyed its own foundations, rooted as they were in the society [it] helped to change" (230).

His argument has three parts. First, he argues that despite the existence of separate broadcasting organizations, television broke down the separateness of the pillars:

Television was bound to have a tremendous influence in a country where not only the doors of the living room were closed to strangers but also the doors of schoolrooms, union meetings, youth hostels, football grounds and dancing schools . . . It confronted the masses with views, ideas and opinions from which they had been isolated . . . [T]here was no way out, no hiding place, except by the difficult expedient of switching the set off. Television viewers could not even switch to a second channel, because there wasn't one . . . Catholics discovered that Socialists were not the dangerous atheists they had been warned about, Liberals had to conclude that orthodox Protestants were not the bigots they were supposed to be (201).

Second, he argues that television journalists shifted substantially in the early 1960s toward a more independent and critical relationship with the leaders of established institutions, to whom they had previously deferred.

Third, a new broadcasting organization (TROS), which was the broadcasting equivalent of the catchall party, was founded at the end of the 1960s: originating from a pirate broadcaster, it provided light entertainment and "was the very negation of the broadcasting system based . . . on giving broadcast time to groups that had something to say" (225).[6] TROS acted as a strong force toward homogenization.

The Dutch case is unique in many ways, of course. Still, it seems likely that each of these factors had close parallels across most of Europe: the role of *television as a common ground*, the development of *critical journalism*, and *commercialization*. These tendencies not only are common to broadcasting across Europe, but are closely related to changes in the print press, changes that to some degree reflect the impact of television on the latter. We shall discuss in this section the first two topics: television as a common ground and the journalist as a "critical expert," and take up in the following section the crucial and complex topic of commercialization.

Television as common ground

Across Europe, broadcasting was organized under political authority and often incorporated principles of proportional representation drawn from the political world. Nevertheless, it is quite plausible that it served as a social and political common ground and had some role in weakening separate ideological subcultures. It was highly centralized, with one to three channels (of television and of radio) in most of the post-World War II period. Most programming was aimed at the entire public, regardless of group boundaries. The production of news was generally bound by the principles of political neutrality and internal pluralism, which separated broadcast journalism from traditions of partisan commentary common in the print press (in the Dutch case, while the pillarized broadcasting organizations produced public affairs broadcasts, news, like sports, was produced by the umbrella organization NOS). Television entertainment, meanwhile, provided a common set of cultural references, whose impact on political culture would be very difficult to document, but certainly might have been quite significant.

Even aside from the content of broadcast programming, the fact that broadcast media developed as "catchall" media, capable of delivering messages across ideological and group boundaries, may have had important political effects, as some of the accounts of the decline of party quoted in the preceding text suggest: it made it possible for political parties to appeal to citizens outside their established social base in a very efficient manner, and thus may have encouraged both the growth of catchall parties and the atrophy of traditional means of communication that were tied to social networks in particular subcommunities. It should also be kept in mind that television was not the only "catchall" medium to expand in this period, particularly in the Democratic Corporatist and Liberal countries. Catchall commercial newspapers were also increasingly central to the communication process. It could be said that in general, the development of the media in the twentieth century led to an increased flow of culture and information across group boundaries, reducing the dependence of citizens on exclusive sources within their particular subcommunities.

"Critical expertise" in journalism

The diffusion of television also coincided with the development of a new journalistic culture that Padioleau (1985), in a comparative study of *Le Monde* and *The Washington Post*, termed a culture of "critical expertise." In both Western Europe and North America (Hallin 1992), there was a significant shift in the 1960s and 1970s from a form of journalism that was relatively deferential toward established elites and institutions, toward a relatively more active, independent form of journalism This shift took place both in electronic and in print media. In the case of Swedish television, for example, Djerf-Pierre (2000; see also Ekecrantz 1997; Olsson 2002) writes:

> The journalist culture of 1965–1985 embraced a new ideal of news journalism, that of critical scrutiny. The dominant approach was now oriented toward exerting influence, both *vis-à-vis* institutions and the public at large . . . [J]our-nalists sought to bridge information gaps in society and to equip their audiences for active citizenship and democratic participation . . . Journalists also had the ambition to scrutinize the actions of policy makers and to influence both public debate on social and political issues and the policies made by public institutions (254).

This shift varied in form and extent, but seems to have been quite generalized across national boundaries in the countries of all of our three models. It involved the creation of a journalistic discourse that was distinct from the discourse of parties and politicians, a conception of the media as a collective watchdog of public power (Djerf-Pierre and Weibull 2000) and a conception of the journalist as representative of a generalized public opinion that cuts across the lines of political parties and social groups. Critical professionals, as Neveu (2002) puts it, "[S]pot blunders in strategy, mistakes in governing, from an in-depth knowledge of issues. They question politicians in the name of public opinion and its requests – identified 'objectively' by the polls – or in the name of suprapolitical values such as morality, modernity or the European spirit."

Why did this change take place? Surely it was to a significant extent rooted in the broader social and political changes discussed previously. If, for example, affluence, political stability, and increasing educational levels led to a general cultural shift toward "postmateri-alist" value of participation and free expression, the rise of critical expertise in journalism might be seen as one effect of this deeper social change. It might be noted that this change was not reflected only in journalism, but also in popular culture more generally. It is reflected, for example, in the growth of political satire on television, in the form of shows such as *That Was the Week that Was* and *Monty Python's Flying Circus* in Britain and *The Smothers Brothers Show* in the United States, comedy programs that relied heavily on political humor. If catchall parties were already being formed in the 1950s – Kirchheimer noted their rise in 1966 – the discourse of a general public opinion made up of individualized voters committed to "suprapolitical" values, which would be crucial to the perspective of critical professionalism in journalism, may predate the latter.[7]

Even if the rise of critical professionalism in the media was in part an effect or reflection of other social forces, however, it seems likely that at some point it began to accelerate and amplify them. It is also possible that a number of factors internal to the media system contributed to the shift in the political role of journalism, and thus in turn to the secularization of European society and to the diminution of differences among political systems. These internal factors include:

1.   Increased educational levels of journalists, leading to more sophisticated forms of analysis, in part by the incorporation into journalism of critical perspectives from the social sciences and humanities.

2.   Increased size of news organizations, leading to greater specialization and greater resources for news gathering and news processing.

3.   Internal development of the growing professional community of journalism, which increasingly develops its own standards of practice.

4.   Development of new technologies of information processing that increase the power of journalists as information producers. This includes the visual techniques of television as well as many developments in printing and in information technology. One interesting example would be polling: Neveu (2002) argues that opinion polling gave journalists increased authority to question public officials, whose claims to represent the public they could independently assess.

5.   Increased prestige of journalists, related to all these factors, to the central position large media organizations came to occupy in the general process of social communication, and probably also to the image of catchall media as representative of the public as a whole. Thus Papathanassopoulos (2001: 512) argues for the Greek case (a bit different, to be sure, because, as we shall see, partisan attachments do survive more strongly in Greece, as in much of Southern Europe):

> One can say that the commercialization and the rapid development of the Greek media market have increased the social and professional status of Greek journalists. In fact, television journalists and especially television news anchorpersons have become public figures. They have adopted the role of authorities, i.e. they present their views and interpret social and political reality. They do this by presenting themselves both as professionals with the right to make judgements and as representatives of the people. By taking on both these roles, they increase their public profile and authority.

Commercialization

The most powerful force for homogenization of media systems, we believe, is commercialization that has transformed both print and electronic media in Europe. In this section we will describe the process and outline the principal causes of commercialization of European media, and in the following section we will examine its consequences for the social and political role of the media. In the case of print media the later part of the twentieth century is characterized by a decline of the party press (in some countries this was already under way by the 1950s, in others, Italy and France most clearly, the party press revived after World War II, then began to decline), an increasing dominance of "omnibus" commercial newspapers, and, in consequence, a separation of newspapers from their earlier rooting in the world of politics. To some degree, this shift was no doubt a result of the broader process of secularization, as readers became less committed politically and less inclined to choose a newspaper on the basis of its political orientation. But it is also clear that the internal development of newspaper markets pushed strongly in this direction. Indeed market forces were beginning to put pressure on the party press early in the twentieth century, when party allegiance was still strongly entrenched in the political culture. The number of newspapers in Sweden, for example, peaked in 1920 (Picard 1988: 18). From that point on, just as in the North American case we explored in Chapter 7, there was a trend toward concentration in newspaper markets, with the result that newspapers increasingly attempted to expand their markets by appealing across traditional group and ideological boundaries. Highly capitalized, advertising-funded commercial papers tended to drive less wealthy, politically oriented papers out of the market, eventually leading to an almost complete eclipse of the party press that dominated the media in these countries for most of the twentieth century.

Even more dramatic than the changes in the print press, however, is the transformation of European broadcasting from an almost purely public service system in 1970 to a system in which commercial broadcasting is increasingly dominant. The "commercial deluge," as it is commonly called, began in Italy, following a 1976 decision of the Italian Supreme Court that invalidated the legal monopoly of public broadcasting allowing private stations to broadcast within local areas. (Even earlier, TROS and Veronica, the latter originating from a pirate radio station and oriented toward the youth culture, had begun operating in the Netherlands, within the public service structure but by a very different logic.) By 1990, most of the rest of Europe had introduced commercial broadcasting and by the end of the century only Austria, Ireland, and Switzerland had no significant commercial television.[8] In most countries commercial broadcasting had a majority of the audience and competition for audience had significantly transformed public broadcasting as well, forcing it to adopt much of the logic of the commercial system.

Beyond the changes in the social structure that we have already outlined, many forces combined to produce this change in the European broadcasting system. In the first place, competing forms of broadcasting emerged, and these siphoned audiences away from the public broadcasters, undercut their legitimacy, and contributed to a change in the perception of media programming, which with the multiplication of channels – by one count a shift from 35 channels in 1975 to 150 in 1994 (Weymouth and Lamizet 1996: 24) – came to seem less like a social institution, a public good provided for and shared by everyone in society, and more like a commodity that could be chosen by individual consumers. The development of the VCR no doubt also contributed to this change of consciousness. The earliest alternative forms of broadcasting were pirate radio stations, the first of which began broadcasting from ships off the coast of Scandinavia in the late 1950s. These were advertising funded and to some degree their popularity was fueled by the growth of a distinct – and globalized – youth culture. In both these characteristics they are clearly connected with the larger cultural trend toward global consumer culture. Pirate radio proliferated substantially in many countries during the 1970s, when it was often connected not only with youth culture but also with the new social movements of that era. The efforts of public broadcasting to suppress pirate radio undercut their image as a champion of political pluralism. Private radio and television stations based in Luxembourg that started broadcasting to neighboring countries in French, German, Italian, and Dutch also undercut public service monopolies, as did Radio Monte Carlo and Radio Capodistria (based in Croatia), which revolutionized Italian radio in the 1970s. The phenomenon of transborder broadcasting, with its tendency to undercut the connection between broadcasting institutions and national political systems, expanded in the 1980s with the growth of cable and direct broadcast satellite TV.

Another important factor was the growth of strong lobbies pressing for change in media policy. The most important of these was the advertising lobby, which pushed hard in many countries for access to electronic media (Humphreys 1996: 172–3). Pilati (1987) stresses that Italian private television stations were born when various commercial and manufacturing companies were making enough money to invest in advertising and public broadcasting was not able to meet this new demand for air time. In many cases advertising interests were joined in the push for commercial broadcasting by media companies hungry to expand into electronic media. To some extent laws limiting concentration in print media encouraged this desire, as many companies could not expand their print empires without running afoul of these limits. Another, very different kind of force that in many cases pushed toward private broadcasting came from social movements (student movements, unions, etc.) that were looking for new opportunities and means to express their voice outside of the established circuits of communication, often turning to pirate broadcasting to obtain that voice.

Also significant was the fact that funding for public broadcasting became increasingly problematic as the market for color television sets became saturated, and natural growth in license fee revenue therefore leveled off. From that point forward, additional license fee revenue could only be obtained by raising the fee, which was of course politically unpopular. This meant that expansion of television beyond the limited number of channels then in operation seemed to depend on the introduction of private broadcasting.

Finally, economic globalization, both in general and in media industries specifically, played an important and many-sided role. As early as 1974, the European Court of Justice ruled that broadcasting was covered as a form of trade under the Treaty of Rome. This decision was reaffirmed on a number of occasions in the early 1980s, in the context of strong shift globally toward liberalizing trade in services – the General Agreement on Trade in Services was ratified in 1994 – and toward defining broadcasting in these terms, rather than as a national social and cultural institution. When the European Commission turned its attention to broadcasting policy in the 1980s – producing the Television without Frontiers Directive in 1989 – it stressed the goal of creating a common European audiovisual market that would facilitate the development of transnational media companies capable of competing with American media conglomerates. Individual European governments, as well, increasingly saw media policy in terms of global competition in the cutting-edge information industries. These policies facilitated the transnationalization of media industries, in which ownership is increasingly internationalized (e.g., the Spanish television channel Tele5 was owned, in 1998, by Berlusconi [25 percent], by the German firm Kirch [25 percent], and by the Bank of Luxembourg [13 percent], with some participation from Bertelsmann), co-production is often necessary to compete in global markets, and in general the forces of the global market tend to displace the national political forces that once shaped the media.

The consequences of commercialization

A broad range of consequences flow from the commercialization of media. Commercialization, in the first place, is clearly shifting European media systems away from the world of politics and toward the world of commerce. This changes the social function of journalism, as the journalist's main objective is no longer to disseminate ideas and create social consensus around them, but to produce entertainment and information that can be sold to individual consumers. And it clearly contributes to homogenization, undercutting the plurality of media systems rooted in particular political and cultural systems of individual nation states that characterized Europe through most of the twentieth century, and encouraging its replacement by a common global set of media practices. Public broadcasting systems, especially, always placed strong emphasis on the goal of giving voice to the social groups and cultural patterns that defined national identity, "sustaining and renewing the society's characteristic cultural capital and cement" (Blumler 1992: 11; Avery 1993; Tracey 1998). Increasingly even public broadcasting systems must follow the logic of global cultural industries.

Commercialization of media has no doubt played some significant role in the "secularization" of European society. As we have seen, secularization has deep roots, and was already well advanced by the time the most dramatic change – the commercialization of broadcasting – occurred. As the case of TROS in the Netherlands suggests, however, commercial forces were beginning to make themselves felt in a variety of ways before the commercial deluge of 1980s: in the shift toward commercial newspapers, through import of American media content and imitation of American practices, through advertising in some European systems, through pirate and transborder broadcasting, and with the breakdown of the public service monopoly in Italy at the end of the 1970s. It is certainly plausible that if Europe was becoming more of an individualist consumer society in the 1960s the growth of television and radio and the commercialization of the press contributed to that trend; and it seems certain that they have intensified the process since the 1980s.

Commercialization also has important implications for the process of political communication. Commercial media create powerful new techniques of representation and of audience creation, which parties and politicians must adopt in order to prevail in the new communication environment. Two of the most important of these techniques – closely related to one another – are personalization and the tendency to privilege the point of view of the "ordinary citizen." In Italian public broadcasting in the 1980s, for example – at a time when commercial television still was not allowed to broadcast news – spokesmen from each significant party appeared to comment on any major political story (Hallin and Mancini 1984). They appeared as representatives of their parties, not as individual characters in a dramatic portrayal of politics: political logic dominated the presentation of news, and the personal characteristics of these politicians were generally as irrelevant as those of the news readers, who were rotated each night and had none of the significance for the news audience of American anchors. By the 1990s Berlusconi could dominate the news because he was a good story, and the narrative logic of commercial news was increasingly dominant in the Italian media scene. In the era of commercial media politicians increasingly become "media stars" who act well beyond the borders of politics: they appear in sport broadcasts, talk shows, and entertainment programs (Mancini 2000). Personalization, it might be noted, is not exclusively a characteristic of television, but of popular commercial media generally: nowhere is it stronger than in the sensationalist press of Britain, Germany, or Austria; and it has increasing importance in print media everywhere.

Another important manifestation of the new logic of commercial media is the tendency to focus on the experience and perspective of the "common citizen." Earlier traditions of European journalism were heavily focused on the perspectives of official representatives of parties, organized groups, and the state (e.g., Hallin and Mancini 1984), while with the shift toward commercial media the perspective of the individual citizens is increasingly privileged (Neveu 1999; see also Blumler and Gurevitch 2001). This results both from changes in news coverage and the development of new forms of infotainment in which public issues are discussed, such as the talk show, where politicians, if they appear at all, are typically relegated to a secondary role, and "common sense," as Leurdijk (1997) puts it, is privileged over political discourse. As many analysts have noted, these changes very likely have contributed to the erosion of the influence of the traditional mass party and the social organizations connected to it.

Commercialization contributes to a shift in the balance of power between the media and political institutions, with the media themselves becoming increasingly central in setting the agenda of political communication. One important manifestation of this tendency is the increased frequency of political scandals, which can be found across both Europe and North America. In the case of Greece:

> . . . media have begun to fight with the politicians for control of the political agenda and have started to make themselves heard in the process of political communication with a constant stream of criticism of politicians and the actions of parties . . . The rise of commercial media may have precipitated this trend

and created a situation where, today, Greek citizens can watch an endless stream of stories about political scandals, rivalry and self-interest. And, as with the media in other liberal democratic countries, Greek media have tried to create stories about political conflict by giving particular attention to politicians who hold controversial views or who oppose the actions of the government (Papathanassopoulos 2000: 58).

These tendencies are not produced solely by commercialization. They are also connected with the rise of critical professionalism, which in many countries took place before the full flowering of commercialization (Djerf-Pierre 2000). Scandals are often driven simultaneously by the desire of journalists to build professional prestige and assert their independence vis-à-vis political actors, and by the desire of media organizations to compete for audience. The rise of scandal politics is also connected with changes in the political system, including the judiciary, which, as we saw in Chapter 5, has become more independent and assertive particularly in Southern Europe. As Waisbord (2000) has pointed out, scandals almost always require the participation of political sources and cannot therefore be explained strictly in terms of the media system. Nevertheless, commercialization tends to give the media both the independent power base and the incentive to assert their own agenda, often at the expense of politicians.

One of the more difficult questions to sort out is whether commercialization has increased or decreased the flow of political information and discussion. European media have traditionally given central attention to politics; in the case of public broadcasting, a "sense of some responsibility for the health of the political process and for the quality of public discussion generated within it" (Blumler 1992: 36) was always a central value, and news and public affairs programming were significantly privileged. Though it is difficult to compare levels of political knowledge across populations, there is some evidence that Europeans know more than Americans about world affairs, even in countries where newspaper readership is low (Dimock and Popkin 1997). One of the central fears expressed by European commentators about "Americanization" of the media is that political information and discussion would be marginalized in a commercial system. Public broadcasting systems have traditionally broadcast the news in the heart of prime time, and in an era when nothing else was on television, news broadcasts had enormous audiences. In a commercial environment this practice is clearly threatened, as manifested in the decision of Britain's regulated commercial broadcaster, ITV, to cancel the country's most popular news program, *News at Ten*, and follow the American practice of broadcasting the news in early fringe time at 6:30 P.M.

At the same time, it is a common assumption that there has been an explosion of information with the expansion of media. One of the arguments of the political scientists quoted in the preceding text about the role of the media in the decline of parties is that "growing availability of political information through the media has reduced the costs of making informed decisions" (Flanagan and Dalton 1990: 242). In some sense it is surely true that there is more information available, at least if we compare across the post-World War II era. Not only have television channels proliferated, but news organizations in general are larger. Newspapers are generally physically larger than in the past; in 1967 *Il Corriere della Sera* had sixteen to twenty-eight pages, while today it has forty to fifty. On the other hand, it seems unlikely that increasingly commercialized media will consistently give the emphasis to public affairs that either the politically connected newspapers of the past or public broadcasting monopolies did.[9]

The existing empirical evidence is fragmentary and not entirely consistent, however, and the patterns are likely to be complex (e.g., Brants and Siune 1998). Rooney (2000), for example, finds a decrease in public affairs content in the *Sun* and *Mirror* in Britain from

33 and 23 percent of news content, respectively, in 1968, to 9 percent in 1998 – consistent with a common view in British media research that commercialization has driven political content out of the British popular press, a development symbolized by the demise of the trade-union supported *Daily Herald* and its replacement by the sensationalist *Sun*. McLaughlan and Golding (2000), however, using a narrower definition of political coverage, find no consistent trend in the content of either the tabloid or broadsheet press in Britain, and point out that "the very essence of tabloid provision continues to be suffused with the political, or if you like, the ideological" (87). Franklin (1997) reports a decline in reporting of Parliament in British broadsheets in the 1990s. Negrine (1998) also reports a decline in parliamentary coverage (British broadsheets had dedicated pages for parliamentary coverage until the 1990s). He also reports declines in political reporting in French and German TV news. Pfetsch (1996) found a decline in reporting of political institutions – government, Parliament, parties – in German TV news, though not a decline in political coverage overall, in part because coverage of political violence increased. Winston (2002) shows that the percent of news items devoted to politics declined from 21.5 percent on the main news bulletin of the BBC1 in 1975 to 9.6 percent in 2001, while the percent of items devoted to crime grew from 4.5 to 19.1. ITN showed similar – slightly larger – shifts. Brants (1998: 322) found that "in most countries commercial television has not marginalized political news. In eight West European countries, almost six out of an average of 13.3 items per newscast in the early 1990s were about politics." Italian newspapers, finally, though they have become more market oriented, have not decreased their political coverage: samples of thirty issues of Italian newspapers in each year showed 80 political stories in 1966, 647 in 1976, 560 in 1986, and 1257 in 1996 (Mancini 2002). Of course, politics is treated differently than in the past, through discourse genres that increase the possibility of dramatization (Bionda et al. 1998; Mancini 2002). In television too the prevalence of current affairs programs has increased, as these programs seem to be popular with Italian viewers (Menduni 1998).

The question of whether political content will decrease with commercialization thus clearly remains open.

Closely related to the question of whether political content will be marginalized in an increasingly commercialized media system is the question of whether commercialization is likely to lead to an alienation of the mass public from political life. Again there are conflicting views. Many have argued that focus of commercial media on private life, the deemphasis of collective political actors, the emphasis on scandal, and the often negative portrayal of political life will tend to undermine the involvement of the public in the political process (e.g., Patterson 1993). Changes in campaign style connected with the rise of commercial media are also often seen as having this effect. Papathanassopoulos (2000: 56) argues that "in adopting television-centered-campaigning the parties have moved away from the traditional emphases on public rallies and personal contacts with party workers, thus lessening opportunities for citizens to participate directly in campaigns and further distancing the parties from voters." Others (e.g., Brants 1998) have argued that the dramatization of politics and the migration of political discussion into "infotainment" venues in which the voice of the ordinary citizen has a greater role is likely to increase popular involvement in politics.

The difficulty of sorting out the effects of commercialization arises partly from the fact that it arose in the context of a complex set of changes in Western societies and interacts with those changes. This is well illustrated by the phenomenon of pirate radio, which was pushed forward by the advertising industry and simultaneously by new social movements with a desire for a greater voice in the public sphere. Much of pirate radio was pervaded by a youth culture that represented both a cultural challenge to an established system of power and a manifestation of the growing global consumer society. It is similarly evident in the way contemporary journalistic practices were influenced both by the rise of critical expertise and by commercialization. We will also argue, in the following section, that commercialization is not necessarily incompatible with a degree of political parallelism and under certain circumstances might even increase partisanship in the media. Despite these complexities it can be said that commercialization has in general weakened the ties between the media and the world of organized political actors that distinguished the Democratic Corporatist and Polarized Pluralist from the Liberal system, and has encouraged the development of a globalized media culture that substantially diminishes national differences in media systems.

Limits and countertendencies of the homogenization process

There is no question that the forces of homogenization are strong, and that considerable convergence has taken place, primarily in the direction of the Liberal Model. It is very reasonable to assume that this trend will continue in the future, as, for example, younger journalists socialized to different conceptions of the media's role replace earlier generations, and as the consequences of commercialization of broadcasting – still relatively new in many European countries – continue to work themselves out. If this trend were to continue unchanged into the future, it is possible to imagine a complete convergence of media systems in the United States and Western Europe toward something close to the Liberal Model. History does not usually move in straight lines, however, and there are many reasons to doubt whether it makes sense to project the trend toward homogenization of the past couple of decades indefinitely into the future.

There are, for one thing, important variations in the political systems of the countries considered here that seem likely to persist despite the changes in political institutions and culture that have clearly taken place. It is common to say that European politics has been to some degree "presidentialized." But parliamentary systems remain different from presidential ones. As Blumler, Kavanaugh, and Nossiter (1996: 59) observe:

> separation of powers in the U.S. government has imposed a continual pressure on the President to court mass opinion through the mass media in order to keep the heat of popular support for his measures . . . In Britain's parliamentary system, however, the Prime Minister and his or her Cabinet can count on party discipline to ensure passage of almost all proposed legislation. . . .

Proportional representation also remains different from a first-past-the-post electoral system and produces a different kind of party system. Constitutional changes could of course lead to homogenization here too – Italy, in particular has been debating such changes. But in most of Europe there is no sign that any such changes are in the offing. The structure of the political systems does not, of course, affect the media system as deeply as it once did, because the mass media have become more differentiated from it. But the news media still interact intensively with the political system. The flow of information and structural organization of news sources seems inevitably different in contrasting systems, and so too the narrative conventions of reporting politics. It seems unlikely that media systems could entirely converge while party and electoral systems remain sharply different.

Legal systems also remain different in important ways. There is no reason to assume, in particular, the "first amendment absolutism" that characterizes the U.S. legal system would ever spread to Europe. And this difference seems likely to have continuing consequences for media systems. It seems likely, for example, that electoral communication will continue to be more regulated in Europe, with much television time allocated according to political criteria and paid advertising restricted (Belgium, Denmark, France, Norway, Portugal, Spain, Sweden, Switzerland, and the United Kingdom currently ban paid political advertising on television) (Farrell and Webb 2000: 107).[10] Stronger regulation of broadcast media in general may well also survive the "commercial deluge." (It is possible, in fact that certain aspects of European regulatory regimes will increasingly affect U.S. regulation, as well as the other way around, as the European market becomes increasingly important for U.S. companies. It may be, for example, that stronger EU regulations on privacy will eventually affect U.S. regulation of the information industry.) The European welfare state has clearly been rolled back as a consequence of the global shift to neoliberalism. But here again many scholars doubt that complete homogenization is a likely outcome of this process. Moses, Geyer, and Ingebritsen (2000: 18), for example, conclude that "the Scandinavian model remains a potent indicator of the limitations of the powers of globalization/Europeanization, the capabilities of individual nations to pursue distinct policy strategies, the capacity of the Left to oppose and successfully counter international market forces, and the ability of social democratic parties to adapt to the demand of a changing international order." The same logic may certainly apply to Scandinavian media systems. Similarly, Blumler and Gurevitch (2001) found that, although there were important signs of convergence between U.S. and British styles of election coverage, the differences between the United States in the amount of campaign coverage actually grew between the 1980s and 1990s, as commercialization intensified in the United States and the culture of public service broadcasting persisted in Britain.

It is also possible that some of the trends that have led to the convergence of media systems would not only slow or stop but even reverse, either in general or in particular countries. There is, for example, some evidence that the decline of political polarization and of ideological differences among parties that has taken place in most if not all of the countries considered here, and which seems clearly to undercut political parallelism in media systems, has been affected by countertendencies in recent years. In the United States, for example, according to Jacobson (2001), partisan consistency in voting and political attitudes declined from the 1950s to 1970s, but has subsequently strengthened. In Europe, Communist and in some cases Fascist parties have declined, as have differences between traditional parties of the left and right. But new extremist parties have arisen on the right in many countries, motivated by opposition to immigration, multiculturalism, and European integration, while Green parties have grown on the left and there are some signs that other parts of the left may persist or even grow. In France in the first round of the 2002 presidential election the right-wing National Front beat out the centrist Socialists, getting 17 percent of the vote, while the Greens and Trotskyists did well on the left.

Homogenization is usually taken to mean a shift toward the neutral journalistic professionalism, of the sort that has been particularly strong in the United States. This, as we have seen, is clearly the prediction of modernization/differentiation theory, which sees media institutions built around the idea of neutral professionalism as the most developed. And indeed there has been a significant trend in this direction. But here there are quite important limitations and countertrends that need to be stressed. Not only do forms of advocacy journalism persist in European countries where they have always been strong, but new forms are also beginning to proliferate, and this is occurring in the Liberal at least as much as in other systems. If there is convergence here, it is not proceeding only in one direction.

In Chapter 5, we saw that advocacy forms of journalism have persisted in the Polarized Pluralist countries, particularly in Italy, Spain, and Greece. In Italy, though the press has become more market oriented since the 1970s, the papers that have led this shift, for example *La Repubblica* and *Il Giornale*, have strong political identies, and attempts to establish neutral papers have failed. In Spain most of the media, print and broadcast alike, became divided during the 1980s and 1990s into two opposing political camps. In Greece, Papatha-nassopoulos (2001) argues that increasingly popular, market-oriented forms of journalism have not eliminated the pattern of political instrumentalization of the news media, but have shifted the balance of power away from politicians and toward the media owners, who have increasingly powerful tools of political pressure. Deregulation and commercialization have produced sensationalism but not neutrality, according to Papathanassopoulos, who quotes Zaharopoulos and Paraschos's (1993: 96) comment that "the vast majority of Greek media are unabashedly partisan, sensational, and political." The same pattern prevails in Italy (Bechelloni 1995; Mancini 2000; Roidi 2001).

In Chapter 6 we saw that in the Democratic Corporatist countries, though there has been an important trend toward neutrality as a journalistic norm and market strategy, political parallelism in the national press persists, and shows no sign of vanishing in the immediate future. In Liberal systems, meanwhile, new forms of advocacy journalism are proliferating. In the United States, politicized talk programs on both radio and cable TV have become increasingly common, and Fox News has differentiated itself from other broadcast networks with a clear political profile, evident in both content and the political preferences of its audience.

The evidence suggests that there is no necessary connection between commercialization of media and neutral professionalism. The shift toward commercialization is likely to create new forms of advocacy journalism and political parallelism, even as it undercuts old ones. Commercialization can, without question, increase pressures toward "catchallism" and therefore toward neutral professionalism. This seems to happen under specific market conditions, however – most strongly in highly concentrated local newspaper markets. Indeed, neutral professionalism seems to flourish best where competitive pressures are *not* particularly intense (Hallin 2000) – in monopoly local newspapers (in the U.S. case espe-cially when competition from other media was less intense and when newspaper companies were not listed on the stock exchange); in public service broadcasting, where the latter has political independence; or, again in the U.S. case, in the government-regulated oligopoly broadcasting that prevailed before deregulation in the 1980s. In other cases commercial pressures can encourage media to differentiate themselves politically and to stress the color and drama of opinion over the gray utility of information. Thus in Chapter 7 we saw that the competitive British press – especially the tabloid press – is much more politicized than the monopoly American press. Under the right political and economic conditions, opinion sells. This is obvious not only in the tabloid press, particularly in Britain, Germany, and Austria, but also in Spanish radio, where the hosts of "tertulias" – political discussion programs – build their popularity on the strong expression of opinions and command princely salaries as a result (Barrera 1995), or in American cable TV, where opinions are also central to the popularity of talk show hosts and increasingly journalists as well (e.g., Rutenberg 2002). The "commercial deluge" of the past twenty years is also accompanied by a dramatic expansion in the number of channels of electronic media, and seems likely for this reason to produce new forms of political parallelism, as the fragmentation of the audience makes catchall strategies less viable, at least for many channels.

Finally, it is important to keep in mind that, as we saw in discussing professionalization in the Liberal systems in Chapter 7, neutral professionalism in the news media was based in part on a separation of journalism from the commercial logic of media industries. As commercialization undercuts this separation, often reducing the autonomy of journalists within media organizations and disrupting the boundaries between news and entertainment, neutral professionalism is likely, not to disappear, but to find itself reduced to one genre among many. This is evident in the growth of "infotainment" genres, sometimes referred to as the "new news" (Taylor 1992), which often depart from the traditional professional ideal of objectivity.

Differentiation and de-differentiation

In the final section of this chapter we return to the question posed in our discussion of differentiation theory in Chapter 4 and in a slightly different way at the beginning of this chapter: Does it make sense to understand change in media systems in Western Europe and North America as a process of "modernization" in the sense of structural-functionalism – as a move toward increased differentiation of the media from other social institutions? Clearly in many ways this theoretical perspective seems to fit. The process of secularization is certainly consistent with differentiation theory. In the early twentieth century many European societies – including those belonging to both our Democratic Corporatist and Polarized Pluralist Models – were characterized by a strong fusion of institutions and identities: ideological, social class, and religious identities were fused in important ways, as were institutions of party, church, trade union, and mass media. In the last decades of the century these connections were substantially dissolved, and the relations of media to political parties as well as to individuals and social groups became much more fluid, much less bound by stable loyalties or organizational connections. As we saw in Chapter 4, Alexander argued that three major forces propelled the process of differentiation of the media: demands for more universalistic information put forward by new social groups against forms of advocacy journalism linked to the preexisting social order; the growth of professional norms and self-regulation, leading toward the development of journalistic autonomy; and, finally, the degree of universalism in national civil cultures, which is connected with rational-legal authority. Our analysis of historical development of the media in the three groups of countries confirm these connections, though the differentiation of media from political groups was also driven by economic factors, whose role in Alexander's theory, as we shall see, is more ambiguous and problematic.

Also consistent with differentiation theory, the media became increasingly central to political and much of social life, which according to differentiation theory is a necessary outcome of the differentiation process. As political parties, for example, become separated from churches, trade unions, and other social groups – as well as from portions of the state they may once have controlled (an increasingly professionalized judiciary, for example) – they increasingly must depend on the media to establish ties with individual voters and other social actors. In general, a differentiated society relies on media to connect actors and institutions no longer connected by more direct ties, according to differentiation theory. These processes took place in all of the countries studied here, but earliest in the Liberal and later in the Democratic Corporatist and Polarized Pluralist systems.

At the same time, there are real problems with differentiation theory and the concept of modernization connected with it as a way of understanding media system change. In Chapter 4 we considered two alternative perspectives to differentiation theory, associated with Habermas and with Bourdieu, both of whom have argued that media history can in some ways be seen as a process of de-differentiation. Our analysis suggests that in important ways they are correct.

Differentiation and the market

One of the central arguments of Habermas and Bourdieu is that the media have lost autonomy in relation to the market and economic system. And indeed, when we turn from the first of the two principal processes of change discussed in this chapter – secularization – to the second – commercialization – the modernization hypothesis of a unilinear shift toward greater differentiation begins to seem increasingly simplistic. As we saw in Chapter 2, Alexander (1981) argues that modernization of the media requires that "there must be differentiation from structures in the economic dimension, particularly social classes." The main meaning he gives to the differentiation of media from "economic structures" has to do with ties of media to class-linked parties and organizations: he argues that trade union-linked papers are historically a hindrance to professionalization and differentiation, though he also mentions highly partisan bourgeois papers in nineteenth-century Germany. He does not address the role of the market in detail, nor that of private media owners. He makes only one comment about media economics, in discussing U.S. media history: "This transition in content [away from partisanship] coincided with the birth of journalistic professionalization and the emergence of newspapers as big business. By the turn of the twentieth century, the notion of the news media as a 'public institution' was, then, beginning to be institutionalized (31)." Clearly this implies that commercialization contributed to or at least was in harmony with differentiation and professionalization.

In important ways this is correct: the development of strong media markets frees media institutions from the kind of dependence on patrons that leads to the pattern of instrumentalization we identified particularly in the history of Polarized Pluralist systems, and size of media organizations is likely connected with the growth of a journalism as a distinct occupational category. Competition for readers and for advertisers, meanwhile, often encourages media to seek audiences across subcultural boundaries, as well as leading to a process of concentration that disrupts older patterns of association between media and social groups, and enhances the power and independence of the large surviving media organizations. Of course, professionalization and differentiation did also occur within other institutional structures, as we have seen in preceding chapters: it occurred strongly in public broadcasting systems in both the Democratic Corporatist and the Liberal countries, and occurred to a substantial degree in party and trade union-linked papers in the Democratic Corporatist countries, in a later stage of their development. Commercialization is not *necessary* to the development of autonomous institutions or professions; obviously the professionalization and autonomy of the judiciary or administrative corps does not depend on their commercialization.

Professionalization in the news media, moreover, though it has developed in a commercial context in many cases, has by no means developed in total harmony with commercialization. It involves a form of differentiation that often takes place within news organizations themselves, as journalists assert the integrity of journalistic criteria *against* purely commercial ones, and their own autonomy against the intervention of owners, marketers, and advertising sales staff. We have seen this form of differentiation in the "separation of church and state" that was institutionalized in U.S. newspapers in the mid-twentieth century, in the journalistic autonomy achieved in much of the French elite press in the post-World War II period, or in the editorial statutes that can be found in some of the Democratic Corporatist systems, as well as in systems of journalistic self-regulation such as press councils, which are intended to uphold professional values to a large extent against the pressures of economic self-interest.

In the U.S. case, there is certainly strong evidence that this form of differentiation has declined – reducing journalistic autonomy and bringing into question the "notion of the news media as a 'public institution,'" which is no longer taken for granted today as it was from about the 1950s through the 1970s (Hallin 2000). Though the U.S. media were always primarily commercial in character, commercial pressures have intensified with deregulation of broadcasting and changes in ownership patterns that have brought newspapers under the influence of Wall Street. Similar changes are clearly under way to varying degrees through-out Europe, most dramatically in the sphere of broadcasting.

Here it is worth going back to the distinction Mazzoleni makes between media logic and political logic. As many have observed, the changes in European media systems have meant that "media logic" has become differentiated from "political logic," and in many ways has become increasingly dominant over the latter. Story selection, for example, is increasingly determined not by political criteria – such as principles of proportional representation – but by journalistic or media-based criteria of what is a "good story." It is important to recognize, however, that this "media logic" that has emerged in the late twentieth century is a hybrid logic: as we have seen, it is rooted in two developments that overlapped historically, and were intertwined in important ways, but are also distinct:

1. the growth of critical professionalism, which was particularly important in the 1960s and 1970s (and even later in some European countries) and probably has slowed down or even been reversed to a degree since that time; and
2. commercialization, which was beginning in the 1960s and 1970s but accelerated in the 1980s and 1990s.

The former fits the story told by differentiation theory much better than the latter. The growth of infotainment as a hybrid form of programming is a good illustration. Luhmann argues that the differentiation of mass media content into three genres – news and current affairs, advertising, and entertainment – each with distinct social functions, is "the most important internal structure of the system of mass media" (2000: 24). But clearly commercialization undercuts this form of differentiation, not only by blurring the boundaries between news and entertainment, in fact, but also those between advertising and the other two, as product placement, for example, increases in entertainment and as news is used to cross-promote other products of media conglomerates.

It is, in sum, quite plausible to argue that the media are becoming less differentiated in relation to the economic system, even as they are becoming more differentiated in relation to the political system. Many would argue that this is part of a general tendency toward de-differentiation in contemporary society: that with the shift toward neoliberalism market logic tends to dominate wide swaths of society – including politics, which increasingly resembles marketing, education, leisure, social services, etc. If an increasingly commercialized media are growing more central to social life they may be an important agent of this broader process of de-differentiation. This is clearly Bourdieu's argument.

Differentiation and the state

We have focused here on the tendency for media to become de-differentiated in relation to the economic system. It is worth adding a few words, however, about the relation of media to the state. The media, as we have seen, have become increasingly differentiated over the course of the twentieth century from organized social and political groups such as parties, trade unions, and churches. Has their relation to the state followed the same course? If we look at the past twenty years, we would clearly say they have become more differentiated from the state as well. Liberalization and deregulation have diminished the role of the state as an owner, funder, and regulator of the media, and journalists have become more assertive in relation to state elites. If we look over a longer historical period, however, the picture is more complicated, and the direction of change looks a lot less linear. In the early days of the newspaper the state played an important role everywhere, printing official gazettes and often taxing, subsidizing, and censoring the media. During the nineteenth century, as we have seen, there was a general shift toward press freedom, which took place at different rates in different countries: the media became separated from the state in important ways, especially in the Liberal and Democratic Corporatist countries, and became rooted either in the market or in civil society, where they were supported by parties and social organizations. With the growth of corporatism and of the welfare state in the mid-twentieth century, which integrated into the state the social groups of civil society on which much of the media depended, it could be said that the media differentiation from the state lessened in important ways. As Ekecrantz (1997: 400) says about Sweden, "strong labor organizations, a regulatory framework negotiated by the state, journalist training within state universities, heavy subsidies to the press as well as tax redemption belong to the picture of journalism as a public institution in Sweden." Obviously Ekecrantz could add public broadcasting. It was in this context, moreover, that the role of the state as the "primary definer" of news content developed. In the Liberal countries corporatism was weaker, but the rise of the national security state during World War II and the Cold War led to the partial integration of the media into the growing state apparatus. In many countries, finally – though most strongly in the Polarized Pluralist countries, where it also continues especially strongly – media owners continued to be important political actors, often with a share of state power, either formally or informally. Here too, then, we should be careful about assuming that a unilinear trend toward differentiation is the "natural" course of media development.

Differentiation and power

It is also worth focusing, finally, on the issue Alexander raises about the differentiation of media from social class, which brings us back to the broad issue of power raised at the end of Chapter 4. For Alexander, the fact that media in the modern, liberal system become part of "big business" does not prevent their differentiation from social class. Much European scholarship, on the other hand, has historically referred to the commercial press as the "bourgeois" press. This is typical in the Scandinavian literature, for example. The displacement of party papers and public broadcasting by commercial media could thus be seen as reinforcing the power of a particular social class over the media system as a whole. As we have seen, the argument that commercial media reflect a class bias in the sense that they tilt toward the political right has also been made strongly by scholars in the Liberal countries (e.g., Murdock and Golding 1977; Westergaard 1977; Curran 1979). Britain's commercial press has always had a particularly strong slant toward the political right. It is also supported by the comparative research of Patterson and Donsbach (1993: 13), who observe that:

> Historically, conservative parties have been overrepresented by news organizations. The press receives an indirect subsidy from business in the form of advertising, which has worked to the benefit of right-wing parties in the past. The data presented in this paper suggest that these parties are still advantaged; as perceived by journalists, there is a closer parallelism between news organizations and conservative parties than liberal ones.

It could be added that this tendency is particularly marked if we set aside public broadcasting and focus on the most commercially viable news organizations. To the extent that this is correct, the commercialization of media currently under way could be expected to strengthen "bourgeois" dominance of political communication. This is one of the arguments of Herman and McChesney (1997) and others writing within the critical political economy tradition.

How is it that Alexander sees trade-union papers as tied to a particular social class, but commercial papers not? We might interpret this as a sort of inversion of Georg Lukacs's conception of the working class as the universal class, as a claim that the bourgeoisie is the universal class whose interests are identical to those of society as a whole. In fact, Alexander's claim is really about professionalization and about the development by the media of a network of connections with a variety of parties, social groups, and sectors of society – not organizational connections, which tend to die out as the media become commercialized, but relations of influence and exchange of information. Clearly it is true that commercial papers in general have tended to distance themselves from earlier narrow connections to conservative parties and to broaden and blur their political identities, as they have sought to capture readers from the party press of the left – and in some cases have been merged with papers that previously had other political orientations.

Whether this tendency has been strong enough to counterbalance the decline of non-commercial papers with diverse political orientations, in the representation of different social classes – or of different social interests more generally – is difficult to say. For much of the twentieth century, the support parties, trade unions, churches, and the like, gave to their own papers partly counterbalanced the support business gave to "conservative liberal" papers through advertising. As the last Social Democratic papers disappear in Northern Europe, what does this mean: Are they no longer needed, because the existing commercial media adequately represent all the major interests in society? Or does this development increase what Lindblom (1977) called "the privileged position of business" in Western societies? This of course is a general issue raised by the global trend toward neoliberalism, of which the specific case of media commercialization is one important facet.

Here again, the relation between commercialization and professionalization is an important issue. Donsbach and Patterson (1993), for example, after noting that news organizations – and they could add particularly commercial ones – tend to support the political right, at least in their editorial positions, go on to argue that this is counterbalanced by the fact that journalists in most countries shade somewhat to the left. Their influence, then, might provide through other means some of the balance lost through the decline of the political press. It is probably true that the rise of "critical professionalism" in the 1960s and 1970s to an important degree counterbalanced the effect of media concentration and the diminution in the political diversity of news organizations that accompanied it, producing greater degrees of internal pluralism to replace declining external pluralism. If, however, commercialization has the effect of eroding journalistic professionalism over the long run, the issue of diversity and political balance will presumably become more pressing.

We cannot, unfortunately, resolve this issue here: as we noted in Chapter 4, research that systematically addresses issues of media and power in a comparative way is almost totally lacking.

Conclusion

The differences among national media systems described in the preceding chapters of this book are clearly diminishing. A global media culture is emerging, one that closely resembles the Liberal Model we explored in Chapter 7. The homogenization of media systems involves, most centrally, the separation of media institutions from the strong ties to the political world that distinguished both the Democratic Corporatist and Polarized Pluralist from the Liberal Model. This transformation has many causes. We have stressed a distinction between forces external to European society, including direct influence from the United States and the impact of technological innovation, and forces that are essentially internal to

European society, though certainly linked to the process of globalization. The most important of these internal forces, we have argued, are "secularization" – that is, the decline of the political faiths connected to organized social groups that once structured much of European politics and culture, and the shift from a collectivist to a more individualist political culture – and commercialization. Although we have made the case that changes in European media systems are driven by deeper processes of social change, we have also argued that media system change has played an independent causal role, as the rise of television, the development of "critical professionalism," and the growth of media markets have transformed the relations between political parties and organized social groups and the individual citizens who once relied upon them.

We have also noted that there are important factors that limit, and in some ways might even reverse, the process of convergence toward the Liberal Model. Differences among national political systems remain substantial and are likely to prevent complete homogenization of media systems for the foreseeable future. And changes in media markets have created countertendencies that can be seen even in the Liberal countries, as, for example, the multiplication of television channels reintroduces external pluralism into the American media system.

We have, finally, posed the question of whether this process of change in the relation between media institutions and the social and political system can be understood in terms of differentiation theory – which is often implicit in the use of the term *modernization*. Differentiation theory fits well in one very important way: The "secularization" of European society involves the decline of social institutions – mass parties and religious and class-based communities – that at one time fused many different social functions, from political representation to the organization of leisure time to socialization and communication; and the mass media have emerged as specialized institutions of communication independent of these groups. Commercialization, on the other hand, is much harder to integrate into the perspective of differentiation theory: commercialization seems clearly to involve significant de-differentiation of the media system in relation to the market, an erosion of the professional autonomy journalists gained in the later part of the twentieth century, and also, possibly, a subordination of the media to the political interests of business that could diminish political balance in the representation of social interests.

Notes

1   Drake and Nicolaidis (1992) similarly show how the transformation of international telecommunications regimes in the 1980s resulted from the production by experts in western countries of new ways of understanding telecommunication.

2   When we presented an early version of our research at the journalism school at the University of Dortmund, our host, Professor Gerd Kopper, stressed that the liberal conception of neutral professionalism was exactly what the students there were taught.

3   Much of this research is summarized in Schlesinger (1999). Schlesinger notes that Europeanized news coverage is produced mainly for a highly elite audience, while the media that address the mass public follow national political agendas.

4   Rieffel (1984: 114) notes the influence of the *Herald-Tribune* on French journalists. An interesting recent example of U.S. influence is the fact the *Le Monde* has begun providing its readers a version of *The New York Times* as a supplement.

5   The business press is the most global sector of the media. This is not surprising because capital is globalized in a way government or other spheres of social life covered by the news media are not. The world business press is also clearly dominated by the style of journalism that prevails in the liberal countries. This is in part because so many key players are based in the liberal countries – the *Financial Times*, Dow Jones, Reuters, Bloomberg. It is probably also connected with the fact that

business journalism has always been largely informational in character, going back to the earliest days of the press. This is to a large extent the function of the press for market participants, to provide the information they need to make decisions. Business papers do also, of course, serve to advance ideas – promoting neoliberalism, for example – and as a forum for debate over political issues. But because the business community – like the countries of the Liberal Model – is characterized by a high degree of consensus on basic ideological assumptions, it is easy for "objective" styles of presentation to become dominant.

6   Rules on the allocation of broadcast slots had also been changed in 1965 to emphasize the number of dues-paying members each broadcast organization had, increasing the importance of building an audience and decreasing the importance of pillar affiliation (Van der Eijk 2000: 311).

7   Marchetti (2000: 31) notes in a discussion of the rise of "investigative reporting" in France: ". . . the depoliticization of the stakes of the political field induced by the 'neoliberal alignment,' particularly of the socialist party . . . contributed to modifying the conditions of political struggle. The weakening of traditional left/right oppositions, the important fact of homogenization of political personnel trained by the schools of power, has shifted the stakes of political struggle toward more strictly moral stakes. . . ."

8   All are small countries next to large countries with the same language. Foreign television has a large audience in all of them – a majority of the audience in the Swiss case – and the market has generally been considered too small, given this competition, to sustain domestic commercial broadcasters at the national level.

9   The question of how much political information is produced, is also different from the question of how much is consumed. Prior (2002) argues that multiplication of television channels makes it easier for citizens to avoid political information, and is therefore likely to increase inequality in political knowledge, even if more information is available overall.

10   "In Britain, advertising is a lower-status occupation compared to the higher status that politicians have traditionally enjoyed, and a legal ban on all political advertising and radio remains in force despite the recent exposure of British broadcasting to market forces in many respects" (Blumler, Kavanaugh, and Nossiter 1996: 59).

References

Alexander, Jeffrey C. (1981). "The Mass News Media in Systemic, Historical and Comparative Perspective." In E. Katz and T. Szecskö, eds., *Mass Media and Social Change*, pp. 17–51. Beverly Hills: Sage.

Avery, Robert (1993). *Public Service Broadcasting in a Multichannel Environment*. New York and London: Longman.

Barnhurst, Kevin and John Nerone (2001). *The Form of News: A History*. New York: Guilford Press.

Barrera, Carlos (1995). *Sin Mordaza: Veinte Años de Prensa en Democracia*. Madrid: Temas de Hoy.

Bechelloni, Giovanni (1995). *Giornalismo o postgiornalismo?* Napoli: Liguori.

Beck, Ulrich (2000). *What is Globalization?* Cambridge: Polity Press.

Bionda, M. L., A. Bourlot, V. Cobianchi and M. Villa (1998). *Lo spettacolo della politica*. Roma: Eri.

Blanchard, Margaret A. (1986). *Exporting the First Amendment: The Press-Government Crusade of 1945–1952*. New York: Longman.

Blumler, Jay G. (1992). *Television and the Public Interest*. London: Sage.

Blumler, Jay G. and Michael Gurevitch (2001). " 'Americanization' Reconsidered: U.K.-U.S. Campaign Communication Comparisons Across Time." In Lance Bennett and Robert M. Entman, eds., *Mediated Politics: Communication in the Future of Democracy*. New York: Cambridge University Press.

Blumler, Jay, Dennis Kavanaugh, and T. J. Nossiter (1996). "Communication versus Politics in Britain." In D. Swanson and P. Mancini, eds., *Politics, Media and Modern Democracy: An International Study of Innovations in Electoral Campaigning and Their Consequences*. Westport, CT: Praeger.

Boyd-Barrett, Oliver (1977). "Media Imperialism: Towards an International Framework for the Analysis of Media Systems." In J. Curran, M. Gurevitch, and J. Woolacott, eds., *Mass Communication and Society*, pp. 116–35. London: Arnold.

Brants, Kess (1998). "Who's Afraid of Infotainment?" *European Journal of Communication* 13: 315–35.

Brants, Kees and Karen Siune (1998). "Politicization in Decline?" in D. McQuail and K. Siune, eds., *Media Policy: Convergence, Concentration and Commerce*, pp. 128–43. London: Sage.

Curran, James (1979). "Capitalism and Control of the Press, 1800–1975." In J. Curran, M. Gurevitch, and J. Woolacott, eds., *Mass Communication and Society*, pp. 195–230. Beverly Hills: Sage.

Dalton, Russell J. and Martin P. Wattenberg (2000). *Parties without Partisans: Political Change in Advanced Industrial Democracies*. New York: Oxford University Press.

Dimock, Michael A. and Samuel L. Popkin (1997). Political Knowledge in Comparative Perspective. In S. Iyengar and R. Reeves, eds., *Do the Media Govern? Politicians, Voters and Reporters in America*, pp. 217–24. Thousand Oaks, CA: Sage Publications.

Djerf-Pierre, Monika (2000). "Squaring the Circle: Public Service and Commercial News on Swedish Television, 1956–99." *Journalism Studies* 1(2): 239–60.

Djerf-Pierre, Monika and Lennart Weibull (2000). *News and Current Affairs Journalism in Sweden 1925–1995*. Working Paper presented at the European Science Foundation Seminar, Changing Media, Changing Europe, Paris, May 25–8.

Donsbach, Wolfgang and Thomas Patterson (1992). "Journalists' Roles and Newsroom Practices: A Cross-National Comparison." Paper presented at 42nd Conference of the International Communication Association, Miami.

Drake, William J. and Kalypso Nicolaïdis (1992). "Ideas, Interests and Institutionalization: 'Trade in Services' and the Uruguay Round." *International Organization* 46(1): 37–100.

Eisenstein, Elizabeth (1983). *The Printing Revolution in Early Modern Europe*. Cambridge: Cambridge University Press.

Ekecrantz, Jan (1997). "Journalism's 'Discursive Events' and Sociopolitical Change in Sweden 1925–87." *Media, Culture & Society* 19(3): 393–412.

Fagen, Richard (1966). *Politics and Communication*. Boston: Little, Brown and Company.

Farrell, David M. and Paul Webb (2000). "Political Parties as Campaign Organizations." In R. J. Dalton and M. P. Wattenberg, eds., *Parties Without Partisans: Political Change in Advanced Industrial Democracies*, pp. 102–12. New York: Oxford University Press.

Flanagan, Scott and Russell J. Dalton (1990). "Parties under Stress." In P. Maier, ed., *The West European Party System*, pp. 232–46. New York: Oxford University Press.

Franklin, Bob (1997). *Newzak and News Media*. London: Arnold.

Galli, G. (1968). *Il comportamento elettorale in Italia*. Bologna: Il Mulino.

Geyer, Robert, Christine Ingebritsen, and Jonathan W. Moses, eds. (2000). *Globalization, Europeanization and the End of Scandinavian Social Democracy?* New York: St. Martins.

Giddens, Anthony (1990). *The Consequences of Modernity*. Stanford: Stanford University Press.

Golding, Peter (1977). "Media Professionalism in the Third World: The Transfer of an Ideology." In J. Curran, M. Gurevitch, and J. Woollacott, eds., *Mass Communication and Society*, pp. 291–308. London: Sage.

Gundle, Stephen (2000). *Between Hollywood and Moscow: The Italian Communists and the Challenge of Mass Culture, 1943–1991*. Durham NC: Duke University Press.

Hallin, Daniel, C. (1992). "Sound Bite News: Television Coverage of Elections, 1968–1988." *Journal of Communication* 42(2): 5–24.

—— (2000). "Commercialism and Professionalism in the American News Media." In J. Curran and M. Gurevitch, eds., *Mass Media and Society*, pp. 218–37. London: Arnold.

Hallin, Daniel C. and Paolo Mancini (1984). "Speaking of the President: Political Structure and Representational Form in U.S. and Italian TV News." *Theory and Society* 13: 829–50.

—— (1994). "Summits and the Constitution of an International Public Sphere: The Reagan-Gorbachev Meetings as Televised Media Events." In D. C. Hallin, ed., *We Keep America on Top of the World: Television Journalism and the Public Sphere*, pp. 153–69. London: Routledge.

Herman, Edward and Robert McChesney (1997). *The Global Media: The New Missionaries of Corporate Capitalism*. London: Cassel.

Humphreys, Peter (1996). *Mass Media and Media Policy in Western Europe*. Manchester: Manchester University Press.

Inglehart, Ronald (1977). *The Silent Revolution: Changing Values and Political Styles among Western Publics*. Princeton: Princeton University Press.

Jacobson, Gary (2001). "A House and Senate Divided: The Clinton Legacy and the Congressional Elections of 2000." *Political Science Quarterly* 116: 5–27.

Katz, Richard and Peter Mair (1994). *How Parties Organize*. London: Sage.

Kirchheimer, Otto (1966). "The Transformation of the West European Party Systems." In J. LaPalombara and M. Weiner, eds., *Political Parties and Political Development*, pp. 50–60. Princeton: Princeton University Press.

Kitschelt, Herbert (2000). "Citizens, Politicians and Party Cartelization: Political Representation and State Failure in Post-Industrial Democracies." *European Journal of Political Research* 37: 149–79.

Leurdijk, Ardra (1997). "Common Sense Versus Political Discourse: Debating Racism and Multicultural Society in Dutch Talk Sows." *European Journal of Communication* 12(2): 147–68.

Lijphart, Arend (1968). *The Politics of Accommodation*. Berkeley: University of California Press.

—— (1977). *Democracy in Plural Societies*. New Haven: Yale University Press.

—— (1999). *Patterns of Democracy: Government Forms and Performance in Thirty-Six Countries*. New Haven: Yale University Press.

Lindblom, Charles E. (1977). *Politics and Markets: The World Political and Economic Systems*. New York: Basic Books.

Lipset, Seymour M. and Rokkan Stein (1967). *Party Systems and Voter Alignments: Cross-National Perspectives*. New York: Free Press.

Lorwin, V. (1971). "Segmented Pluralism: Ideological Clevages and Political Cohesion in the Smaller European Democracies." *Comparative Politics* 3(2): 141–77.

Luhmann, Niklas (2000). *The Reality of the Mass Media*. Stanford, CA: Stanford University Press.

Lukes, Stephen (1974). *Power: A Radical View*. London: Macmillan.

Mair, Peter (1997). *Party System Change: Approaches and Interpretations*. Oxford: Clarendon Press.

Mair, Peter, ed. (1990). *The West European Party System*. Oxford: Oxford University Press.

Mancini, Paolo (2000a). "How to Combine Media Commercialization and Party Affiliation: The Italian Experience." *Political Communication* 17(4): 319–24.

—— (2000b). *Il sistema fragile: I mass media in Italia tra politica e mercato*. Roma: Carocci.

—— (2000c). "Political Complexity and Alternative Models of Journalism: The Italian Case." In J. Curran and M.-J. Park, eds., *De-Westernizing Media Studies*, pp. 265–78. London: Routledge.

—— (2002). "Parliament and the News." Paper presented at the annual meeting of the American Political Science Association, Boston.

Mannheimer, Renato and Giacomo Sani (1987). *Il mercato elettorale*. Bologna: Il Mulino.

Marchetti, Dominique (2000). "Les Révélations du 'Journalisme d'Investigation.' " *Actes de la recherche en sciences sociales*, 131–2.

Mazzoleni, Gianpietro (1987). "Media Logic and Party Logic in Campaign Coverage: The Italian General Election of 1983." *European Journal of Communication* 2(1): 81–103.

McLachlan, Shelly and Peter Golding (2000). "Tabloidization and the British Press: A Quantitative Investigation into Changes in British Newspapers, 1952–1997." In C. Sparks and J. Tulloch, eds., *Tabloid Tales: Global Debates Over Media Standards*, pp. 75–90. Oxford: Rowman and Littlefield.

McQuail, Denis (1994). *Mass Communication Theory. An Introduction*. London: Sage.

Menduni, Enrico (1998). "Televisione e radio." In Istituto di Economia dei Media, ed., *L'industria della comunicazione in Italia. Quarto rapporto Iem*. Milano: Guerrini e Associati.

Murdock, Graham and Peter Golding (1977). "Capitalism, Communication and Class Relations." In J. Curran, M. Gurevitch, and J. Woollacott, eds., *Mass Communication and Society*, pp. 12–43. London: Sage.

Negrine, Ralph (1998). *Parliament and the Media: A Study of Britain, Germany and France*. London: Chatham House.

Negrine, Ralph and Stylianos Papathanassopoulos (1996). "The 'Americanization' of Political Communication." *Harvard International Journal of Press/Politics* 1(2): 45–62.

Neveu, Erik (1999). "Politics on French Television: Toward a Renewal of Political Journalism and Debate Frames?" *European Journal of Communication* 14(3): 379–409.

—— (2001). *Sociologie du journalisme*. Paris: La Découverte.

—— (2002). "The Four Generations of Political Journalism." In R. Kuhn and E. Neveu, eds., *Political Journalism. New Challenges. New Practices*. London: Routledge.

Nieuwenhuis, J. (1992). "Media Policy in The Netherlands: Beyond the Market." *European Journal of Communication* 7(2): 195–218.

Olsson, Tom (2002). "The Right to Talk Politics in Swedish Journalism 1925–1995." In M. Hurd, T. Olsson, and P. Åker, eds., *Storylines: Media, Power and Identity in Modern Europe. Festschrift for Jan Ekecrantz*. Stockholm: Hjalmarson and Högberg.

Ortega, Félix and M. Luisa Humanes (2000). *Algo Mas Que Periodistas: Sociología de una Profesión*. Barcelona: Editorial Ariel.

Padioleau, Jean G. (1985). *Le Monde et Le Washington Post: Précepteurs et Mousquetaires*. Paris: Presses Universitaires de France.

Panebianco, Angelo (1988). *Political Parties: Organization and Power*. Cambridge: Cambridge University Press.

Papathanassopoulos, Stylianos (2000). "Election Campaigning in the Television Age: The Case of Contemporary Greece." *Political Communication* 17: 47–60.

—— (2001a). "Media Commercialization and Journalism in Greece." *European Journal of Communication* 16(4): 505–21.

—— (2001b). "The Decline of Newspapers: The Case of the Greek Press." *Journalism Studies* 2(1): 109–23.

Patterson, Thomas C. (1993). *Out of Order*. New York: A. Knopf.

Patterson, Thomas E. and Wolfgang Donsbach (1993). "Press-Party Parallelism: A Cross-National Comparison." Paper presented at the annual meeting of the International Communication Association, Washington, DC.

Pfetsch, Barbara (1996). "Convergence Through Privatization? Changing Media Environments and Televised Politics in Germany." *European Journal of Communication* 11(4): 427–51.

Picard, Robert G. (1988). *The Ravens of Odin: The Press in the Nordic Nations*. Ames: Iowa State University Press.

Pilati, Antonio (1987). *Il nuovo sistema dei media*. Milano: Edizioni di Comunità.

Plasser, Fritz (2000). "American Campaign Techniques Worldwide." *Harvard International Journal of Press/Politics* 5(4): 33–54.

Prior, Markus (2002). "Liberated Viewers, Polarized Voters: The Implications of Increased Media Choice for Democratic Politics." *The Good Society* 11(3).

Pye, Lucian W., ed. (1963). *Communications and Political Development*. Princeton: Princeton University Press.

Rieffel, Rémy (1984). *L'Élite des Journalistes: Les Hérauts de L'Information*. Paris: Presses Universitaires de France.

Roidi, Vittorio (2001). *La fabbrica delle notizie*. Bari: Laterza.

Rooney, Dick (2000). "Thirty Years of Competition in the British Tabloid Press: The Mirror and the Sun 1968–1988." In C. Sparks and J. Tulloch, eds., *Tabloid Tales: Global Debates over Media Standards*, pp. 91–109. Oxford: Rowman and Littlefield.

Rutenberg, Jim (2002). "Cable TV Serves Business News with Opinions." *The New York Times*, April 3: C1.

Salokangas, Raimo (1999). "From Political to National, Regional and Local." In *Nordicom Review* 20(1): 31–76.

Sani, Giacomo (1980). "The Political Culture of Italy: Continuity and Change." In G. Almond and S. Verba, eds. *The Civic Culture Revisited*. New York: Sage.

Schiller, Herbert I. (1969). *Mass Communications and American Empire*. Boston: Beacon Press.

—— (1973). *The Mind Managers*. Boston: Beacon Press

—— (1976). *Communication and Cultural Domination*. White Plains, NY: International Arts and Sciences Press.

Schlesinger, Philip (1999). "Changing Spaces of Political Communication: The Case of the European Union." *Political Communication* 16(3): 263–79.

Schou, Søren (1992). "Postwar Americanisation and the Revitalisation of European Culture." In M. Skovmand and K. C. Schroder, eds., *Media Cultures: Reappraising Transnational Media*, pp. 142–58. London and New York: Sage.

Schudson, Michael (1995). "Question Authority: A History of the News Interview." In *The Power of News*. Cambridge, MA: Harvard University Press.

Splichal, Slavko and Colin Sparks (1994). *Journalists for the 21st Century*. Norwood, NJ: Ablex.

Swanson, David and Paolo Mancini, eds. (1996). *Politics, Media and Modern Democracy*. Westport: Praeger.

Taylor, Paul (1992). "Political Coverage in the 1990s: Teaching the Old News New Tricks." In Twentieth Century Fund, *The New News v. the Old News*. New York: Twentieth Century Fund.

Thogmartin, Clyde (1998). *The National Daily Press of France*. Birmingham, AL: Summa Publications.

Tracey, Michael (1998). *The Decline and Fall of Public Service Broadcasting*. New York: Oxford University Press.

Trigilia, C. (1981). "Le subculture politiche territoriali." In *Sviluppo economico e trasformazioni socio-politiche dei sistemi territoriali a economia diffusa, Quaderni della Fondazione Feltrinelli*, 16.

Tunstall, Jeremy (1977). *The Media Are American*. London: Constable.

van der Eijk, Cees (2000). "The Netherlands: Media and Politics between Segmented Pluralism and Market Forces." In R. Gunther and A. Mughan, eds., *Democracy and the Media*, pp. 303–42. Cambridge: Cambridge University Press.

Waisbord, Silvio (2000). *Watchdog Journalism in South America: News, Accountability and Democracy*. New York: Columbia University Press.

Weaver, David H., ed. (1998). *The Global Journalist: News People Around the World*. Cresskill, NJ: Hampton Press.

Westergaard, John (1977). "Power, Class and the Media." In J. Curran, M. Gurevitch, and J. Woollacott, eds., *Mass Communication and Society*, pp. 15–115. London: Sage.

Weymouth, Anthony and Bernard Lamizet, eds. (1996). *Markets and Myths: Forces for Change in the Media of Western Europe*. New York: Longman.

Wigbold, Herman (1979). "Holland: The Shaky Pillars of Hilversum." In A. Smith, ed., *Television and Political Life: Studies in Six European Countries*, pp. 191–231. London: Macmillan.

Winston, Brian (2002). "Towards Tabloidization? Glasgow Revisited, 1975–2001." *Journalism Studies* 3(1): 5–20.

Zaharopoulos, Thimios and Manny E. Paraschos (1993). *Mass Media in Greece: Power, Politics and Privatization*. Westport, CT: Prager.

Chapter 11

Robert McChesney

THE MEDIA SYSTEM GOES GLOBAL

BY THE END OF the 1990s a major turning point was reached in the realm of media. Whereas media systems had been primarily *national* before the 1990s, a *global* commercial media market has emerged full force by the dawn of the twenty-first century. "What you are seeing," states Christopher Dixon, director of media research for the stockbroker PaineWebber, "is the creation of a global oligopoly. It happened to the oil and automotive industries earlier this century; now it is happening to the entertainment industry."[1] In the past, to understand any nation's media situation, one first had to understand the local and national media and then determine where the global market — which largely meant imports and exports of films, TV shows, books, and music — fit in. Today one must first grasp the nature and logic of the global commercial system and then determine how local and national media deviate from the overall system. The rise of a global commercial media system is closely linked to the rise of a significantly more integrated "neoliberal" global capitalist economic system. To some extent, the rise of a global media market is encouraged by new digital and satellite technologies that make global markets both cost-effective and lucrative. It is also encouraged by the institutions of global capitalism — the World Trade Organisation (WTO), the World Bank, the International Monetary Fund (IMF) — as well as those governments, including that of the United States, that advance the interests of transnational corporations (TNCs). Moreover, during the past thirty years, media and communication more broadly have become a much more significant sector for business activity.[2] And this is just the beginning. As Ira Magaziner, the Clinton administration's Internet policy adviser put it in 1998, worldwide electronic commerce will be "the primary economic driver over the next 25 years."[3]

The rise to dominance of the global commercial media system is more than an economic matter; it also has clear implications for media content, politics, and culture. In many ways the emerging global media system is an extension of the U.S. system described in chapter 1 [of the original publication], and its culture shares many of the attributes of the U.S. hypercommercial media system. This makes sense, as the firms that dominate U.S. media also dominate the global system and the system operates on the same profit maximizing logic. But there are also some important distinctions. On the one hand, a number of new firms enter the picture as one turns to the global system. On the other hand, and more important, a number of new political and social factors enter the discussion. There are scores of governments, and regional and international organizations that have a say in the regulation of media and communication. There are also a myriad of languages and cultures, which makes establishing a global version of the "U.S. system" quite difficult. But even if the U.S. media system and culture will not be punch-pressed onto the globe, the trajectory is toward vastly greater integration, based on commercial terms and dominated by a handful of transnational media conglomerates.

In this chapter I briefly chronicle the rise of the global media system and its core attributes. It is a system dominated by fewer then ten global TNCs, with another four or five dozen firms filling out regional and niche markets. I examine the activities and holdings of the three most important global media firms — Time Warner, Disney, and News Corporation — in detail. I then consider what the rise of the global media means for traditional notions of cultural imperialism, and for culture and journalism writ large. In my view, the general thrust of the global commercial media system is quite negative — assuming one wishes to preserve and promote institutions and values that are conducive to meaningful self-government. Such a global media system plays a central role in the development of "neoliberal" democracy; that is, a political system based on the formal right to vote, but in which political and economic power is resolutely maintained in the hands of the wealthy few.

The rise of the global media system

The global markets for film production, TV show production, book publishing, and recorded music have been oligopolistic markets throughout much of their existence. Although there are important domestic companies in many of these industries, the global *export* market is the province of a handful of mostly U.S.-owned or U.S.-based firms. These not only remain important markets but are also tending to grow faster than the global economy. The motion picture and TV show production industries are absolutely booming at the global level.[4] The major film studios and U.S. TV show production companies (usually the same firms) now generate between 50 and 60 percent of their revenues outside the United States.[5] A key factor that makes these global oligopolies nearly impenetrable to newcomers is the extent of their distribution systems.[6] The rational choice for someone wishing to enter this market is either to buy one of the existing giants or, if one does not have a spare $10 or $20 billion or does not wish to spend it, to set up as an "independent" and forge a link with one of the existing giants.[7] The global film industry is the province of seven firms, all of which are part of larger media conglomerates. Likewise, the global music industry is dominated by five firms, all but one of which (EMI) are part of larger media TNCs.[8] These five music giants earn 70 percent of their revenues outside of the United States.[9]

What distinguishes the emerging global media system is not transnational control over exported media content, however, so much as increasing TNC control over media distribution and content within nations. Prior to the 1980s and 1990s, national media systems were typified by nationally owned radio and television systems, as well as domestic newspaper industries. Newspaper publishing remains a largely national phenomenon, but the face of television has changed almost beyond recognition. The rise of cable and satellite technology has opened up national markets to scores of new channels and revenue streams. The major Hollywood studios — all part of global media conglomerates — expect to generate $11 billion alone in 2002 for global TV rights to their film libraries, up from $7 billion in 1998.[10] More important, the primary providers of these channels are the media TNCs that dominate cable television channel ownership in the United States and have aggressively established numerous global editions of their channels to accommodate the new market.[11] Neoliberal "free market" policies have opened up ownership of stations as well as cable and satellite systems to private and transnational interests. As the *Wall Street Journal* notes, "the cable colonialists continue to press on in Europe, Asia and Latin America, betting on long-term profit."[12] Likewise, the largest media TNCs are invariably among the main players in efforts to establish digital satellite TV systems to serve regional and national markets.[13]

Television also is rapidly coming to play the same sort of dominant cultural role in Europe, Asia, and worldwide that it has played in the United States for two or three generations. After reviewing the most recent research, one observer noted in early 1998: "Europe hasn't caught up to American TV consumption levels, but Europeans are spending more time than ever watching television."[14] In 1997 French children aged four to ten years old watched on average nearly two hours of television per day, up 10 percent from the previous high in 1996; but this remains only one-half the amount of TV watching for children in the United States.[15]

The close connection of the rise of the global media system to the global capitalist political economy becomes especially clear in two ways. First, as suggested above, the global media system is the direct result of the sort of "neoliberal" deregulatory policies and agreements (e.g., NAFTA and GATT) that have helped to form global markets for goods and services. (It is worth noting that the actual negotiations surrounding communication issues in these international trade agreements are so complex, and the language employed in the deals is so technical and legalistic, that one expert estimates that no more than a few dozen people in the entire world — mostly lawyers — can intelligibly explain the media and cultural terms they include. A less inclusive discourse over global media policy would be difficult to imagine.)[16] At the global level, for example, the WTO ruled in 1997 that Canada could not prohibit Time Warner's *Sports Illustrated* from distributing a Canadian edition of the magazine.[17] In Australia, for another example, the High Court ruled against the legality of Australian domestic media content quotas in April 1998, stating that "international treaty obligations override the national cultural objectives in the Broadcasting Services Act."[18]

Although there is considerable pressure for open media markets, this is a sensitive area. There are strong traditions of protection for domestic media and cultural industries. Nations ranging from Norway, Denmark, and Spain to Mexico, South Africa, and South Korea, for example, have government subsidies to keep alive their small domestic film production industries.[19] Over the coming years it is likely that there will be periodic setbacks to the drive to establish an open global media market. In the summer of 1998 culture ministers from twenty nations, including Brazil, Mexico, Sweden, Italy, and Ivory Coast, met in Ottawa to discuss how they could "build some ground rules" to protect their cultural fare from "the Hollywood juggernaut." Their main recommendation was to keep culture out of the control of the WTO.[20] A similar 1998 gathering sponsored by the United Nations in Stockholm recommended that culture be granted special exemptions in global trade deals.[21] In India, in 1998, a court issued an arrest warrant for Rupert Murdoch for failing to appear in court to defend himself on the charge that his Star TV satellite service broadcast "obscene and vulgar" movies.[22]

Nevertheless, the trend is clearly in the direction of opening markets to TNC penetration. Neoliberal forces in every country argue that cultural trade barriers and regulations harm consumers, and that subsidies even inhibit the ability of nations to develop their own competitive media firms.[23] There are often strong commercial media lobbies within nations that perceive they have more to gain by opening up their borders than by maintaining trade barriers. In 1998, for example, when the British government proposed a voluntary levy on film theater revenues (mostly Hollywood films) to provide a subsidy for the British commercial film industry, the British commercial broadcasters reacted warily, not wishing to antagonize their crucial suppliers.[24] In November 1998 the British government declared the proposal dead after lobbying pressure from British commercial broadcasters.[25]

The European Union (EU) and European Commission (EC) provide an excellent case study of the movement of media policy making toward a largely procommercial position, and of the complexities involved in such a position. Historically, European nations have enjoyed prominent and well-financed national public broadcasters as well as a variety of other mechanisms to protect and promote domestic cultural production. The EU and EC are scarcely commissioned to advance the interests of U.S.-based media TNCs, but they are devoted to establishing strong European firms and a regional open commercial market. "If the European market doesn't become a single market," an Italian film director stated, "there's no way it can compete against America."[26] The powerful European media giants want the EU to advance their interests in the same way the U.S. government invariably lobbies and pushes for the interests of its media TNCs.[27] In 1998, for example, the EC officially moved to break up the European distribution company co-owned by Viacom, Seagram, and MGM–United Artists, arguing that it gave U.S. film producers too much ability to overwhelm potential European competitors.[28]

The EU and EC also see their mission as encouraging more competitive media markets between European firms.[29] Pressure from the EU Competition Commission was a factor in derailing the prospective merger between Reed Elsevier and Wolters Kluwer in 1998.[30] Accomplishing competitive markets, while helping build strong pan-European firms, sometimes produces conflict, as in 1998 when the EU opposed the efforts of Bertelsmann and Kirch to merge their German digital TV operations. In this case, some voices in the European business community argued that the EU was undermining the "emergence of a strong European business."[31] But the EU and EC, like regulators everywhere, are less likely to act on behalf of the public interest if it is aligned against the entirety of the business community. So it was with the Bertelsmann–Kirch deal — the dominant European media groups as well as Rupert Murdoch were urging the EU to block the merger, since they all wanted to have a shot at the German TV market as well.[32] Bertelsmann, too, was rumored not to be displeased that the deal was kiboshed, as it cripples the debt-laden Kirch and leaves Bertelsmann with an even better chance of dominating German digital television — all by itself.[33]

The nature of the EU system's media policies and values were revealed in several other developments in the late 1990s. To address the concern that U.S.-based media firms would quickly overwhelm Europe unless regulations to protect European content were enacted, the EU nearly passed a law in 1997 requiring that 50 percent of TV content be European-made. This drive fell short after a "ferocious" lobbying campaign by the largest European media interests, who are linked with U.S. media firms and dependent upon U.S. fare. Eventually the wording of the law was watered down to become virtually meaningless.[34] The EU system has been more effective in spreading commercial values; on two occasions in 1997 the European Court of Justice ruled that member states could not prohibit cable TV channels that featured advertising aimed at children, even though this violated national statutes.[35] Even when, in response to massive pressure from health authorities and educators, the EU banned tobacco advertising and sports sponsorship in 1998, there was a reasonable chance the law could be overturned by the European Courts of Justice.[36]

Increasingly lost in the shuffle are the fates of European public broadcasters. As the political power of public broadcasters recedes in Europe, the market-oriented EU and EC find the traditional notion of public service media, meaning nonprofit media with public subsidy, something of a square peg. By 1998, for example, a coalition of European commercial broadcasters and publishers were lobbying the EU to stop state subsidies of public broadcasters, when the public broadcasters were using the funds to enter into commercial television ventures.[37] (I will discuss this tension and what it means for public service broadcasting in greater length in chapter 5.) An indication of the shifting terrain of European policy making came in June 1997 when the European Summit found it necessary to include a protocol to the EU treaty formally acknowledging that public service broadcasters had a right to exist.[38] A generation earlier such a protocol would have been considered not just unnecessary but absurd.

Advertising is the second way that the global media system is linked to the global market economy. Advertising is conducted disproportionately by the largest firms in the world, and it is a major weapon in the struggle to establish new markets. The top ten global advertisers alone accounted for some 75 percent of the $36 billion spent by the one hundred largest global marketers in 1997.[39] For major firms like Procter & Gamble and Nike, global advertising is a vitally important aspect of their campaigns to maintain strong growth rates.[40] In conjunction with the "globalization" of the economy, advertising has grown globally at a rate greater than GDP growth in the 1990s.[41] The most rapid growth has been in Europe, Latin America, and especially East Asia, although the economic collapse of the late 1990s has slowed what had earlier been characterized as "torrid ad growth."[42] Advertising in China is growing at annual rates of 40 to 50 percent in the 1990s, and the singularly important sector of TV advertising is expected to continue to grow at that rate, at least, with the advent of sophisticated audience research that now delivers vital demographic data to advertisers, especially TNC advertisers.[43]

It is this TNC advertising that has fueled the rise of commercial television across the world, accounting, for example, for over one-half the advertising on the ABN-CNBC Asia network, which is co-owned by Dow Jones and General Electric.[44] And there is a world of room for growth, especially in comparison to the stable U.S. market. In 1999, the United States still accounted for nearly one-half of the world's approximately $435 billion in advertising.[45] Even in the developed markets of western Europe, for example, most nations still spend no more than one-half the U.S. amount on advertising per capita, so there remains considerable growth potential.[46] Were European nations, not to mention the rest of the world, ever to approach the U.S. level of between 2.1 and 2.4 percent of the GDP going toward advertising — where it has fluctuated for decades — the global media industry would see an almost exponential increase in its revenues.[47] As it is, European commercial television is growing at more than a 10 percent annual rate, twice the U.S. average.[48]

The advertising agency business itself has consolidated dramatically on a global basis in the 1990s, in part to better deal with the globalization of product markets and also to better address the plethora of commercial media emerging to serve advertisers. The largest advertising organizations now include several major brand agencies and countless smaller formerly independent agencies in nations around the world. The largest ad organization, Omnicom (1997 revenues: $4.2 billion), has fourteen major agencies in its portfolio, including BBDO Worldwide and DDB Needham Worldwide.[49] Omnicom dominates the global advertising agency industry along with two other massive giants — WPP Group (1997 revenues: $3.6 billion), and Interpublic Group (1997 revenues: $3.4 billion). They have a combined income greater than that of the ad organizations ranked fourth through fourteenth; and the size of ad organizations falls precipitously after one gets past the first fourteen or so. For example, number fifteen (Carlson Marketing, 1998 revenues: $285 million) does less than half the business of the firm ranked number fourteen, Cordiant Communications. And the fiftieth-largest advertising organization in the world — Testa International (1997 revenues: $60 million) — does around 1.5 percent of the business of the Omnicom Group.[50]

The wave of global consolidation among advertising agencies is far from over. The four most active ad agency acquirers spent $1.25 billion to buy other agencies in 1997, up over 250 percent from what they spend in 1996. Industry surveys suggest that most agency executives expect the agency merger and acquisition boom to increase in momentum in coming years.[51] Interpublic budgeted $250 million in 1998 for the purchase of other advertising companies.[52] The consolidation is encouraged by globalization, as the largest advertisers increasingly prefer to work with a single agency worldwide.[53] When Citibank consolidated its global advertising into one agency in 1997, an observer noted that "they want to have one brand with one voice — that's their mantra."[54] "We're not going to get a shot at [major clients]," one agency owner said, "without being global."[55] Global consolidation is also encouraged because the larger an ad agency, the more leverage it has getting favorable terms for its clients with global commercial media.[56] An agency needs worldwide "critical mass" to be competitive, the president of the French Publicis stated when Publicis purchased the U.S. Hal Riney and Partners in 1998.[57] The largest advertising organizations are scurrying about purchasing almost all of the remaining viable independent agencies around the world.[58] Even Japan, until recently effectively off-limits to foreign ad agencies, is being incorporated into the global networks of these giant agencies, as its main advertisers want global expertise for their brands.[59] In 1998 Omnicom and the WPP Group each purchased stakes in major Japanese agencies.[60] In combination, all of this suggests increased advertising influence over media operations.

But the most important corporate concentration concerns the media industry itself, and here concentration and conglomeration are the order of the day. There is increased global horizontal integration in specific media industries. Book publishing, for example, has undergone a major shakeout in the late 1990s, leading to a situation in which a handful of global firms dominate the market. "We have never seen this kind of concentration before with global ownership and the big getting bigger," a mergers and acquisitions lawyer who specializes in publishing deals stated in 1998.[61] But much more striking have been the vertical integration and conglomeration of the global media market. In short order the global media market has come to be dominated by the same eight TNCs that dominate U.S. media, as I presented in chapter 1, plus Bertelsmann, the German-based conglomerate. The dominant advertising firms are featherweights in comparison to the first tier of media firms, all of which rank among the few hundred largest publicly traded firms in the world in terms of market value. They are General Electric (#1), AT&T (#16), Disney (#31), Time Warner (#76), Sony (#103), News Corp. (#184), Viacom (#210), and Seagram (#274).[62] Bertelsmann would certainly be high on the list, too, were it not one of the handful of giant firms that remain privately held. In short, these firms are at the very pinnacle of global corporate capitalism. This is also a highly concentrated industry; the largest media firm in the world in terms of annual revenues, Time Warner (1998 revenues: $28 billion), is some fifty times larger in terms of annual sales than the world's fiftieth-largest media firm.[63] But what distinguishes these nine firms from the rest of the pack is not merely their size but the fact that they have global distribution networks.

I spelled out the rapidity with which these giants have emerged in the 1990s in chapter 1. There, too, I explained the strong pressure for firms to get larger and larger (and fewer and fewer). Likewise, and probably lost to most Americans who do not travel abroad, the media giants have moved aggressively to become global players. Time Warner and Disney, for example, still get the vast majority of their revenue in the United States, but both firms project non-U.S. sales to be a majority of their revenues within a decade, and the other media giants are all moving to be in a similar position. The point is to capitalize on the potential for growth — and not get outflanked by competitors — as the U.S. market is well developed and only permits incremental growth. As Viacom CEO Sumner Redstone puts it, "companies are focusing on those markets promising the best return, which means over-seas."[64] Frank Biondi, former chair of Seagram's Universal Studios, says "ninety-nine percent of the success of these companies long term is going to be successful execution offshore."[65] Another U.S. media executive stated that "we now see Latin America and the Asia-Pacific as our twenty-first century."[66] Sony, to cite one example, has hired the investment banking Blackstone Group to help it identify media takeover candidates worldwide.[67]

But this point should not be exaggerated. Non-U.S. markets, especially markets where there are meddlesome governments, are risky and often require patience before they pro-duce profit. The key to being a first-tier media powerhouse is having a strong base in the United States, by far the largest and most stable commercial media market. That is why Bertelsmann is on the list; it ranks among the top U.S. recorded music, magazine publishing, and book publishing companies. It expects to do 40 percent of its $16 billion in annual business in the United States in the near future.[68] "We want to be a world-class media company," the CEO of the U.K.'s Pearson TV stated, "and to do that, we know we've got to get bigger in America."[69]

It is also mandatory to be a conglomerate, for the reasons presented in chapter 1. The essence of the first-tier firms is their ability to mix production capacity with their distribu-tion networks. These nine firms control four of the five music firms that sell 80 percent of global music. The one remaining independent, EMI, is invariably on the market; it is worth considerably more merged with one of the other five global music giants that are all part of huge media conglomerates, or to another media TNC that wants a stake in the music market.[70] All of the major Hollywood studios, which dominate global film box office, are connected to these giants too. The only two of the nine that are not major content producers are AT&T and GE's NBC. The former has major media content holdings through Liberty Media and both of them, ranking among the ten most valuable firms in the world, are in a position to acquire assets as they become necessary. Such may soon be the case for GE. NBC was forced to scale back its expansion into European and Asian television in 1998, in part because it did not have enough programming to fill the airwaves.[71]

The global media market is rounded out by a second tier of four or five dozen firms that are national or regional powerhouses or have strong holds over niche markets, such as business or trade publishing. About one-half of these second-tier firms come from North America; most of the rest, from western Europe and Japan. Each of these second-tier firms is a giant in its own right, often ranking among the thousand largest firms in the world and doing over $1 billion per year in business. The list of second-tier media firms from North America includes, among others, Dow Jones, Gannett, Knight-Ridder, Newhouse, Comcast, the New York Times, the Washington Post, Hearst, McGraw Hill, Cox Enterprises, CBS, Advance Publications, Hicks Muse, Times-Mirror, Reader's Digest, Tribune Company, Thomson, Hollinger, and Rogers Communication. From Europe the list of second-tier firms includes, among others, Kirch, Havas, Mediaset, Hachette, Prisa, Canal Plus, Pearson, Carlton, Granada, United News and Media, Reuters, Reed Elsevier, Wolters Kluwer, Axel Springer, Kinnevik, and CLT. The Japanese companies, aside from Sony, remain almost exclusively domestic producers. I will discuss the handful of "third world" commercial media giants below.[72]

This second tier has also crystallized rather quickly; across the globe there has been a shakeout in national and regional media markets, with small firms getting eaten by medium firms and medium firms being swallowed by big firms. Many national and regional con-glomerates have been established on the back of publishing or television empires, like Denmark's Egmont Group.[73] The situation in most nations is similar to the one described in the United States in chapter 1: a smaller number of much larger firms dominate the media in comparison to the situation only ten or twenty years ago. Indeed, as most nations are smaller than the United States, the tightness of the media oligarchy can be even more severe. In Britain, for example, 90 percent of the newspaper circulation is controlled by five firms, including Murdoch's News Corporation, while mergers have turned British cable into a fiefdom dominated by three firms.[74] In Canada, vocal right-winger Conrad Black — who owns 437 newspapers globally in an empire that generated revenues of $2.2 billion in 1997 — owns 61 of that nation's 101 daily newspapers, and over one-half of Canada's newspaper circulation.[75] The second-largest chain controls another one-quarter of Canadian newspaper circulation.[76] The situation may be most stark in New Zealand, where the newspaper industry is largely the province of the Australian-American Murdoch and the Irish Tony O'Reilly, who also dominates New Zealand's commercial radio broadcasting and has major stakes in magazine publishing. Two of the four terrestrial (over-the-air) television channels are owned by the Canadian CanWest. Murdoch controls pay television and is negotiating to purchase one or both of the two public TV networks, which the government is aiming to sell.[77] In short, the rulers of New Zealand's media system could squeeze into a closet.

Moreover, as the New Zealand example implies, the need to go beyond national borders applies to second-tier media firms as well as first-tier giants. Australian media moguls, following the path blazed by Rupert Murdoch, have the mantra "expand or die." As one puts it, "you really can't continue to grow as an Australian supplier in Australia."[78] Mediaset, the Berlusconi-owned Italian television power, is desperately seeking to expand in Europe and Latin America.[79] Perhaps the most striking example of second-tier globalization is provided by Hicks, Muse, Tate and Furst, the U.S. radio-publishing-TV-billboard-movie theater power discussed in chapter 1 that has been constructed almost overnight. In 1998 Hicks Muse spent well over one billion dollars purchasing media assets in Mexico, Argentina, Brazil, and Venezuela.[80]

In combination, these sixty or seventy giants control much of the world's media: book publishing, magazine publishing, music recording, newspaper publishing, TV show production, TV station and cable channel ownership, cable/satellite TV system ownership, film production, motion picture theater ownership, and newspaper publishing.[81] They are also the most dynamic element of the global media network. But the system is still very much in formation. New second-tier firms are emerging, especially in lucrative Asian markets, and there will probably be further upheaval among the ranks of the first-tier media giants. And firms get no guarantee of success merely by going global. The point is that they have no choice in the matter. Some, perhaps many, will falter as they accrue too much debt or as they enter unprofitable ventures. But the chances are that we are closer to the end of the process of establishing a stable global media market than we are to the beginning of the process. And as that happens, there is a distinct likelihood that the leading media firms in the world will find themselves in a very profitable position. That is what they are racing to secure.

Corporate growth, oligopolistic markets, and conglomeration barely reveal the extent to which the global media system is fundamentally noncompetitive in any meaningful economic sense of the term. As I mentioned in chapter 1, many of the largest media firms share major shareholders, own pieces of each other, or have interlocking boards of directors. When *Variety* compiled its list of the fifty largest global media firms for 1997, it observed that "merger mania" and cross-ownership had "resulted in a complex web of interrelationships" that will "make you dizzy."[82] The global market strongly encourages firms to establish equity joint ventures in which the media giants each own a part of an enterprise. In this manner, firms reduce competition and risk, and increase the chance of profitability. As the CEO of Sogecable, Spain's largest media firm and one of the twelve largest private media companies in Europe, put it to *Variety*, the strategy is "not to compete with international companies but to join them."[83] In 1998, for example, Prisa, another large Spanish media conglomerate, merged its digital satellite television service with the one controlled by state-owned telecommunications firm Telefonica to establish a monopoly in Spain.[84] Almost all of the second-tier companies have joint ventures or important relationships with each other and with first-tier media giants. Indeed, it is rare for first-tier media giants to launch a new venture in a foreign country unless they have taken on a leading domestic media company as a partner. The domestic firm can handle public outreach and massage the local politicians.

News Corporation heir Lachlan Murdoch expressed the rational view when explaining why News Corporation is working more closely with Kerry Packer's Publishing and Broadcasting Ltd., the company that with News Corp. effectively controls much of Australian media. It's better, contends Murdoch the younger, if we are not "aggressively attacking each other all the time."[85] In the global media market the dominant firms compete aggressively in some concentrated oligopolistic markets, are key suppliers to each other in other markets, and are partners in yet other markets. As the headline in one trade publication put it, this is a market where the reigning spirit is to "Make profits, not war."[86] In some respects, the global media market more closely resembles a cartel than it does the competitive marketplace found in economics textbooks.

The holy trinity of the global media system

The nature of the global media system seems less abstract when one examines the recent growth, activities, and strategies of its three most important TNCs: Time Warner, Disney, and News Corporation. Time Warner and Disney are the two firms with the largest media and entertainment operations. News Corporation is in contention with Viacom for the status of fourth largest, with sales around one-half those of Time Warner and Disney, but under Rupert Murdoch it has led the way in media globalization. These global empires were mainly constructed in the 1990s, and they are a long way from completion.

Time Warner is the outgrowth of the 1989 merger of Time and Warner Communications and the 1996 acquisition of Turner Broadcasting. It did around $28 billion in business in 1998, and its sales are expected to continue to grow at double-digit rates for the foreseeable future. With two hundred subsidiaries worldwide, Time Warner is also a strikingly dominant global player in virtually every important media sector except newspaper publishing and radio broadcasting. Time Warner's challenge is to develop its *synergies* (the process of taking a media brand and exploiting it for all the profit possible), that is, to mesh its extremely lucrative parts to increase the size of the profit whole.[87] It has an unparalleled combination of content production and distribution systems to work with.

Here are some of Time Warner's holdings:

- majority interest in the U.S. WB television network;
- largest cable broadcasting system operator in U.S., controlling twenty-two of the one hundred largest markets;
- controlling interest in cable TV channels CNN, Headline News, CNNfn, CNN International, TNT, TBS, Turner Classic Movies, CNNSI, Cartoon Network, Court TV, HBO, HBO International, and Cinemax;
- partial interest in cable TV channel Comedy Central;
- minority stake in U.S. satellite TV service Primestar;
- Warner Bros. film studios, one of the half-dozen studios that dominate the global market;

- Warner Bros. TV production studios, one of largest TV show production companies in the world;
- New Line film studios;
- the largest U.S. magazine publishing group, including *Time*, *People*, *Sports Illustrated*, and *Fortune*;
- Warner Music Group, one of the five firms that dominate the global recorded music industry;
- leading global book publisher, with 42 percent of sales outside the U.S.;
- 150 Warner Bros. retail stores;
- the Atlanta Hawks and Atlanta Braves U.S. professional sports teams;
- Hanna-Barbera animation studios;
- 10 percent stake in France's Canalsatellite, a digital TV service;
- 100 percent of Citereseau and 49 percent of Rhone Cable Vision, two French cable television system companies;
- 90 percent of Time Warner Telecom, which offers telephone service over Time Warner cable lines;
- 37 percent stake in Road Runner, the cable Internet Access service;
- one of the largest movie-theater-owning companies in the world, with over one thousand screens, all outside the U.S.;
- 20 percent of Midi Television, first private South African television network;
- over 40 percent stake in Towani, a joint venture with Toshiba and Japan's Nippon Television to produce movies and TV programs for Japanese market and export;
- 4.5 percent stake in Enic, owner of four European football teams, and, in fifty-fifty joint venture with Time Warner, proprietor of a worldwide chain of Warner Bros. restaurants;
- 23 percent stake in Atari;
- 14 percent stake in Hasbro;
- minority stakes in the following non-U.S. broadcasting joint ventures: Germany's N-TV, European music channel VIVA, and Asian music channel Classic V;
- 31 percent stake in U.S. satellite television company Primestar;
- 25 percent stake in Japanese cable company Titus;
- 19 percent stake in Japanese cable company Chofu;
- 50 percent stake in Columbia House record club.

Yet even this formidable list fails to do justice to Time Warner's global reach. CNN International is the dominant global TV news channel, broadcasting in several languages to some two hundred nations.[88] HBO is a global powerhouse as well, having expanded successfully into both eastern and western Europe, Latin America, and most of Asia. As one observer notes, HBO's International division "gobbles up new countries."[89] The Warner Bros. film studios coproduces films with Australian, German, French, Japanese, and Spanish companies, often times not in English.[90] Warner Bros. International Television Production has joint ventures to coproduce TV series with partners in Canada, France, Germany, and Britain.[91] Even the U.S.-based magazine division is going global, with non-U.S. editions of its publications and planned acquisitions of European magazines.[92]

What really distinguishes Time Warner, and what gives it such leverage in the global market, are two related things. First, in addition to arguably *producing* more media content than any other firm, Time Warner also has the world's largest library of music, films, TV shows, and cartoons to exploit. This makes Time Warner extremely attractive to national media firms for joint ventures or simply major contracts, such as it has with Canal Plus, the satellite television power in France, Spain, and Italy.[93] Second, Time Warner has perhaps more recognizable media *brand names* than any firm in the world. Branding is considered the most crucial determinant of market success and the one factor that can assure success in the digital world, with its myriad of choices — even though the choices are controlled by a small number of owners. Branding also lends itself to extensive licensing and merchandising of products related to media characters, channels, and programming. Time Warner considers its *Looney Tunes* cartoons alone a $4 billion worldwide brand; Batman is a mere $1 billion worldwide brand. With 150 Warner Bros. retail stores and scores of licensing agreements, merchandising has become a multi-billion-dollar segment of Time Warner's annual income — and what is more, it is among the fastest-growing branches of its global operations.

But nobody understands branding and merchandising better than Disney, which runs neck-and-neck with Time Warner for the honor of being the world's largest media firm. With some 660 Disney retail stores worldwide as well as merchandising and licensing deals with numerous manufacturers and retailers, Disney is evolving into what one industry observer characterizes as "the ultimate global consumer goods company."[94] Disney has moved aggressively into China; it has seven stores in Hong Kong and plans to open several more on the mainland before the century ends.[95] Disney has also carefully intertwined its media brands with its retail activities, and has done so on a global basis. There are major Disney theme parks in Japan and France as well as in the United States, a Disney passenger cruise ship line, and the company is launching DisneyQuest, a chain of "location-based entertainment" stores — that is, high-tech video arcades — centered around Disney brands.[96] Disney has even launched a planned community near its Disney World resort in Orlando, Florida, replete with Disney-run schools and social services. Disney is the master of synergies. Its animated films routinely generate vastly more income and profit from merchandising and other sources than they do from box-office receipts.

Here are some of Disney's holdings:

- the U.S. ABC television and radio networks;
- ten U.S. TV stations and twenty-eight radio stations;
- U.S. and global cable TV channels Disney Channel, ESPN, ESPN2, ESPNews, ESPN International, and major stakes in Lifetime, A&E, E! Entertainment, and History Channels;
- a stake in Americast, an interactive TV joint venture with several U.S. telephone companies;
- 43 percent of InfoSeek, an Internet portal service;
- major film studios, Miramax, Touchstone, and Walt Disney Pictures;
- TV production and distribution through Buena Vista;
- magazine publishing through its Fairchild and Chilton subsidiaries;
- book publishing holdings including Hyperion Press;
- music recording, including the Hollywood, Mammoth, and Walt Disney labels;
- world's largest theme parks and resorts, including Disneyland, Disney World, and a stake in EuroDisney;
- Club Disney, chain of children's restaurants and entertainment locations;
- Disney cruise line;
- DisneyQuest, chain of high-tech arcade game stores;
- controlling interest in Anaheim Mighty Ducks and Anaheim Angels, U.S. professional sports teams;
- 660 Disney stores worldwide;
- 50 percent stake in Super RTL, a joint venture with Bertelsmann;
- 20–33 percent stakes in the following commercial media companies: Eurosport TV

network, the Spanish Tesauro SA, the German terrestrial channel RTL2, the German cable TV channel TM3, and the Brazilian TVA, a pay-TV company;

- 33 percent stake in Patagonic Film, Argentine film studio.

Disney, like Time Warner, has globalized its production and has signed production and distribution deals with firms in France, Japan, and Latin America, to mention but a few.[97] Disney's Miramax is launching a European film studio to be based in Britain.[98] Disney also has distributed its Disney TV Channel in numerous nations around the world, customizing it to local cultures and languages. Most important, Disney's ESPN International has become the world leader in televised sports. It is broadcast on twenty networks in twenty-one languages to 155 million TV households in 182 nations outside the United States. It is even available in Antarctica.[99]

Sport is arguably the single most lucrative content area for the global media industry, a point understood best of all by Rupert Murdoch, the swashbuckling CEO of News Corp. Sport was crucial in making his British Sky Broadcasting (BSkyB) the most successful satellite TV service in the world and in making the U.S. Fox TV network a full-fledged competitor of ABC, NBC, and CBS. Murdoch, more than any other figure, has been the visionary of a global corporate media empire. Using as a base his newspaper empires, first in his native Australia where he controls 70 percent of the daily circulation, and later in Britain where he is the largest newspaper publisher, Murdoch has expanded into film, publishing, and, especially, television worldwide.[100] He has established a major film studio in Australia to serve the global market.[101] Murdoch remains the most aggressive media mogul, and he has turned to joint ventures to expand his empire without using much of his own capital. "We don't see ourselves as a large corporation," Murdoch informed a closed meeting of investors in 1997. "We see ourselves as tiny compared to the world-wide opportunities for media." Murdoch has devoted inordinate attention to developing media properties in Asia and Latin America, even though News Corp. will receive the majority of its income from the United States for at least another decade. "He views these investments in multiyear terms," states a securities analyst, "even multigenerational."[102]

Here are some of News Corp.'s holdings:

- the U.S. Fox television network;
- twenty-two U.S. television stations, covering 40 percent of the U.S. population;
- Fox News Channel, U.S. and international TV network;
- 50 percent stake in fx, fxM, Fox Sports Net, Fox Kids Worldwide, Family Channel TV channels;
- 33 percent stake in Golf TV Channel;
- film studio Twentieth Century Fox;
- Twentieth Television, U.S. and international TV production and distribution group;
- over 130 daily newspapers, including *The Times* (of London) and the *New York Post*, controlling 70 percent of Australia's newspaper circulation;
- 23 magazines;
- 40 percent stake in United Video Satellite Group, publisher of *TV Guide* and inter-active TV technology company;
- 30 percent stake in Echostar, U.S. satellite television company;
- book publishing, including Harper-Collins;
- the Los Angeles Dodgers professional baseball team;
- minority stake in the New York Knicks and the New York Rangers;
- option to purchase 40 percent stake in Los Angeles Kings NHL hockey team and 10 percent of Los Angeles Lakers NBA basketball team;

- controlling interest in British Sky Broadcasting (BSkyB) satellite TV service;
- through BSkyB, 32.5 percent stake in British Interactive Broadcasting, interactive television service;
- numerous Sky TV channels distributed across Britain and parts of Europe including Sky News;
- partial stake in Music Choice Europe TV channels;
- Latin American TV channels El Canal Fox and Fox Sport Noticias;
- 30 percent stake in Latin Sky Broadcasting satellite TV service to Latin America, joint venture with AT&T-TCI, Televisa, and Globo;
- following additional Latin American TV holdings: 20 percent stake in Cinecanal, pay-TV service; 12 percent stake in Telecine, Brazilian pay TV service;
- 66 percent stake in Munich TV station TM-3;
- 50 percent stake in German Vox TV network;
- controlling interest in Italian pay-TV venture, Stream;
- minority stake in Taurus, holding company that owns German Kirch media group (pending);
- Fox TV Channel (the Netherlands);
- the following European radio interests: 71 percent stake in Sky radio; 42 percent stake in Radio 538; 28 percent stake in Sky radio Sweden;
- 80 percent stake in New Zealand's Natural History Unit, the world's leading producer of nature and wildlife documentaries;
- Heritage Media, leading U.S. direct marketing company, with 1996 revenues over $500 million;
- partial stakes in two eastern European telecommunication companies: PLD Telekom (30.2 percent) and PeterStar (11 percent);
- Asian Star TV satellite TV service;
- pan-Asian TV channels: ESPN and Star Sports (four Asian channels), Channel V music channel (four Asian channels) joint venture with major record companies, Star World, Star Plus, Star Movies (nine Asian channels);
- 50 percent stake in Indian TV channels Zee TV, El TV, and Zee Cinema;
- partial stake in Indian cable TV company Siti Cable;
- partial stake in Indonesian pay TV venture Indovision and Film Indonesia pay TV channel;
- 11.375 percent stake, with Sony, Fuji TV, and Softbank, in Japan SkyPerfecTV Broadcasting satellite TV system;
- Star Chinese Channel, broadcast across Taiwan;
- 45 percent interest in Phoenix Chinese Channel, satellite TV service for mainland China;
- partial interest in Golden Mainland Productions, TV joint venture with Taiwan Sports Development;
- Australian TV channel FoxTel;
- controlling interest in New Zealand's Independent Newspapers Ltd., controls 52 percent of New Zealand's newspaper circulation, and owns 40 percent of New Zealand's Sky Television.
- partial interest in ChinaByte, website joint venture with China's *People's Daily*;
- India Sky Broadcasting, satellite TV service;
- 50 percent stake, Australian National Rugby League;
- British First Division soccer team, Manchester United (pending approval).

The defining feature of Murdoch's global push is the establishment of satellite television systems, along with the channels and programming to be displayed on them. By 1998 Murdoch claimed to have TV networks and systems that reached more than 75 percent of the world's population. As Murdoch contends, "The borderless world opened up to us by the digital information age will afford huge challenges and limitless opportunities."[103] The archetype will be BSkyB, which not only dominates British pay television but also has launched film and program production facilities and has channels to be broadcast not only in Britain but also on European TV systems and eventually across the world.[104] Murdoch's two other main TV "brands" are the Fox channels, connected to his U.S. TV network, cable channels, and major film and TV production studios, and his Star Television service, which News Corp. purchased in 1993, for all of Asia.

The list above barely gives a sense of how quickly Murdoch's News Corporation has made Asian television its fiefdom. In India, for example, it has equity stakes of either 50 or 100 percent in eight different networks, constituting 45 percent of the nation's total viewership in cable and satellite homes. News Corp. has six networks in China, and its Phoenix joint venture has already been cleared in 36.2 million Chinese cable TV households. In Taiwan, News Corp. has seven channels and dominates the market.[105]

In 1997, when Prince Al-Waleed invested $400 million to purchase a 5 percent stake in News Corp., he commented that "News Corp. is the only real global media company that covers the world."[106] Whether News Corp. ever fulfills its ambitions remains to be seen, and it faces numerous obstacles along the way. In India, for example, the government in 1997 cracked down on foreign ownership of media after Murdoch hired scores of former government employees to be his top local executives.[107] News Corp. has enjoyed tremendous successes and its persistence has paid off just about everywhere it has gone. But in China, Murdoch got in hot water in 1993 by remarking that new communication technologies "were a threat to totalitarian regimes everywhere."[108] And as firms like News Corp. expand through mergers and acquisitions, they run the risk of taking on large levels of debt that leaves them exposed, especially if there is a business recession.

There is no indication that Murdoch is slowing down his march across the planet. He negotiated, albeit unsuccessfully, in 1998 to purchase stakes in leading media companies in Germany, Italy, and Argentina.[109] In 1998 Murdoch established an Italian-based subsidiary, News Corp. Europe, to coordinate News Corp.'s expansion into continental television, especially in Italy, Germany, Spain, and France. As one business analyst put it, "It's D-Day and the invasion has begun."[110] Murdoch has shown a remarkable capacity to use his media properties to curry the favor of political leaders, and use that favor to advance his interests. In chapter 1 I reviewed his massive U.S. lobbying armada. It is no less impressive elsewhere. His British newspapers' surprise support for Tony Blair in the 1997 election has put him in the prime minister's very good graces, to the extent that Blair spoke on Murdoch's behalf to the Italian government when Murdoch was negotiating to buy Mediaset in 1998.[111] This conduct has not settled well with all Britons. "We have a Prime Minister," Nick Cohen observed in the *New Statesman*, "who cannot control his tongue when Rupert Murdoch's posterior passes by."[112]

All of the media giants are emulating News Corp.'s strategy of getting bigger and going global with a vengeance. In the current political environment, the global media giants are in position to make dramatic strides in short order. Thus the world is being remade before our eyes by the executives of gigantic corporations, in dogged pursuit of profit.

Global media culture

When turning to the implications of the emerging global media system for journalism, politics, entertainment, and culture, the same caveats provided for the discussion of U.S.

commercial media culture in chapter 1 apply again. Although fundamentally flawed, the system produces much of value for a variety of reasons. Commercial entertainment can be very appealing and often plays on very attractive themes. In addition, the global media system can be at times a progressive force, especially as it enters nations that had been tightly controlled by corrupt crony media systems, as in much of Latin America, or nations that had significant state censorship over media, as in parts of Asia. But, as we will see, this progressive aspect of the globalizing media market should not be blown out of proportion; the last thing the media giants want to do anywhere is rock the boat, as long as they can do their business. The global commercial media system is *radical*, in the sense that it will respect no tradition or custom, on balance, if it stands in the way of significantly increased profits. But it ultimately is politically *conservative*, because the media giants are significant beneficiaries of the current global social structure, and any upheaval in property or social relations, particularly to the extent it reduced the power of business and lessened inequality, would possibly — no, probably — jeopardize their positions. Indeed, in this regard, the logic and trajectory of global media culture is quite similar to that of the U.S. product.

It may be a bit misleading to call the emerging system "global." As India proved with News Corporation, nations can erect huge barriers against the intrusion of transnational media corporations, whether for political, cultural, or economic reasons. As mentioned at the outset of this chapter, there is widespread concern that regulations and subsidies are necessary to protect local content.[113] Therefore, to make sense of any particular national media scene, one must take into account local laws and regulations, as well as the contours of the domestic commercial media industry. Nevertheless, the momentum is clearly in the opposite direction. Even China has put its media on a largely commercial basis, and is in the process of opening its doors to media TNCs in a manner unthinkable only two or three years ago.[114] In addition, the global commercial media system is far more developed in some parts of the world than in others. As a profit-driven enterprise, it devotes most of its attention to the wealthier sectors. In the so-called developing world, the system is accordingly oriented toward middle- and upper-class consumers. In India, this relevant market contains perhaps at the outside 300 or 400 million people — a large number, to be sure, but not overwhelming in a nation of almost one billion. Not surprisingly, an area like sub-Saharan Africa receives minimal global media attention in comparison to almost anywhere else in the world. Nor does this mean sub-Saharan nations (or the poor of India) enjoy a wealth of indigenous media, for these poorest populations have scarcely any public funds to develop media.

Presented in this manner, the logical question traditionally has been: Does the global media system represent the highest form of "cultural imperialism"? Or to put it another way: Are the largely U.S.-owned and/or U.S.-based media giants inculcating the world's peoples with western consumer values and undermining traditional cultures and values?[115] (One thinks of Disney CEO Michael Eisner's delight when someone presented him with a photograph of a woman from Timbuktu wearing a cap for Disney's Anaheim Mighty Ducks hockey team. "Now that's the definition of global reach!" Eisner enthused.)[116] The answers to these questions are yes and sort of. One of the problems with the way the issue often has been framed is that it regards culture in a static manner and assumes that corporate commercial culture equals "American" culture. As the *Economist* put it, "people who see America as a cauldron of self-obsessed, TV-centred, have-it-all sensation" fail to understand "that the country still contains deeper hungers and a respect for cultural attitudes which address them."[117] "There is nothing particularly American," the *Economist* noted in reference to the themes of Hollywood blockbuster films, "about boats crashing into icebergs or asteroids that threaten to obliterate human life."[118] The flip side of this reductionism toward U.S. culture is to regard non-U.S. cultures as pristine.

In addition, viewing the global media system in terms of national geopolitical domination may have made some sense in the 1960s and 1970s, but it is no longer an especially satisfactory construct. It is true that the U.S. government remains the steadfast advocate of the transnational media corporations worldwide. Media and computer software — the "copyright" industries — are the leading exports of the United States, to the tune of $60 billion in 1997.[119] This figure has doubled during the course of the 1990s.[120] The U.S. government therefore harasses and threatens with sanctions nations that do not respect media firms' copyrights.[121] It also uses its diplomatic leverage to get barriers to media imports reduced. President Clinton, for example, during his June 1998 China trip, pressured the Chinese government to increase its quota for U.S. films from 10 to 20 within two years.[122] In 1998, the U.S. government led the fight in the negotiations among the largest economic powers over the new multilateral agreement on investment — a bill of rights for global investors to protect them from national government regulations — to see that the MAI included all media, communication, and "cultural" activities within its province.[123] In that same year the U.S. government pressured the WTO to declare the Internet a "duty-free area," so as to encourage its commercial development.[124] In addition, the U.S. government has further relaxed its anemic antitrust standards for media mergers and acquisitions, thus permitting them to become "stronger worldwide player[s]."[125] The U.S. government even subsidizes a program to train bureaucrats and business persons around the world in how to construct commercial broadcasting systems.[126]

It is also true that the expansion of media TNCs generally greases the wheels for global markets in general — which has long been a general aim of the U.S. and other western governments. It is notable that in 1998 a leading member of the U.S. business community argued that the United States should relax its efforts to establish a global commercial media market and accept that nations might have legitimate concerns about "cultural imperialism." Such a tack, he argued, would undercut the movements against global free trade and "even bolster America's ability to export its ideas and ideals for the long haul."[127] But regardless of what the U.S. government does, U.S. firms have always enjoyed a tremendous advantage in the global media market because their huge domestic market gives them economies of scale such that their media exports can be sold at rates well below cost of production for a smaller nation. They also have the advantage of the principal international language, English. It is telling that in 1998 several leading French film directors began working in English, as that was understood as the only way "to reach a wider international audience."[128] U.S. firms can also take advantage of their historic ability to define the terms of commercial entertainment.[129] Naturally there is a strong taste for U.S. commercial entertainment around the world: in the global marketplace, the U.S. is the 500-pound gorilla.[130]

But the impetus behind the global media system is far more corporate and commercial expansion than national geopolitics, and, as the system evolves, the material basis for providing "American" entertainment lessens. On the one hand, the "geopolitical" element of the global communication system prior to the 1990s was connected to some extent to the ideological aspect of the cold war, which is no longer a pressing concern. On the other hand, the system is moving away from direct attachment to a particular nation-state. The British film industry enjoyed a boom of sorts in the late 1990s, but did so through a series of deals with the major Hollywood studios that provided both financing and the global distribution networks necessary for success.[131] When Time Warner, for example, is earning over half its income outside the United States, when its shareholders come from all over the world, and when its production is globalized, it will still have important ties to the United States and the U.S. government; but those ties will be weakened. It will be bad business for a U.S.-based media giant to be nationalistic. "Today, the media's responsibility for helping us see the world in all its complexity is greater than ever," Time Warner CEO Gerald Levin stated in

1998. "Yet too often we are left with a superficial impression of a global village that resembles an American suburb, in which the values and viewpoints fit into familiar categories."[132] Moreover, the always dubious notion that the product of the corporate media firms represents the essence of U.S. culture appears ever less plausible as the media system is increasingly concentrated, commercialized, and globalized.

The global media system is better understood, then, as one that advances corporate and commercial interests and values, and denigrates or ignores that which cannot be incorporated into its mission. Four of the eight largest media firms are headquartered outside of the United States, but all of them — Bertelsmann, News Corp., Sony, and Seagram — are major U.S. players, indeed owning three of the major Hollywood film studios. They rank among the seventy largest foreign firms operating in the United States, based on their U.S. sales, and all but Bertelsmann rank in the top thirty.[133] There is no discernible difference in the firms' content, whether they are owned by shareholders in Japan or Belgium or have corporate headquarters in New York or Sydney. Bertelsmann CEO Thomas Middelhoff bristled when, in 1998, some said it was improper for a German firm to control 15 percent of the U.S. book publishing market. "We're not foreign. We're international," Middelhoff said. "I'm an American with a German passport."[134] Bertelsmann already generates more income from the United States than from any other nation;[135] Middelhoff's immediate goal is to boost the U.S. percentage of Bertelsmann's revenues from 31 to 40 percent.[136] "The soul of the whole entertainment business is in the U.S.," stated Bertelsmann's second-ranking executive.[137] Indeed the output of the global media giants is largely interchangeable, as they constantly ape each other's commercial triumphs.

In this light, the notion that the transnational media conglomerates ultimately will fail because people tend to prefer their local media and cultures appears wide of the mark. For one thing, the evidence is mixed, and people's tastes are malleable. There is significant indication that Hollywood-type fare is popular worldwide, and that the taste for it is growing with increased exposure. In France, arguably Europe's most culturally nationalistic nation, U.S. films account for 60 percent of box-office revenues. In Britain, U.S. films account for 95 percent of the box-office revenue.[138] In April 1998, for example, U.S. films dominated the lists of top ten box-office movies for most European nations: in France, seven of ten; in Britain, nine of ten; in Spain, ten of ten; in Italy, nine of ten; and in Germany, nine of ten. In 1996 the United States claimed 70 percent of the EU film market, up from 56 percent in 1987. Growth was comparable in Japan.[139] Indeed the trade deficit between the EU nations and the United States in films, television programs, and videos has grown steadily in the 1990s, and stood at nearly $6 billion in 1996.[140] The German market, by far Europe's largest, provides a further indicator of Hollywood dominance. Of its fifty top grossing films in 1997, forty-two were made by first-tier global media giants.[141] Nine of Germany's ten leading video rentals and nine of its top ten best-selling videos in 1997 were also produced by the Hollywood giants.[142]

Moreover, as the global media system spreads its tentacles and deepens its reach, there is reason to believe this will then shape popular tastes toward that with which they are becoming more familiar. Variety editor Peter Bart concluded in 1998, based upon his conversations with Hollywood executives, that "there's also growing evidence that the world filmgoing audience is fast becoming more homogeneous." Whereas "action" movies had once been the only sure-fire global fare — and comedies had been considerably more difficult to export — by the late 1990s comedies like My Best Friend's Wedding and The Full Monty were doing between $160 and 200 million in non-U.S. box office.[143] A 1998 survey of thirty-five thousand consumers in thirty-five countries, conducted by the venerable Roper Starch Worldwide research group, provided "additional evidence that consumers around the world are more similar than different." As Martha Farnsworth Riche, former director of the U.S.

Census Bureau who consulted on the study, put it, certain factors once deemed crucial to understanding consumer behavior, particularly overseas, had become less important. "People aren't all that different. Their tastes are very similar," Riche stated. "When selling Whirlpools in Korea," for example, "you've got to make sure that you don't use the taboo color, but the cultural stuff is just a wrinkle."[144]

At the same time, there is countervailing evidence. Although U.S. films dominate the European market, the box office revenues of European films in Europe are beginning to rebound, especially with the rise of the multiplex theater. In music, non-U.S. fare has been the most rapidly growing element of the global market.[145] The CEO of a Spanish media firm only stated what is virtually received wisdom across the media industries: "The most successful content in most countries is local content."[146]

But this is hardly a contradiction. To the extent that most audiences prefer locally made fare if it is of adequate quality, the global media giants, rather than flee in despair, have globalized their production.[147] This globalization of production is spurred by economic and political factors, such as the desire to establish stronger relationships with domestic broadcasters who may be required to air locally produced content.[148] When U.S. magazine publishers expand overseas they cheerfully adjust the content and language to appeal to Germans, Japanese, or Russians.[149] As the discussion above of the "holy trinity" suggests, all of the media TNCs are establishing production on a global basis.[150] Universal Pictures, for example, spent much of 1997 "busily forging international acquisition and co-production deals with a raft of filmmakers in Europe, Latin America and Asia." As *Variety* notes, "there's moolah to be made from foreign films."[151] Time Warner has found that it can enhance the appeal of its Warner Bros. films in Asia by having local musicians do a song in the native language for the film's promotional campaigns in each nation.[152] Indeed, the media TNCs' global television channels all emphasize a mixture of English-language material with a heavy dose of local languages and programming as well as programming dubbed in local languages. Time Warner's Cartoon Network is dubbed in numerous languages, including those of smaller nations like Sweden and Denmark.[153]

Animation is, in fact, ideal for dubbing; hence the children's television and entertainment market is more easily dominated by the media TNCs.[154] Viacom's Nickelodeon has a commanding presence in Latin America and parts of Europe, and launched a major expansion into Asia in 1998.[155] "For all children, the Disney characters are local characters and this is very important. They always speak local languages," a Disney executive stated. The Disney strategy, he added, is to "think global, act local."[156] This principle applies beyond animation, however, to the entire global media system: "The right mix for Western media," Rupert Murdoch informed a United Nations conference on television in the autumn of 1997, "is taking the best international programming and mixing it with local content. Localization is playing an increasingly crucial role."[157] In the case of Latin America, then, its TV media capital has become Miami, where English- and Spanish-language fare easily co-exist.[158]

The traditional notion of media or cultural imperialism also tended to regard the existing non-TNC domestic commercial media as some sort of oppositional or alternative force to the global market. That was probably a dubious notion in the past, and it does not hold true at all today. Throughout the world, media consolidation and concentration have taken place in national markets, leaving a handful of extremely powerful media conglomerates dominating regional and national markets. These firms have found a lucrative niche teaming up with the global media giants in joint ventures, offering the "local" aspect of the content, and handling the local politicians. As the head of Norway's largest media firm put it, "We want to position ourselves so if Kirch or Murdoch want to sell in Scandinavia, they'll come to us first."[159]

The notion of non-U.S. or non-TNC media firms being "oppositional" to the global system is no less far-fetched when one turns to the "Third World." Mexico's Televisa, Brazil's Globo, Argentina's Clarin, and the Cisneros group of Venezuela, for example, rank among the sixty or seventy largest media firms in the world.[160] They have extensive ties and joint ventures with the largest media TNCs, as well as with Wall Street investment banks.[161] These firms tend to dominate their own national and regional media markets, which are experiencing rapid consolidation in their own right.[162] The commercial media powerhouses of the developing world tend, therefore, to be primary advocates for — and beneficiaries of — the expansion of the global commercial media market.[163] And these Third World media giants, like other second-tier media firms elsewhere, are also establishing global operations, especially to nations that speak the same languages.[164] And within each of their home nations these media firms have distinct probusiness political agendas that put them at odds with large segments of the population.[165] In short, the global system is best perceived as one that best represents the needs of investors, advertisers, and the affluent consumers of the world. In wealthy nations this tends to be a substantial portion of the population; in developing nations, a distinct minority.

All of these trends converge in the global music industry. Music has always been the least capital-intensive of the electronic media and therefore the most open to experimentation and new ideas. U.S. recording artists generated 60 percent of their sales outside of the United States in 1993; by 1998 that figure was down to 40 percent.[166] Rather than fold their tents, however, the five media TNCs that dominate the world's recorded music market are busy establishing local subsidiaries across the world, in places like Brazil where "people are totally committed to local music."[167] Sony, for example, has led the way in establishing distribution deals with independent music companies from around the world.[168] In places like India and Japan, there has been a huge expansion of interest in traditional western pop music, combined with a maintenance of domestic musical traditions and the rise of local pop traditions that merge elements of each.[169]

This development of new and exciting forms and genres of popular music underscores the point that commercial culture is a complex process that does not always lend itself to categorical analysis. In one sense these developments demonstrate just how flexible capitalism and commercialism can be in allowing new trends and even "countercultural" patterns in the pursuit of profit.[170] But this point should not be exaggerated. Commercial imperatives put distinct (and often quite negative) limits on the nature and range of what music gets produced, as the long U.S. experience with the corporate music industry reveals.[171] (I discuss this point in chapter 1.) And to the extent that Viacom's global MTV Networks, which reach 300 million homes or one-quarter of the world's TV households, influence music, commercialism is clearly in the driver's seat.[172] As one trade publication noted approvingly, MTV provides a "seamless blend of hip music and sponsors' messages."[173]

The corporate media culture is hardly the result of some abstract value-free media market that "gives the people what they want." Highly concentrated, it gives the dominant corporations market power to give their shareholders what they can make the most profit from. That means linking media fare to all sorts of products and merchandising, as described in the discussion of the "holy trinity" above. As one observer noted, Hollywood films now have so many promotional tie-ins and deals that their competition "extends from theaters to fast-food chains to grocery aisles."[174] Disney and McDonald's have a ten-year exclusive agreement to promote each other's products in 109 nations, a relationship so detailed that the *Wall Street Journal* termed the two firms "McDisney."[175] Music labels, for example, increasingly link musical genres to clothing fashions that can also be exploited. The rise of "hip-hop" clothing in the middle 1990s has increased music industry revenues by as much as 20 percent.[176] On the other hand, and most important, the media firms devote their activities to providing advertisers with the audiences and content they want. Hence, aside from sports with its "killer" demographics of middle- and upper-class males aged eighteen to forty-nine, the other main focus of the global media system is children's television programming and its product-conscious audience.[177]

The hallmark of the global media system is its relentless, ubiquitous commercialism. At the most explicit, TV shopping channels are one of the primary growth areas around the world.[178] Similarly, "infomercials" are positively booming on global commercial television systems. Mike Levey, the U.S. "king of the infomercial," sells goods in sixty countries and in fourteen languages. Virtually unknown in his own land, Levey has become a television superstar, the "heartthrob to the world."[179] Advertising not only dominates media, it is beginning to be used on telephone and paging systems.[180] In this commercially saturated environment, audiences barely raised their eyebrows when former Soviet premier Mikhail Gorbachev did a TV commercial for Pizza Hut in 1997.[181] In Japan, where the commercial competition to influence the teen market is intense, agencies now exist that will hire teenagers to undertake surreptitious "word-of-mouth" advertising for their corporate clients to create an artificial "buzz" about them.[182] Although media scholars can study and debate the exact nature of media effects upon people, it should be no surprise that account after account in the late 1990s documents the fascination, even the obsession, of the world's middle-class youth with consumer brands and products.[183]

Being a global market also influences the nature of film content, since the U.S. market only accounts for about 40–45 percent of Hollywood studio revenues. This may be the one area where Americans can sense how a global media market changes things; otherwise, the rest of the world is getting a taste of what has been the U.S. situation for generations.[184] Of course, globalization has some positive attributes; for example, it makes films less likely to portray Arabs or Asians in a racist manner that would undercut crucial markets. (Sometimes this effort to avoid giving offense reaches almost comic dimensions. For example, the world hockey championships in *D2*, the Disney *Mighty Ducks* sequel, depicted the thuggish "bad guys" as being from *Iceland* — a nation with probably fewer movie theaters than most U.S. suburban shopping malls!) Hollywood films are also more likely to employ international casts so as to have global box office appeal.[185] But globalization has also meant that violent films (and TV shows) receive massive attention, "while comedy and drama languish."[186] As has been well documented, violent "action" fare is the genre that crosses borders most easily and makes the most commercial sense. The result is, when filmgoers are exposed to more and more "action" films and begin to develop a taste for them, the studios piously claim they are "giving the people what they want." Violent fare also has a certain de-evolutionary logic to it. Over time, films and TV programs need to become ever more grisly to attract attention.[187] Even animal documentaries have found a worldwide niche because they feature numerous "kill sequences" and blood fights among the animals.[188]

Global media and neoliberal democracy

With this hypercommercialism and corporate control comes an implicit political bias regarding the content of the media system. Consumerism, the market, class inequality, and individualism tend to be taken as natural and often benevolent, whereas political activity, civic values, and antimarket activities tend to be marginalized or denounced. This does not portend mind-control or "Big Brother," for it is much more subtle than that. (For example, Hollywood films and television programs may not present socialism in a favorable light, and will rarely criticize capitalism as an economic system overall, but they frequently use particular businesses or business persons to serve as the "bad guys." Since businesses of one kind or another rank high on many peoples' lists of disreputable operators, to avoid using them as "bad guys" in entertainment would leave the studio to resort to science fiction.)[189] Indeed, the genius of the commercial media system is the general lack of overt censorship. As George Orwell noted in his unpublished introduction to *Animal Farm*, censorship in free societies is infinitely more sophisticated and thorough than in dictatorships because "unpopular ideas can be silenced, and inconvenient facts kept dark, without any need for an official ban."[190] The logical consequence of a commercial media system is less to instill adherence to any ruling powers that be — though that can and does of course happen — than to promote a general belief that politics is unimportant and that there is little hope for organized social change.

As such, the global media system buttresses what could be termed "neoliberal" democracy, that is, the largely vacuous political culture that exists in the formally democratic market-driven nations of the world. As I mentioned in the introduction, neoliberalism operates not only as an economic system but as a political and cultural system as well. Neoliberalism works best when there is formal electoral democracy, but when the population is diverted from the information, access, and public forums necessary for meaningful participation in decision making. As neoliberal theorist Milton Friedman put it in his seminal *Capitalism and Freedom*, because profit making is the essence of democracy, any government that pursues antimarket policies is being antidemocratic, no matter how much informed popular support they might enjoy. Therefore it is best to restrict governments to the job of protecting private property and enforcing contracts, and to limit political debate to minor issues. The real matters of resource production and distribution and social organization should be determined by market forces.[191]

Equipped with this peculiar understanding of democracy, neoliberals like Friedman had no qualms over the military overthrow of Chile's democratically elected Allende government in 1973, because Allende was interfering with business control of Chilean society. After fifteen years of often brutal and savage dictatorship — all in the name of the free market — formal democracy was restored in 1989 with a constitution that made it vastly more difficult, if not impossible, for the citizenry to challenge the business-military domination of Chilean society. That is neoliberal democracy in a nutshell: trivial debate over minor issues by parties that basically pursue the same probusiness policies regardless of formal differences and campaign debate. Democracy is permissible as long as the control of business is off-limits to popular deliberation or change; that is, so long as it isn't democracy.

Neoliberal democracy therefore has an important and necessary by-product — a depoliticized citizenry marked by apathy and cynicism. If electoral democracy affects little of social life, it is irrational to devote much attention to it. The United States provides the preeminent model of "neoliberal" democracy and shows the way for combining a capitalist economy with a largely toothless democratic polity. Sometimes these points are made explicit. Jaime Guzmán, principal author of Chile's 1980 constitution, believed that private property and investors' rights needed to be off-limits to popular debate or consideration, and he crafted Chile's "democracy" accordingly. Consider Guzmán's thoughts. "A democracy can only be stable when in popular elections . . . the essential form of life of a people is not at play, is not at risk," Guzmán explained. "In the great democracies of the world, the high levels of electoral abstention do not indicate, as many erroneously interpret them, a supposed distancing of the people from the reigning system." Noninvolvement by the bulk of the population is in fact a healthy development. Guzmán concludes that in the best form of capitalist democracy, "if one's adversaries come to power, they are constrained to pursue a course of action not very different than that which one would desire because the set of alternatives that the playing field imposes on those who play on it are sufficiently reduced to render anything else extremely difficult."[192]

Chile is held up as the greatest neoliberal success story in Latin America, perhaps even the world. As the *New York Times* put it, Pinochet's coup "began Chile's transformation from a backwater banana republic to the economic star of Latin America." And while there has been strong overall economic growth over the past decade, Chile has also seen a widening of economic inequality such that it ranks seventh worst in a World Bank study of economic stratification in sixty-five nations. But what is the caliber of political and social life in this neoliberal miracle? Prior to the 1973 coup, Chile was legendary for the intense politicization of its population, reflected by voter turnouts as high as 95 percent of the adult population. One U.S. researcher found in 1970 that Chilean teenagers were among the three least alienated, most optimistic groups of youth on earth. In the 1990s Chile is a very different nation. As one observer puts it, "Chile is perhaps the one place on earth where idolatry of the market has most deeply penetrated." In the most recent elections 41 percent of the population either did not vote, defaced their ballots, or left them blank. Voter participation among Chileans under twenty-five was considerably lower. By the canons of neoliberalism, then, Chile is a success both economically and politically.[193] Chile has seen its political life reduced to a placid, tangential spectator sport.

This hollowing out of democracy is a worldwide phenomenon in the age of the uncontested market. As a Greek peasant put it following Greece's 1996 elections: "The only right we have is the right to vote and it leads us nowhere." The very term democracy has been turned on its head so its very absence in substance is now seen as what constitutes its defining essence. The *Washington Post* noted that modern democracy works best when the political "parties essentially agree on most of the major issues."[194] Or, more bluntly, as the *Financial Times* put it, capitalist democracy can best succeed to the extent that is about "the process of depoliticising the economy."[195] (Is it even necessary to note that in a genuine democracy, the matter of who controls the economy and for what purposes would be at the *center* of political debate and consideration?)

Let me be clear about my argument. I am not stating that the global media or commercial media are solely or even primarily responsible for the type of depoliticized and demoralized political environment that exists in the United States or that has developed in Chile. My argument is that this depoliticization responds most directly to the rise of the market and commercial values to preeminence in those societies. But I am obviously generalizing; in any given nation any number of other important factors are going to influence the nature and trajectory of its political culture, and that is true for both the United States and Chile as well. That being said, however, the global commercial media system is integrally related to neoliberal democracy with its attendant depoliticization at two levels. At the broadest institutional level, the rise of a global commercial media system has been the result of and necessary for the rise of a global market for goods and services dominated by a few hundred TNCs. Both the global commercial media system and the growth and emergence of this "global" economy are predicated upon probusiness neoliberal deregulation worldwide. On the other hand, the marketing networks offered by global media system are essential for the creation of global and regional markets for TNC goods and services. To the extent, therefore, that the neoliberal global economic order thrives upon a weak political culture, the global media system is a central beneficiary as well.

But the global media system plays a much more explicit role in generating a passive, depoliticized populace that prefers personal consumption to social understanding and activity, a mass more likely to take orders than to make waves. Lacking any necessarily "conspiratorial" intent, and merely following rational market calculations, the media system simply exists to provide light escapist entertainment. In the developing world, where public relations and marketing hyperbole are only beginning to realize their awesome potential, and where the ruling elites are well aware of the need to keep the rabble in line, the importance of commercial media is sometimes stated quite candidly. In the words of the late Emilio

Azcarraga, the billionaire head of Mexico's Televisa: "Mexico is a country of a modest, very fucked class, which will never stop being fucked. Television has the obligation to bring diversion to these people and remove them from their sad reality and difficult future."[196]

The global journalism of the corporate media system reinforces these trends, with devastating implications for the functioning of political democracies. Here the trends mirror the collapse of U.S. journalism discussed in chapter 1. Again, I do not wish to exaggerate the decline of journalism to the extent that I imply the existence of some previous glorious golden age that most certainly did not exist. Privately owned press systems historically have been conservative forces, and for logical reasons: they tended to reflect the values of their owners. That bias remains: in 1998 Sweden's three largest newspapers, all Swedish-owned, take explicit "free market" editorial positions, despite the fact that Sweden continues to have significant support for prolabor, welfare state, and socialist politics.[197]

But as in the United States, journalism worldwide is deteriorating, as it has become an important profit source for the media giants.[198] Because investigative journalism or coverage of foreign affairs makes little economic sense, it is discouraged as being too expensive.[199] On the one hand, there is a relatively sophisticated business news pitched at the upper and upper-middle classes and shaped to their needs and prejudices. CNN International, for example, presents itself as providing advertisers "unrivalled access to reach high-income consumers."[200] But even in "elite" media there is a decline. The *Economist* noted that in 1898 the first page of a sample copy of the *Times* of London contained nineteen columns of foreign news, eight columns of domestic news, and three columns on salmon fishing. In 1998 a sample copy of the *Times*, now owned by Rupert Murdoch, had one international story on its front page: an account of actor Leonardo DiCaprio's new girlfriend. "In this information age," the *Economist* concluded, "the newspapers which used to be full of politics and economics are thick with stars and sport."[201] On the other hand, there is an appalling schlock journalism for the masses, based upon lurid tabloid-type stories. For the occasional "serious" story, there is the mindless regurgitation of press releases from one source or another, with the range of debate mostly limited to what is being debated among the elite. "Bad journalism," a British observer concluded in 1998, "is a consequence of an unregulated market in which would-be monopolists are free to treat the channels of democratic debate as their private property.[202]

As with entertainment, at times the media giants generate first-rate journalism, but it is a minuscule fraction of their output and often causes just the sort of uproar that media firms prefer to avoid. It is also true that some well-organized social movements and dissident political views can get coverage in the world of commercial journalism, but the playing field is far from level. And, as John Keane noted, "in times of crisis" — meaning when antibusiness social movements gain *too much* political strength — "market censorship tends to become overt."[203]

Just how bogus this commercial journalism is, when measured by any traditional notion of the communication requirements necessary for a democracy, becomes especially clear when one looks at China. There, a full-scale dictatorship with a long tradition of suppressing dissident or prodemocratic political viewpoints has no particular problem with business news or tabloid journalism, the two main products of the so-called "free press."[204] The Chinese government media has lost most of its subsidy, and has turned to advertising as the primary means of support, with all that that suggests about content. So far the marriage of commercial media and communism has been considerably less rocky than most analysts had anticipated.[205] Indeed, it appears increasingly that the Chinese government can co-exist with the corporate media giants quite comfortably. Chinese president Jiang Zemin went so far as to praise the 1997 U.S. film *Titanic* in a speech before the National Peoples Congress. "Let us not assume we can't learn from capitalism."[206]

The relationship of the media giants to China is highly instructive about their commitment to democracy as well. In 1997, when Disney had the temerity to produce *Kundun*, a film biography of the Dalai Lama, Disney's numerous media projects in China were "frozen" by the Chinese government.[207] Disney responded by working with the Chinese government to show them how to use public relations to ride out the controversy. Disney even hired super-lobbyist Henry Kissinger to go to China and "to keep China open to the Walt Disney Company."[208] The advertising that Disney was contractually obligated to provide for *Kundun* virtually eliminated any reference to Disney.[209] In the summer of 1998, Disney appointed a special executive, John J. Feenie, to coordinate its Chinese activities. Feenie observed that Disney had made "great strides toward smoothing things over with the Chinese" and it hoped to distribute more films and even build a theme park in China. Disney CEO Michael Eisner "is very serious about wanting meaningful progress in that market," Feenie stated.[210] Eisner finally made a visit to Beijing to meet the head of state in December 1998, and indications were that Disney would soon be able to resume its Chinese operations.[211] The message is clear: Disney, and any other firm that is attempting to maximize profit, will never again produce a film like *Kundun* concerning China. Nor will such a firm countenance the caliber of journalism that could significantly undermine the firm's capacity to maximize profit.

Far more striking have been the activities of Rupert Murdoch and News Corporation in China. Since Rupert Murdoch fell into the Chinese leadership's bad graces by suggesting in 1993 they would not survive the rise of satellite communication, he has bent over backwards to appease them. In 1995 he eliminated the BBC from his Star Television bouquet because the Chinese leaders thought the BBC too critical of their activities. Then, in 1996, he launched an Internet joint venture with the Chinese *People's Daily* newspaper. He also published what one critic termed a "fawning biography" of Chinese leader Deng Xiaoping, written by no less an authority than Deng Xiaoping's youngest daughter.[212] Then in 1998 Murdoch's HarperCollins canceled its contract to publish former Hong Kong governor Chris Patten's book, which was expected to be highly critical of the Chinese government. Murdoch personally ordered the cancellation — leading the HarperCollins editor to resign in protest — describing the Patten book as "boring" and beneath his standards. (Those standards had apparently been determined after the publication of the Deng Xiaoping biography.) After an extraordinary public brouhaha, Murdoch and News Corporation apologized for the cancellation and reached a settlement with Patten, but his book would be published by another press.[213] (It may be worth noting that this incident was ignored in the newspapers and news media owned by News Corporation.)[214] Following this episode, Murdoch was appointed to be one of fourteen "captains of industry" who would advise the new Hong Kong government on how to lure international investment.[215]

But Murdoch hardly will be deterred by a little bad publicity. Mandarin-language Phoenix Television, in which News Corp. has a 45 percent stake, signed major deals to gain clearance on Chinese cable television systems in 1997 and 1998, with the tacit approval of the Chinese leadership.[216] And industry observers claim Phoenix "has made significant progress in capturing advertising."[217] As the *Financial Times* put it, Phoenix "enjoys rare access into China, which has been denied to other foreign broadcasters."[218] In May 1998 Murdoch won another major victory when his Chinese partners in Phoenix Television won effective control of Hong Kong's second (of two) terrestrial broadcast stations.[219] Some sense of Phoenix's "journalism" came when a Phoenix reporter prefaced a question to Chinese premier Zhu Rongji with the words: "You are my idol."[220] In December 1998, Murdoch had a well-publicized visit with Jiang Zemin, worthy of a head of state. As a result, observers noted that Murdoch's fortunes were "rising fast in the East."[221] In stunning contrast, at the exact moment Murdoch was breaking bread with the Chinese leadership, three of China's foremost prodemocratic activists — who advocated free elections, new political parties, free speech, and independent trade unions — were given long prison sentences in the toughest crackdown on political dissidents since 1989.[222]

Compare this corporate behavior with that of Baruch Ivcher, the Peruvian whose TV station's numerous exposés of the Fujimori government's corruption and criminal activity led to the seizure of his station and caused him to flee Peru.[223] Or compare Murdoch and Eisner to Jesús Blancornelas, the Mexican newspaper editor who has faced assassination attempts for refusing to back down on his investigation into that nation's drug trade and its links to the highest echelons of Mexican society.[224] Or compare Murdoch and Eisner to Larisa Yudina, the Russian editor savagely murdered in a contract killing, whose crime was reporting the corruption of her local government.[225] Across the world there are numerous examples of heroic journalists, risking life and limb to tell the truth about the powers that be. The Brussels-based International Federation of Journalists reports forty-one journalists murdered worldwide in the line of duty in 1997, and 474 since 1988.[226] The U.S.-based Committee to Protect Journalists reported twenty-six journalists murdered worldwide in 1997, with another 129 cases of journalists wrongly imprisoned for going about their work.[227] But only in rare instances are these murdered and imprisoned journalists in the direct employ of the media giants.[228] One might posit that thugs and tyrannical governments are afraid to mess with reporters from powerful media corporations, so they concentrate on hassling the small fry. But if that was the case, why don't the types of stories that these martyrs were investigating get sustained attention in the corporate giants' media? The truth is that Baruch Ivcher, Jesús Blancornelas, Larisa Yudina, and their ilk may be courageous journalists valiantly advancing the public interest, but they lack what it takes to become successful in the brave (new) world of commercial journalism.[229]

It was ironic, indeed, when the World Bank in 1998 attributed the economic crisis in Asia to the lack of a "freer, more aggressive and more critical news media in the region" that would "put a brake on government corruption and so-called crony capitalism." The bank's own policies had been instrumental in assuring that no such media and no such journalism could possibly exist.[230]

Conclusion

As with the United States, it does not have to be this way. The "wild card" in the global media deck are the people of the world — people constituted as organized citizens rather than as passive consumers and couch potatoes. It may seem difficult, especially from the vantage point of the United States and other wealthy nations, to see much hope for public opposition to the global corporate media system. As one Swedish journalist noted in 1997, "Unfortunately, the trends are very clear, moving in the wrong direction on virtually every score, and there is a desperate lack of public discussion of the long-term implications of current developments for democracy and accountability."[231] And, as discussed above, this political pessimism is precisely the type of political culture necessary for a neoliberal economic order to remain stable.

But there are indications that progressive political forces in nations around the world are increasingly making media issues part of their political platforms. (I discuss some of these activities in the conclusion.) As the global media system is increasingly intertwined with global capitalism, their fates go hand in hand. And despite much blathering about the "end of history" and the triumph of the market in the commercial media and among western intellectuals, the actual track record is quite dubious. Asia, the long celebrated tiger of twenty-first-century capitalism, is now mired in an economic depression. Latin America, the other vaunted champion of market reforms since the 1980s, has seen what a World Bank official terms a "big increase in inequality."[232] The ecologies of both regions are little short of disastrous. "The international economy, outside of the United States and Europe — perhaps 50% of the world," one economist noted in 1998, "is already experiencing a downturn that is worse than any that has occurred since the 1930s."[233] If this generates anything remotely like the political responses that emerged in the 1930s, all bets will be off concerning the triumph of neoliberalism and the global media market.

Notes

1   Emma Duncan, "Wheel of Fortune," *Economist*, Nov. 21, 1998, "Technology and Entertainment Survey," p. 4.
2   Michael J. Mandel, "The New Business Cycle," *Business Week*, March 31 1997, pp. 58–68.
3   Brushan Bahree, "U.S. Will Ask WTO to Keep Internet Free," *Wall Street Journal*, Feb. 19, 1998, p. B20.
4   Martin Peers, "Movie Biz Enjoys Global Warming," *Variety*, Apr. 7–13, 1997, pp. 1, 32.
5   Henry-Goldblatt, "The Universal Appeal of Schlock," *Fortune*, May 12, 1997, p. 32.
6   Alice Rawsthorn, "Film Industry Focuses on Distribution Scene," *Financial Times*, Oct. 4–5, 1997, p. 5.
7   Alice Rawsthorn, "Put to the Screen Test," *Financial Times*, Aug. 30–31, 1997, p. 7; Adam Dawtrey, "Polygram Sets Sail for American Market," *Variety*, Dec. 15–21, 1997, pp. 11, 40.
8   Adam Sandler, "BMG's Potent Portfolio Boosts Market Share," *Variety*, Dec. 15–21, 1997, pp. 38, 78.
9   Adam Sandler, "Seagram Making a Music Monolith," *Variety*, May 25–31, 1998, p. 10.
10   Alice Rawsthorn, "Film Rights Revenue Set for Growth," *Financial Times*, Apr. 30, 1998, p. 5.
11   Michael Williams, "NBC Europe Enters Spain, Eyes France," *Variety*, Sept. 8–14, 1997, p. 33.
12   Robert Frank and Matthew Rose, "A Massive Investment in British Cable TV Sours for U.S. Firms," *Wall Street Journal*, Dec. 17, 1997, p. A1.
13   Gail DeGeorge and Elisabeth Malkin, "Satellite TV: Still a Fuzzy Picture," *Business Week*, Dec. 29, 1997, p. 50E4; Louise McElvogue, "Digging for Gold in Latin America," *Television Business International*, Sept. 1997, p. 92.
14   Miriam Hils, "Tube Time on the Rise in Europe," *Variety*, Jan. 5–11, 1998, pp. 41, 48.
15   Marie-Agnes Bruneau, "Report Reveals French Kids Spend More Time Watching Television," *European Television Analyst*, Apr. 23, 1998, p. 14.
16   See Ted Magder, "Franchising the Candy Store: Split-run Magazines and a New International Regime for Trade in Culture," *Canadian-American Public Policy*, no. 34 (Apr. 1998), esp. pp. 15–22, 35–51.
17   John Urquhart and Brushan Bahree, "WTO Body Orders Canada to Change Magazine Role," *Wall Street Journal*, July 1, 1997, p. B8; Joseph Weber, "Does Canadian Culture Need This Much Protection?" *Business Week*, June 8, 1998, p. 37.
18   Liz Fell, "Trade Treaty Override Quotas," *Television Business International*, June 1998, p. 14.
19   Mary Sutter, "At Last, Mexican Film Industry Finds Coin," *Variety*, Mar. 23–29, 1998, p. 50; Hanna Lee, "Samsung Ups Local Pic Coin," *Variety*, May 4–10, 1998, p. 27; Mary Sutter, "Mexico Fires Up Film Fund," *Variety*, Mar. 23–29, 1998, p. 16; John Hopewell, "Spain Eyes TV for $100 Mil Film Fund," *Variety*, May 11–17, 1998, p. 41; James Ulmer, "Norwegian Cinema Rides New Wave," *Variety*, May 18–24, 1998, p. 26; Marlene Edmunds, "Danes Tap into Double Subsidy," *Variety*, Apr. 20–26, 1998, p. 17; Bryan Pearson, "South African Gov't Grant Boosts Local Filmmakers," *Variety*, June 29–July 12, 1998, p. 11.
20   Craig Turner, "19 Nations Join to Counter Spread of U.S. Culture." *Capital Times* (Madison, Wis.), July 1, 1998, p. 1A.
21   "Culture Wars," *Economist*, Sept. 12, 1998, p. 97.
22   John Lippmann, " 'Big Bad Mama,' 'Stripped to Kill' Spell Trouble for Murdoch in India," *Wall Street Journal*, July 7, 1998, p. B1.
23   "Home Alone in Europe," *Economist*, Mar. 22, 1998, p. 74.
24   Adam Dawtrey, "Brit Pic Policy Goosed by Report's Proposals," *Variety*, Mar. 30–Apr. 5, 1998, p. 20.
25   Adam Dawtrey, "U.K. Gov't Scotches Proposal for Pix Tax," *Variety*, Nov. 30–Dec. 6, 1998, p. 10.
26   David Rooney, "Italy Moves Closer to Euro Primetime," *Variety*, Jan. 26–Feb. 1, 1998, p. 16.

27   Alice Rawsthorn, "More Support for Music Industry Urged," *Financial Times*, Jan. 14, 1998, p. 8.

28   Edmund L. Andrews, "European Commission May Revoke Exemption for U.S. Movie Studios," *New York Times*, Feb. 18, 1998, p. C7; Alice Rawsthorn and Emma Tucker, "Movie Studios May Have to Scrap Joint Distributor," *Financial Times*, Feb. 6, 1998, p. 1.

29   Emma Tucker, "EU Tells Telecoms Groups to Isolate Cable TV," *Financial Times*, Dec. 17, 1997, p. 3; Neil Buckley and John Gapper, "Publishing Merger Plan Probed by Brussels," *Financial Times*, Dec. 12, 1997, p. 15. Emma Tucker, "German Groups to Halt Digital TV Promotion," *Financial Times*, Dec. 16, 1997, p. 3.

30   Martin DuBois, "Reed Elsevier and Wolters Kluwer End Merger Plans after Concerns at EU," *Wall Street Journal*, Mar. 10, 1998, p. A19.

31   John Gapper and Emma Tucker, "Bad Reception in Brussels," *Financial Times*, Apr. 28, 1998, p. 14.

32   Samer Iskander, "New Campaign on Pay-TV Deal," *Financial Times*, May 5, 1998, p. 3; Frederick Studemann, "Murdoch Set to Lift German TV Interests," *Financial Times*, June 15, 1998, p. 20.

33   Wilfried Ahrens, "Van Miert Ban Opens Way to a Monopoly," *Television Business International*, June 1998, p. 16.

34   Emma Tucker, "EU Media Initiative Bogged Down," *Financial Times*, Mar. 13, 1997, p. 3; Emma Tucker, "TV Law Finds the Off-switch," *Financial Times*, Apr. 17, 1997, p. 3.

35   "Broadcasting across Borders," *Financial Times*, July 15, 1997, p. 11; "TV Restrictions Unlawful," *Financial Times*, June 3, 1997, p. 25.

36   Michael Smith, "New Defeat for Tobacco Advertising," *Financial Times*, Apr. 23, 1998, p. 2; Suzanne Bidlake, "Europe to Halt Tobacco Ads Sponsorships," *Advertising Age*, May 18, 1998, p. 56.

37   Andy Stern, "EC Faces Static on Pubcast Funding Cuts," *Variety*, Oct. 26–Nov. 1, 1998, p. 77; Andy Stern, "Coalition Fights EU on Pub Subsidies," *Variety*, Nov. 16–22, 1998, p. 29.

38   Thierry Leclercq, "Europeans Give Blessing to Public Service," *Television Business International*, July–Aug. 1997, p. 13.

39   "Top 100 Global Marketers by Ad Spending outside the U.S.," *Advertising Age International*, Nov. 9, 1998, p. 16.

40   Richard Tomkins, "P&G to Get Ahead by Marketing," *Financial Times*, June 5, 1997, p. 21; Sally Goll Beatty, "Bad-Boy Nike Is Playing the Diplomat in China," *Wall Street Journal*, Nov. 10, 1997, pp. B1, B10.

41   Cardona, "Coen: Ad Spending in '98 Will Outpace Overall Economy."

42   Laurel Wentz and Jon Herskovitz, "Asian Economic Turmoil Douses Torrid Ad Growth," *Advertising Age*, Dec. 8, 1997, p. 18; Laurel Wentz, "Happy New Year? Asia Drops Long Shadow over Forecast," *Advertising Age International*, Jan. 1998, pp. 3, 6.

43   Janine Stein and Mansha Daswani, "Counting China," *Television Business International*, Dec. 1997, pp. 30–31.

44   Louis Lucas, "Business Television in Asia Receiving Mixed Signals," *Financial Times*, Dec. 11, 1997, p. 14.

45   Vanessa O'Connell, "Ad-Spending Forecast for Next Year Is Cut Slightly but Growth of 5.5% Is Still Seen," *Wall Street Journal*, Dec. 8, 1998, p. B9

46   Juliana Koranteng, "Top Global Ad Markets," *Advertising Age International*, May 11, 1998, pp. 15–19.

47   Stuart Elliott, "Billion Here, Billion There, and Soon Your Estimate on 1998 U.S. Ad Spending Reaches $200.3 Billion," *New York Times*, June 24, 1998, p. C8.

48   Diane Mermigas, "Scandinavia's SBS Has Eye on Prize," *Electronic Media*, Oct. 12, 1998, p. 50.

49   "Omnicom Group," *Advertising Age*, Apr. 27, 1998, p. s22.

50   "World's Top 50 Advertising Organizations," *Advertising Age*, Apr. 27, 1998, p. s10.

51   Sally Beatty, "Merger Boom Is Expected in Ad Industry," *Wall Street Journal*, May 21, 1998, p. B10.

52   Sally Goll Beatty, "Interpublic Plans Acquisitions, Starting Off with Hill Holliday," *Wall Street Journal*, Feb. 25, 1998, p. B9.

53   Helen Jones, "The Search Is On for a Global Message," *Financial Times*, Nov. 11, 1998, p. viii; Rekha Balu, "Heinz Places Ketchup in Global Account," *Wall Street Journal*, Sept. 9, 1998, p. B8.

54   Mercedes M. Cardona and James B. Arndorfer, "Citibank's Global Plum Lands at Y&R," *Advertising Age*, Aug. 11, 1997, p. 4.

55   Stuart Elliott, "The Consolidation Trend Reaches the Industry's Second Tier as Lois/USA Acquires a Smaller Rival," *New York Times*, May 21, 1998, p. C6.

56   Alison Smith, "Strength through Unity," *Financial Times*, Nov. 10, 1997, p. 15.

57   Alice Z. Cuneo and Bruce Crumlet, "Publicis' Levy Views Riney Buy as a Start," *Advertising Age*, May 18, 1998, pp. 3, 60.

58   See, for example, Mercedes M. Cardona, "Agency Groups Scramble for Top Tier," *Advertising Age*, Feb. 2, 1998, p. 44; Stuart Elliott, "In a Further Push into Latin America, DDB Needham Is Buying a Stake in a Brazilian Agency," *New York Times*, June 16, 1997, p. C12; Rebecca A. Fannin, "DDB Needham Takes Majority Interest in Brazil Hot Shop DM9," *Advertising Age*, June 16, 1997, p. 12.

59   Norihiko Shirouzu, "Madison Avenue Looks to Japanese Market," *Wall Street Journal*, July 6, 1998, p. A20.

60   Alexandra Harney, "Omnicom Arm Buys Stake in Japan's Nippo," *Financial Times*, Aug. 20, 1998, p. 20; John William and Alexandra Harney, "WPP Takes 20% Stake in Japanese Ad Agency," *Financial Times*, July 31, 1998, p. 17.

61   Doreen Carvajal, "Book Publishers Seek Global Reach and Grand Scale," *New York Times*, Oct. 19, 1998, p. C1.

62   "The Top 100 Companies," *Business Week*, July 13, 1998, p. 53.

63   "FT 500," *Financial Times*, special section, Jan. 22, 1998, p. 3.

64   Martin Peers, "Showbiz Bullish on the Future," *Variety*, Apr. 6–12, 1998, p. 7.

65   Frank Rose, "There's No Business like Show Business," p. 98.

66   James Brooke, "American Publishers Add Readers in Booming Latin America," *New York Times*, May 11, 1998, p. C1.

67   Eben Shapiro, "Sony Says It's Weighing Digital Moves and Hires Blackstone Group to Assist," *Wall Street Journal*, Nov. 21, 1997, p. B6.

68   Patrick M. Reilly and Greg Steinmetz, "Bertelsmann to Buy Random House," *Wall Street Journal*, Mar. 24, 1998, p. B1.

69   Cynthia Littleton and Martin Peers, "All American Raises Brit Flag," *Variety*, Oct. 6–12, 1997, p. 36.

70   Alice Rawsthorn, "Playing in a Minor Key," *Financial Times*, Nov. 22–23, 1997, p. 22.

71   Kyle Pope, "NBC Is Expected to Sharply Scale Back Its TV Programming in Europe and Asia," *Wall Street Journal*, Apr. 16, 1998, p. B14; Steve McClellen, "NBC Gets Help from Geographic," *Broadcasting and Cable*, Apr. 27, 1998, p. 31.

72   This second tier is presented in detail in Herman and McChesney, *Global Media*, chap. 3.

73   Debra Johnson, "Solid Foundation," *Television Business International*, June 1988, pp. 28–36.

74   "Hot Wires," *Economist*, June 20, 1998, p. 78.

75   Joseph Weber, "The Murdoch of the North," *Business Week*, Aug. 3, 1998, p. 64.

76   Anthony DePalma, "Merger Would Create Canada's 2nd-Largest Newspaper Group," *New York Times*, Dec. 10, 1998, p. C5.

77   Paul Smith, "Murdoch Eye on Cash Cow TV2," *Variety*, May 11–17, 1998, p. 170; Paul Smith, "Study Favors Sale of TVNZ," *Variety*, June 15–21, 1998, p. 29.

78   Don Groves and Mark Woods, "Expand or Die," *Variety*, May 4–10, 1998, p. A1.

79   Elena Cappuccio and Lucy Hillier, "Mediaset Develops Its International Strategy," *European Television Analyst*, May 8, 1998, p. 1.

80   Alejandro Bodipo-Memba and Jonathan Friedland, "Chancellor Sets Pact for Purchase of Radio Centro," *Wall Street Journal*, July 13, 1998, p. B6; Carlos Tejada, "Hicks Muse to Pay $700 Million for 30% of Argentine Media Firm CEI Citicorp," *Wall Street Journal*, May 28, 1998, p. B9; Allen R. Myerson, "Polishing His Game," *New York Times*, May 25, 1998, pp. C1, C2; Ken Warn and William Lewis, "Hicks Muse in Argentine Telecoms Purchase," *Financial Times*, May 28, 1998, p. 15; Pamela Druckerman, "Hicks Muse, GE to Invest in Brazil," *Wall Street Journal*, Nov. 24, 1998, p. A14.

81   This is covered in detail in Herman and McChesney, *Global Media*.

82   Martin Peers, "The Global 50," *Variety*, Aug. 25–31, 1997, p. 31.

83   John Hopewell, "Running with the Big Dogs," *Variety*, Mar. 23–29, 1998, p. 40.

84   Al Goodman, "Spanish Digital TV Services To Merge After Costly Fight," *New York Times*, July 23, 1998, p. C5.

85   Don Groves, "Heir Power," *Variety*, Sept. 8–14, 1997, p. 8.

86   Lee Hall and Jim McConville, "Time Warner, News Corp.: Make Profits, Not War," *Electronic Media*, July 28, 1997, pp. 3, 38.

87   "Ted Turner's Management Consultant," *Economist*, Mar. 22, 1997, p. 86.

88   Karen Anderson, "CNNI's Money Makers," *Cable and Satellite Express*, May 8, 1997, p. 6.

89   Thea Klapwald, "Int'l Division Gobbles Up New Countries," *Variety*, Nov. 3–9, 1997, p. 56; see also Don Groves, "Hooks and 'Faith' Helped Delivery," *Variety*, June 9–15, 1997, p. 63; John Nadler, "HBO Gets Sat Hookup," *Variety*, Apr. 7–13, 1997, p. 66; Cathy Meils, "HBO Goes Sat for Slovak Launch," *Variety*, Mar. 17–23, 1997, p. 35; Vladimir Dutz, "HBO Takes First Steps with Romanian Service," *TV East Europe*, Jan. 1998, p. 1.

90   "Nippon, Time Warner Join Toshiba to Produce Movies," *Wall Street Journal*, July 13, 1998, p. B6; Adam Dawtrey, "Warners Intl. Favors Local Flavor," *Variety*, May 26–June 1, 1997, p. 19; Paul Karon, "WB, Village Ink Prod'n Pact," *Variety*, Dec. 15–21, 1997, p. 20; Rex Weiner, "H'Wood's Euro Fever," *Variety*, May 19–25, 1997, pp. 1, 70.

91   "Warner Bros. Develops Co-production Deals," *Television Business International*, May 1998, p. 10.

92   Rebecca A. Fannin, "Every Title a Pearl," *Advertising Age International*, May 1997, p. 116; Maggie Brown, "A Whiff of the Exotic," *Financial Times*, Sept. 8, 1997, p. 11.

93   See Nicole Vulser, "Time Warner to Buy 10% Stake in Canalsatellite," *Cable and Satellite Express*, Nov. 20, 1997, pp. 1, 2; Andrew Jack, "Warner to Purchase 10% of Canal Satellite," *Financial Times*, Nov. 18, 1997, p. 20; John Hopewell, "WB Creates Spanish Axis," *Variety*, Jan. 5–11, 1998, p. 28; John Hopewell and Elizabeth Guider, "Sogecable, WB in Pact," *Variety*, July 14–20, 1997, p. 33.

94   Diane Mermigas, "Strong Profit Picture for Animation," *Electronic Media*, Dec. 22–29, 1997, p. 14.

95   Don Groves, "Tough Going: Sino the Times," *Variety*, Dec. 1–7, 1997, pp. 1, 86.

96   John Voland, "Disney Sets Sites on New Game," *Variety*, Aug. 11–17, 1997, pp. 7, 8.

97   Michiyo Nakamoto, "Walt Disney Presents: A Japanese Story," *Financial Times*, July 17, 1997, p. 5; Bruce Orwall, "Disney's Miramax Signs Pay-TV Pact with Canal Plus," *Wall Street Journal*, May 16, 1997, p. B6; Andrew Paxman, "It's a Smaller World Already for Disney in Mexico," *Variety*, Mar. 17–23, 1997, p. 32.

98   Christopher Parkes, "Disney Hires Once More, to Keep the Brits A'Coming," *Financial Times*, Nov. 4, 1997, p. 5.

99   Andy Fry, "On Top of Their Game," *Variety*, Jan. 19–25, 1998, special section, "ESPN Intl. at 15," p. A1.

100   "Let Battle Commence," *Economist*, Apr. 26, 1997, pp. 60, 63.

101   Don Groves, "Fox Oz Studios Eye Int'l Biz," *Variety*, Aug. 25–31, 1997, p. 18; Don Groves, "Bowing Complex Courts New Strategies," *Variety*, Sept. 15–21, 1997, pp. 21, 27.

102   John Lippmann, "News Corp.'s Murdoch Is Shopping to Expand Empire," *Wall Street Journal*, Apr. 16, 1997, p. B10.

103   John Gapper, "News Corporation Raises Coverage," *Financial Times*, Sept. 15, 1997, p. 23.

104   Julian Clover, "Sky Launches Nordic Package," *European Television Analyst*, Mar. 12, 1997, p. 5; Erich Boehm, "BSkyB Eyes Move into U.K. Film Market," *Variety*, Apr. 21–27, 1997, p. 8.

105   Gary Davey, "Star TV," *Asia Research* (a Goldman Sachs publication), Oct. 24, 1997, pp. 5–13.

106   Robert Frank, "Prince Waleed Invests $850 Million in News Corp. Netscape, Motorola," *Wall Street Journal*, Nov. 25, 1997, p. B4.

107   Jonathan Karp, "India May Pull Plug on News Corp.'s TV," *Wall Street Journal*, Sept. 2, 1997, p. A15; Anil Wanravi, "Star in a Storm," *Television Business International*, Oct. 1997, pp. 82–83.

108   Tony Walker and Raymond Snoddy, "Murdoch Woos China on Satellite TV," *Financial Times*, May 16, 1997, p. 1.

109   John Gapper, "Murdoch Eyes Media in an Integrated Europe," *Financial Times*, Apr. 7, 1998, p. 8; Hilary Clarke and Dawn Hayes, "Murdoch Eyes Kirch Stake," *Independent*, June 7, 1998; *Financial Times*, June 15, 1998, p. 20; Beatriz Goyoaga, "Murdoch, Cisneros Eyeing CEI," *Variety*, May 4–10, 1998, p. 41.

110   "News Corp. Plants Flag in Europe, Kick-starts Italian DTH," *TV International*, Nov. 30, 1998, p. 1; John Gapper and Paul Betts, "Murdoch Gains Some Ground in Continental Europe," *Financial Times*, Nov. 14, 1998, p. 25.

111   Robert Preston and James Blitz, "Magnate Finds Premier He 'Could Do Business With,' " *Financial Times*, Mar. 25, 1998, p. 9.

112   Nick Cohen, "The Death of News," *New Statesman*, May 22, 1998, p. 20.

113   Mike Galetto, "How to Protect Local Content in a Global Era?" *Electronic Media*, Dec. 1, 1997, p. 22.

114   Kathy Chen, "China's Reforms Reach Culture Sector," *Wall Street Journal*, Dec. 16, 1997, p. A14.

115   For thoughtful discussions of the issue of cultural and media imperialism see the contributions to the following two excellent books: Peter Golding and Phil Harris, eds., *Beyond Cultural Imperialism: Globalization, Communication and the New International Order* (London: Sage, 1997); Daya Kishan Thussu, ed., *Electronic Empires: Global Media and Local Resistance* (London: Arnold, 1998).

116   Frank Rose, "There's No Business like Show Business," p. 90.

117   "Movers and Shakers," *Economist*, May 9, 1998, p. 86.

118   "Culture Wars," p. 98.

119   Christopher Stern, "U.S. Ideas Top Export Biz," *Variety*, May 11–17, 1998, p. 50.

120   Paul Fahri and Megan Rosenfeld, "American Pop Penetrates Worldwide," Oct. 25, 1998, p. A1.

121   James Wilson, "Film Piracy Move on Honduras," *Financial Times*, Jan. 23, 1998, p. 6.

122   Alice Rawsthorn and James Harding, "Clinton Will Lobby China to Let Hollywood Show Its Wares," *Financial Times*, June 18, 1998, p. 4.

123   Rosanna Tamburri, "Canada Considers New Stand against American Culture," *Wall Street Journal*, Feb. 4, 1998, p. A18.

124   Bahree, "U.S. Will Ask WTO to Keep Internet Free," p. B20.

125   Rance Crain, "Cozy Doesn't Cut It for Marketers Playing the Game on Global Scale," *Advertising Age*, Jan. 26, 1998, p. 24.

126   David Hatch, "Program Teaches American Way of Life," *Electronic Media*, Jan. 19, 1998, pp. 83, 90.

127   The writer is the dean of the Yale School of Management, a former investment banker, and a former official for international trade in the U.S. Department of Commerce. See Jeffrey E. Garten, " 'Cultural Imperialism' Is No Joke," *Business Week*, Nov. 30, 1998, p. 26.

128   Michael Williams, "Sacre Bleu! Gallic Pix Speak English," *Variety*, Dec. 14–20, 1998, p. 9.

129   "A World View," *Economist*, Nov. 29, 1997, pp. 71–72.

130   Andrew Paxman, "Latins Hot for U.S. TV," *Variety*, Mar. 31–Apr. 6, 1997, p. 62; Laurel Wentz, "Pan-Asian TV Survey Represents Baby Step for Regional Research," *Advertising Age International*, Oct. 1997, p. 13.

131   Alice Rawsthorn, "From Bit Part to Star Billing," *Financial Times*, Jan. 31–Feb. 1, 1998, p. 7.

132   Cynthia Littleton, "Is It Global Village of the Suburbs?" *Variety*, June 15–21, 1998, p. 6.

133   *Forbes*, July 27, 1998, pp. 167–70.

134   Dugan, "Boldly Going Where Others Are Bailing Out," p. 46.

135   Marc Gunther, "Bertelsmann's New Media Man," *Fortune*, Nov. 23, 1998, p. 176.

136   Thane Peterson and Richard Siklos, "Cautious Company, Risk-Taking CEO," *Business Week*, Nov. 9, 1998, p. 147.

137   Patrick M. Reilly, "Bertelsmann Picks Zelnick, 41, to Head BMG Entertainment Music, Video Unit," *Wall Street Journal*, July 28, 1998, p. B5.

138   "Home Alone in Europe," p. 74.

139   "Culture Wars," p. 97.

140   "Why Rupert Murdoch Is Polite," *Economist*, Apr. 11, 1998, p. 39.

141   "Box Office Winners," *Variety*, June 8–14, 1998, p. 10.

142   Ibid., p. 14.

143   Peter Bart, "Can H'wood Afford Superstars?" *Variety*, Apr. 20–26, 1998, p. 4.

144   Stuart Elliott, "Research Finds Consumers Worldwide Belong to Six Base Groups That Cross National Lines," *New York Times*, June 25, 1998, p. C8.

145   Adam Dawtrey, Michael Williams, Miriam Hils, David Rooney, and John Hopewell, "Euro Pix Revel in Plextasy," *Variety*, Apr. 27–May 3, 1998, pp. 1, 70–72.

146   Andrea Campbell, "Telefonica Alliance Hunts for Argentine Media Bargains," *Financial Times*, Mar. 12, 1998, p. 16.

147   David Rooney, "Mediaset Stays Home," *Variety*, Sept. 22–28, 1997, p. 103.

148   Benedict Carver, "Hollywood Going Native," *Variety*, Feb. 23–Mar. 1, 1998, pp. 9, 57.

149   Constance L. Hays, "Even Titles Are Flexible as U.S. Magazines Adapt to Foreign Ways," *New York Times*, Aug. 4, 1997, p. C7.

150   Cacilie Rohwedder, "Ein Popcorn, Bitte: Hollywood Studios Invade Europe," *Wall Street Journal*, Nov. 5, 1997, pp. B1, B11; Alice Rawsthorn, "Hollywood Turns Focus on Europe," *Financial Times*, Feb. 16, 1998, p. 19; Alice Rawsthorn, "PolyGram's Uncertain Future Threatens Europe Rising Star," *Financial Times*, May 13, 1998, p. 14; John Hopewell and Benedict Carver, "Reuther Taps Euro Partners for WB Co.," *Variety*, Mar. 16–22, 1998, p. 5; Eric Boehm, "British Sky B'casting Bows Pic Production Arm," *Variety*, May 25–31, 1998, p. 21; Jon Hersovitz, "Japanese Pic Gets Disney Coin," *Variety*, Apr. 27–May 3, 1998, p. 18; Sarah Walker, "The Localisation of Hollywood," *Television Business International*, Oct. 1998, pp. 30–46; Cathy Meils, "WB Poland Boosts Local Pic Prod'n," *Variety*, Nov. 16–22, 1998, p. 19; Benedict Carver, "Sony Launches Hong Kong Unit," *Variety*, Oct. 5–11, 1998, p. 19.

151   Don Groves, "U Locks in the Locals," *Variety*, Jan. 19–25, 1998, p. 22.

152   Louise Lee, "To Sell Movies in Asia, Sing a Local Tune," *Wall Street Journal*, Sept. 22, 1998, pp. B1, B4.

153   Julian Clover, "Cartoon Network Expands Nordic Feed," *Cable and Satellite Express*, Jan. 15, 1998, p. 7.

154   Julian Clover, "Fox Kids Breaks Language Barrier," *Cable and Satellite Express*, Feb. 12, 1998, p. 7.

155   Steve Donohue, "Nickelodeon Bound for Asia," *Variety*, July 20, 1998, pp. 10, 42.

156   Cited in Herman and McChesney, *Global Media*, p. 43.

157   In Galetto, "How to Protect Local Content in a Global Era?" p. 22.

158   Felicia Levine and Cheryl Kane Heimlich, "Latin Cable Arms Flex Miami's Post Edge," *Variety*, May 19–25, 1997, pp. 52–53.

159   Herman and McChesney, *Global Media*, p. 53.

160   Andrew Paxman, "Trimming for the 21st Century," *Variety*, Dec. 9–14, 1997, pp. 51, 58, 70.

161   See, for example, Raymond Colitt, "Fund Aims at LatAm Media," *Financial Times*, Dec. 17, 1997, p. 24; Jonathan Friedland, "Citicorp Group Makes Move in Argentina," *Wall Street Journal*, Oct. 20, 1997, p. A17; Nuno Cintra Torres, "SIC, Globo, TV Cabo Form Pay-TV Alliance," *Cable and Satellite Express*, Sept. 11, 1997, pp. 1, 2.

162   Tim Westcott, "Cisneros Jumps Ahead," *Television Business International*, Jan./Feb. 1998, pp. 85–86. This is true across the world, not just in the Third World. See, for example, Marlene Edmunds, "Mergers Make Sense," *Variety*, Feb. 9–15, 1998, pp. 61, 64.

163   Mary Sutter, "They Might Be Moguls," *Advertising Age International*, Feb. 9, 1998, p. 9.

164   Raymond Colitt, "Venezuela's Unfolding Television Drama," *Financial Times*, Mar. 24, 1998, p. 22; Michael Kepp, "Globo Signs Portugal Pay-TV Pact," *Television Business International*, Mar. 1998, p. 14; Jonathan Friedland and Joel Millman, "Led by a Young Heir, Mexico's Televisa Puts New Stress on Profits," *Wall Street Journal*, July 10, 1998, pp. A1, A8.

165   Andrea Mandel-Campbell, "Clarin Faces Argentine Media War," *Financial Times*, Jan. 20, 1998, p. 19.

166   Adam Sandler, "U.S. Sounds Lost in Translation," *Variety*, Mar. 23–29, 1998, pp. 27, 102.

167   Jonathan Wheatley, "Brazil Keeps Watch for Music Pirates," *Financial Times*, Dec. 4, 1997, p. 5.

168   Alice Rawsthorn, "Records Sold All around the World," *Financial Times*, Mar. 12, 1998, p. 19.

169   Paul Raeborn, "The World Beat Goes On," *Business Week*, June 23, 1997, pp. 166E2, 166E4; Alice Rawsthorn, "Music Groups Dream of Capturing Global Market," Aug. 23–24, 1997, p. 2; Mark Nicholson, "India Spices Up Its Youth Music Market," *Financial Times*, Nov. 10, 1997, p. 15.

170   See Thomas Frank, *The Conquest of Cool: Business Culture, Counterculture, and the Rise of Hip Consumerism* (Chicago: University of Chicago Press, 1997).

171   See Fred Goodman, *Mansion on the Hill*.

172   Mermigas, "Surf and Groove," p. 20.

173   "On-Air Opportunities," *Television Business International*, Jan./Feb. 1998, p. 49.

174   Andrea Adelson, "The Battle of Summer Blockbusters Extends from Theaters to Fast-food Chains to Grocery Aisles," *New York Times*, June 9, 1997, p. C25.

175   Richard Gibson and Bruce Orwall, "New Mission for Mickey Mouse, Mickey D," *Wall Street Journal*, Mar. 5, 1998, pp. B1, B5; Louise Kramer, "McD's, Disney: Year-old Pact Is a Happy Deal," *Advertising Age*, May 11, 1998, p. 24.

176   Soren Baker, "A Beat Becomes a Profitable Fashion," *New York Times*, Aug. 18, 1997, p. C7.

177   Jeffrey D. Zbar, "Kids' Networks Mature into Global Programming Force," *Advertising Age International*, Mar. 1997, p. i6; Dominic Schreibet, "A Global Battle," *Television Business International*, Sept. 1997, pp. 36–37.

178   Mike Galetto, "Univision, HSN Venture May Be a Gem," *Electronic Media*, Nov. 17, 1997, pp. 10, 52.

179   Tim Carvell, "A Star Is Born in the Wee Hours," *Fortune*, May 26, 1997, pp. 36–38.

180   John Blau, "Sell It like It Is," *Communications Week International*, Apr. 7, 1997, pp. 12–16; Bernhard Weaver, "Ads in the Ether on PCS Phones, Pagers," *Mediaweek*, Mar. 31, 1997, pp. 34–36.

181   Julie Wolf and Ernest Beck, "Gorbachev Plugs Pizza Hut," *Wall Street Journal*, Dec. 3, 1997, p. B13.

182   Bethan Hutton, "Winning Word-of-Mouth Approval," *Financial Times*, Sept. 8, 1997, p. 10.

183   Bernard Wysocki, Jr., "In the Emerging World, Many Youths Splurge, Mainly on U.S. Goods," *Wall Street Journal*, June 26, 1997, pp. A1, A11. Erik Eckholm, "Delectable Materialism Catching On in China," *New York Times*, Jan. 10, 1998, pp. A1, A4.

184   For an argument that global market concerns have influenced Hollywood film content since the 1920s, see Ruth Vasey, *The World according to Hollywood* (Madison: University of Wisconsin Press, 1997).

185   Annette Insdorf, "Like the World, Casting Is Going Multinational," *New York Times*, Nov. 8, 1998, arts and entertainment section, p. 13.

186   Mark Woods, "Action Shows Pack a Punch in Asia," *Variety*, May 26–June 1, 1997, p. 48.

187   Les Brown, "TV Violence Leaves Striking Impression," *Television Business International*, Nov. 1997, p. 4.

188   Louise McElvogue, "Making a Killing out of Nature," *Television Business International*, Nov. 1997, p. 52.

189   "HMOs, the New Nasties," *Economist*, July 11, 1998, p. 34.

190   Quoted in John Pilger, *Hidden Agendas* (London: Vintage, 1998), p. 486.

191   Milton Friedman, *Capitalism and Freedom* (Chicago: University of Chicago Press, 1962), pp. 7–36; see also David Kelley and Roger Donway, "Liberalism and Free Speech," in *Democracy and the Mass Media*, ed. Judith Lichtenberg (New York: Cambridge University Press, 1990), pp. 95–96.

192   Jaime Guzmán, "El Camino Político," *Estudios Públicos* 42 (Autumn 1991): 375–78. The article originally appeared in *Realidad* 1 (Dec. 1979): 13–23, and is translated in Patrick Barrett, "Forging Compromise: Business, Parties, and Regime Change in Chile" (Ph.D. dissertation, University of Wisconsin–Madison, 1997), esp. pp. 314–15.

193   All the material in this paragraph comes from Marc Cooper, "Chile: Twenty-Five Years after Allende," *Nation*, Mar. 23, 1998, pp. 11–23.

194   Cited in Serge Halimi, "When Market Journalism Invades the World," presented at "Is Globalisation Inevitable and Desirable?" conference sponsored by London School of Economics, London, May 7, 1997.

195   John Thornhill, "Russia's Unfinished Revolution," *Financial Times*, May 30, 1996, p. 13.

196   Cited in *Multinational Monitor*, Oct. 1996, p. 13.

197   Robert L. Pollock, "A Socialist 'Third Way' Turns Out to Be a Dead End," *Wall Street Journal*, June 17, 1998, p. A16.

198   Jane Birch, "Package Deal," *Television Business International*, Nov. 1997, pp. 31–32.

199   Louise McElvogue, "Not in My Back Yard," *Television Business International*, Nov. 1997, pp. 16–22.

200   CNN International advertisement, *Advertising Age International*, June 29, 1998, p. 6.

201   "Here Is the News," *Economist*, July 4, 1998, p. 13.

202   Nick Cohen, "Death of News," p. 20.

203   John Keane, *The Media and Democracy* (Cambridge, Mass.: Polity Press, 1991), pp. 91–92.

204   James Harding, "Gang of Four Found on Mars," *Financial Times*, Dec. 6–7, 1997, p. 7; Robert S. Greenberger, "Interim Pact with China Is Reached on Access for Financial-News Providers," *Wall Street Journal*, Oct. 27, 1997, p. B10.

205   Elisabeth Rosenthal, "A Muckraking Program Draws 300 Million Daily," *New York Times*, July 2, 1998, p. A8.

206   Alan Riding, "Why 'Titanic' Conquered the World," *New York Times*, Apr. 26, 1998, section 2, pp. 1, 28.

207   Joyce Barnathan, Matt Miller, and Dexter Roberts, "Has Disney Become the Forbidden Studio?" *Business Week*, Aug. 4, 1997, p. 51.

208   Bernard Weinraub, "Disney Hires Kissinger," *New York Times*, Oct. 10, 1997.

209   Dan Cox, "Disney Trumps Sony with China Card," *Variety*, Dec. 8–14, 1997, p. 3.

210   "Disney's Appointment of a China Executive Signals New Thrust," *Wall Street Journal*, June 8, 1998, p. B2.

211   Christopher Parkes, "Disney Hints at Better Ties with Beijing," *Financial Times*, Dec. 14, 1998, p. 6.

212   Eric Alterman, "Murdoch Kills Again," *Nation*, Mar. 23, 1998, p. 7; Silverstein, "His Biggest Takeover," p. 29.

213   "HarperCollins Settles Row with Patten and Apologizes," *Wall Street Journal*, Mar. 10, 1998, p. A13.

214   "Murdoch Hunt," *Financial Times*, Mar. 2, 1998, p. 19.

215   Maureen Sullivan, "Murdoch, Welch on Advisory Board," *Variety*, Oct. 12–18, 1998, p. 36.

216   Craig S. Smith, "China Television Appeals to Beijing as Broadcaster Nears End of Its Funds," *Wall Street Journal*, Feb. 27, 1998, p. B6.

217   John Gapper, "News Corp Joins Hong Kong Book Row," *Financial Times*, Feb. 28 / Mar. 1, 1998, p. 5.

218   Louise Lucas, "Hong Kong's ATV Won by Pro-Beijing Interests," *Financial Times*, May 27, 1998, p. 4.

219   Janine Stein, "ATV Sale Prompts Censorship Fears," *Television Business International*, June 1998, p. 11.

220   James Kynge and John Gapper, "Murdoch Mends Fences with Beijing," *Financial Times*, Dec. 12–13, 1998, p. 1.

221   Don Groves, "Star Shines Bright in East," *Variety*, Dec. 21, 1998–Jan. 3, 1999, p. 37.

222   Erik Eckholm, "Beijing, Toughening Crackdown, Gives 2 Activists Long Sentences," *New York Times*, Dec. 22, 1998, pp. A1, A6; James Kynge, "Third China Dissident Gets Jail Sentence," *Financial Times*, Dec. 23, 1998, p. 4.

223   Andrew Paxman, "TV Mogul Out to Retake Peru Broadcast Empire," *Variety*, Mar. 23–29, 1998, p. 68.

224   Sam Dillon, "After a Murder Attempt, an Editor Is Unbowed," *New York Times*, Mar. 7, 1998, p. A4.

225   Celestine Bohlen, "Slain Editor Makes Moscow Take Notice," *New York Times*, June 12, 1998, p. A11.

226   "Killing the Messengers," *Economist*, July 4, 1998, p. 41.

227   Committee to Protect Journalists, *Attacks on the Press in 1997* (New York: Committee to Protect Journalists, 1998).

228   Felicity Barringer, "In a Country Run by the Military, a Station Manager Sees Talk Radio as a Democratic Duty," *New York Times*, Nov. 30, 1998, p. C9.

229   Sally Bowen, "Peruvian TV at Centre of Legal Drama," *Financial Times*, Sept. 23, 1997, p. 8; Calvin Sims, "Crusading TV Station Is the City's Daytime Drama," *New York Times*, July 22, 1997, p. A4.

230   Paul Lewis, "Call to Arms: A Free Media Can Do Battle with Graft," *New York Times*, Oct. 11, 1998, p. 11.

231   Tor Wennerberg to Edward S. Herman, private correspondence, Aug. 18, 1997.

232   Raymond Colitt, "Latin America Reforms 'Fail to Cut Income Disparities,' " *Financial Times*, Nov. 13, 1997, p. 7.

233   Robert Brenner, "From Neoliberalism to Depression," *Against the Current*, Dec. 1998, p. 22.

Chapter 12

Daya Kishan Thussu

MAPPING GLOBAL MEDIA FLOW
AND CONTRA-FLOW

IN HIS MAGISTERIAL WORK *The Information Age*, Manuel Castells has argued that flows dominate contemporary life: 'our society is constructed around flows', he writes, 'flows of capital, flows of information, flows of technology, flows of organisational interactions, flows of images, sounds, and symbols' (Castells, 2000: 442). In an increasingly networked global society such flows have shown extraordinary growth in direction, volume and velocity. My aim in this chapter is to attempt a mapping of media flows, both as mainstream commercial commodities to be consumed by heterogeneous global audiences, and as alternative messages and images – emanating from a wide range of actors – from anti- and alter-globalisation activists to revisionist radicals circulating on an emerging 'alternative Internet' (Atton, 2004).

My focus is on the global flows and contra-flows of visual media, mainly television and film, as, despite the exponential growth of the Internet in the last decade, it was being used only by about 15 per cent of the world's population in 2006, while television and film had a much larger audience base. The chapter proposes a typology to divide the main media flows into three broad categories: global, transnational and geo-cultural. It then goes on to examine what it terms as the 'dominant flows', largely emanating from the global North, with the United States at its core; followed by contra-flows, originating from the erstwhile peripheries of global media industries – designated 'subaltern flows'. While celebrating the global circulation of media products from a wider range of hubs of creative and cultural industries, the chapter emphasises the disparities in the volume and economic value of such flows in comparison to the dominant ones and cautions against the tendency to valorise the rise of non-Western media, arguing that they may reflect a refiguring of hegemony in more complex ways.

Multi-vocal, multi-directional, multimedia

In the late 1990s, the UNESCO *World Culture Report* argued that media globalisation had increased Western cultural influence but noted that it also triggered possibilities of other models based on 'different cultural, institutional and historical backgrounds . . . such alternatives are likely to multiply in the era of globalisation, in spite of appearances, which may paradoxically witness greater diversity than uniformity' (UNESCO, 1998: 23).

The global media landscape in the first decade of the twenty-first century represents a complex terrain of multi-vocal, multimedia and multi-directional flows. The proliferation of satellite and cable television, made possible by digital technology, and the growing use of online communication, partly as a result of the deregulation and privatisation of broadcasting and telecommunication networks, have enabled media companies to operate in increasingly transnational rather than national arenas, seeking and creating new consumers worldwide. With the exception of a few powers such as the United States, Britain and France, whose media (particularly broadcasting, both state-run and privately operated) already had an international dimension, most countries have followed a largely domestic media agenda within the borders of a nation-state.

Gradual commercialisation of media systems around the world has created new private networks that are primarily interested in markets and advertising revenues. Nationality scarcely matters in this market-oriented media ecology, as producers view the audience principally as consumers and not as citizens. This shift from a state-centric and national view of media to one defined by consumer interest and transnational markets has been a key factor in the expansion and acceleration of media flows: from North to South, from East to West, and from South to South, though their volume varies according to the size and value of the market.

The US-led Western media, both online and offline, and in various forms – information, infotainment and entertainment – are global in their reach and influence (Bagdikian, 2004; Boyd-Barrett, 2006; Thussu, 2006). Given the political and economic power of the United States, its media are available across the globe, if not in English then in dubbed or indigenised versions. As its closest ally, Britain – itself a major presence in global media, particularly in the field of news and current affairs – benefits from the globalisation of Americana. The only non-Western genre with a global presence is Japanese animation (and this would not have been possible without the economic underpinnings of the world's second largest economic power). These represent what might be termed as 'dominant media flows'. Though some peripheral countries have emerged as exporters of television programmes and films (Sinclair et al., 1996), the USA continues to lead the field in the export of audio-visual products. From news and current affairs (CNN, Discovery) through youth programming (MTV), children's television (Disney), feature films (Hollywood), sport (ESPN) to the Internet (Google), the United States is the global behemoth. One result of the privatisation and proliferation of television outlets and the growing glocalisation of US media products is that American film and television exports witnessed nearly a five-fold increase between 1992 and 2004 (see Figure 12.1).

The convergence of television and broadband has opened up new opportunities for the flow of media content. As US-led Western media conglomerates have regionalised and localised their content to extend their reach beyond the elites in the world and to create the 'global popular', many Southern media organisations have benefited from synergies emerging from this glocalisation process. Some have skilfully used their position within a media conglomerate, drawing on technological and professional expertise to grow into global operators. In addition, the globalisation of Western or Western-inspired media has contributed to the creation of professional careers in media and cultural industries. The localisation of media content and the out-sourcing of digital media for transnational corporations – from Hollywood post-production to animation and digital data management – have provided the impetus for the formation of important global hubs for creative industries: by 2006, for example, India had emerged as a key destination for out-sourcing media content (UNESCO, 2005a).

A second layer of international media players may include both private as well as state-sponsored flows. The Indian film industry (popularly referred to as Bollywood) and the Latin American telenovelas are the two major examples of transnational global flows that operate in a commercial environment. The South Africa-based, pan-African network M-Net is another example of such transnational and regional communications. Among the state-supported flows we can include Euronews, the 24/7 multilingual news consortium of Europe's public service broadcasters, TV5 and Radio France Internationale, aiming at the francophone market. Other transnational actors may include the Arab news network Al-Jazeera, the pan-Latin American TV channel Televisora del Sur ('Television of the South', Telesur) based in Venezuela, and the round-the-clock English-language global television channel, Russia Today (RTTV), intended to provide news 'from a Russian perspective', launched in 2005. The expansion of CCTV-9, the English language network of China Central Television, reflects the recognition by the Beijing authorities of the importance of the English language as the key to success for global commerce and communication and their strategy to bring Chinese public diplomacy to a global audience. These originators of transnational media flows have a strong regional presence but are also aimed at audiences outside their primary constituency. These can be categorised as representing 'subaltern flows' (see Table 12.1). As one recent study of Al-Jazeera concluded: 'The information age is upon us and in the decades ahead we can expect only more Al-Jazeeras, adding to an ever greater torrent of information, as regional ideas spread around the world and become global' (Miles, 2005: 426).

A third category of geo-cultural media caters to specific cultural-linguistic audiences, which may be scattered around the world. The Chinese television channel Phoenix and the pan-Arabic entertainment network MBC are examples of media representing what may be labelled as 'geo-cultural flows', aimed largely at diasporic populations, which may not necessarily be defined solely by language – for example, a network such as India's Zee TV is watched by second-generation British Asians who may not have competency in Hindi. The emerging transnational and geo-cultural networks both represent contra-flows and may operate in both dimensions.

The extension of satellite footprints and the growth of Direct-to-Home (DTH) broadcasting have enabled Southern media networks to operate across the globe, feeding into and

Table 12.1 A typology of media flows

Dominant flows	Contra-(subaltern) flows	
Global	*Transnational*	*Geo-cultural*
Hollywood	'Bollywood'	Phoenix
MTV	Al-Jazeera	Zee TV
Disney	Telenovelas	TRT-International
CNN	TV5	Al-Hayat
Discovery	Telesur	Baidu.com
BBC	Radio France Internationale	MBC
ESPN	CCTV-9	NHK World TV
Google	RTTV	islamonline.net
CNBC	Euronews	Roj TV
Wall Street Journal	M-Net	
Japanese animation	Korean films	

developing the emergent 'diasporic public spheres' (Appadurai, 1996). With the acceleration of movements of populations around the world, primarily as a result of economic globalisation, major geo-cultural markets based on languages such as Spanish, Mandarin, Hindi, Arabic, Turkish and French are becoming increasingly prominent in transnational communication. Here again a combination of state-supported and privatised media flows is discernible. The state-run Turkish Radio and Television (TRT) has been operating an international channel TRT-INT as well as TRT-AVRASYA TV (later renamed as TRT-TÜRK) specifically for Central Asia. The Chinese portal Baidu.com and the Islamic website islamonline.net are two prominent cases of online networks based on geo-cultural and/or linguistic affinities. For some geo-cultural groups, such flows may be crucial for identity affirmation: the Kurdish satellite channel Roj TV, for example, is an important constituent in the diasporic lives of the world's largest 'stateless' population.

State-supported initiatives have also been an important contributing factor for the globalisation of cultural products. In South Korea, for example, state policies of a quota system for local films and support for such events as the Pusan International Film Festival, have put Korean cinema on the world map. In India, one example of this public–private convergence is the Frames, an annual 'global convention' showcasing the Indian film and entertainment industry. Organised by the Federation of Indian Chambers of Commerce and Industry (FICCI) every year since 2001, it attracts delegates from across the world. The creation of such bodies as the India Brand Equity Foundation – a public–private partnership between the Ministries of Commerce and Industry and the Confederation of Indian Industry with the primary objective, 'to build positive economic perceptions of India globally' – is another example of this public–private synergy (IBEF, 2005). When in 2005, TV18, an Indian television channel, joined hands with Zee Network to launch an English-language news channel, South Asia World, aimed at the UK and USA, the Indian Prime Minister Manmohan Singh welcomed this development in an advertisement aired on the channel.

Global media flows as 'dominant flows' of Americana

The global trade in cultural goods (films, television, printed matter, music, computers) almost tripled between 1980 and 1991, from $67 billion to $200 billion (UNESCO, 1998; UNESCO, 2000) and has grown at a rapid pace with the liberalisation of these sectors across the world. The United States is the leading exporter of cultural products and the entertainment industry is one of its largest export earners. UNESCO's 2005 report on *International Flows of Selected Goods and Services* estimates that the global market value of the cultural and creative industries was $1.3 trillion and was rapidly expanding. According to the report, between 1994 and 2002 international trade in cultural goods increased from $38 billion to $60 billion (UNESCO, 2005a) and, as Table 12.2 demonstrates, the trade, as with other sectors of global commerce, is heavily weighted in favour of the industrialised world, with Europe having more than 60 per cent of the share of global exports of books, newspapers, periodicals and recorded media, as against Africa's almost negligible share.

The United States leads the global export market in media products: according to the US government's Bureau of Economic Analysis, receipts for film and television tape rentals, covering 'the right to display, reproduce and distribute US motion pictures and television programming abroad', have shown a steady increase from $2.5 billion in 1992 to $10.4 billion in 2004 (US Government, 2005) (see Figure 12.1).

In terms of regional distribution, Europe continues to be the largest market for American film and television content: in 2004, the value of exports was $6.7 billion, more than 60 per cent of all US exports in the sector, while the Middle East accounted for a mere

Table 12.2 Exports of selected media products, 2002

Region	Books		Newspapers and periodicals		Recorded media	
	Value $ million	Global share %	Value $ million	Global share %	Value $ million	Global share %
Europe	6,599	61	3,096	70	11,344	61
North America	2,317	21	1,041	24	3,426	19
Asia	1,489	14	144	3	3,364	18
Latin America & Caribbean	310	3	78	2	246	1
Africa	35	0.3	6	0.1	20	0.1

Source: UNESCO, 2005a, figures rounded up, for 2002.

$114 million (see Table 12.3). American television programmes are broadcast in over 125 countries and yet the disparity between American exports of television programming and films and imports of these products is striking. As Table 12.4 demonstrates, in 2004 the US imported TV programmes and films worth $341 million, while exports were worth more than 30 times that at $10,480 million. With its largest trading partner – Europe – US exports ($6,787 million) were worth 120 times its imports from the continent ($56 million). This disparity is consistent with recent trends in the trade in television. The balance of trade in television programmes between the EU and the USA more than tripled between 1989 and 1993 and the EU sustained a trade deficit 15 times the total value of their exports for 1995 to 2000 in this sector to North America (UNESCO, 2005a: 47).

The opening up of the audio-visual market both to pan-European and international operators has changed the television landscape in Europe, with a twenty-fold increase in the number of channels available to European audiences in the past decade and a half – from 93 in

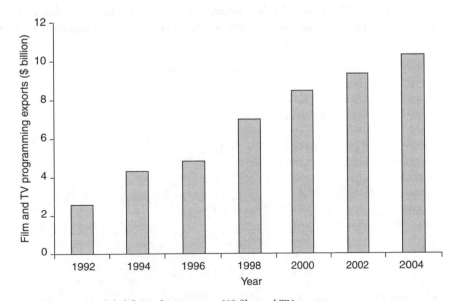

Figure 12.1 Growing global flow of Americana: US film and TV exports.

Source: US Government, 2005

Table 12.3 US exports of film and TV programmes, 2004, by region

Region	Value of film and TV exports ($ million)
Europe	6,787
Asia and Pacific	1,835
Latin America	757
Africa	124
Middle East	114
All countries	**10,480**

Source: US Government, 2005.

1990 to more than 1,700 in 2005, with entertainment channels showing the most robust growth. This has substantially increased the US presence on European television, especially in film-based programming, which is often dubbed into local languages. One reason for this, it has been argued, is that no 'lingua franca' unites European television viewers in front of their screens, and if there is a media 'cultura franca', it is based on American-style popular enter-tainment forms – soaps, game shows, talk shows, hospital and detective series – but prefer-ably with nationally specific themes and settings (Richardson and Meinhof, 1999: 174–5). Empirical research conducted in the late 1990s examining the origin of films and TV series broadcast on 36 public and commercial channels in six European countries confirmed that, despite support from the European Union to develop a pan-European television industry, US programming dominated the airwaves across Europe (de Bens and de Smaele, 2001).

While US-based companies remain undisputed leaders in selling TV programmes around the world (accounting for more than 70 per cent of all sales), Britain leads the world in the export of television formats. In 2003 Britain sold formats to the value of nearly $1 billion, accounting for 45 percent of international format sales by hours and 49 per cent by titles (Clarke, 2005). Britain holds a prominent position within the global creative industries and is Europe's largest media exporter: in 2004, it sold TV programmes worth

Table 12.4 US exports/imports of film and TV programmes to selected countries, 2004

	Export ($ million)	Import ($ million)
Britain	1,820	34
Germany	970	2
France	914	14
Japan	894	27
Canada	861	29
Netherlands	725	2
Spain	645	1
Italy	560	1
Mexico	284	9
Brazil	197	6
All countries	**10,480**	**341**

Source: US Government, 2005.

$1,513 million. According to the UK Government Department of Culture, Media and Sport, the creative industries grew in Britain by an average of 6 per cent annually between 1997 and 2003 and their exports totalled $20.3 billion in 2003 (DCMS, 2005).

One key reason for US domination of the global entertainment market is its film industry: Hollywood films are shown in more than 150 countries worldwide and dominate market share in most countries (Miller *et al.*, 2005) (see Table 12.5). In the 1970s Hollywood earned one-third of its revenue from overseas: by 2005 more than half of its revenues came from foreign markets. According to the Motion Picture Association, in 2004 the worldwide box office was worth $25.24 billion, with the world's top ten grossing films being produced by Hollywood.

A study by the European Audiovisual Observatory on cinema admissions in 34 European countries for 1996–2004 found that the top ten films in this period were all Hollywood films. In the same period, the top five European films by admission were all English-language films, four of which had been financed by Hollywood companies. Within the EU overall, nearly 72 per cent of films shown in 2004 were from Hollywood, over 25 per cent were European, and just over 2 per cent of market share belonged to the rest of the world (European Audiovisual Observatory, 2005). For countries with a limited or non-existent audio-visual domestic industry, the dependence on Hollywood is even more striking. According to UNESCO, more than one-third of the countries in the world do not produce any films at all, while Africa as a whole (constituting 53 countries) has only produced just over 600 films in its history – fewer than India produces every year (UNESCO, 2005a: 47). Even in countries with developed local film production networks and markets, US films represent a majority of imports, as Table 12.6 shows, and given the global increase in TV channels dedicated to film, it is unlikely that the dependence on Hollywood will decrease.

Table 12.5 Film market share, selected countries, 2004

		Foreign films %	
	Domestic films %	Hollywood	Other
India	93	7*	—
USA	83	10†	7
China	55	45*	—
South Korea	54	41	5
France	39	47	14
Japan	38	62*	—
Germany	24	76*	—
Italy	20	62	18
Spain	14	78	8
Britain	12	84	4
Russia	12	81	7
Canada	4	90	6
Australia	1	89	10

Source: European Audiovisual Observatory, 2005, figures for
    2004, rounded up.

Notes:

* Not specified.

† European co-production.

Table 12.6 US film imports in major film-producing countries

Country	Latest data year	Total film imports	US imports (%)
Israel	2003	173	87
India	2003	198	80
Australia	2003	245	73
Mexico	2003	267	64
Spain	2004	461	55
Russia	2004	446	54
Germany	2004	363	37
Italy	2004	349	36
Japan	2004	470	28
France	2004	556	24
Egypt	2003	300	22

Source: European Audiovisual Observatory/national statistics and *Screen Digest*, 2005.

The extensive reach of US-based media, advertising and telecommunications networks contributes to the global flow of consumerist messages, helping the US to use its 'soft power' to promote its national economic and political interests (Nye, 2004). With its ability to transcend linguistic and geographical boundaries, transnational television is particularly important in relation to media flows. Television is central to a 'global mass culture', one dominated 'by the image, imagery, and styles of mass advertising' (Hall, 1991: 27). The flow of international television programmes from the West (mainly the US) to other parts of the world, documented by two UNESCO-sponsored studies (Nordenstreng and Varis, 1974; Varis, 1985) has become more pronounced in the era of multi-channel television, though there is a small but significant contra-flow from the non-Western world, as discussed below. The UNESCO studies conducted amid heated debates about the New World Information and Communication Order during the 1970s and 1980s suggested that there was generally a one-way traffic, mainly in entertainment-oriented programming, from the major Western-exporting nations to the rest of the world.

In the era of globalisation, the one-way vertical flow has given way to multiple and horizontal flows, as subaltern media content providers have emerged to service an ever growing geo-cultural market. However, as trade figures demonstrate, the circulation of US media products continues to define the 'global'. But how these products are consumed in a cross-cultural context poses a contested range of responses, made more difficult due to the paucity of well-grounded empirical studies. Some have argued that the global–national–local interaction is producing 'heterogeneous disjunctures' rather than a globally homogenised culture (Appadurai, 1990). Others have championed the cause of cultural hybridity, a fusion formed out of adaptation of Western media genres to suit local languages, styles and conventions (Robertson, 1992; Martin-Barbero, 1993; Kraidy, 2005).

On the other hand, critical theorists have argued that the transnational corporations, with the support of their respective governments, exert indirect control over the developing countries, dominating markets, resources, production and labour. In the process they undermine the cultural autonomy of the countries of the South and create a dependency on both the hardware and software of communication and media: 'transnational corporate cultural domination' is how one prominent scholar defined the phenomenon (Schiller, 1992: 39). Galtung also argued that information flows maintain and reinforce a dependency syndrome: the interests, values and attitudes of the dominant elite in the 'peripheries' of the

South coincide with those of the elite in the 'core' — the North. The core–periphery relations create institutional links that serve the interests of the dominant groups, both in the centre and within the periphery (Galtung, 1971). In this analysis of global flows, the audience and media content was largely ignored: that the content can be interpreted differently by different audiences and that the so-called periphery may be able to innovate and improvise on the core was discounted. Theoretical debates have largely been confined to how the rest of the world relates to, adopts, adapts or appropriates Western media genres. There is relatively little work being done on how the 'subaltern flows' create new transnational configurations and how they connect with gradually localising global 'dominant flows'.

Localisation of global Americana

Glocalisation is central to the acceleration of Western or Westernised media flows across the globe. What seems to be emerging is a glocal media product, conforming to what Sony once characterised as 'global localisation': media content and services being tailored to specific cultural consumers, not so much because of any particular regard for national cultures but as a commercial imperative. Glocalisation strategies exemplify how the global can encompass both the transnational and geo-cultural by co-opting the local in order to maintain the dominant flow. This localisation trend is discernible in the growth of regional or local editions of Western or more specifically American newspapers or magazines; the transmission of television channels in local languages and even producing local programming, as well as having local language websites.

Major US studios are increasingly using local production facilities in Europe, Asia and Latin America. Columbia TriStar, Warner Brothers and Disney have set up international TV subsidiaries to produce English-language co-productions, to be followed by country-specific programming. Sony has contributed to local-language film production in Germany, Hong Kong, France and Britain, and television programming in eight languages. Global media companies are particularly keen to consolidate their position in the world's two largest markets: China and India. Cartoon Network has indigenised operations in India, producing series based on the Hindu religious epics, the *Ramayana* and the *Mahabharat*, while Disney Consumer Products has established more than 1,800 'Disney Corners' in Chinese department stores. Disney Publishing grew ten-fold in the 11 years after the launch of *Mickey Mouse Magazine* in China (Disney, 2005). In 2005 CNN started a round-the-clock English-language news operation in collaboration with the Indian television software company TV18, reaching a global south Asian audience.

STAR TV, part of media mogul Rupert Murdoch's News Corporation, has aggressively adopted the policy of indigenisation in offering localised channels, including: STAR Chinese Channel (for Taiwan), STAR Japan, STAR Plus and STAR News (the latter two for India) and VIVA Cinema for the Philippines. ESPN-STAR Sports, the result of STAR's agreement with ESPN to provide coverage of pan-Asian and international sport events, is Asia's most widely watched channel. Among the business television channels, too, Asia is a priority area. By 2006, CNBC Asia, CNBC-TV18 (India) and Nikkei-CNBC (Japan) were available in more than 34 countries across the Asia-Pacific region. CNBC also had an alliance with China Business Network, a subsidiary of the Shanghai Media Group. In the Middle East, Western or Westernised TV platforms such as Orbit, Viacom's pay-TV joint venture Showtime and Murdoch's Star Select are increasingly localising their content to go beyond the expatriate constituency in the Gulf region. This 'Arabisation' includes using subtitles for American programming and moderating language and depictions of nudity and sex.

In Latin America localised Americana is well represented by such American brands as MTV Latin America, Canal Fox, CNN En Español, Fox Kids Network and Fox Sports Americas. In America's own 44 million strong Hispanic market a key player, Telemundo, is owned by NBC. In Africa, South-Africa-based pay TV networks M-Net and MultiChoice, both having a pan-African audience, broadcast American content, including that from Discovery, Hallmark, CNN and Cartoon Network.

In print media the localisation process is well established. *Newsweek* has a network of local-language publications in Japanese, Korean, Spanish, Arabic and Polish. The regional editions of major US business publications such as the *Asian Wall Street Journal*, *Far Eastern Economic Review*, *Fortune Asian* and *Fortune China* have a small but influential pan-Asian readership. In India, *Time* and *Fortune* magazines have distribution agreements with *India Today*, the country's most widely read publication, with a weekly circulation in 2006 of 1.4 million. In Latin America, US players are present in significant numbers, with *The Wall Street Journal Americas* published as a supplement in leading newspapers in nine Spanish-speaking countries, and weekly in eight countries, including three Portuguese-language newspapers in Brazil. *Time* also produces a pan-regional newspaper supplement in Latin America in Portuguese and Spanish. *América Economía*, a Dow Jones publication, is Latin America's leading pan-regional business magazine, published bi-weekly in Spanish and Portuguese. *Fortune* also has a Latin American edition, *Fortune Americas*, with a readership of 1.5 million.

Apart from the news publications mentioned above, many international media brands publish multiple international editions of magazines like *Reader's Digest*, *Esquire* and *Good Housekeeping*. *National Geographic*, which specialises in wildlife, the environment and travel adventure, had 27 local-language editions in 2006 and a combined circulation worldwide of more than 9 million. This localised Americana is supported by regionalised advertising, increasingly using regional and national languages and cultural values to sell consumer and other products through the different media.

In many traditional societies, interactions with mediated Western culture can produce complex results. Martin-Barbero has argued that people 'first filter and reorganise what comes from the hegemonic culture and then integrate and fuse this with what comes from their own historical memory' (1993: 74). This plurality of interpretation of media messages exists within a broader new-liberal ideological framework. It could be argued that localised Americana is promoting a globalised, 'Westernised' elite that believes in the supremacy of the market and liberal democracy, as defined by the West. The global business channel CNBC notes candidly that 'strong affinity with high net worth individuals and CEOs means our viewers exert both tremendous consumer and commercial influence' (NBC, 2005).

'Subaltern' contra-flows: anti-hegemonic or pro-Americana?

In parallel with the globalisation of Americana – whether in its original or hybridised version – new transnational networks have emerged, contributing to what one commentator has called 'Easternisation and South–South flows' (Nederveen Pieterse, 2004: 122). There is evidence that global media traffic is not just one way – from the West (with the USA at its core) to the rest of the world, even though it is disproportionately weighted in favour of the former. These new networks, emanating from such Southern urban creative hubs as Cairo, Hong Kong and Mumbai, and trading in cultural goods (Curtin, 2003), represent what could be called 'subaltern flows'. Over the last ten years the media world has witnessed a proliferation of multilingual growth of content emanating from these regional creative centres (Banerjee, 2002). The availability of digital technology, privatised and deregulated broadcasting and satellite networks has enabled the increasing flow of content from the global

South to the North, for example, the growing international visibility of telenovelas or Korean and Indian films, as well as regional broadcasting, such as the pan-Arabic Middle East Broadcasting Centre (MBC), the pioneering 24/7 news network Al-Jazeera, or the Mandarin language Phoenix channel, which caters to a Chinese diaspora.

Non-Western countries such as China, Japan, South Korea, Brazil and India have become increasingly important in the circulation of cultural products, as indicated by Table 12.7. Japanese animation, film, publishing and music business was worth $140 billion in 2003, with animation, including *manga* (comics), *anime* (animation), films, videos and merchandising products bringing in $26 billion, according to the Digital Content Association of Japan (JETRO, 2005). South Korea has emerged as a major exporter of entertainment – film, television soap operas, popular music and online games – with television dramas such as *Jewel in the Palace* being extremely popular in China, prompting commentators to speak of a Korean wave (the '*Hallyu*') sweeping across east and southeast Asia (Shim, 2006).

One reason for the growing visibility of such products is the physical movement of people from one geographical location to another, brought about by a process of 'deterritorialisation', which García Canclini described as 'the loss of the "natural" relation of culture to geographical and social territories' (1995: 229). According to a report of the UN Global Commission on International Migration, the world had nearly 200 million migrants in 2005, partly as a result of globalisation of commerce and communication. Though migration is generally associated with the working classes, increasing internationalisation of a professional workforce, employed by the transnational corporations, international nongovernmental organisations and multilateral bureaucracies, as well as a growing number of foreign students, has ensured greater mobility of middle-class populations around the world (UN, 2005).

Transnational satellite broadcasters and online media companies have tapped into these emergent geo-cultural and linguistic groups (Karim, 2003; Chalaby, 2005). In Britain, South Asian channels including Zee, Sony, Star and B4U, are available on Sky's digital network, while in the USA, such platforms as Echostar DISH system and DirecTV provide a range of programmes for various diasporic groups. MBC is one of the most widely viewed channels in the Arab world, claiming an audience of 130 million viewers and helping to shape a new kind of Arab identity, based on language and culture rather than nationality.

Table 12.7 Export of cultural goods by selected non-Western countries, 2002 ($ million)

Countries	Books	Newspapers and periodicals	Recorded media
China*	668	40	510
Japan	108	34	371
Russia	240	15	59
Mexico	120	33	146
South Korea	72	4	175
India	43	13	191
Brazil	12	11	11
Turkey	8	2	13
South Africa	19	2	8
Egypt	6	1	0.3

Note

* Includes Hong Kong and Macao.

Source: UNESCO, 2005a, figures for 2002, rounded to nearest million.

The Qatar-based Al-Jazeera, which, since its launch in 1996 has redefined journalism in the Arab world, is a prominent example of contra-flow in global media products. By 2006, this pan-Arabic 24/7 news network was claiming to reach 50 million viewers across the world, undermining the Anglo-American domination of news and current affairs in one of the world's most geo-politically sensitive areas. If the live broadcast of the 1991 US military action against Iraq contributed to making CNN a global presence, the 'war on terrorism' catapulted Al-Jazeera into an international broadcaster whose logo can be seen on television screens around the world. In the region, satellite networks have led to what one commentator has called 'the structural transformation of the Arab public sphere' (Lynch, 2006). That public sphere also has an Islamist agenda; Al-Jazeera has been labelled by its critics as 'the voice of Bin Laden', having aired his taped messages. For the wider world, it has provided an alternative source of information emanating from a news-rich arena and as its services are available in English, its presence is likely to become more important in global news discourse.

Private media corporations have been more successful in accelerating the contra-flow in media products. Since they do not necessarily represent a particular country, they have contributed to creating geo-linguistic or geo-cultural identities, for example the Hong Kong-based Mandarin-language, Phoenix Chinese Channel, which is part of News Corporation. In the decade since it hit the airwaves in 1996, Phoenix has emerged as a key example of a geo-cultural television news and entertainment network which has made its presence felt among Chinese-speaking communities around the world (more than 35 million Chinese people live outside China). Phoenix sees itself as 'the window to the world for the Chinese global community' and says it 'seeks to promote a free flow of information and entertainment within the Greater China region' (Phoenix website).

Transnational telenovelas

Another key example of transnational 'subaltern flow' is the Latin American soap opera, the telenovela, which is increasingly becoming global in its reach (Large and Kenny, 2004; Martínez, 2005; Rosser, 2005). The transnationalisation of telenovelas has been made possible through Televisa in Mexico, Venevisión in Venezuela, and Globo TV in Brazil – the leading producers of the genre. The Brazilian media giant TV Globo (exporting 26,000 hours of programmes annually to 130 countries) and Mexico's Televisa (the world's largest producer of Spanish-language programming, which in 2004 earned $175m from programming exports, largely from telenovelas), are also the two primary exporters of this popular genre of television across the globe (Rosser, 2005).

By 2005 the telenovela had developed into a $2 billion industry, of which $1.6 billion was earned within the region and $341 million outside, being broadcast in 50 languages and dialects and reaching 100 countries from Latin America to southern and eastern Europe, to Asia, Africa and the Arab world (Martínez, 2005). Apart from being a commercial success, telenovelas can also help in the construction of a transnational 'hispanic' identity, as the Venezuelan scholar Daniel Mato has suggested (Mato, 2005). The appeal of the genre lies in the melodramatic and often simplistic narrative which can be understood and enjoyed by audiences in a wide variety of cultural contexts (Sinclair, 1999). Bielby and Harrington have argued that this reverse flow has influenced soap operas back in the US, leading to 'genre transformation' especially in day-time soaps (Bielby and Harrington, 2005).

The success of telenovelas outside the 'geo-linguistic market' of Spanish and Portuguese consumers, shows the complexity of media consumption patterns. Such telenovelas as *The Rich Also Cry* were very successful in Russia in the 1990s, while Sony developed its first telenovela in 2003 – *Poor Anastasia* for the Russian network, CTC (Martínez, 2005). The genre has become popular even in Western Europe: a German company has produced their own telenovela, *Bianca: Road to Happiness*, shown in 2004 on the public channel ZDF. In India, Sony has successfully adapted the popular Colombian telenovela, *Betty la Fea* into Hindi as *Jassi Jaissi Koi Nahin*, which became one of the most popular programmes on Indian television (Large and Kenny, 2004). The transnationalisation of telenovelas is an indication of contra-flow in television content. As one commentator has noted:

> In all, about two billion people around the world watch *telenovelas*. For better or worse, these programmes have attained a prominent place in the global market-place of culture, and their success illuminates one of the back channels of globalization. For those who despair that Hollywood or the American television industry dominates and defines globalization, the *telenovela* phenomenon suggests that there is still room for the unexpected.
>
> (Martínez, 2005)

'Bollyworld'

Given its size and diverse social and cultural antecedents, India is among the few non-Western countries to have made their presence felt in the global cultural market. Particularly significant is India's $3.5 billion Hindi film industry which, in terms of production and viewership, is the world's largest: every year a billion more people buy tickets for Indian movies than for Hollywood films. More films are made in India each year than in Hollywood, but their influence is largely confined to the Indian subcontinent and among the South Asian diaspora, though in recent years many 'cross-over' films have changed this situation (Kaur and Sinha, 2005). The unprecedented expansion of television in the 1990s and early 2000s was a boost for the movie industry, with the emergence of many dedicated film-based pay-channels. In addition, advancements in digital technology and the growth of broadband have ensured that Indian films are regularly shown outside India, dominating the cinema of South Asia and the South Asian diaspora as well as constructing a popular culture based on 'Bollywood'.

The globalisation of Bollywood has ensured that Indian films are increasingly being watched by an international audience as well as a wider diasporic one: Hindi films are shown in more than 70 countries and are popular in the Arab world, in central and southeast Asia and among many African countries. This has made it imperative for producers to invest in subtitling to widen the reach of films, as well as privileging scripts which interest the overseas audience. Indian film exports witnessed a twenty-fold increase in the period 1989–99 – by 2004 exports accounted for nearly 30 per cent of the industry earnings (FICCI, 2004; UNESCO, 2005a). Plans for joint ventures between Indian film producers and Hollywood giants received a boost with the decision of the Indian government, announced in 2000, to allow foreign companies to invest in the film industry. One result of such interest is that diasporic film makers such as Mira Nair (director of *Monsoon Wedding*) and the British-based Gurvinder Chaddha (director of such internationally successful 'British-Asian' films as *Bend It Like Beckham* and *Bride and Prejudice*) have acted as a bridge between Western and Indian popular cinema.

In 2004 PricewaterhouseCoopers valued the entertainment and media sector in India at $7 billion and it was expected to grow at about 14 per cent over the next five years to reach over $10 billion by 2009 (FICCI, 2004). By 2005, such neologisms as 'Bollyworld' were being used – referring to an Indian cinema 'at once located in the nation, but also out of the nation in its provenance, orientation and outreach' (Kaur and Sinha, 2005: 16).

Hybridity as hegemony

These prominent examples of 'subaltern' and 'geo-cultural' media flows may give a false impression that the world communication has become more diverse and democratic. A careful analysis of the reality of global media flows and contra-flows demonstrates a more complex process, however. The imbalance between the 'dominant' and the 'subaltern' and 'geo-cultural' global media flows reflects the 'asymmetries in flows of ideas and goods' (UNDP, 2004: 90). Despite the growing trend towards contra-flow as analysed in this book, the revenues of non-Western media organisations, with the exception of Japanese animation, are relatively small and their global impact is restricted to geo-cultural markets or at best to small pockets of regional transnational consumers. None of the Latin telenovelas has had the international impact comparable with US soaps such as *Dallas* or the cult following of *Friends* or *Sex and the City*, and, despite the growing presence of Indian films outside India, its share in the global film industry valued in 2004 at $200 billion was still less than 0.2 per cent.

At the same time, 'dominant flows' are becoming stronger. It is no coincidence that the world's biggest television network MTV (reaching 418 million households in 2005) is American, as are CNN International (260 million households worldwide) and Discovery Channel (180 million households worldwide). In 2004, out of the world's top five entertainment corporations, according to *Fortune* magazine, four were US-based: Time Warner (2004 revenue: $42.8 billion); Walt Disney (2004 revenue: $30.7 billion); Viacom (2004 revenue: $27.05 billion); and News Corporation (2004 revenue: $20.8 billion). Wal-Mart was for the fourth year running the world's largest corporation, with a revenue in 2004 of nearly $288 billion and profit of $10.2 billion. Not surprisingly, US-based companies – 181 in total – dominated the list (*Fortune*, 2005). Voice of America claims to have 100 million weekly listeners for its 44 languages; AP reaches 8,500 international subscribers in 121 countries, while APTN is a major television news agency. The world's top three largest business newspapers and magazines are American: *The Wall Street Journal* (2005 global circulation 2.3 million), *Business Week* (1.4 million) and *Fortune* (1.1 million). The world's top three magazines too are American: *Reader's Digest* (2005 global circulation, 23 million), *Cosmopolitan* (9.5 million) and *National Geographic* (8.6 million), as are the two major international news magazines: *Time* (2005 global circulation: 5.2 million) and *Newsweek* (4.2 million). The world's top three advertising agencies in 2005 were all based in the US: Young & Rubican (gross worldwide income $9.25 billion), The Ogilvy Group ($6.48 billion) and J. W. Thompson ($5.05 billion) (Thussu, 2006).

The question of how contra is contra and against whom also acquires salience. With its slogan 'News from the South', the pan-Latin American 'anti-hegemonic' news network Telesur promises to be an alternative to CNN. 'It's a question of focus, of where we look at our continent from', Jorge Botero, Telesur's news director told the BBC. 'They look at it from the United States. So they give a rose-tinted, flavour-free version of Latin America. We want to look at it from right here' (quoted in Bruce, 2005). It has been dubbed as *al-Bolivar* – a combination of Al-Jazeera and the Latin American hero. The French government has announced a 24-hour international TV news network, the French International News Channel (CFII) that aims to be the French-language CNN – 'CNN à la Française'. 'France must . . . be on the front line in the global battle of TV pictures' was how President Jacques Chirac justified the network, a joint venture between state-owned broadcaster France Télévisions and commercial television company TF1 (AFP, 2005). These examples, however, are exceptions rather than the rule – both are state-sponsored flows and their impact on global communication is yet to be felt.

In ideological terms, commercial contra-flows champion free-market capitalism, supporting a privatised and commodified media system. One should therefore avoid the temptation to valorise them as counter-hegemonic to the dominant Americana. Subaltern flows are unlikely to have a significant impact on the American hegemony of global media cultures, which, arguably, has strengthened not weakened given the localisation of media content, despite the supposed decentring of global media. This can also bode ill for local cultural sovereignty, as one UN report noted: 'the unequal economic and political powers of countries, industries and corporations cause some cultures to spread, others to wither' (UNDP, 2004: 90). Moreover, as Americana expands and deepens its hegemony, a hybridised and localised media product can provide the more acceptable face of globalisation and therefore effectively legitimise the ideological imperatives of a free-market capitalism.

Towards a new cartography of global communication

Media flows have a close relationship with economic power: traditionally, trade has followed television. According to a 2003 Goldman Sachs report, over the next few decades Brazil, Russia, India and China, the so-called BRIC economies, could become much larger forces in the world economy. A 'new geography of trade', with East Asia, and China in particular taking the lead, is already having 'a significant impact on international trade flows' (UNCTAD, 2005: 153).

By 2005, South Korea was leading the world in broadband penetration, with nearly a quarter of its population having access to broadband, while China had emerged as the world's largest television market, overtaking the United States. China also had the world's largest number of mobile phone users and had become the largest exporter of IT products (OECD, 2005). In communication hardware too China had made impressive progress: the China Great Wall Industry Corporation, a major satellite company, had launched 30 satellites since 1990.

The global expansion of India's informational technology industry has created the phenomenon of 'offshore outsourcing'. According to the National Association of Software Service Companies (NASSCOM), the apex body of India's IT industry, the sector has witnessed an annual growth rate of more than 25 per cent, earning $17.2 billion in export revenue for 2005 (NASSCOM, 2006). As a UNESCO report noted:

> Today the value of Indian cultural and creative industries is estimated at $4.3 billion. This sector is growing at an annual rate close to 30 per cent and analysts forecast that exports may continue to grow by 50 per cent in the coming years. An important factor in this impressive performance is that Indian companies are succeeding in bringing international audiences to the cinemas, in addition to the traditional diaspora communities of the USA, the United Kingdom and the Middle East. This strategy includes expansion to non-traditional countries, both industrialised and emerging, such as Japan and China.
>
> (UNESCO, 2005a: 44)

Though large population countries such as China and India are yet to fully integrate into the global market, changes in the media and communication industries in these two countries have been remarkable, making them the second and the fourth largest users of the Internet in absolute terms. Such demographic shifts may lead to the decline of English dominance on the Internet, as other languages, including non-European ones, proliferate. In 2006, Chinese was the second largest language of online communication (UNESCO, 2005b). India and China, a British Council report notes, 'probably now hold the key to the long-term future of English as a global language' (Graddol, 2006). In the long run, what John Hobson in his important book has called 'oriental globalisation' is likely to become more important, given the rapid economic rise of the world's two largest populated countries with old histories and new geo-political ambitions (Hobson, 2004)

Media flows and contra-flows form part of the wider struggle over information flows which define power relations in the global information economy. In the era of 'full-spectrum dominance' and the 'global information grid', a hybridised, glocal Americana is likely to circulate with faster velocity, greater volume and higher economic value. It is no coincidence that on the logo of the Pentagon's Information Awareness Office, the motto is 'Scientia est potentia – knowledge is power'. Despite the massive movement of media across continents, cultures and communities, one should not lose sight of the fact that 'soft' media power is firmly underpinned by 'hard' political and economic power.

References

AFP (2005) 'France enters "battle of the images" with "French CNN" ', Agence France Presse. Paris, November 30.

Appadurai, Arjun (1990) 'Disjuncture and difference in the global cultural economy', Public Culture, 2 (2): 1–24.

Appadurai, Arjun (1996) Modernity at Large: Cultural Dimensions of Globalisation. Minneapolis: University of Minnesota Press.

Atton, Chris (2004) An Alternative Internet: Radical Media, Politics and Creativity. Edinburgh: Edinburgh University Press.

Bagdikian, Ben (2004) The New Media Monopoly (7th edn). Boston: Beacon Press.

Banerjee, Indrajit (2002) 'The locals strike back? Media globalization and localization in the new Asian television landscape', Gazette, 64 (6): 517–35.

Bielby, Denise and C. Lee Harrington (2005) 'Opening America? The telenovelaization of US soap operas', Television & New Media, 6 (4): 383–99.

Boyd-Barrett, Oliver (2006) 'Cyberspace, globalization and empire', Global Media and Communication, 2 (1): 21–41.

Bruce, Iain (2005) 'Venezuela sets up "CNN rival" '. BBC News, 28 June.

Castells, Manuel (2000) The Rise of the Network Society: The Information Age: Economy, Society and Culture, vol. 1 (2nd edn). Oxford: Blackwell.

Chalaby, Jean (ed.) (2005) Transnational Television Worldwide – Towards a New Media Order. London: I. B. Tauris.

Clarke, Stewart (2005) 'UK leader in global format sales', Television Business International, April.

Curtin, Michael (2003) 'Media capital: towards the study of spatial flows', International Journal of Cultural Studies, 6 (2): 202–28.

DCMS (2005) Creative Industries Economic Estimates: Statistical Bulletin, October. London: Department of Culture, Media and Sport.

De Bens, Els and Hedwig de Smaele (2001) 'The inflow of American television fictions on European broadcasting channels revisited', European Journal of Communication, 16 (1): 51–76.

Disney (2005) Annual Report, 2005. New York: Disney Corporation.

European Audiovisual Observatory (2005) Focus 2005: World Film Market Trends. Strasbourg: European Audiovisual Observatory.

FICCI (2004) The Indian Entertainment Industry: Emerging Trends and Opportunities. Mumbai: Federation of Indian Chambers of Commerce and Industry in association with Ernst & Young.

Fortune (2005) Fortune Global 500, August.

Galtung, Johan (1971) 'A structural theory of imperialism', Journal of Peace Research, 8 (2): 81–117.

García Canclini, Nestor (1995) Hybrid Cultures: Strategies for Entering and Leaving Modernity. Minneapolis: University of Minnesota Press.

Graddol, David (2006) English Next: Why Global English May Mean the End of 'English as a Foreign Language'. London: British Council.

Hall, Stuart (1991) 'The local and the global: globalization and ethnicity', in A. King (ed.), Culture,

Globalization and the World-System — Contemporary Conditions for the Representation of Identity. London: Macmillan.

Hobson, John M. (2004) *The Eastern Origins of Western Civilisation*. Cambridge Cambridge University Press.

IBEF (2005) *Entertainment and Media*. New Delhi: India Brand Equity Foundation. Available at http://www.ibef.org.

JETRO (2005) 'Japan animation industry trends', *Japan Economic Monthly*, June.

Karim, H. Karim (ed.) (2003) *The Media of Diaspora: Mapping the Global*. London: Routledge.

Kaur, Raminder and Ajay Sinha (eds) (2005) *Bollyworld: Popular Indian Cinema Through a Transnational Lens*. New Delhi: Sage.

Kraidy, Marwan (2005) *Hybridity, or, the Cultural Logic of Globalisation*. Philadelphia: Temple University Press.

Large, Kate and Jo Anne Kenny (2004) 'Latino soaps go global', *Television Business International*. January.

Lynch, Marc (2006) *Voices of the New Arab Public: Iraq, Al-Jazeera, and Middle East Politics Today*. New York: Columbia University Press.

Martin-Barbero, Jesus (1993) *Communication, Culture and Hegemony: From Media to Mediations*, trans. E. Fox. London: Sage.

Martínez, Ibsen (2005) 'Romancing the globe', *Foreign Policy*, November.

Mato, Daniel (2005) 'The transnationalization of the telenovela industry, territorial references, and the production of markets and representations of transnational identities', *Television & New Media*, 6 (4): 423–44.

Miles, Hugh (2005) *Al-Jazeera: How Arab TV News Challenged the World*. London Abacus.

Miller, Toby, Nitin Govil, Richard Maxwell and John McMurria (2005) *Global Hollywood* (2nd edn). London: British Film Institute.

NASSCOM (2006) *NASSCOM Strategic Review 2006*. Mumbai: National Association of Software Service Companies.

NBC (2005) *Annual Report, 2004*. New York: National Broadcasting Corporation.

Nederveen Pieterse, Jan (2004) *Globalization or Empire?* London: Routledge.

Nordenstreng, Kaarle and Tapio Varis (1974) *Television Traffic — A One-Way Street? A Survey and Analysis of the International Flow of Television Programme Material*, Reports and Papers on Mass Communication, no. 70. Paris: UNESCO.

Nye, Joseph (2004) *Power in the Global Information Age: From Realism to Globalization*. London: Routledge.

OECD (2005) *Science, Technology and Industry Scoreboard*. Paris: OECD.

Phoenix website: http://www.phoenixtv.com.

Richardson, Kay and Ulrike Meinhof (1999) *Worlds in Common? Television Discourse and a Changing Europe*. London: Routledge.

Robertson, Roland (1992) *Globalization: Social Theory and Global Culture*. London: Sage.

Rosser, Michael (2005) 'Telenovelas, the next instalment', *Television Business International*, December.

Schiller, Herbert (1992) *Mass Communications and American Empire* (2nd edn). New York: Westview Press.

Shim, Doobo (2006) 'Hybridity and the rise of Korean popular culture in Asia', *Media, Culture & Society*, 28 (1): 25–44.

Sinclair, John (1999) *Latin American Television: A Global View*. Oxford: Oxford University Press.

Sinclair, John, Elizabeth Jacka and Stuart Cunningham (eds) (1996) *New Patterns in Global Television — Peripheral Vision*. Oxford: Oxford University Press.

Thussu, Daya Kishan (2006) *International Communication: Continuity and Change* (2nd edn). London: Arnold.

UN (2005) *Migration in an Interconnected World: New Directions for Action*. Report of the Global Commission on International Migration. Geneva: United Nations Publications.

UNCTAD (2005) *Trade and Development Report 2005*. Geneva: United Nations Conference on Trade and Development.

UNDP (2004) *Cultural Liberty in Today's Diverse World: Human Development Report 2004*, United Nations Development Programme. Oxford: Oxford University Press.

UNESCO (1998) *World Culture Report 1998: Culture, Creativity and Markets*. Paris: United Nations Educational, Scientific and Cultural Organization.

UNESCO (2000) *International Flows of Selected Cultural Goods 1980–1998*, UNESCO Institute for Statistics. Paris: United Nations Educational, Scientific and Cultural Organization.

UNESCO (2005a) *International Flows of Selected Cultural Goods and Services 1994–2003*, UNESCO Institute for Statistics. Paris: United Nations Educational, Scientific and Cultural Organization.

UNESCO (2005b) *Measuring Linguistic Diversity on the Internet*. Paris: United Nations Educational, Scientific and Cultural Organization.

US Government (2005) *US International Services: Cross-border Trade in 2004*. Washington: US Bureau of Economic Analysis, October.

Varis, Tapio (1985) *International Flow of Television Programmes*, Reports and Papers on Mass Communication, no. 100. Paris: UNESCO.

Chapter 13

Jeremy Tunstall

ANGLO-AMERICAN, GLOBAL, AND EURO-AMERICAN MEDIA VERSUS MEDIA NATIONALISM

"GLOBALIZATION" DOES NOT ADEQUATELY describe today's worldwide pattern of media exporting and importing. Media trade varies from very direct sales to more ambiguous transactions, such as TV format sales, or piracy.

Although Anglo-American media have been world leaders since before 1900, today's leading media force is Euro-American. The European and American continents are the main importers, as well as exporters, of media. But the world's people spend very much more time with their own media than with imported media.

English language, Anglo-American media already led the world's media in 1900. Until 1913 Britain was probably still the world's leading media power. From 1914 to 1918 the U.S. media became the leading partner in the Anglo-American media. Through the twentieth century this Anglo-American combination depended upon several key, but gradually changing, factors.

By 1913 the United States already had a larger population (97.6 million) than did any western European country. This was crucial in the media industries, where scale economies tend to take an extreme form. In 1918 the United States had just become the leading producer of films; in film additional audience millions can often be reached at the low additional cost of printing more copies. This fact meant that film was always likely to be a winner-takes-all industry.

Around 1900 in much of western Europe, and in Japan, the press was still only just emerging from state control; but in both the United States and Britain newspapers experienced very few governmental constraints.

In the United States the commercial element (including advertising) continued to predominate. Nevertheless the Anglo-American media also included important not-for-profit elements. Reuters (British) and the Associated Press (U.S.) were leading wholesalers of news around the world through the twentieth century, and neither was a conventional commercial enterprise. The London-based BBC was the most successful international radio broadcaster of the years 1940–2000, and it also was not-for-profit.

In 1913 the U.S. population was over twice that of Britain's; by 2005 the U.S. population was nearly five times that of the United Kingdom. But the trend toward ever-increasing U.S. dominance within English-language media occurred gradually and relatively smoothly.

In practice the U.S. media were able to infiltrate the British empire and later the (British) Commonwealth in pursuit of export markets. Already in the 1920s Hollywood was the dominant film power in India.

In recent decades, as the United Kingdom has become an increasingly weaker player within the Anglo-American media, other countries in which all, or most, of the population speak English as their first language have become more significant. By 2005 the United States, the United Kingdom, Canada, Australia, New Zealand, and Ireland had a combined population of 417 million (about 90 percent of whom spoke English as their main language). In recent decades the United States media industries have been able to use not only the United Kingdom, but also these other four English-speaking countries, as junior partners in the Anglo media enterprise.

Today the United Kingdom, Canada, Australia, New Zealand, and Ireland all have film industries that operate in partnership with Hollywood. This includes Hollywood offshore productions in all five countries and the production of Hollywood TV series and New York TV commercials in Canada. These five countries also have some of the most Americanized of the world's media systems. These are the main locations where Hollywood products are sold without the need for translation. The United Kingdom, Canada, Australia, New Zealand, and Ireland can be seen as leading examples of media globalization; these nations' newspaper presses also exhibit high levels of market concentration and foreign ownership.

Anglo-American media exert world influence through their status as mother-tongue speakers of the world's leading international language. Although many other countries (especially in Asia and Africa) have their own versions of the English language, it is the United States, with some British help, that develops the concepts and usages that enter the conceptual frameworks of international trade and of many other international activities and organizations. English is in practice the main working language not only of the European Union but also of the United Nations.

Small- and large-population countries: globalized and nonglobalized media

"Globalization," another term of U.S. origin, became more and more heavily used during the 1990s; politicians, journalists, and public relations people were prominent as proponents and definers of globalization. Academics also in the 1990s used the term in thousands of academic papers and in the titles of hundreds of books.[1]

Most definitions of globalization gave a prominent place to finance (including banking) and to communications (including both telecommunications and mass media). Clearly finance, banking, and credit do operate on a much more global basis than in the past. This does have some impact on mass media; for example, foreign acquisition and ownership of media companies is now more widely tolerated. Nevertheless, a solely financial focus can be misleading. Just as much "global trade" is in fact between neighboring countries inside the European Union, so "global media exports" from Hollywood also rely financially mainly on the affluent markets of western Europe, Japan, Canada, and Australia.

Telecommunications (not mass media) has the most global potential—since the Internet, consumer credit, and plain old phone calls use telecommunications networks. Many of these global transactions focus on trade names and numbers and on cash amounts. The network aspect of globalization has been stressed by Manuel Castells and by Armand Mattelart.[2] The potential global reach of telecommunications was obvious to the thousands of Americans who worked for NASA in the 1960s; as NASA's funding was reduced in the 1970s, many NASA personnel went into telecommunications. One of the main public relations arguments for the break-up of AT&T was that smaller and more commercial telecom companies would be better able to exploit the global potential for the United States.[3]

The global potential for mass media is again strong,[4] especially if we focus only on technologies—such as space satellite systems. However, the global *export* potential for mass media content—movies, TV series, news stories—is inevitably lower. Words and cultural assumptions are central to most major forms of mass media, including movies and pop songs. And most people around the world prefer most of the time to be entertained and informed by people from their own culture and nation.

One of the oddities of the globalization literature is that there are relatively few references to population size or to the differences between large and small population nation-states. There are, however, marked differences between, for example, China and Jamaica. China has a population of over 1,300 million and supplies most of its own TV, print, and other media output in, of course, Mandarin and a few other Chinese languages. Jamaica has less than three million people and, like its big neighbor the United States, speaks English; not surprisingly, Jamaica is a massive importer of media, although even here "globalized" is not really the correct term. Jamaica's media intake includes huge amounts of material from its close neighbor the United States, some 500 miles away.

Population size has a central place in the arguments found in this book. Some 42 percent of the world's population live in China and three Indian subcontinent countries (India, Pakistan, and Bangladesh). In none of these countries do media imports from the United States or western Europe have a big market share. This is also true of six other countries—Indonesia, Japan, Brazil, Mexico, Nigeria, and Russia—each of which has a population of over 100 million people. Taking these 10 countries together, probably not more than 10 percent of their entire audience time is spent with foreign media.

The most globalized media systems—the systems that do the most importing—fall into three categories. One group is small-population countries in sub-Saharan Africa (where most imports are from the United States, United Kingdom, and France). Second, in the Caribbean and Central America, small countries do a lot of importing, mainly from their big neighbors, the United States and Mexico. Third, the best export market for the United States in financial terms continues to be Europe; the smaller-population European countries do the most importing—not only from the United States but also from their bigger neighbors such as France, Germany, and the United Kingdom.

Direct and indirect media exports

Some media exports are very direct, but other exports are so indirect as perhaps not to qualify as exports.

The media product that is *exported without any alteration* is the most direct and least ambiguous. Examples include a Hollywood movie or TV series going to another English-speaking country or a German production going to another German-speaking country. Here there is usually no need for translation and also no (or minimal) editing. In this most direct case, the importing country's audience sees the same product that the audience in the exporting country sees. But this does not ensure an identical impact; Australians may not experience a Hollywood TV series in the same way that an American audience does. A Swiss-German audience will be well aware that a German TV series carries German, and not Swiss, accents, values, and characters.

A *translated or edited* version of a Hollywood product is needed in all non-English-speaking markets. In general the wealthier TV markets dub the sound by employing local actors;[5] this in itself subtly alters the film or TV series, especially if, for example, a Texas accent in the Hollywood product is dubbed into a German regional accent such as Bavarian.

In less affluent and smaller countries, foreign language imports are usually subtitled. These words under the picture are typically a much-shortened version of the spoken dialogue; this process of abbreviation can lose certain subtleties and also split the audience's attention between subtitles and pictures. Both forms of translation make quite radical changes, and there may also be editing—for example, to remove or shorten scenes that are regarded as too obscene, too sexy, too boring, or too obscure.

Versioning is another variety of both editing and translation. Not uncommonly an importing TV network buys eight hours of a TV mini-series but then edits it down to perhaps five hours. Often one purpose is to conceal from the audience that the series is a 100 percent import; this can be done by using a local national performer who appears on screen and/or does the (translated) commentary. Such versioning can make a Japanese series about the Pacific seem like a British or French series about the Pacific. Or a production that was originally 90 percent American can be made to seem a 50/50 co-production.

Foreign financing can include a very wide range of situations. Ownership (in whole or in part) sounds fairly unambiguous; but some foreign owners of newspapers, magazines, or satellite TV channels claim not to interfere with the local editorial team. This may seem to be wise business practice, but a foreign owner will normally "interfere" to the extent of selecting the top local personnel, while also establishing the broad financial guidelines. In many cases foreign ownership will go much further; for example, a foreign edition of an American (or French) magazine will probably operate on some specific ratio of local content to American (or French) material from the main edition.

Foreign commissioning of television programming is a common practice of export versions of American satellite channels that are seeking to become more local. An American channel operator such as Discovery does seek to commission good quality local material, but it also enforces some of its own key editorial guidelines—for example, historical characters may appear in period costume, but will not be allowed to speak.

A script-sale or format sale in practice usually involves a smaller editorial input from the exporter. One cheap device for a new channel is to purchase the scripts of an American or British comedy or soap opera; the purchased script will then be rewritten into the local language and culture. These arrangements often last only for one or two seasons.

Format sales are especially common in game and reality shows.[6] The sum of money that changes hands is relatively modest; an "importing" TV network, by buying the format for its national market, acquires access to useful production details and advice. However, the key ingredient of many such shows is the "host"—often an already popular local comedian or entertainment star.

Copying of a genre or editorial formula probably does not involve a contractual sale, and the end-product may be only very loosely related to any single existing model. For example, if an African or Asian TV network is about to make its first hospital drama, it may well look at episodes of American, British, Mexican, or Indian hospital dramas; but the key influences could come from nearer to home in the form of a well-known hospital novel or from a hospital radio series.

Finally, *media policies or media systems* may be imported. Such imports may be very important, but particular examples are likely also to be ambiguous. Many countries in the 1980s and 1990s moved their radio and TV systems toward a greater commercial emphasis and away from various kinds of "public" broadcasting. However, these trends, toward privatization and commercializing and Americanizing the national media, typically led to revised systems that were still significantly different from supposed American models. Often such adoption of foreign media policies and media systems is most strongly influenced not by

America or Europe, but by the example of close neighbors, whose popular media output may be leaking across the border. Both India and Israel initially decided not to introduce television; but India changed its mind because of nearby Pakistani transmissions, and Israel changed its policy because of nearby Arab TV.

Euro–American, eastern Asian, southern Asian, and Arab media

This book argues that the world splits into four major media regions, which are largely self-sufficient. Each of these four is based on geography, on religious and cultural tradition, and on one main language or one main group of languages.

Euro-America (the whole of America, north and south, and most of Europe) is the largest and most affluent of these groupings. Euro-America (minus Russia) has some 27 percent of the world's population. It includes most of the world's leading media exporters—not only the United States, but also Brazil, Mexico, France, Germany, and the United Kindom. Europe and Latin America include most of the United States' best media export markets. Although the predominant flow is eastward across the Atlantic, there is a substantial (but smaller) reverse flow into the United States—especially from Mexico, France, Germany, and the United Kingdom (and from Japan). There is substantial European ownership of U.S. media, as well as substantial U.S. ownership of European media. Euro-America relies on common European-based history, culture, and religion. Euro-America is the home not only of large numbers of English and Spanish speakers but also of other major world languages, including French, German, and Portuguese. There is even a degree of common regulation, as the Justice Department in Washington cooperates with the competition Directorate in Brussels.

Many European and American television executives meet their transatlantic colleagues three times each year at MIP-TV (International TV Program Market) in France, at MIPCOM (International Film and Program Market for TV, Video, Cable and Satellite) also in France, and at NATPE (National Association of TV Programming Executives) in Las Vegas.[7] All three annual sales conventions are dominated by Europeans, Americans, and Latin Americans.

China has some 20 percent of the world's population and has become a major media power. China does do some importing of media, but it balances modest American imports with imports from culturally (and geographically) closer places such as Taiwan, Hong Kong, and South Korea. In China a simultaneous TV audience of 200 million people is common-place. China is, of course, protected by its unique history, culture, and cuisine and by the Mandarin language.

India alone has 17 percent of the world's population; India possesses the leading mass media industries of southern Asia, and much of its output leaks across the borders into Pakistan and Bangladesh. When these latter two countries are added, southern Asia has nearly 22 percent of the world's population. India possesses the world's most complex national media system, which really involves a collection of 10 separate-language media systems. Since its independence in 1947, India has done little media importing.

A fourth distinctive media grouping is the *Arabic-language media*, which stretch from Morocco on the Atlantic to the Persian Gulf. This grouping consists of 20 countries, whose media intake is mainly in Arabic; again, of course, there is a distinctive cultural history, a distinctive religion, and a language that foreigners find very difficult. The Arabic-speaking countries (including Sudan) had a combined population of only about 346 million in 2005.

These four regional groupings (Euro-America, China, southern Asia, and the Arab countries) currently have about 74 percent of the world's population.

Among these four big groupings the Europeans are the most avid media importers. Globalization does not seem the most apt description. Europe is perhaps the leading example of American media exporting. But rather than refer to either Americanization or globalization, this book will regard the combined Euro-American media as world leaders.

National and regional media are stronger than international media

Foreigners visiting big cities such as Beijing, Delhi, Paris, or Berlin have little difficulty in observing the relevant national media, as well as American and other international channels available in hotel bedrooms. But in the larger-population countries where most of the world's people live, the main tension tends to be between national media (based in the capital or largest city) and big regional media (based in the leading cities of the larger regions).

Domestic, or nonglobal and non-American, media in fact exist in many countries at four different levels. First are the *national media* coming from the biggest city and using the main national language. Second are the *regional media* based in that region and often using the regional language, as well as reflecting regional policies and politicians. Third are often the *local media*, such as newspapers and radio stations, which may appeal to a smaller minority, distinct from the regional media and language. Fourth are often the foreign media coming from a *neighboring nation-state*; often a language group straddles an international frontier—for example, people in both eastern India and in Bangladesh speak the same Bengali language. Added together, these four different categories of domestic media typically attract much bigger audiences than do the current crop of Euro-American imports.

New technology has helped to make media available from far-off places. But technology has also made possible a huge increase in local FM radio stations, and new printing systems make it easier to produce local newspapers. Even in the United States, where the national media are strong, many people rely heavily on nonnational media (local radio, a local newspaper, and local TV news-weather-sport-crime) and follow their local teams on regional sports networks.

Even in small population countries the majority of audience time goes to national media. In larger population countries the national, regional, local, and across-the-border media typically achieve audience between 6 and 12 times those of global or American media.

Notes

1   David Held and Anthony McGrew (eds.), *The Global Transformations Reader*, Oxford: Polity Press, 2003 ed.

2   Manuel Castells, *The Rise of the Network Society*, Oxford: Blackwell, 2000; Armand Mattelart, *Networking the World, 1794–2000*, Minneapolis: University of Minnesota Press, 2000.

3   An interesting book from this period is Joseph Pelton, *Global Talk*, Boston: A.W. Sijthoff, 1981.

4   Terhi Rantanen, *The Media and Globalization*, London: Sage, 2005; Symposium: "What Is Global About Global Media?" *Global Media and Communication*, Vol.1/1, April 2005: 9–62.

5   Bob Jenkins, "Mind Your Language," *Television Business International*, September 2001: 49–51.

6   Marie-Agnès Bruneau, "When Is a Format Not a Format?" *Television Business International*, January/February 2000: 44–51.

7   Timothy J. Havens, "Exhibiting Global Television: On the Business and Cultural Functions of Global Television Fairs," *Journal of Broadcasting and Electronic Media*, Vol. 47/1, March 2003: 18–35.

PART 4

Dominant and alternative discourses

Chapter 14

Herbert I. Schiller

NOT YET THE POST-IMPERIALIST ERA

A PART FROM THE PERSISTENT explanatory and semantic efforts in recent years to minimize or discredit the idea of cultural domination (Ang, 1985; Liebes & Katz, 1990), changing conditions make it desirable to reassess the original thesis.

Two governing circumstances strongly influenced the early elaboration of the theory of cultural dominance in the mid-1960s. The first was the then-existing world balance of forces.

Twenty-five years ago, the international order could be divided into three major groups. The most powerful of these was the so-called First World, including essentially those countries that were grounded in private propertied relations and whose production was undertaken by capitalist enterprise. The Second World comprised those nations that were organized along state ownership of property lines and that called themselves socialist. The last category (in every sense) was the Third World, containing those countries that had just emerged from the collapsed European colonial empires. In the case of Latin America, these nations continued to suffer economic exploitation although they had been nominally independent for over a century. In most of the Third World states, national liberation movements still existed, and the social structures had not yet been completely captured by new, privileged elites.

In this general map, the United States was by far the most powerful individual state in the First World and in the other two categories as well. Although the Soviet Union, after the Second World, claimed superpower status on the basis of possessing nuclear weapons, its economic and technological position was decidedly subordinate.

The other determining feature of this period in the cultural realm was the rapid development of television and its capability for transmitting compelling imagery and messages to vast audiences.

These geopolitical and technological conditions provided the social landscape for the era's cultural domination perspective. The essential assumptions undergirding it were (and are) few and relatively straightforward: Media-cultural imperialism is a subset of the *general* system of imperialism. It is not freestanding; the media-cultural component in a developed, corporate economy supports the economic objectives of the decisive industrial-financial sectors (i.e., the creation and extension of the consumer society); the cultural and economic

spheres are indivisible. Cultural, no less than automobile, production has its political economy. Consequently, what is regarded as cultural output also is ideological and profit-serving
to the system at large. Finally, in its latest mode of operation, in the late twentieth century,
the corporate economy is increasingly dependent on the media-cultural sector.

The thesis assumed that the state socialist (Second) World was, if not immune to
Western cultural-informational pressure, at least to some degree insulated from it and
would, under certain circumstances, support limits on its advance. The Third World, in
contrast, was seen as an extremely vulnerable and deliberate target of American cultural
exports. At the same time, it also was viewed as a potentially organizable force—not yet
frozen in class relationships—that might give leadership to a comprehensive restructuring of
the world information system. The movement for a new international information order
was one vehicle for such a mobilization.

The charge that American-produced cultural commodities—television programs in
particular—were overwhelming a good part of the world hardly needed documentation. But
the data were there (Nordenstreng & Varis, 1974).

Changes in the international geopolitical arena

Twenty-five years later, some of this map has changed. Most importantly, the Second World
(the socialist "camp") has all but disappeared. With the (temporary?) exceptions of China,
Albania, North Korea, Vietnam, and Cuba, there is no longer a state socialist sphere in the
global arena.

The Eastern European states, along with the Soviet Union, are in varying stages of
capitalist restoration. Rather than providing an oppositional pole to the First World, they are
now eager adherents to that world, as well as its supplicants. They offer national space to the
marketing and ideological message flows of their former adversaries.

In a material sense, the strength and influence of the First World, especially that of its
most powerful members, are less restrained than they were in the preceding period. This is
observable not only with regard to the erstwhile socialist bloc but even more so with respect
to the people and nations of Africa, Asia, and Latin America.

Actually, the condition of the Third World vis-à-vis the North (Western Europe, Japan,
and the United States) is one of near-desperation. Now under the control of elites that accept
and benefit from the workings of the world market economy, the African, Asian, and Latin
American nations are deeply in debt and stalled for the most part in efforts for improvement.
Most of the Third World nations seem more helpless than ever to resist the demands of their
creditors and overseers. Despite some variability in this condition and occasional balking by a
recalcitrant ruling group, the general situation reveals practically an abandonment of the
challenging economic and cultural positions this group advanced not so long ago.

The role of television in the global arena of cultural domination has not diminished in
the 1990s. Reinforced by new delivery systems—communication satellites and cable networks—the image flow is heavier than ever. Its source of origin also has not changed that
much in the last quarter of a century. There is, however, one significant difference. Today,
television is but one element, however influential, in an all-encompassing cultural package.

The corporate media-cultural industries have expanded remarkably in recent decades
and now occupy most of the global social space. For this reason alone, cultural domination
today cannot be measured by a simple index of exposure to American television programming. The cultural submersion now includes the English language itself, shopping in
American-styled malls, going to theme parks (of which Disney is the foremost but not
exclusive example), listening to the music of internationally publicized performers, following

news agency reports or watching the Cable News Network in scores of foreign locales, reading translations of commercial best sellers, and eating in franchised fast-food restaurants around the world. Cultural domination means also adopting broadcasting systems that depend on advertising and accepting deregulatory practices that transform the public mails, the telephone system, and cable television into private profit centers (Engelhardt, 1990).

Alongside this all-service-supplying cultural-media environment, the relative economic and political power of the United States continues to diminish. This suggests that American cultural domination is not guaranteed in perpetuity. Yet irrefutably that domination has been preeminent for the last four decades and remains so to this date, though subsumed increasingly under transnational corporate capital and control. The cultural primacy that the ruling national power in the world economy historically exercised may now be changing.

The commanding position of American media products in the post-World War II era, the expertise derived from more than a century of successful marketing activity, and the now near-universal adoption of English as the international lingua franca still confer extraordinary influence on U.S.-produced cultural commodities. How long this influence can be sustained while American systemic power declines is an open question. But in any case, American *national* power no longer is an exclusive determinant of cultural domination.

The domination that exists today, though still bearing a marked American imprint, is better understood as *transnational corporate cultural domination*. Philips of the Netherlands, Lever Brothers of Britain, Daimler-Benz of Germany, Samson of Korea, and Sony of Japan, along with some few thousand other companies, are now the major players in the international market. The media, public relations, advertising, polling, cultural sponsorship, and consultants these industrial giants use and support hardly are distinguishable from the same services at the disposal of American-owned corporations. Still, a good fraction of these informational-cultural activities continue to be supplied by American enterprises.

These developments leave most of the peoples and nations in the world more vulnerable than ever to domination—cultural, military, and economic. Former oppositional forces have collapsed.

Unsurprisingly, at this moment, there seems a barely contained euphoria in Washington and other centers where capital rules. George Bush, speaking at the United Nations General Assembly in New York in October 1990, proclaimed "a new era of peace and competition and freedom." He saw "a world of open borders, open trade and, most importantly, open minds" (Transcript of President's address to U.N. General Assembly, 1990, p. A-6).

How aptly expressed are the current objectives of the for-the-moment unrestrained global corporate order—open borders, which can be transgressed; open trade, which enables the most powerful to prevail; open minds, which are at the mercy of the swelling global flows of the cultural industries. At least for now, the celebratory mood seems justified. Still, the currently triumphant corporate juggernaut is not on an open freeway with no stop lights and road checks. Possible sources of slowdown will be considered later.

Cheerful surveyors of the current scene

Not all view the developments described above with skepticism or dismay. Indeed, some see the phenomena that now characterize daily life in a very large, and growing, part of the world as evidence that cultural domination no longer exists, or that what appears as domination actually fosters resistance to itself.

The idea of cultural diversity, for example, enjoys great popularity among many cultural observers. The central assumption—that many diverse cultural tendencies and movements operate, with no one element dominating—is the familiar pluralist argument, now applied to the cultural field. A more recent construct is the notion of "globalization." In this proposition, the world is moving, however haltingly, toward a genuinely global civilization. There is also the very widely accepted hypothesis of an "active audience," one in which viewers, readers, and listeners make their own meaning from the messages that come their way, often to the point of creating resistance to hegemonic meanings. Most comprehensive of all is the postmodern perspective. Whatever else this approach offers, it insists that systemic explanations of social phenomena are futile and wrong-headed. Mike Featherstone, editor of *Global Culture*, writes:

> Postmodernism is both a symptom and a powerful cultural image of the swing away from the conceptualization of global culture less in terms of alleged homogenizing processes (e.g. theories which present cultural imperialism, Americanization, and mass consumer culture as a proto-universal culture riding on the back of Western economic and political domination) and more in terms of the diversity, variety and richness of popular and local discourses, codes and practices which resist and play-back systemicity and order (Featherstone, 1990, p. 2).

Each of these presently prevailing ideas asserts that:

1.   Imperialism no longer exists. (A variant is that U.S. imperialism, in particular, is a spent force.)
2.   A new global community is now emerging—global civil society, so to speak—that is independent of the interstate system. It is busily constructing alternative linkages and networks that provide space for new cultural environments.
3.   Finally, it is of little consequence if cultural outputs from one source occupy a preponderant share of an audience's attention, because individuals reshape the material to their own tastes and needs. In this schema, the individual receptor takes precedence over the cultural producer.

How do these propositions stand up when examined against the actual context of observable conditions?

Imperialism's vital signs are unimpaired

Is imperialism dead? Is the United States a declining imperialist power? These are two separate though connected questions.

Imperialism, understood as a system of exploitative control of people and resources, is alive and well. At the same time, opposition and resistance to imperialism are far more intense now than at the end of the nineteenth century. The existence of 125 new nations testifies to the fact that many relations of domination have been broken. But powerful means of control still exist. Most of the African, Asian, and Latin American nations continue to experience economic, financial, and even military domination.

Although the term "imperialism" rarely appears in Western media, the word seems to befit the deployment of more than 400,000 U.S. troops in Saudi Arabia. It is also a signal that people's efforts to arrange their affairs without regard for the interests of current controllers (of oil, real estate, or good geographical bases) will be met with overpowering force. Moreover, the Middle East situation reveals another aspect of contemporary imperialist strategy: the ability to mobilize international organizations—now that the Soviet presence has been integrated into the West—for imperialist aims. President Bush explained it this way: "Not since 1945 have we seen the real possibility of using the United Nations as it was designed, as a center for international collective security" (Transcript of President's address to U.N. General Assembly, 1990, p. A-6).

A good part of the world's population lives in desperation, often below the subsistence level. A recent dispatch from Mexico City starkly described the appalling conditions in the capital city of the country directly south of the United States (Guillermoprieto, 1990). Hundreds of millions of people on all continents are similarly affected.

When efforts are made—as they continuously are—to radically change these awful conditions, invariably there is foreign intervention to maintain the arrangements that offer advantage to one or another global governors and their local surrogates, the so-called national elites. In recent years, Central and South America serve as models of this process. Chile, Guatemala, El Salvador, the Dominican Republic, Nicaragua, and Cuba have felt the force of U.S. intervention—economic, military, ideological—when they have tried to create new living conditions. Similar treatment has been meted out across Africa—e.g., Angola, Mozambique, Zaire—and Asia as well—e.g., Vietnam, Afghanistan.

The U.S. military deployment in Saudi Arabia is only the most recent instance of imperialism. This action takes place amidst growing contradictions, however. The relative position of the United States in the world economy seems to be declining, yet it embarks on a costly and potentially disastrous adventure to maintain control of an economically and strategically valuable region and a source of colossal profitability.

One explanation, one most pleasing to officialdom, is that American power is still dominant. It is expressed best by Joseph Nye, a former top-level State Department official and currently a professor of international relations at Harvard University:

> Obviously, we have strengths and weaknesses. . . . But the mistake many ana-
> lysts were making was to take a single anecdote illustrating American weakness,
> such as a decline in auto sales or the fact that the Germans concluded a deal
> with Gorbachev, and extrapolating from that to some very broad general con-
> clusions that we were going down the tubes. We still have a lot more strengths
> than weaknesses (Nye, 1990, p. 1).

Interestingly, Nye finds some of these strengths in what he calls "soft power." "Soft power—the ability to co-opt rather than command—rests on intangible resources: culture, ideology, the ability to use international institutions to determine the framework of debate" (p. A-33). Soft power, as Nye defines it, is essentially the control of communications and definitional power. This is cultural imperialism with a semantic twist.

Nye may be overly sanguine about the capabilities of "soft power" to do the job, but he is not totally off the mark, especially with respect to "hard power." *Fortune*'s 1990 list of "The Global 500," the 500 biggest industrial corporations in the world, reveals that "The U.S. leads all countries, with 167 companies on the list. That's more than Japan, West Germany, and Canada combined. . . . Americans are No. 1 in 14 of the 25 industries on the Global 500." Still, the magazine notes, "Impressive as these figures are, U.S. dominance is slowly giving way. In 1980, 23 U.S. companies made the top 50, compared with only 5 Japanese. Now there are 17 American and 10 Japanese."

But other factors must be considered in evaluating the present strength or weakness of the American global imperial position. One momentous development is the break-up of Communist Eastern Europe and the accelerating restoration of capitalist forms and practices there and in the Soviet Union. Removed thereby is an oppositional pole that served to severely limit, though not fully check, the exercise of American power in the postwar years.

One (possibly too extravagant) reading of this situation is that "Washington may enjoy a greater freedom of action in foreign affairs than at any time since the end of World War II" (Toth, 1990, p. A-6).

Certainly, the Saudi Arabian intervention would have been inconceivable a few years ago. In any case, whatever the extent of the expanded range of American power, for the poorer people and countries in the world, the new situation is a disaster (Ramirez, 1990). The unrestrained use of what is called "low intensity warfare," against desperate people, now moves closer to realization as American military power no longer has to be concerned with Soviet counterforce (Klare, 1990). Whether it can disregard the financial cost of such undertakings is another matter.

Domination is further strengthened by the enfeeblement of the Non-Aligned Movement of the nations of Africa, Asia, and Latin America, established in Belgrade in 1961. Its present weakness can be attributed, in large part, to the enormous growth of transnational corporate power in the last twenty years, the collapse of the nonmarket sector of the world, and its own internal class stratification. Today, the ruling strata in the periphery have nowhere to turn except to the reservoirs of corporate capital. And they are doing just that.

Once assertive and insisting on national sovereignty, governments on all continents— Brazil, India, Mexico—headed by their dominant classes are enlisting the support of Western banks and the flow of Western-Japanese capital. One-time stalwarts of independence have demonstrated their new accommodationist outlook by engaging in sweeping denationalizations and privatizations.

Some still believe that these vast regions soon will be the vanguard of a new revolutionary upsurge (Amin, 1990). Perhaps, if the time frame is long enough, this will prove true. But in the meantime, their integration into the world market economy moves ahead. As part of their integration, the people are exposed to the drumbeat of corporate consumerism, no matter how limited the ordinary individual's spending power. The consumerist virus is an inseparable element in the rising global volume of marketing messages. This virus will impair the ability of leaders, still unborn, to act for the national community's social benefit.

A new hope for overcoming the deepening economic and social disparities around the world is seen in what is called the trend to globalization. This development, according to Featherstone (1990), one of its proponents, "emphasizes the autonomy of the globalization process, which should be seen not as the outcome of inter-state processes, but to operate in *relative* independence of conventionally designated societal and social-cultural processes." Contributing to this movement are "the increase in the number of international agencies and institutions, the increasing global forms of communication, the acceptance of unified global time, the development of standard notions of citizenship, rights and conception of humankind" (p. 6). It is emphasized that "the focus on the globe is to suggest that a new level of conceptualization is necessary." This new conceptualization can be comprehended in what it wants to dispose of: the center-periphery model of analysis and the very notion of intense social conflict. "From the vantage point of the late twentieth century it seems that the era of revolution is now finally over" (p. 4).

In short, globalization is defined to exclude domination, cultural control (soft or hard), and social revolution. The growth of the global institutions enumerated above is supposed to make these relationship and processes irrelevant, if not obsolete.

Globalism or corporate transnationalism?

It is indisputable that extranational cultural and political relationships have expanded spectacularly in recent decades. But what has been the engine of this growth? Is it a multifacted outpouring of impulses toward a still-distant but slowly emerging world order? Do the forms and structures, however embryonic, indicate a looming era of universality?

It would be comforting to believe this. It would also be profoundly delusionary. The genuine character of the globalization drive can be appreciated by examining the fate of United Nations structures in the last fifteen years and the apparent reversal of their prospects since the Iraq-Kuwait imbroglio.

Until the fall of 1990, the experiences of the World Health Organization (WHO), the Food and Agriculture Organization (FAO), and, especially, the United Nations Educational, Scientific and Cultural Organization (UNESCO)—the entity established to encourage education, science, and culture on a world scale—tell a uniform story. Each of these organizations, as well as the United Nations itself, has been harshly attacked by the U.S. government and the American media. Each has been financially disabled for pursuing goals unacceptable to powerful American interests, i.e., the media, right-wing anti-abortion and anti-environmental groups, and the military-industrial complex. In mid-1990, the United States owed $750 million to the U.N. overall, exclusive of unpaid dues to WHO and FAO (*The New York Times*, September 13, 1990, p. A-10).

Such massive withholding of funds has crippled major health, agricultural, and educational programs worldwide. UNESCO has been a special target of Washington's anger because it served as a forum—nothing more—to express the complaints of 125 nations against the prevailing international information order. The United States withdrew from UNESCO in 1984 and has remained outside that organization since (Preston, Herman & Schiller, 1989).

Now, however, a new era seems to be opening up. It was inaugurated with U.N. support (thus far) for the U.S.-initiated embargo of Iraq and the American military deployment in Saudi Arabia. A newfound appreciation of the international organization has emerged in Washington and across the American media.

Does this suggest a better-late-than-never response to global organization and international cooperation? More realistically, what the new spirit reveals is the current U.S.–U.S.S.R. accommodation, achieved on the collapse of the Soviet economy and consequent Soviet eagerness to acquiesce in whatever initiatives its former adversary may propose—embargoes, aid termination to Angola and Cuba, unification of Germany and its adherence to NATO.

Equally important in this era of seemingly widespread international agreement is the indebtedness and paralyzing weakness of the Third World and its resultant inability to express any serious opposition to current developments. This species of "internationalism," based on either the weakness or the opportunism of most of the participants, can hardly be viewed as a movement toward global equilibrium and social peace.

The actual sources of what is being called globalization are not to be found in a newly achieved harmony of interests in the international arena. To the contrary, the infrastructure of what is hopefully seen as the first scaffolding of universalism is supplied by the transnational corporate business order, actively engaged on all continents, in all forms of economic and cultural organization, production, and distribution. Many of the actual international structures that monitor these activities are staffed and managed or advised by personnel on leave from the major (mostly American) companies in the system (D. Schiller, 1985).

This worldwide system now enlists American, Japanese, German, Korean, Brazilian, English, and other nationally based but globally engaged corporations. These private giant economic enterprises pursue—sometimes competitively, sometimes cooperatively—historical capitalist objectives of profit making and capital accumulation in continuously changing market and geopolitical conditions.

The actual practices of individual companies vary from one national setting to another, and there is no general coordination of the system at large. (This does not mean that there is an absence of uncoordinated ensemble action. Capital flight, for example, demonstrates how many groups and companies, acting independently when there is a perceived threat to their interests, can cripple the economy from which the capital flows). Still, with different specific interests and objectives, and often rival aims, harmonization of the global business system is out of the question. Yet the *generalized interest* of some thousands of super-companies is not that different. In their quest for both markets and consumers, they adopt fairly similar practices and institutional processes—technological, economic, political, and cultural. They are at one in maintaining the existing global hierarchy of power, though individual positions in that hierarchy constantly change. They utilize the communication and telecommunication systems, locally and globally, to direct their complex and geographically dispersed operations. They have pressed for and obtained privatization of communication facilities in one national locale after another, enabling them to have the greatest possible flexibility of decision making and allowing them a maximum of social unaccountability. They fill the media circuits with their marketing messages. Their combined efforts in the places they exercise the greatest influence have produced the consumer society, of which the United States stands as model.

Although the super-companies are owned for the most part by national groups of investors and are based in specific national settings, national concerns are not necessarily primary in the calculations and decisions of these enterprises. As the chief executive of Fiat, Italy's largest industrial corporation, pointed out: "Reasoning in nationalist terms does not make sense anymore" (Greenhouse, 1990, p. C-11). This seems to be the case for at least some of the transnational corporate companies.

How this works itself out in the world-at-large is still unclear, and not all transnationals behave identically. Still, the question of national sovereignty has become quite murky in the intersection of national interest and the profit-driven activities of these economic colossuses.

Insofar as the visible slippage of the U.S. economy in the global hierarchy of advantage is concerned, American companies' constant search for low-cost sites of production has contributed considerably to this condition. Yet there is one sector in which American dominance remains, if not intact, at least very considerable: the media-cultural arena.

U.S. media–cultural dominance

American films, TV programs, music, news, entertainment, theme parks, and shopping malls set the standard for worldwide export and imitation. How long this dominance can endure alongside a receding economic primacy is uncertain. Already, many U.S. media enterprises have been acquired by Japanese (film and TV), German (publishing and music distribution), British (advertising), and other competing groups. Yet even when this occurs, the new owners, at least for the time being, usually are intent on keeping American creative and managerial media people in executive positions.

American cultural domination remains forceful in a rapidly changing international power scene. It is also undergoing transformation. This occurs by acquisition and, more importantly, by its practices being adopted by the rest of the transnational corporate system. What is emerging, therefore, is a world where alongside the American output of cultural product are the practically identical items marketed by competing national and transnational groups.

For some time, critics of media-imperialism theory have offered, as evidence of the doctrine's fatal flaw, the emergence of new centers of media production. Brazil, in particular, is hailed as a strikingly successful example of this development. Its achievement in television production and export is supposed to demolish the notion of a single center of cultural domination (Rogers & Antola, 1985; Straubhaar, 1989; Tracy, 1988).

In reality, according to the work of Brazilian researcher Omar Souki Oliveira (1990), Brazilian TV now broadcasts a minimum of U.S. programming. The biggest audiences watch and prefer Brazilian shows, which are widely exported abroad. Globo, the main Brazilian private TV network, currently exports shows to 128 countries. "Its productions outnumber those of any other station [sic] in the world." Oliveira writes that one American researcher (Straubhaar, 1989) has concluded that Brazilian television programs have been "Brazilianized almost beyond (American) recognition." Other U.S. researchers (Rogers & Antola, 1985) see Brazil's exports as "reverse media imperialism." A third observer (Tracey, 1988) writes that "in Brazil one sees a television devoted to national culture."

In Oliveira's reading of the same evidence, Brazilian programming is "the creolization of U.S. cultural products. It is the spiced up Third World copy of Western values, norms, patterns of behavior and models of social relations." He states that "the overwhelming majority of Brazilian soaps have the same purpose as their U.S. counterparts, i.e. to sell products"—and, it should be emphasized, to sell goods made by the same transnational corporations who advertise in Brazil as well as in the United States. The "local" sponsors are Coca-Cola, Volkswagen, General Motors, Levi's, etc.

"In most Brazilian soaps," Oliveira finds, "the American lifestyle portrayed by Hollywood production reappears with a 'brazilianized face.' Now we don't see wealthy Anglos any more, but rich white Brazilians enjoying standards of living that would make any middle class American envious." Oliveira concludes: "Glamorous as they [TV series] are—even outshining Hollywood—their role within Brazilian society isn't different from that of U.S. imports. Unfortunately, the refinements applied to the genre were not to enhance diversity, but domination."

Domination is precisely what cultural imperialism is all about. With that domination comes the definitional power, Nye's "soft power," that sets the boundaries for national discourse.

Meanwhile, despite the developments already noted, the global preeminence of American cultural product is being not only maintained but extended to new locales. U.S. media incursions into Eastern Europe and the Soviet Union are assuming the dimension of a full-scale takeover, albeit shared with German and British media conglomerates.

American-owned and -styled theme parks, with their comprehensive ideological assumptions literally built into the landscape and architecture, are being staked out across Europe and Japan. "Euro-Disneyland will open its first park at Marne la Vallee in 1992, with a second possible in 1996. Anheuser-Busch [the second-largest theme park owner after Disney] has launched a theme park development in Spain, and other U.S. corporations are exploring projects elsewhere in Europe" (Sloan, 1990, p. D-3).

It must be emphasized that the corporate takeover of (popular) culture for marketing and ideological control is not a patented American practice, limited exclusively to U.S. companies. It is, however, carried to its fullest development in the United States. Cultural-recreational activity is now the very active site for spreading the transnational corporate message, especially in professional sports, where American practice again provides the basic model.

In the United States, practically no sports activity remains outside the interest and sponsorship of the big national advertisers. The irresistible lure of big sponsorship money has become the lubricant for a sport's national development. Accordingly, sports events and games have become multi-billion-dollar businesses, underwritten by the major corporations who stake out huge TV audiences. The hunt for sports events that can be made available to advertisers now includes university and, in increasing instances, high-school games. Assuming the mantle of moral concern, *The New York Times* editorialized: "College athletic departments have abandoned any pretense of representing cap and gown and now they roam the country in naked pursuit of hundreds of millions of television dollars" (Bright lights, big college money, 1990, p. A-22).

Unsurprisingly, the practice has become internationalized. A report from Italy describes the frenzied pursuit, by the largest Italian corporations, to own soccer and basketball franchises. "A growing trend in Italy . . . [is] the wholesale takeover of a sport by the captains of industry in search of new terrain from which to promote a corporate product or image" (Agnew, 1990, p. 14). The new patrons of Italian sports include the agro-chemicals giant Montedison, which also owns the widely read Rome daily *Il Mesaggero*; the Agnelli family, owners of the giant Fiat company, who also own the successful Juventus soccer club; and Silvio Berlusconi, the Italian TV and film mogul, who owns the AC Milan soccer club and other teams.

Recent developments in East Germany illustrate the extent to which sports have become a venue of corporate image promotion and an aggressive marketing instrument. *Business Week* ("Look Out" Wimbledon, 1990) reports that

> the women's Grand Prix tennis tournament scheduled for the final week of September [1990] is moving from Mahwah, New Jersey to Leipzig, East Germany . . . the tournament [is] the first successful effort to lure big corporate sponsors into a major tourney behind the old Iron Curtain . . . a number of heavyweight sponsors . . . include Volkswagen, Isostar, Sudmilch, Kraft-General Foods and American Airlines.

Major sports are now transmitted by satellite to global audiences. The commercial messages accompanying the broadcast, ringing the stadia, and often worn on the uniforms of the athletes constitute a concerted assault of corporate marketing values on global consciousness.

The total cultural package and the "active audience"

The envelopment of professional and amateur sports for transnational corporate marketing objectives and ideological pacification is a good point at which to return to another one of the arguments contradicting the cultural imperialist concept. This is the belief in the existence of an "active audience," a view supported by a good number of Anglo-U.S. communications researchers.

According to this view, the audience is supposed to make its own meaning of the messages and images that the media disseminate, thereby playing a relatively autonomous role that is often interpreted as resistance to these messages and meanings (see Budd, Entman, & Steinman, 1990; H. Schiller, 1989). Active-audience theorizing has been largely preoccupied with the analysis of individual cultural products—a program or a TV series, a movie, or a genre of fiction. The theory follows closely in the tradition of "effects" research, though not necessarily coming to the same conclusions.

Leaving specific studies aside, it can be argued that one overarching condition invalidates, or at least severely circumscribes, the very idea of an active audience, to say nothing of one resisting a flow of messages. This is the current state—impossible to miss—of Western cultural enterprise. How can one propose to extract *one* TV show, film, book, or even a group, from the now nearly seamless media-cultural environment, and examine it (them) for specific effects? This is not to say there are no *generalized* effects—but these are not what the reception theorists seem to be concerned with.

Cultural/media production today has long left the cottage industry stage. Huge conglomerates like Time-Warner, with nearly $20 billion in assets, sit astride publishing, TV production, filmmaking, and music recording, as well as book publishing and public classroom education. Theme park construction and ownership, shopping malls, and urban architectural design also are the domain of the same or related interests.

In this totalizing cultural space, who is able to specify the individual source of an idea, value, perspective, or reaction? A person's response, for example, to the TV series *Dallas* may be the outcome of half-forgotten images from a dozen peripheral encounters in the cultural supermarket. Who is to say what are the specific sites from which individual behavior and emotions now derive?

In 1990, even actual war locales become the setting for the marketing message. *Business Week* ("Publicity?" 1990) announces: "Welcome to the New World Order, Marketing Dept. where companies are using history-making events as occasions to promote their products." The magazine explains: "With U.S. troops digging in their heels in Saudi Arabia, companies all around the country are vying to supply them with everything from nonalcoholic beer to video cassettes . . . if a soldier is going to be photographed sipping a cold drink or playing poker, most marketers agree that he or she might as well be using their product." In this new world of pervasive corporate message making, the dispatch of over 450,000 troops provides an opportunity to cultivate this or that taste for consumption, along with a powerful patriotic backdrop for the company and the product. How does the audience engage this spectacle of democracy and consumption?

There is much to be said for the idea that people don't mindlessly absorb everything that passes before their eyes. Yet much of the current work on audience reception comes uncomfortably close to being apologetics for present-day structures of cultural control.

Meaningful resistance to the cultural industries

There is good reason to be skeptical about the resistance of an audience, active or not, to its menu of media offerings. Yet this does not mean that the cultural conglomerates and the social system they embody are without an opposition. It is a resistance, however, that differs enormously from the kind of opposition that is supposed to occur in reinterpreting the message of a TV sitcom.

Some may believe in the end of history and others may insist that the era of revolution is finally over and that social (class) conflict is obsolete. The daily newspaper headlines tell a different story (though of course they don't explain it). What *is* apparent is that aroused people, if not their leaderships, all around the world are protesting their existing living conditions.

In the United States itself, still the most influential single unit of the world market economy, numerous oppositional elements force at least minimal acknowledgment, and some limited accommodation, from the governing crowd. For example, the congressional fight over the national budget in the fall of 1990 was essentially a class conflict, however obscured this was in its media coverage. To be sure, the class most directly affected—the working people—was largely absent from the deliberations. But the main question at issue was which class would be compelled to shoulder the burden of America's deepening crisis. This debate, and others underway, reveal the fragile condition of the dominating power in the country.

Between 1980 and 1990, the wealthiest I percent saw their incomes rise by 75 percent, while the income of the bottom 20 percent actually declined. The richest 2½ million Americans' combined income nearly equaled that of the 100 million Americans at the bottom of the pyramid (Meisler, 1990).

It is the still growing disparities between the advantaged and the disadvantaged countries, as well as the widening gap *inside* the advantaged and disadvantaged societies, that constitute the fault line of the still seemingly secure world market economy. To this may be added the ecological disaster in the making, which is the inevitable accompaniment of the market forces that are roaring triumphantly across the continents.

A routine headline in the Western media reads: "Indonesia: The Hottest Spot in Asia." Elaborating, *Business Week* ("Indonesia: The Hottest Spot," 1990) rhapsodizes: "With a 7% growth rate, a population of 182 million—the world's fifth largest—and a wealth of natural resources, Indonesia is poised to be the region's new success story." As the twentieth century winds down, success presumably is achieved by adopting the long-standing Western industrialization model, profligate with resource use and wastage, and exploiting the work force to satisfy foreign capital's search for the maximum return.

Indonesia, with an average wage of $1.25 *a day*, is an irresistible site. The chairman of the American Chamber of Commerce in Indonesia explains: "Indonesia will have a cheap labor supply well into the 21st century. . . . Nobody else in Asia except China can offer that." Not unexpectedly, "The income gap between affluent business people and the millions of impoverished who eke out a living in the villages and Jakarta's teeming slums is widening" (p. 45).

The Indonesian "success story," and others like it, are hardly confirmation for the end-of-social-conflict perspective. Much more convincing is the expectation that the next century will be the truly revolutionary era, accomplishing what the twentieth began but could not finish. In any case, communication theory, tied to the assumptions of political or cultural pluralism, harmonization of interests between the privileged and the deprived, resistance to domination residing in individualized interpretation of TV or film shows, or, overall, the long-term viability of capitalist institutions, is and will be unable to explain the looming social turbulence.

Certainly, there are no grounds for complacency about the prospects of the First and Third Worlds (the latter now including the once-Second World states) in the years ahead. Yet Western communication researchers seem intent on holding on to these assumptions. James Curran, surveying the English and continental research scene over the last fifteen years, concludes that

> a major change has taken place. The most important and significant overall shift has been the steady advance of pluralist themes within the radical tradition, in particular, the repudiation of the totalizing, explanatory framework of Marxism, the reconceptualization of the audience as creative and active and the shift from the political to a popular aesthetic. . . . A sea change has occurred in the field, and this will reshape—for better or worse—the development of media and cultural studies in Europe (1990, p. 157–8).

The same tendencies are well advanced, if not dominant, in the United States, though they have not totally swept the field as they seem to have done in England. There is still more than a little life left in those who look at the material side of the economy in general and the cultural industries in particular. Expressing this perspective is David Harvey, in his comprehensive approach to *The Condition of Postmodernity* (1989). Reviewing the same years that Curran surveyed, from the 1970s on, and relying on many of the same basic sources (though not as focused on the field of communication research), Harvey also finds that "there has been a sea-change in cultural as well as in political-economic practices since around 1972" (p. vii). He concludes that these changes, and the rise of postmodernist cultural forms, "when set against the basic rules of capitalist accumulation, appear more as shifts in surface appearance rather than as signs of the emergence of some entirely new post-capitalist or even post-industrial society" (p. vii).

Yet these "shifts in surface appearance" have contributed greatly to the capability of the corporate business system to maintain, and expand, its global reach. For this reason, the acknowledgment of and the struggle against cultural imperialism are more necessary than ever if the general system of domination is to be overcome.

References

Agnew, P. (1990, September 4). Italy's sport madness has a very business like basis. *International Herald Tribune*, p. 14.

Amin, S. (1990). The future of socialism. *Monthly Review, 42*(3), 10–29.

Ang, I. (1985). *Watching "Dallas": Soap opera and the melodramatic imagination.* London: Methuen.

Bright lights, big college money (1990, September 13). *The New York Times*, p. A-22.

Budd, M., Entman, R. M., & Steinman, C. (1990). The affirmative character of U.S. cultural studies. *Critical Studies in Mass Communication, 7*, 169–184.

Curran, J. (1990). The new revisionism in mass communication research. *European Journal of Communication, 5*, 135–164.

Engelhardt, T. (1990). Bottom line dreams and the end of culture. *The Progressive, 54*(10), 30–35.

Featherstone, M. (Ed.). (1990). *Global culture.* London: Sage.

The global 500, the world's biggest industrial corporations. (1990, July 30). *Fortune*, p. 265.

Greenhouse, S. (1990, October 5). Alliance is formed by Fiat and French company. *The New York Times*, p. C-11.

Guillermoprieto, A. (1990, September 17). Letter from Mexico City. *The New Yorker*, 93–104.

Harvey, D. (1989). *The condition of postmodernity.* Oxford: Basil Blackwell.

Indonesia: The hottest spot in Asia. (1990, August 27). *Business Week*, pp. 44–45.

Klare, M. T. (1990). Policing the gulf—and the world. *The Nation, 251*(12), 1, 416, 418, 420.

Liebes, T., & Katz, F., (1990). *The Export of meaning: Cross-cultural readings of "Dallas."* New York: Oxford University Press.

Look out Wimbledon, here comes Leipzig. (1990, September 24). *Business Week*, p. 54.

Meisler, S. (1990, July 24). Rich-poor gap held widest in 40 years, *Los Angeles Times*, p. A-11.

Nordenstreng, K., & Varis, T. (1974). Television traffic—A one-way street. *Reports and papers on mass communication*, No. 70. Paris: UNESCO.

Nye, J. S., Jr. (1990, October 3). No, the U.S. isn't in decline. *The New York Times*, p. A-33.

Oliveira, O. S. (1990, October 8–10). *Brazilian soaps outshine Hollywood: Is cultural imperialism fading out?* Paper presented at the meetings of the Deutsche Gesellschaft für Semiotik Internationaler Kongress, Universität Passau.

Preston, W., Jr., Herman, E., & Schiller, H. (1989). *Hope & Folly: The United States and Unesco, 1945–1985.* Minneapolis: University of Minnesota Press.

Publicity? Why it never even occurred to us. (1990, September 24). *Business Week*, p. 46.

Ramirez, A. (1990, September 14). 2 American makers agree to sell Soviets 34 billion cigarettes. *The New York Times*, p. A-14.

Rogers, E., & Antola, L. (1985). Telenovelas: A Latin American success story. *Journal of Communication, 35*(4), 24–35.

Schiller, D. (1985). The emerging global grid: Planning for what? *Media, Culture and Society, 7*, 105–125.

Schiller, H. I. (1989). *Culture, Inc.: The corporate takeover of public expression.* New York: Oxford University Press.

Sloan, A. K. (1990, August 22). Europe is ripe for theme parks. *Los Angeles Times*, p. D-3.

Straubhaar, J. (1989, May 25–29). *Change in assymetrical interdependence in culture: The Brazilianization of television in Brazil*. Paper presented at the International Communication Association, San Francisco.

Toth, R. C. (1990, September 12). With Moscow crippled, U.S. emerges as top power. *Los Angeles Times*, p. D-3.

Tracy, M. (1988, March). Popular culture and the economics of global television. *Intermedia*, 19–25.

Transcript of President's address to U.N. General Assembly. (1990, October 2). *The New York Times*, p. A-6.

Chapter 15

Joseph D. Straubhaar

BEYOND MEDIA IMPERIALISM: ASYMMETRICAL INTERDEPENDENCE AND CULTURAL PROXIMITY

I N THE 1960s AND 1970s, critics analyzed unequal media flows and structural inequalities of cultural production in terms of media imperialism and dependency, but more recently these approaches have been criticized as overly simplistic. Building on the concept of dependent development (Cardoso, 1973; Salinas & Paldán, 1979), this article reinterprets the term *asymmetrical interdependence* (Galtung, 1971) to refer to the variety of possible relationships in which countries find themselves unequal but possessing variable degrees of power and initiative in politics, economics, and culture.

The idea is that one must analyze the structural context, problems, and constraints of the world's media (as dependency theory points out) while analyzing the development of increasingly independent cultural industries, including the cycles of technological changes that frequently change structural relations. In addition, beyond the structural relationships that the dependency literature leads us to examine, we must look at how media are received by the audience as part of cultures and subcultures that resist change. Building on some of the ideas in reception analysis (Fiske, 1987), we propose that audiences make an active choice to view international or regional or national television programs, a choice that favors the latter two when they are available, based on a search for cultural relevance or proximity. These audience preferences lead television industries and advertisers to produce more programming nationally and to select an increasing proportion of what is imported from within the same region, language group, and culture, when such programming is available (Pool, 1977).

Media imperialism

During the 1960s and 1970s, several observed patterns in the structure and role of international mass media led to a charge that the United States and a few other First World nations dominated media to their advantage. Most particularly, several ideas promoted by the United States were challenged: that there should be a relatively free flow of news and cultural products (television, movies, music, advertisements), that entertainment was a primary function of media, and that commercially operated media would benefit most countries' development.

Several key problems were identified. Several studies (Beltran, 1978; Nordenstreng & Varis, 1973) identified what was increasingly perceived as a one-way flow of television from a few countries of the First World to the rest of the world, while other studies (Boyd-Barrett, 1980) observed a similar one-way flow of news controlled by the four large news agencies (AP, UPI, Agence France Presse, and Reuters). The spread of the commercial model of media, foreign investment in media, and the power of multinational advertisers were seen to threaten the use of media for nationally determined, development-oriented purposes (Beltran & Fox de Cardona, 1979; Janus, 1981).

Two primary bodies of theory developed to explain these patterns. The first, cultural dependence, builds on the idea of dependency theory, which looks primarily at the ideological role of media as part of the cultural superstructure that results from the economic relations of dependency. In this pattern, the peripheral or Third World countries depend on the industrialized world for capital, technology, and most manufactured goods, while exporting low-cost primary products or cheap manufactures, which add little benefit to the local economy (Hamelink, 1983). The role of culture is to make Third World residents content with their lot. This idea is similar to (but in many formulations less sophisticated than) Gramsci's concept of hegemony, in which elites and sometimes others compete to use media and other cultural or informational structures to set a dominant ideology (Gramsci, 1971).

Some versions of cultural dependency are more complex, particularly those recognizing that growth and development can take place even in a dependent context (Cardoso, 1973; Evans, 1979). Such treatments are more aware of class conflict (within the domestic elites that operate media), of separate national agendas by media personnel, and of the need to analyze cases separately and historically (Salinas & Paldán, 1979). Control of domestic media structures and the ideological role of advertising and imported news and media products are primary concerns. This view still sees structures and economic factors as determinant and does not give much attention to the audience's interaction with the text or content of the cultural products. For that reason, we find even the dependent development approach somewhat too deterministic to adequately explain current realities in the Third World and in the smaller First and Second World nations.

The second important body of theory, media imperialism, is somewhat less structural and Marxist in orientation and tends to focus on imbalances of power and media flows (Boyd-Barrett, 1980; Lee, 1980). Lee, in particular, defined indicators or levels of media imperialism that could be empirically examined. He focused on flow of television, foreign investment, adoption of foreign models, and impact on cultures (1980). Critics particularly noted that he missed some of the connections between the larger context of dependency and media, particularly the influence of advertising (Mattos, 1984). Boyd-Barrett (1980) also relied on a largely empirical definition; he considered media imperialism essentially an unbalanced set of relationships between countries in the sphere of media. Both authors realized that analysis should rest largely on a variety of unequal relationships and recognized a continuum of possibilities, not just a dichotomous state of dependency or dominance.

Lee (1980) critiqued both dependency theory and what he termed product–life cycle theory. Pool (1977) and Read (1976) had argued that the expansion of U.S. media into international sales and investment could be better understood as a natural logic of a business cycle than as the result of systemic imperialism or an intention to dominate. They argued that media flows followed a cycle that consisted of the development of an appealing product, the expansion of its production, a continued expansion into export, and an eventual peak as markets and audiences became saturated. At that point, Pool predicted, local producers would begin to compete with U.S. and European productions, and audiences would tend to prefer their own culture in media products when they were available.

Active audiences and class

Pool's prediction (1977) about audience preferences for national culture flew in the face of then-current wisdom about the production value-based attractiveness of U.S. and European programming. It also contradicted dependency theory's theoretical assumption that foreign elites and internationalized national elites who cooperated with them would push acceptance of foreign programming or at least of foreign models that would carry values supportive of the population's absorption into the world economy, as discussed below (Cardoso, 1973).

Two growing bodies of theory and research that support parts of Pool's prediction are uses and gratifications research, which focuses on the active role of the audience in selecting media inputs (Blumler & Katz, 1974), and the part of cultural studies that has focused on the active role of the audience in interpreting television programs (Fiske, 1987). Fiske, perhaps the major proponent of the active audience concept from within the latter tradition, argues that the audience is composed of a wide series of groups, not a homogenous mass, and that "these audiences actively read television in order to produce from it meanings that connect with their social experience" (1987, p. 84).

This builds on Hall (1982) and others who argued that social class is the major factor in producing socially determined readings of television. This primacy of social class is a very useful notion for explaining developments in audience choices and interpretations of television in Latin America. Nevertheless, researchers in this tradition also note that class can be overemphasized, that how audiences fit within institutional settings and subcultures is also important (Morley, 1980), and that class is one major factor among socially and historically situated people (Fiske, 1987). These researchers also looked at how actual viewers might resist or reinterpret the dominant ideologies, or preferred readings, contained in television texts (Fiske, 1987; Morley, 1980). The reading of television texts is mediated by audiences' incorporation into active oral cultures (Fiske, 1987), by active discussion among viewing groups, families, and others to create meanings (Katz & Liebes, 1984). An increasing literature ties such theories and methods to audiences in the Third World (Garcia Canclini, 1988; Martín-Barbero, 1988), particularly in Brazil (as will be reviewed more extensively below).

Commercialization and transnationalization

As the world economy expands, becoming increasingly a world capitalist system (Wallerstein, 1979), there is a consistent pressure toward the commercialization of media systems. This was visible first in Latin America, which tends to follow U.S. commercial models due to extensive, dependent ties of trade and investment (Beltran & Fox de Cordona, 1979; Fox, 1975), but the pattern can be seen elsewhere in the Third World as well, particularly in Asia. Western Europe, at least the countries in the European Economic Community, is also responding to pressure by both would-be advertisers and the EEC itself to open up and standardize rules for advertising. Some countries, such as France, are opening up more private ownership of broadcast media. Changes in Eastern Europe also indicate a movement in several countries toward allowing increased advertising and possibly even private ownership of broadcasting stations.

This could be seen as an increase in dependency or as an increased assertion of imperialist interests; yet both descriptions seem to oversimplify what is actually taking place. Some Latin American scholars have described these changes as primarily a transnationalization of their economies, with a consequent transnationalization of media—that is, increasing integration in the world economy and increasing dominance by transnational companies (Janus, 1981). This approach, too, seems to underestimate the relative power of a number of Third World media enterprises in their national settings and in the world market.

Cultural industries

A more open framework can be found in some interpretations of the concept of cultural industries. Building on the literature of the Frankfurt School as well as on dependency theory, McAnany (1984) describes how the commercial Brazilian television industry has grown beyond the limits originally predicted by dependency theory but continues to be constrained by structural problems of a limited, at least partially dependent economy, and continues to operate within organizational commercial media models imported from the United States.

There seems to be a current tendency virtually worldwide to create commercial cultural industries that reveal both the effects of U.S. influence and also, as we will argue, interdependence in international relations and extensive adaptation of imported forms at the national level. This apparent tendency to adopt and adapt commercial media models, cultural forms, and genres requires more theorization. Some writers, including Oliveira (1990), see relatively little innovation or change in the cultural industry forms and products that a country like Brazil has adapted from the United States. However, other former imperialism theorists (Mattelart & Mattelart, 1990), looking at Brazilian television productions (particularly its evening serials, *telenovelas*), see change that has built on the cultural industry created by TV Globo and Brazilian state support. Earlier (1981) I traced the process whereby U.S. companies transplanted soap operas to Latin America and also analyzed the transformations in form and content that resulted in the *telenovela*, which most Latin American critics now consider a distinct cultural industry product (Marques de Melo, 1988).

Asymmetrical interdependence

It is clear that cultural imperialism and dependency theories have sharpened the debate and focused attention on several key issues, particularly international relationships, economic relations, and class conflicts. However, somewhat more flexible and complex paradigms are now required to apprehend the current development of national media and world media flows. Relationships remain highly unequal, but in many cases—as we will see in the case of Brazil—development may move beyond what was envisioned under the concept of dependent development (although that concept remains an excellent point of departure).

This approach to cultural industries recognizes the limits placed on many nations' media systems by operating within subordinate positions in the world economy, but it also recognizes and gives analytical emphasis to the distinct dynamics of each nation's or industry's historical development. Key national issues include conflicts between domestic and transnational elites, interests of key national elites, entrepreneurial competition, the agendas and actions of key production personnel, and the effects of state intervention, particularly as policy-maker, provider of infrastructure, and advertiser (Mattelart & Mattelart, 1990; Mattos, 1982; Straubhaar, 1984; Vink, 1988). These dynamics have resulted in a continuum of media development that ranges from rather complete dependency to dominant interdependence. (Even the United States has discovered that it is not independent.) This range of relationships might be called forms of asymmetrical interdependence.

Using Brazil and, more generally, Latin America as a case in point, we will examine the conditions and changes over time in relative dependency. We will look at constraints that result from conditions of dependency and the effects of U.S. media expansion. We will also examine how these conditions have affected the growth of indigenous institutions and what distinct developments have taken place locally.

Expanding the institutional/structural framework, we will also assert the importance to media development, particularly in television, of certain technological changes. These include decreasing audio and video technology costs that allow for increased local production, and, more broadly, the development of the technique required to use that hardware to create cultural products. Other changes include new video technologies that fragment audiences along class lines but also permit ever more decentralized production. Finally, building on the active audience literature, we will examine significant changes in how the role of the audience is seen within supposedly dependent situations, moving from a view of a passive, dominated audience to one of an active audience, conditioned by class, age, gender, and interests, and tending to prefer and select local or national cultural content that is more proximate and relevant to them.

Dependency in the Third World media

Before going beyond dependency analysis, we must recognize that existing conditions of dependence or unequal interdependence constrain many nations not only in the Third World but even in Western and Eastern Europe. Both theoretically and empirically, dependency and dependent development paradigms isolate a number of crucial issues and factors.

To begin with, smaller nations have limited markets. There are fewer people to create wealth to support media; even wealthy but small European states such as Belgium or the Netherlands do not have the resources to produce full schedules of national production, particularly when multichannel television technologies such as direct satellite broadcasting (DBS) or cable arrive. Wealth per capita is often very low in the Third World, so that even large nations such as India have limited resources for production, again particularly when trying to fill multiple channels. Dependency theorists attribute this lower level of wealth to exploitation by the industrialized countries in the form of low prices paid for the primary products produced by poorer countries, blocks against or lack of support for industrialization in the poorer Third World, debt, and high prices charged for capital equipment (Cardoso, 1973; Oliveira, 1989).

In many poorer countries of Latin America, Asia, and Africa, whatever limited industrialization exists may be narrowly focused on a few exports and controlled by multinational interests without regard for providing a financial or organizational platform for media growth. Even countries seeking to commercialize may not find enough potential advertisers with a stake in the market to contribute much to finance production. Furthermore, skewed or severely unequal distributions of income in many countries limit the number of potential consumers who might attract advertising investment to the media in poorer nations (World Bank, 1990).

The greatest growth in television production in Third World countries seems to take place in those nations that can build upon other flourishing cultural industries or noncommercial cultural establishments. Commercial television in India and Egypt built on substantial cinema and music industries. Television in Brazil built on radio, theater, and, to a lesser degree, cinema (Milanesi, 1978). Many smaller nations, particularly in the Third World, have very limited cultural industries, too small to reinforce each other and exchange artists, writers, directors, actors, and musicians.

This context of dependency was particularly important in the early history of most Third World broadcasting, particularly television, in the 1950s and 1960s. The costs of starting radio and television broadcasting were actually higher then than now. Luis Fernando Santoro, a producer of both broadcast and alternative political video productions in Brazil, estimated that, except perhaps for cameras, production equipment in 1990 costs approximately one-quarter to one-third of what it cost in the early 1970s; furthermore, the equipment, including cameras, is now more portable, flexible, and useful, making possible a greater volume of production (personal communication, September 3, 1990). In many cases, higher program production costs in the early days of television were also due to the lack of trained personnel and the lack of simple program formats to work with. These higher costs for local production led to a high degree of importation, particularly in the 1960s, when many countries were just beginning television operations. (In the 1950s, the lack of recording and playback technologies such as kinescope and videotape at many television stations actually led to a predominance of local, live production.) By the later 1970s, these conditions were beginning to change, leading in some cases to a gradual increase in television production (Antola & Rogers, 1984; Tunstall, 1977).

Product life cycle revisited

A number of authors, including Read (1976), have observed that the origins of the U.S. film industry set in place a number of patterns that enabled both films and television programs from U.S. producers to enjoy early and continued export success. The variety of immigrant ethnic groups in the U.S. market encouraged production for a broad popular culture. This production was successful in building on the large North American market; the industry structures grew rapidly. The result was a vast scale for U.S. cultural industries compared to the rest of the world, industrial rationalization in the film studio system, and the accumulation of financial and personnel resources. U.S. cultural industries also showed innovation in genre and content. Considerable development of film genres in the 1920s, 1930s, and 1940s was accompanied by export success. In parallel, there was the development of radio genres in the 1930s and 1940s, with a great deal of music exportation, then the adaptation of radio genres to television. The combination of the film and radio industrial bases led to further development of TV genres in the 1950s and 1960s, with a boom in television exports in the 1960s—as a product life cycle theory might predict.

However, as Guback and others have pointed out, the international success of the U.S. film and television industry was not based solely on the attractiveness of the U.S. cultural products. The industry also used monopolistic distribution schemes to ensure their dominance of the world market. The Motion Picture Export Association of America (MPEAA) cartel represented an unusual cooperation between competitors. It gained U.S. government permission to ignore U.S. anti-trust regulations in setting prices and coordinating sales overseas (Guback & Varis, 1986).

Again as a product life cycle theory might predict, U.S. exports of television seemed to peak in the late 1960s or early 1970s; they began to decline during the 1970s and 1980s in some countries in response to local competition (Pool, 1977; Tracey, 1988; Tunstall, 1977). However, not all Third World countries were equally able to begin to compete with U.S.-produced television programs. The results of the conditions of dependency outlined above, such as low income resources, lack of industrial infrastructure, lack of support by weak governments, inappropriate models for production, and lack of trained personnel, keep a number of poorer countries from developing much local or national production, even if their audiences might prefer more national programs.

The role of technological change

Recent writing on technological changes in video media has often assumed that technology would simply reinforce the unequal flow of media between countries by adding a new set of channels favoring U.S. exports over other television possibilities (Mattelart & Schmucler, 1985). In fact, videocassette recorders, cable TV, and home satellite dishes open new channels for the flow of U.S. feature films and, to lesser degree, U.S. television programs and music videos (Boyd, Straubhaar, & Lent, 1989).

The first major cross-border satellite-to-cable TV flows of programming took U.S. cable channels into Canada and the Caribbean. This programming had an extensive impact in English-speaking Canada (Raboy, 1990), the English-speaking Caribbean (Hoover & Britto, 1990), and Belize (Johnson & Oliveira, 1987), but it had less impact in the Spanish-speaking Caribbean, where it tended to be used only by English-speaking elites (Straubhaar, 1989).

Next, Armed Forces Radio-TV Service (AFRTS) became available worldwide over C-Band throughout the 1980s. For many dish owners and hotels throughout the Third World it was one of the few satellite signals available (although CNN is now putting its signal on more satellite channels with broader geographic coverage). My anecdotal evidence from Brazil indicates that while political and diplomatic elites have had increasing access to such services and have been affected by their coverage of events during the 1990 Gulf conflict, for example, there is little indication that CNN or AFRTS had or are gaining much of a mass audience.

CNN is now increasingly available on cable systems or other multichannel delivery systems in some major Latin American cities. However, research in Santo Domingo and São Paulo indicates that actual viewing is limited to a small fraction of the elite, due to lack of general audience interest and the required fluency in English (Straubhaar, 1989). The Korean version of AFRTS, U.S. Armed Forces Korean Network (AFKN), which was until recently broadcast on VHF frequencies for the American military, did acquire a substantial Korean "shadow audience", particularly among students (Choi, Straubhaar, & Tamborini, 1988).

Experiences to date with satellite-delivered cable TV or DBS programming in Europe indicates that there will be considerable resistance by non-native speakers of English to receiving satellite channels consisting largely of U.S. television (Tracey, 1988). For instance, Sky Channel made very few inroads in the European market, except in the smaller countries where cable systems were relatively hungry for new material (Boyd & Straubhaar, 1988).

The Third World's historical dependence on imports from First World countries for television production, transmission, computer effects, etc., (Mattelart & Schmucler, 1985) is changing slightly. For example, although hardware development still takes place in a few First World countries, hardware manufacturing is finally diversifying. Mature technologies are moving to the East Asian and the Latin American newly industrializing countries (NICs) for manufacturing. Brazil, South Korea, and a few others now produce VCRs, satellite dishes, microcomputers, and minor production equipment; a number of countries produce television sets. Nonetheless, most Third World countries, including almost all of Latin America, still import most of their television hardware (L. F. Santoro, personal communication, September 3, 1990).

But the manufacture of hardware may not be a key issue, aside from the desirability of gaining jobs for the national economy. If one takes a larger view of technology—looking at how it is employed rather than where it comes from—one can see an even larger absorption of mature technologies into the Third World. Some poorer Third World countries are still struggling to absorb radio production and diffuse radio receivers to all their population. In Latin America, increasing majorities of the population have both radio and television at home. Those who do not have television at home tend to see it frequently in public places.

In Latin America, the larger countries have already absorbed and dominated the use of television production technology, for the smaller and poorer countries, the process is being made much easier by sharp decreases in the cost of production technology along with increases in portability, ease of use, flexibility, etc. Equipment is much easier to operate and use in field production, making it easier for smaller commercial broadcasters, independent producers, and political and social groups to get involved in television and video production (Santoro, 1989; personal communication, September 3, 1990).

For example, major broadcasters in Brazil, especially TV Globo, have used television production increasingly efficiently and creatively since the 1960s. The 1980s have seen a growth in independent producers, the creation of video and broadcast programs by alternative and political groups, and increased production at the local and provincial levels, particularly in news. Domination of the technology comes later in smaller Third World countries, such as the Dominican Republic and Bolivia, where the decrease in production technology and transmission costs led to a profusion of television stations in the 1980s and to considerable increase in local production (Prada & Cuenco, 1986).

We may conclude that in the Third World, changes in technology have facilitated both an increased flow of First World television programs and an increase in national production. While VCRs, cable TV, and direct satellite reception bring more U.S. and European television to elites, the decreased cost and increased flexibility in television production technology have facilitated an increase in both the numbers and the diversity of television producers in Latin America. While we do not have equivalent information on production in the Mideast, Asia, and Africa, it seems likely that the same logic would be at work there.

Brazilian television programming

From the late 1960s through the 1980s, a number of countries that had large enough markets, including Brazil, began to produce more national programming to compete with U.S. and other imports. Although income in Brazil is very badly skewed, with the wealthiest 10% dominating around 50% of income (World Bank, 1990), Brazil's total gross national product supports a number of fairly strong cultural industries, including television. Although the military government's policy focused primarily on national security, it did shift resources toward television and other media. In particular, the government supplied the microwave and satellite telecommunication infrastructure to create national television networks and financed much of television's growth through extensive government advertising (Mattos, 1982).

The television industry in Brazil was clearly influenced by U.S. models, at a number of levels. Most basically, the notion of commercial media imbedded within a capitalist economy was modeled on the U.S. system and was influenced by the needs and preferences of U.S. manufacturers and advertisers who operated in Brazil. More important, perhaps, the Brazilian elites accepted a role for Brazil in the world economy and structured an explicitly capitalist model of development in which television and advertising were to create consumer demand to fuel growth (Herold, 1988; Oliveira, 1990). There were several attempts to create commercial television networks in the 1960s, including TV Rio, TV Excelsior, and TV Tupi, which proved more important in developing genres than in building institutional structures (Macedo, Falcão, & Mendes de Almeida, 1988). Television station management and network development remained relatively personalistic and political until the birth of TV Globo in 1964–1965. Although its owner, Roberto Marinho, maintained political control, he showed a new willingness to hire professional programmers and managers and delegate power to them.

Direct U.S. investment in Brazilian television began in 1964, when Time-Life created a joint venture with TV Globo, although Time-Life's programming advice was almost immediately discarded. In 1969, the government intervened to expel Time-Life, but several employees from the joint venture, including one American who switched nationalities to stay on (Joe Wallach), helped set up an efficient, U.S.-style network administration. Perhaps more important, though, was the hiring of several key Brazilians who were trained in advertising, Walter Clark and Jose Bonifacio, to create a vision of commercial television that fit the Brazilian market (Straubhaar, 1981). These key program decision-makers adapted both genre models and network operation models to Brazilian market realities. The result was the mediation and adaptation of aspects of the American model via Brazilian elites who then reinvented their own version of capitalist, commercial media. This process can be considered a form of dependent development, particularly initially, but let us consider the transformation and adaptation of institutional, technological, and genre models.

TV Globo introduced a number of local innovations within the commercial television form. It created an extensive vertical integration of all aspects of television, including research, production, and commercialization, and a horizontal integration of a number of media—radio, newspapers, magazines, book publishing, music recording, record printing and distribution, computer technology, telecommunications (the latter under a series of holding companies owned by the Marinho family). In this way, television programs could be linked with music, and hence record sales; specialty audience programs could be spun off into related magazines.

TV Globo also began to show and mention commercial products on various programs in return for a negotiated fee (Ramos, 1987). For example, from 1983 to 1990, a number of *telenovelas* on TV Globo carried in-program propaganda for a major Brazilian bank, Banco Itaú. In the *telenovela Tieta* in 1989–1990, a modern and colorful branch of Banco Itaú was frequently shown in the middle of a small, rather traditional northeast Brazilian town. The series showed the bank branch opening, characters doing frequent business and using credit cards, etc.

These developments may well represent what Brazilians often call "savage capitalism": capitalism without the regulatory restraints found in most First World countries. In the United States, for example, the two practices mentioned above would be restrained by FCC multiple ownership rules and rules against subliminal advertising (Head & Sterling, 1990). But the key point is that Brazilian commercial media take specific forms beyond their original U.S. models, responding to the unique aspects of their home market, culture, economy, and regulatory environment.

TV Globo enjoyed a quasi-monopoly from 1968 until the late 1970s, when other networks were encouraged by the military government to compete with it. Even now it enjoys the results of a "virtuous cycle" of growth: strong programming, which draws a large audience (often a 60–80% share), which draws most of the advertising (up to 70% of the advertising investment in television), which permits extensive reinvestment, which funds strong programming, and so on.

Genre adaptation/development

As in other Latin American countries, television genres in Brazil developed slowly over the 1950s and 1960s. In fact, although countries developed their own specific styles, particularly in music and comedy, there was a remarkable degree of interchange and influence, particularly in *telenovelas*. Limits on recording technology made it difficult for Latin American countries to export programs within the region, but talent, scripts, and ideas were exchanged. Scripts were often sold across borders, adapted, and, in the case of Brazil, translated (Straubhaar, 1982). Although there was not yet a regional market for programming, a base for such a market was being formed by the development of common genres.

Many of these genres have strong roots in both U.S. and European models. For the *telenovela*, for example, experts in Latin America argue about the influence of French serial novels, U.S. radio and television soap operas, and both colonial and post-independence (late nineteenth and twentieth century) regional literary traditions (Ortiz, Simões Borelli & Ortiz Ramos, 1988; Sodré, 1972). Variety shows, particularly the 4- to 8-hour marathons on Sunday afternoons and evenings, often include game show segments that seem to be copied from those in the United States.

An initial dependence on the basic U.S. commercial model has been transformed into a relatively greater interdependence within a world marketplace, with the production of programs that can compete in both national and regional markets with U.S. productions. Some critics feel that other, noncommercial forms of development would be preferable (Herold, 1988; Oliveira, 1990); in any case, the development of commercial genres and their success in the national, regional, and even world marketplaces represents a step beyond traditional dependence into an (admittedly commercialized) interdependence within the capitalist world system.

Of the commerical forms that have developed into Latin American genres, perhaps the most important are *telenovelas*, prime-time serials with a common cast and a series of subplots, like soap operas, but that run for 5–10 months, five to six evenings a week, with distinct beginnings, plot developments, and endings (Antola & Rogers, 1985; Ortiz et al., 1988; Straubhaar, 1981). Although focusing on romantic themes, they also now include historical themes and social and political commentary, and are sometimes based on prominent national or regional works of literature. In Brazil, for instance, several have developed from novels by Jorge Amado. According to Vink (1988), Brazilian *telenovela* writers have their own agendas that express diverse political and social ends.

In 1975, following the logic of its own product life cycle, TV Globo began to export *telenovelas* (Marques de Melo, 1988), a process that is discussed further below. Globo now has stronger competitors, TV Manchete and Sistema Brasileira de Televisão, which have also begun to move beyond the Brazilian market into exporting.

Variety shows are perhaps less distinct as a genre than *telenovelas*, but Latin American variety shows as a genre are far more stabilized than their U.S. cousins. The most consistent are the long variety shows that dominate Sundays on many Latin American television stations, combining music, comedy, games, discussions, dancing, amateur try-outs, and the patter of the host. Variations common in many countries include morning and noon-time shows, which include somewhat more talk and discussion.

In many Latin American countries, the line between music programs and variety is often fuzzy. Increasingly, however, live music programs or programs of regional, North American, and European music videos are seen as a particularly low-cost way to attract an audience. Particularly in countries with strong popular music traditions, like the Dominican Republic with *merengue* or Brazil with *samba*, these types of music can offer poor countries or small stations a way to compete.

Comedy tends to have a national focus, since much of it is current and topical. But forms analogous to U.S. sitcoms have developed, particularly in Mexico and Brazil, with regular casts of characters and more reliance on plot as opposed to simple gags.

Action or dramatic series, as opposed to *telenovelas*, have been quite rare in Latin America. Brazil tried to develop series in the late 1970s and early 1980s but found the form too expensive when compared to the almost equal attraction of *telenovelas* for the general audience. Series, particularly action series, remain a strong point for U.S. exports. Mini-series have also been developed in several countries, frequently with exportation clearly in mind. TV Globo has exported over a dozen mini-series to a variety of countries.

News programs are regularly produced almost everywhere in Latin America. However, the greater resources of the major networks in the larger countries is reflected by their use of their own national and international correspondents instead of national and foreign news agencies. There is also a great deal of programming in public affairs, particularly low-cost discussion and interview programs.

Audience preferences and change

The development of the genres discussed above reflected a judgment from within Latin American cultural industries that their audiences preferred at least some nationally produced genres. In Brazil, long before academic audience researchers discovered the fact, this was clearly marked by audience research conducted for TV Globo by Research Director Homero Icaza Sanchez (Straubhaar, 1981; Vink, 1988). TV Globo's programming strategy reflected this preference by filling prime time with *telenovelas*, music, and comedy; creating increasing quantities of national programming for mornings and afternoons; and pushing U.S. imports into off-hours and a few prime-time slots reserved for the U.S. genres, such as a few action series and periodic feature films, that retained an audience.

This pattern is reflected in the trends in the audience hours[1] in São Paulo devoted to different categories of programming from 1963 to 1987. The audience for U.S. programs, series, films, and cartoons increased from 36% in 1963 to 47% in 1971 and gradually declined after that to a low of 29% in 1983, as audience viewing time shifted toward national genres, such as *telenovelas*, variety shows, news, music, and comedy. After 1983, between 66 and 71% of São Paulo audience hours were devoted to national programming (Straubhaar, 1990). This receptivity for national programming supports Pool's (1977) prediction that, other things being equal, audiences will choose their own cultural products when they can.

However, the preference for national culture is not uniform, and it can be shown to be related to social class. Work in Latin America shows a distinctly greater receptivity toward national and local culture by the "popular classes"—the lower-middle class, working class, and poor (Garcia Canclini, 1988; Martín-Barbero, 1988). Martín-Barbero and Garcia Canclini both emphasize popular loyalties to folk media, music, handicrafts, etc., but Vink (1988) demonstrates that popular classes have greater affinity for national and local television production as well.

Bourdieu (1984) distinguished economic class and cultural capital (based on education and family background) as components of the larger notion of class. Earlier we noted that elites tend to have greater access to new media, such as VCRs, cable TV, and satellite dishes, which tend to carry more U.S. programming. This access is largely based on purchasing power, or economic class. However, class also directly affects preferences for particular program genres of particular origins. Dependency theorists predicted an internationalization of the bourgeoisie, the elites, and upper middle classes (Salinas & Paldán, 1979). New research seems to point to a greater traditionalism and loyalty to national and local cultures by lower or popular classes, who show the strongest tendency to seek greater cultural proximity in television programs and other cultural products. They seem to prefer nationally or locally produced material that is closer to and more reinforcing of traditional identities, based in regional, ethnic, dialect/language, religious, and other elements.

A study in São Paulo (Straubhaar, 1990), summarized in Table 15.1,[2] reflects the considerable differences in preferences for television genres among persons of different educational or cultural capital. Preference for U.S. programs, such as mini-series, series, and music, tends to be stronger among the better educated. Preference for international films, which are largely from the United States, is also stronger among the better educated. In contrast, preference for national variety shows and regionally produced Mexican comedies tends to be stronger among the less educated. Although educational/cultural capital differences in preferences were stronger than age or gender differences, those were also notable. So it seems that the desire for cultural proximity that leads lower classes and middle classes (in terms of education) toward national culture may not be as strong for elites, who seem much more internationalized, as dependency theory would predict.

Transnational media corporations

One of the clearest examples of the need to shift paradigms from dependent development to asymmetrical interdependence is provided by the growth of European, Asian, Mideastern,

Table 15.1 São audience preference for television genres, by education
Tell me how much you like the following types of television programs (percentage is based on the positive [liked & liked a lot] responses by consumers)

	Education			
	No schooling	*Primary*	*Secondary*	*University*
Genre	*% N = 9*	*% N = 37*	*% N = 35*	*% N = 27*
U.S. programs				
Mini-series	22	40	46	41
Series	22	37	43	48
Rock music	20*	32*	49*	58*
Intl. programs				
Films	30*	68*	60*	84*
Mexican comedies	22*	18*	17*	4*
Cartoons	56	54	62	39
Japanese heroes	22*	22*	14*	4*
Brazilian programs				
Telenovelas	80	66	63	56
Mini-series	44	38	60	59
Comedies	78	66	66	48
Variety shows	44***	66***	34***	27***
Pop music	80*	78*	91*	77*
Rock music	40*	30*	46*	62*
News	20***	84***	89***	93***
Debates	40*	54*	69*	85*
Films	56**	50**	71**	73**
Political ads	33**	40**	71**	73**
Sports	11**	57**	83**	60**

* $P < .05$. **$P < .01$. ***$P < .001$ based on chi-square test.

and Latin American transnational media corporations (TNCs). Dependent development theorists envisioned that major Third World countries would succeed in import substitution, often in cooperation with First World multinational companies, and develop and grow within their own markets (Evans, 1979; Salinas & Paldán, 1979). However, the more theoretically challenging phenomenon is the growth of non-U.S., indeed, non-First World, media TNCs in world and regional markets. The ability of some Third World media companies to compete with U.S., European, and Japanese cultural exporters reflects considerable growth in their size as industries, their production capacity and sophistication, and their development of programming genres. Together these factors add up to a relative increase in these companies' independence of action within the world market and the relative interdependence of that market as a whole. Their success also reflects diverse audience tastes and a search for cultural proximity and relevance.

Brazil was one of the first Third World countries to succeed in substituting its own television production for U.S. imports, beginning in the early 1970s, as indicated by the decline to 29 percent of viewing time spent on imported programs in 1983 (Straubhaar, 1990). Similarly, Brazil was one of the first Third World countries to move into regional and world market exports. However, film, music, and television exports from Argentina, Cuba, Egypt, Hong Kong, India, and Mexico have also been prominent in various regional markets since the 1950s and 1960s, so Brazil is not an isolated example.

The Latin American market for television serves as an interesting example of both the possibilities and limits for Third World cultural industries. The volume of trade in television programs between countries within the region is steadily increasing. Studies comparing the early 1970s with the early 1980s noticed such an increase, particularly in *telenovelas* (Rogers & Antola, 1985; Varis, 1984). But there has also been an increase in the flow of variety shows, comedy, music, and possibly news footage/wire copy among Latin American countries (Chen, 1987).

Mexico is the major exporter within the region, exporting a number of *telenovelas*, comedies (such as *El Chapulin Colorado* and *Chavez*), variety shows (such as *Siempre en Domingo*), music programs, and, to some countries, news (by Televisa, the private quasi-monopoly television broadcaster). Brazil, Argentina, and Venezuela also compete in the regional market, primarily with *telenovelas*, plus some variety shows (such as TV Globo's *Fantastico*) and music (both full-length programs and music videos). Colombia, Puerto Rico, and Peru have also participated in the market to lesser degrees with *telenovelas*. Television productions for U.S. Hispanics, particularly variety shows and music, are also being sold in Latin America.

A relatively clear segmentation of program genres exists within the Latin American region. Almost all Latin American countries, even the smallest, now produce an increasing amount of television. For example, in Bolivia, local production is 30–35% (Prada & Cuenco, 1986) and in the Dominican Republic around 40% (Straubhaar & Viscasillas, 1991). Most of this national production consists of live variety shows, panel discussions, news, live music, and simple format comedies—all of which are relatively inexpensive to produce and several of which depend, like panels and debates, on local topicality. At the next level, where a greater degree of interdependence is being shown, a smaller group of regional exporters produces *telenovelas*, more polished variety shows, music videos, and somewhat more highly polished comedies. Finally, there is still a considerable market throughout Latin America for U.S. action series and for feature films, cartoons, and documentaries from the United States, Europe, Japan, and, occasionally, Latin America or elsewhere in the Third World. Asian action series (kung fu, samurai dramas, etc.) and feature films have made major inroads. Similar processes of nationalization and regionalization can be seen in the Mideast, in South Asia, and in the Chinese-language regional market in Asia. There are some signs that major television producers are increasing their exports beyond Latin America. Televisa in Mexico exports *telenovelas*, variety shows, comedies, music, news, and feature films to the Hispanic market in the United States (Valenzuela, 1985). TV Globo has been successful in exporting *telenovelas* and mini-series to a variety of countries in Europe, Eastern Europe, Asia, and Africa, including China, Cuba, and the Soviet Union. TV Globo's programs have been particularly popular in Portugal and Italy (Marques de Melo, 1988; Mattelart & Mattelart, 1990).

Dominican Republic television programming

Because Brazil functions primarily as an exporter within the regional market, importing only a few comedies and occasionally programs from Mexico, Brazil is not the best example of how the Latin American regional market behaves. A better example is the Dominican Republic and its audience's reception of national, regional, and U.S. genres.

As Table 15.2 shows, the audience in Santo Domingo for regionally produced genres, such as comedies, *telenovelas*, series, music, and sports, is strong.[3] Regional programs, particularly Mexican comedies and *telenovelas*, are also notably more popular with less educated, lower-class audiences, as suggested by the foregoing discussion of class divisions in audiences' taste. Audiences exist for U.S. genres as well, and some of them are also divided by class, with better educated people tending to prefer particular U.S. genres. The strongest preferences, across classes, are for Dominican programming. This pattern reflects several key trends: the rise in production and audience preference for national programming, the rise of a market for regional programming, and the continued role of the United States as an exporter in Latin America. The Dominican audience shows clearly a second layer of the search for cultural proximity; although audiences, particularly in the middle and popular classes, prefer national material, when they cannot find it in certain genres, they then tend to prefer regional Latin American productions, which are *relatively* more culturally proximate or similar than are those produced in the United States.

Conclusion

Latin America, and Brazil in particular, seems to exemplify several developments that portend a shift away from simple dependency and toward a greater, but still asymmetrical, interdependency. National cultural industries, particularly television, have grown tremendously in their capacity as production structures, reflected in the genres they produce and increasingly export. Audiences in many countries are also clearly expressing a preference both for national production and, particularly in the smaller countries, for intraregional exports, seeking great cultural proximity at both levels.

Regional exporters are working within an increasingly integrated commercially based Latin American TV market. There are major exporters, such as Brazil and Mexico, and intermediate exporters, such as Venezuela, Colombia, and Argentina. There are net importers, like Bolivia and the Dominican Republic. Among the regional genres that are exported, chief are *telenovelas*. That seems to reflect a trend of the rise of soap operas everywhere: In Brazil, they are becoming more complex and cinematic; in Mexico and India, they seem more romantic and also more didactic (Singhal & Rogers, 1989). In Japan and Hong Kong, soap operas are often combined with martial arts action.

Other genres are beginning to compete in regional and world markets. For instance, in Brazil, for children, there is now a tendency to import both cartoons and action series

Table 15.2 Santo Domingo audience preference for television genres, by education
Tell me how much you like the following types of television programs? (percentage is based on the positive [liked & liked a lot] responses by consumers)

Genre	Education		
	Primary or less % N = 35	*Secondary* % N = 36	*University* % N = 49
U.S. programs			
Series	52	35	34
Rock music	24	18	13
Films in English	25**	15**	50**
Films	68	74	73
News in English	09	13	15
Cartoons	55*	30*	45*
Sports	46	25	38
Documentary	29*	42*	66*
Regional Latin American programs			
Mexican comedies	67*	39*	26*
Telenovelas	38*	41*	17*
Series	35	23	26
Music	46	31	62
World sports	48*	42*	49*
Dominican programs			
Comedies	77	61	57
AM variety shows	17	22	27
Noon variety shows	64*	47*	27*
Sunday variety show	56	62	48
Merengue	80	72	66
Music	59	55	44
Debates/panels	33*	38*	64*
Natl. news	78	85	81
Natl. sports	50	46	44
Children's	41*	30*	10*

* $P < .05$. **$P < .01$ based on chi-square test.

from Asia as well as the United States. The particular examples in Brazil are from Japan—super heroes called "Jaspion", "Changeman", etc.—but elsewhere Chinese kung fu series are also becoming popular. There are also increased world flows of feature films, music, comedy, and sports.

Nevertheless, the increasing interdependence of the world television market seems to bear a strong regional flavor. That makes sense, given distinct regional cultural patterns such as those found in Latin America, Europe, the Mideast, East Asia, South Asia, and parts of Africa. Language groups, such as Spanish in Latin America or Chinese in East Asia, tend to reinforce regionality. But, as the success of Brazilian programming dubbed into Spanish throughout Latin America shows, there are regional similarities beyond language (although the similarity of the Spanish and Portuguese languages makes dubbing easier and more acceptable).

Television production is growing within Latin America at both the national and regional levels precisely because there are audiences receptive to both. The Brazilian case shows how strong the preference is for national programming, when the domestic market is large enough to support 10–12 hours a day of production on the major channel and when the cultural industries are developed to produce it. Within, Brazil, the desire for yet more cultural proximity is leading toward an expressed desire for increased regionalization in news and entertainment to express and satisfy regional cultures (L.F. Santoro, personal communication, September 3, 1990). The case of the Dominican audience shows clearly a second layer of the search for cultural proximity: a preference first for national material, and, when that cannot be filled in certain genres, a tendency to look next to regional Latin American productions, which are relatively more culturally proximate or similar than are those of the United States.

Thus we see a qualitative change in world media relations. Although the United States still dominates world media sales and flows, national and regional cultural industries are consolidating a relatively more interdependent position in the world television market. Reflecting and contributing to that industrial change, audiences are seeking greater cultural relevance or proximity from both national and regional television programs. We would expect to see similar changes toward nationalization and regionalization of industries and audiences in music, magazine production, film, and other media. The process remains complex, however. While some national producers gain greater interdependence in some genres with some audiences, some producers and genres fail, and some audiences continue to prefer internationalized productions from outside both nation and region. We simply suggest a larger gamut of possibilities, from dependence to relative interdependence, in media relations.

Notes

1   Audience hours are a weighted ratings measure that represents the proportion of an audience's total viewing time spent watching programs in a particular genre or program format (Straubhaar, 1981).
2   The table is based on in-depth interviews with a quota sampling of 120 adults (over 15) conducted in December 1989–March 1990. For further methodological detail, see Straubhaar (1990).
3   The table is based on in-depth interviews with a quota sampling of 120 adults (over 15) conducted in January–March 1988. Further methodological detail is available from the author.

References

Antola, A., & Rogers, E. M. (1984). Television flows in Latin America. *Communication Research*, *11*, 183–202.

Beltran, L. R. (1978). TV etchings in the minds of Latin Americans: Conservatism, materialism, and conformism. *Gazette*, *24*(1), 61–85.

Beltran, L. R., & Fox de Cardona, E. (1979). Latin America and the United States: Flaws in the free flow of information. In K. Nordenstreng & H. I. Schiller (Eds.), *National Sovereignty and International Communications* (pp. 33–64). Norwood, NJ: Ablex.

Blumler, J. G., & Katz, E. (Eds.). (1974). *The uses of mass communications: Current perspectives on gratifications research*. Beverly Hills: Sage.

Bourdieu, P. (1984). *Distinction: A social critique of the judgement of taste*. Cambridge, MA: Harvard University Press.

Boyd, D. A., & Straubhaar, J. D. (1988). Developmental impact of the home video cassette recorder on third world countries. *Journal of Broadcasting and Electronic Media*, *29*(1), 5–21.

Boyd, D. A., Straubhaar, J. D., & Lent, J. A. (1989). *Videocassette recorders in the Third World*. New York: Longman.

Boyd-Barrett, O. (1980). *The international news agencies*. Beverly Hills: Sage.

Cardoso, F. H. (1973). Associated dependent-development: Theoretical and practical implications. In A. Stepan (Ed.), *Authoritarian Brazil* (pp. 142–178). New Haven, CT: Yale University Press.

Chen, S.-L. (1987). *The flow of television programs from the United States to Latin America: A comparative study of two weeks' television schedules in 1973 and in 1983*. Unpublished master's thesis, Michigan State University, East Lansing.

Choi, J., Straubhaar, J., & Tamborini, R. (June 1, 1988). *American Armed Forces television in Korea and its shadow viewers: Who views what for what reasons with what impact?* Paper presented at the meeting of the International Communication Association, New Orleans.

Evans, P. (1979). *Dependent development: The alliance of multinational, state, and local capital in Brazil*, Princeton, NJ: Princeton University Press.

Fiske, J. (1987). *Television culture*. New York: Methuen.

Fox, E. (1975). Multinational television. *Journal of Communication*, *25*(2), 122–127.

Galtung, J. (1971). A structural theory of imperialism. *Journal of Peace Research*, No. 2, 81–117.

Garcia Canclini, N. (1988). Culture and power: The state of research. *Media, Culture and Society*, *10*, 467–498.

Gramsci, A. (1971). *Selections from the prison notebooks*. New York: International Publishers.

Guback, T., & Varis, T. (1986). *Transnational communication and cultural industries*, No. 92. Paris: UNESCO Reports and Papers on Mass Communication.

Hall, S. (1982). The rediscovery of ideology: Return of the repressed in media studies. In M. Gurevich, T. Bennett, J. Curran & J. Woollacott (Eds.). *Culture, Society & The Media* (pp. 56–90). London: Methuen.

Hamelink, C. J. (1983). *Cultural autonomy in global communications*. New York: Longman.

Head, S. W., & Sterling, C. H. (1990). *Broadcasting in America* (6th ed.). Boston: Houghton Mifflin.

Herold, C. M. (1988). The "Brazilianization" of Brazilian television: A critical review. *Studies in Latin American Popular Culture*, *7*, 41–58.

Hoover, S., & Britto, P. (June 25–July 1, 1990). *Communication, culture and development in the Eastern Caribbean: Case studies in new technology and culture policy*. Paper presented at the meeting of the International Communication Association, Dublin.

Janus, N. (1981). Advertising and the mass media in the era of the global corporation. In E. McAnany & J. Schnitman, & N. Janus (Eds.), *Communication and social structure: Critical studies in mass media research* (pp. 287–316). New York: Praeger.

Johnson, J. D. & Oliveira, O. S. (1987). *Media evaluations and levels of television exposure in Belize*. Paper presented at the Eastern Communication Association Conventions, Syracuse, NY.

Katz, E., & Liebes, T. (1984). Once upon a time in Dallas. *Intermedia*, *12*(3), 28–32.

Lec, C.-C. (1980). *Media imperialism reconsidered*. Beverly Hills: Sage.

Macedo, C., Falcão, A., & Mendes de Almeida, C. J. (1988). *TV ão vivo—depoimentos*. São Paulo: Brasiliense.

Marques de Melo, J. (1988). *As telenovelas da Globo*. São Paulo: Summus.

Martín-Barbero, J. (1988). Communication from culture: The crisis of the national and the emergence of the popular. *Media, Culture and Society*, *10*, 447–466.

Mattelart, M., & Mattelart, A. (1990). *The carnival of images: Brazilian television fiction*. New York: Bergin & Garvey.

Mattelart, A., & Schmucler, H. (1985). *Communication and information technologies: Freedom of choice for Latin America?* Norwood, NJ: Ablex.

Mattos, S. (1982). *The Brazilian military and television*. Unpublished master's thesis, University of Texas, Austin.

Mattos, S. (1984). Advertising and government influences on Brazilian television. *Communication Research*, *11*, 203–220.

McAnany, E. (1984). From modernization and diffusion to dependency and beyond: Theory and practice in communication for social change in the 1980's. In V. Sigman (Ed.), *Communication in the Third World* (pp. 1–14). Urbana: College of Agriculture, University of Illinois.

Milanesi, L. A. (1978). *O paraiso via EMBRATEL*. Rio de Janeiro: Paz e Terra.

Morley, D. (1980). *The "Nationwide" audience: Structure and decoding*. London: British Film Institute.

Nordenstreng, K. & Varis, T. (1973). *Television traffic: A one way street?* Reports, papers on Mass Communication #70 Paris: UNESCO.

Oliveira, O. S. (1989). Media and dependency: A view from Latin America. *Media Development* No. 1, 10–13.

Oliveira, O. S. (June 25–July 1, 1990). *Brazilian soaps outshine Hollywood: Is cultural imperialism fading out?* Paper presented at the meeting of the International Communication Association, Dublin.

Ortiz, R., Simões Borelli, S. H., & Ortiz Ramos, J. M. (1988). *Telenovela: história e produção.* São Paulo: Brasiliense.

Pool, I. de S. (1977). The changing flow of television. *Journal of Communication, 27*(2), 139–149.

Prada, R. R., & Cuenco, N. T. (1986). *La television en Bolivia.* La Paz: Quipus.

Raboy, M. (1990). *Missed opportunity. The story of Canada's broadcasting policy.* Montreal: McGiu University Press.

Ramos, R. (1987). *Gra-finos na Globa—culture e merchandising nas novelas* (2nd ed.). Petropolis, Brazil: Vozes.

Read, W. H. (1976). *America's mass media merchants.* Baltimore: Johns Hopkins University Press.

Rogers, E. M. & Antola, L. (1985). Telenovelas: A Latin American success story. *Journal of Communication, 35,* 24–35.

Salinas, R., & Paldán, L. (1979). Culture in the process of dependent development: Theoretical perspectives. In K. Nordenstreng & H. I. Schiller (Eds.), *National sovereignty and international communications* (pp. 82–98). Norwood, NJ: Ablex.

Santoro, L. F. (1989). *A imagem nas mãos—o video popular no Brasil.* São Paulo: Summus.

Singhal, A., & Rogers, E. M. (1989). *India's information revolution.* New Delhi and Newbury Park, CA: Sage.

Sodré, M. (1972). *A communicacão do grotesco.* Petropolis, Brazil: Editora Vozes.

Straubhaar, J. D. (1981). *The transformation of cultural dependency: The decline of American influence on the Brazilian television industry.* Unpublished doctoral dissertation, Fletcher School of Law and Diplomacy, Tufts University.

Straubhaar, J. (1982). The development of the telenovela as the pre-eminent form of popular culture in Brazil. *Studies in Latin American Popular Culture, 1,* 138–150.

Straubhaar, J. D. (1984). Brazilian television: The decline of American influence. *Communication Research, 11*(2), 221–240.

Straubhaar, J. D. (May 25–29, 1989). *The uses and effects of cable TV in the Dominican Republic.* Paper presented at the meeting of the International Communication Association, San Francisco.

Straubhaar, J. D. (June 25–July 1, 1990). *Social class and audience responses to television and new video technologies in Brazil and the Dominican Republic: Toward a concept of cultural proximity.* Paper presented at the meeting of the International Communication Association, Dublin.

Straubhaar, J. D., & Viscasillas, G. M. (1991). Class, genre, and the regionalization of television programming in the Dominican Republic. *Journal of Communication, 41*(1), 53–69.

Tracey, M. (1988). Popular culture and the economics of global television. *Intermedia, 16*(3), 9–25.

Tunstall, J. (1977). *The media are American.* Beverly Hills: Sage.

Valenzuela, N. A. (1985). *Organizational evolution of a Spanish-language television network: An environmental approach.* Unpublished doctoral dissertation, Department of Communication, Stanford University.

Varis, T. (1984). The international flow of television programs. *Journal of Communication, 34*(1), 143–152.

Vink, N. (1988). *The telenovela and emancipation.* Amsterdam: Royal Tropical Institute.

Wallerstein, I. (1979). *The capitalist world-economy.* Cambridge: Cambridge University Press.

World Bank. (1990). *World development report.* New York: Oxford University Press.

Chapter 16

Lina Khatib

COMMUNICATING ISLAMIC FUNDAMENTALISM AS GLOBAL CITIZENSHIP

DEBATES ON GLOBALIZATION have carried with them variable, often conflicting, views on the relationship between the global and the local. On one hand, globalization has been seen as the intensification of relations between different cultures in a time-space compression (Robertson 1997). On the other hand, it has been looked at as the expansion of cultures into the global realm (Featherstone 1995). Both those views articulate the idea that the global and the local are constantly interacting. The result of this interaction has often been seen as either a homogenization of cultures, resulting in cultural integration or unification, or a heterogenization, not only in the sense that cultures are diverse but also that they may clash (Huntington 1996).

At the heart of all this lies a debate about the position of the nation in a globalized world. Some argue that the nation and nationalism are becoming obsolete, with connections being made between cultures and individuals across national boundaries, resulting in cosmopolitanism where the individual becomes a citizen of the world (Naussbaum 1994). Others argue that the nation is in fact strengthened in this context, with individuals holding on to their national identity to protect its existence in the face of usurping global forces (Dorris 1994). In other words, this view looks at the global as a threat to the local. In this context, I am using the term *local* to refer to national rather than subnational (Mann 2000) affiliation.

However, the world today is witnessing the emergence of new forms of affiliation that transcend the nation yet that do not necessarily mean that the nation is under threat. Those new affiliations can be seen as a new kind of nationalism, or patriotism. This "new patriotism" describes the existence of intersecting affiliations, local, global, regional, and religious. This article discusses a particular case of new patriotism, that of Islamic fundamentalism as an example of global (not cosmopolitan) citizenship. The article argues that Islamic fundamentalism articulates itself within, and not in opposition to, processes of globalization, defined here as "those processes, operating on a global scale, which cut across national boundaries, integrating and connecting communities and organizations in new space-time combinations, making the world in reality and in experience more interconnected" (Hall 1992, 299).

Attention will be paid to the role of the Internet as an identity tool communicating this global citizenship, as the Internet is a means of self-definition for Islamic fundamentalist movements worldwide (Beck 2000). The Internet is discussed as a means of constituting, representing, and influencing the existence and growth of various Islamic fundamentalist groups in a global context.

In what follows, I will start with justifying my choice of Islamic fundamentalism as new patriotism, followed by a definition of the term *Islamic fundamentalism* as used in this article. I will then explore Islamic fundamentalism in the local (defined as national) and regional realms, followed by a discussion of the Internet as an identity tool. Then, I will discuss Islamic fundamentalist groups' use of the Internet to communicate their global identity. Finally, I will conclude with an analysis of Islamic fundamentalism as a glocal force.

Why Islamic fundamentalism?

In "Identity Blues," Ien Ang (2000) looks at cultural identities as being historically grounded but also as being transformable. She argues that identities are not essential, but instead, that at the level of experience, identities "*feel* natural and essential" (p. 2). She says that the focus on identities as constructions diverts attention away from the political realities of identities that are expressed as essentialist (like Islamic fundamentalism). This results in a pathological outlook on those "essentialist" identities while romanticizing the "constructed," open ones. One reason for this romanticization of identity, she says, is that the idea of open identities is often ascribed to new social movements, from feminism to multicultural movements—movements that have been seen as progressive and future-orientated. She cites Calhoun's argument that this idea is problematic because it

> groups together what seem to the researchers relatively "attractive" move-ments, vaguely on the left, but leaves out other contemporary movements such as the new religious right and fundamentalism, the resistance of white ethnic communities against people of color, various versions of nationalism, and so forth. (Calhoun 1994, 22, cited in Ang 2000, 3)

Hall (1992) argues that globalization entails the formation of new identifications that are simultaneously global and local. However, he singles out the Islamic fundamentalist identity as being the result of the "tension between Tradition and Translation" (p. 312), or between "ethnicity" and "global homogenization" (p. 313). However, while Islamic funda-mentalist movements have often been looked at as being oppositional to global processes, they articulate their identities in a similar manner to the new social movements'. By that I mean that both constitute a new patriotism, conceptualized as the formation of new "linkages between . . . delocalized political communications, and revitalized political com-mitments," and at the same time provide a means for the production of locality for com-munities in multiple ethnoscapes (Appadurai 1996, 196). Islamic fundamentalism today, namely after the September 11 attack on the World Trade Center in 2001, has been invoked as a threat to globalization, a closed, localized force that challenges our nonessentialist, fluid identities. However, I argue that Islamic fundamentalism is a relativizing force within processes of globalization, not aiming at negating global reality but at shaping it. By that I mean that Islamic fundamentalism is "a way of asserting a particular (group) identity, which in turn is a prime method of competing for power and influence in the global system" (Beyer 1994, 4). In doing so, Islamic fundamentalism transcends nations but is not necessarily oppositional to the nation. The articulation of an Islamic fundamentalist identity is essential-ist à la Ang, but that identity itself is fluid and is constructed differently in different contexts.

Islamic fundamentalism is experienced locally, but is at the same time a global movement. I will discuss these ideas and their relationship with communication in the sections to follow; but to understand those perspectives, it is first necessary to view Islamic fundamentalism in a historical context.

Defining Islamic fundamentalism

There has been a considerable degree of disagreement over the term *Islamic fundamentalism*. Although in this article I am using the term to refer to various Islamic groups and traditions, it has to be stressed that each should be looked at in a specific historical context (e.g., there is a difference between the fundamentalism of Saudi Arabia and that of Iran; Tehranian 2000). The term has been defined from various angles and to describe diverse and unrelated movements within a fractured political landscape (Agha 2000; Hall 1992). The term can refer to "the growth of Islam as a religious force and a political ideology and . . . to the desire to reinstate the Islamic legal code" (White, Little, and Smith 1997, 7). The term can also refer to "the emotional, spiritual and political response of Muslims to an acute and continuing social, economic and political crisis that has gripped the Middle East" (Ehteshami 1997, 180). However, it has also been defined as a challenge to America's position as a global power and its hegemonic interests, a term used by the United States as a shorthand to discredit opponents as irrational and irresponsible (Saikal 2000). At the same time, it has been seen as a challenge to Western ideologies in general like secularism (Mowlana 2000). It has also sometimes been defined (erroneously) as synonymous with terrorism (White, Little, and Smith 1997). The term has caused such controversy that it has been proposed that it should be avoided altogether. This is because it "has become a psychological scapegoat for those who refuse to acknowledge and take responsibility for the real international and intercultural problems" (Tehranian 2000, 217). Those multiple definitions can be traced to the difficulty of aligning contradictory or "dislocated" identities "into one, overarching 'master identity' on which a politics could be securely grounded" (Hall 1992, 280).

There are three characteristics that link the various Islamic fundamentalisms, and which form the basis for the use of the term in this article. First, Islamic fundamentalism does not refer to movements that are religious only, but also to political ones that aim at establishing a "polity of believers" (Hamzeh 1998). Second, Islamic fundamentalists believe in Islamic authenticity, juxtaposed with what is seen as Western hegemony, which in turn is believed to threaten this authenticity. Western hegemony is not confined to Western countries; it also applies to secular people in the Muslim world who are seen as even worse than the "foreign infidels" (Faksh 1997, 9). They are seen as "representing the interests of the . . . formerly . . . colonial powers" (Taheri 1987, 16). Finally, fundamentalist groups seem to agree on the necessity of Jihad (holy war) to preserve and expand the Muslim community. However, the groups differ in their interpretation and application of Jihad. While some see Jihad as nonviolent, others like the Islamic Jihad Organization view Jihad as being military.

In this article I am using the term loosely to refer to "a diverse set of competing political opinions held within the Muslim community" (Ehteshami 1997, 179). In short, my use of the term emanates from the fact that other terms (Islamists, extremists, fanatics, etc.) are no less damaging, and also carry their own complications. Thus, I am using *Islamic fundamentalism* in the political sense, to refer to groups that use Islam as a basis to achieve political power. In doing so I will be concentrating on a set of Islamic fundamentalist groups connected (directly or indirectly) through the Internet with al-Qaida, the group led by Osama bin Laden that has gained notoriety after having been blamed for the September 11 attacks.

Islamic fundamentalism and nationalism

From this we can see that Islamic fundamentalism is an example of "the ambiguous expression [of] assimilation into the universal . . . and simultaneously for . . . adhering to the particular, the reinvention of difference" (Wallerstein 1984, 166–67). On one hand, Islamic fundamentalism recognizes its "difference" from the West, and articulates it to replace Western hegemony with its own "hegemony" or, as Robins (2000) puts it, "to create a global civilization on different basis from that which is being elaborated by the symbolic analysts of the West" (p. 200). Fundamentalism's "shifting hegemony" provides "alternative visions of the global situation" (Friedman 1994, 201) that aim at "the formation of a single world culture" that transcends the nation (Friedman 1994, 100). Islamic fundamentalism's ideal, the establishment of a polity of believers (or *umma*) conflicts with the idea of the nation-state. For example, Sayyid Qutb—an Egyptian fundamentalist guru with a following among al-Qaida members—has been quoted as saying that a "Muslim's nationality is his [*sic*] religion" (quoted in Faksh 1997, 10). Indeed, Qutb has himself engaged in an active opposition to the past Egyptian president Nasser's nationalist-secularist regime, which ended in Qutb's execution in 1966.

On the other hand, Islamic fundamentalism has not always been oppositional to the nation. Islamic fundamentalism was mobilized in the 1920s to expel the British from Egypt and rally against the Soviets in Afghanistan. More recently, it has been used by Hizbollah to expel the Israelis from South Lebanon. These examples illustrate how "being" (or rather, "becoming") Islamic fundamentalist is not a matter of subsuming cultural/national difference, but rather of "constituting a *discursive device* which represents difference as . . . identity" (Hall 1992, 297).

On another level, the Islamic fundamentalist identity recognizes the national nature of conflicts yet projects them beyond the nation. An example is Palestinian group Hamas, which targets its activities against Israel and yet engages in rallying support in other countries (like Britain), where it hails the suffering of Palestinians as a global issue rather than a localized one. As we can see, Islamic fundamentalism's fluid identity has taken different forms according to the historical context, moving from being nationalist to a challenge to nationalism to a mixture of both. The spread of fundamentalism as a "national" form "divorced from territorial states" (Appadurai 1996, 169) has prompted Appadurai to label its identity "postnational." He also uses the term to refer to fundamentalism's emergence as an alternative form "for the organization of global traffic in resources, images and ideas." However, while Appadurai also maintains that this implies that nation-states have become obsolete, the above discussion alerts us that we cannot make generalizations about Islamic fundamentalism as being essentially oppositional to the nation, and as seeing the concept of the nation-state as hegemonic and anti-Islam.

Islamic fundamentalism as a regional force

Islamic fundamentalism does not only have a local character but is also regional. Islamic fundamentalism as a regional force is seen in the Islamic world, but is perhaps most visible in the Arab world (although that view is currently being challenged with the increasing exposure of groups in places like Kenya, Indonesia, and Chechnya). The Arab world has gone through stages in which its regional identity has been put forward and withdrawn. During the rule of Egypt's Nasser, for example, there was a resurgence of pan-Arabism. This can be seen as a reaction to colonial (British, French, Italian) presence in the region, as well as to the formation of the state of Israel in 1948. However, Nasser failed at establishing Arab unity. This is because, first, pan-Arabism underwent tensions between the demands of the state and those of collective action (Smith 1997), and second, because the different political regimes within it are ultimately national (Fanon 1994).

Moreover, the advocacy of a national identity (whether local or regional) has been in conflict with the views of many Islamic fundamentalists in the Arab world who argue for an Islamic identity (Al-Ahsan 1992). The existence of Islamic fundamentalists in the Arab world and elsewhere can be seen as an example of the failure of the nation-state system to create a truly national identity (whether local or regional). However, what seemed to partly resolve this identity crisis in the Arab world is the problem with Israel, as Arab countries have attempted to unite against this common enemy (Al-Ahsan 1992). Yet this unity was short-lived, catalyzed by Egypt's and Jordan's signing of peace agreements with Israel. Not only did the peace treaties go against popular opinion across the Arab world, they also added to the dismay of Islamic fundamentalist groups, who regard Jihad against Zionism as one of their motives. In this sense, Islamic fundamentalism has arisen as a kind of substitute for a failing Arab identity.

Today, Islamic fundamentalism can also be looked at as a global force articulating the three sides of globalization: the material (flow of trade, local/global happenings and reper-cussions), the spatio-temporal (interregional meetings across time and space), and the cognitive (transformation of power relations beyond the nation) (Held and McGrew 2000). Al-Qaida (literally, the base) is an example of the multiple construction of Islamic funda-mentalist identity "across different, often intersecting and antagonistic, discourses, practices and positions" (Hall 1996a, 4). Al-Qaida is a network of movements operating worldwide, with converging yet variable political agendas. The movements are united in their oppos-ition to Western hegemony, yet the way they implement this antagonism differs in different contexts. While the movements agree in opposing Israel, for example, not all of them engage in anti-Israeli missions (such missions seem to be conducted mainly by the Islamic Jihad and Hamas in Palestine). The movements thus are global in the sense that they function within a disembedded institution (interestingly, al-Qaida does not have a recog-nized physical base), "linking local practices with globalized, social relations" (Giddens 1990, 79).

Hall (1996a) argues that identities are constituted through representation: the Internet is a "system of cultural representation" (p. 292) that mirrors "the weakening of homo-geneous identities, and the multiplicity of identities which we are able to live in and inhabit" (Hall 2003). The Internet narrates the Islamic fundamentalist imagined community, reflect-ing the groups' principles and aims, and representing their shared experiences (Hall 1992).

The Internet as an identity tool

The Internet has been argued to be a medium of possibility, where the individual can go beyond his or her social self (Turkle 1996; Hjarvard 2002). It also blurs the boundaries between the spaces in which those who are connected exist (Freeman 1999). Cyberspace has created communities that are not necessarily physically or nationally bound but which transcend the sacred boundaries of home and nation (Morley 1999). However, that is not to imply that the Internet is detached from the realities of the social world. On the contrary, as Shohat (1999) argues, cyberspace is another space and not a substitute space. Existing local and global power relations are thus extended to this (new) space, rather than being displaced from the physical one. Cyberspace is another zone in which conflicts are carried out and that is connected with the corporality of its users.

Today, after the September 11 attacks, we are becoming more aware of the connections between Islamic fundamentalism and cyberspace, with more unearthing of Islamic fundamentalist cyberactivities (such as al-Qaida's messages on its Web site al-Neda [www.alneda.com] supporting the attack and calling for an all-out war between Islam and the West [OutThere News 2002]). However, even before the attacks, this relationship had already been cemented and recognized. The Internet has been a site of political struggle through the use of chat rooms, e-mail, and various Web sites. Not only have people with clashing political opinions battled over the Internet, political conflicts have been carried further through practices like hacking and raids on ISPs. For example, the Lebanese group Hizbollah's Web site was hacked in 2001 after Hizbollah captured three Israeli soldiers at the border in South Lebanon (Scheeres 2001). Its Lebanese service provider, Destination, also had its home page hacked by a group of Israeli teenagers (Weisman 2001). Six days before September 11, FBI and other agents raided InfoCom Corporation in Texas, crashing five hundred Web sites with Arab or Muslim connections (Whitaker 2001).

The events of September 11 catalyzed more cyberwar activities. Al-Neda's messages to rally support against the United States prompted its hacking by an American in 2002 (Di Justo 2002). Visitors to the Web site today are greeted with the slogan "Hacked, Tracked and Now Owned by the USA." However, as we will see in the next section, other militant groups still have a presence on the Internet.

The next section examines the various ways Islamic fundamentalist groups use the Internet to articulate their global/local identity. This covers political, commercial, ideological, linguistic, and communicative/interactive uses of Web sites. The analysis poses the following questions: How is the Internet used by Islamic fundamentalist groups to express conflicting ideologies toward the nation? How is the Internet used to communicate a Pax Islamica in and outside of the Middle East? How is it used to respond to a changing political climate? What kinds of cyberwars are taking place and among whom?

To answer those questions, the article will analyze the Web sites' commercial and fundraising activities, organizational and communicative uses, choice of languages, selection of news published, and interactive sections and hyperlinks with other sites. This will be done through the use of textual analysis, comprising discourse and thematic analysis, combined with network analysis. Those methods are important due to the complex nature of the Internet and the structure of Web sites. The combination of methods helps reveal the structure in the Web sites' interaction, as the units of analysis in this research project (the Web sites) are embedded within a system of related sites (Garton, Haythornthwaite, and Wellman 1997; Jackson 1997). The analysis will concentrate on the sites' content but will also refer to their design and structure and how those factors are linked with the related groups' activities in the social world. Due to the vast number of Web sites related to Islamic fundamentalist groups, the project will limit itself to thirteen sites connected with the al-Qaida network through hyperlinks.

Communicating Islamic fundamentalism

The use of the Internet by Islamic fundamentalist groups reflects an outward vision combined with a global target audience, while also paying attention to local issues. The Internet has many uses for the groups. It is used to post messages about the groups' mission statements. It is used to relay photographs, audio and video messages, and footage about the groups' activities. It is often used to post the latest news related to the groups and their affiliates. It acts as a convenient way for collecting money donations. It allows group members and supporters to find out about the groups' latest actions. It also allows them to communicate via e-mail and chat rooms. The Internet is also used by the groups to sell books, tapes, CDs, and other materials. The groups can also use the Internet to respond to current political situations.

The groups' Web sites differ in their design and ease of use: some are mainly text-based (like JihaaɗulKuffarin, www.jihaadulkuffarin.jeeran.com), while others are more sophisticated, resembling multilayered news portals (like Taliban Online, www.muslimthai.com/talibanonline). Some Web sites are directly affiliated to specific Islamic fundamentalist groups, like the Lebanese Hizbollah (www.hizbollah.org), the Afghani Taliban (Taliban Online), the Pakistani Tanzeem-e-Islami (www.tanzeem.org), the Palestinian Hamas (under the name Palestine Information Center, www.palestine-info.co.uk), the Chechen al-Mujahidoun (under the name Qoqaz.net, www.qoqaz.net; and also Qoqaz.com, www.qoqaz.com), and al-Muhajiroun (a Salafi Islamic fundamentalist group connected to the Taliban, www.almuhajiroun.com).

Other Web sites are slightly more ambiguous about their affiliations, such as JihaaɗulKuffarin, which is connected to the Islamic Group (Jamaّa Islamiyya) led by the Egyptian Sheikh Omar Abd-el-Rahman, and Supporters of Shareeah (www.shareeah.com), which is the site of Sheikh Abu Hamza al-Masri and his followers in Britain. Other Web sites do not have any overt affiliations, such as Jannah (www.jannah.org), as-Sahwa (www.as-sahwah.com), Beware of Shiaism (www.bewareofshiaism.8k.com), and Maktabah Al-Ansar (www.maktabah.net); however, they are connected through hyperlinks to other recognized sites like Shareeah.

I will now move to a brief description of the content of the Web sites discussed and how it reflects their global/local identity or new patriotism.

The expression of conflicting ideologies toward the nation

Globalization is characterized by the transformation of power relations, where the established (new) world order is challenged by forces like Islamic fundamentalist groups (Held and McGrew 2000). On one hand, the groups' Web sites pay attention to local issues in the countries in which the groups operate. On the other hand, the Web sites advocate a kind of global ethics that links the groups together in their aims and goals (such as the establishment of a Pax Islamica) (European Community Studies Association [ECSA] 2003). This multifocal approach reflects how the Islamic fundamentalist identity "is perceived as a shattered repertoire of mini-roles, instead of a nucleus of hypothetical sense of self" (Canclini 1998, quoted in Network EICOS 2003).

The Web sites' adherence to the nation can be seen in the way they pay attention to particular issues in particular nation states. Thus, Tanzeem is mainly concerned with Pakistan; Qoqaz.net and Qoqaz.com with Chechnya; Taliban with Afghanistan, presenting information about the Taliban, the history of Afghanistan, and a list of Taliban enemies (including the United States); and Hizbollah with Lebanon, reporting the latest attacks by Israel on villages in the South. This localization can be seen in the sites' mission statements, which contain sections highlighting their accomplishments, military and civilian. Hamas contains a "Glory Record," summarizing a list of the group's anti-Israeli activities both inside and outside Palestine, starting from 1988 and ending in 1994. Hizbollah contains video clips of the group's attacks on Israeli targets and photographs of victims of Israeli violence in Lebanon and Palestine.

At the same time, the Islamic fundamentalist global outlook illustrates an antagonism toward the nation, with sites like Shareeah declaring that one cannot be a British Muslim because national affiliation contradicts the concept of *umma*. The sites seem to recognize the heterogeneity in the articulation of how Islam is understood in light of interweaving political beliefs and practices like nationalism (Eade 2003). Hence, some sites like as-Sahwah contain articles interpreting Islam as antinationalist, like "A Muslim's Nationality and His Belief" by Sayyid Qutb.

The sites also mirror the groups' global scope of operation and cooperation. Articles on JihaadulKuffaarin contain the Jamaa Islamiyya's position on various international events, with headlines like "Mujaahideen Attack Russian Army Base in Dagestan [Chechnya]," "Arab Veterans of the Afghan War," and "The Moro Jihaad: Continuous Struggle for Islaamic [sic] Independence in Southern Philippines." Taliban Online boasts headlines like "There is Taliban-like movement in Iraq's Kurdish area" and "Anti-Americanism alive in a friendly country" (referring to Kuwait). Shareeah has a "Projects" section, containing items with titles such as "Department of Education Schools for Girls" and "Food Distribution Program" (in Afghanistan). However, the links to the body of the sections are inactive, leaving such "projects" ambiguous.

However, one way in which the sites link together the local and the global is through their language use. The Web sites use English as their primary language, with Arabic being the second most popular. Web sites like Shareeah, Hizbollah, and Taliban Online use both languages. While the use of English can be seen as an example of "hegemonic globalization" (ECSA 2003), it can also be interpreted as reflecting the groups' "growing mobility across frontiers" (Robins 2000, 195). Shareeah also has an option in Bosnian, while Hamas's Web site, the Palestine Information Center, uses Malawi, Urdu, Persian, and Russian, in addition to Arabic and English. The Web sites thus seem to aim at an audience beyond the Arab world. They also hint at the fact that the members and supporters of the various groups belong to several nationalities or live in different countries. Yet the sites' outlooks are localized through the inclusion of Arabic terms within English language sentences (umma, zakaah, shaheed). This can be seen as an illustration of how "global encounters and inter-actions are producing inventive new cultural forms" (Robins 2000, 196). The sites are also localized in their subject matter, as the content of mirror sites in different languages sometimes differs. While Hizbollah's Web site seems to offer identical information in Arabic and English, Shareeah's Bosnian option takes you to another Web site altogether with more specific information related to Bosnia. This suggests that the groups' primary affiliation remains to the countries in which they are based.

The communication of a Pax Islamica

The Web sites reveal the solidarity of vision among the groups as they converge in their agreement on the establishment of a Pax Islamica. This Pax Islamica is communicated through the Web sites' statements on the necessity of Jihad, their commercial activities, and their interactive sections and hyperlinks. The agreement on Jihad can be seen on JihaadulKuffaarin, which contains an article claiming that the notion of Jihad refers to qital (military fighting) and not linguistic or other forms of Jihad. This is mirrored on al-Muhajiroun's Web site, which in its Q&A section affirms that "jihad as divine terrorism is obligatory in Islam." Tanzeem-e-Islami's mission statement declares that the group is replacing Sayyid Abdul A 'al Maududi's Jamaat-e-Islami in Pakistan and continuing its Jihadi mission. Hamas contains biographies (along with photographs) of major Hamas figures, beginning with its founder Sheikh Ahmad Yassin, and clearly describes the group as Jihadi. Shareeah's mission statement traces its allegiance to Islamic fundamentalist groups in Egypt and to people like the late Hassan Banna and Sayyid Qutb, two of the early founders of the Islamic movement in Egypt who are known for their pro-Jihad views. While al-Muhajiroun describes the group as a mere Islamic movement with no overt mentioning of politics, the group is affiliated to the Taliban, also known for their agreement on Jihad.

The Web sites also allow the groups to engage in a global flow of trade to materially sustain this Pax Islamica (Held and McGrew 2000). As Appadurai (1996) argues, electronic-ally mediated communication creates "virtual neighborhoods" that "are able to mobilize ideas, opinions, moneys, and social linkages that often directly flow back into lived neigh-borhoods" (p. 195). The sites engage in limited commercial activities to help sustain their funds. Shareeah offers users a section dedicated to downloading lectures and Quran interpretations for free, but it also sells lectures and *khutbas* on tape, video, and CD. Topics covered are global in scope, with titles including "About the Jihad in Bosnia," "Afghanistan, the Return of Islam," and "Intifada, Blessed Hijacking, the Tricks of Shaytan [devil]." The site also offers books, with titles like "Defence of Muslim Lands by Shaheed [martyr] Abdullah Azzam" (in Chechnya).

Some Web sites also invite the supporters to donate money, either indirectly like as-Sahwah's call for Muslims to give *zakaah*, although the site does not explain where the money donated would go to. Others blatantly ask for donations, like Indonesian group Laskar Jihad (Jihad Troopers) which had been connected to al-Qaida. Its Web site has been noted as stating, "It takes a lot of fund, equipments [*sic*], and facilities for the daily needs of the Laskar and refugees. Consequently this becomes a responsibility of Moslem society as a whole for the glory of Islam and its believers" (Scheeres 2001). Shareeah also has a section that asks for donations to be made through sending checks to its provided London address. Hall (1992) argues that such "global consumerism" creates "the possibilities of 'shared identities'—as 'customers' for the same goods, 'clients' for the same services, 'audiences' for the same messages and images—between people who are far removed from one another in time and space" (p. 302).

The Pax Islamica is also supported through the Web sites' interactive sections. Stuart Hall argues that the Internet has enabled the formation of a global consciousness through its expansion of "the possibilities of sharing conversations across . . . different divides" (Hall 2003). Most fundamentalist Web sites enable this via providing e-mail addresses through which visitors can contact the webmasters and the groups behind the sites. This is important for maintaining contact between visitors of the Web sites and the groups. The sites also give the supporters a chance to meet through cyberspace. Al-Muhajiroun offers—besides e-mail—members' mobile phone numbers (in the United Kingdom), fax numbers, and a London mailing address, while as-Sahwah contains a discussion board where people can post their opinions.

The Internet's time-space compression is best demonstrated by Taliban Online, which seems to be the most technologically sophisticated Web site analyzed. The site includes a no-registration-required chat room: the user just needs to choose a nickname to join the conversation, and there are no private chat rooms. The site also contains a "Support us!" section, which has three options: an option enabling the user to add Taliban Online as a link to another Web site of their choice, an option with information about the site designed to be downloaded for mIRC chat, and a "tell a friend via e-mail" option.

Another way in which the Internet helps sustain this Pax Islamica is through the Web sites' hyperlinks. The hyperlinks reflect the groups' local and global political affiliations as well as ideological expressions. Hizbollah's hyperlinks, for example, are centered on institu-tions within Lebanon that are connected with the group, but the site itself is hyperlinked from Tanzeem. Taliban Online is hyperlinked to few Web sites, including al-Muhajiroun and al-Neda, both of which are inactive. Shareeah contains a large number of hyperlinks divided into sections like "News Sites," "Discussion Boards," "Dawa Sites (Non/Muslims)," and "Chat Sites." Most of the hyperlinks mentioned are active, but some are those to Web sites that do not exist anymore or that have been closed down. It also has hyperlinks copied from Jannah, a news portal. Jannah's hyperlinks include sections like Business, Education, and Community, but also sites like Tanzeem and Hizb-ut-Tahrir (a site run by a Jihadi political party based in Palestine, www.hizb-ut-tahrir.org). The latter two are also hyper-linked to each other. In addition, Tanzeem is hyperlinked to the Algerian F.I.S. (www.fisalgeria.org), the Lebanese Al-Moqawama al-Islamiyya (the Islamic Resistance Support Association run by Hizbollah, www.moqawama.tv), the international Muslim Brothers (Al-Ikhwan al-Muslimoun, www.ummah.net/ikhwan), and the Pakistani branch of the group (www.ikhwan.org.pk). The availability of the Web sites listed here has fluctuated over time.

Hyperlinks are important because they enable the site visitors to find out about other affiliate groups and therefore to further increase their global connections. The hyperlinks' international scope is another way in which the various Islamic fundamentalist groups maintain and communicate their global presence. The content of the Web sites thus challenges the notion of Islamic fundamentalism as having an essentially localist nature. In fact, the groups utilize new media effectively and thus are able to form a global network that goes in tune with their global outlooks and aims.

The response to changes in the political climate

The groups use their Web sites to respond to global and local politics. The Web sites are thus an example of how local happenings can also have global repercussions and vice versa (Eade 2003). For example, after the September 11 attacks, Taliban Online claimed that the Taliban do not support the attacks and that Osama bin Laden denied any involvement. After the raid by British police on the Finsbury Park mosque in London in January 2003, where Abu Hamza preaches, his Web site Shareeah covered the story on its homepage, defending the mosque as a mere place of worship, and ignoring the terrorist allegations that the raid was based on. The Web sites' presentation of such alternative news can be seen as an attempt at decentralizing a West-focused flow of information (Network EICOS 2003). The presenta-tion of alternative news is, as Kevin Robins (2000) argues, an "aspiration to create a space within global culture" (p. 200).

The groups also aim at strengthening their position in global politics through the use of interactive sections, namely opinion polls. Taliban Online's Survey, for example, has posed questions like, "Do you believe the Taliban will defeat Army of disbelievers by the Grace of Mighty Allah?" referring to American presence in Afghanistan. The survey claims that 98.8 percent of votes (equaling, according to the site, 3,768,982 votes) said yes. In this way, the Internet functions as a tool for "speaking" from "positions within the global distribution of power"; as Hall argues, "Because these positions change and alter, there is always an engagement with politics as a 'war of position' " (Hall 1996b, 237).

Cyberwars

The Internet has been a theatre for the groups' political actions. It has been alleged that the September 11 attacks were coordinated mainly through e-mail (Norton-Taylor 2001). It has also been alleged that some of the groups' Internet chat rooms had been circulating rumors of an assault before the missile attack on an Israeli airliner in Kenya in December 2002 took place (Butcher 2002). The response to this increased exposure of the Internet as a tool in the hands of terrorists has varied from posting messages on the groups' Web sites appealing for information about potential terrorists (as the British MI5 did in October 2001, posting "contact us" messages on Qoqaz.com) (Norton-Taylor 2001), to surveillance and retention of e-mail records (Byrne 2002), to actual closing down of sites. During the course in which this article has been written, the al-Muhajiroun Web site was hacked (allegedly by the United States) and repaired. Al-Muhajiroun and al-Neda sites were among the links available on Taliban Online, but the Links section on Taliban Online later stated that it is Under Construction. The site had also been linked to another titled Beware of Shiaism, which contains anti-Shiite information in English and Urdu. This overtly reveals how the groups seem to use the Internet to fight with one another (as the Taliban belong to the Sunni sect). However, Figure 16.1 shows how the groups are at the same time indirectly hyperlinked to Hizbollah, a Shiite group, which reveals the contradiction in their appeal.

The Internet is also used by the groups to respond to attacks outside cyberspace. Shareeah's articles are compiled in an online magazine titled *al-Jihaad*. After the raid on the Finsbury Park mosque, and with rumors that the British government is going to close down the Web site (Rant on website 2003), al-Jihaad posted a disclaimer on its first page, stating: "Supporters of Shareeah does not take responsibility for all the content contained in these articles. And neither to claim to agree with all of the content contained in these articles or that it is representative of our views and beliefs." The articles present in al-Jihaad are listed under a "Contributed" section to refer that their writers are not the people behind the Web site, and have titles like "Tyrani [*sic*] in Pakistan," "Anti Israel Reports," and "Stupid Bush." Shareeah was later closed down following the British government's decision to try to expel Abu Hamza from Britain due to his controversial preaching at Finsbury Park.

The fluid nature of the Internet has also been utilized by the groups to avoid being forced to disappear from cyberspace through hacking. The Web site of Azzam Publications (www.azzam.com, a Chechen site linked to Qoqaz.net) has now been closed down (allegedly by the United States), but just before that it published a news posting containing fifteen points informing the site users of what to do after the Web site disappears. The posting urged users to copy material from the Web site and publish it on their own Web sites and through discussion boards and e-mail lists. It also advised them to access the site "via proxies or anonymous services, such as http://www.safeweb.com or http://www.anonymizer.com." The posting also encouraged users to utilize the Internet to disseminate information and news about Jihad (Shareeah also encourages visitors to publicize its existence), and informed them that Azzam's products would be available to buy from Maktabah Al-Ansar Bookshop.

Indeed, Maktabah's Web site is selling the products (books, audio and video material,

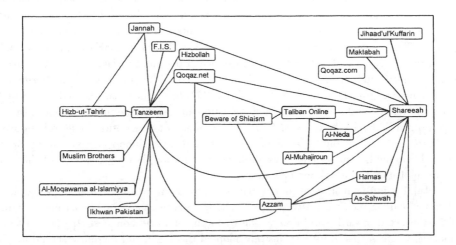

Figure 16.1 Hyperlinks between Islamic fundamentalist Web sites.

posters, as well as items like perfume and clothing), while Azzam Publications News Postings can now be accessed on as-Sahwah. The case of Azzam illustrates the difficulty of controlling content on the Internet and the range of possibilities available for the groups to exist in cyberspace.

The instantaneous nature of the Internet means that the groups can immediately adjust their web presence according to the political climate. Shareeah's site, for example, contained a link to al-Neda, which disappeared following the raid on the Finsbury Park mosque. As-Sahwah's "Zakaah Calculator" and the "Click to Give Zakaah" option also disappeared after the raid.

Implications

The Internet has been celebrated as a place of dialogue, perhaps too optimistically as stated by Nathan Gardels (2000): "As the realm of the global mind grows, it will necessarily enroach on all enclosed spaces—political, national ethnic, linguistic or psychological. Openness and transparency are its bywords; closure of any kind entails the risk of isolation and failure" (p. 2). Ronfeldt and Arquilla (2000) are also prematurely celebratory about the workings of cyberspace when they describe it as a space allowing "peace through knowledge" rather than "peace through strength." They argue for increased freedom of information on the Internet, as that is seen as an essential element toward achieving this peace. Such views neglect other players in the socio-political realm like Islamic fundamentalism—players that are part of the "global mind" but are excluded because of their pathological associations.

However, now attention is being paid to Islamic fundamentalism as a global player that destabilizes the existing political status quo. Toffler and Toffler (2000) describe it as a "global gladiator." They point out that such "new forces, now are linked by the Internet, global telecom nets and other advanced technologies . . . and they come accompanied by . . . fund raisers . . . media manipulators and volunteer computer hackers" (p. 26). The change that forces like Islamic fundamentalism will bring, they argue, is a change in the political representational system, whereby the United Nations will become obsolete as nations are undermined. Thus, the debate seems to center around the idea that Islamic fundamentalism (and Islam in general) is necessarily oppositional to the nation.

But this denies Islamic fundamentalism its role in the building of nations as mentioned earlier in this article, and also undermines the existence of Islamic fundamentalist nations like Iran. Of course, Islamic fundamentalist groups, like the Muslim Brotherhood that has branches in more than seventy countries under different names, are advocating a Pax Islamica. The Internet for these groups provides what Sloterdijk (2000) terms a "portable homeland" (p. 16), a tool that enables the existence of the multispatial self—an ethnospace. Islamic fundamentalism then is a force that is "located within and beyond the borders of the nation-state" (Moallem 1999, 324). Barber (1992) has argued that Islamic fundamentalism is an example of the fragmentation of the nation into smaller groups. He argues that this is in contrast with what he terms *McWorld*, or "an emergent, transnational cultural uniformity" (Grosby 1997, 82). But the situation is more complex than homogeneity/heterogeneity. I see Islamic fundamentalism as an example of glocalization, bearing elements of the local and the global in its outlook and operation.

Islamic fundamentalism is not a nativist movement merely "entailing a 'localist' character" (Abaza and Stauth 1990, 218). Abaza and Stauth argue that "the Islamic religious ethic is directed toward world domination by means of world conquest" (p. 210). Islamic fundamentalism seems to have exclusively adopted this ethic, and therefore should not be confused with other Islamic movements, such as that of the Nation of Islam in the United

States, which is a separatist movement, aiming at isolating the Muslim community from the "existing social order" (Kepel 1997, 54), even though the two movements share certain aspects like "bottom-up Islamization" that offers services to the community to attract common members of society (p. 72). Islamic fundamentalism's advocacy of jihad is also characteristic of its global nature. In the early days of Islam when jihad in the name of religion was declared, the aim was not only to protect the Islamic umma and to "redraw boundaries" (Barber 1992) but to expand it so that the whole world (if possible) would be Muslim.

The existence of several Islamic fundamentalist groups across the globe adds to the globalism of this network. Some groups are in opposition, such as the Jamaa Islamiyya and the Ahbash in Lebanon; however, the groups themselves do not see a need to unite under one name. Al-Muhajiroun argues that "Allah (SWT) obliges groups to exist in order to maintain unity. Groups are a method of uniting the Muslims rather than dividing them." I argue that the existence of several groups is necessary for the protection of the transforming Islamic fundamentalist identity and its survival vis-à-vis opposition by global powers like the United States. The existence of several groups in different countries is also necessary to cater for the local issues the groups encounter in the countries they exist in.

Castells sees the Islamic fundamentalist identity as a resistant one and describes it as an expression of "*the exclusion of the excluders by the excluded*" (1997, 9). He sees the Islamic fundamentalist identity as being defensive against the dominant institutions/ideologies. He argues that the world is divided between the "Net and the Self" (1997, 3) where there is an opposition between "abstract universal instrumentalism" (the global) and "historically rooted, particularistic identities" (the local). While he argues that the Net "emerges from interconnected developments in new communication technologies . . . the emergence of mediated 'real virtuality' " (Saukko 2000), he casts Islamic fundamentalism as local and as resistant to the Net.

This is somewhat similar to arguments on cosmopolitanism and patriotism as oppositional. Martha Naussbaum's (1994) procosmopolitanism argument in *Boston Review*, which advocates being a "citizen of the world," has generated various responses from thinkers like Barber (1994) and Dorris (1994), who argue that this global citizenship is too demanding and overwhelming, and Beitz (1994) and Wallerstein (1994), who say that cosmopolitanism need not reject patriotism but that the two can be sustained together. This article has shown that none of those arguments can be simplistically applied to Islamic fundamentalism. It may have resistant characteristics, but it is not oppositional to global forces. It is neither an example of cosmopolitanism nor of patriotism but articulates a new patriotism that is relational and negotiative within the processes of globalization.

References

Abaza, Mona, and Georg Stauth. 1990. Occidental reason, Orientalism, Islamic fundamentalism: A critique. In *Globalization, knowledge and society*, edited by Matrin Albrow and Elizabeth King, 209–30. London: Sage.

Agha, Olfat Hassan. 2000. Islamic fundamentalism and its image in the western media: Alternative views. In *Islam and the west in the mass media*, edited by Kai Hafez, 219–34. Cresskill, NJ: Hampton Press.

Al-Ahsan, Abdullah. 1992. *Ummah or nation? Identity crisis in contemporary Muslim society*. Leicester, UK: The Islamic Foundation.

Ang, Ien. 2000. Identity blues. In *Without guarantees: In honour of Stuart Hall*, edited by Paul Gilroy, Lawrence Grossberg, and Angela McRobbie, 1–13. London: Verso.

Appadurai, Arjun. 1996. *Modernity at large: Cultural dimensions of globalization*. Minneapolis: University of Minnesota Press.

Barber, Benjamin R. 1992. Jihad vs. McWorld. *Atlantic Monthly*, March. Retrieved 23 January 2003 from http://www.theatlantic.com/politics/foreign/baberf.htm.

——. 1994. Constitutional faith. *Boston Review* 19 (5): 14–15.

Beck, Ulrich. 2000. What is globalization? In *The global transformations reader: An introduction to the globalization debate*, edited by David Held and Anthony McGrew, 99–103. Cambridge, UK: Polity Press.

Beitz, Charles. 1994. Patriotism for cosmopolitans. *Boston Review* 19 (5): 23–4.

Beyer, Peter. 1994. *Religion and globalization*. London: Sage.

Butcher, Mike. 2002. Cyber hype. *The Guardian*, 5 December. Retrieved 23 January 2003 from http://www.guardian.co.uk/online/story/0,3605,853535,00.html.

Byrne, Ciar. 2002. Anti-terrorist measures "threatens web freedom." *The Guardian*, 6 September. Retrieved 23 January 2003 from http://media.guardian.co.uk/newmedia/story/0,7496,786913,00.html.

Castells, Manuel. 1997. *The power of identity*. Oxford, UK: Blackwell Publishers.

Di Justo, Patrick. 2002. How al-Qaida site was hijacked. *Wired News*, 10 August. Retrieved 23 January 2003 from http://www.wired.com/news/culture/0,1284,54455-2,00.html.

Dorris, Michael. 1994. No place like home. *Boston Review* 19 (5): 18.

Eade, John. 2003. Local/global processes and the Islamisation of urban space. School of International Migration and Ethnic Relations (IMER), Malmo: Malmo University. Retrieved 16 May 2003 from http://www.imer.mah.se/hemsida_forskning/paper_john_eade.pdf.

Ehteshami, Anourshiravan. 1997. Islamic fundamentalism and political Islam. In *Issues in world politics*, edited by Brian White, Richard Little, and Michael Smith, 179–99. London: Macmillan Press.

European Community Studies Association. 2003. Interculturalism, globalization and cultural identity. Retrieved 16 May 2003 from http://www.ecsanet.org/dialogue/contributions/Paun.doc.

Faksh, Mahmud A. 1997. *Fundamentalism in Egypt, Algeria and Saudi Arabia*. London: Praeger.

Fanon, Frantz. 1994. On national culture. In *Colonial discourse and post-colonial theory: A reader*, edited by Patrick Williams and Laura Chrisman, 36–52. London: Harvester Wheatsheaf.

Featherstone, Mike. 1995. *Undoing culture: Globalization, postmodernism and identity*. London: Sage.

Freeman, Nick. 1999. See Europe with ITC: Stock footage and the construction of geographical identity. In *Alien identities: Exploring difference in film and fiction*, edited by Deborah Cartmell et al., 49–65. London: Pluto Press.

Friedman, Jonathan. 1994. *Cultural identity and global process*. London: Sage.

Gardels, Nathan. 2000. Comment: The global mind. *New Perspectives Quarterly* 17 (1): 2–3.

Garton, Laura, Caroline Haythornthwaite, and Barry Wellman. 1997. Studying online social networks. *Journal of Computer-Mediated Communication*, 3 (1). Retrieved 23 February 2003 from http://jcmc.huji.ac.il/vol3/issue1/garton.html.

Giddens, Anthony. 1990. *The consequences of modernity*. Cambridge, UK: Polity Press.

Grosby, Steven, 1997. The future of nationality: A few, mostly theoretical considerations. *International Journal on World Peace* 14 (4): 81–96.

Hall, Stuart. 1992. The question of cultural identity. In *Modernity and its futures*, edited by Stuart Hall, David Held, and Tony McGrew, 273–326. Cambridge, UK: Polity Press.

——. 1996a. Introduction: Who needs "identity"? In *Questions of cultural identity*, edited by Stuart Hall and Paul du Gay, 1–17. London: Sage.

——. 1996b. The meaning of new times. In *Stuart Hall: Critical dialogues in cultural studies*, edited by David Morley and Kuan-Hsing Chen, 233–37. London: Routledge.

——. 2003. Interview by Martin Jacques. Retrieved 16 May 2003 from http://www.usyd.edu.au/su/social/papers/hall1.html.

Hamzeh, A. Nizar. 1998. The future of Islamic movements in Lebanon. In *Islamic fundamentalism: Myths and realities*, edited by Ahmad S. Moussalli, 249–73. Ithaca, NY: Ithaca Press.

Held, David, and Anthony McGrew. 2000. The great globalization debate: An introduction. In *The global transformations reader: An introduction to the globalization debate*, edited by David Held and Anthony McGrew, 1–45. Cambridge, UK: Polity Press.

Hjarvard, Stig. 2002. Mediated encounters: An essay on the role of communication media in the creation of trust in the "global metropolis." In *Global encounters: Media and cultural transformation*, edited by Gitte Stald and Thomas Tufte, 69–84. Luton, UK: University of Luton Press.

Huntington, Samuel P. 1996. *The clash of civilizations and the remaking of world order*. New York: Simon & Schuster.

Jackson, Michele. 1997. Assessing the structure of communication on the World Wide Web. *Journal of Computer-Mediated Communication* 3 (1). Retrieved 23 February 2003 from http://jcmc.huji.ac.il/vol3/issue1/jackson.html.

Kepel, Gilles. 1997. *Allah in the west: Islamic movements in America and Europe*. Cambridge, UK: Polity Press.

Mann, Michael. 2000. Has globalization ended the rise and rise of the nation-state? In *The global transformations reader: An introduction to the globalization debate*, edited by David Held and Anthony McGrew, 136–47. Cambridge, UK: Polity Press.

Moallem, Minoo. 1999. Transnationalism, feminism, and fundamentalism. In *Between woman and nation: Nationalisms, transnational feminisms, and the state*, edited by Caren Kaplan, Norma Alarcon, and Minoo Moallem, 320–48. London: Duke University Press.

Morley, David. 1999. Bounded realms: Household, family, community, and nation. In *Home, exile, homeland: Film, media, and the politics of place*, edited by Hamid Naficy, 151–68. New York: Routledge.

Mowlana, Hamid. 2000. The renewal of the global media debate: Implications for the relationship between the west and the Islamic world. In *Islam and the west in the mass media*, edited by Kai Hafez, 105–18. Cresskill, NJ: Hampton Press.

Naussbaum, Martha. 1994. Patriotism and cosmopolitanism. *Boston Review* 19 (5): 3.

Network EICOS. 2003. Cultural identity: Development and sustainability. Program of Interdisciplinary Studies of Communities and Social Ecology. Retrieved 16 May 2003 from http://www.eicos.psycho.ufrj.br/ingles/ing1%20_ident_cultural/identidadecultural.htm.

Norton-Taylor, Richard. 2001. MI5 posts terror appeal on Arab web sites. *The Guardian*, 26 October. Retrieved 23 January 2003 from http://media.guardian.co.uk/attack/story/0,1301,581273,00.html.

OutThere News. 2002. Al-Qaeda a year after 9/11: Triumphant, frustrated and watching Wall Street. September. Retrieved January 23 2003 from http://www.megastories.com/attack/alqaeda/analysis020906.shtml.

Rant on website of hate. 2003. *The Sun*, 22 January.

Robertson, Roland. 1997. Glocalization: Time-space and homogeneity-heterogeneity. In *Global modernities*, edited by Mike Featherstone, Scott Lash, and Roland Robertson, 25–44. London: Sage.

Robins, Kevin. 2000. Encountering globalization. In *The global transformations reader: An introduction to the globalization debate*, edited by David Held and Anthony McGrew, 195–201. Cambridge, UK: Polity Press.

Ronfeldt, David, and John Arquilla. 2000. From cyberspace to the Noosphere: Emergence of the global mind. *New Perspectives Quarterly* 17 (1): 18–25.

Saikal, Amin. 2000. Islam and the west? In *Contending images of world politics*, edited by Greg Fry and Jacinta O'Hagan, 164–77. London: Macmillan Press.

Saukko, Paula. 2000. The interconnected self: Problems and possibilities in an emergent ideal. Unpublished manuscript.

Scheeres, Julia. 2001. Blacklisted groups visible on web. *Wired News*, 19 October. Retrieved January 23 2003 from http://www.wired.com/news/politics/0,1283,47616-2,00.html.

Shohat, Ella. 1999. By the bitstream of Babylon: Cyberfrontiers and diasporic vistas. In *Home, exile, homeland: Film, media, and the politics of place*, edited by Hamid Naficy, 213–32. New York: Routledge.

Sloterdijk, Peter. 2000. From agrarian patriotism to the global self. *New Perspectives Quarterly* 17 (1): 15–18.

Smith, Michael. 1997. Regions and regionalism. In *Issues in world politics*, edited by Brian White, Richard Little, and Michael Smith, 69–89. London: Macmillan Press.

Taheri, Amir. 1987. *Holy terror: The inside story of Islamic terrorism*. London: Sphere Books Limited.

Tehranian, Majid. 2000. Islam and the west: Hostage to history? In *Islam and the west in the mass media*, edited by Kai Hafez, 201–18. Cresskill, NJ: Hampton Press.

Toffler, Alvin, and Heidi Toffler. 2000. Global gladiators challenge the power of nations. *New Perspectives Quarterly* 17 (1): 26–7.

Turkle, Sherry. 1996. *Life on the screen: Identity in the age of the internet*. London: Weidenfeld and Nicholson.

Wallerstein, Immanuel. 1984. *The politics of the world economy*. Cambridge. UK: Cambridge University Press.

Wallerstein, Immanuel. 1994. Neither patriotism nor cosmopolitanism. *Boston Review* 19 (5): 15–16.

Weisman, Robyn. 2001. Teen hackers crash Hizbollah ISP. *NewsFactor Network*, 22 January. Retrieved 23 January 2003 from http://www.newsfactor.com/perl/story/6880.html.

Whitaker, Brian, 2001. US pulls the plug on Muslim websites. *The Guardian*, 10 September. Retrieved 23 January 2003 from www.guardian.co.uk/elsewhere/journalist/story/0,7792,549590,00.html.

White, Brian, Richard Little, and Michael Smith. 1997. Issues in world politics. In *Issues in world politics*, edited by Brian White, Richard Little, and Michael Smith, 1–23. London: Macmillan Press.

Chapter 17

John D. H. Downing

AUDIENCES AND READERS OF ALTERNATIVE MEDIA: THE ABSENT LURE OF THE VIRTUALLY UNKNOWN

THERE IS A DISTINCTLY disturbing gulf between our currently fragmentary knowledge or debates concerning how audiences and readers use[1] alternative media, and the mass of descriptions and theorizations of alternative media at last now becoming available. The welcome surge in research attention includes Atton (2001), Downing (2001), Fairchild (2001), Gumucio Dragon (2001), Halleck (2001), Land (1999), Rodríguez (2001), Soley (1999), and was instanced in 2002 by the 70 papers delivered in the second 'OurMedia' pre-conference and the Community Media Section panels at the IAMCR (International Association for Media and Communication Research) Barcelona conference.

I am taking a fairly wide definition of alternative media here, though focusing principally on the politically radical. I am not, however, including for the purposes of this discussion those alternative sectors whose media products cater for the affluent or very affluent, such as ski hobby magazines or oil industry bulletins. Such parameters are always porous, to be sure, and in addition there are excellent arguments for avoiding tidy definitions (Rodríguez, 2001: 21–3) of alternative media, which always risk requiring them to be evaluated by standards peculiar to large-scale mainstream media – and by which they are bound to fail! A huge extra spiral in this problem of producing a tidy definition of alternative media is the multiplicity of formats and technologies involved (see Downing, 2001: Part II).

It is a paradox, however, that so little attention has been dedicated to the user dimension, given that alternative-media activists represent in a sense the most active segment of the so-called 'active audience'. One would imagine that they above all would be passionately concerned with how their own media products were being received and used.

The gap is definitely an urgent one to fill, not least (1) given global trends to giant media corporations and the international growth of anticorporate sentiment and action, all of which create a particularly important setting for understanding small-scale oppositional media; but also in any case (2) considering the multiple social roles of myriads of alternative media, constantly expanding on the Internet and elsewhere, but not necessarily limited to those with an ostensibly radical agenda.

We need to flag as well (3) the actual and potential roles of extreme rightist alternative media (Downing, 2001: 88–96, 2002) and their appeal. The Nazi newspapers *Völkischer Beobachter* and *Der Stürmer* in the 1920s and 1930s (Kershaw, 1983; Showalter, 1982), and

Radio-Télévision Libre des Mille Collines during the 1994 Rwandan genocide (Chrétien, 1995; Human Rights Watch, 1999: *passim*), serve as chilling examples of what is possible at this end of the alternative media spectrum. For while some people will cynically sniff at the impact of leftist alternative media, and therefore at their uses, hopefully few would be so unwise, given the history of the 20th century alone, as to dismiss how people may respond to ultrarightist ones. Not that these are limited to agents of mass repression and genocide, as per the two cases cited. The studies in Kintz and Lesage (1998), for example, illustrate the importance of rightist religious media in the contemporary USA.

Usage of this considerable spectrum of alternative media therefore represents a huge gap in our research knowledge, one with direct implications for the study of labor and other social movements, community formation, minority–majority ethnic relations,[2] transitional political regimes, the arts and the Internet, to name only some of the most obvious. For those considering engaging in this minimally developed audience and readership[3] research, the prolegomena that follow are designed in order to encourage and guide researchers, raising as they do key conceptual and methodological questions.

We will commence then by analyzing reasons for the virtual absence of alternative-media user research. We will then proceed to note two initial research priorities. The first will be to incorporate the play between alternative-media uses with their frequent focus on challenging the structures of power, and mainstream-media uses, with their more typical focus on hegemonic integration. The second will be to propose a political ethics of listening. The former priority will be discussed with a variety of examples, mostly from the experience of soviet-style polities, the latter much more summarily. We will then proceed to typify mainstream-media user research by way of establishing a 'listening' contrast with the demands of alternative-media user research. We will conclude by exploring four further research priorities, namely to focus on the mesh between alternative-media users and (1) social and political movements; (2) oppositional consciousness; (3) the conditions of reception; and (4) the variety of communication technologies, genres and formats in alternative as compared to mainstream media.

The weak appetite for user research within alternative media

As we suggested above, if media activists are so disenchanted with mainstream media neglect of their concerns that they expend great energy making their own media, is it not predictable that they should be absorbed with knowing their own users' reactions?

But the answer is, not so much as this logic proposes. One of the good reasons is the colossal effort needed, especially when activists are unpaid, to launch *and sustain* many alternative media projects, leaving little over for user research. To this we may sometimes add political repression that deters people from even admitting to using alternative media; sometimes the intense 24/7 dynamic of an ongoing political crisis that leaves no time for longer-term study of the users; sometimes large demonstrations in support that prove beyond any doubt a strong measure of public enthusiasm.[4] Let us also, though, explore the bad reasons.

While, not surprisingly, the ethos of commercial user research holds rather little interest for alternative-media activists, sometimes its casual ideological dismissal creates problems. One result may be a cavalier attitude to basic financial realities, which can mean that the project goes bust for entirely avoidable reasons, or staggers along but without achieving its feasible goals.

A second case consists of alternative media that strive just to sustain a distinctive orthodoxy and therefore not to engage with casual bystanders or opponents (e.g. religious or political zealot newspapers, ethnic separatist publications). So long as the faithful stay loyal, the locked circuit continues.

A third example is where activists have effectively colonized an alternative media outlet and it has become their entire, sometimes quasi-messianic, *raison d'être*. While their world-view may be secular and pluralistic, they nonetheless represent a particular cultural niche, perhaps a generational one,[5] which effectively closes off access to groups alternative to themselves. Cable television access centers in the USA in the 1990s and 2000s quite often had what looked like a tenure system for local producers, who represented a variety, to be sure, but the identical variety – and people – year after year. Just because people think their voice is not represented does not mean they are interested in other voices than their own.

A fourth case is where public support is unmistakably tangible during a period of acute political contention, but misleads the activists into seeing it as more widespread and durable than it is, so that they take it for granted beyond the point they should.

Indeed, we might be inclined to pursue this disconnect a step further. Is it not the case that the wooden, even leaden, language of some alternative media and their sometimes unappealing appearance (see Downing, 1980: 180–99; Violi, 1977) gives us immediate pause as we wonder how *could* those supposedly organic intellectuals be sincerely interested in their users?

Yet on this issue we need a note of methodological caution: the language and aesthetics of alternative media can be more complex questions than superficial comparisons with mainstream media aesthetics would suggest. Let us examine briefly Gramsci's *L'Ordine Nuovo* and Soviet *samizdat* as cases in point, the first in regard to language, the second in regard to 'look'.

During Italy's Red Biennium in 1919–20, Turin auto workers, then the most pivotal sector of the Italian industrial working class, did not simply strike but actually took over the running of the factories, displacing for a while the supposedly essential management. *L'Ordine Nuovo* (*The New Order*) was one of the newspapers that circulated in the factories, but it was pretty tough reading (Williams, 1975). Agnelli senior, Fiat's founder, assumed a dissident member of his engineering staff had to be writing it, such was its intellectual acuity. Yet at the time and in the conditions, it was not simply shrugged off as a series of ivory tower *pronunciamentos*, struggle with its language was probably at the very least what a number of insurrectionary auto workers had to do.

We could, in graphical layout terms, compare early Soviet *samizdat* media. These were simply typed sheets with neither margins nor spaces at the top and bottom of the page, because of the difficulty of getting hold of blank typing paper in any quantity without attracting KGB attention, and were also typed using carbon copy-sheets between nine further pages. This meant the lower copies were very blurry and hard to read. Nonetheless, they passed from hand to hand like hot cakes, despite the severe repression that would attend their discovery by the authorities.

In other words, notwithstanding the fact that there are alternative-media instances which evince a really profound lack of interest in their users, we should not, without attention to the context, rush to negative judgment of seemingly unattractive alternative-media aesthetics and writing style, and their impact on users.

To sum up, however: the various reasons, good or bad, for alternative-media activists not to engage in user research do offer a valuable role, if they choose to adopt it, to politically engaged academic media researchers with the needed time and resources. There is, however, an important intellectual and ethical caveat about how the academics judge their role:

> . . . audience images are *always* inscribed: the institutional according to insti-
> tutional goals; the academic according to methodological and other scientific

> (theoretical) discourses; and the audience's image according to cultural codes for good taste and decent lifestyles, that is, according to moral hierarchies in the culture. (Hagen, 1999: 145, my emphasis)

This quotation is not intended to plant a Total Relativism flag on the terrain of alternative-media research, denying there are real people using media. It is simply to emphasize the degree of reflexive self-critique with which academic researchers should deploy their methods, and the respect they should maintain for alternative-media users they research.

Two contrasting but complementary views of audience agency

A pivotal difference that research into alternative-media use confronts was posed in principle by Indymedia Italia, which, on 16 March 2002, organized a Reclaim Your Media march in Rome, along with Radio *Onda Rossa*.[6] They developed a telling watchword for the demonstration's placards: 'Don't hate the media! Become the media!' In other words, they said, we can all become media communicators: in Italian socialist terminology of the 1970s, the subjects (agents) of struggle can become the subjects of information (Downing, 2001: 278).

To clarify this perspective, let us contrast it with the postmodernist analysis of audience agency developed by Abercrombie and Longhurst (1998). They argue that with the diffusion of commodity-exchange-based spectacle via television and other media, the world has recently added an extra cultural dimension in which, in our habitual role of *being* audiences, we are typically also 'performing *for* an imagined audience' (1998: 96, my emphases). Yet our 'narcissistic' responses as performers/audiences lead mostly to 'a dedicated interest in clothes, perfume, hair-style, home furnishing, cars, houses, music, food . . . the management of appearance' (1998: 93).

Their attempt to construct a mass psychology of media-modernity tends to lead, however, not to any focus on the extension of the public's potential to communicate independently – despite their obvious sympathy with amateur musicians (1998: 162–6) and their emphasis on ludic agency in fandom (1998: 154–6) – but ultimately only to attention to highly bounded consumer culture options. They do note the distinction, following Lawrence Grossberg, between 'everyday life' for affluent consumers in an affluent economy and 'daily life' for the majority of the world's public (1998: 167–8), but the 'daily' media realities and audience agency depicted in the 50 alternative media case-studies provided by Gumucio Dragon (2001) are clearly not pivotal to their vision. The common Nigerian pidgin response to being asked how you are – 'Patch de patch' (= 'I'm sewing a new patch to hold the old one, surviving by the skin of my teeth') – conveys a lifestyle and set of options quite outside their chosen radius.

Their wish to move beyond a pure and reductionist binary of power-resistance is perfectly reasonable, for that basic agenda and an interest in the ludic is as valid for analyzing politics and culture in the global South as anywhere else. But the authors effectively sideline rather than complicate (their avowed intent) the stubborn continuing question of sharp power differentials, which is a little surprising and rather a pity given their explicitly heavy debt (1998: 82–5) to Guy Debord's and the Situationists' notion of the advanced bourgeois society of the spectacle.

In the contrasted problematic of 'us the objects' becoming 'we the subjects' of media communication, the relationship between alternative communicators and audiences/readers/users may at first blush appear to be merely a constantly circulating switch of hats. As media activists researching alternative-media users we the subjects would not be investigating a sociological category, a niche market, or an election target group – objects – but simply ourselves wearing our other hat. This would not magically cancel all differences between researchers and researched in language, cultural capital, ethnicity, gender, experience or anything else, but it could substantially reduce the 'knowledge-for-manipulation' factor that characterizes conventional research on media-users, for the demographics-robots of the commercial sector and the *Hochkultur* elite of public broadcasting have always shared an icily remote relationship to actual media users.[7]

Nonetheless, we need to be cautious if we move in this 'object-to-subject' elision. Historically, the Soviet utilization of worker and farmer correspondents (*rabselkory*), closely linked to the Soviet institution of the 'wall' newspaper (Gorham, 1996; Kelly, 2002; Lenoe, 1999), was superficially similar to Indymedia Italia's vision of 'becoming the media', one in which differences between media users, media makers and therefore audience researchers virtually melted away into insignificance. Wall newspapers were mostly written entirely by local volunteers, not professional journalists, and displayed on walls, or notice-boards or display stands, in specific localities – a factory, an office, a school, a hospital, after 1928 in a collective farm administration building. Developed originally in the early 1920s by Russian Communist enthusiasts as a grassroots initiative, then quickly blessed by the Party authorities in order to cope with newsprint shortages, and thereafter becoming a mediascape fixture, the wall newspaper consisted typically of very short reports on the local institution of around 50 words each, sometimes getting as far in literary terms as agitational doggerel and satirical anecdotes. On the face of it, this was indeed the public becoming the media, and thus, in a sense, who needed researchers into media uses in this tight nexus?

In reality the wall-newspaper and *rabselkory* phenomenon, reproduced throughout Eastern Europe, China, Vietnam and North Korea during the Soviet era, wore a very different complexion. 'Blessing' by the Party authorities, locally speaking, meant not only their approval for starting it, but editorial control and guidance by Party cells and the Communist Youth organization, and the ever-present potential for unwelcome attention from State censorship offices. In practice, in the Russian case at least, the contents seem often to have been a blend of official propaganda communiqués, critiques set firmly within Party policy confines of particular managers' behavior or local work-policies, and local trivia or gossip (sometimes seasoned with personal venom). In periods of the tightest repression, even some of this variety was flattened out, though in the post-Stalin Thaw period the wall newspaper enjoyed a short-lived resurgence of energy.

The institution of people's correspondents during the Sandinista regime in Nicaragua (1979–89) owed much to a certain rather under-informed and populist image of the *rabselkory* tradition, derived via Cuba. As Rodríguez (2001: 65–81) notes, however, the early promise of this grassroots movement in opening up the voices of the public began to deteriorate after some years, largely in response to the Sandinista leadership's determination to have 'politically reliable' correspondents in place in the context of the US-funded guerrilla war against the regime. In China too after 1949, big character posters (*dazibao*) were also at times vehicles of popular expression, but at others, or sometimes simultaneously, methods of mass mobilization by one elite fraction against another. Certainly when they were closer to being the former, they were only permitted for as long as it suited the tactics of the winning fraction of the elite (Downing, 2001: 170–2). Thus Soviet, Maoist and comparable experiences are well worth studying, but in order to learn from past transmutations of a democratic media ideal how perhaps to avoid such pitfalls in future. They were never true exemplars.

Much more lively instances of democratic media agency are the British examples of anarchist press reader-writers reviewed by Atton (2001: 103–28). He carefully depicts the considerable variety evidenced in his sample of publications, including even within a single publication: 'In terms of content *Green Anarchist* is an odd blend of the colloquially pragmatic (often expressed confrontationally), the densely theoretical and at times the simply baffling' (2001: 124). His brief comments on a self-selected sample of 50 *SchNEWS* readers' responses to the weekly (2001: 128–32), suggest that for them its main merits were honesty and credibility, the fact no money-making was involved in the newspaper's production, and the networking of information concerning protest actions and oppositional cultural events. He is however careful to stress the great variety of the readers' motivations and uses.

An important lesson in this regard may also be drawn from the specific experience of People's Radio (*Radio Popolare*) in Milan over nearly 30 years, where virtually from the inception of the station its leading activists were very conscious of certain pragmatic realities (Downing, 2001: 275–86). Those with the time to devote unpaid or barely paid to the station were mostly those with sufficient financial resources of one kind or another not to have to work, very often students (in Italy, undergraduate study is quite often pursued over the best part of a decade). In turn, students' more academic language-style and allusions did not necessarily enable them to communicate easily with a diverse audience. Furthermore, in a city with a growing migrant worker public from Arab and other nations, not to mention issues of gender or age, media communicators were not simply interchangeable members of a single social class. Rather than proceed by presupposing this implausible fusion, the station's leaders sought to bring these contradictory factors into open debate as a means to try to keep them from surreptitiously balkanizing and disrupting the radio station's operation.

Thus neither the attractive directness of 'becoming the media' nor Abercrombie and Longhurst's sidelining of the continuing thorny dilemmas of responding to corporate, trans-national and state power refracted in media, provide us with sufficiently solid analytical ground by themselves on which to base research into alternative media users and uses. The former simply wipes out Abercrombie and Longhurst's acknowledgment of our multiple levels of interaction with and attractions to mainstream media – alternative media users rarely switch off from mainstream media, and certainly grew up with them. Their point is crucial, but they simply juxtapose a prior power/resistance audience dimension to the new 'diffused-audience' dimension they put forward, without engaging with their mutual imbrication and its implications.

In the analysis of alternative media uses, incorporating this mesh into our models is the first priority. But there are others.

Further priorities, social-ethical and analytical

We need to be alert to another dimension if we are to 'become the media', namely the dimension of social-ethical concern not to translate our commitment as alternative-media activists into a dystopia of incessant and compulsive public communication, where the question will not be the usual one of who will keep the corporate media owners under surveillance (*quis custodiet ipsos custodes?*), but who will actually have the stamina to listen to this myriad of popular communicators pounding out their messages? As Charles Husband (1996) has argued, a purely sending mode of communication need only produce a Tower of Babel. *Listening*, literally and figuratively, needs also to be central to the alternative media process and must be the ethical dimension at the heart of our models. For Habermas, attending carefully to the interlocutor's intentions and meanings represents a yardstick by which we may measure our democratic practice. For Husband, the issue is not simply one of measurement, but an imperative.

We need to admit in all frankness that there have been only too many examples of people, like instances from US cable access cited earlier, who started alternative media ostensibly to allow 'other voices' but actually only to express their own, and where the term 'dialogic' has definitely been honored far more in the breach than in its observance. Husband (1996) proposes a (third-order) human right 'to be understood', but in dialogic media this has to entail careful attention to public audiences/readers, for they too have the right to have media activists listen to and engage with their experiences, their dreams and their nightmares, and not simply to be communicated *at*.

How to hew to this 'listening' principle needs to be the topic of extensive analysis of practical experience, for which there is no space here. But it is fundamental.

Before exploring four further research priorities in this sphere, we will proceed in the section that immediately follows to typify some primary elements in conventional mainstream-media user research, and thus establish a basic template with which to conceptualize the contrasting dimensions of alternative-media user research. This contrastive approach is inspired in part by Eliasoph's (1997) illuminating study of how news priorities and practices at a Pacifica Network alternative radio station in the USA were thrown into relief by comparing them with the station's mainstream counterparts.

Conventional research on media users

Most user research, especially if at all current, is not available to the general public, but is a market commodity strictly reserved for contracted firms. It is based, obviously, on demographics, and at its simplest correlates eyeballs (or ears) and wallets. Why the public may like or not like a particular program or song is a secondary question that may also be researched if profit may plausibly be made from doing so. The research may be quantitative, or qualitative (e.g. the famous Hollywood focus groups),[8] or both. But only to that point does it assess the public's *involvement*, the mainsprings of its media uses. For media executives the shifting news or programming balance is perpetually between the tried and tested and the decreasingly flavorsome, and to monitor this does not require scouring the public's thinking and emotions in detail. What they will apparently switch on to suffices.

Indeed it is an open secret that the standard methods of broadcast audience measurement are riddled with flaws (Meehan, 1984, 1993); nonetheless there has to be some common currency between media executives and advertising buyers for them to be able to sign contracts with each other. Their normal acceptance of ratings is based on mutual financial convenience, not on scientific precision.

To understand mainstream media producers' and journalists' relation to users, one level down from the corporate executives, it is useful to begin from Hagen's (1999: 133) deployment of a distinction she draws from the social psychology of organizational management, namely 'single-loop' and 'double-loop' learning. In mainstream media the former would denote an *image* of media users that professional communicators derive from each other within their own closed circles, while the latter would signify audience-images they might draw from external sources. Hagen provides an excellent summary of empirical studies that demonstrate the typical reliance of professionals within established media on each others' judgment (1999: 133–5), in other words their determinedly single-loop learning practices. Husband's assertion of the centrality of listening receives only the faintest of echoes.

There are also intensive media marketing modalities. The vast promotional system, the star system, the fan clubs, the Oscars, the Emmys, major annual film festivals, and all their national analogues outside the USA, play significant roles as well. But they are all about stimulating consumer markets, not about understanding audiences/readers,[9] and certainly not about the public's social agency.

In other words, the history of mainstream media-user research up to the present is firmly anchored within this marketing dynamic: expensive, initially secret, quantified, but actually very loosely estimated broadcast ratings, based on particular programs and products; a star system; giant promotional budgets which for a blockbuster film may equal or surpass its production costs; focus groups whose role is to warn of box-office disaster; and producers' 'single-loop' learning. Academic research still often pursues the commercial research paradigm, although since the 1980s there has been a small wave of ethnographic-style studies – accompanied by a torrent of hypothesizing – investigating details of audience uses.

Commercial research studies and most of their academic counterparts are radically different from the world of alternative media. The passion for *engaging* with media users is certainly absent and, in addition, the substance of mainstream media content is tendentially very different.

Let us now proceed to a discussion of the four key factors in alternative-media reception proposed above, beginning with their relation to social movements.

Alternative media and social movements

Not all such media are part and parcel of such movements, either in fact or by intention. But often they are and when they are, whether the movements are in full flood or in abeyance or somewhere in between, standard research assumptions about the public, audiences, readership and users must alter significantly. Not only is the established relation between communicator and user potentially not in play in the case of social movement media, but we are no longer just in the realm of stable television viewers, settled audiences, habitual decisions, 'program flow', the daily newspaper reading ritual, drive-time radio, the TV screen as everyday distraction in bar and airport.

Like the definition of alternative media, so too social movements have suffered from reductive definitions, beginning with the mob model favored by 19th-century commentators, on to the rational actor model influenced by facets of the US Civil Rights movement, and in the 1980s and 1990s to the 'new social movement' model based on readings of the feminist, peace and ecological movements (Atton, 2001: 80–102; Cohen, 1985). More recently, debates have opened more widely, for example around the notion of 'contentious politics' (see Aminzade et al., 2001), and seek to address facets of social and political movements still typically left un-examined by academic research, such as emotion, space, time, religious and secular dimensions. Other recent work includes studies of solidarity movements (Giugni and Passy, 2001). The snare of reductiveness is as acute in social movement research as it is in the attempt to produce a single set definition of alternative media, not surprisingly since they have some of the same multi-faceted and tendentially unpredictable qualities.

So much so that it would be pointless in this short compass to try to capture more than a few key points in the relation between the two. One such however is the question of time, which I will subdivide into (a) the genealogy of social movements, (b) the role of specific events in their life-cycle, and (c) the difference between ephemeral and long-running alternative media.

Major 20th-century social movements such as the South African anti-apartheid movement and the US Civil Rights movement were very far from flashes in the pan. They were decades in the making, in the case of the anti-apartheid movement going back at least to the protests led by Gandhi a century ago and the foundation of the (predecessor to the) African

National Congress in 1912. Media and communication networks of resistance developed very painstakingly and slowly in symbiosis with those struggles, so that to evaluate alternative-media uses over such a period requires a longitudinal or historical study, only feasible today by oral history methods[10] that conventional audience research practically never even considers undertaking. Yet to grasp the roles of these media over the *longue durée*, no alternative offers itself.

Obviously some social movements are much younger than these, and it is correspondingly easier to research their media, but social movements do not explode into life overnight even if they seem to do so to external observers. Study of alternative-media users in movements' gestation periods addresses one facet; of users when movements are in full flood, another; and of users during periods of abeyance, a third. An example of the first would be the early phase of US lesbian and gay movements (Morris and Braine, 2001: 23–5), and of the third, the persistence of the US feminist movement.

The second time-dimension, to which McAdam and Sewell (2001) draw particular attention, is the pivotal role of particular events in the growth of social movements. In the anti-apartheid movement inside and outside South Africa, the 1960 Sharpeville Massacre, the first Soweto uprising of 1976 and the second of 1983, were such events, catalyzing broader and broader involvement against the regime. Social movements are not steadily evolutionary, and insofar as this is central to their understanding, equally central are alternative-media representations of major turning points, and their impact – or maybe absence of impact – among oppositional forces. Their meaning hangs on their immediate and continuing representation. Media user research especially needs to be able to evaluate alternative-media effectiveness at these crucial points in time.[11]

The third time-dimension is that which distinguishes, approximately at least, between what we might call one-shot alternative media such as graffiti, song, performance art or political cartoons, and ongoing alternative media of which perhaps one of the most signal instances is the US political weekly *The Nation*, in existence since 1865. Both may be associated with very long-running social movements, or with shorter-term ones, but obviously function differently in temporal terms. Ephemeral alternative media are typically much closer to artistic than to journalistic models, and seek to make an instant and hopefully lasting imprint by concentrating a great deal into a very compressed and often pungent format. Long-running alternative media, whatever their content, have more formally in common with mainstream media, although obviously the political cartoonist's work often overlaps the two formats.

In this time-context, notions of memory overlap considerably with alternative-media formats and uses. On the one hand, memory as an accumulation of exposure to ongoing counter-hegemonic definitional frameworks, information, images and debates; on the other, memory as the repository of single arresting images and experiences, in some cases the encapsulation of a whole iceberg of critique. And also memory as the agora of competing critiques and counter-critiques, among them the superficial, the misconceived, the searching, the silly.

These are just some examples of how the temporal dimension needs to be taken into account in research on alternative-media users when they are enmeshed in social movements, either closely or on the periphery.

Alternative media and the question of consciousness

However, as insisted already, we must acknowledge that these more hegemonic media habits interact with alternative-media uses, both in terms of their prior communicative accumulation and simultaneously. People do not categorically switch off mainstream media in the present moment, however intense that moment, nor can they elect simply to erase their accumulated mainstream media inheritance by some magical act of will. It is normal for there to be a dynamic mental co-habitation among users between the two types of media source and their variants.

One index of this is the question of credibility of alternative news sources. For some, there is always the nagging doubt that these ragtag and bob-tail media can possibly have gotten it right. For others, there is a rigid rejection of all mainstream media as polluted sources. Both responses in their different ways betray the hegemony of mainstream media, the first rather obviously, the second in its fear of complexity.

Addressing the question of consciousness, not least oppositional consciousness, is fundamental in this regard. Acknowledging its messiness, that it is pushed and pulled by many vectors simultaneously, that it is unstable over time, is equally so. Mansbridge (2001: 240–1) argues that oppositional consciousness requires identifying with an unjustly subordinated group, recognizing a group identity of interest in doing so, understanding the injustice as systemic, and accepting the need for and efficacy of collective action. She also argues that it forms an oppositional culture in both an additive and an interactive process (2001: 249), where a variety of motivations are in play within the group. We might add to this list a fifth dimension, namely having a strategy or strategies to address the injustice. Mansbridge's discussion of the relations between individual and group consciousness and culture stops short of a thorough exploration, and tends to posit individual-versus-group as straightforwardly binary categories.

However, there is also typically a core–periphery dimension to be taken into account in alternative-media user research within oppositional cultures, with some super-committed and highly conscious and others more tangentially so. To take a disquieting example from an ultra-rightist movement, Billig (1978) found that the neo-Nazis leading the National Front in 1970s Britain focused their propaganda against people of color because they found that gained them white recruits, although their own personal convictions, which they kept rather quiet in public pronouncements, were that Jews represented by far the greatest danger. This is also an explicitly manipulative instance, but the phenomenon is common of partial versus thoroughgoing commitment to a cause. Over time, too, individuals and groups in a social movement may move for a variety of reasons more closely to the core or out toward the periphery.

Thus the questions researchers ask alternative-media users need to be *infinitely* more complex than those posed in commercial surveys. Some of the qualitative research conducted by media and cultural studies researchers is more likely to bring illuminating results.[12] But simply asking people which are their favorite programs or what kind of sports news they prefer does not engage with most media users at any profound level, whereas many alternative media, in ways too numerous to list, and not only in explicitly political ways, do.

Indeed one pivotal dimension of research on consciousness in social movements has typically been poorly handled, namely a focus on emotion and its relation to social involvement. The rational-actor model of social movements excluded it, the mob model demonized it, and the 'new social movement' literature, insofar as it addressed it, mostly harnessed it to questions of identity-politics. But as Aminzade and McAdam argue (2001: 17–18), in the understanding of social movements, emotion is directly relevant both to collective mobilization and the onset of individual activism. They do not pose emotion as operating in a binary opposition to rationality, but rather as frequently spurring more rational forms of collective action than heretofore. These emotions may be both reactive (to particular situations or events) and at the same time deeply connected to national cultural patterns (relation to family, or government, for example).

For research on alternative-media users, the emotive and affective dimension is crucial.

Partly as a heritage of the simplistic definitions of consciousness and culture characteristic of early Marxist analysis and their long influence within leftist movements, a counter-information model of alternative media has often predominated (e.g. Baldelli, 1972). People are starving for the truth, they are being lied to, they are going out to kill and be killed in war, so our job is to feed them factual vitamins instead of cardboard capitalist ideology. Under dictatorships and even other regimes, not least in the USA during its aggressive 'world policing' administrations, this vision is very far from dotty in and of itself, but it is *always* radically insufficient. Gobbets of truth by and of themselves may simply breed cynicism and fatalism. We are not simply jigsaws waiting for the crucial pieces.

The conditions of alternative-media reception

Next in this very introductory discussion we need to note how the conditions of reception, not least questions of space and location, must be factored in to alternative-media user research. Quite often, the situations in which alternative media are used will very from the stable home or office environment associated with broadcasting, VCR/DVD and computer use. They may include all sorts of collective gatherings, school and college classes, voluntary clubs, solidarity groups, religious groups, underground organizations, labor union auspices, demonstrations and outdoor assemblies. Or they may be individually used.

Bennett (1990: 133–48), in her study of theatre audiences, rightly lays tremendous emphasis on the huge differences that the location of a dramatic performance has on its forms of reception (to take a patent example, whether in a Victorian gilt-and-plush multi-balcony theatre or in the street). The impact is likely to be, not least, on how free people feel to express their reactions and debate with each other in response to what they have witnessed or are in the very process of witnessing. Sheltered spaces, where people feel safe from violent police or fascist intervention as they watch an illegal film or video and conduct subversive political discussion, are another very obvious example of this issue.

In his discussion of theatre audiences, Brecht (Downing, 2001: 62) raised by implication the further, simpler issue of the standard cultural expectations people bring to different kinds of public spectacle. His example was the difference between the energy and confidence with which people will shout their support or critiques of particular plays in sporting contests, and the disciplined timidity with which people will feel free to intervene while they watch a play on stage. His observation is not culturally universal however. Black and Latino cinema audiences in the USA often comment noisily upon the film as it is running, and this cultural practice may well be widespread elsewhere.

However, in the case of international solidarity movements and their media (Giugni and Passy, 2001), the situation is more complex still. There are likely to be at least four audiences, each one using the movements' media and press releases/conferences in very varying contexts. One is the solidarity movement itself, often operating under liberal democratic conditions, that is, under police surveillance but permitted open activity. The second is the opposition movement in the nation or nations with whom solidarity is expressed, including its political prisoners. The third is the foreign regime and its embassies, or the transnational corporations, or both, against whom the movement is protesting. The fourth is the domestic government and corporate elite, which may have a variety of interests in play in the countries with whose publics human rights movements are acting in solidarity. Whatever is said publicly by foreign or domestic governmental or corporate paid spokespeople to dismiss as uninformed, ineffective or lunatic the efforts of domestic opposition or international solidarity, we know only too well now from archives and political memoirs that in private, elite discussions of those efforts are often conducted in entirely different tones. We also need to acknowledge both the boost to political prisoners, and the frequent overflow of political activism among the solidarity militants on to associated political issues.

Taking a quite different level in the analysis of the conditions of reception, let us conclude this section by noting the empowering impact upon fresh alternative-media users of their new experience. Rodríguez's (2001: 109–28) account of the tremendous impact on women in a poverty-stricken Bogotá neighborhood of the videos they themselves made about their lives, and Couldry's (2000: 155–74) account of English activists' media strategies and understandings, both nicely illustrate this. The examples are highly local in these cases, but they return us in the most direct way, though hopefully seasoned and cautioned by the discussion above, to the Indymedia Italia watchword: 'Don't hate the media! Become the media!'

Indeed, for Rodríguez, emphasis upon – and consequently the validation of – local audiences and users, is a defining characteristic of most alternative media. The central argument of her book is that beginning at *this* level of the conditions of reception is essential, if we are to avoid the generic error of framing alternative media process in terms of mainstream media process, thereby glissading past their actual modes of impact (and maybe not even spotting the latter at all).

Technologies, genres and formats: variety and connections

Much too much mainstream media-user research – and this could be an unintended problem with the generic term 'user' – tends silently to conflate technologies, genres and formats. News becomes all of television, fiction becomes all of cinema, media become simply broadcasting and print, we even allude to 'the' Internet as a single phenomenon. Or we pursue the opposite track with regard to advertising, as somehow out on its own, and in a different way so too with popular music, or videogames, and by so doing we conceptually sever their intertextual relations with the total media ecology.

Yet if this is a problem with research into mainstream media uses, it would be far more so with alternative media, which span a gigantic spectrum from performance art, graffiti and dance through to Internet and satellite use, and from the construction of alternative news services to the creation of satire and visual shock, whether on lamp posts or transmittable computer files. No researcher or even large project can possibly engage with this spectrum simultaneously. The research challenges and opportunities are tremendous, but the consequent need for caution in making generalizations is even more essential than in mainstream user research.

An example of the need for caution is Khiabany's stimulating and informative comparison of British Leninist and non-sectarian leftist publications, which proposes that the former 'have survived longer and have attracted more readers than did the attempt to construct a broader and more commercially sophisticated alternative' (2000: 462). Survival here is defined as pivotal, and a narrow focus as proven to be most attractive to alternative media users. Yet by these criteria parish magazines too would star, and while marketing and distribution energy is not automatically successful, its absence may not be either. Khiabany's crisp conclusions beg too many questions, although they would be an excellent jumping-off point for further research.

Conclusions

This has been a preliminary foray into this terrain, and has focused frequently on alternative-media uses in social movement mobilizations. There are many other kinds of alternative media just in this category, notably media of migrant workers and of political refugees, as well as media of settled minority-ethnic and indigenous groups, women's movement media from the suffragists onwards, lesbian and gay media, labor media. Reactionary and fascist media, local issue media, minority-ethnic media, religious media, hobby media, sharply different from each other in content, represent still further categories.

A further question, also suitable for extended separate treatment, is the Internet. For some, it represents the very apotheosis of the 'alternative' in its dizzying range and in its interactivity, and both these are solid issues, even if sometimes hyped to screeching point. Yet, on another level, the Internet's diversity tremendously complicates the issue of 'What is alternative?', inasmuch as the current weakness of widely accepted and toughminded criteria for evaluating its sources risks devaluing the currency (or cachet) of the alternative and the different.

Nor have we engaged in depth with the tension between Abercrombie and Longhurst's emphasis on the ludic in the sphere of audience agency, and emphasis on power and oppositional movements. These may be alternative dimensions, but their existence and operation need urgently to be analytically interrelated, not to become some pointless theoretical zero-sum game.

This complex terrain – much more complex, as has been shown, than commercial media-user research bothers to register – is in urgent need of careful, sensitive exploration by communication researchers, in conjunction with cultural anthropologists, cultural geographers, historians and the more innovative among political scientists and sociologists. For the reasons set out above, and despite the inevitable limitations of our academic problematics, it is likely to be academic researchers or no one who will engage with these matters. Yet especially in our corporate-media-saturated world, they are crucial to address.

Notes

1   I deliberately employ the word 'media user(s)' rather than media 'consumers', in part because of the passivity implicit in the latter term, and in part because of my skepticism as to the utility of applying the discourse of consumption, effectively derived from the reductionist model of the consumer in economics, to the cultural process. Barker (1998: 186) puts it wittily: 'such terms suggest a rising intake of media calories, a digestive stuffing of the senses and mind . . . the "heavy viewer" who "consumes" all the time is understood to be accumulating deposits of message-fat . . .'. Furthermore the term entirely obliterates distinctions between types of media and media format and the varied purposes to which people put them. 'Media users' is appropriately agnostic rather than reductive. On the other hand, the individualist bias in the 'uses and gratifications' tradition (Elliott, 1974) is not one to which I subscribe.

2   The most interesting work to date, small as it is in volume, has been done on minority-ethnic users of minority-ethnic media. Outstanding in this regard have been the studies by Naficy (1993) and those collected by Cunningham and Sinclair (2000/2001). The focus in this article is tendentially on social movement media, but in no way is designed to exclude the numerous other forms of alternative media.

3   I use 'readership' to include Web and Internet use as well as print media use, inasmuch as both mostly involve alphanumeric symbols, and in modern times are principally an individual activity. The 'new tyranny of the visual image' is a myth beloved of nostalgic anti-modernists: what do they make of millennia of religious painting and sculpture? Have their ears fallen off too?

4   The San Francisco Bay Area support for KPFA in 1999–2000 and the Lisbon support for Rádio Renascença in 1975 are two cases in point (Downing, 2001: 258–61, 343–9).

5   E.g. in France the *soixante-huitards*, in Italy the *sessantottini*, in Russia the *shyestidyesatilyetniki*, i.e the 1968-ists or the Sixties folk.

6   See www.italy.indymedia.org (consulted 1 September 2002).

7   As Hellman (1999: 125) puts it, 'Whilst traditional arguments based on "what-the-audience-needs"

have partly been replaced by arguments based on "what-the-audience-wants", commercial broadcasters have also compromised their populist programme policies, resulting in a *rapprochement* between the two policy discourses.' In terms of serious interest in the public's involvement in media-making, neither side can claim significant credit at any point in its history.

8   The ending of the film *Fatal Attraction* was changed at the cost of $US3 million to have the psychotic seductress female lead shot to death, because the chosen focus groups were outraged she met with no punishment for her vicious attempts to break up her lover's family.

9   I refer to the official fan clubs and their utilization. Jenkins (1992) and others have explored the social agency in autonomously constructed fandom.

10 Payne (1996) and Egerton (1994) provide model and moving accounts of the growth of the Civil Rights movement based in significant part on oral histories, though both unfortunately focus little on its media or communication dimensions.

11 Lahusen (2001) has a useful discussion of celebrity rallies as mobilizing mega-events.

12 This is not to assert that survey methods can never be applied to this research area. That would be a theological claim. On the other hand, alternative media with a very shifting social base would present practical problems in this regard.

References

Abercrombie, N. and B. Longhurst (1998) *Audiences: A Sociological Theory of Performance and Imagination*. London: Sage.

Aminzade, R.R., J.A. Goldstone, D. McAdam, E.J. Perry, W.H. Sewell Jr, S. Tarrow and C. Tilly (eds) (2001) *Silence and Voice in the Study of Contentious Politics*. Cambridge: Cambridge University Press.

Aminzade, R.R. and D. McAdam (2001) 'Emotions and Contentious Politics', pp. 14–50 in R.R. Aminzade, J.A. Goldstone, D. McAdam, E.J. Perry, W.H. Sewell Jr, S. Tarrow and C. Tilly (eds) *Silence and Voice in the Study of Contentious Politics*. Cambridge: Cambridge University Press.

Atton, C. (2001) *Alternative Media*. London: Sage.

Baldelli, P. (1972) *Informazione e Controinformazione*. Milan: Mazzotta Editore.

Barker, M. (1998) 'Critique: Audiences "Я" Us', pp. 184–91 in R. Dickinson, R. Harindranath and O. Linné (eds) *Approaches to Audiences: A Reader*. London: Edward Arnold.

Bennett, S. (1990) *Theatre Audiences: A Theory of Production and Reception*. London: Routledge.

Billig, M. (1978) *Fascists: A Social Psychological View of the National Front*. London: Academic Press.

Chrétien, J.-P. (1995) 'Rwanda: la propagande du génocide', pp. 22–55 in Reporters Sans Frontières, *Les Médias de la Haine*. Paris: Éditions La Découverte.

Cohen, J. (1985) 'Strategy of Identity: New Theoretical Paradigms and Contemporary Social Movements', *Social Research* 52: 663–716.

Couldry, N. (2000) *The Place of Media Power: Pilgrims and Witnesses of the Media Age*. London: Routledge.

Cunningham, S. and J. Sinclair (eds) (2000/2001) *Floating Lives: The Media and Asian Diasporas*. Brisbane: University of Queensland Press and Lanham, MD: Rowman and Littlefield.

Downing, J. (1980) *The Media Machine*. London: Pluto Press.

Downing, J. (2001) *Radical Media: Rebellious Communication and Social Movements*. Thousand Oaks, CA: Sage.

Downing, J. (2002) 'International Communication and the Extremist Right', pp. 137–46 in Manjunath Pendakur and Roma Harris (eds) *Citizenship and Participation in the Information Age*. Aurora, ON: Garamond Press.

Egerton, J. (1994) *Speak Now Against the Day: The Generation before the Civil Rights Movement in the South*. Chapel Hill, NC: University of North Carolina Press.

Eliasoph, N. (1997) 'Routines and the Making of Oppositional News', pp. 230–53 in D. Berkowitz (ed.) *Social Meanings of News: A Text-Reader*. Thousand Oaks, CA: Sage.

Elliott, P. (1974) 'Uses and Gratifications Research: A Critique and a Sociological Alternative', pp. 248–68 in J.G. Blumler and E. Katz (eds) *The Uses of Mass Communication*. London: Sage.

Fairchild, C. (2001) *Community Radio and Public Culture*. Cresskill, NJ: Hampton Press.

Giugni, M. and F. Passy (eds) (2001) *Political Altruism? Solidarity Movements in International Perspective*. Lanham, MD: Rowman and Littlefield.

Gorham, M. (1996) 'Tongue-tied Writers: The *Rabselkor* Movement and the Voice of the New Intelligentsia', *Russian Review* 55: 412–29.

Gumucio Dragon, A. (2001) *Making Waves*. New York: Rockefeller Foundation.

Hagen, I. (1999) 'Slaves of the Ratings Tyranny? Media Images of the Audience', pp. 130–50 in P. Alasuutari (ed.) *Rethinking the Media Audience*. London: Sage.

Halleck, D.D. (2001) *Hand-held Visions*. New York: Fordham University Press.

Hellman, H. (1999) 'Legitimations of Television Programme Policies: Patterns of Argumentation and Discursive Convergences in a Multi-channel Age', pp. 105–29 in P. Alasuutari (ed.) *Rethinking the Media Audience*. London: Sage.

Human Rights Watch (1999) *Leave None to Tell the Story: Genocide in Rwanda*. New York: Human Rights Watch.

Husband, C. (1996) 'The Right to be Understood: Conceiving the Multi-ethnic Public Sphere', *Innovation* 9(2): 205–11.

Jenkins, H. (1992) *Textual Poachers: Television Fans and Participatory Culture*. London: Routledge.

Kelly, C. (2002) ' "A Laboratory for the Manufacture of Proletarian Writers": The *Stengazeta* (Wall Newspaper), *Kul'turnost'* and the Language of Politics in the Early Soviet Period', *Europe-Asia Studies* 54(4): 573–602.

Kershaw, I. (1983) 'Ideology, Propaganda, and the Rise of the Nazi Party', pp. 162–81 in P.D. Stachura (ed.) *The Nazi Machtergreifung*. London: George Allen and Unwin.

Khiabany, G. (2000) '*Red Pepper*: A New Model for the Alternative Press?', *Media, Culture & Society* 22(4): 447–63.

Kintz, L. and J. Lesage (eds) (1998) *Media, Culture and the Religious Right*. Minneapolis: University of Minnesota Press.

Lahusen, C. (2001) 'Mobilizing for International Solidarity: Moral Crusades and Mega-events', pp. 177–95 in M. Giugni and F. Passy (eds) *Political Altruism? Solidarity Movements in International Perspective*. Lanham, MD: Rowman and Littlefield.

Land, J. (1999) *Active Radio: Pacifica's Brash Experiment*. Minneapolis: University of Minnesota Press.

Lenoe, M.E. (1999) 'Letter-writing and the State: Reader Correspondence with Newspapers as a Source for Early Soviet history', *Cahiers du Monde Russe* 40(1–2): 139–69.

Mansbridge, J. (2001) 'Complicating Oppositional Consciousness', pp. 238–64 in J. Mansbridge and A. Morris (eds) *Oppositional Consciousness: The Subjective Roots of Social Protest*. Chicago, IL: University of Chicago Press.

McAdam, D. and W.H. Sewell Jr (2001) 'It's About Time: Temporality in the Study of Social Movements and Revolutions', pp. 89–125 in R.R. Aminzade, J.A. Goldstone, D. McAdam, E.J. Perry, W.H. Sewell Jr, S. Tarrow and C. Tilly, *Silence and Voice in the Study of Contentious Politics*. Cambridge: Cambridge University Press.

Meehan, E.R. (1984) 'Ratings and the Institutional Approach: A Third Answer to the Commodity Question', *Critical Studies in Media Communication* 1(2): 216–25.

Meehan, E.R. (1993) 'Commodity Audience, Actual Audience: The Blindspot Debate', in J. Wasko, V. Mosco and M. Pendakur (eds) *Illuminating the Blindspots: Essays Honoring Dallas W. Smythe*. Norwood, NJ: Ablex Publishing.

Morris, A. and N. Braine (2001) 'Social Movements and Oppositional Consciousness', pp. 20–37 in J. Mansbridge and A. Morris (eds) *Oppositional Consciousness: The Subjective Roots of Social Protest*. Chicago, IL: University of Chicago Press.

Naficy, H. (1993) *The Making of Exile Cultures: Iranian Television in Los Angeles*. Minneapolis: University of Minnesota Press.

Payne, C. (1996) *I've Got the Light of Freedom*. Berkeley, CA: University of California Press.

Rodríguez, C. (2001) *Fissures in the Mediascape*. Cresskill, NJ: Hampton Press.

Showalter, D. (1982) *Little Man, What Now? Der Stürmer in the Weimar Republic*. London: Archon Books.

Soley, L. (1999) *Free Radio: Electronic Civil Disobedience*. Boulder, CO: Westview Press.

Violi, P. (1977) *I Giornali dell' Estrema Sinistra: I Tranelli e le Ambiguità della Lingua e dell' Ideologia*. Milano: Aldo Garzanti Editore.

Williams, G. (1975) *Proletarian Order: Antonio Gramsci, Factory Councils and the Origins of Communism in Italy 1911–1921*. London: Pluto Press.

PART 5

Communication and power

Chapter 18

Armand Mattelart

AN ARCHAEOLOGY OF THE GLOBAL ERA: CONSTRUCTING A BELIEF

Into the Global Age . . . (Giddens, 1999)
As in any serious discussion, words are sovereign. (Braudel, 1979)

Translated from the French by Susan Taponier with Philip Schlesinger

FEW TERMS HAVE BEEN stretched as far or proved to be as infinitely extend-able as the word 'globalization'. Few terms have come into widespread use at such a 'global speed', as Paul Virilio would say, taken over from English by every other language on earth. And few terms have been so widely disseminated in a context of such widespread social atopia, without any prior inventory of its possible significance or time for scrutiny by citizens, thus leaving an aura of doubt concerning the conditions and meaning of its source. It is a notion that refers not just to an actual process but also to a project, not just to fragments of reality but also to firmly established beliefs. Indeed, the terms governing interdependence have profoundly changed. National systems, whether technological, economic, cultural, socio-political, civilian or military, are all permeated by a logic that transcends and reconfigures them.

The project would have us believe that self-regulated trade is the necessary path, the Caudine Forks of 'prosperity for all' or 'happiness for everyone'. This is what gives the notion of globalization the configuration of a new totalizing ideology, lending support and legitimacy to the neoliberal scheme. Incorporating all individual societies into the world is now reduced to incorporating them into a social and productive system, based on what is conventionally known as integrated, global capitalism. The ideology of corporate global-ization is indissolubly linked to the ideology of worldwide communication. Together, they form the matrix both for the symbolic management of the worldwide scheme and for the further, unacknowledged reality of a world ruled by the logic of social and economic segregation.

This technoglobal newspeak operates like a latter-day *lingua franca*, making its pro-nouncements as if they were self-evident truths requiring no discussion. It stipulates how we must talk about the present and future. It endows the historical process of world unification with its own particular features. It transmutes a phenomenon with multiple dimensions both symbolic and real into a single body of beliefs. In the end, it blurs our grasp of what is at stake in the complex new forms of contemporary interaction and transaction between economies, societies and cultures. In this article, I propose to unearth the archaeology of some of the expressions of this *pensée unique* (one-sided thinking), in keeping with the intellectual project I have been pursuing since the second half of the 1980s (Mattelart, 1994, 1999, 2001). This archaeology appears all the more necessary to make the politics of the contemporary era intelligible as words convey beliefs which summon symbolic forces, a *mana* which forces action in one direction within the limits it imposes and prohibits our going in the opposite direction. Whether we like it or not, these beliefs conceal uncertainties that weigh on the process by which the world is being rearranged and, at the same time, they keep history on a path that far from represents our universal best interests.

Forgetting history

History is bunk. A glance through the panegyric discourse and meta-discourse concerning our entry into the global era seems to suggest that this observation, once uttered by Henry Ford on the threshold of his industrial triumph, is now making a conspicuous come-back. Global integration is being achieved through a multi-secular movement divested of any memory of conflict and, hence, of any grasp of what is now at stake. The historian Marc Ferro, a disciple of Fernand Braudel, is right to warn us against repressing the historical view:

> The end of this millennium is dominated by the idea that we have entered a new historical era, that of globalization. But isn't this simply an optical illusion? The movement in the direction of world unification appeared long ago, even though it has recently been extended and expanded at an accelerated pace. (Ferro, 1999: 28)

Historians are not the only ones to remind us of the need to take a long-term view of this process. Some economists have expressed a similar concern. Robert Boyer, the leading economist of the so-called 'regulatory' school, insists on the fact that history seldom repeats itself in an identical fashion and that the contemporary situation of the global economy represents an original configuration. He speaks of 'true' and 'false' novelty with regard to globalization, and argues that we must urgently transcend the 'retrospective analyses of economists and most researchers in social science which deal at best with a period of one or two decades' in order to 'take the long-term view of capitalism into account' (Boyer, 2000: 32). Pierre Bourdieu and Loïc Wacquant have expressed a similar need for caution:

> The globalization of material and symbolic exchange and the diversity of cultures are not products of the 20th century, they are co-extensive with human history, as Emile Durkheim and Marcel Mauss already pointed out in their *Note on the notion of civilisation*. (Bourdieu and Wacquant, 2000: 7)

We might add that the concept of interdependence, which sounds like a recent invention, was in fact forged at the end of the 19th century. It is actually a metaphor borrowed from biology, which used it to designate the close ties linking the cells of an organism to each other. The metaphor was developed at the time by the advocates of what was called 'world-ism' or 'worldwide solidarism' to signify the 'new meaning of the world' which, in their view of the evolution of international life, was already emanating from the planet-wide network of underwater cables and communication routes. The notion of interdependence was at the root of the new project of creating an 'international community', first achieved in the League of Nations, and simultaneously lent legitimacy to the national plans for creating the welfare state.

One thing is certain: defective memory has encouraged the return of an eschatology with a religious connotation, drawn from the writings of the theologian and palaeontologist Pierre Teilhard de Chardin, the early inventor of the notion of 'planetization' (Teilhard de Chardin, 1955). Marshall McLuhan, who was a convert to Catholicism, was already steeped in Teilhard's writings when he launched the cliché of the 'global village', the modern version of the old Christian myth of the 'great human family' that keeps coming back in new garb (McLuhan, 1962). One can find repeated references to Teilhard de Chardin, the thinker of the noosphere and of 'cosmic totality', among the authors who originally constructed the notion of the 'global society', such as Zbigniew Brzezinski. Since the sudden arrival of the Internet, however, there has been a qualitative leap in the use of Teilhard's name through intensive appropriation by the techno-libertarian crusaders of cyberspace (Lévy, 2000). He has even been claimed as a kind of patron saint by American Net-war strategists, who introduced the concept of 'noopolitics' in a report prepared for the Pentagon under the aegis of the famous think-tank, the Rand Corporation (Arquilla and Ronfeldt, 1999).

Amnesia provides the foundation for a modernity without substance. Instead of a genuine social project, techno-mercantile determinism has instituted endless, unlimited communication, the heir to the notion of ongoing, limitless progress. In the process, the old scheme to westernize the world has been recycled along with the coming of the so-called knowledge-based society. 'The educated person of the future will have to expect to live in a globalized world, which will be a westernized world', proclaims the management theoretician Peter Drucker (1990) in his book on 'post-capitalist society', a society free from friction. The diffusion theory of linear progress, first formulated by 19th-century classical ethnology and updated a century later by the sociologies of modernization and westernization in the fight against 'underdevelopment' of the 1960s and the first half of the 1970s, has resurfaced with a new liberal Darwinist twist, on the pretext that today's technology has made 'universal knowledge' accessible to that whole world. The cultural models of modernity can only branch out from the centre towards the periphery. It is a modernity in line with a Euro-American centre, which anticipates the future of the rest of the world, provided it faithfully follows the canonical stages of the evolutionary process through which adult nations have already passed. The global age, which both *ingénues* and cynics view as the end of imperialism, has hardly put an end to the ethnocentrism of the age of empires. The obvious fiasco of development strategies in the 1970s had, or so one assumed, sealed the fate of the schematic steps of historical maturation: history – modernization – progress. Corporate thinking ignores the fact that, in the meantime, new critical ways of understanding the formation of modernity have been developed – starting in the 1980s – which compel us to question the processes whereby global flows are being appropriated by individual cultures and territories. In arguing that the information revolution has resulted in a new westernization of the world, Drucker makes a case for a broad alliance between managers and intellectuals, which he considers the main prerequisite to successfully achieving the plan for a planetary society guided by the knowledge industry:

> They [managers and intellectuals] are opposites; but they relate to each other as poles than as contradictions. They surely need each other. The intellectual's world, unless counterbalanced by the manager, becomes one in which everybody does his own thing but nobody achieves anything. (Drucker, 1990: 215)

Thus, the old demons of anti-intellectual populism surreptitiously rear their ugly heads.

The refusal to join historians in 'seeing the future in the mirror of the past' means deliberately overlooking the underlying moments of conflict that have built up the imaginary picture that we carry in our minds of planetary society and consciousness. Indeed, from the 15th century to the present, it is possible to track the dream of world unity as variously coming under the sign of a religion, an empire, an economic model or the struggle of the oppressed. There has been a profusion of plans and schemes for reorganizing and 'pacifying' the planet. In the early 18th century, Abbot Saint-Pierre imagined a world government, a conception that was to haunt every plan for world integration until the Treaty of Versailles and the founding of the League of Nations (1919). In 1776, Adam Smith spoke of a universal mercantile republic and a single worldwide factory. In 1794, in the midst of the French Revolution, Condorcet drew up plans for a universal republic of the sciences, taking his inspiration from the *New Atlantis* by Francis Bacon, the founder of the experimental method. In the first quarter of the 19th century, the followers of Claude Henri de Saint-Simon formulated the first doctrine of 'Universal Association' through technological networks. Throughout this long history, the generosity of exchange often fell back into the tyranny of *la pensée unique*, just as utopias were in danger of withering in prison. The 'discovery' of a New World, opened up the prospect of dialogue and, thanks to 16th-century Spanish scholastic theologians such as Francisco de Vitoria who justified the *jus communicationis* (the right to communicate), paved the way to modern international public law, but ended in massacres and the negation of Native Amerindian culture. Yet, four centuries later, the self-same international public law made it possible to indict General Pinochet for genocide. The philosophy of the Enlightenment sketched out a plan for the joint control of nature and provided a justification for the great colonial enterprises. The international thrust of true socialism was diluted as it gave way to nationalism. Free trade turned into an imperialist nightmare. To an unusual degree, the promise of redemption by building a universal community veered into damnation of the 'wretched of the earth', to borrow the expression of the Martinique-born writer Frantz Fanon.

Each of these historical moments has contributed successive notions of universality and of our relationship to others, which in turn were reflected in utopias that emphasized either technological networks or social networks in the service of building a 'supranational social bond' or both.

To exorcise the technoglobal representation of the world's destiny that forces us to adopt the short-term view and allow ourselves instead a clear picture of our *devoir de mémoire* (duty to remember), we might well go back and read through some of the essays by the Argentine writer Jorge Luís Borges on the Holy Grail of the 'universal library', 'Babel' or 'The Congress', on the impossible quest for a 'planet-wide organization'. Or yet again, 'The Analytical Language of John Wilkins' which recounts the equally quixotic quest for the 'principles of a world language', undertaken at the time of the great intellectual restoration, which translate into a 'thought chart' enabling all creatures to be ordered and classified, the same utopian scheme at work in all the ensuing projects to develop a 'universal language', including the new language of 'computerese'.

Let us shift our gaze from this brief look at the founding moments of the project for world integration and unification and take up a vantage point in the more recent past. This angle is just as essential, for it has resulted in the one-dimensional discourse announcing the entry of human societies into the global age and the development of the 'end-of' thesis, responsible for the insidious infiltration of an ideology that prefers to remain nameless.

The 'end-of' thesis

In the early 1970s, the manufacturing of an imaginary related to a new era in history was already well under way. By 1977, an IBM advertisement declared: 'Information age: there's growing agreement that it's the name of the age we live in.' As the processes of deregulation and privatization were stepped up, the image of the information age encountered that of the 'global age'. In March 1994 in Buenos Aires, Albert Gore, the then Vice-President of the United States, announced his plan for a Global Information Infrastructure, holding out to the 'great human family' the prospect of a new Athenian agora on a planetary scale. The notion of the New Economy appeared for the first time in official speeches that same year. In February 1995, the G7 countries met in Brussels where they ratified the notion of the Global Information Society, along with the decision to speed up the pace of telecom market deregulation. We had come full circle, ending the long conceptual flight forward during which – bearing the stamp of determinism – the field of ideas about technological change was formed.

The process had begun in the wake of the Second World War. The Cold War set the stage, overseeing the construction of concepts intended to announce, if not explain, that humanity had reached the threshold of a new information age and, hence, of a new universalism. There were three successive sources of this discourse: first, the social sciences, then forecasting techniques and, finally, geopolitics.

The first step involved decreeing the death of the previous age of 'ideology', which, according to its gravediggers, was consubstantial with the 19th century and the first half of the 20th century, and of 'mass society'. That was precisely the task assigned to the participants at a meeting in Milan in September 1955 on the topic of 'The Future of Freedom' sponsored by the Congress for Cultural Freedom. The latter organization was founded in Berlin in 1950 and, apparently unbeknownst to the meeting's organizers, financed by the CIA under the cover of a private foundation. The list of participants included the economist Friedrich A. von Hayek, Raymond Aron, who had just published *L'Opium des intellectuels*, and the American sociologists Daniel Bell, Seymour Martin Lipset and Edward Shils. The agenda referred to a series of endings, among them the end of ideology, the end of politics, the end of classes and of class struggle, as well as the end of protesting intellectuals and the end of political commitment. The idea was put forward that 'sociological analysis' was in the process of sweeping away the prejudices of 'ideology', testifying to the new legitimacy of the 'Western liberal intellectual' (Shils, 1955, 1960; Lipset, 1960). Another recurring thesis, first expressed in 1940 by the American philosopher James Burnham, who had broken from the Trotskyist Fourth International, played into the hands of the 'end-of' discourse: the managerial revolution and the irresistible rise of organization men, bearing with them the new society, the managerial society that prefigured the convergence of the capitalist and Communist systems (Burnham, 1941).

In 1960, Daniel Bell, director of the international seminar program of the Congress for Cultural Freedom, published *The End of Ideology*. Between 1965 and 1968, he chaired the Commission on the Year 2000, set up by the American Academy of Arts and Sciences, during which he worked on the concept of the 'post-industrial society'. In 1973, he brought out *The Coming of the Post-Industrial Society* in which he correlated his earlier thesis of the end of ideology with the concept of the 'post-industrial society'. The latter, also called the 'information society' or 'knowledge-based society', would be free from ideology. Bell was making a prediction; hence the subtitle of the book: *A Venture of Social Forecasting*. It is worth coming back briefly to this text, particularly in view of the fact that a new edition has just been brought out with a 30,000-word preface by the author, on the occasion of the publication of Manuel Castells's magnum opus on the 'network society'. Castells pays tribute to his American colleague, by the way, while taking him out of context. Even Bell himself, in his eagerness to demonstrate the validity of *The Coming* in the age of the Internet, presents his ideas out of context in the new preface, thereby offering further proof of how little regard is shown for history when the point is to celebrate the future (Bell, 1999).

Bell extrapolates from observable structural trends in the United States to construct an ideal model of society, a society featuring the rise of new elites whose power lies in the new 'intellectual technology' geared to decision-making and by the pre-eminence of the 'scientific community', a 'charismatic', universally oriented, disinterested community, 'without any ideology'; a hierarchical society, governed by a centralized welfare state in charge of planning change (hence his insistence on methods for monitoring and evaluating technological changes); a society allergic to network thinking and the topic of 'participatory democracy', an issue that cable television had, however, already put on the US agenda at the time. In such a society, where the economy is gradually shifting towards 'technical and professional services', growth will be linear and exponential. The prevailing 'history– modernity–progress' view is in keeping with mathematical information theory and the westernized-evolutionary model sketched out in 1960 by Walt W. Rostow in his 'Non-Communist Manifesto' concerning the 'stages of economic growth'.

Uncertainty about growth and the 'crisis of governability of western democracies', diagnosed by the Trilateral Commission, the informal headquarters for representatives of the political and intellectual world of the triad (Japan, Western Europe and North America), soon made the hypotheses of the initial projected schema of the information society look shaky (Crozier et al., 1975). Though this scientistic vision was flagrantly contradicted by subsequent events, it nevertheless succeeded in establishing the idea that organizational doctrines had supplanted politics. The new society was functional and would be run according to the principles of scientific management. Among his illustrious precursors, Bell mentions Claude-Henri de Saint-Simon, Frederic Winslow Taylor and Robert McNamara, former head of the Ford Motor Company, who oversaw the rationalization of Pentagon operations in the early 1960s, and later became president of the World Bank.

The professional forecasters

The idea that objective methods existed to explore the future gained legitimacy during the 1960s, and a market for the production of future-oriented scenarios developed. Professional forecasters offered their services to companies and governments, eager for advice and ready to pay for it. Through them, the general public became familiar with the new techno-information age.

One of them was Herman Kahn, director of the Hudson Institute, which made a number of forecasts under the aegis of the Commission on the Year 2000, headed by Bell. Kahn predicted, among other things, that Argentina and Spain would arrive side by side at the threshold of the post-industrial society and that, in the coming post-industrial (and therefore post-scarcity) society, people would work no more than 5–7 hours a day, four days a week, 39 weeks a year. The leading voice among forecasters was the independent consult-ant Alvin Toffler, author of the bestsellers *Future Shock* (1970) and *The Third Wave* (1979). A former Marxist, Toffler clearly indicated the role that anticipatory scenarios were designed to play: it was necessary to generate a desire for the future among the citizenry in order to avoid the 'trauma of future shock'. He publicized his expectations for the foreseeable future, including interactive democracy, the end of 'mass' media, customization, the return of the consumer, pluralism, full employment and flexibility. Above all, he predicted the end of that 'dangerous anachronism', the nation-state, which would be swept away by the 'matrix organization' of global companies. Instead of pitting the rich against the poor, or capitalism against communism, the new dichotomy would oppose the Archaic to the Modern. At the time, 'interactive democracy' meant the 'wired cities' still on the drawing boards that were taken over by think-tanks and transformed into laboratories for experiments in technocommunitarian ideology.

The precocious determination, revealed by the wave of forecasting, to give political legitimacy to the idea of a real 'information society', here and now, overcame any doubts one might have had about its epistemological soundness. By the 1970s, it was a *fait accompli*, with strategies for achieving economic recovery being formulated through information technologies in the major industrial countries. There was an increasing tendency to assimilate information in statistical terms (as data) and to recognize it as such only when a technology capable of processing it was available. As a result, a purely instrumental concept of the information society took hold. Along with the vagueness of the concept, which was supposed to indicate the new destiny of the world, came a gradual fading of the socio-political stakes involved.

Soft power networks

By the end of the 1960s, Zbigniew Brzezinski, a specialist in the problems of communism, in his analyses of the worldwide consequences of the convergence of data processing and telecommunications, was explicitly presenting a geopolitical grid that lent legitimacy to the notion of the information society as a global society. In fact, his book on the technotronic revolution published in 1969 can be read as the final outcome of 'end-of' discourse, expressed as a strategy for worldwide hegemony. His central thesis went like this: President J.F. Kennedy was the first president of the global era, because he viewed the entire world as a domestic policy problem; since the United States controlled world networks, it was the 'first global society in history', the one that 'communicates the most'; the 'global society' model represented by the US foreshadows the destiny of the other nations; the new universal values flowing from the US will inevitably captivate the imagination of humanity as a whole, which will then imitate them. The moral of the story: the time of gunboat diplomacy was over; the notions of imperialism, Americanization and a *Pax Americana* were obsolete; long live the new 'network diplomacy'. In 1974, two years before his appointment as national security advisor to James Carter, Brzezinski proposed setting up a special inter-ministerial body to manage the 'economic-political-international machinery' or 'global system', which would report to the Vice-President and be in charge of 'global matters'. The plan did not materialize, however, until the Clinton administration, which created an ad hoc Under-Secretary of State position.

With the expression 'network diplomacy', we find ourselves projected three decades into the future. In 1996, the political analyst Joseph S. Nye and Admiral William A. Owens, both of them advisers to the Clinton administration, said exactly the same thing when they introduced the notion of soft power as the basis of the new doctrine of 'global security':

> Knowledge, more than ever before, is power. The one country that can best lead the information revolution will be more powerful than any other. For the foreseeable future, that country is the United States. . . . The information edge is equally important as a force multiplier of American diplomacy, including soft power – the attraction of American democracy and free markets. (Nye and Owens, 1996)

Conclusion: only modern communications, first and foremost the Web, can 'encourage the expansion of a peaceful community of democracies, which will be the best guarantee of a safe, free, prosperous world'. The notion of 'soft power' was launched by Nye in a book bearing the telling title *Bound to Lead: The Changing Nature of American Power*, published a year after the fall of the Berlin Wall. It was defined as:

> . . . the ability to achieve desired outcomes in international affairs through attraction rather than coercion. It works by convincing others to follow, or getting them to agree to, norms and institutions that produce the desired behavior. Soft power can rest on the appeal of one's ideas or on the ability to set the agenda in ways that shape the preferences of others. If a state can make its power legitimate in the perception of others and establish international institutions that encourage them to channel or limit their activities, it may not need to expend as many of its costly traditional economic and military resources. (Nye, 1990: 12)

In contrast to this definition, it is helpful to remember the warning issued as early as 1931 by Aldous Huxley: 'In an age of advanced technology, the greatest danger to ideas, culture and the mind may well come from an enemy with a smiling face rather than from an adversary who inspires terror and hatred' (Ramonet, 2000).

There is another leitmotif at the core of the doctrine of soft power, which tends to eliminate any sense of responsibility: the interdependence of nations, the increase in the number of players and stakes involved, and the weakening of hierarchies across the world makes the notion of power so 'complex, volatile and interactive' (Nye uses all of these terms) that it loses all consistency. The world system has no head, and therefore none of the players in the global scenario can be held accountable for their actions. In *Mythologies*, Roland Barthes described the bourgeoisie as a 'limited company'. The same name could well apply to today's 'global business class', as global leaders like to describe themselves.

As everyone knows, the year that the Berlin Wall came down also gave fresh impetus to the 'end of history' discourse, in a new version devised by Francis Fukuyama, in the light of the victory of free-market democracy.

Global security or the 'revolution in military affairs'

The concept of soft power reflects the hidden side of globalization doctrines, namely the thinking of the military establishment. A new doctrine arose in connection with the Gulf War, and was later consolidated with regard to the war in Bosnia and the implosion of Africa. The new strategic idea that enshrined the position of the United States as the 'lonely superpower' to use Samuel Huntington's expression, or head of the 'system of systems', was an updated notion of 'American national interests' at a time when US information domin-ance was becoming obvious. Pentagon experts, inspired in part by Admiral Owens, immedi-ately dubbed this new geo-strategic outlook resulting from the disappearance of the 'global enemy', i.e. the communist bloc, a 'revolution in military affairs'.

The doctrinal revision aimed at redefining 'military control in an uncontrollable world' where the players in the 'global system' have increased in number, along with their modes of action. According to its proponents, wars of agrarian and industrial civilization in the era of information war were a relic of the past, requiring careful doses of intervention and absten-tion. War, which acquired legitimacy in the name of humanitarian universalism, thus had a number of targets, from which America's overriding national interests would choose. The

US should avoid intervening in local wars, in which belligerents solved their problems by hacking each other to death. In any case, when intervention did occur, it should be limited to the commitment to bringing into play the resources of cyberwar, namely, control of the skies. Ideally, the US alone should decide on the military operations, including those outside the European-Atlantic zone, within the scope of NATO, which they tried to turn into a virtually autonomous security organization. At the bottom of the ladder were the countries destined to remain fatally 'unconnected', the irretrievable 'failed states', still mired in agrarian or industrial conflicts. State organization in these countries was decomposing and was obviously incapable of fulfilling the geo-economic tasks assigned to it by the new world order (Joxe, 1996). What was new was the fact that the military was starting to use geo-economic criteria for decision-making. It was promoting an offensive strategy of peaceful enlargement of the world market as a paradigm, in place of the defensive strategy of containment adopted during the polar opposition of the Cold War years. Hence, the revolution in military affairs assigned prime importance to extending the realm of free trade, revealing the close links it was developing among the control of information networks, the universalist model of market democracy and the so-called 'global security' strategy intended to ensure the stability of the planet viewed strictly through the prism of the new liberalism. The concentration of geopolitical power in the hands of the lonely superpower was the logical counterpart to economic globalization, defined as nothing less than decentralization at the planetary level.

Since the fall of the Berlin wall, experts in the military establishment have delighted in celebrating the 'revolution in military affairs'. The antiseptic wars in the Gulf and Kosovo seemed to confirm this vision, with its traces of technological determinism, until the attacks on 11 September 2001, when they were forced to observe that the macro system of remote surveillance via spy satellites and planetary eavesdropping had not been able to anticipate the terrorist actions, since old-fashioned human information gathering methods ('humint', as they call it in intelligence circles) had been relegated to the dustbin. Similarly, the doctrine of zero casualties from among their own ranks appeared totally outdated when formulating a counterattack on a faceless enemy.

The rise of management metaphors

In a tribute to the new legitimacy of geo-economic reasoning, a number of metaphors bloomed to designate the global company, such as 'hologram-firm' or 'amoeba-firm'. A global company was composed of relationships and information, a paradigm of the fluid, 'circulating' society. It was free of the complex modes of Fordist compartmentalized, hierarchical organization and could adopt the credo of company flexibility, employee autonomy and the 'good-citizen firm'. The watchword of this new form of organization was 'integration'. First of all, this meant the integration of geographical levels: the local, national and international levels would no longer be compartmentalized, but would instead interact with each other and be thought about simultaneously. Integration also meant combining design, production and marketing. It meant joining together activities that were once separate (the giant mergers of software and hardware firms, of contents and containers, come to mind). This cluster of convergences generated its own neologisms, such as 'glocalize', a term invented by Japanese management theorists to describe local–global circularity, and 'co-producer' or 'prosumer', which designated the consumer's new interactive function. The word 'integration' naturally refers explicitly to a 'holistic' or better still, 'cybernetic' philosophy, whereby the world is organized into large economic units. This new 'management-speak' had only one obsession: the death of the infamous nation-state (Ohmae, 1985, 1995).

This system-oriented view distilled its own imaginary. The 'network-based company' was another name for the 'postmodern company', an immaterial, abstract unity, a world of forms, symbols and information flows. The more aesthetically inclined management gurus unabashedly quoted the most scholarly references from Derrida, Lyotard and Foucault to lend legitimacy to the new fluid order of so-called 'dissipative' structures (Cooper, 1989). What stands out clearly in this hazy picture of the entrepreneurial world is the dissipation of the stakes involved in restructuring the world economy, the failure to mention the appearance of neo-Tayloristic methods applied in the face of stiff competition and the quiet acceptance of the shameful exploitation of workers making electronic devices on assembly lines in tax-free zones. It confused words with realities, since only a few companies could be properly called 'global firms'. 'The global firm is more of a project than a reality'. It also ignored the fact that 'globalization deepens the specific features of each economy and greater globalization need not be an impediment to diverse production models which take the particular social and economic aspects of the various countries into account' – in short, that 'complex hybrids' exist (Boyer, 2000: 21).

The weightlessness of the postmodern corporation and the Net economy do not offer any protection against reality. With the attacks on the World Trade Center and the Pentagon, the techno-libertarian myth of the end of the nation-state has suddenly been cracked at the seams by the force of renewed patriotism and state intervention.

The global democratic marketplace and freedom of commercial speech

Globalization walks hand in hand with deregulation. The debate on culture, information and communication has gone beyond UNESCO and shifted to technical organizations, the first and foremost of which is the GATT or General Agreement on Tariffs and Trade, renamed the World Trade Organization in 1995. In administrative terminology, these areas now come under the heading of 'services'.

A new version of free speech and choice appeared in response to initial controversies surrounding deregulated advertising and television. The very definition of the citizen's right of free speech was now competing against 'freedom of commercial speech', which was claimed to be a new 'human right'. This has generated a recurring tension between the empirical law of the marketplace and the rule of law, between the absolute sovereignty of consumers and that of citizens, guaranteed by their parliaments. It was in this context that the neo-populist notion of a global democratic marketplace, the cornerstone of free trade legitimacy, arose.

The management language (not to say the language of states that are accomplices to their own dispossession) used to describe the information society is the outcome of this ideological project: the definition of cultural diversity is transmuted into offering a plurality of services to sovereign consumers; the cultural term 'work' has been supplanted by the market notions of 'service' and 'product'. In 1998, a European Directive was issued concerning the protection of personal data, to the indignation of global marketeers who consider building databanks to be one of the main driving forces of targeted e-commerce. The objections to the Directive raised by information industry pressure groups were based on the same 'philosophy' of the freedom of commercial speech: 'Restrictions laid down in the name of protecting privacy should not be allowed to prevent legitimate business from being carried on electronically both inside and outside our borders' (Eurobit et al., 1995). Here Pierre Legendre's analysis takes on its full significance: management doctrine is indeed the 'technical version of politics' (Legendre, 1992: 26).

Lobbies immediately denounced legitimate objections to the market concept of freedom as an attempt to restore censorship: there should be no restrictions on the freedom to communicate. The movement of cultural and information flows should be regulated only by the consumer's free will in a free marketplace of products. With this axiom, any attempt at formulating national and regional public policies in this domain lost its legitimacy. There was no point in debating whether or not the state should play a role in organizing information and communication systems with a view to protecting citizens' free speech from the logic of market and technological segregation, nor was there any reason to examine how organizations in civil society might act as decisive pressure groups to demand arbitration from public authorities on this issue.

Clearly, the claim of full rights to freedom of commercial speech was an attempt to push back the limits imposed by society to 'using the public sphere for public relations purposes', as Habermas would say. The notion of the freedom of commercial speech, as a principle of world organization, is indissolubly linked to the old principle of the free flow of information, which American diplomats began using at the start of the Cold War, but which was actually developed during the middle of the Second World War (Mattelart, 1995). The business management doctrine of globalization is a recycled version of this principle, which equates freedom itself with freedom to trade. Hence, any position that holds that the principle of the free flow of information is not synonymous with justice and equality among people is considered obsolete, if not altogether antediluvian.

In the GATS (General Agreement on Trade in Services) negotiations which were slated to begin at the third WTO conference, known as the Millennium Round, organized in Seattle, Washington from 30 November to 3 December 1999, one of the issues was to make sure the doctrine of free trade was not applied to all types of goods and services. The aim was to have not only culture but also health, education and the environment recognized as universal public goods.

The search for the global standard

The search for a 'global standard' has stepped up the production of possible scenarios for future society. By 'publicizing' a future free from the weight of 'centralization', 'territoriality' and 'materiality', these scenarios plainly seek to hasten its arrival. The bestsellers by Nicholas Negroponte (1995) or Bill Gates (1995) are typical of this logistical system, which has been given the task of supporting the promise of le grand soir of 'friction-free capitalism'. 'The digital' turns into a 'natural force'; there is no way of 'stopping' it or 'holding it back'. Its power lies in 'decentralizing', 'globalizing', 'harmonizing' and 'empowering' (Negroponte, 1995). The verb 'globalize', like its ally 'communicate', has become intransitive, testifying to the implosion of thought.

As for think-tanks, they have become the purveyors of 'organic' system-bound intellectuals and salesmen of deregulation. In a January 2000 interview in Le Monde de l'économie, one of the heads of the Cato Institute summed up his 'liberal philosophy' this way:

> The 20th century has been nothing but one long state-oriented parenthesis. We are responding to the issue of poverty by saying that, the freer the economy, the more jobs it creates, the better it pays its employees, the fewer poor people it creates. State intervention is only necessary for the army, the police and the law. Everything else can be managed by the private sector. As far as I'm concerned, the new economy is clearly in tune with this project for freedom. (Boaz, 2000: III)

This think-tank, specializing in monitoring public policy, belongs to the most radical libertarian current in the neo-liberal family, precisely because of its anti-government stance. It has only one doctrine regarding network regulation: the application of common business law. The role of the state should be restricted to creating an environment conducive to free trade.

Free-market fundamentalists are by no means the sole proponents of this vision, as the discussion on digital convergence has shown. At the present time, an attempt is being made to merge the regulatory systems applied to audiovisual communication and telecommunications and make both of them subject to a 'simplified' standard dictated by 'market forces'. This is tantamount to putting telephonic communication on an equal footing with cultural products, and the latter would thereby cease to be given special treatment.

The new messianism

Globalization also goes hand in hand with megalomania. Discourse on the values of the global firm and the market totality exudes overweening self-confidence: 'Where conquest has failed, business can succeed.' The global business community has continually claimed for itself the messianic role of midwife of world peace. In fact, the organizers of the economic forum in Davos (transferred from this Swiss city to New York after 11 September 2001), where the business elite comes together every year, have defined their undertaking as a 'sort of global social conscience', but only after first recalling its 'apolitical' nature. In an astonishing interview broadcast by the TV channel Arte in November 1997 as part of a documentary film, Ted Turner, the founder of CNN, pushed this new-millennium position to an extreme:

> We have played a positive role. Since CNN was set up, the Cold War has ended, the conflicts in Central America are over, there is peace in South Africa, etc. People can see how stupid war is. But nobody wants to look stupid. With CNN, information circulates throughout the world and nobody wants to look like a jerk. So, they make peace, because it's smart. (Laffont, 1997)

Two years later, this determinism with its crusader-like tone was especially piquant in light of the *realpolitik* of the Allied Forces in ex-Yugoslavia.

The rudimentary discourse used to give legitimacy to the ideology of corporate globalization is an affront to the real complexity of our interconnected world. Its increasing social legitimacy has been indissolubly linked to conceptual destabilization resulting from the deregulation of the information and communication systems. That is exactly the point Gilles Deleuze and Félix Guattari were making when they denounced the use of 'communication universals', the most basic of which is the notion of globalization. As they wrote:

> The absolute low-point of shamefulness was reached when data processing, marketing, design and advertising, all the communication disciplines, took over the word 'concept' itself and said: this is our business. . . . It is profoundly depressing to learn that 'concept' now designates a service and computer engineering society. (Deleuze and Guattari, 1991: 15)

Deleuze saw this semantic expropriation as a further sign supporting his definition of the new society as a 'control society': a society in which the company serves as a paradigm and control is exercised in the short term, in rapid yet ongoing, unlimited turnover, replacing the mechanisms of the disciplinary societies revealed by Michel Foucault.

The asymmetrical planet

By announcing the arrival of the Global Information Infrastructure to the 'great human family', the then Vice-President of the United States, Albert Gore, was holding out the dazzling prospect to underdeveloped countries of escaping from their problems, along with a 'new Athenian age of democracy forged in the forums that this network is going to create' (Gore, 1994). Experience has shown, however, that communication networks not only link people together, but often widen the gap between economies, societies and cultures along the lines taken by 'development' (Braudel, 1979; Wallerstein, 1983).

In 1999, the United Nations Development Programme (UNDP) made a critical assessment of globalization, confirming the growing marginalization of most of the world's countries from the standpoint of information technology. Ninety-one percent of Internet users were found in the OECD countries, which comprise the 29 richest countries in the world and represent 19 per cent of the world's population. More than half of them were in the United States, which accounts for only 5 per cent of the world's population. To finance computer connections for the planet's cyberspace misfits, the UN proposed the shock therapy of a 'byte tax', a sort of network tax, equivalent to the 'Tobin tax' on financial transactions worldwide proposed by French anti-globalization social movements (UNDP, 1999).

The World Report on Culture published by UNESCO for the year 2000 presents a telling picture of enormous disparities in new technology equipment. In the industrialized world, for every 10,000 inhabitants, the study documented the existence of 1,822 cellular phones (compared to 163 among the other [majority] portion of the planet), 444 faxes (compared to 13), 1,989 personal computers (compared to 113) and 2,000 Internet addresses (compared to 4.7). More than 50 percent of the earth's inhabitants do not have a telephone line, or even electricity. In order to access basic telecommunication services, there must be one telephone for every hundred people, whereas a quarter of the world's population has yet to reach that point. As if that were not enough, the cost of Internet access is directly proportionate to the density of the country's Net-user population. Whereas the average cost of 20 hours of Internet connection in the United States is $30, it jumps to well over $100 in countries with few Net users.

The world economy can best be described as an 'archipelago' or 'techno-apartheid' global economy, due to the growing dichotomies within it, which are also found, in their own way, inside the rich countries themselves. The gap becomes a gulf when the potential for information technology development is used as a veneer for an economic model that many countries and social groups today correctly perceive as unbridled. In a similar context, the way the digital era is reconfiguring the physiognomy of cities offers further testimony. Increasingly, we find fortified centres, veritable enclaves along the lines of private towns in the United States, and companies where the employees live closed in upon themselves on planned sites linked by new information technologies, in opposition to the vast no-man's land of the information-poor and excluded. The neo-liberal fundamentalists readily admit that this is the world's unavoidable new deal, invoking a magical figure of 20/80, which means that the global economy model can benefit only 20 per cent of the world's population, whereas the fate of everyone else will remain precarious. People are being openly encouraged to believe that the former plan for a modern world based on the desire to end inequality and injustice is a thing of the past. It is a 'stupefying period of mass mystification', says Alain Joxe; the 'ideologists of global laissez-faire' are concealing the de facto 'exclusion of those condemned to death by economic war'. Joxe, an expert on war and peace studies, concludes: 'The war against the poor, and even the genocide of the poor, is the agenda of modernity' (Joxe, 1997: 24).

Contrary to the geo-techno-economic vision of a world supposedly held together by free trade, there are signs everywhere that given socio-cultural systems are being unhitched from the drive towards a unified economic field. The dissociation between the two is an ongoing source of conflict and tension that feeds the various networks of planetary disorder which take on their own form of globalization. In contrast to new hybrid landscapes, some assertions of cultural difference respond to the threat of creeping homogeneity by refusing otherness, even though they are inextricably linked to the common reconstruction of identity-affirming processes in the age of global flows.

A global system with new global actors

By taking to the streets in the 1990s to protest against the rule of the market, new social movements on a worldwide scale revealed the harshness of the notion of globalization that was coming dangerously close to achieving a consensus. The protest movement was a salutary awakening of citizens who brought to the fore terms such as domination, power struggle and inequality, which had been called into question by the project for neo-liberal flexibility.

As the stakes became planetary in scope, they ignited equally far-reaching protests. The new political deal came into focus most clearly in Seattle, at the time of the mobilization (a genuinely global event) of non-governmental organizations, trade unions and associations against the drive towards, and danger of, a wholly market-oriented world. While less spectacular, in 1998 the concerted action of 600 organizations in some 70 countries, linked together by the Internet, had already succeeded in interrupting the MAI (Multilateral Agreement on Investment) negotiations on the deregulation of unbridled investment. For three years, one example of using the Internet to lodge protests was in the back of every-one's mind: the 'information guerrilla' action in Mexico's Chiapas region by the neo-Zapatistas and Sub-Commander Marcos. Downstream, this emblematic experiment gave food for thought about social movements to theorists of the global network society (Castells, 1996). Upstream, it called forth a Net-war strategy at the Pentagon, where new forms of political activism were eagerly monitored (Swett, 1995; Arquilla and Ronfeldt, 1998).

The unification of the economic sphere presents a major challenge when it comes to choosing the form of protest. It requires that social organizations, anchored in a historically situated territory but capable of broadening their scope beyond national boundaries, discover what binds them to other realities and struggles. Searching for multilevel articulations was one of the main tasks of the global movements gathered in the two first World Social Fora of Porto Alegre, Brazil, in 2001 and 2002. They testify to the different forms of social interaction emanating from the grassroots, pervading national societies and ultimately achieving true global reach.

Buoyed by the high visibility and efficient communication of the cyber-mobilization of the new social networks on a worldwide scale, groups from one end of the political spectrum to the other soon began proclaiming the arrival of a 'global civil society'. In examining how that notion was manipulated, however, one must be more circumspect, especially as the notion of 'civil society' itself carries with it a long history of ambiguities. Such extrapolation generally ignores the complex ways in which the nation-state has been reconfigured in its articulation with national civil society, both of them being faced with the logic of global system integration. It masks a refusal to think about the state outside of the ready-made idea of the 'end of the nation-state'.

Like it or not, the territory of the nation-state remains the place where the social contract is defined. It has by no means reached the degree of obsolescence suggested by the crusade in favour of deterritorialization through networks. It takes the nearsightedness of techno-libertarians to support this kind of globalizing populism, which avails itself of the simplistic idea of a somewhat abstract and evil state in opposition to that of an idealized civil society – an area of free exchange between fully sovereign individuals. Despite all the talk that relativizes the position of the nation-state, negotiations between states continue to be necessary as a counterforce to the deviations of ultra-liberalism. One of the tasks of organized civil society is indeed to ensure that the state is not robbed of its regulatory function. That is precisely what the sociologist Anthony Giddens, promoted to advisory status by Tony Blair, has rejected in his search for a 'third way', tinged with a Christian communitarian spirit, to rebuild worldwide social democracy (Giddens, 1999). What he calls the 'global age' functions as a kind of determinism. The corollary to his univocal celebration of the mythical power of a global civil society shaped by new social movements is the disempowerment of public authorities. This type of meta-discourse can only be formulated within a national situation in which ultra-liberalism has already swept away social achievements and reduced state intervention to a minimum. Once again, the 'global' keeps showing its 'local' face.

To conclude, I would say that the current confusion surrounding words, concepts and notions relating to the global age, which appear to make sense and generate consensus in the most varied cultural and political contexts, forces us to remain on our epistemological guard. Long study trips to China, the Indian Ocean islands and the Middle East during the past year have prompted me to emphasize the visible wish of citizens throughout the world to reappropriate the process of worldwide integration by starting with the idea of a 'regional cultural community'. In spite of numerous political tensions, such attempts to build large geo-cultural entities (with their own specific features) are an essential response to the plan for a globalization that can grasp culture only in instrumental terms. Of these attempts, which I have observed in every cultural area, what pleased me the most was the fact that they not only reached across physical borders but also across academic disciplines. Geographers, anthropologists, historians, economists as well as life scientists and many others have all been invited to think and rethink the new world of networks. On the fringe of global events, on the fringe of the new totalizing theories about the future of the world led by a techno-globalizing ideology, an alternative way is being paved to build a viable planet for everyone.

It is significant that the United Nations placed the year 2001 under the auspices of the 'Dialogue between Civilizations' proposed by President Khatami of Iran, who was seeking thereby to counter Samuel Huntington's thesis on the inevitable 'clash of civilizations'. The call for dialogue seems increasingly like a premonition, in the light of the spectre of the crusade and holy war following the 11 September terrorist attacks.

To date, the most important narrative accounts of a social utopia have talked about 'nowhere'. The slow rebuilding of a utopian vision on the threshold of the 21st century needs its *genius loci*, the spirit of each place, the singularity of places. No doubt, this is the only way to accomplish a new vision of the universe and of the universal.

References

Arquilla, J. and D. Ronfeldt (1998) *The Zapatista Social Netwar in Mexico*. Santa Monica, CA: Rand Corporation.

Arquilla, J. and D. Ronfeldt (1999) *The Emergence of Noopolitik: Toward an American Information Strategy*. Santa Monica, CA: Rand Corporation.

Bell, D. (1960) *The End of Ideology*. Glencoe, IL: Free Press.

Bell, D. (1973) *The Coming of Post-Industrial Society: A Venture in Social Forecasting*. New York: Basic Books.

Bell, D. (1999) 'Foreword', in *The Coming of Post-Industrial Society*, 3rd edn. New York: Basic Books.

Boaz, D. (2000) 'Entretien', *Le Monde de l'économie* (Paris) 25 Jan.

Bourdieu, P. and L. Wacquant (2000) 'La Nouvelle Vulgate planétaire', *Le Monde diplomatique* March.

Boyer, R. (2000) 'Les Mots et la réalité', in S. Cordellier (ed.) *Mondialisation au-delà des mythes*. Paris: La Découverte.

Braudel, F. (1979) *Le Temps du monde, vol. III, Civilisation matérielle, économie et capitalisme XVe–XVIIIe siècle*. Paris: Armand Colin. (English trans., *Civilisation and Capitalism: 15th–18th Century, vol. III*. London: Collins, 1984).

Brzezinski, Z. (1969) *Between Two Ages: America's Role in the Technetronic Era*. New York: Viking Press.

Burnham, J. (1941) *The Managerial Revolution*. Bloomington: Indiana University Press.

Castells, M. (1996) *The Rise of Network Society*. Oxford: Blackwell.

Cooper, R. (1989) 'Modernism, Post-Modernism and Organizational Analysis: The Contribution of Jacques Derrida', *Organizational Studies* 10(4).

Crozier, M., S. Huntington and J. Watanuki (1975) *The Crisis of Democracy: Report on the Governability of Democracies to the Trilateral Commission*, Preface by Z. Brzezinski. New York: New York University.

Deleuze, G. and F. Guattari (1991) *Qu'est-ce que la philosophie?* Paris: Minuit.

Drucker, P. (1990) *Post-Capitalist Society*. New York: Harper Business.

Ferro, M. (1999) 'Le Futur au miroir du passé', *Le Monde diplomatique* September.

Gates, B. (1995) *The Road Ahead*. New York: Viking Penguin.

Giddens, A. (1999) *The Third Way: The Renewal of Social Democracy*. Cambridge: Polity Press.

Gore, A. (1994) 'Remarks Prepared for Delivery by Vice-President Al Gore to the International Telecommunications Union', Buenos Aires, 21 March. Washington, DC: Department of State.

Joxe, A. (1996) *Le Débat stratégique américain 1995–1996: révolution dans les affaires militaires*. Paris: Cirpes.

Joxe, A. (1997) 'La Science de la guerre et la paix', Lecture at the Autonomous University of Mexico, Centre for Interdisciplinary Studies, mimeo, January.

Laffont, F. (1997) *'La Planète CNN'*, documentary film, *Arte* channel, Paris, 14 November.

Legendre, P. (1997) *La Fabrique de l'homme occidental*. Paris: Editions Arte.

Lévy, P. (2000) *World Philosophie*. Paris: Odile Jacob.

Lipset, M.S. (1960) *Political Man: The Social Basis of Politics*. New York: Doubleday.

McLuhan, M. (1962) *The Gutenberg Galaxy*. Toronto: Toronto University Press.

Mattelart, A. (1994) *L'Invention de la communication*. Paris: La Découverte (English trans., *The Invention of Communication*. Minneapolis and London: University of Minnesota Press, 1996).

Mattelart, A. (1999) *Histoire de l'utopie planétaire: de la cité prophétique à la société globale*. Paris: La Découverte.

Mattelart, A. (2000) *Networking the World: 1794–2000*. Minneapolis: University of Minnesota Press.

Mattelart, A. (2002) *Histoire de la société de l'information* [The Information Society]. Paris: La Découverte. London: Sage

Mattelart, T. (1995) *Le Cheval de Troie audiovisuel: le rideau de fer à l'épreuve des radios et télévisions transfrontières*. Grenoble: PUG.

Negroponte, N. (1995) *Being Digital*. New York: Vintage.

Nye, J.S. (1990) *Bound to Lead: The Changing Nature of American Power*. New York: Basic Books.

Nye, J.S. and W.A. Owens (1996) 'America's Information Edge', *Foreign Affairs* 75(2).

Ohmae, K. (1985) *The Triad Power*. New York: Free Press.

Ohmae, K. (1995) *The End of the Nation State: The Rise of Regional Economies*. London: Harper-Collins.

Ramonet, I. (2000) 'Un délicieux despotisme', *Le Monde diplomatique* March.

Rostow, W.W. (1960) *The Stages of Economic Growth: A Non-Communist Manifesto*. Cambridge: Cambridge University Press.

Shils, E. (1955) 'The End of Ideology?', *Encounter* 5(5).

Shils, E. (1960) 'Mass Society and Its Culture', *Daedalus* spring.

Swett, C. (1995) *Strategic Assessment: The Internet*. Washington, DC: Department of Defense.

Teilhard de Chardin, P. (1955) *Le Phénomène humain*. Paris: Seuil.

UNDP (1999) *Rapport mondial sur le développement humain*. Geneva: UNDP.

Wallerstein, I. (1983) *Historical Capitalism*. London: Verso.

Chapter 19

Harold D. Lasswell

THE THEORY OF
POLITICAL PROPAGANDA

PROPAGANDA IS THE MANAGEMENT of collective attitudes by the manipulation of significant symbols. The word attitude is taken to mean a tendency to act according to certain patterns of valuation. The existence of an attitude is not a direct datum of experience, but an inference from signs which have a conventionalized significance. We say that the voters of a certain ward resent a negro candidate, and in so doing we have compactly summarized the tendency of a particular group to act toward a particular object in a specific context. The valuational patterns upon which this inference is founded may be primitive gestures of the face and body, or more sophisticated gestures of the pen and voice. Taken together, these objects which have a standard meaning in a group are called significant symbols. The elevated eyebrow, the clenched fist, the sharp voice, the pungent phrase, have their references established within the web of a particular culture. Such significant symbols are paraphernalia employed in expressing the attitudes, and they are also capable of being employed to reaffirm or redefine attitudes. Thus, significant symbols have both an expressive and a propagandist function in public life.

The idea of a "collective attitude" is not that of a super-organic, extra-natural entity. Collective phenomena have too often been treated as if they were on a plane apart from individual action. Confusion has arisen principally because students have been slow to invent a word able to bear the connotation of uniformity without also implying a biological or metaphysical unity. The anthropologists have introduced the notion of a pattern to designate the standard uniformities of conduct at a given time and place, and this is the sense of the word here intended. Thus the collective attitude, as a pattern, is a distribution of individual acts and not an indwelling spirit which has achieved transitory realization in the rough, coarse facts of the world of sense.

Collective attitudes are amenable to many modes of alteration. They may be shattered before an onslaught of violent intimidation or disintegrated by economic coercion. They may be reaffirmed in the muscular regimentation of drill. But their arrangement and rearrangement occurs principally under the impetus of significant symbols; and the technique of using significant symbols for this purpose is propaganda.

Propaganda as a word is closely allied in popular and technical usage with certain others. It must be distinguished from education. We need a name for the processes by which techniques are inculcated—techniques of spelling, letter-forming, adding, piano-playing, and lathe-handling. If this be education, we are free to apply the term propaganda to the creation of valuational dispositions or attitudes.

The deliberative attitude is capable of being separated from the propagandist attitude. Deliberation implies the search for the solution of a besetting problem with no desire to prejudice a particular solution in advance. The propagandist is very much concerned about how a specific solution is to be evoked and "put over." And though the most subtle propaganda closely resembles disinterested deliberation, there is no difficulty in distinguishing the extremes.

What is the relation between propaganda and the changing of opinions through psychiatric interviews? Such an interview is an intensive approach to the individual by means of which the interviewer gains access to the individual's private stock of meanings and becomes capable of exploiting them rather than the standard meanings of the groups of which the individual is a member. The intimate, continuing relationship which is set up under quasi-clinical conditions is quite beyond the reach of the propagandist, who must restrict himself to dealing with the individual as a standard member of some groups or sub-groups which he differentiates upon the basis of extrinsic evidence.[1]

Propagandas may be classified upon the basis of many possible criteria. Some are carried on by organizations like the Anti-Cigarette League which have a definite and restricted objective; others are conducted by organizations, like most civic associations, which have a rather general and diffused purpose. This objective may be revolutionary or counter-revolutionary, reformist or counter-reformist, depending upon whether or not a sweeping institutional change is involved. Propaganda may be carried on by organizations which rely almost exclusively upon it or which use it as an auxiliary implement among several means of social control. Some propagandas are essentially temporary, like the boosters' club for a favorite son, or comparatively permanent. Some propagandas are intra-group, in the sense that they exist to consolidate an existing attitude and not, like the extra-group propagandas, to assume the additional burden of proselyting. There are propagandas which are manned by those who hope to reap direct, tangible, and substantial gains from them; others are staffed by those who are content with a remote, intangible, and rather imprecise advantage to themselves. Some are run by men who make it their life work, and others are handled by amateurs. Some depend upon a central or skeleton staff and others rely upon widespread and catholic associations. One propaganda group may flourish in secret and another may invite publicity.

Besides all these conceivable and often valuable distinctions, propagandas may be conveniently divided according to the object toward which it is proposed to modify or crystallize an attitude. Some propagandas exist to organize an attitude toward a person, like Mr. Coolidge or Mr. Smith; others to organize an attitude toward a group, like the Japanese or the workers; others to organize an attitude toward a policy or institution, like free trade or parliamentary government; and still others to organize an attitude toward a mode of personal participation, like buying war bonds or joining the marines. No propaganda fits tightly into its category of major emphasis, and it must be remembered that pigeon-holes are invented to serve convenience and not to satisfy yearnings for the immortal and the immutable.

If we state the strategy of propaganda in cultural terms, we may say that it involves the presentation of an object in a culture in such a manner that certain cultural attitudes will be organized toward it. The problem of the propagandist is to intensify the attitudes favorable to his purpose, to reverse the attitudes hostile to it, and to attract the indifferent, or, at the worst, to prevent them from assuming a hostile bent.

Every cultural group has its vested values. These may include the ownership of property or the possession of claims to ceremonial deference. An object toward which it is hoped to arouse hostility must be presented as a menace to as many of these values as possible. There are always ambitious hopes of increasing values, and the object must be made to appear as the stumbling block to their realization. There are patterns of right and wrong, and the object must be made to flout the good. There are standards of propriety, and the object must appear ridiculous and gauche. If the plan is to draw out positive attitudes toward an object, it must be presented, not as a menace and an obstruction, nor as despicable or absurd, but as a protector of our values, a champion of our dreams, and a model of virtue and propriety.

Propaganda objects must be chosen with extreme care. The primary objects are usually quite distinct. Thus war propaganda involves the enemy, the ally, and the neutral. It involves leaders on both sides and the support of certain policies and institutions. It implies the control of attitudes toward various forms of participation—enlistment, bond buying, and strenuous exertion. These, and similar objects, are conspicuously entangled in the context of the total situation, and the propagandist can easily see that he must deal with them. But some are contingently and not primarily implicated. They are important in the sense that unless precautions are taken attention may be inconveniently diverted to them. The accumulating unrest of a nation may be turned by social revolutionaries into an outburst against the government which distracts the hostility of the community from the enemy, and breakdown ensues. War propaganda must therefore include the social revolutionist as an object of hostility, and all propaganda must be conceived with sufficient scope to embrace these contingent objects.

The strategy of propaganda, which has been phrased in cultural terms, can readily be described in the language of stimulus-response. Translated into this vocabulary, which is especially intelligible to some, the propagandist may be said to be concerned with the multiplication of those stimuli which are best calculated to evoke the desired responses, and with the nullification of those stimuli which are likely to instigate the undesired responses. Putting the same thing into terms of social suggestion, the problem of the propagandist is to multiply all the suggestions favorable to the attitudes which he wishes to produce and strengthen, and to restrict all suggestions which are unfavorable to them. In this sense of the word, suggestion is not used as it is in individual psychology to mean the acceptance of an idea without reflection; it refers to cultural material with a recognizable meaning.

Whatever form of words helps to ignite the imagination of the practical manipulator of attitudes is the most valuable one. Terminological difficulties disappear when we turn from the problem of choosing propaganda matter to discuss the specific carriers of propaganda material. The form in which the significant symbols are embodied to reach the public may be spoken, written, pictorial, or musical, and the number of stimulus carriers is infinite. If the propagandist identifies himself imaginatively with the life of his subjects in a particular situation, he is able to explore several channels of approach. Consider, for a moment, the people who ride the street cars. They may be reached by placards posted inside the car, by posters on the billboards along the track, by newspapers which they read, by conversations which they overhear, by leaflets which are openly or surreptitiously slipped into their hands, by street demonstrations at halting places, and no doubt by other means. Of these possible occasions there are no end. People walk along the streets or ride in automobiles, trams, and subways, elevated trains, boats, electrical or steam railways; they congregate in theatres, churches, lecture halls, eating places, athletic parks, concert rooms, barber shops and beauty parlors, coffee-houses and drug stores; people work in offices, warehouses, mills, factories, and conveyances. An inspection of the life patterns of any community reveals the web of mobility routes and congregating centres through which interested fact and opinion may be disseminated.

Propaganda rose to transitory importance in the past whenever a social system based upon the sanctions of antiquity was broken up by a tyrant. The ever-present function of propaganda in modern life is in large measure attributable to the social disorganization which has been precipitated by the rapid advent of technological changes. Impersonality has supplanted personal loyalty to leaders. Literacy and the physical channels of communication have quickened the connection between those who rule and the ruled. Conventions have arisen which favor the ventilation of opinions and the taking of votes. Most of that which formerly could be done by violence and intimidation must now be done by argument and persuasion. Democracy has proclaimed the dictatorship of palaver, and the technique of dictating to the dictator is named propaganda.

Note

1   Advertising is paid publicity and may or may not be employed in propaganda.

Chapter 20

Joseph S. Nye Jr.

PUBLIC DIPLOMACY AND SOFT POWER

POWER IS THE ABILITY to affect others to obtain the outcomes you want. One can affect others' behavior in three main ways: threats of coercion ("sticks"), inducements and payments ("carrots"), and attraction that makes others want what you want. A country may obtain the outcomes it wants in world politics because other countries want to follow it, admiring its values, emulating its example, and/or aspiring to its level of prosperity and openness. In this sense, it is important to set the agenda and attract others in world politics, and not only to force them to change through the threat or use of military or economic weapons. This soft power—getting others to want the outcomes that you want—co-opts people rather than coerces them.[1]

Soft power rests on the ability to shape the preferences of others. At the personal level, we all know the power of attraction and seduction. Political leaders have long understood the power that comes from setting the agenda and determining the framework of a debate. Soft power is a staple of daily democratic politics. The ability to establish preferences tends to be associated with intangible assets such as an attractive personality, culture, political values and institutions, and policies that are seen as legitimate or having moral authority. If I can get you to want to do what I want, then I do not have to force you to do what you do *not* want.

Soft power is not merely influence, though it is one source of influence. Influence can also rest on the hard power of threats or payments. And soft power is more than just persuasion or the ability to move people by argument, though that is an important part of it. It is also the ability to entice and attract. In behavioral terms, soft power is attractive power. In terms of resources, soft power resources are the assets that produce such attraction. Whether a particular asset is an attractive soft power resource can be measured through polls or focus groups. Whether that attraction in turn produces desired policy outcomes has to be judged in each particular case. But the gap between power measured as resources and power judged by the outcomes of behavior is not unique to soft power. It occurs with all forms of power. Before the fall of France in 1940, for example, Britain and France had more tanks than Germany, but that advantage in military power resources did not accurately predict the outcome of the battle.

This distinction between power measured in behavioral outcomes and power measured in terms of resources is important for understanding the relationship between soft power and public diplomacy. In international politics, the resources that produce soft power arise in large part from the values an organization or country expresses in its culture, in the examples it sets by its internal practices and policies, and in the way it handles its relations with others. Public diplomacy is an instrument that governments use to mobilize these resources to communicate with and attract the publics of other countries, rather then merely their governments. Public diplomacy tries to attract by drawing attention to these potential resources through broadcasting, subsidizing cultural exports, arranging exchanges, and so forth. But if the content of a country's culture, values, and policies are not attractive, public diplomacy that "broadcasts" them cannot produce soft power. It may produce just the opposite. Exporting Hollywood films full of nudity and violence to conservative Muslim countries may produce repulsion rather than soft power. And Voice of America (VOA) broadcasts that extol the virtues of government policies that are seen by others as arrogant will be dismissed as mere propaganda and not produce the soft power of attraction.

Governments sometimes find it difficult to control and employ soft power, but that does not diminish its importance. It was a former French foreign minister who observed that Americans are powerful because they can "inspire the dreams and desires of others, thanks to the mastery of global images through film and television and because, for these same reasons, large numbers of students from other countries come to the United States to finish their studies" (Vedrine and Moisi 2001, 3).

Soft power is an important reality. Those self-styled realists who deny the importance of soft power are like people who do not understand the power of seduction. They succumb to the "concrete fallacy" that espouses that something is not a power resource unless you can drop it on a city or on your foot.[2] During a meeting with President John F. Kennedy, senior statesman John J. McCloy exploded in anger about paying attention to popularity and attraction in world politics: " 'world opinion?' I don't believe in world opinion. The only thing that matters is power." But as Arthur Schlesinger noted, "like Woodrow Wilson and Franklin Roosevelt, Kennedy understood that the ability to attract others and move opinion was an element of power" (McCloy and Schlesinger, as quoted in Haefele 2001, 66). The German editor Josef Joffe once argued that America's soft power was even larger than its economic and military assets. "U.S. culture, low-brow or high, radiates outward with an intensity last seen in the days of the Roman Empire—but with a novel twist. Rome's and Soviet Russia's cultural sway stopped exactly at their military borders. America's soft power, though, rules over an empire on which the sun never sets" (Joffe 2001, 43). But cultural soft power can be undercut by policies that are seen as illegitimate. In recent years, particularly after the invasion of Iraq, American soft power has declined. For example, a 2007 BBC opinion poll reported that across twenty-five countries, half of those polled said the United States played a mainly negative role in the world (New York Times 2007).

The development of public diplomacy

The soft power of a country rests primarily on three resources: its culture (in places where it is attractive to others), its political values (when it lives up to them at home and abroad), and its foreign policies (when they are seen as legitimate and having moral authority). Culture is the set of practices that create meaning for a society, and it has many manifestations. It is common to distinguish between high culture such as literature, art, and education, which appeals to elites; and popular culture, which focuses on mass entertainment. After its defeat in the Franco-Prussian War, the French government sought to repair the nation's shattered prestige by promoting its language and literature through the Alliance Francaise created in 1883. "The projection of French culture abroad thus became a significant component of French diplomacy" (Pells 1997, 31). Italy, Germany, and others soon followed suit. World War I saw a rapid acceleration of efforts to deploy soft power, as most of those governments established offices to propagandize their cause. The United States not only established its own office but was a central target of other countries. During the early years before American entry into the war, Britain and Germany competed to create favorable images in American public opinion.

The United States was a relative latecomer to the idea of using information and culture for the purposes of diplomacy. In 1917, President Woodrow Wilson established a Committee on Public Information directed by his friend, the newspaperman George Creel. In Creel's words, his task was "a vast enterprise in salesmanship, the world's greatest adventure in advertising" (Rosenberg 1982, 79). Creel insisted that his office's activities did not constitute propaganda and were merely educational and informative. But the facts belied his denials. Among other things, Creel organized tours, churned out pamphlets on "the Gospel of Americanism," established a government-run news service, made sure that motion picture producers received wartime allotments of scarce materials, and saw to it that the films portrayed America in a positive light. The office aroused suspicions sufficient enough that it was abolished shortly after the return of peace.

The advent of radio in the 1920s led many governments into the arena of foreign-language broadcasting, and in the 1930s, communists and fascists competed to promote favorable images to foreign publics. In addition to its foreign-language radio broadcasts, Nazi Germany perfected the propaganda film. As Britain's Foreign Secretary Anthony Eden realized about the new communications in 1937, "It is perfectly true, of course, that good cultural propaganda cannot remedy the damage done by a bad foreign policy, but it is no exaggeration to say that even the best of diplomatic policies may fail if it neglects the task of interpretation and persuasion which modern conditions impose" (as quoted in Wagnleitner 1994, 50).

By the late 1930s, the Roosevelt administration was convinced that "America's security depended on its ability to speak to and to win the support of people in other countries" (Pells 1997, 33). President Roosevelt was particularly concerned about German propaganda in Latin America. In 1938, the State Department established a Division of Cultural Relations, and supplemented it two years later with an Office of Inter-American Affairs that, under Nelson Rockefeller, actively promoted information about America and its culture to Latin America. In 1939, Germany beamed seven hours of programming a week to Latin America, and the United States about twelve. By 1941, the United States broadcast around the clock.

After America's entry into the war, the government's cultural offensive became global in scope. In 1942, Roosevelt created an Office of Wartime Information (OWI) to deal in presumably accurate information, while an intelligence organization, the Office of Strategic Service, included among its functions the dissemination of disinformation. The OWI even worked to shape Hollywood into an effective propaganda tool, suggesting additions and deletions to many films and denying licenses to others. And Hollywood executives were happy to cooperate out of a mixture of patriotism and self-interest. Well before the cold war, "American corporate and advertising executives, as well as the heads of Hollywood studios, were selling not only their products but also America's culture and values, the secrets of its success, to the rest of the world" (Pells 1997, xiii). Wartime soft power resources were created partly by the government and in part independently. What became known as the Voice of America grew rapidly during World War II. Modeled after the BBC, by 1943 it had twenty-three transmitters delivering news in twenty-seven languages.

With the growth of the Soviet threat in the cold war, public diplomacy continued to expand, but so did a debate about the extent to which it should be a captive purveyor of government information or an independent representative of American culture. Special radios were added such as Radio Liberty and Radio Free Europe, which used exiles to broadcast to the Eastern bloc. More generally, as the cold war developed, there was a division between those who favored the slow media of cultural diplomacy—art, books, exchanges—which had a "trickle down effect," and those who favored the fast information media of radio, movies, and newsreels, which promised more immediate and visible "bang for the buck." Although the tension has never fully been resolved to this day, public diplomacy of both sorts helped to erode faith in communism behind the Iron Curtain.[3] When the Berlin Wall finally went down in 1989, it collapsed under the assault of hammers and bulldozers, not an artillery barrage.

With the end of the cold war, Americans were more interested in budget savings than in investments in soft power. From 1963 to 1993, the federal budget grew fifteen-fold, but the United States Information Agency (USIA) budget grew only six and a half times larger. The USIA had more than 12,000 employees at its peak in the mid-1960s but only 9,000 in 1994 and 6,715 on the eve of its takeover by the U.S. State Department (U.S. Department of State n.d.). Soft power seemed expendable. Between 1989 and 1999, the budget of the USIA, adjusted for inflation, decreased 10 percent. While government-funded radio broadcasts reached half the Soviet population every week and between 70 and 80 percent of the populace of Eastern Europe during the cold war, at the beginning of the new century, a mere 2 percent of Arabs heard the VOA (Blinken 2003, 287). Resources for the USIA mission in Indonesia, the world's largest Muslim nation, were cut in half. From 1995 to 2001, academic and cultural exchanges dropped from forty-five thousand to twenty-nine thousand annually, while many accessible downtown cultural centers and libraries were closed (Johnson and Dale 2003, 4). In comparison, the BBC World Service had half again as many weekly listeners around the globe as did the VOA. Public diplomacy had become so identified with fighting the cold war that few Americans noticed that with an information revolution occurring, soft power was becoming more rather than less important. Government policies reflected popular attitudes. For example, the percentage of foreign affairs articles on the front page of U.S. newspapers dropped by nearly half (Hiatt 2007). Only after September 2001 did Americans begin to rediscover the importance of investing in the instruments of soft power.

Public diplomacy in an information age

Promoting positive images of one's country is not new, but the conditions for projecting soft power have transformed dramatically in recent years. For one thing, nearly half the countries in the world are now democracies. The competitive cold war model has become less relevant as a guide for public diplomacy. While there is still a need to provide accurate information to populations in countries like Burma or Syria, where the government controls information, there is a new need to garner favorable public opinion in countries like Mexico and Turkey, where parliaments can now affect decision making. For example, when the United States sought support for the Iraq war, such as Mexico's vote in the UN or Turkey's permission for American troops to cross its territory, the decline of American soft power created a disabling rather than an enabling environment for its policies. Shaping public opinion becomes even more important where authoritarian governments have been replaced. Public support was not so important when the United States successfully sought the use of bases in authoritarian countries, but it turned out to be crucial under the new democratic conditions in Mexico and Turkey. Even when foreign leaders are friendly, their leeway may be limited if their publics and parliaments have a negative image of the United States. In such circumstances, diplomacy aimed at public opinion can become as important to outcomes as the traditional classified diplomatic communications among leaders.

Information is power, and today a much larger part of the world's population has access to that power. Long gone are the days when "small teams of American foreign service officers drove Jeeps to the hinterlands of Latin America and other remote regions of the world to show reel-to-reel movies to isolated audiences" (Ross 2003, 252). Technological advances have led to a dramatic reduction in the cost of processing and transmitting information. The result is an explosion of information, and that has produced a "paradox of plenty" (Simon 1998, 30–33). Plenty of information leads to scarcity of attention. When people are overwhelmed with the volume of information confronting them, it is hard to know what to focus on. Attention rather than information becomes the scarce resource, and those who can distinguish valuable information from background clutter gain power. Editors and cue-givers become more in demand, and this is a source of power for those who can tell us where to focus our attention.

Among editors and cue-givers, credibility is the crucial resource and an important source of soft power. Reputation becomes even more important than in the past, and political struggles occur over the creation and destruction of credibility. Governments compete for credibility not only with other governments but with a broad range of alternatives including news media, corporations, nongovernmental organizations (NGOs), intergovernmental organizations, and networks of scientific communities.

Politics has become a contest of competitive credibility. The world of traditional power politics is typically about whose military or economy wins. Politics in an information age "may ultimately be about whose story wins" (Arquila and Ronfeldt 1999). Governments compete with each other and with other organizations to enhance their own credibility and weaken that of their opponents. Witness the struggle between Serbia and NATO to frame the interpretation of events in Kosovo in 1999 and the events in Serbia a year later. Prior to the demonstrations that led to the overthrow of Slobodan Milosevic in October 2000, 45 percent of Serb adults were tuned to Radio Free Europe and VOA. In contrast, only 31 percent listened to the state-controlled radio station, Radio Belgrade (Kaufman 2003). Moreover, the domestic alternative radio station, B92, provided access to Western news, and when the government tried to shut it down, it continued to provide such news on the Internet.

Reputation has always mattered in world politics, but the role of credibility becomes an even more important power resource because of the "paradox of plenty." Information that appears to be propaganda may not only be scorned, but it may also turn out to be counterproductive if it undermines a country's reputation for credibility. Exaggerated claims about Saddam Hussein's weapons of mass destruction and ties to Al Qaeda may have helped mobilize domestic support for the Iraq war, but the subsequent disclosure of the exaggeration dealt a costly blow to American credibility. Similarly, the treatment of prisoners at Abu Ghraib and Guantanamo in a manner inconsistent with American values led to perceptions of hypocrisy that could not be reversed by broadcasting pictures of Muslims living well in America. In fact, the slick production values of the new American satellite television station Alhurra did not make it competitive in the Middle East, where it was widely regarded as an instrument of government propaganda. Under the new conditions of the information age, more than ever, the soft sell may prove more effective than the hard sell. Without underlying national credibility, the instruments of public diplomacy cannot translate cultural resources into the soft power of attraction. The effectiveness of public diplomacy is measured by minds changed (as shown in interviews or polls), not dollars spent or slick production packages.

The dimensions of current public diplomacy

In 1963, Edward R. Murrow, the noted broadcaster who was director of the USIA in the Kennedy administration, defined public diplomacy as interactions not only with foreign governments but primarily with nongovernmental individuals and organizations, and often presenting a variety of private views in addition to government views (as cited in Leonard 2002). Skeptics who treat the term *public diplomacy* as a mere euphemism for propaganda miss the point. Simple propaganda often lacks credibility and thus is counterproductive as public diplomacy. Good public diplomacy has to go beyond propaganda. Nor is public diplomacy merely public relations campaigns. Conveying information and selling a positive image is part of it, but public diplomacy also involves building long-term relationships that create an enabling environment for government policies.

The mix of direct government information with long-term cultural relationships varies with three dimensions of public diplomacy, and all three are important (Leonard 2002). The first and most immediate dimension is daily communications, which involves explaining the context of domestic and foreign policy decisions. After making decisions, government officials in modern democracies usually devote a good deal of attention to what and how to tell the press. But they generally focus on the domestic press. The foreign press has to be an important target for the first stage of public diplomacy. The first stage must also involve preparation for dealing with crises. A rapid response capability means that false charges or misleading information can be answered immediately. For example, when Al Jazeera broadcast Osama bin Laden's first videotape on October 7, 2001, U.S. officials initially sought to prevent both Al Jazeera and American networks from broadcasting further messages from bin Laden. But in the modern information age, such action is not only as frustrating as stopping the tide, but it runs counter to the value of openness that America wants to symbolize. A better response would be to prepare to flood Al Jazeera and other networks with American voices to counter bin Laden's hate speech. While Al Jazeera and other foreign networks are hardly free of bias, they also need content. As their Washington bureau chief invited, "Please come talk to us, exploit us" (as quoted in Blinken 2003).

The second dimension is strategic communication, which develops a set of simple themes much as a political or advertising campaign does. The campaign plans symbolic events and communications over the course of the next year to reinforce central themes or to advance a particular government policy. Special themes focus on particular policy initiatives. For example, when the Reagan administration decided to implement NATO's two-track decision of deploying missiles while negotiating to remove existing Soviet intermediate-range missiles, the Soviet Union responded with a concerted campaign to influence European opinion and make the deployment impossible. The United States's themes stressed the multilateral nature of the NATO decision, encouraged European governments to take the lead when possible, and used nongovernmental American participants effectively to counter Soviet arguments. Even though polls in Germany showed residual concerns about the policy, they also showed that the German public was pro-American by a two-thirds majority. As former secretary of state George Schultz later concluded, "I don't think we could have pulled it off if it hadn't been for a very active program of public diplomacy. Because the Soviets were very active all through 1983 . . . with peace movements and all kinds of efforts to dissuade our friends in Europe from deploying" (as quoted in Tuch 1990).

The third dimension of public diplomacy is the development of lasting relationships with key individuals over many years through scholarships, exchanges, training, seminars, conferences, and access to media channels. Over time, about seven hundred thousand people, including two hundred heads of governments, have participated in American cultural and academic exchanges, and these exchanges helped to educate world leaders like

Anwar Sadat, Helmut Schmidt, and Margaret Thatcher. Other countries have similar programs. For example, Japan has developed an interesting exchange program bringing six thousand young foreigners from forty countries each year to teach their languages in Japanese schools, with an alumni association to maintain the bonds of friendship that develop.[4]

Each of these three dimensions of public diplomacy plays an important role in helping to create an attractive image of a country that can improve its prospects for obtaining its desired outcomes. But even the best advertising cannot sell an unpopular product. Policies that appear as narrowly self-serving or arrogantly presented are likely to prohibit rather than produce soft power. At best, longstanding friendly relationships may lead others to be slightly more tolerant in their responses. Sometimes friends will give you the benefit of the doubt or forgive more willingly. This is what is meant by an enabling or a disabling environment for policy.

A communications strategy cannot work if it cuts against the grain of policy. Actions speak louder than words, and public diplomacy that appears to be mere window dressing for hard power projection is unlikely to succeed. In 2003, former speaker of the House of Representatives Newt Gingrich attacked the State Department for failing to sell America's policy (Gingrich 2003). But selling requires paying attention to your markets, and on that dimension, the fault did not rest with the State Department. For example, Gingrich complained about America's removal from the UN Human Rights Commission in 2001. But that was in retaliation for America's failure to pay its UN dues (a policy that originated in the U.S. Congress) and the unilateral policies of the new Bush administration (that often originated in other executive departments despite the warnings of the State Department). As Republican Senator Charles Hagel noted, after 9/11 many people in Washington were suddenly talking about the need for renewed public diplomacy to "get our message out." But, he pointed out, "Madison Avenue-style packaging cannot market a contradictory or confusing message. We need to reassess the fundamentals of our diplomatic approach. . . . Policy and diplomacy must match, or marketing becomes a confusing and transparent barrage of mixed messages" (Hagel 2003).

Effective public diplomacy is a two-way street that involves listening as well as talking. We need to understand better what is going on in the minds of others and what values we share. That is why exchanges are often more effective than mere broadcasting. By definition, soft power means getting others to want the same outcomes you want, and that requires an understanding of how they are hearing your messages and adapting them accordingly. It is crucial to understand the target audience. Yet research on foreign public opinion is woefully underfunded.

Preaching at foreigners is not the best way to convert them. Too often, political leaders think that the problem is simply that others lack information, and that if they simply knew what we know, they would see things our way. But all information goes through cultural filters, and declamatory statements are rarely heard as intended. Telling is far less influential than actions and symbols that show as well as tell. That is why the Bush administration initiatives on increasing development assistance or combating HIV/AIDS were potentially important before they vanished under the burdens of Iraq. It is interesting that provision of Tsunami relief to Indonesia in 2004 helped to reverse in part the precipitous slide in America's standing in Indonesian polls that began after the Iraq war.

Broadcasting is important but needs to be supplemented by effective "narrowcasting" via the Internet. While the Internet reaches only the elites in many parts of the world where most people are too poor to own a telephone (much less a computer), its flexibility and low cost allows for the targeting of messages to particular groups. It also provides a way to transfer information to countries where the government blocks traditional media. And the

Internet can be used interactively and in combination with exchanges. Face-to-face communications remain the most effective, but they can be supplemented and reinforced by the Internet. For example, a combination of personal visits and Internet resources can create both virtual and real networks of young people who want to learn about each other's cultures. Or the United States might learn a lesson from Japan and pay young foreigners to spend a year teaching their language and culture in American schools. The alumni of these programs could then form associations that would remain connected over the Internet.

Some countries accomplish almost all of their public diplomacy through actions rather than broadcasting. Norway is a good example. It has only 5 million people, lacks an international language or transnational culture, is not a central location or hub of organizations or multinational corporate brands, and is not a member of the European Union. Nonetheless, it has developed a voice and presence out of proportion to its modest size and resources "through a ruthless prioritization of its target audiences and its concentration on a single message—Norway as a force for peace in the world" (Leonard 2002, 53). The relevant activities include conflict mediation in the Middle East, Sri Lanka, and Colombia, as well as its large aid budget and its frequent participation in peace-keeping missions. Of course, not all Norwegian actions are consistent in their message. The domestic politics of whaling sometimes strikes a discordant note among environmentalists, but overall, Norway shows how a small country can exploit a diplomatic niche that enhances its image and role.

Not only do actions need to reinforce words, it is important to remember that the same words and images that are most successful in communicating to a domestic audience may have negative effects on a foreign audience. When President Bush used the term *axis of evil* to refer to Iraq, Iran, and North Korea in his 2002 State of the Union address, it was well received domestically. However, foreigners reacted against lumping together disparate diplomatic situations under a moralistic label. Similarly, while declaring a "war on terrorism" helped mobilize public and congressional support after 9/11, many foreign publics believed that the United States was making cooperative efforts against terrorism more difficult, particularly when the idea of a war of indefinite duration could be used to incarcerate prisoners at Guantanamo without full legal rights. In 2006, the British Foreign Office prohibited its diplomats from using the phrase because they believed that it played into Al Qaeda's narrative of global jihad (Nye 2007).

Even when policy and communications are "in sync," wielding soft power resources in an information age is difficult. For one thing, as mentioned earlier, government communications are only a small fraction of the total communications among societies in an age that is awash in information. Hollywood movies that offend religious fundamentalists in other countries or activities by American missionaries that appear to devalue Islam will always be outside the control of government. Some skeptics have concluded that Americans should accept the inevitable and let market forces take care of the presentation of the country's culture and image to foreigners. Why pour money into VOA when CNN, MSNBC, or Fox can do the work for free? But such a conclusion is too facile. Market forces portray only the profitable mass dimensions of American culture, thus reinforcing foreign images of a one-dimensional country.

Developing long-term relationships is not always profitable in the short term, and thus leaving it simply to the market may lead to underinvestment. While higher education may pay for itself, and nonprofit organizations can help, many exchange programs would shrink without government support. Private companies must respond to market forces to stay in business. If there is no market for broadcasting in Serbo-Croatian or Pashtu, companies will not broadcast in those languages. And sometimes private companies will cave in to political pressures from foreign governments if that is better for profits—witness the way Rupert

Murdoch dropped the BBC and its critical messages from his satellite television broadcasts to China in the 1990s.

At the same time, postmodern publics are generally skeptical of authority, and governments are often mistrusted. Thus, it often behooves governments to keep in the background and to work with private actors. Some NGOs enjoy more trust than governments do, and though they are difficult to control, they can be useful channels of communication. American foundations and NGOs played important roles in the consolidation of democracy in Eastern Europe after the end of the cold war. Similarly, for countries like Britain and the United States, which enjoy significant immigrant populations, such diasporas can provide culturally sensitive and linguistically skilled connections. Building relationships between political parties in different countries was pioneered by Germany, where the major parties have foundations for foreign contacts that are partly supported by government funds. During the Reagan administration, the United States followed suit when it established the National Endowment for Democracy, which provided funds for the National Democratic Institute and the International Republican Institute, as well as trade unions and chambers of commerce, to promote democracy and civil society overseas.

American companies can also play an important role. Their representatives and brands directly touch the lives of far more people than government representatives do. Some public-spirited businesspeople have suggested that companies develop and share sensitivity and communications training for corporate representatives before they are sent abroad. Companies can also take the lead in sponsoring specific public diplomacy projects such as "a technology company working with Sesame Workshop and a Lebanese broadcaster to co-produce an English language children's program centered on technology, an area of American achievement that is universally admired" (Reinhard 2003, 30).

Another benefit to indirect public diplomacy is that it is often able to take more risks in presenting a range of views. It is sometimes domestically difficult for the government to support presentation of views that are critical of its own policies. Yet such criticism is often the most effective way of establishing credibility. Part of America's soft power grows out of the openness of its society and polity and the fact that a free press, Congress, and courts can criticize and correct policies. When the government instruments avoid such criticism, they not only diminish their own credibility but also fail to capitalize on an important source of attraction for foreign elites (even when they are fiercely critical of government policies). In fact, some observers have suggested that the United States would get a better return on its investment if it turned Alhurra into an international C-SPAN that broadcasts seminars, town meetings, and congressional debates.

The military can sometimes play an important role in the generation of soft power. In addition to the aura of power that is generated by its hard power capabilities, the military has a broad range of officer exchanges, joint training, and assistance programs with other countries in peacetime. The Pentagon's international military and educational training programs include sessions on democracy and human rights along with military training. In wartime, military psychological operations ("psyops") are an important way to influence foreign behavior. An enemy outpost, for example, can be destroyed by a cruise missile or captured by ground forces, or enemy soldiers can be convinced to desert and leave the post undefended. Such psyops often involve deception and disinformation that is effective in war but counterproductive in peace. The dangers of a military role in public diplomacy arise when it tries to apply wartime tactics in ambiguous situations. This is particularly tempting in the current ill-defined war on terrorism that blurs the distinction between normal civilian activities and traditional war. The net result of such efforts is to undercut rather than create soft power [see Table 20.1].

Finally, it is a mistake to see public diplomacy simply in adversarial terms. Sometimes

Table 20.1 Soft power sources, referees, and receivers

Sources of soft power	Referees for credibility or legitimacy	Receivers of soft power
Foreign policies	Governments, media, nongovernmental organizations (NGOs), intergovernmental organizations (IGOs)	Foreign governments and publics
Domestic values and policies	Media, NGOs, IGOs	Foreign governments and publics
High culture	Governments, NGOs, IGOs	Foreign governments and publics
Pop culture	Media, markets	Foreign publics

there is a competition of "my information versus your information," but often there can be gains for both sides. German public diplomacy during the cold war is a good example. In contrast to French public diplomacy, which sought to demonstrate independence from the United States, a key theme of German public diplomacy was to portray itself as a reliable ally in American eyes. Thus, German and American policy information goals were mutually reinforcing. Political leaders may share mutual and similar objectives—for example, the promotion of democracy and human rights. In such circumstances, there can be joint gains from coordination of public diplomacy programs. Cooperative public diplomacy can also help take the edge off suspicions of narrow national motives.

In addition, there are times when cooperation, including enhancement of the public image of multilateral institutions like NATO or the UN, can make it easier for governments to use such instruments to handle difficult tasks like peacekeeping, promoting democracy, or countering terrorism. For example, during the cold war, American public diplomacy in Czechoslovakia was reinforced by the association of the United States with international conventions that fostered human rights. In 1975, the multilateral Helsinki Conference on Security and Cooperation in Europe (CSCE) legitimized discussion of human rights behind the Iron Curtain and had consequences that were unforeseen by those who signed its Final Act. As former CIA director Robert Gates concluded, despite initial American resistance, "the Soviets desperately wanted the CSCE, they got it, and it laid the foundations for the end of their empire" (as quoted in Thomas 2003, 257).

Conclusions

Power in a global information age, more than ever, will include a soft dimension of attraction as well as the hard dimensions of coercion and inducement. The ability to combine hard and soft power effectively is "smart power." The United States managed to deploy smart power throughout much of the cold war. It has been less successful in melding soft and hard power in the period since 9/11. The current struggle against transnational terrorism is a struggle over winning hearts and minds, and the current overreliance on hard power alone is not the path to success. Public diplomacy is an important tool in the arsenal of smart power, but smart public diplomacy requires an understanding of the role of credibility, self-criticism, and the role of civil society in generating soft power. Public diplomacy that degenerates into propaganda not only fails to convince, but can undercut soft power.

Notes

1   I first introduced this concept in *Bound to Lead: The Changing Nature of American Power* (Nye 1990). It builds on what Peter Bachrach and Morton Baratz (1963) called the "second face of power." I developed the concept more fully in *Soft Power: The Means to Success in World Politics* (Nye 2004).
2   The term is from Steven Lukes (2005).
3   See Yale Richmond (2003). Also, see Nye (2004, chap. 2).
4   See David McConnell (forthcoming).

References

Arquila, John, and D. Ronfeldt. 1999. *The emergence of neopolitik: Toward an American information strategy.* Santa Monica, CA: RAND.

Bachrach, Peter, and Morton Baratz. 1963. Decisions and nondecisions: An analytical framework. *American Political Science Review* 57 (September): 632–42.

Blinken, Anthony J. 2003. Winning the war of ideas. In *The battle for hearts and minds: Using soft power to undermine terrorist networks,* ed. Alexander T. J. Lennon, Cambridge, MA: MIT Press.

Gingrich, Newt. 2003. Rogue State Department. *Foreign Policy,* July, p. 42.

Haefele, Mark, 2001. John F. Kennedy, USIA, and world public opinion. *Diplomatic History* 25 (1): 66.

Hagel, Senator Chuck. 2003. Challenges of world leadership. Speech to the National Press Club, June 19, Washington, DC.

Hiatt, Fred. 2007. The vanishing foreign correspondent. *Washington Post,* January 29.

Joffe, Josef. 2001. Who's afraid of Mr. Big? *The National Interest* 64 (Summer): 43.

Johnson, Stephen, and Helle Dale. 2003. How to reinvigorate U.S. public diplomacy. *The Heritage Foundation Backgrounder,* No. 1645, April 23, p. 4.

Kaufman, Edward. 2003. A broadcasting strategy to win media wars. In *The battle for hearts and minds.* Washington, DC: Center for Strategic and International Studies.

Leonard, Mark. 2002. *Public diplomacy.* London: Foreign Policy Centre.

Lukes, Steven. 2005. *Power: A radical view.* 2nd ed. London: Palgrave.

McConnell, David. Forthcoming. Japan's image problem and the soft power solution: The JET Program as cultural diplomacy. In *Soft power in flux: National assets in Japan and the United States,* ed. Yasushi Watanabe and David McConnell. Armonk, NY: M. E. Sharpe.

New York Times. 2007. Global view of U.S. worsens, poll shows. January 23.

Nye, Joseph. 1990. *Bound to lead: The changing nature of American power.* New York: Basic Books.

——— . 2004. *Soft power: The means to success in world politics.* New York: Public Affairs.

——— . 2007. Just don't mention the war on terrorism. *International Herald Tribune.* February 8.

Pells, Richard. 1997. *Not like us.* New York: Basic Books.

Reinhard, Keith. 2003. Restoring Brand America. *Advertising Age,* June 23, p. 30.

Richmond, Yale. 2003. *Cultural exchange and the cold war.* University Park: Pennsylvania State University Press.

Rosenberg, Emily, 1982. *Spreading the American dream.* New York: Hill & Wang.

Ross, Christopher. 2003. Public diplomacy comes of age. In *The battle for hearts and minds.* Washington, DC: Center for Strategic and International Studies.

Simon, Herbert A. 1998. Information 101: It's not what you know, it's how you know it. *Journal for Quality and Participation.* July–August, pp. 30–33.

Thomas, Daniel C. 2001. *The Helsinki Effect: International Norms, Human Rights, and the Demise of Communism.* Princeton, NJ: Princeton University Press.

Tuch, Hans N. 1990. *Communicating with the world: U.S. public diplomacy overseas,* chap. 12. New York: St. Martin's.

U.S. Department of State. n.d., *History of the Department of State during the Clinton presidency (1993–2001)*. Washington, DC: Office of the Historian, Bureau of Public Affairs.

Vedrine, Hubert, and Dominique Moisi. 2001. *France in an age of globalization*. Washington, DC: Brookings Institutions Press.

Wagnleitner, Reinhold. 1994. *Coca colonization and the cold war*. Chapel Hill: University of North Carolina Press.

Chapter 21

Monroe Price

TOWARD A FOREIGN POLICY OF INFORMATION SPACE

FOR SEVERAL DECADES PRIOR to the war on terrorism and prior to the events of September 11, 2001, there was no articulated US foreign policy of media space. Significant shards and important pieces of such a policy existed, as we will see, but little realization that these elements ought to cohere and be rendered more effective. The White House, through various administrations, showed no need for strong direction to make such a policy central to the achievement of US objectives. With the end of the cold war, long-standing US government efforts to help shape global public opinion on matters signifi-cant to national security had essentially been privatized. Respect for the United States Information Agency (USIA), the prime instrument for this function and descendant of the World War II Office of War Information, had declined, and it was robbed of its autonomy and merged into the State Department in 1999. On the other hand, Hollywood and Madison Avenue, CNN, and the Motion Picture Association of America, were celebrated as extremely effective carriers and projectors of US values.

All of this changed, at least temporarily, when fuel-laden airplanes crashed into the World Trade Center and the Pentagon. After September 11, it became the accepted wisdom that US national security turned on the effect that ideas and images, perceptions and beliefs, that could slowly coalesce into unanticipated danger would have on governments and a new global demography. Now a coherent and effective policy was seen as urgent. In November 2001, when Charlotte Beers was confirmed as the Under Secretary for Public Diplomacy in the US Department of State, she was immediately put in charge of a campaign to change "hearts and minds" globally and, in her articulation of the issues, to "rebrand" the United States and communicate its strengths more effectively around the world. She became part of a high-level team in the George W. Bush administration that would coordinate with British and other counterparts and shape a strategy for managing information affecting public opinion abroad.

Here, I try to place these intensified efforts in context. I have demonstrated, in previous chapters, the stake one state or group of states has in the media laws and policies in another state that foster political consequences. State strategies and techniques quite obviously differ depending on each country's history, position as receiver and sender of imagery, internal political and belief structure, and geopolitical ambitions and realities. In this chapter, I focus on the United States to ask a question less discussed, namely how a power or superpower brings together and renders coherent and effective its goals and objectives.[1] In doing this, I focus on several areas where different levels of information foreign policy have developed. I examine skirmishing in the Department of State to establish more directed and integrated policies and then turn to peacekeeping operations in Bosnia-Hercegovina as a zone where policies of forceful intervention into radio and television were tested.

Based on these experiences and others, including actions in the area of copyright, technical assistance, and trade, I ask whether there is a set of practices in the United States that could be characterized as its foreign policy with respect to global media space.[2] The United States, in this sense, serves as an example, but only as an example. For many states, an information and media-related foreign policy has evolved, though rarely explicitly. External attitudes toward media structures and the flow of images reflect many changes, only most immediately the concern about terrorism and national security. Among these are the shifts caused by the end of the cold war, the expansion of the free trade paradigm, the search for new alliances and new enemies, and changing approaches toward global involvement and humanitarian intervention. A study of emerging "foreign policies of media structures" (and US policies in particular) rests on the history of scholarship concerning international communications systems and the interplay between American power and the worldwide distribution of information and imagery.[3]

International Public Information Group

There is an imperfect but ambitious precedent for the making of a foreign policy of media space. It occurred within the US State Department during the Clinton administration. On April 30, 1999, the White House issued Presidential Decision Directive 68. The Directive sought to consolidate approaches concerning the use and shaping of information policies internationally. In the usual lulling terms of such directives, the document stated that the goals were "to improve [the] use of public information communicated to foreign audiences . . . [so as] to improve our ability to prevent and mitigate foreign crises, and to promote understanding and support for United States foreign policy initiatives around the world." The document went on to say, "Dramatic changes in the global information environment . . . require that we implement a more deliberate and well-developed international public information strategy in promoting our values and interests."

The drafters of the directive intended a far more aggressive use of information strategies where there is potential or actual conflict, including "effective use of our nation's highly-developed communications and information capabilities to address misinformation and incitement, mitigate inter-ethnic conflict, [and] promote independent media organizations." Achieving the capacity to utilize US information assets more efficiently would become "a critical foreign policy objective." Something in the way of "rapid-response" was envisaged. Under the policy, US international public information strategy would take on a heightened quasi-military rhetoric. It would include contingency plans, catalog the potential for information-based US responses, and predict the resources required for meeting US public information goals. The government would be affirmative in "preventing and mitigating foreign crises" while advancing US national interests. The directive imposed a duty to "use information assets—including those that reflect new and emerging technologies—in an innovative and proactive manner."

The directive found its bureaucratic embodiment in a new implementing structure. At the State Department, the Under Secretary for Public Diplomacy was made head of a newly formed International Public Information Group, the IPIG, whose mandate was directed at information abroad rather than at home. This Information Group was to have members from the State Department, USAID, the National Intelligence Council, the National Security Council, the Department of Defense, and the Joint Chiefs of Staff. The composition of this group, particularly the inclusion of members of the intelligence and military community, was designed to reflect the importance of media structure to foreign policy and national security.

Neither the words of the directive nor the composition of the group alone is sufficient to indicate the potential implications for a foreign policy of information space. The directive has, however, a more than usually explicit provenance and a franker articulation prior to its promulgation than is usually the case. While the fashioning of the directive was the work of more than one person, its essence sprang from the mind of an unusual young policy advocate, Jamie Frederic Metzl, a foreign policy specialist who had long campaigned for a redefinition of US capabilities in the information field and had written extensively about his objectives.

As part of the staff of the National Security Council, Metzl became involved in considering the reorganization of public diplomacy functions within and outside the State Department and the consolidation of the United States Information Agency under congressional direction. He wrote about the project for *Daedalus*.[4] He applauded the redefinition of public diplomatic functions and the forging of a closer relationship between substantive foreign policy decisions and the capacity to persuade key elements of a decentralized global public opinion of the desirability and efficacy of a US national interest initiative.[5]

Other critics had seen the controversial reorganization—in which the United States Information Agency was absorbed into the State Department—as flawed. They thought that the vestigial USIA would become less objective, less credible, more subject to direction by political leadership in the Department. Metzl, however, considered that, under the right conditions, the consolidation presented positive opportunities. The reorganization could begin a process of "reinvigorating the United States foreign policy establishment" by bringing public diplomacy and traditional diplomacy closer together. To engage internationally as effectively as possible in a decentralized world, a shift in foreign policy focus would be needed "towards a new vision, a new model, and a new culture."[6] Force, he appreciated, always required justification. "Without winning the struggle to define the interpretation of state actions, the physical acts themselves become less effective."

In his *Daedalus* article, which I cite because of its unusual openness about the issues at stake, Metzl also described the need to reach beyond governments and touch hearts and minds more directly. "With the rapid expansion and decentralization of information systems, including the growth of the Internet, satellite television and the sharp reduction in the costs of international communications, information assets have come to play an even greater role in defining the legitimacy of the use of force."[7] The particular impact of these new technologies, combined with other vectors of change, would redefine the relative importance of centralized and decentralized power as an object of persuasion. "How much effort should the United States put into relations with other governments compared to efforts to interact directly with foreign populations or with multilateral organizations or to facilitate nongovernmental contacts between sectors of the United States and foreign societies?"[8] Metzl called for a change in emphasis at the State Department for public persuasion rather than a system based on country contacts. His driving claim was that it must be a key element of US foreign policy to mesh public diplomacy with national interest decisions, and to have public diplomacy involved early in policy making as well as in a critical part of the execution of policy.

Fresh from his work helping to bring the International Public Information Group into existence, Metzl became its first director and had several opportunities to try to implement his philosophy. A useful example occurred in the period after the 1999 NATO military intervention in Kosovo. Under the prodding of IPIG, the United States took the lead in establishing a "ring around Serbia," a peripheral group of transmitters that pumped alternate voices into targeted parts of the former Yugoslavia. This aspect of "information intervention" provided a mode of distribution for reinforced Serbian language programming of the Voice of America, the BBC, the US surrogate, RFE/RL (a meshing of the former Radio Free Europe and Radio Liberty), and Deutsche Welle. The US government persuaded the leadership in Republika Srpska to allow transmitters there to be retooled for the Serbian information action. The "ring around Serbia" also included transmitters in Romania and Croatia that broadcast targeted messages into Serbia.

The concentration of energy, the ambition of the Information Group idea, and the implications for standard State Department practices attracted criticism. One basis was the fear that the Group would seek to manipulate American public opinion as well as opinion abroad. The argument was "that government cannot send one message to the international press corps and another to domestic media."[9] A different sense of concern arose from the very mode and comprehensiveness of the foreign policy objectives. *The Washington Times* sounded an alert based on what it claimed to be a leaked version of the character of the new policy group.[10] The draft charter apparently indicated that the Group would control all "international military information" to influence "the emotions, motives, objective reasoning and ultimately the behavior of foreign governments, organizations, groups, and individuals."[11] Both the political left and right were concerned that the IPIG was intermixing military and civil foreign strategy considerations in a way that posed problems for the future.

In the 1990s, a sense of supportive urgency for the IPIG mandate was lacking. The cold war was over; propaganda seemed obsolete. But Metzl's philosophy, in its most extended form, anticipated the actions taken after 2001 by the Bush administration in its campaign to win "hearts and minds." Underlying the approach of the IPIG was the idea that the very means of distribution of information become a critical aspect of the way the United States represents itself in the world. And to accomplish such an integrated goal a foreign policy is necessary concerning media structures and the content and use of information space globally. Certain forms of global distribution of information will be more amenable to the exercise of "soft power" than others. In the wake of September 11, Charlotte Beers and her new apparatus scampered for new avenues to capture attention and to begin the process of reinforcing US policy through public diplomacy. The IPIG, to the extent it embraced Metzl's approach, recognized the special requirements of a decentralized information environment, where nongovernment organizations help shape public opinion across national lines. There, he thought, the critical element of any governmental effort would be flexibility and the capacity to adapt.

Such a foreign policy of media space began with the recognition that the institutions for delivering information had changed. During the time of monopoly state broadcasting authorities, with their substantial control over information space, the process of public diplomacy could be limited to influencing those broadcasters or trying to circumvent them. Now, the apparent shapelessness of transnational information networks, and especially the Internet, as it became a more significant means of immediate changes in information flow, compelled a different situational response. Any government engaged in these processes must be far more proactive as it deals with information distribution.

The point is not only that, as Metzl had put it, "foreign public opinion has become harder to influence as once jealously guarded state monopolies on information dissemination to home populations have been broken down by satellite dishes, telephones, fax and Internet links in all but the most repressive countries."[12] These dramatic changes could be turned to advantages. They did not mean that weak and powerful states no longer could use "public diplomacy" to achieve central national goals. Rather, as subsequent events demonstrated, effective public diplomacy required a wholesale rethinking of organization at home and modes of distribution abroad. States hoping to retain advantages in traditional areas of power, including military and economic, "must engage this decentralized environment in new and creative ways in order to retain these advantages . . . To retain current levels of relevance into the next century, governments must recognize and internalize this [communications] transformation."[13]

The influence of the IPIG or of its underlying philosophy was never fully realized. The United States was not yet ready for so integrated a media-related foreign policy, at least not so explicitly, and not during peacetime. Still, it was, at least for the moment, administration policy that the greater the emphasis on public diplomacy, the greater the need for a far more comprehensive rethinking of the way in which information is distributed and received internationally. There was, again temporarily, recognition that developing a global media policy integrated into foreign policy required elaborate notions of how information is distributed.

Information intervention

The approach to media after the World Trade Center and Pentagon attacks dramatized an obvious fact: that sensitivity to media abroad (as well as at home) becomes more visible and actions to affect such media more tangible and directed when war, or conflict that raises the threat of war, is involved. At such a time, the geopolitical stakes in the patterns of distribution of information are too high to be left solely to a market, often fictive, in which governments do not actively participate. In the 1990s, proposals began to be made, as they would be again a decade later in connection with the campaign against terrorism, for concerted action by the international community to forestall use of broadcast media that promoted or accentuated devastating, often genocidal, conflict.[14] These proposals commonly pointed to the explosive mobilizing role *Radio-Television Libre des Milles Collines* (RTLM) played in the Rwandan genocide with its repetitious and explicit incitement for Hutu to slaughter Tutsi. That became the textbook example where preventive intervention by the international community should have been deemed suitable and necessary.

Alison des Forges has written passionately about the maddeningly slow development of US foreign policy toward the Rwandan media space. Before the genocide, NGOs sought US assistance in jamming as a preventive measure. Though knowledgeable State Department officials agreed with the need, requests were denied on the ground that jamming went against the principles of freedom of expression and respect for national sovereignty. Des Forges points out that the United States had already engaged in jamming radios in arenas of combat, namely during the 1991 Persian Gulf War and in 1994 in Haiti.[15] "The State Department lawyers could have drawn on this precedent, given that the genocide was being executed during a war. They did not do so, almost certainly because the policy decision had already been made not to intervene and they knew that they were serving merely to endorse it."[16] With the crisis deepening, on May 4, 1994, the Pentagon concluded that jamming was an "ineffective and expensive mechanism."[17] The failure to stem the genocide in Rwanda would become a precedent for more rapid response in the future and a rallying cry for those who believed earlier intervention in the media space of Rwanda would have helped lessen the conflict.

What has emerged from Rwanda to the war in Afghanistan is a rich but insufficiently examined approach to critical elements of a foreign policy of media space which, together, can be called "information intervention." Information intervention includes a broader range of intermediary or information-related techniques available to the UN, NATO, or the United States as they engage in avoiding conflict, in conflict itself, and in peacekeeping operations. Both as a humanitarian and practical matter, proponents of information interventions consider it wise to avoid a stark choice between the extremes of massive, armed humanitarian intervention and mere symbolic action.

In war itself, as was exemplified in Serbia in 1999 and in Afghanistan in 2001, the elimination, through bombing, of domestic broadcast systems has become more customary, indeed frighteningly so. But what about interventions short of war? What media steps can be taken that lead to conflict avoidance or the encouragement of stability? The same Jamie Metzl who had been the young architect of the Information Policy Information Group has also written about the questions of blocking and interrupting transmissions, monitoring of local transmissions, or so-called peace broadcasting (the insertion of a channel of information that is "objective" and has as its goal defusing conflict).[18] He has argued that though sovereignty objections might be lodged to such aggressive nonforcible intervention, especially in internal strife, preventing such civil conflicts from becoming regional conflagrations is in the general interest. Permitting limited radio and television jamming in defense of human rights, while not a solution to all ills, still could be "a potentially effective and relatively low-risk tool for countering dangerous messages that incite people to violence." In 1958, President Eisenhower included in an address to the United Nations a proposal, for the monitoring of inflammatory communications. "I believe that this Assembly should . . . consider means for monitoring the radio broadcasts directed across national frontiers in the troubled Near East area. It should then examine complaints from these nations which consider their national security jeopardized by external propaganda."[19] Ultimately, as Metzl concluded, information intervention would be "one of a larger set of intermediate actions between neglect and armed intervention," that can increase the capacity of tools available for responding to potential conflict or genocidal calls to violence.

An example: information intervention in Bosnia

Information intervention foreign policy can be divided into three segments: (1) attitudes toward the use of media pre-conflict (as in Rwanda), where war, instability, and massive human rights violations could be predicted; (2) attitudes toward manipulation of information in time of war (as in Aghanistan and the Gulf War); and (3) a foreign policy toward management of media in the wake of conflict when peacekeeping operations are initiated.[20] Here I focus on peacekeeping in Bosnia-Hercegovina because so many elements of information intervention played themselves out there. Bosnia-Hercegovina is significant for many reasons. One is that the ordinary foreign policy of supporting indigenous media was overtaken, in a time of crisis, by a desire to weaken embedded nationalist parties and strengthen the electoral prospects of candidates favored by the United States. Precedents established there became significant later in Kosovo and in Afghanistan. The creation of a machine of media-related peacekeeping would make a lasting impact on US policies toward the press and broadcasters in conflict zones.

Under the Dayton Accords, the NATO-led Stabilization Force (Sfor) and the Office of High Representative (OHR), together with the Organization for Security and Cooperation in Europe (OSCE) and a wide variety of nongovernmental organizations, took steps to reshape and reform the media space in Bosnia-Hercegovina, recognizing the critical relationship of altering media as part of reconstructing society. It became clear that a new approach was emerging, with vastly important constitutional, political, and structural implications. All of a sudden, the kind of machinery of administration over media was put in place that had not been seen as an imposition of the international community for almost half a century.[21]

NATO and the Office of High Representative (OHR) employed various modes, after the Dayton Accords, of creating a political environment with what might be deemed the desired democratic outcome. Control of the media continued to be important because hard-line Bosnian Serb "Srpska Radio Televizija Pale" (SRT Pale, after the city of transmission), controlled by Radovan Karadzic, was seen as fanning discord, creating the potential for renewed conflict and engendering opposition to the NATO mission. Responding to this challenge, NATO and OHR made a decision to address SRT aggressively. At its May 1997 semiannual meeting to review the progress of Dayton's implementation, the Steering Board of the Peace Implementation Council passed the Sintra Declaration, which stated that the High Representative "has the right to curtail or suspend any media network or programme whose output is in persistent and blatant contravention of either the spirit or letter of the Peace Agreement."[22] This extraordinary provision of the Declaration established the right of the Stabilization Force and the OHR to block media outlets throughout Bosnia-Hercegovina. It also provided the framework Sfor used to justify its later seizure of television towers in Republika Srpska.

On August 14, US Senator Carl Levin, the ranking Democrat on the Senate Armed Services Committee, suggested that American planes jam SRT signals while simultaneously transmitting "broadcasts that depict the true reasons for [the Serbian people's] isolation and poor standing in the international community" as a way of leavening their attitudes. Bosnian Serb leaders were furious. The Bosnian Serb information minister, Miroslav Toholj, stated that, "Any United States administration operation to jam SRT will be considered an act of war and will be treated as such." Only days later, in defiance of pressure by the OHR to broadcast the warning of the Sintra Declaration, SRT ran a report comparing Sfor with the Nazis and referred to them as "occupying forces." With the logo "SS-for" instead of Sfor, the broadcast alternated images of Sfor soldiers with World War II German storm troopers.

In a response on August 23, the new High Representative, Carlos Westendorp, sent a letter demanding that SRT broadcast, that day, an OHR statement explaining the inter-nationally imposed obligations for the broadcaster included in the Sintra Declaration. In the letter, Westendorp wrote, "If this is not done, I am prepared to use my powers, including those stemming from the Sintra Declaration." This was essentially a threat to impose a protectorate over SRT. Westendorp called the broadcast comparing Sfor to Nazis "absolutely unacceptable." He suggested Sfor might take action by seizing television towers to stop the Pale media propaganda against the peace forces in Bosnia-Hercegovina. SRT promptly submitted to Westendorp's demand, and broadcast the statement before the deadline. However, immediately afterward, SRT announced that the High Representative's actions exceeded the bounds of the Dayton Accords and rebroadcast the clip comparing Sfor to the Nazis.

On August 22, in the next step of what became the transformation of SRT, US troops seized a television broadcast tower in Udrigovo, a northeastern town, under the pretense that they were trying to prevent possible clashes between supporters of Karadzic and supporters of Biljana Plavsic, a more moderate Bosnian Serb leader whom the international community and the United States backed in forthcoming elections. Political outcomes were surely a major element of the activities. But this desire had to be housed in a claim of neutrality. "Our aim is not to influence which programme will be broadcast via the transmit-ter. All we want is to prevent conflicts, but we will use any force deemed necessary at any attempt of violence," said Chris Riley, a Stabilization Force spokesman.

What followed was a negotiation resulting in a document known as the Udrigovo Agreement.[23] Sfor handed the tower back to the SRT authorities in Pale but on conditions designed to balance the information environment.[24] The Agreement required that the media of the Serb Republic stop producing inflammatory reports against Sfor and the other international organizations implementing the Dayton Accords, that SRT Pale would regularly provide an hour of prime time programming to air political views other than those of the ruling party, that SRT Pale provide Westendorp with a daily half hour of prime time programming to introduce himself and talk about recent developments, and that the Serb Republic agree to abide by all the rules being established by the international community's Media Support Advisory Group.[25]

Against a background of increased conflict on the airwaves of Republika Srpska, and the raised stakes for political control as the election drew nearer, the appeal for international jamming of SRT Pale gained currency. In fact the United States dispatched three Air Force EC-130 Commando Solo planes capable both of broadcasting information and jamming existing radio and television signals. These aircraft had been used for similar purposes in Haiti, Panama, and Grenada (and would be used again for jamming and transmission purposes in Afghanistan). US officials claimed that the primary role of the electronic warfare planes would be to broadcast "fair and balanced news and information" to the local population. Voice of America (VOA) broadcasts to Bosnia-Hercegovina also stated that the planes had the capability to jam pro-Karadzic transmissions. VOA reported the US belief that Karadzic supporters had violated the Udrigovo Agreement that mandated softened rhetoric against Plavsic and NATO peacekeeping troops.

The VOA broadcasts during this critical time also included an interview with Pentagon spokesman Dave Arlington who stated, "Commander Sfor controls the airwaves in Bosnia-Hercegovina, OK, so he is well within his mandate to be able to broadcast, and he will be the guy that's managing the frequencies and the broadcasts there within the theater." This contention made clear what had been only obliquely suggested before, namely that Sfor considered that it had ultimate authority over broadcasting in Bosnia-Hercegovina. This disturbed not only the Karadzic faction, but other political entities as well, all of whom became more vocal against what they called "media colonization." Western press freedom organizations also protested possible jamming. The planes were not put into immediate service but were held in readiness at bases in Italy.

More pressure to affect the flow of information in an election period resulted in the internationally brokered Belgrade Agreement designed to give more airtime for the station favoring Biljana Plavsic, the more moderate Serbian leader. The agreement stated: "President Biljana Plavsic and President Momcilo Krajisnik agree that the unified media environment of the Republika Srpska and free access to media by all participants in elections is vital for [elections to be] held in a democratic manner. They agree that news programmes be broadcast daily from studios in Pale and Banja Luka [the Plavsic station] alternately."

Hope for a harmonious implementation of the Belgrade Agreement was dashed almost immediately. A September 25 press release from the OHR said that SRT Pale was continuing to broadcast, as news, political announcements "devoid of any balance or alternative opinion." SRT Pale refused to soften its editorial content. On September 26, the chief prosecutor of the International Criminal Tribunal for the Former Yugoslavia, Louise Arbour, gave a press conference in Sarajevo, which was covered by SRT. The Bosnian Serb leadership had always maintained that the Tribunal was not a legitimate juridical body but rather designed to denigrate the reputation of the Serbs. Consistent with this view, an SRT Pale announcer introduced Arbour's press conference with a commentary claiming that the Tribunal was a political instrument and that it was prejudiced against the Serbs.

The United Nations, with substantial US involvement, considered this a breach of prior understandings, including the Udrigovo Agreement, and demanded that SRT Pale make a public apology on television. On September 30, SRT Pale did so, stating, "Serb-Radio-TV in this way wishes to apologize unreservedly for its misrepresentation of a news conference given by the prosecutor of The Hague Tribunal, Louise Arbour. We will read out a statement to this effect made by the prosecutor. The statement will be followed by the complete and unedited footage of the news conference given by Judge Arbour last Friday, during her visit to Bosnia-Hercegovina." Despite SRT Pale's apology, Sfor troops seized control of certain SRT transmitters the next day (October 1), thereby preventing SRT Pale from transmitting further broadcasts. Western governments also claimed that SRT Pale's repeated broadcast comparing Sfor troops to Nazis constituted a threat to the safety of the Sfor soldiers and therefore needed to be silenced.

Sensitive to the potential for condemnation of the seizure, Sfor and OHR announced that SRT Pale could regain access to the transmission network and resume operations, but only if strict conditions were met. SRT Pale would be obliged to agree to "criteria for its reconstruction and reorganization, as well as for editorial control of broadcasting, as suggested by the Office of the High Representative in Bosnia-Hercegovina and the international community." In protest of the silencing of their station, employees at SRT Pale went on strike. They then held a meeting with twenty local radio stations in the Serb Republic and sent an appeal to the international community to "lift the blockade of the SRT transmitters."

The High Representative dictated the criteria SRT Pale needed to meet in order to go back on the air. He demanded that all politicians withdraw from SRT's board of directors and give up their right to control the station. In a letter, the High Representative went on to say that a "transitory international director-general" and two deputies would be appointed by the OHR to head SRT Pale.[26] He also stated that the OHR would draft a statute and editorial charter for the station, that SRT Pale would be obliged to broadcast programs requested by officials from the international community without editing or commentary, and that a team of journalists and editors would be brought in to train personnel and supervise the programming of SRT Pale. He added further that the international representatives would evaluate the SRT journalists and editors and that "only those who are positively evaluated will be able to get a job again."

On October 10, the editor of SRT Pale announced, "the international community is planning to introduce a protectorate over Serb Radio-Television and to destroy it."[27] Both Krajisnik and the Bosnian Serb prime minister at the time, Gojko Klickovic, rejected Westendorp's demands and challenged the OHR's legal basis for seizing the TV transmitters and reorganizing the board of directors of SRT Pale. Meanwhile, the staff of SRT, deprived of their normal distribution methods and allegedly on strike, kept trying to devise ways to get around the NATO blockade, and much to the chagrin of Sfor (the NATO troops), they did so. The staff of SRT Pale also disabled signals transmitting programming supporting Plavsic. SRT Pale then used special military vehicles fitted with broadcasting and jamming equipment to transmit its programs on the pirated frequency in contravention of the NATO blockade. NATO responded immediately by deploying one of its Commando Solo electronic warfare planes to jam the mobile SRT Pale broadcasts. The plane also transmitted a message to Serbs in eastern Bosnia-Hercegovina that the Pale authorities were responsible for the interruption of regular SRT Banja Luka programming.

On the same day, a mysterious explosion destroyed a transmitter in Bijeljina that was key to SRT Pale's ability to circumvent the NATO blockade. SRT Pale's broadcasting ability effectively was destroyed. Several days later, Western diplomats in Sarajevo suggested broadcasting SRT Banja Luka to eastern Bosnia-Hercegovina via a US satellite. By October 31, this was done and Serbs in eastern Bosnia-Hercegovina could watch only SRT Banja Luka.[28]

This brief history demonstrates the use of information intervention instrumentally to affect the outcome of a key election. This could be justified on the grounds that the distribution of media power was severely biased toward the encouragement of conflict and, as well, was in the hands of the state. Sfor and the Office of High Representative could determine that it was proper to weaken the undergirding of the nationalist politicians and supporting the media power of those who, to a greater extent, supported a more democratic society. Bosnia-Hercegovina saw the use of almost all the instruments of information intervention. The international community provided assistance to rebuild the infrastructure of existing media, established an alternate media network, set requirements for the electoral regulation, forced "corrective" and official broadcasts, jammed broadcasts and transformed the staff and leadership of broadcasting entities. Internationally designed and staffed media regulation bureaucracies, some tied to elections and some not, were all introduced in Bosnia-Hercegovina. Finally, the Office of High Representative attempted to rationalize the process and created a comprehensive new regulatory scheme for a post-NATO pluralistic unified multi-ethnic state.

The law of information intervention

What was the basis for the intervention by the United States and the international community in Bosnia-Hercegovina's media and information space? A part of foreign policy is articulating justifications, and as the international community increasingly uses media-related intervention as part of its peacekeeping arsenal, greater attention must be paid to its legal framework.[29] The idea of supporting one side in an election over another, or one set of parties over another, or of creating a whole new political class may be a superb one, but it fits with difficulty into acceptable forms of media subvention. Various groups within Bosnia-Hercegovina questioned whether the international community had the legal power to reshape the information space in Bosnia-Hercegovina. Outside press organizations, some from Europe and the United States, expressed grave reservations as to whether the international community's actions in Bosnia-Hercegovina were consistent with international norms.

The legal justification for media intervention in Bosnia-Hercegovina is nowhere clearly stated and the United States and other parties neither sought nor articulated such a legal justification as they responded to practical realities. But it matters what legal principles are invoked. If the United States and its Western allies acted as "occupiers," then a particular body of international norms would govern their powers and the limits on them.[30] If they acted, on the other hand, under a consent regime, then the shape of their authority would be governed, in large part, by the conditions of their particular entry into Bosnia-Hercegovina.[31]

The United States and its allies belligerently occupied Germany and Japan after World War II.[32] The Allies refashioned the radio broadcasting systems in Germany and Japan, as part of the larger mission in constructing a democratic society in the former Axis nations.[33] In Germany, the Allies split up and decentralized the dominant media outlets in order to prevent a dominant national voice from arising.[34] In Japan, the US government sought to eradicate all elements of militarism and nationalism from the national voice.[35] The first Memorandum of the Allies asserting that Allied actions reestablished freedom of speech and press required that news be true to facts, be faithful to the policies of the Allied Powers, and refrain from skeptical criticisms of the Allied Forces.[36]

In Bosnia, the international community set in place a legal system governing all media, established licensing requirements, and invested in a public service broadcasting network with a governing board that meticulously attempted to reflect the various segments of the society. Institutions and legal systems were introduced to emphasize and encourage harmony and unification not separation. But Bosnia is not Japan or Germany and under current norms the term "occupiers" does not describe the status of the international presence in Bosnia. The historic examples provided by occupation strategies in Japan and Germany may inform, but they do not justify the actions of the Office of High Representative or Sfor.[37] Occupiers have the power to act in lieu of a sovereign, though those actions are constrained by the duty to serve as a surrogate for the local sovereign and to do so in accord with internationally established standards.[38]

In the Bosnian context, exploring the legal basis of intervention, other than occupation, must start with the General Framework Agreement for Peace, the Dayton Accords themselves. The significance of the Dayton Accords was that essentially the Republic of Bosnia-Hercegovina, the Republic of Croatia, and the Federal Republic of Yugoslavia all consented to let the international community enter Bosnia-Hercegovina. In other words, the powers of NATO, the OSCE, and the Office of High Representative, to the extent they arose from the Dayton Accords, came from the parties to the Accord, not from the use of force or from other international doctrines. The powers thus described were, however, extensive. For example, Annex 6 of the Dayton Accords provides that the parties "shall secure to all persons within their jurisdiction the highest level of internationally recognized human rights and fundamental freedoms," including freedom of expression. Restructuring the media, including displacing some media outlets and building new ones, was deemed, in a radical sense, as securing freedom of expression.[39]

In the Accords, Annex 10 recognizes that fulfillment of each party's obligation under the terms of the treaty requires "a wide range of activities" including the establishment of political and constitutional institutions in Bosnia-Hercegovina, and the creation of a High Representative whose duties are "to facilitate the Parties' own efforts and . . . coordinate the activities of the organizations and agencies involved in the civilian aspects of the peace settlement." This general architectural commitment could be read to include the kinds of powers that Sfor and NATO exercised in reshaping the media of Bosnia-Hercegovina.

In Annex 1-A, the Agreement on the Military Aspects of the Peace Settlements, each party recognizes that NATO would establish a multinational military implementation force (first known as IFOR and then as Sfor) "composed of ground, air, and maritime units from NATO and non-NATO nations, deployed in Bosnia-Hercegovina . . . to help ensure compliance" with the Accords. The Annex authorizes IFOR to "take such actions as required, including the use of necessary force . . . to ensure its own protection." In Annex 3, the parties agree to ensure "free and fair elections in . . . a politically neutral environment" and, in that connection, they ensure "freedom of expression and of the press." The Parties invite the OSCE to "supervise, in a manner to be determined by the OSCE and in cooperation with other international organizations the OSCE deems necessary, the preparation and conduct" for specific elections, including the elections involved in the post-Dayton media disputes.

The Accords are, thus, a charter of authority, a specific and bounded invitation to particular actors in the international community to participate in the peace process in explicitly limited ways. They grant the international community three important fonts of power. The first font of power is election-specific and flows from Annex 3 of the Dayton Accords.[40] Many of the aspirations embodied in the Dayton Accords and much of the international community's involvement in Bosnia-Hercegovina concern the political process and the indispensable involvement of media in this process. The authority of the international community in this area lies with the OSCE.

The second font of power involves the authority of the military to accomplish its mission and to protect and preserve itself. If troops were endangered as a result of inflammatory media statements, authority to act could be inferred. This power stems from Annex 1-A and other portions of the Dayton Accords and is in some sense self-evident, but its apparent simplicity masks difficult questions surrounding the authority of individuals and groups to take specific actions in Bosnia-Hercegovina. In some instances NATO troops acted as a result of military command decisions. NATO troops were not subject to the direct authority of the High Representative, though the OHR had coordinating responsibilities.

The third font of power is the broadest. It stems from the executive power of the OHR itself and, as we have seen, overlaps with the other two fonts of power. The Accords were parsimonious in assigning specific powers to the OHR and, as a consequence, the OHR's powers sometimes grew organically, due to broad interpretations of the Accords mandated by the circumstances on the ground. With respect to media, however, the OHR emerged as an idealized "information intervention unit" backed by the support of the international community. OHR encapsulated the contradictions, the constitutional dramas, and the struggle over standards that determined what actions to take towards media. It was the OHR that became the receptacle for international hopes.

In its Bonn Statement, the Peace Implementation Council "reiterate[s] its firm commitment to establish free and pluralistic media throughout Bosnia and Hercegovina." More important, it "support[s] the High Representative's overall media and telecommunications strategy." This broad focus on the OHR as manager of the Bosnian media strategy emerged from the Sintra Declaration. The Contact Committee, the six-country coordinating committee of NATO powers, expressed confidence in the OHR and its role in regulating media in Bosnia-Hercegovina in the Sintra Declaration. The Declaration is an example of the formulation of law as a post hoc clarification of power and extension of authority necessitated by circumstances on the ground.

In Bosnia-Hercegovina, finally, the international community intervened by establishing a new media regime and relicensing all existing broadcasters. Ultimately, law reform plays a key part in legitimating and facilitating change. Law becomes the vehicle for articulating goals and establishing the machinery for meeting those goals. In Bosnia-Hercegovina, whatever the original authority for intervention, the OHR, in an effort to create a moral plural medium, found it necessary to develop a system of media regulation that was clear, transparent, and available to all the actors in the region.[41]

This case study of the role of the international coalition in shaping the Bosnian domestic media space helps us understand the context, limitations, and techniques of information intervention. It illustrates how the international community struggles to define and implement a policy, including developing justifications for initiating an intervention or increasing the scope and bite of existing interventions.

In spring 1998, Sfor handed the seized towers to the newly elected Bosnian government with one explicit condition, namely that Sfor had a right to retake the transmitters at any time.[42] On April 14, 1998, the Serb Republic Prime Minister, Milorad Dodik, and Sfor Commander, Eric Shinseki, signed a memorandum of understanding in which Sfor agreed to stop "provid[ing] security protection for TV transmitters belonging to Serb Radio and TV."[43] The episode of transmitter seizure was over. A graphic incident, the enactment of a specific set of integrated foreign policies to affect the media and information space of Republika Srpska and Bosnia-Hercegovina, had concluded at least as to one episode of it.

Elements of an information foreign policy

I have suggested, in my discussion of the US State Department's International Public Information Group, that a foreign policy of media space had to be flexible, involve many tools, and respond to local needs. If this approach is plausible, we should be able to identify and describe an ensemble of methods used to implement such a policy. In the next chapter, I look at a major historic piece of such an articulated policy, namely the deployment of state-sponsored broadcasters like the Voice of America. But a foreign policy of media space incorporates many elements that have percolated in earlier parts of this book. It includes the use or management of media to prevent conflict, to conduct war, or to engage in peacekeeping. An information-related foreign policy incorporates issues of trade in cultural policy, media-related assistance to change regime structures abroad, and, generally, the persuasion of a global audience of the value of national policies. New information technologies have created novel media-related foreign policy questions, such as structuring new governance needs on the Internet,[44] regulating "terrorism,"[45] gaming,[46] or issues of copyright.[47]

I have also already mentioned many techniques employed in implementing such a foreign policy: providing subsidies for favored forms of media; sponsoring the export of legal and policy models regarding media structures (and rewarding those states that adopt the favored model); expanding or altering state-sponsored international broadcasting; using the World Trade Organization and related mechanisms as means to force changes in media-related trade practices; reinvigorating the international copyright regime to affect domestic intellectual property regimes; developing regional agreements, treaties, and customary international law as measures to shape or limit state media law enactments; increasing "information intervention" by the international community especially in postconflict situations; encouraging an international environment that fosters new technology (including addressing the digital divide). The United States has such a signature role that fragments or elements of such a foreign policy in all these areas are more explicit than elsewhere.

Trade and media policies

Of course, one increasingly important component of a multilateral policy concerning media structures are trade agreements. Debates concerning the World Trade Organization have been a major forum for describing the relationship between trade, flow of programs, and concepts of identity. It was a post-cold war slogan for Western democracies to advance a "dual transition to democracy and market economy," and the foreign policy of many Western democracies was designed to assist in this conjunction.[48] The compatibility of the two objectives was supported by the logic that in time, countries with strong civil societies and institutions can manage and reduce domestic conflict and will be more stable. Also "nations that deregulate and privatize their economies are much more likely to achieve economic growth and be competitive in the global economy. A participatory political system supported by a rule of law culture and democratic institutions will enable sustained economic growth over time."[49] Trade, and especially trade in information, produces democracy, stability, and peace.

In the 1980s and 1990s, during the Uruguay Round, the United States forcefully advanced measures extending the idea of an all-encompassing international economy, grounded in free trade. For much of the 1990s the question was whether broadcasting and cultural production should be subject to its sweeping religion. The international debate focused on whether information is a "commodity," whether there should be cultural exemptions, and how broad those exemptions should be. Regional agreements dealt with whether there could be changes in foreign ownership restrictions for the media and whether national quotas, protecting national program producers, should be retained.[50] As new rounds of negotiations were planned for the first decade of the twenty-first century, both Canada and Europe (especially France) sought alliances that would help them resist free trade rules for cultural products.[51] They did this, they claimed, to protect cultural industries vital to their social and democratic development, and possibly even to their survival as a nation.[52] Large monetary stakes are involved—cultural products are the second largest export item of the United States.[53] Although some rounds of the dispute have been settled, the struggle continues.[54]

The US position has been that free trade generally benefits consumers worldwide and provides incentives for workers and firms who are more productive and efficient. For media products, as for tires, steel, or chewing gum, the system as a whole (and presumably most countries) is better off when resources now used in comparatively inefficient sectors are moved to economic activities where they hold a comparative advantage. C. Edwin Baker has written an extensive and sweeping critique of the free trade position that notwithstanding the fact that media products (including newspapers and magazines as well as television and film) are integral to the formation of public opinion and political discourse, they should be treated no different from other consumer goods.[55]

Marc Raboy has also set forth the case for the competing, so-called protectionist approach. His concern rests on the determination that:

> The mass media, cultural industries and communication and information technologies have become the major catalysts for cultural activity, mass consumption and participation in public life. . . . Access to the resources that facilitate communication can be seen as part of the basic building blocks of citizenship and raises policy issues that are central to the development of civil society.[56]

Much of the world, often including the United States itself, sees Western (usually US) programming as being message laden and at least as persuasive politically as the programming of the state-sponsored international broadcasters. MTV, CNN, and the treasured library of US film are persistent carriers of a specific culture, effective ambassadors of a point of view about the individual in society and ultimately, therefore, of ideas of allegiance and political values. Advocacy of free trade means easier access, it might be argued, for these perspectives to compete in a global "collision of cultures."

There is a related idea. One must look at the First World as developing two distinct but related products. Major developed societies, including, of course, United States and Japan, have shaped an entertainment industry with global aspirations, manufacturing software, news, films, television series, and other elements of content. Developed societies generally have not only facilitated the achievement of this industrial goal but shaped two other, equally important export products: a style of trade-regulated regulation and a set of doctrines or ideologies of democratization that facilitate an attitude toward trade. The export of models of regulation serves as a policy housing to facilitate the export of goods. The export of ideology functions to legitimate the infrastructure for trade. Indeed, much of this book has been about the export of regulatory doctrine from the United States and the West.[57]

Copyright

National policies toward international intellectual property agreements are also a measure of attitudes concerning media and information space. TRIPs (Agreement on Trade-Related Aspects of Intellectual Property Rights) relies on national treatment and nondiscrimination principles to set minimum standards for international protection of intellectual property.[58] The agreement, which took effect as an element of the WTO process, established something closer to a global approach to global rules.

Copyright—itself a mode of affecting the flow of information and imagery—is an area where multilateral negotiations over rules that limit or shape national policies have intensified. In the last century, the scope of intellectual property rights was largely a matter for national definition though within an international framework. Now, reliance on an adequate degree of protection in distant markets, without support of international policy, seems increasingly less possible, and there have been several efforts to augment the working of the Berne Convention, the great older international effort that established standards for its members. The Convention itself never adequately adjusted to new technologies or the extraordinary changes that arise from a global spread of information and media.

Neil Weinstock Netanel has eloquently written of the impact of the TRIPs Agreement on this state of affairs. "In a seeming blink of an eye, international bodies applying international law have effectively become the arbiters of domestic copyright law."[59] Globalization of copyright might, in Netanel's view, be a superior outcome, because of his view that intellectual property serves fundamentally to underwrite a democratic culture. By according creators of original expression a set of exclusive rights to market their literary and artistic works, "copyright fosters the dissemination of knowledge, supports a pluralist, nonstate communications media, and highlights the value of individual contributions to public discourse." If authoritarian states and developing countries are compelled to institute a full-fledged Western system of quasi-proprietary copyright, "TRIPs effectively unleashes copyright's democratising force, even if the Agreement's primary goal is the furtherance of trade."[60]

The point here is not whether Netanel is right or not (expanded copyright protection restricts the public domain, for example) but rather the intricate relationship between one country's foreign policy toward another's copyright laws and the potential effect on political systems. Bruce Lehman, then US Commissioner of the Patent Office, articulated a part of the reasoning behind intellectual property protection's connection with foreign policy. In one congressional hearing, he put administration attitudes pithily, "people from my office are [daily] in several countries in the world, often times along with representatives from the United States Trade Representatives Office, or from the State Department . . . making it very clear to foreign governments that there will be a price to pay if they do not respect our intellectual property rights."[61] For him, and the information industry in the United States, what constituted adequate enforcement by China, Mexico, or other countries was a foreign policy issue.

An overly rigorous copyright enforcement policy, paradoxically, can hamper efforts in developing countries to nourish "free and independent media" and halt the spread of parasitic start-ups. These start-ups often depend on the bounty of Western programming and have little immediate capacity to pay. Even so, they challenge existing, often state-financed, broadcasters. In the Internet era the expansion of intellectual property protection is viewed, by some, as problematic, and possibly inconsistent with the democratic potential of the new medium.[62] Thus, while meticulous arrangements further certain aspects of US foreign policy (those related to trade), they may not always work to support the immediate and instrumental development of plural and abundant media in transitional societies. Places where a viable economy to sustain media in a Western marketplace fashion does not exist are places where copyright niceties are likely to be ignored. If there is a foreign policy need for plural media—during a period in which multiple voices are desirable—then raising the cost of entry is counterproductive.[63]

Technical assistance

Box 1

Media assistance and transition states

1. **Consolidating democracies (Estonia, Czech Republic, Hungary, Poland, Latvia, Lithuania, and Slovenia)** A strong political and social consensus exists. There is a relatively high level of government decentralization. Government has passed acceptable media laws, private media flourishes, and citizens gain access to a variety of different sources of information from both broadcast and print media. Associations lobby on behalf of journalists.

2. **Unstable states/divided states (Albania, Armenia, Bulgaria, Croatia, Georgia, Macedonia, Montenegro, and Romania)** Powerful ethnic/clan divisions and loyalties sharply impede nation building and divide citizens at the local level. "Liberal" media laws may exist, but politics still control media regulation. State media are not independent from the governing political party, although reform efforts could have started. Print media generally plentiful.

3. **Weak states/weak societies (Moldova, Russia, and Ukraine)** A stagnant or contracting economy, a lack of proactive support from a generally passive and/or disinterested government, and an increasingly cynical public hamper democratic transition. In the case of Russia, the government, under President Vladimir Putin, is actually taking a more active role in trying to manage independent media. This includes challenging private media more often in court, arresting so-called media barons, and writing policy that may result in more restrictive media laws.

4. **Consolidating authoritarian states (Azerbaijan, Belarus, Kazakhstan, increasingly Kyrgyzstan, Serbia, Turkmenistan, and Uzbekistan)** Elections used, but increasingly represent little more than plebiscitary endorsements of state power; society remains almost completely state dependent, monoculture economic development (oil, cotton, etc.) with prime businesses in the hands of a political/business elite. National broadcast media completely controlled by the state; local broadcast media in the pockets of local politicians. Media laws—even if on books—are not followed, as government takes extreme measures to control, censure, and even shut down any independent voices.

5. **Failed states (Serbia, Tajikistan, and international protectorates of Bosnia and Kosovo)** Economic stagnation and weak governance, civil war, and ethnic conflict have interrupted transitions. Basic questions of identity, community, and control of boundaries remain unresolved. Government's capacity to control policy and provide services is limited. Media are either in an embryonic state, receiving complete support from international community (e.g., Kosovo broadcast media), or professional journalists are working but are hampered by authoritarian regime, as in Serbia under Milosevic. Networking among media outlets is essential in media defending themselves against a powerful state apparatus.

In chapter 2, I touched upon financial assistance and other forms of technical aid to media as a means of addressing stability issues and achieving desirable outcomes in terms of regime structure. The United States and Europe in the 1990s mounted many efforts to foster transitions to democracy and these continue into the new century.[64] The goal was to establish a media sector supportive of democracy, one that would have a substantial degree of editorial independence, was financially viable, reflected diverse and plural voices, and provided information necessary for citizenship to be meaningful.[65] Technical assistance is a basic tool of foreign policy.

I start with a time-fixed categorization of transition or transition-related states in Central and Eastern Europe prepared at the turn of the millennium for USAID.[66] It provides insights into problems in delivering media assistance. The five categories in box 1 are in the form of descriptions, almost report cards, but the manner in which the categories are articulated have implications for the policy directions of the external "assisting" state.[67]

A number of elements are interesting in this description of the world, or at least in this description of Central and Eastern Europe. Categories are formulated in order to explain different media assistance priorities and then to use those priorities to shape future action. Thus, for example, USAID may conclude that aid to media has a lower priority or is unnecessary in states characterized as "consolidating democracies." It might limit forms of assistance to those considered worthwhile in consolidating authoritarian states. The description suggests areas in which previous assistance patterns were probably helpful (the consolidated democracies) and areas where instability implies the need for immediate attention. The presentation is one in which there is no built-in sense of automatic progressivity. Failed states and weak or unstable states demonstrate the tentative nature of transformation and the complex factors that are involved in shifting toward a more democratic culture. Failed states may also require wholesale international intervention, of the kind that occurred in Bosnia-Hercegovina. The description of the qualities of a consolidated democracy provides at least a partial list of media-related goals. Assistance should include ways of encouraging "strong political and social consensus," a decentralized government that has passed acceptable media laws, presumably fairly administered, a diversity of information sources, and the capability of journalists to lobby for change.[68]

The document lists barriers. These include the existence of weak economies where, as a consequence of the lack of economic support and independence, media would be too dependent on local politicians and others with "narrow interests." In such a weak economy, "publishers and editors are forced to accept the demands of local governors and less-than-honest business interests that run underground economies." A second barrier to the development of independent media is "outdated, socialist or communist-style media regulations." A third factor of concern, listed by USAID as a barrier to the nurturing of a transformative media is the "political vulnerability" and instability of governments. Because of deep insecurity, such governments invoke "fear, [and] harass, imprison, and sometimes kill dissenting journalists and media managers." And weak governments might also lack the political will "to break up state media monopolies." Less basic, but still a factor, is "substandard equipment in both broadcast and print media, which creates a substandard product." Without better programming, independent media would be "unable to compete with the usually better financed State media." The USAID document notes that "disquietingly," in a number of countries independent media has "made great strides and then slipped back, as a result of changing economic and political circumstances."

This set of USAID categorizations is studiously agnostic about the inevitability of change, inherently pessimistic, perhaps, about the potential for change. It recognizes the complexity of world events as chastening and limiting. But the diagnostic aspect of this approach to technical assistance implies a direction for foreign policy: the relationship between a "stage" or status of society and the mode of technical or media assistance that might contribute to the democratization process. Dr. Beata Rozumilowicz, in a study of media assistance across widely varying regime types,[69] linked stages to forms of fulfillment of foreign policy. As to what might be called a pre-transition stage, for example, Dr. Rozumilowicz suggested that foreign policy might include a series of steps, as outlined in box 2.

Box 2
Pre-transition media support measures

1. Identifying the soft-liners or reformers within the ruling regime and providing them with material, informational, and moral support in disseminating their opinions and views.
2. Persuading the regime to recognize an opposition (either structured or unstructured) through diplomacy or economic measures (tying such actions to financial loans, packages, or debt remission).
3. Providing a targeted opposition group (directly, indirectly, or through regime support) with resources that will allow them to disseminate their opinions and views.
4. Persuading the regime to allow greater levels of open criticism without fear of reprisal (tying such actions to financial loans, packages, or debt remission).
5. Attempting to minimize reprisals when they occur (again, as above).
6. Upgrading the use of international broadcasting.
7. Providing constructive media infringement critiques (or more general human rights critiques).
8. Developing multilateral efforts to assist move toward the next stage.
9. Identifying a future civil society or potentially active civil sector and, in like manner to the other groups above, providing it with support.

These elements of a media-related foreign policy, taken together as "technical assistance," sound neutral and virtually mechanical. But the bases for determining what assistance should be provided can be electric in controversy in the target community and far from neutral in its administration. Its theoretical grounding is often connected to difficult issues of political theory and communications policy. A foreign policy of technical assistance for media reform is a mix of idealism and realpolitik, of advocacy of principle and extension of national interest. Each element of assistance (financial aid, organizational assistance, and legal reform) touches on choices concerning the meaning of democracy and the role of media in the enhancement of a political process. Each element assumes a structure of laws and administration in which assistance is embedded.

Mostly, this discussion of the dynamics of transitions has been about the policies of states, especially the United States, and the public international community. But it would be wrong to ignore the importance, in policy setting and implementation of nonstate actors. A great deal has been written about globalization from above, "the restructuring of the world economy on a regional and global scale through the agency of the transnational corporation and financial markets."[70] But increasingly important, both the formulation of policy and its implementation, is the rise of transnational social forces concerned with environmental protection, human rights, peace, and human security from below.[71]

Benedict Kingsbury has made a broader point about the relationship of state activity and the "dense matrix of transnational interactions involving other states, intergovernmental institutions, corporations, and a whole range of cross-border groups and networks that are slowly evolving into a transnational civil society." Participants in the human rights decision-making process include individual states but also individual participants, NGOs, intergovernmental organizations (IGOs), and other voluntary associations. This means that the formulation and implementation of human rights standards now involves more than the state; it involves many non-state interests as well.[72]

Ten years after they have begun, these processes of media assistance are being subjected to resistance and criticism even as they continue to expand.[73] Concerns extend to administration and execution, such as lack of coordination among donor governments and lack of an implementing strategy. Differences between European and US assistance patterns may turn, for example, on the extent public service broadcasting should be favored as compared to private commercial media. Sustainability of newly encouraged media initiatives is also a serious problem. In addition there are doubts about the theoretical basis for the activity of shaping civil society itself.[74] Critics argue about the capacity of external governments to implant the elements of democratic society.

The receptivity of target societies to aspects of media reform has also become more complex, with reactions ranging from active rejection to an integrating acceptance. After a decade of efforts to plant democracies in relatively hostile terrains, and in an environment affected more and more by new technologies, the grounding, organization, and implementation of media assistance is in need of more systematic examination, study, and possibly revision. Still, "media reform" remains an important technique by which the media structures of a target society are influenced by external efforts.

Conclusion

Government responses following September 11 reinforce an emerging realization: that there are information foreign policies everywhere. In Armenia, there is an information foreign policy concerning Azerbaijan. In India, there is an information foreign policy concerning Pakistan. In Turkey, there is an information foreign policy concerning the use of media by Kurds abroad.

Governments, democratic and authoritarian, have long concerned themselves with the impact of competing narratives on their capacity to function in a complex world order. Prior to the Gorbachev era in the Soviet Union and to the fall of the Berlin Wall, the United States and the West had a foreign policy toward the use of information and media that (especially in retrospect) was clearly articulated and implemented. This was a policy specific to the cold war, its institutions and technologies. But now the scale has changed and the stakes have altered. There have been repeated instances where the United States and other countries cite the need to influence media, ranging from presidential statements concerning hearts and minds in the Middle East to ambassadorial urgings in the Balkans. This is an approach to information space that seeks, in a wholly new context, to maintain stability, further democratic values, and, to some extent, limit the use of media for infringing human rights.

The extraordinary power of modern information techniques, yielding an enhanced role of imagery, news, and culture in world politics, has turned what may have once been deemed an arguably domestic set of preoccupations into an international concern. Governments are no longer passive, if they ever were, in the light of changing media realities. Altered structures and roles for the media result in modified responses by governments. What appears in the media establishes political priorities. Governments, as a matter of course, will as always seek to influence what media report. More than that, they increasingly understand that they have a stake in the process by which information and cultural signals are developed and communicated and the machinery through which that occurs.

These reactions, as events move from the ad hoc to platforms of consistency, from the anecdotal to the deliberate, become elements of policy, and should be discussed as such, whether or not the governments involved explicitly recognize what is occurring. Indeed, this process of turning the occasional to the frequent is one possible outgrowth of the often-empty notion that "media are global." What once constituted primarily the domestic concern of local regulatory activities, such as the use of Internet by groups labeled terrorists by other states, the propounding of hate speech, general determination of free expression levels, and attitudes towards investment and ownership, now have external consequences and are increasingly subject to international norms and bilateral and multilateral pressure. Ironically, while countries are increasingly frustrated at the task of controlling the flow of information into their own boundaries, they try, unilaterally or multilaterally, to affect the mix of information that streams around the world through satellite and the Internet.

Notes

1   See, for instance, John Tomlinson, *Cultural Imperialism: A Critical Introduction* (Baltimore: Johns Hopkins University Press, 1991); Herbert Schiller, *Information Inequality: The Deepening Social Crisis in America* (New York: Routledge, 1996); George Gerbner, Hamid Mowlana, and Herbert I. Schiller, eds., *Invisible Crises: What Conglomerate Control of Media Means for America and the World* (Boulder, CO: Westview Press, 1996). It would be ostrich-like not to recognize the role of the United States as superpower and as the home of major exporters of entertainment programming and corporate distributors of imagery. Much global redefinition and reaction is by states vis à vis the United States (or the idea of the United States) and much, as well, is about United States policy with respect to the rest of the world.

2   Edward Herman and Noam Chomsky have written about US mass media coverage and its relationship to foreign policy. Edward S. Herman and Noam Chomsky, *Manufacturing Consent: The Political Economy of the Mass Media* (New York: Pantheon, 1988).

3   See, for example, Hamid Mowlana, *Global Information and World Communication: New Frontiers in International Relations* (London: Sage, 1997); R. Fortner, *International Communication: History, Conflict and Control of the Global Metropolis* (Belmont, CA: Wadsworth, 1993); Anthony Appadurai, *Modernity at Large: Cultural Dimensions of Globalization* (Minneapolis: University of Minnesota Press, 1996).

4   Jamie Frederic Metzl, "Popular diplomacy," *Daedalus* 128, no. 2 (spring 1999): 187.

5   One could tie aspects of Metzl's strategy to Gramscian notions, namely that "military force was not necessarily the best instrument to retain power for the ruling classes, but that a more effective way of wielding power was to build a consent by ideological control of cultural production and distribution." Thussu, *International Communication*, p. 68.

6   Metzl, "Popular democracy," p. 187.

7   Ibid., p. 178.

8   Ibid., p. 186.

9   Joel Bleifuss, "The first stone," *In These Times*, Mar. 20, 2000, p. 2.

10   Ibid.

11   Ibid.

12   Metzl, "Popular diplomacy," p. 182.

13   Ibid., p. 192.

14   Jamie F. Metzl, "Information intervention: When switching channels isn't enough," *Foreign Affairs* (Nov.–Dec. 1997): 15.

15   Jamie F. Metzl, "Rwandan genocide and the international law of radio jamming," *American Journal of International Law* 91, no. 4 (Oct. 1997), p. 1, cited in Alison des Forges, "Silencing the voices of hate in Rwanda," in Monroe E. Price and Mark Thompson, *Forging Peace: Intervention, Human Rights, and the Management of Media Space* (Edinburgh: Edinburgh University Press, 2002).

16   Alison des Forges, *Leave None to Tell the Story: Genocide in Rwanda* (New York: Human Rights Watch, 1998).

17   Frank G. Wisner, Memorandum for Deputy Assistant to the President for National Security Affairs, National Security Council, May 5, 1994. See also, "Intelligence briefing memo" from INR/AA— Janean Mann to AF—Ms. Render, of May 3, 1994, and Chas. W. Freeman Jr., "Memorandum for Director Joint Staff," May 3, 1994; cited in Aes Forges, op.cit., note 15 *supra*.

18   The quotes are from his article in *Foreign Affairs*. Metzl has also contributed his views in the *Human Rights Quarterly*. See Jamie Frederic Metzl, "Metzl response to Ball, Girouard, and Chapman," *Human Rights Quarterly* 19 (1997): 4; Jamie Frederic Metzl, "Information Technology and Human Rights," *Human Rights Quarterly* 18 (1996): 4; Mark Thompson, "Defining information intervention: An interview with Jamie Metzl" in Price and Thompson, eds., *Forging Peace: Intervention, Human Rights, and the Management of Media Space* (Edinburgh: Edinburgh University Press, 2002).

19   *Department of State Bulletin* 39: 337–42 at p. 339. 1958 Statement to the UN, August 1958.

20   For media participation in US overseas interventions, see the following writing on the Gulf War: W. Lance Bennett and David L. Paletz, eds., *Taken by Storm: The Media, Public Opinion, and United States Foreign Policy in the Gulf War* (Chicago: University of Chicago Press, 1994); Philip M. Taylor, *War and the Media: Propaganda and Persuasion in the Gulf War* (Manchester: Manchester University Press, 1998). For the related subject of cyberwar, see John Arquilla and David Ronfeldt, "Cyberwar and netwar: New modes, old concepts of conflict," *Rand Research Review*, fall 1995.

21   For a fuller account, see Mark Thompson and Daniel De Luce, "Escalating to success? The media intervention in Bosnia and Herzegovina," in Price and Thompson, eds., *Forging Peace*. A more extensive discussion of the issues raised in the text can be found at Monroe E. Price, "Information intervention: Bosnia, the Dayton Accords, and the seizure of broadcasting transmitters," *Cornell International Law Journal* 33 (2000): 67.

22   See "Political declaration from ministerial meeting of the steering board of the Peace Implementation Council Sintra, 30 May, 1997." Online [Nov. 27, 2000], available: *http://www.hrt.hr/arhiv/dokumenti/dok/sintra_eng.html*.

23   Memorandum of Agreement for Release of Udrigovo Tower (CQ334489), Sept. 2, 1997 (hereinafter Udrigovo Agreement). Online [Jul. 2001], available: *http://www.ohr.int/press/p970902a.htm*. See also NATO/Sfor Briefing, Sept. 3, 1997. Online [Apr. 26, 2001], available: *http://www.nato.int/Sfor/trans/1997/t970903a.htm*. A summary of the Agreement is presented at 59 Bulletin, Office of the High Representative, Sept. 5, 1997. Online [Jul. 2001], available: *http://www.ohr.int/bulletins/b970905.htm#5*.

      The Agreement was formally signed by Commander of Multinational Division (North) Major-General David Grange, the SRT editor-in-chief, Drago Vukovic, and the Deputy Minister of Interior (and chairman of the board for SRT), General Karisik.

24   "Serb broadcasts resume in North after Sfor handover," BBCSWB, Sept. 5, 1997, available in LEXIS, News Library [Bosnian Serb Radio, Pale, in Serbo-Croat, Sept. 1, 1997].

25   See Udrigovo Agreement, 59 Bulletin, Office of the High Representative, Sept. 5, 1997. Online [Jan. 17, 2001] available: *http://www.ohr.int/bulletins/b970905.htm#5*.

26   "Bosnian Serbs reject demands on SRT," BBC Summary of World Broadcasts, Oct. 17, 1997. World Broadcast Information; Bosnia-Herzegovina; WBI/0042/WB. Source: Beta News Agency, Belgrade, in Serbo-Croat (Oct. 10, 1997).

27   "SRT editor rejects attempts to set up 'protectorate,' " BBC Summary of World Broadcasts (Oct. 17, 1997). World Broadcast Information; Bosnia-Herzegovina; WBI/0042/WB. Source: Beta news agency, Belgrade, in Serbo-Croat (10 Oct. 97).

28   Ever resourceful, Karadzic's faction in Pale figured out yet another way to continue broadcasting. On November 4, they set up an "electronic media" center in eastern Bosnia-Hercegovina, this time in Foca. This "technical and information center" had the capability of broadcasting SRT Pale programs to a significant portion of eastern Bosnia-Hercegovina. This time, because the action did not interfere with the transmission of Banja Luka television, NATO and the OHR did not take action.

29   See Krug and Price, "A module for media intervention: Content regulation in post-conflict zones," in *Forging Peace*; Barry E. Carter and Phillip R. Trimble, eds., *International Law*, 2nd ed. (Boston: Little Brown, 1995), p. 1381.

30   See generally Eyal Benvenisti, *The International Law of Occupation* (Princeton: Princeton University Press, 1993).

31   See, for example, Indar Rikye et al., *The Thin Blue Line: International Peace Keeping and Its Future* (New Haven: Yale University Press, 1974): pp. 24–30.

32   Compare Sharon Korman, *The Right of Conquest* 177 (Oxford: Clarendon Press, 1996), with Benvenisti, *The International Law of Occupation*, pp. 91–93.

33   Donna E. Arzt, "Nuremberg, denazification and democracy: The hate speech problem at the international military tribunal," *New York Law School Journal of Human Rights* 12 (1995): 689, 727; Benvenisti, *The International Law of Occupation*, p. 91.

34   Arzt, "Nuremberg, Denazification and Democracy."

35   William J. Sebald and C. Nelson Spinks, *Japan: Prospects, Options, and Opportunities* (Washington: American Enterprise Institute for Public Policy Research, 1967), p. 17.

36   See, Berlin (Potsdam) Conference, chapter II, sub. A. pt. 10 (1945), reprinted in "The Department of State, Germany 1947–1949, the story in documents" 49 (1950).

37   See, for example, Regulations Respecting the Laws and Customs of War on Land (annexed to 1907

Hague Convention IV), (Oct. 18, 1907), art. 42, 36 Stat. at 2306 [hereinafter Hague Regulations]. There has been debate about the use of the term "occupation" to describe activities of the international community in Bosnia-Hercegovina and debate, as well, over use of the power of the occupier to justify media and information intervention.

38   Hague Regulations, art. 43. The article in its entirety states: "The authority of the legitimate power having in fact passed into the hands of the occupant, the latter shall take all the measures in his power to restore and ensure, as far as possible, public order and [civic life], while respecting, unless absolutely prevented, the laws in force in the country." Ibid.

39   See S.C. Res. 713, U.N. SCOR (1991); S.C. Res. 743, U.C. SCOR (1992); S.C. Res. 770, U.N. SCOR (1992); S.C. Res. 816, U.N. SCOR (1993); S.C. Res. 1031, U.N. SCOR (1995); Dayton Accords, art. IX.

40   See ibid. Annex III. Mary Fulbrook, *The Divided Nation: A History of Germany*, 1918–1990 (Oxford: Oxford University Press, 1992); See also Nigel Foster, *German Law and Legal System* (London: Blackstone Press, 1993).

41   For a valuable review, see "Media and democratization in Bosnia and Herzegovina," *www.imcbih.org*; and International Crisis Group, "Media in Bosnia and Herzegovina: How international support can be more effective," *www.crisisweb.org*.

42   General Accounting Office, "Bosnia peace operation: Mission, structure, and transition strategy of NATO's Stabilization Force" (Letter Report, 10/08/98, GAO/NSIAD-99–19), Online [January 2002] available: *http://www.fas.org/man/gao/nsiad-99–019.htm*.

43   "Serbs and Sfor agree to return transmitters," BBCSWB (Apr. 17, 1998), available in LEXIS, News Library [Radio St. John, Pale, in Serbo-Croat, Apr. 14, 1998].

44   Brian Loader, ed., *The Governance of Cyberspace: Politics, Technology and Global Restructuring* (London: Routledge, 1997).

45   See Thomas Friedman, "Digital defense," *New York Times*, Jul. 27, 2001. ("Bush missile defense plan is geared to defending the country from a rogue who might fire a missile over our walls. But the more likely threat is from a cyberterrorist who tries to sabotage our webs. The more tightly we get woven together, the more we become dependent on networks, the more a single act of terrorism can unleash serious chaos.") See also Mark T. Pasko, "Re-defining national security in the technology age: The encryption export debate," *Journal of Legislation* 26 (2000): 337.

46   Mark G. Tratos, "Symposium: Gaming on the Internet" *Stanford Journal of Law, Business, and Finance* 3 (1997): 101.

47   See, for example, Jessica Litman, *Digital Copyright: Protecting Intellectual Property on the Internet* (Buffalo, NY: Prometheus Books, 2001); Susan Mort, "The WTO, WIPO and the Internet: Confounding the borders of copyright and neighboring rights," *Fordham Intellectual Property, Media and Entertainment Law Journal* 8: (1997): 173.

48   See, as an example of this literature, Stephan Haggard and Robert R. Kaufman, *The Political Economy of Democratic Transitions* (Princeton: Princeton University Press, 1995).

49   Brian Atwood, "Midwife to democracy: The not-so-ugly American," *New Perspectives Quarterly* 13 (1996): 20. "We promote democracy because it is the right thing to do and because it enhances global stability and economic growth. A stable, growing world economy creates American jobs, keeps America out of war." Atwood was the administrator of the US Agency for International Development.

50   NAFTA followed the earlier United States–Canada Free Trade Agreement, Jan. 2, 1988, *International Law Materials* 27 (1988): 281, at art. 2005, in not covering trade in cultural products. North American Free Trade Agreement, Dec. 17, 1992, *International Law Materials* 32 (1993): 289, p. 2106, annex 2106.

51   The US position has a long history. From about 1975 to 1983, a highly emotional dispute between the United States and many developing nations burst forth over the distribution of information from the North to the South. A New World Information and Communication Order, inscribed in the MacBride Report, became an object of US scorn, and ultimately led to US abandoning the United Nations Educational Social and Cultural Organization (UNESCO) which had sponsored and promoted the MacBride Report. See Colleen Roach, "American textbooks v NWICO History," in George Gerbner, ed., *The Global Media Debate: Its Rise, Fall, and Renewal*, (Westport, CT: Ablex Publishing, 1993), pp. 35, 43–46.

52   See M. E. Footer and C. B. Graber, "Trade liberalisation and cultural policy," *Journal of International Economic Law* 3 (2000): 115–44; P. Schlesinger, "From cultural defence to political culture: Media, politics and collective identity in the European Union," *Media, Culture and Society* 19 (1997): 360–91.

53   Thomas M. Murray, "The United States dispute over GATT treatment of audiovisual products and the limits of public choice theory," *Maryland Journal of International Law and Trade* 21 (1997): 203, at n. 13. Steven S. Wildman and Stephen E. Siwek, *International Trade in Films and Television Programs* 1 (Washington: American Enterprise Institute, 1988).

54   An important round resulted in a World Trade Organization panel and appellate board decision holding that Canadian laws protecting its magazine industry violate older provisions of GATT, a legal attack adopted by the United States after Canada had carefully assured that its policy would not be covered by NAFTA. World Trade Organization Report of the Appellate Body, *Canada Certain Measures Concerning Periodicals*, Jun. 30, 1997, available in 1997 WL 398913.

55   See C. Edwin Baker, *Media, Markets, and Democracy* (Cambridge: Cambridge University Press, 2001). See, for example, Robin L. Van Harpen, Note, "Mamas, don't let your babies grow up to be cowboys: Reconciling trade and cultural independence," *Minnesota Journal of Global Trade* 4 (1995): 165, 187–89; Fred H. Cate, "The First Amendment and the international free flow of information," *Virginia Journal of International Law* 30 (1990): 371, 407. Examining the rhetoric of the debate, Baker notes, "Interestingly, despite the similarity of many of the issues—that is, national attempts to assure a rich local communications order in the face of global market forces—the United States routinely invoked First Amendment values—freedom of information and freedom of the press—to attack UNESCO while changing to an economic parlance to oppose Europe and Canada in the dispute about cultural products."

56   Marc Raboy, *Communication and Globalization—A Challenge for Public Policy* (Toronto: University of Toronto Press, forthcoming).

57   See Oliver Boyd-Barrett, "Media imperialism: Towards an international framework for the analysis of media systems," in J. Curran, M. Gurevitch, and J. Woollacott, eds, *Mass Communications and Society* (London: Edward Arnold, 1997) p. 117. (Calling media imperialism, "the process whereby the ownership, structure, distribution or content of the media in any one country are singly or together subject to substantial external pressures from the media interests of any other country or countries, without proportionate reciprocation of influence by the country so affected.")

58   According to the World Trade Organization, TRIPs is "to date the most comprehensive multilateral agreement on intellectual property." It covers: "copyright and related rights (i.e., the rights of performers, producers of sound recordings and broadcasting organizations); trademarks including service marks; geographical indications including appellations of origin; industrial designs; patents including the protection of new varieties of plants; the layout-designs of integrated circuits; and undisclosed information including trade secrets and test data." Its activities lie in setting standards, enforcement, and settling disputes. See *http://www.wto.org/english/tratop_e/trips_e/trips_e.htm* for more information. See the World Intellectual Property Organization (WIPO) Web site for information on numerous international treaties governing IPR, *http://www.wipo.int/about-wipo/en/index. html?wipo_content_frame*=http://www.wipo.int/about-wipo/en/gib.htm.   John   H.   Barton, "Economics of TRIPs: International trade in information-intensive products," *George Washington International Law Review* 33 (2001): 473.

59   Neil Weinstock Netanel, "Asserting copyright's democratic principles in the global arena," *Vanderbilt Law Review* 51 (Mar. 1998): 217; see also Marci A. Hamilton, "The TRIPs agreement: Imperialistic, outdated, and overprotective," *Vanderbilt Journal of Transnational Law* 29 (1996): 613, 620–33.

60   Netanel contends that "the notion that upward harmonization under TRIPs will contribute to global democracy is seriously misguided. Copyright's constitutive value for democratic development depends heavily on local circumstances. Indeed, copyright may sometimes impede democratisation unless substantial limits are placed on copyright holder rights."

61   Bruce Lehman, Testimony at Hearing of the International Economic Policy and Trade Committee of the House International Relations Committee, May 21, 1998.

62   J. H. Reichman and David Lange, "Bargaining around the TRIPs agreement: The case for ongoing public-private initiatives to facilitate worldwide intellectual property transactions," *Duke Journal of Comparative and International Law* 9 (1998): 11.

63   There are solutions, consistent with copyright protection, for encouraging programming in such contexts. These include benign neglect of copyright violations or subsidy.

64   The literature on transitions and assistance is vast. See, for example, Geoffrey Pridham, ed., *Transitions to Democracy: Comparative Perspectives from Southern Europe, Latin America and Eastern Europe* (Aldershot, UK: Dartmouth, 1995); Adam Przeworski, *Sustainable Democracy* (Cambridge: Cambridge University Press, 1995); Juan J. Linz and Alfred C. Stepan, *Problems of Democratic Transition and Consolidation: Southern Europe, South America, and Post-Communist Europe* (Baltimore: Johns Hopkins

University Press, 1996). A trenchant review of the critical literature is contained in Amy L. Chua, "Markets, democracy, and ethnicity: Toward a new paradigm of law and development," *Yale Law Journal* 108 (1998): 1.

65   See Ann Hudock, *The Role of Media in Democracy: A Strategic Approach* (Washington: USAID Center for Democracy and Governance, 1999).

66   "Independent media development," USAID, Bureau for Europe and Eurasia, Office of Democracy and Governance (Oct. 4, 2000).

67   The listing was made before the death of Croatian President Franjo Tudjman and the fall of former Serbian President, Slobodan Milosevic.

68   See Monroe E. Price and Peter Krug, *The Enabling Environment for Free and Independent Media* (Washington: US Agency for International Development, Office of Democracy and Governance, 2002). Online [January 2002] available: *http://www.usaid.gov/democracy/pdfs/pnacm006.pdf*.

69   The study was done together with the author of this book. See Price, Rozumilowicz, and Verhulst, *Media Reform*.

70   Richard Falk, "The nuclear weapons advisory opinion and the new jurisprudence of global civil society," *Transnational Law and Contemporary Problems* 7 (1997): 333, 335.

71   See Julie Mertus, "From legal transplants to transformative justice: Human rights and the promise of transnational civil society," *American University International Law Review* 14 (1999): 1342.

72   See Benedict Kingsbury, "The concept of compliance as a function of competing conceptions of international law," *Michigan Journal of International Law* 19 (1994): 345, 357 (discussing new "liberal" theories of international law). Mertus, "From legal transplants to transformative justice," pp. 1347–48.

73   A much-cited, strongly opinionated study is Janine Wedel, *Collision and Collusion: The Strange Case of Western Aid to Eastern Europe 1989–1998* (New York: St. Martins, 1998); see also Frances H. Foster, "Information and the problem of democracy: The Russian experience," *American Journal of Comparative Law* 44 (1996): 243.

74   See, for example, Marina Ottoway and Thomas Carothers, eds., *Funding Virtue: Civil Society Aid and Democracy Promotion* (Washington: Carnegie Endowment for International Peace, 2000).

PART 6

Cultures of global communication

Chapter 22

Elihu Katz and Tamar Liebes

READING TELEVISION: TELEVISION AS TEXT AND VIEWERS AS DECODERS

THE STUDY OF TELEVISION is the study of effect. Research on ownership patterns, ratings research, and content analysis are all oriented primarily to assessment of the influence of senders on receivers in indirect ways. Owners are assumed to be selling their ideologies and products; audiences are assumed by their mere presence to be mesmerized; texts are *assumed* to imprint the messages perceived by content analysts. These are substitutes for the study of actual effects on audiences, because proving effects is so difficult. It is much easier to count heads or to count acts of violence or to identify the power structure which controls the media than to make certain that the audience is awake, that the owners actually have a message, and that the message is getting through. However, what possible justification can there be for studying the corporate deals between American and overseas broadcasters or the patterns of flow of American programs in the world without trying to ascertain whether the overseas audiences of these programs *are* getting the message that the text allegedly carries?

As long as one focuses on the influence of television within a particular society, it may be reasonable to assume that the message perceived by professional critics and content analysts is the message that gets through to the audience; perhaps one knows intuitively—as a member of society—what the powerholders really want. *Verstehen* has a chance, perhaps, *within* a society in which both researchers and subjects are members. Even then, the case is not strong. Domestic audiences are not homogenous entities. The ethnic and cultural communities that make up most societies, not to speak of the aggregates of age, education, gender, and class, are all different enough to raise the possibility that decodings and effects vary widely within any given society.

Content analysis and the study of effect

But content analysis is clearly an essential prerequisite for defining what's on television. Such analysis constitutes a basis for the construction of hypotheses about viewer decodings and effects, thus making it possible to compare readings within the community of analysts and between the community of analysts and the communities of audiences. While we would argue strongly against the possibility of inferring effects from content analysis alone, we do not wish to belittle the role of the content analyst. In this, we dissociate ourselves from the empiricism of mass-media research, which too often assumed that any text was simply projective and could serve to gratify any social or psychological need. This is the counter-part of the no less arrogant position of certain critical theorists who assumed that their text was the one that imposed itself unequivocably on the audience (Fejes, 1984; Liebes, 1989; Schroder, 1987).

Though content analysis is a central concern, communications research is by no means of one piece. There are several different methodological strands. The critical theorists, and more recently structuralists and semiologists with humanistic and philosophical orientations, obviously lean to the qualitative and the latent. Mainline communications researchers—as social scientists—have focused on manifest content in a quantitative way. But the more important difference is in the definition of the unit of analysis. Compared with qualitative analyses, studies employing quantitative methods tend to be much more microscopic, focusing on small units. Ironically, this microscopic orientation leads to less interest in the boundaries of a program or a genre and more interest in the supertext of television as a tantalizing medium which delivers incidents of violence, messages about the ethnic types that qualify as heroes and villains, rankings of different occupations, instructions about the behavior expected of the several sex and class roles, and toutings of the values of consumerism and success (Browne, 1984; Houston, 1985; Gerbner, Gross et al., 1979). The qualitative orientation, by contrast, stresses genre, sometimes individual programs, emphasizing themes and their interrelations, such as the relationship between civilization and wilderness in the Western. The two types of analysis do converge, at least to a certain extent, on the study of genre. Two genres, in particular, have occupied communications research almost from the beginning: the news and family drama.

The news, of course, has long been the subject of students of political communication (Galtung and Ruge, 1970), although it has recently attracted the interest of students of the sociology of rhetoric and narrative structure as well (Tuchman, 1973; Molotch and Lester, 1974; Gitlin, 1980; Glasgow University Media Group, 1976; Dahlgren, 1985; Gans, 1979; Graber, 1984; Hartley, 1982; Robinson and Levy, 1986). Analysis of daytime family serials dates to the early days of radio (Herzog, 1941; Arnheim, 1942–43; Warner and Henry, 1948) and has experienced a major revival in the television era (Katzman, 1972; Greenberg, 1982; Cassata and Skill, 1983; Cantor and Pingree, 1983; Newcomb, 1974; Braudy, 1982; Cavell, 1982; Booth, 1982; Eco, 1985; Allen, 1985), gradually widening the circle to include sociologists, literary scholars, semiologists, film scholars, etc. The fact that television resides in the bosom of the family and that it was long considered the daytime companion of housewives (now joined by students and professors) makes the soap opera an obvious object of fascination for the study of involvement, decoding, gratifications, and effects. The recent upsurge of feminism has added further interest, inasmuch as these daytime programs are thought to be relevant for, and to provoke, reflection and debate over the issue of family roles (Modleski, 1984).

With expansion of the American daytime serial into prime time and its subsequent export to other countries, new dimensions were added to the fascination with the television soap opera. The allegation of cultural imperialism was made, and students of international communication began to take interest. Looking at the soap opera in this new comparative context, scholars took note of the indigenous development of prime-time family stories in many countries. In line with the earliest communications research, these recent studies also assert that the soap is a conservative agent of socialization to familistic values, disconnecting viewers from the political arena while reassuring them that the world will continue to turn. Some studies have begun to rethink the soap opera as a locus for the discussion of social issues and the focusing of social conflict. Internationally, soap operas are seen as mobilizing ethnic and national identities and as capable of promoting social and economic change (Bombardier, 1985).

On the content analysis of *Dallas*

Dallas is surely one of the most studied texts in the history of television. This is probably due to its worldwide status as a best-seller and perhaps because it is perceived as the beginning of a new genre in American television, combining the afternoon soap with other prime-time forms. The analysts are literary scholars and professional critics of various ideological inclinations. Integrating their very different versions of the themes and messages of *Dallas* will give us a base from which to proceed. The diversity of critical readings will immediately reveal how farfetched it is to assume that there is one dominant reading that will produce a single, monolithic effect. And if the critics treat the narrative so polysemically, why not the viewers?

The debate centers on whether *Dallas* is anomic and unprincipled or conservative and patriarchal. Thus, Michael Arlen (1980), the critic, treats *Dallas* as an expression of our modern anarchic era. For him—speaking, presumably, for cosmopolitan readers—it is a chaotic comedy of manners. We enjoy the Ewings, says Arlen, because, like us, they improvise both morals and actions as they go along. There are no fixed values to guide behavior, and there is no knowing what anybody will do next.

Unlike Arlen, Gillian Swanson (1982), a feminist critic of *Dallas*, is not amused. For her, the story is about the failure of women's liberation. Far from being unpredictable and creative, Swanson sees the Ewings operating within a patriarchal system in which reward or punishment can be expected for the woman who conforms to or deviates from the stereotypical role assigned to her. Inevitably, women who strive to achieve professional independence or emotional fulfillment outside their roles as wives and mothers have to pay. For Swanson, there are no surprises here, only the one hegemonic principle lurking everywhere.

Mander (1983) couples this family principle with modern lawlessness. She sees the program as reflecting a change in American society in which the myth of mobility is sacrificed to the *Godfather* myth of corrupt, self-contained family networks that hold the key to success. Modern life may seem anarchic and unexpected, but, in fact, it is governed by the oldest rules, which Banfield (1958) calls "amoral familism." It is the family against the world, where particularism and ascription dictate who is in and who is out, and no institutional restraints bridle family imperialism. This formulation shifts the *Dallas* narrative generically from Arlen's anomic anti-soap to the gangster or Mafia genres in which crime—that is, the breaking of norms—is a central theme. This new focus can be well illustrated by the issues that arouse most public interest, ranging from "Who killed Kristen?" to "Who shot J. R.?" to "Who set Southfork on fire?"

In yet another look at *Dallas*, Newcomb (1982) reads the story nostalgically as a modern Western in which shootouts take place not in the bar on Main Street but over the telephone and in the boardrooms of Dallas skyscrapers. Elaborating on this notion, Y. Nir (1984) points to the title sequence that juxtaposes the big-city office buildings with the open fields and oil rigs of the old Wild West where the unions are still weak, income tax is low, and oil millionaires are thriving. For Newcomb, Dallas is a place where national monopolies and bureaucratic rules have not yet stamped out the original American values of initiative and individuality.

Our reading is different still, based on kinship relations among the Ewings and between the Ewings and their rival dynasties (see Figure 22.1). Clearly these relations involve two

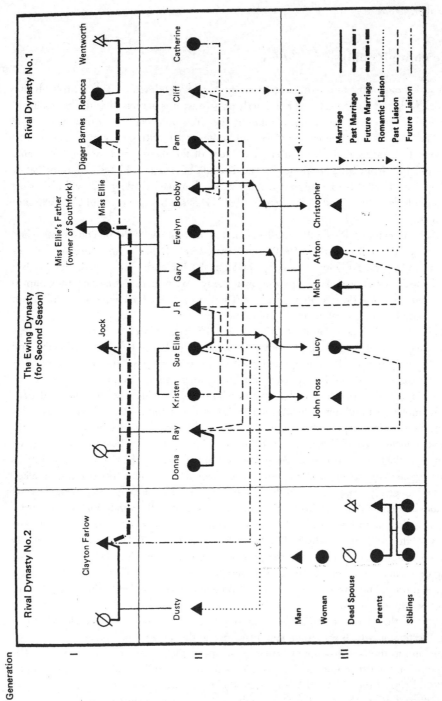

Figure 22.1 The *Dallas* family tree.

N.B. *The parentage of John Ross and Christopher is problematic. The father of John Ross is either J. R. or Cliff. Christopher – later adopted by Bobby and Pam – is probably J. R. and Kristen's biological son.*

competing principles. The vertical line from generation to generation (grandfather-father-son) is based on loyalty and harmony; it is a sacrosanct structure. Horizontal relations within generations, however, are based on treachery, where everybody is fair game for everybody else: siblings, spouses, friends, business partners, etc. We disagree with Michael Arlen's proposal that *Dallas* is anomic and unpredictable. It *is* based on contradiction, but it is systematic contradiction in that one principle (loyalty) inheres in the vertical strand of the kinship system, and another principle (treachery) inheres in the horizontal. Moreover, it is impossible to understand the story without taking account of both principles, since the justification for the back-stabbing on the horizontal line is continually rationalized in terms of the loyalty on the vertical line. The source of women's strength can also be derived from a glance at the chart. Women derive their power from their joint affiliation in rival dynasties, that is, in being intermediaries, spies, or double agents between their families of orientation and families of procreation. Only Sue Ellen is powerless in this sense.

A second theme in our content analysis has to do with the permeability of the institution of the family to the norms of business, and vice versa. The insulation between these institutions that allows family to function as relief from economics is altogether absent in *Dallas*. The success of marriage is dependent almost wholly on exchange (Liebes and Katz, 1988); true love is either absent or without sexual consummation. Self-interest prevails at the most intimate moments, as is evident throughout the horizontal line. And the opposite is true as well. Emotion is exported from primary relations into the world of business, transforming fair business practice into a total war with no holds barred. Economic power is wielded in the name of private passion, as when J. R. buys up all the oil in Texas in order to destroy father and son of a rival dynasty at whose ranch Sue Ellen and baby John Ross have sought refuge.

This diversity of interpretations makes clear that professional readers are hardly of one mind. Classical content analysis (Berelson, 1952) could not tolerate such unreliability, but the new literary theory is quite hospitable to such diversity (Fish, 1980). Depending on the mood and the theoretical perspective of the analyst, J. R. becomes a metaphor for a chauvinist patriarch, a modern swinger, a city gangster, a lone rider of the Wild West, and a dutiful son and treacherous brother.

But it would be equally wrong to conclude that the text is so open that the range of headings is infinite. In fact, these readings have the text in common. All of these analysts note the breakdown of society into an earlier (or later) state in which the family is the central (remaining) institution, incorporating economic and political functions, and is at war with other families. The readings differ, perhaps, concerning the stability of the family; Mander and Swanson see it as strongly paternalistic while Arlen sees it as an experimental laboratory. The point is that the text evokes certain shared perceptions—at least among members of the same culture—which are then assimilated and evaluated within the analysts' different frames of reference. Arlen's frame is ironic, Newcomb's is nostalgic, Swanson's and Mander's are serious and even angry, ours is primordial. It is obvious that the effect implied in Swanson's analysis is different from Arlen's; the former is hegemonic, aimed at keeping women down, while the latter invites play and experimentation.

We have found that viewers' decodings also vary, but within the limits of the text. If professional critics and scholars do not tell the same story, even among themselves, why should we expect viewers to see a single story or to be affected by a monolithic message about which even the experts disagree? The absurdity of this expectation is all the more clear when some of the viewers concerned are not even members of the analysts' culture and not even of the so-called modern world.

The export of American television

It follows, therefore, that the study of audience decodings of American television programs is even more acutely needed overseas than it is domestically. What *do* Zairians make of the Ewings? Until very recently nothing at all was known about meaning perceived by overseas viewers of American television programs. The emphasis of intercultural communications research was almost exclusively on institutional aspects, on audience ratings, and on occasional studies of effect (particularly in the area of economic development), but nothing at all was known about the meanings perceived in imported programming.

A number of studies (e.g., Tunstall, 1977; Head, 1974; Dorfman and Matelart, 1975) deal with the transfer of the technology, the organizational forms, the ideologies, and the programs of Western broadcasting to the capitals of the new nations of Asia, Africa, and South America. *Broadcasting in the Third World* (Katz and Wedell, 1977) deals at some length with the irony of a process whereby television is introduced, in part, to promote culturally authentic self-expression but rather quickly digresses to transmitting what then was called *Kojak*, what today is called *Dallas*. The process begins from the moment the prime minister announces that the great day of the first broadcast is near at hand (thanks to the combined efforts of the Treasury, Western technical assistance, and local talent). Then follows the realization that most of the promised four to five hours per day must be purchased abroad; the odyssey of the director of programs charged with purchasing material that will "open a window on the world", the realization that the only programs available to fill the voracious appetite of a television broadcasting station as internationally defined are mass-produced, long-running American series and serials. At about the time of the study, British broadcasters were waking up to the idea that one-off programs or short series of four or five episodes, the pride of British television, could not hope to compete in the export market. The director of programs needs as much time to preview a one-off program as to preview the whole of *I Love Lucy*. The one-off solves his problem for a single Monday evening; *I Love Lucy* solves his problem forever.

Like Tunstall, the authors of *Broadcasting in the Third World* noted the patterns of international flow of American programs and analyzed the outcry against this new brand of alleged imperialism. The book focused on the transplantation of ideas and practices at the level of the organization. Extensive studies of the audience, apart from collecting simple surveys of the popularity of programs, were not attempted. These surveys, however, suggested that local productions often outdraw much more elegant imports, but no thought was given to the possibility that local programs might be better. It was *assumed* that the programs conceived in the capitals of the West were equally well understood and that their messages were getting through. Indeed, the book speculates at some length on the functions and dysfunctions of such programs for political integration, for modernization, and for cultural continuity. However, "What, for example, are the gratifications derived from viewing *Ironside* in Bangkok or from listening to American pop music in Nigeria? What is understood of *Peyton Place* or *Mission Impossible* in rural areas where electricity has only just arrived? Is the idealization of the American way of life really perceived by the viewers in a conscious way? What picture of the world does the imported staccato-style news format of radio and television bulletins present to the peasant farmer?" (Katz and Wedell, 1977, p. ix)

These questions are equally valid for Europe. In Europe, as in the Third World, very little was known about how imported programs are decoded. Dutch or French readings of *Dallas* should be as interesting as those of Thailand or Nigeria—so should American readings. But on the whole, prior to *Dallas*, little thought had been given to perceived meanings. In the best case this was because no adequate research method was available for doing so and certainly no adequate supply of funds; in the worse case, it was because it did not occur to anybody to ask. Both the best and the worst reasons leave unchallenged the assumption that the presumed message of the foreign producers is getting through.[1]

Decodings of *Dallas* overseas

Curiously, *Dallas* changed all this. Researchers in a number of different countries decided, quite independently, to study the meaning of the program for foreign audiences. It is not so difficult to explain how this happened. For one thing, there was the striking fact that *Dallas* had captured the world: scholars, no less than journalists, asked themselves why. They also seized upon the opportunity to come to grips with what might be a good test of cultural imperialism. Unlike *Kojak* and other previous best-sellers, *Dallas* is the undisguised story of a family. However remote its cultural setting, viewers were invited to examine their own interpersonal relations and values in the light of those on the screen. When they did so, researchers thought that something might be happening.

Ang (1985) in Holland and Herzog-Massing (1986) in Germany explain the pleasure of viewing *Dallas* in terms of psychological needs whose origins are in social structure. While Dutch viewers are said by Ang to suffer from a lack of inherent meaning in a life that modern society has rendered meaningless, German fans of *Dallas* are perceived by Herzog as repressed by a patriarchal family structure. It is interesting that the two studies explain the attraction of the program in opposite ways: one as an antidote to the absence of structure, the other as an antidote to too much of it.

Herzog analyzes fans of the program in terms of both interviews and projective tests to reveal fantasies about the glamor of richness, corruption, and adultery which are taboo in the conservative German society. For Ang, in her analysis of forty letters from fans responding to the advertisement she placed in a women's magazine, the pleasure of viewing is generated by the need to be reassured that life has a meaning after all. She describes viewing as a rebellion against the superficiality and rootlessness of a life cut off from tradition and lacking in any integrating values. For Dutch fans, *Dallas* does not serve as escapist fantasy but transmits the sense of the tragedy in life. Admittedly, says Ang, it is not very feminist to identify with the masochism of Sue Ellen and Pamela, but it is not altogether antifeminist either. Inasmuch as feminist politics can only promise a utopian future at the expense of pain and unease in the present, such identification supplies a way to endure the present.

This interim solution wherein the unfortunate social role of women leads women to find comfort in the troubles of the soap opera echoes the early radio studies of Herzog (1941) and Warner and Henry (1948). In her new study, however, Herzog-Massing (1986) finds viewers using the program subversively. German viewers of *Dallas* show great admiration for J. R.—what Gitlin (1983) calls "the id unbound." But they can do so, says Herzog, only after declaring that their allegiance is with Miss Ellie, the virtuous mother. Miss Ellie's function, according to Herzog, is to reinforce the superego and set boundaries to her son's mischief. Identifying with her legitimizes German viewers' admiration for J. R.

The type of involvement generated by *Dallas* may result, paradoxically, from the fact that it is not considered serious artistically and, perhaps, also because of its perceived distance from viewers' reality. In her study of women viewers in Denmark from the middle and working classes, Hjort (1986) found that *Dallas* allows the expression of emotions like love and hate in a liminal context, removed from one's life to neutral ground. The Danish series *Daughters of the War*, on the other hand, is regarded by viewers as more realistic and, therefore, is more likely to invoke critical evaluation both about the accuracy of its reality and about its artistic quality. In their critical statements, Danish viewers articulate their aesthetic pleasure by comparing the slower tempo and more profound images of *Daughters* with the speed and superficiality of *Dallas*. Attention to an element such as tempo is a good illustration of the metalinguistic or attributional aspect of viewers' critical abilities and implies awareness of possibly more subtle elements of cultural imperialism. The staccato tempo of American advertising, adopted as a formula for *Sesame Street* and then exported worldwide, has been debated at the BBC and elsewhere for the hidden message of its form.

An increasing number of countries are producing their own serials (Tracey, 1985), and it is, therefore, of interest that such local productions may be more likely to be judged in terms of their reality than imported programs from which viewers feel more culturally distant. This does not mean that the local program is necessarily perceived as more real, even though this seems to be the case for Danish viewers of *Daughters*. It is certainly not the case for American viewers in our study, who insisted that *Dallas* was not real because they compared it with the reality they know first-hand.[2] This is unlike both Hjort's Danish viewers, who seem to enjoy the nowhere-no-time unreality of the program, and the more traditional Israeli viewers in our study, who take for granted that *Dallas* reveals America or the rich or the modern world. In other words, cultural distance reduces the preoccupation with the question of reality, and proximity causes viewers to measure critically how real it really is.

Another example of this phenomenon is reported by Stolz (1983) about *Dallas* viewers in Algeria. Again, the reality of the Ewings is unquestioned and, therefore, invites translation into local terms. Rather than a reflection of modern capitalism, for Algerians *Dallas* is a reminder of the reality they are fast losing. It is reminiscent of the traditional values of a world where one's basic allegiance is to the extended family, where it is normal for three generations to live under the same roof, where the pater familias is king, where a cousin would do all he can to help, and where a state bureaucracy is regarded suspiciously as an enemy to be fought by family solidarity. Thus, what Mander (1983) considers a post-modern story of a Mafia family is recognized by Algerians as a premodern family tale where universalistic principles of fairness, of equality, of opportunity do not obstruct the showing of favoritism to a relative, showing hostility to another clan, or cheating the alien bureaucracy. *Protektzia* is not labeled as corruption but taken for granted as the way society operates.

Even if *Dallas* may be read as compatible with the values of a society based on principles of ascription rather than the modern ones of achievement, Stolz (1983) believes that it contributes, nevertheless, to the erosion of traditional cultures by changing the leisure-time agenda. In Algeria, viewing *Dallas* became everybody's favorite entertainment, displacing such a popular pastime as gathering to listen to grandmother's folktales.

An altogether original approach to viewers' perception of *Dallas*—indeed, almost a formal ethnosemiotics of the program—is proposed by Livingstone (1987a). A small sample of British viewers was asked to indicate the extent of similarity among characters in *Dallas*, and the same procedure was followed for viewers of *Coronation Street*, the British serial about daily life in a working-class neighborhood. Employing a multidimensional scaling method, Livingstone measured (and then validated) the "goodness of fit" between the resultant ranking of the characters in *Dallas* and a number of value dimensions, of which morality and power were the best fits. Moreover, these two dimensions were found to be orthogonal, that is, good and bad were *not* correlated with strong and weak. It was different in *Coronation Street* where the good tended to be weak and the bad tended to be strong. Moreover, Livingstone found that viewers perceive the *Dallas* women as divided among strong and weak (although they concentrate on the weak side), whereas *Coronation Street* women are perceived as more matriarchal in character, not the mix of irrationality, softness, or weakness usually attributed to television women. From the orthogonal relationship between power and morality in *Dallas*, Livingstone was also able to suggest that the dramatic tension in the story is not between strong-and-weak and good-and-bad but between all four combinations of morality and power. This, of course, makes for a greater number of possibilities and surprises.

Convergence on the study of decoding

There is yet another reason explaining the flurry of studies on the decoding of *Dallas*: this has to do with the coincidence in time of certain developments within communications research and the appearance of the program. The division of labor in communications research was such that some had been studying the texts of popular culture while others were studying their effects on audiences, including popularity ratings, uses, and gratifications. The former ascribed influence to the text without knowing anything about the audience, while the latter, more surprisingly perhaps, did not know anything about the text. Blumler et al. (1986) have pronounced this anomaly "a dialogue of the deaf." The students of texts believed that the reader role and reader reaction were determined by the text, while the gratificationists believed that the text existed only in the eye of the beholder; therefore, why look to the text at all?

In recent years these extreme positions are being abandoned, and there is a growing convergence of interest among theoretical traditions on the process of interaction between readers and texts. This convergence makes bedfellows not only of functionally oriented audience research and Marxist-oriented critical studies but also, even more surprisingly, of so-called reader-response theory in literature studies. It is of some interest to trace the ways in which the three traditions transformed themselves—each in its own way—after finding themselves at dead ends.

The clearest case is that of critical studies. Having long assumed that the texts of popular culture inscribe themselves hegemonically in the defenseless minds of their readers, critical theorists realized that their theory left no room at all for social change. How to explain feminism, for example, if culture is totally mobilized to maintain the status quo? In recent years, therefore, critical theorists—such as the Cultural Studies group in England—have made room for alternate readings, thus acknowledging that the ordinary viewer, not only the theorist, may know how to read oppositionally. This realization led critical theorists to the empirical study of reader decodings (Morley, 1980).

As critical theorists became aware that they were studying texts without readers, gratifications researchers came to realize that they were studying readers without texts. The idea that readers, listeners, and viewers can bend the mass media to serve their own needs had gone so far that almost any text—or, indeed, no text at all—was found to serve functions such as social learning, reinforcing identity, lubricating interaction, providing escape, etc. But it gradually became clear that these functions were too unspecified: these studies did not say *what* was learned, which aspect of identity was reinforced, what was talked about, where one went for escape, etc. This more specific set of questions reopened the larger issue of which kinds of communications serve these more substantive purposes.

It is more than trivial to differentiate between viewers who use *Dallas* as a guide to reality and those who use it as an aesthetic game. Such concerns did, in fact, characterize the early days of gratifications research when the radio soap opera, the quiz program, or Kate Smith's war-bond marathon were studied for the specifics of the interaction between listeners of particular social backgrounds and very specific attributes of the program. The study of decoding by gratifications researchers is as much a return to an earlier formulation as something new. The reinstatement of text in mainline communications research also speaks to the long-standing anxiety of gratifications theorists that the receiver, more than the sender, is responsible for the message.

It is striking that literary theorists began to take interest in reader decodings more or less at the same time. Unconnected with either of the other branches of communications research, literary theorists moved from the idea that qualified readers are defined and positioned by authors to the idea that readers, no less than authors, create the text. Like gratifications theory, literary theory of this brand also went through the throes of asking whether there is a text, any text, that constrains the reader's reading (Fish, 1980) and reemerged with the idea of interaction between types of readers and types of texts, even to the point of conducting empirical studies of readers (Radway, 1985).

The new convergence on reader decodings clearly implies an active reader—selecting, negotiating, interpreting, discussing, or, in short, being involved. But this image of the reader—and, a fortiori, this image of the television viewer—does not sit well with those theories of communications research that emphasize the passivity of the viewer. Researchers such as Csikzentmihalyi and Kubey (1981) insist—based on a method which signals respondents to jot down what they are doing and feeling when the beeper sounds—that television is consumed in a semi-dazed state, and unlike other activities, dazes its participants even more. The psychoanalytically oriented film theorists seem to be saying something similar in proposing that the television viewer regresses to an infantile state in which the teasing flow of the supertext stimulates and frustrates. Gerbner et al. (1979), too, approaches the viewer as a passive recipient, not so much because he is anesthetized by television, but because he is its victim; shut in and nurtured by the medium to the exclusion of other sources of influence, heavy viewers learn the television message ritualistically and hegemonically, not by negotiation.

The convergence on the study of decoding is, therefore, a challenge to these theories. Perhaps the viewers are more active and more independent than these researchers suggest— more like gratificationists have assumed. Perhaps this activity characterizes only certain sorts of programs—such as *Dallas* and the moon landings. The empirical study of viewer decodings should help us find out.

We have tried to point out in this chapter that the flurry of research on the decoding of *Dallas* overseas has roots both in the text itself—the phenomenon of *Dallas*—and in new or newly revived theories of the active viewer. What follows should be seen, therefore, as an exercise in the study of viewer involvement in the process of consuming television. It will contribute, we hope, to a clearer conceptualization of the different types of decodings and their connections with different types of involvement on the one hand, and different types of uses and effects on the other.

Notes

1   Ironically, there is another similarity between Europe of the moment and the Third World of ten years ago. Confronted with an explosion in the number of hours of broadcasting as a result both of the deregulation of national broadcasting systems and of new media technology, European broadcasting appears to be going in several different directions at once. The Italians—at least in the first phase of deregulation—were scrambling to import whatever lurid reruns they could find, exactly as the Third World nations did when they realized they were committed to broadcasting many more hours than they could produce. The French, on the other hand, more constrained by an ethic of authenticity, are resolved to produce for themselves, but their most famous self-production so far is the intentional imitation of *Dallas*. Based on careful research into the organization, content, and

audience reactions to *Dallas*, the French have imported not an American program but an American concept for a program, along with the American way of manufacturing it. This is what the Chianciano Television Festival of 1983 admiringly entitled "Europe Fights Back."

2   It is likely that both Danes and Americans are right. The Danish program reflects a specific social and historical period, whereas *Dallas* is more of an invention. Michael Arlen (1980) argues that the show is carefully stripped of any clues to the constraints of an "outside world," resembling the "smooth pebbles" of fairy tales.

References

Allen, Robert C. 1985. *Speaking of Soap Opera*. Chapel Hill: Univ. of North Carolina Press.

Ang, Ien. 1985. *Watching* Dallas. London and New York: Methuen.

Arlen, Michael. 1980. *Camera Age: Essays on Television*, 38–50. New York: Farrar, Strauss and Giroux.

Arnheim, Rudolf. 1943. "The World of Daytime Serial." In P. Lazarsfeld and F. Stanton (eds.), *Radio Research*. New York: Duell, Sloan, and Pearce.

Banfield, Edward C. 1958. *The Moral Basis of a Backward Society*. Glencoe: Free Press.

Berelson, B. 1952. *Content Analysis in Communication Research*. New York: Free Press.

Blumler, Jay, Michael Gurevitch and Elihu Katz. 1986. *"Reaching Out: A Future for Gratifications Research."* In Karl E. Rosengren, Lawrence A. Wenner, Philip Palm-green (eds.), *Media Gratifications Research: Current Perspectives*. Newbury Park, Calif.: Sage.

Bombardier, Denise. 1985. "Television as an Instrument of Cultural Identity: The Case of Quebec." In Everett Rogers and Francis Balle (eds.), *The Media Revolution in America and Western Europe*. Norwood: Ablex.

Booth, Wayne. 1982. "The Company We Keep: Self-Making in Imaginative Art, Old and New." *Daedelus* 111/4: 33–59.

Braudy, Leo. 1982. "Popular Culture and Personal Time." *The Yale Review* 71 (41): 481–488.

Browne, Nick. 1984. "Reflections of Desire in 'The Rules of the Game': Reflections on the Theater of History" *Quarterly Review of Film Studies* 7/3: 251–262.

Cantor, Muriel, and Suzanne Pingree. 1983. *The Soap Opera*. Beverly Hills: Sage.

Cassata, Mary B., and Tom Skill. 1983. *Life on Daytime Television*. Norwood, N.J.: Ablex.

Cavell, Stanley. 1982. "The Fact of Television" *Daedalus* 111/4: 75–96.

Csikszentmihalyi, Mihaly, and Robert Kubey. 1981. "Television and the Best of Life: A Systematic Comparison of Subjective Experience." *Public Opinion Quarterly* 45: 317–328.

Dahlgren, Peter. 1985. "Media, Meaning and Method: A Post Rational Perspective." *The Nordicom Review of Nordic Mass Communication Research*, vol. 2.

Dorfman, Morris, and A. Matelart. 1975. *How to Read Donald Duck: Imperialist Ideology and the Disney Comic*. New York: International General.

Eco, Umberto. 1985. "Innovation and Repetition: Between Modern and Post Modern Aesthetics." *Daedalus* 774/4: 161–184.

Fejes, F. 1984. "Critical Mass Communications Research and Media Effects: The Problem of the Dis-appearing Audience." *Media, Culture and Society* 6: 219–232.

Fish, Stanley. 1980. *Is There a Text in This Class? The Authority of Interpretive Communities*. Cambridge: Harvard Univ. Press.

Galtung, Johan, and Marie H. Ruge. 1970. "Structure of Foreign News." In Jeremy Tunstall (ed.), *Media Sociology*, 259–298. London: Constable.

Gans, Herbert. 1979. *Deciding What's News*. New York: Pantheon Books.

Gerbner, George, Larry Gross, et al. 1979. "The Demonstration of Power." *Journal of Communication* 29: 177–196.

Gitlin, Todd. 1980. *The Whole World Is Watching*. Berkeley: Univ. of California Press.

Gitlin, Todd. 1983. *Inside Prime Time*. New York: Pantheon Books.

Glasgow University Media Group. 1976. *Bad News*. London: Routledge and Kegan Paul.

Graber, Doris. 1984. *Processing the News: How People Tame the Information Tide*. New York: Longman.

Greenberg, Bradley S. 1982. *Life on Television*. Norwood, N.J.: Ablex.

Hartley, John. 1982. *Understanding News*. London and New York: Methuen.

Head, Sydney. 1974. *Broadcasting in Africa*. Philadelphia: Temple Univ. Press.

Herzog, Herta. 1941. "On Borrowed Experience—An Analysis of Listening to Daytime Sketches." *Studies in Philosophy and Social Science*. The Institute of Social Research.

Herzog-Massing, Herta. 1986. "Decoding *Dallas*." *Society* 24/1: 74–77.

Hjort, Anne. 1986. *When Women Watch Television. How Danish Women Perceive the American Series* Dallas *and the Danish Series* Daughters of the War. Copenhagen: Media Research Department, Danish Broadcasting Corporation.

Houston, Beverle. 1985. "Viewing Television: The Metapsychology of Endless Consumption." *Quarterly Review of Film Studies* 9: 183–195.

Katz, Elihu, and George Wedell. 1977. *Broadcasting in the Third World*. London: Macmillan.

Katzman, Nathan. 1972. "Television Soap Operas: What's Been Going On Anyway?" *Public Opinion Quarterly* 36: 200–212.

Liebes, Tamar. 1989. "On the Convergence of Theories of Mass Communication and Literature Regarding the Role of the Viewer." In Brenda Dervin (ed.), *Progress in Communication Sciences*. Norwood, N.J.: Ablex.

Liebes, Tamar, and Elihu Katz. 1988. "*Dallas* and Genesis: Primordiality and Seriality in Popular Culture." In James Carey (ed.), *Media, Myths, and Narratives: Television and the Press*, 113–125. Newbury Park, Calif.: Sage.

Livingstone, Sonia. 1987a. "The Implicit Representation of Characters in *Dallas*: A Multi-Dimensional Scaling Approach." *Human Communication Research* 13(3): 399–440.

Mander, Mary. 1983. "*Dallas*: The Mythology of Crime and the Moral Occult." *Journal of Popular Culture* 17: 44–48.

Modleski, Tania. 1984. *Loving with a Vengeance: Mass Produced Fantasies for Women*. London and New York: Methuen.

Molotch, Harvey, and Marilyn Lester. 1974. "News as Purposive Behavior." *American Sociological Review* 39/1: 101–112.

Morley, Dave. 1980. *The "Nationwide" Audience*. London: British Film Institute.

Newcomb, Horace. 1974. *TV, The Most Popular Art*. New York: Anchor Books.

Nir, Yeshayahu. 1984. "JR, the Kennedys and Arik Sharon." *Hotam* (Summer).

Radway, Janice. 1985. *Reading the Romance. Women, Patriarchy and Popular Culture*. Chapel Hill: Univ. of North Carolina Press.

Robinson, John P., and Mark R. Levy. 1986. *The Main Source: Learning from Television News*. Beverly Hills: Sage.

Schroder, Kim C. 1987. "Convergence of Antagonistic Traditions? The Case of Audience Research." *European Journal of Communication* 2: 7–32.

Stolz, Joelle. 1983. "Les Algeriens regardent *Dallas*." *Les Nouvelles Chaines*. Paris: Presse Universitaire de France, and Institut Universitaire d'Etudes du Development.

Swanson, Gillian. 1982. "*Dallas*." *Framework* 14: 32–35; 15: 81–85.

Tracey, Michael. 1985. "The Poisoned Chalice? International Television and the Idea of Dominance." *Daedalus* 114/4: 17–56.

Tuchman, Gaye. 1973. "Making News by Doing Work." *American Journal of Sociology* 79/1: 110–131.

Tunstall, Jeremy. 1977. *The Media Are American*. London: Constable.

Warner, Lloyd W. and William Henry. 1948. "The Radio Daytime Serial: A Symbolic Analysis." *Genetic Psychology Mongraphs* 38: 3–71.

Chapter 23

Arjun Appadurai

DISJUNCTURE AND DIFFERENCE IN THE GLOBAL CULTURAL ECONOMY

THE CENTRAL PROBLEM OF today's global interactions is the tension between cultural homogenization and cultural heterogenization. A vast array of empirical facts could be brought to bear on the side of the 'homogenization' argument, and much of it has come from the left end of the spectrum of media studies (Hamelink, 1983; Mattelart, 1983; Schiller, 1976), and some from other, less appealing, perspectives (Gans, 1985; Iyer, 1988). Most often, the homogenization argument subspeciates into either an argument about Americanization, or an argument about 'commoditization', and very often the two arguments are closely linked. What these arguments fail to consider is that at least as rapidly as forces from various metropolises are brought into new societies they tend to become indigenized in one or other way: this is true of music and housing styles as much as it is true of science and terrorism, spectacles and constitutions. The dynamics of such indigenization have just begun to be explored in a sophisticated manner (Barber, 1987; Feld, 1988; Hannerz, 1987, 1989; Ivy, 1988; Nicoll, 1989; Yoshimoto, 1989), and much more needs to be done. But it is worth noticing that for the people of Irian Jaya, Indonesianization may be more worrisome than Americanization, as Japanization may be for Koreans, Indianization for Sri Lankans, Vietnamization for the Cambodians, Russianization for the people of Soviet Armenia and the Baltic Republics. Such a list of alternative fears to Americanization could be greatly expanded, but it is not a shapeless inventory: for polities of smaller scale, there is always a fear of cultural absorption by polities of larger scale, especially those that are near by. One man's imagined community (Anderson, 1983) is another man's political prison.

This scalar dynamic, which has widespread global manifestations, is also tied to the relationship between nations and states, to which I shall return later in this essay. For the moment let us note that the simplification of these many forces (and fears) of homogenization can also be exploited by nation-states in relation to their own minorities, by posing global commoditization (or capitalism, or some other such external enemy) as more 'real' than the threat of its own hegemonic strategies.

The new global cultural economy has to be understood as a complex, overlapping, disjunctive order, which cannot any longer be understood in terms of existing center-periphery models (even those that might account for multiple centers and peripheries). Nor is it susceptible to simple models of push and pull (in terms of migration theory) or of surpluses and deficits (as in traditional models of balance of trade), or of consumers and producers (as in most neo-Marxist theories of development). Even the most complex and flexible theories of global development which have come out of the Marxist tradition (Amin, 1980; Mandel, 1978; Wallerstein, 1974; Wolf, 1982) are inadequately quirky, and they have not come to terms with what Lash and Urry (1987) have recently called 'disorganized capitalism'. The complexity of the current global economy has to do with certain fundamental disjunctures between economy, culture and politics which we have barely begun to theorize.[1]

I propose that an elementary framework for exploring such disjunctures is to look at the relationship between five dimensions of global cultural flow which can be termed: (a) ethnoscapes; (b) mediascapes; (c) technoscapes; (d) finanscapes; and (e) ideoscapes.[2] I use terms with the common suffix scape to indicate first of all that these are not objectively given relations which look the same from every angle of vision, but rather that they are deeply perspectival constructs, inflected very much by the historical, linguistic and political situatedness of different sorts of actors: nation-states, multinationals, diasporic communities, as well as sub-national groupings and movements (whether religious, political or economic), and even intimate face-to-face groups, such as villages, neighborhoods and families. Indeed, the individual actor is the last locus of this perspectival set of landscapes, for these landscapes are eventually navigated by agents who both experience and constitute larger formations, in part by their own sense of what these landscapes offer. These landscapes thus, are the building blocks of what, extending Benedict Anderson, I would like to call 'imagined worlds', that is, the multiple worlds which are constituted by the historically situated imaginations of persons and groups spread around the globe (Appadurai, 1989). An important fact of the world we live in today is that many persons on the globe live in such imagined 'worlds' and not just in imagined communities, and thus are able to contest and sometimes even subvert the 'imagined worlds' of the official mind and of the entrepreneurial mentality that surround them. The suffix scape also allows us to point to the fluid, irregular shapes of these landscapes, shapes which characterize international capital as deeply as they do international clothing styles.

By 'ethnoscape', I mean the landscape of persons who constitute the shifting world in which we live: tourists, immigrants, refugees, exiles, guestworkers and other moving groups and persons constitute an essential feature of the world, and appear to affect the politics of and between nations to a hitherto unprecedented degree. This is not to say that there are not anywhere relatively stable communities and networks, of kinship, of friendship, of work and of leisure, as well as of birth, residence and other filiative forms. But it is to say that the warp of these stabilities is everywhere shot through with the woof of human motion, as more persons and groups deal with the realities of having to move, or the fantasies of wanting to move. What is more, both these realities as well as these fantasies now function on larger scales, as men and women from villages in India think not just of moving to Poona or Madras, but of moving to Dubai and Houston, and refugees from Sri Lanka find themselves in South India as well as in Canada, just as the Hmong are driven to London as well as to Philadelphia. And as international capital shifts its needs, as production and technology generate different needs, as nation-states shift their policies on refugee populations, these moving groups can never afford to let their imaginations rest too long, even if they wished to.

By 'technoscape', I mean the global configuration, also ever fluid, of technology, and of the fact that technology, both high and low, both mechanical and informational, now moves at high speeds across various kinds of previously impervious boundaries. Many countries now are the roots of multinational enterprise: a huge steel complex in Libya may involve interests from India, China, Russia and Japan, providing different components of new technological configurations. The odd distribution of technologies, and thus the peculiarities of these technoscapes, are increasingly driven not by any obvious economies of scale, of political control, or of market rationality, but of increasingly complex relationships between money flows, political possibilities and the availability of both low and highly-skilled labor. So, while India exports waiters and chauffeurs to Dubai and Sharjah, it also exports software engineers to the United States (indentured briefly to Tata-Burroughs or the World Bank), then laundered through the State Department to become wealthy 'resident aliens', who are in turn objects of seductive messages to invest their money and know-how in federal and state projects in India. The global economy can still be described in terms of traditional 'indicators' (as the World Bank continues to do) and studied in terms of traditional comparisions (as in Project Link at the University of Pennsylvania), but the complicated technoscapes (and the shifting ethnoscapes), which underlie these 'indicators' and 'comparisions' are further out of the reach of the 'queen of the social sciences' than ever before. How is one to make a meaningful comparision of wages in Japan and the United States, or of real estate costs in New York and Tokyo, without taking sophisticated account of the very complex fiscal and investment flows that link the two economies through a global grid of currency speculation and capital transfer?

Thus it is useful to speak as well of 'finanscapes', since the disposition of global capital is now a more mysterious, rapid and difficult landscape to follow than ever before, as currency markets, national stock exchanges, and commodity speculations move megamonies through national turnstiles at blinding speed, with vast absolute implications for small differences in percentage points and time units. But the critical point is that the global relationship between ethnoscapes, technoscapes and finanscapes is deeply disjunctive and profoundly unpredictable, since each of these landscapes is subject to its own constraints and incentives (some political, some informational and some techno-environmental), at the same time as each acts as a constraint and a parameter for movements in the other. Thus, even an elementary model of global political economy must take into account the shifting relationship between perspectives on human movement, technological flow, and financial transfers, which can accommodate their deeply disjunctive relationships with one another.

Built upon these disjunctures (which hardly form a simple, mechanical global 'infrastructure' in any case) are what I have called 'mediascapes' and 'ideoscapes', though the latter two are closely related landscapes of images. 'Mediascapes' refer both to the distribution of the electronic capabilities to produce and disseminate information (newspapers, magazines, television stations, film production studios, etc.), which are now available to a growing number of private and public interests throughout the world; and to the images of the world created by these media. These images of the world involve many complicated inflections, depending on their mode (documentary or entertainment), their hardware (electronic or pre-electronic), their audiences (local, national or transnational) and the interests of those who own and control them. What is most important about these mediascapes is that they provide (especially in their television, film and cassette forms) large and complex repertoires of images, narratives and 'ethnoscapes' to viewers throughout the world, in which the world of commodities and the world of 'news' and politics are profoundly mixed. What this means is that many audiences throughout the world experience the media themselves as a complicated and interconnected repertoire of print, celluloid, electronic screens and billboards. The lines between the 'realistic' and the fictional landscapes they see are blurred, so that the further away these audiences are from the direct experiences of metropolitan life, the more likely they are to construct 'imagined worlds' which are chimerical, aesthetic, even fantastic objects, particularly if assessed by the criteria of some other perspective, some other 'imagined world'.

'Mediascapes', whether produced by private or state interests, tend to be image-centered, narrative-based accounts of strips of reality, and what they offer to those who experience and transform them is a series of elements (such as characters, plots and textual forms) out of which scripts can be formed of imagined lives, their own as well as those of others living in other places. These scripts can and do get disaggregated into complex sets of metaphors by which people live (Lakoff and Johnson, 1980) as they help to constitute narratives of the 'other' and proto-narratives of possible lives, fantasies which could become prologemena to the desire for acquisition and movement.

'Ideoscapes' are also concatenations of images, but they are often directly political and frequently have to do with the ideologies of states and the counter-ideologies of movements explicitly oriented to capturing state power or a piece of it. These ideoscapes are composed of elements of the Enlightenment world-view, which consists of a concatenation of ideas, terms and images, including 'freedom', 'welfare', 'rights', 'sovereignty', 'representation' and the master-term 'democracy'. The master-narrative of the Enlightenment (and its many variants in England, France and the United States) was constructed with a certain internal logic and presupposed a certain relationship between reading, representation and the public sphere (for the dynamics of this process in the early history of the United States, see Warner, 1990). But their diaspora across the world, especially since the nineteenth century, has loosened the internal coherence which held these terms and images together in a Euro-American master-narrative, and provided instead a loosely structured synopticon of politics, in which different nation-states, as part of their evolution, have organized their political cultures around different 'keywords' (Williams, 1976).

As a result of the differential diaspora of these keywords, the political narratives that govern communication between elites and followings in different parts of the world involve problems of both a semantic and a pragmatic nature: semantic to the extent that words (and their lexical equivalents) require careful translation from context to context in their global movements; and pragmatic to the extent that the use of these words by political actors and their audiences may be subject to very different sets of contextual conventions that mediate their translation into public politics. Such conventions are not only matters of the nature of political rhetoric (viz. what does the aging Chinese leadership mean when it refers to the dangers of hooliganism? What does the South Korean leadership mean when it speaks of 'discipline' as the key to democratic industrial growth?).

These conventions also involve the far more subtle question of what sets of communicative genres are valued in what way (newspapers versus cinema for example) and what sorts of pragmatic genre conventions govern the collective 'readings' of different kinds of text. So, while an Indian audience may be attentive to the resonances of a political speech in terms of some key words and phrases reminiscent of Hindi cinema, a Korean audience may respond to the subtle codings of Buddhist or neo-Confucian rhetorical strategy encoded in a political document. The very relationship of reading to hearing and seeing may vary in important ways that determine the morphology of these different 'ideoscapes' as they shape themselves in different national and transnational contexts. This globally variable synaesthesia has hardly even been noted, but it demands urgent analysis. Thus 'democracy' has clearly become a master-term, with powerful echoes from Haiti and Poland to the Soviet Union and China, but it sits at the center of a variety of ideoscapes (composed of distinctive pragmatic configurations of rough 'translations' of other central terms from the vocabulary of the Enlightenment). This creates ever new terminological kaleidoscopes, as states (and the groups that seek to capture them) seek to pacify populations whose own ethnoscapes are in motion, and whose mediascapes may create severe problems for the ideoscapes with which they are presented. The fluidity of ideoscapes is complicated in particular by the growing diasporas (both voluntary and involuntary) of intellectuals who continuously inject new meaning-streams into the discourse of democracy in different parts of the world.

This extended terminological discussion of the five terms I have coined sets the basis for a tentative formulation about the conditions under which current global flows occur: *they occur in and through the growing disjunctures between ethnoscapes, technoscapes, finanscapes, mediascapes and ideoscapes*. This formulation, the core of my model of global cultural flow, needs some explanation. First, people, machinery, money, images, and ideas now follow increasingly non-isomorphic paths: of course, at all periods in human history, there have been some disjunctures between the flows of these things, but the sheer speed, scale and volume of each of these flows is now so great that the disjunctures have become central to the politics of global culture. The Japanese are notoriously hospitable to ideas and are stereotyped as inclined to export (all) and import (some) goods, but they are also notoriously closed to immigration, like the Swiss, the Swedes and the Saudis. Yet the Swiss and Saudis accept populations of guestworkers, thus creating labor diasporas of Turks, Italians and other circum-mediterranean groups. Some such guestworker groups maintain continuous contact with their home-nations, like the Turks, but others, like high-level South Asian migrants, tend to desire lives in their new homes, raising anew the problem of reproduction in a deterritorialized context.

Deterritorialization, in general, is one of the central forces of the modern world, since it brings laboring populations into the lower class sectors and spaces of relatively wealthy societies, while sometimes creating exaggerated and intensified senses of criticism or attachment to politics in the home-state. Deterritorialization, whether of Hindus, Sikhs, Palestinians or Ukrainians, is now at the core of a variety of global fundamentalisms, including Islamic and Hindu fundamentalism. In the Hindu case for example (Appadurai and Breckenridge, forthcoming) it is clear that the overseas movement of Indians has been exploited by a variety of interests both within and outside India to create a complicated network of finances and religious identifications, in which the problems of cultural reproduction for Hindus abroad has become tied to the politics of Hindu fundamentalism at home.

At the same time, deterritorialization creates new markets for film companies, art impressarios and travel agencies, who thrive on the need of the deterritorialized population for contact with its homeland. Naturally, these invented homelands, which constitute the mediascapes of deterritorialized groups, can often become sufficiently fantastic and one-sided that they provide the material for new ideoscapes in which ethnic conflicts can begin to erupt. The creation of 'Khalistan', an invented homeland of the deterritorialized Sikh population of England, Canada and the United States, is one example of the bloody potential in such mediascapes, as they interact with the 'internal colonialisms' (Hechter, 1974) of the nation-state. The West Bank, Namibia and Eritrea are other theaters for the enactment of the bloody negotiation between existing nation-states and various deterritorialized groupings.

The idea of deterritorialization may also be applied to money and finance, as money managers seek the best markets for their investments, independent of national boundaries. In turn, these movements of monies are the basis of new kinds of conflict, as Los Angelenos worry about the Japanese buying up their city, and people in Bombay worry about the rich Arabs from the Gulf States who have not only transformed the prices of mangoes in Bombay, but have also substantially altered the profile of hotels, restaurants and other services in the eyes of the local population, just as they continue to do in London. Yet, most residents of Bombay are ambivalent about the Arab presence there, for the flip side of their presence is the absence of friends and kinsmen earning big money in the Middle East and bringing back both money and luxury commodities to Bombay and other cities in India. Such commodities transform consumer taste in these cities, and also often end up smuggled through air and sea ports and peddled in the gray markets of Bombay's streets. In these gray markets, some members of Bombay's middle-classes and of its lumpenproletariat can buy some of these goods, ranging from cartons of Marlboro cigarettes, to Old Spice shaving cream and tapes of Madonna. Similarly gray routes, often subsidized by the moonlighting activities of sailors, diplomats, and airline stewardesses who get to move in and out of the country regularly, keep the gray markets of Bombay, Madras and Calcutta filled with goods not only from the West, but also from the Middle East, Hong Kong and Singapore.

It is this fertile ground of deterritorialization, in which money, commodities and persons are involved in ceaselessly chasing each other around the world, that the mediascapes and ideoscapes of the modern world find their fractured and fragmented counterpart. For the ideas and images produced by mass media often are only partial guides to the goods and experiences that deterritorialized populations transfer to one another. In Mira Nair's brilliant film, *India Cabaret*, we see the multiple loops of this fractured deterritorialization as young women, barely competent in Bombay's metropolitan glitz, come to seek their fortunes as cabaret dancers and prostitutes in Bombay, entertaining men in clubs with dance formats derived wholly from the prurient dance sequences of Hindi films. These scenes cater in turn to ideas about Western and foreign women and their 'looseness', while they provide tawdry career alibis for these women. Some of these women come from Kerala, where cabaret clubs and the pornograpic film industry have blossomed, partly in response to the purses and tastes of Keralites returned from the Middle East, where their diasporic lives away from women distort their very sense of what the relations between men and women might be. These tragedies of displacement could certainly be replayed in a more detailed analysis of the relations between the Japanese and German sex tours to Thailand and the tragedies of the sex trade in Bangkok, and in other similar loops which tie together fantasies about the other, the conveniences and seductions of travel, the economics of global trade and the brutal mobility fantasies that dominate gender politics in many parts of Asia and the world at large.

While far more could be said about the cultural politics of deterritorialization and the larger sociology of displacement that it expresses, it is appropriate at this juncture to bring in the role of the nation-state in the disjunctive global economy of culture today. The relationship between states and nations is everywhere an embattled one. It is possible to say that in many societies, the nation and the state have become one another's projects. That is, while nations (or more properly groups with ideas about nationhood) seek to capture or co-opt states and state power, states simultaneously seek to capture and monopolize ideas about nationhood (Baruah, 1986; Chatterjee, 1986; Nandy, 1989). In general, separatist, transnational movements, including those which have included terror in their methods, exemplify nations in search of states: Sikhs, Tamil Sri Lankans, Basques, Moros, Quebecois, each of these represent imagined communities which seek to create states of their own or carve pieces out of existing states. States, on the other hand, are everywhere seeking to monopolize the moral resources of community, either by flatly claiming perfect coevality between nation and state, or by systematically museumizing and representing all the groups within them in a variety of heritage politics that seems remarkably uniform throughout the world (Handler, 1988; Herzfeld, 1982; McQueen, 1988). Here, national and international mediascapes are exploited by nation-states to pacify separatists or even the potential fissiparousness of all ideas of difference. Typically, contemporary nation-states do this by exercising taxonomical control over difference; by creating various kinds of international spectacle to domesticate difference; and by seducing small groups with the fantasy of self-display on some sort of global or cosmopolitan stage. One important new feature of global cultural politics, tied to the disjunctive relationships between the various landscapes discussed earlier, is that state and nation are at each's throats, and the hyphen that links them is now less an icon of conjuncture than an index of disjuncture. This disjunctive relationship between nation and state has two levels: at the level of any given nation-state, it means that there is a battle of the imagination, with state and nation seeking to cannibalize one another. Here is the seed-bed of brutal separatisms, majoritarianisms that seem to have appeared from nowhere, and micro-identities that have become political projects within the nation-state. At another level, this disjunctive relationship is deeply entangled with the global disjunctures discussed throughout this essay: ideas of nationhood appear to be steadily increasing in scale and regularly crossing existing state boundaries: sometimes, as with the Kurds, because previous identities stretched across vast national spaces, or, as with the Tamils in Sri Lanka, the dormant threads of a transnational diaspora have been activated to ignite the micro-politics of a nation-state.

In discussing the cultural politics that have subverted the hyphen that links the nation to the state, it is especially important not to forget its mooring in the irregularities that now characterize 'disorganized capital' (Lash and Urry, 1987; Kothari, 1989). It is because labor, finance and technology are now so widely separated that the volatilities that underlie movements for nationhood (as large as transnational Islam on the one hand, or as small as the movement of the Gurkhas for a separate state in the North-East of India) grind against the vulnerabilities which characterize the relationships between states. States find themselves pressed to stay 'open' by the forces of media, technology, and travel which had fueled consumerism throughout the world and have increased the craving, even in the non-Western world, for new commodities and spectacles. On the other hand, these very cravings can become caught up in new ethnoscapes, mediascapes, and eventually, ideoscapes, such as 'democracy' in China, that the state cannot tolerate as threats to its own control over ideas of nationhood and 'people-hood'. States throughout the world are under siege, especially where contests over the ideoscapes of democracy are fierce and fundamental, and where there are radical disjunctures between ideoscapes and technoscapes (as in the case of very small countries that lack contemporary technologies of production and information); or between ideoscapes and finanscapes (as in countries such as Mexico or Brazil where international lending influences national politics to a very large degree); or between ideoscapes and ethnoscapes (as in Beirut, where diasporic, local and translocal filiations are suicidally at battle); or between ideoscapes and mediascapes (as in many countries in the Middle East and Asia) where the lifestyles represented on both national and international TV and cinema completely overwhelm and undermine the rhetoric of national politics: in the Indian case, the myth of the law-breaking hero has emerged to mediate this naked struggle between the pieties and the realities of Indian politics, which has grown increasingly brutalized and corrupt (Vachani, 1989).

The transnational movement of the martial-arts, particularly through Asia, as mediated by the Hollywood and Hongkong film industries (Zarilli, forthcoming) is a rich illustration of the ways in which long-standing martial arts traditions, reformulated to meet the fantasies of contemporary (sometimes lumpen) youth populations, create new cultures of masculinity and violence, which are in turn the fuel for increased violence in national and international politics. Such violence is in turn the spur to an increasingly rapid and amoral arms trade which penetrates the entire world. The worldwide spread of the AK-47 and the Uzi, in films, in corporate and state security, in terror, and in police and military activity, is a reminder that apparently simple technical uniformities often conceal an increasingly complex set of loops, linking images of violence to aspirations for community in some 'imagined world'.

Returning then to the 'ethnoscapes' with which I began, the central paradox of ethnic politics in today's world is that primordia, (whether of language or skin color or neighborhood or of kinship) have become globalized. That is, sentiments whose greatest force is in their ability to ignite intimacy into a political sentiment and turn locality into a staging ground for identity, have become spread over vast and irregular spaces, as groups move, yet stay linked to one another through sophisticated media capabilities. This is not to deny that such primordia are often the product of invented traditions (Hobsbawm and Ranger, 1983) or retrospective affiliations, but to emphasize that because of the disjunctive and unstable interplay of commerce, media, national policies and consumer fantasies, ethnicity, once a genie contained in the bottle of some sort of locality (however large) has now become a global force, forever slipping in and through the cracks between states and borders.

But the relationship between the cultural and economic levels of this new set of global disjunctures is not a simple one-way street in which the terms of global cultural politics are set wholly by, or confined wholly within, the vicissitudes of international flows of technology, labor and finance, demanding only a modest modification of existing neo-Marxist models of uneven development and state-formation. There is a deeper change, itself driven by the disjunctures between all the landscapes I have discussed, and constituted by their continuously fluid and uncertain interplay, which concerns the relationship between production and consumption in today's global economy. Here I begin with Marx's famous (and often mined) view of the fetishism of the commodity, and suggest that this fetishism has been replaced in the world at large (now seeing the world as one, large, interactive system, composed of many complex sub-systems) by two mutually supportive descendants, the first of which I call production fetishism, and the second of which I call the fetishism of the consumer.

By production fetishism I mean an illusion created by contemporary transnational production loci, which masks translocal capital, transnational earning-flows, global management and often faraway workers (engaged in various kinds of high-tech putting out operations) in the idiom and spectacle of local (sometimes even worker) control, national productivity and territorial sovereignty. To the extent that various kinds of Free Trade Zone have become the models for production at large, especially of high-tech commodities, production has itself become a fetish, masking not social relations as such, but the relations of production, which are increasingly transnational. The locality (both in the sense of the local factory or site of production and in the extended sense of the nation-state) becomes a fetish which disguises the globally dispersed forces that actually drive the production process. This generates alienation (in Marx's sense) twice intensified, for its social sense is now compounded by a complicated spatial dynamic which is increasingly global.

As for the fetishism of the consumer, I mean to indicate here that the consumer has been transformed, through commodity flows (and the mediascapes, especially of advertising, that accompany them) into a sign, both in Baudrillard's sense of a simulacrum which only asymptotically approaches the form of a real social agent; and in the sense of a mask for the real seat of agency, which is not the consumer but the producer and the many forces that constitute production. Global advertising is the key technology for the worldwide dissemination of a plethora of creative, and culturally well-chosen, ideas of consumer agency. These images of agency are increasingly distortions of a world of merchandising so subtle that the consumer is consistently helped to believe that he or she is an actor, where in fact he or she is at best a chooser.

The globalization of culture is not the same as its homogenization, but globalization involves the use of a variety of instruments of homogenization (armaments, advertising techniques, language hegemonies, clothing styles and the like), which are absorbed into local political and cultural economies, only to be repatriated as heterogeneous dialogues of national sovereignty, free enterprise, fundamentalism, etc. in which the state plays an increasingly delicate role: too much openness to global flows and the nation-state is threatened by revolt – the China syndrome; too little, and the state exits the international stage, as Burma, Albania and North Korea, in various ways have done. In general, the state has become the arbiter of this *repatriation of difference* (in the form of goods, signs, slogans, styles, etc.). But this repatriation or export of the designs and commodities of difference continuously exacerbates the 'internal' politics of majoritarianism and homogenization, which is most frequently played out in debates over heritage.

Thus the central feature of global culture today is the politics of the mutual effort of sameness and difference to cannibalize one another and thus to proclaim their successful hijacking of the twin Enlightenment ideas of the triumphantly universal and the resiliently particular. This mutual cannibalization shows its ugly face in riots, in refugee-flows, in state-sponsored torture and in ethnocide (with or without state support). Its brighter side is in the expansion of many individual horizons of hope and fantasy, in the global spread of oral rehydration therapy and other low-tech instruments of well-being, in the susceptibility even of South Africa to the force of global opinion, in the inability of the Polish state to repress its own working-classes, and in the growth of a wide range of progressive, transnational alliances. Examples of both sorts could be multiplied. The critical point is that both sides of the coin of global cultural process today are products of the infinitely varied mutual contest of sameness and difference on a stage characterized by radical disjunctures between different sorts of global flows and the uncertain landscapes created in and through these disjunctures.

Notes

A longer version of this essay appears in *Public Culture* 2 (2), Spring 1990. This longer version sets the present formulation in the context of global cultural traffic in earlier historical periods, and draws out some of its implications for the study of cultural forms more generally.

1   One major exception is Fredric Jameson, whose (1984) essay on the relationship between postmodernism and late capitalism has in many ways inspired this essay. However, the debate between Jameson (1986) and Ahmad (1987) in *Social Text* shows that the creation of a globalizing Marxist narrative, in cultural matters, is difficult territory indeed. My own effort, in this context, is to begin a restructuring of the Marxist narrative (by stressing lags and disjunctures) that many Marxists might find abhorrent. Such a restructuring has to avoid the dangers of obliterating difference within the 'third world', of eliding the social referent (as some French postmodernists seem inclined to do) and of retaining the narrative authority of the Marxist tradition, in favor of greater attention to global fragmentation, uncertainty and difference

2   These ideas are argued more fully in a book I am currently working on, tentatively entitled *Imploding Worlds: Imagination and Disjuncture in the Global Cultural Economy*.

References

Ahmad, A. (1987) 'Jameson's Rhetoric of Otherness and the "National Allegory"', *Social Text* 17: 3–25.

Amin, S. (1980) *Class and Nation: Historically and in the Current Crisis*. New York and London: Monthly Review.

Anderson, B. (1983) *Imagined Communities: Reflections on the Origin and Spread of Nationalism*. London: Verso.

Appadurai, A. (1989) 'Global Ethnoscapes: Notes and Queries for a Transnational Anthropology', in R.G. Fox (ed.), *Interventions: Anthropology of the Present*. Santa Fe: School of American Research, 191–210.

Appadurai, A. and Breckenridge, C.A. (forthcoming) *A Transnational Culture in the Making: The Asian Indian Diaspora in the United States*. London: Berg.

Barber, K. (1987) 'Popular Arts in Africa', *African Studies Review* 30(3).

Baruah, S. (1986) 'Immigration, Ethnic Conflict and Political Turmoil, Assam 1979–1985', *Asian Survey* 26(11).

Chatterjee, P. (1986) *Nationalist Thought and the Colonial World: A Derivative Discourse*. London: Zed Books.

Feld, S. (1988) 'Notes on World Beat', *Public Culture* 1(1): 31–7.

Gans, Eric (1985) *The End of Culture: Toward a Generative Anthropology*. Berkeley: University of California.

Hamelink, C. (1983) *Cultural Autonomy in Global Communications*. New York: Longman.

Handler, R. (1988) *Nationalism and the Politics of Culture in Quebec*. Madison: University of Wisconsin.

Hannerz, U. (1987) 'The World in Creolization', *Africa* 57(4): 546–59.

Hannerz, U. (1989) 'Notes on the Global Ecumene', *Public Culture* 1(2): 66–75.

Hechter, M. (1974) *Internal Colonialism: The Celtic Fringe in British National Development, 1536–1966*. Berkeley and Los Angeles: University of California.

Herzfeld, M. (1982) *Ours Once More: Folklore, Ideology and the Making of Modern Greece*. Austin: University of Texas.

Hobsbawm, E. and Ranger, T. (eds) (1983) *The Invention of Tradition*. New York: Columbia University Press.

Ivy, M. (1988) 'Tradition and Difference in the Japanese Mass Media', *Public Culture* 1(1): 21–9.

Iyer, P. (1988) *Video Night in Kathmandu*. New York: Knopf.

Jameson, F. (1984) 'Postmodernism, or the Cultural Logic of Late Capitalism', *New Left Review* 146 (July–August): 53–92.

Jameson, F. (1986) 'Third World Literature in the Era of Multi-National Capitalism', *Social Text* 15 (Fall): 65–88.

Kothari, R. (1989) *State Against Democracy: In Search of Humane Governance*. New York: New Horizons.

Lakoff, G. and Johnson, M. (1980) *Metaphors We Live By*. Chicago and London: University of Chicago.

Lash, S. and Urry, J. (1987) *The End of Organized Capitalism*. Madison: University of Wisconsin.

McQueen, H. (1988) 'The Australian Stamp: Image, Design and Ideology', *Arena* 84 Spring: 78–96.

Mandel, E. (1978) *Late Capitalism*. London: Verso.

Mattelart, A. (1983) *Transnationals and Third World: The Struggle for Culture*. South Hadley, MA: Bergin and Garvey.

Nandy, A. (1989) 'The Political Culture of the Indian State', *Daedalus* 118(4): 1–26.

Nicoll, F. (1989) 'My Trip to Alice', *Criticism, Heresy and Interpretation (CHAI)*, 3: 21–32.

Schiller, H. (1976) *Communication and Cultural Domination*. White Plains, NY: International Arts and Sciences.

Vachani, L. (1989) 'Narrative, Pleasure and Ideology in the Hindi Film: An Analysis of the Outsider Formula', MA thesis, The Annenberg School of Communication, The University of Pennsylvania.

Wallerstein, I. (1974) *The Modern World-System* (2 volumes). New York and London: Academic Press.

Warner, M. (1990) *The Letters of the Republic: Publication and the Public Sphere*. Cambridge, MA: Harvard.

Williams, R. (1976) *Keywords*. New York: Oxford.

Wolf, E. (1982) *Europe and the People Without History*. Berkeley: University of California.

Yoshimoto, M. (1989) 'The Postmodern and Mass Images in Japan', *Public Culture* 1(2): 8–25.

Zarilli, P. (Forthcoming) 'Repositioning the Body: An Indian Martial Art and its Pan-Asian Publics' in C.A. Breckenridge, (ed.), *Producing the Postcolonial: Trajectories to Public Culture in India*.

Chapter 24

Karim H. Karim

RE-VIEWING THE 'NATIONAL' IN 'INTERNATIONAL COMMUNICATION': THROUGH THE LENS OF DIASPORA

> I have lived that moment of the scattering of the people that in other times and other places, in the nations of others, becomes a time of gathering.
>
> *Homi Bhabha, 'DissemiNation' (1990)*

THE THEORETICAL AND METHODOLOGICAL frameworks used in the study of international communication have generally conformed to the conceptualisation of the world as a community of nation-states. Even those theorists who have attempted to valorise the role of non-state actors have not completely escaped the implicit worldview of a system of discrete and sovereign countries within which non-state participants conduct cross-border communication. However, according to several forecasts made in the mid-1990 (e.g. Hobsbawm 1990, pp.182–83; Appadurai 1996, p.18), the intensification of globalising tendencies seemed to be making nation-states irrelevant.

One of the key features of globalisation has been the increasing role of supranational bodies like the World Trade Organisation in regulating relations between states. But the legitimation of these entities necessarily takes place at the national level through legislation passed by the governments of member countries. Whereas states have given up some of their powers, they do maintain a substantial degree of agency.[1] Furthermore, following the terrorist attacks of September 11, 2001, national borders have become much more significant than in previous times.

However, a world divided into nation-states is a fairly recent phenomenon from the perspective of the long history of humankind. For thousands of years, communications between city states, kingdoms, empires and other polities had varying levels of formality, with much of the contact between individuals and entities such as trading associations, guilds and religious organisations remaining outside government control. For example, the pilgrimage activities of Islam, Christianity, Hinduism and Buddhism and the intercontinental trade along the Silk Route and across the Mediterranean and Indian oceans was conducted with minimal inter-governmental regulation.

The international system has its roots in the Peace of Westphalia signed by several European powers in 1648. It laid that basis for inter-governmental relations between states which were posited as exercising exclusive sovereignty over the persons and resources in the specific territories which they controlled. With this, the relatively porous borders hardened and were mutually recognised by signatories of the treaty. However, it was not until the 19th century that either rules for multilateral relations between states or international organisations began to emerge. It is significant for students of international communication that among the earliest multilateral agreements dealt with the regulation of cross-border communications such as the postal service, the telegraph and intellectual property (Hamelink 1994, pp.6–16).

By the beginning of the 20th century, the international system had spread from Europe to every other part of the world – mainly through colonisation. Hard borders had been drawn to divide all the land masses of the planet into individual states.

Imaginary nations

Every nation is imaginary. It is willed into existence by belief and action. The European concept of the nation-state was loosely based on the idea of a shared ethnicity of the population that lived within a particular territory (Renan 1990; Smith 1989). The Greek word *ethnos*, from which 'ethnic' is derived, means 'nation'. Notions of nation-state have involved the coalescence of ethnicity and territory to imply the existence of an ancestral homeland belonging to a particular *volk* or people who have kinship ties that are reflected in a common culture and language.

But this idea has been consistently problematic. Rather than unite particular peoples within a specific land mass, national borders have more often divided tribes and linguistic groups. Boundaries are often drawn as a result of conquest or diplomatic compromise between ruling elites and thus usually reflect conditions of historical contingency, not demarcations of 'pure ethnicities'. Due to the inherent tendency of human beings to migrate as well as to intermarry, there have rarely existed territories that are 'ethnically pure', despite the attempts by some to 'cleanse' them. Cultural and linguistic particularities may be eliminated over time through the assimilation of variant groups, but new waves of migration tend to ensure diversity within national populations.

Anthony Smith, a leading scholar on the concept of the nation, notes that contemporary states often maintain themselves with an adherence to a distinctive mythology, symbolism and culture associated with an ancient homeland. In order to do this they often have to mobilise masses to believe in the authenticity of this symbolism through educational and mass communication systems (Smith 1989, p.361). Benedict Anderson's influential work, *Imagined Communities: Reflections on the Origin and Spread of Nationalism* (1983), indicates that the contemporary national imagination began forming in the 19th century with the advent of the novel, to which readers in an entire country could relate. In this way they began to develop a common socio-political consciousness even though they had never met each other.

The roots of the contemporary global system of nation-states are to be found in colonialism. What began in Europe was extended to cover the planet: the sway of Spanish, Portuguese, British, French, German, Italian, Dutch and Russian expansion was imprinted on the world. European forms of governance were replicated around the world. This included the separation of related peoples' identities and relationships by marking out fixed (although not completely immutable or impermeable) national borders, which were to be maintained even after independence. Colonial educational systems helped ensure that this global arrangement was accepted by all peoples as 'natural' (Blaut 1993).

Transnational media's emergence in the 19th century, in the form of news agencies, occurred within the colonial context. The British Reuters, the French Havas and the German Wolff agencies divided the world among themselves by operating a news cartel which involved exclusive presence in the respective spheres of colonial influence. Transnational telegraph, telephone and transportation links to colonies were constructed to serve colonial metropolises. Formal telecommunications linkages between neighbouring countries in Africa or Asia ruled by rival colonising powers were rare; direct connections between southern continents were almost non-existent. Media content in the form of news and entertainment materials flowed largely from North to South, further reinforcing northern worldviews.

The colonial arrangements of global space were therefore linked to the configuration and the exercise of power. Much of this spatialisation was engendered by what Edward Said (1978). calls the 'imaginative geography' of European orientalist science that supported the imperialist enterprise; it presented justifications for the conquest and colonisation of non-European territories. Media materials produced in the North further reinforced orientalist worldviews. Even though the influence of this cultural imperialism did not produce a completely monolithic global culture, it did disseminate the products of northern cultures extensively and intensively in the South.

National mass media systems emphasised the concept of the nation-state as the primary and natural form of polity. They played this role with the continual highlighting of national symbols ranging from the prominent portrayal of national leaders in regular news bulletins to the frequent retelling of tales gleaned from the national mythology in dramatic programs (to say nothing of the ubiquity of the national flag and references to national institutions). Images of the map of the country in relation to others clearly demarcate the citizens of countries as Canadians, Kenyans, Indians etc. A nation becomes a naturalised political, geographic and ethno-cultural entity which is distinct from all other nations in the imagination of not only its own residents but those of others. (The system of nation-states exists by mutual recognition among states.)

But this modernist imaginary appears to have become muddled with postmodernist ambiguities that crept in during the last decades of the 20th century. The increased recognition of ethno-cultural diversity within national borders under policies of multiculturalism has seriously challenged the idea of a nation as ethnoculturally homogenous. Multiculturalism is redefining the nation as comprising an ethnically pluralist populace, but one that is (or should be) united in a common adherence to a set of core civic values. In practical terms, this new approach seeks to contain conflicts between competing ethnic groups in a country and effectively harness their skills as well as their intellectual and economic resources. Nevertheless, the primary cultural values of dominant ethnic groups within particular states remain hegemonic even as some aspects of minorities' cultural heritage are incorporated into the national symbolic landscape, particular forms of racial discrimination are outlawed, and certain measures are instituted to enable greater minority participation in the public sphere.

The acknowledgement of ethno-cultural minorities within nation-states has occurred mainly due to the need for manual and skilled labour, not only in northern countries but also in those like Malaysia that have embarked on ambitious programs of technologically transforming their economies. Long-standing ethnic diversity, which was often not valued previously, is now often seen as a vital national asset and showcased to the world. The public imagery and imaginaries of many nations presently include a multi-ethnic population and a diversity of cultures.

This transformation of the concept of the nation is occurring in an era in which the means of transnational communication are affording individuals and groups the ability increasingly to remain in contact across countries and continents. The Internet, satellite television and telephonic systems, among other media, provide for intricate linkages among members of ethnic groups living in various parts of the world, making their cultural assimilation into national populations more difficult. These diasporas, or 'transnations' as Arjun Appadurai terms them, stretch out across borders through the means of contemporary global communications. Speaking from the US but echoing what is true for a large number of countries, Appadurai notes, 'No existing conception of Americaness can contain this large variety of transnations' (1996, p.172). They live in America but also straddle many other nation-states.

Like the nation-state, diasporas are frequently described as 'imagined communities' (De Santis 2003; Tsaliki 2003). This characterisation, borrowing from Benedict Anderson, underlines, on the one hand, the improbability of experiencing first-hand contact with the entire group and, on the other, the adherence of its members to similar beliefs, symbols and myths. It emphasises the diasporic connections facilitated by various media and the simultaneous consumption of the same content by members of a transnational group. However, as with membership in any ethnic community, one's identification with a particular diaspora is based on an imaginary of a shared ancestry that may be difficult to substantiate.[2]

Diasporas are also often viewed as nations that have become deterritorialised, drawing from the concept of nation as linked to a group's placement within a particular geographic location. This notion, which is integral to the mythical lore of many groups, establishes strong emotional links to a particular landscape that serve to exclude others' overlapping territorial claims. Forced or voluntary migrations diminish the physical links of those who leave the homeland; but they take with them the mythical and linguistic allusions to the ancestral territory, which they invoke in nostalgic reminiscences. Some hold on to a hope of eventual return. This creates the demand for cultural products that maintain and ritually celebrate the links of the diaspora with the homeland.

The dispersed settlements of transnations exchange symbolic goods and services, including media content, among each other, thus sustaining global networks. Homeland politics forms a major topic for the media of some diasporas, especially those consisting largely of first-generation migrants. Ties to the former country remain strong in these cases and individuals seek out the most current information, especially in times of crisis. Hassanpour (2003) and Santianni (2003) show how media are used to mobilise support for the homeland causes of the Kurds and Tibetans, respectively. The increasing ease of air travel around the world is encouraging peripatetic tendencies among diasporics, some of whom frequently travel back and forth returning with video recordings of travels in the old country – which are watched in ritualised ways by the migrant community (Kolar-Panov 2003).

The challenge that diaspora poses for the traditional concept of the nation-state becomes a significant problematic for international communication studies' dominant paradigm of the community of nation-states.

Diaspora, nation and mobility

The word 'diaspora' is derived from the Greek *diaspeirein*, which suggests the scattering of seeds. It has traditionally referred to the Jewish dispersal outside Israel but is now applied to a growing list of migratory groups. An ongoing debate about what 'diaspora' should denote has accompanied the current attention to this topic. Whereas some scholars have argued in favour of identifying a closed set of characteristics in order to develop social scientific parameters for the study of diasporas (e.g. Cohen 1997), others have acknowledged its use in a broader range of human dispersals (Tölöyan 1996; Cunningham & Sinclair 2000). All diasporas do not have homeland myths at the centre of their consciousness, contrary to William Safran's suggestion (1991).

The term is frequently conceptualised as being limited to powerless transnational ethnic communities; but the 'black Atlantic' (Gilroy 1993) includes politically marginalised communities in North America and Britain as well as the ruling elites in many Caribbean states. Often viewed through the lens of migration from the southern to the western hemisphere, 'diaspora' tends to be limited to 'non-white' peoples who remain distinct as minorities in their new countries of residence. But even though some European immigrants like the Irish may find it relatively easy to assimilate into 'white' host countries, their cultural identity frequently remains resilient – especially in music and dance forms. Peoples of European origins are increasingly the objects of diaspora studies (see Kolar-Panov 2003; Tsaliki 2003; and King 2003). The dispersal of Aboriginal groups *within* North American countries has been conceptualised in terms of diaspora (Alia 2003), as has been the transnational migration of Muslims (Mandaville 2003).

Diasporas have pre-existed nation-states, and nomads have pre-existed diasporas. Even though the migrations of many diasporas are singular events and only in one direction, the very act of taking one's belongings and moving to another place of dwelling is an expression of nomadism. The latter may be interspersed with short or long periods of sedentarism in the lives of individuals and groups. Some diasporic lifespans are marked by continual movements, often back and forth for differing lengths of time between the old and new homes. Of course, such peripatetic travels are not limited merely to diasporas but seem to be a feature of the increasingly mobile contemporary world (Clifford 1997, pp.1–13) – like nomads looking for better pastures, we move in search of more promising career or business opportunities.

Nomadism and sedentarism are key mechanics in the human demarcation of space; most importantly, these two modes of life determine how we make home. Archeological and historical evidence tells us of early transcontinental migrations, including those from the Caucasus to Europe and to central and southern Asia, from northern Africa to central and southern parts of the continent, from north-eastern Asia over the ancient ice bridge traversing the Baring Strait into North and later South America or, alternatively, by small sea vessels across the Pacific Ocean. History is punctuated by a series of migrations.

As human civilisation became increasingly sedentary, the clashes between two modes of life grew. There appears to be a structural conflict between those who have chosen sedentary lifestyles and those who continue to be nomads. The former is manifested in the building of villages, towns and cities as well as in the cultivation of crops and the appropriation of territory for other aspects of the sedentary economy. It is a culture of boundaries and of land and bodies of water as property.

Nomadic peoples need large spaces to traverse – they peregrinate with their animals between summer and winter pastures, often cutting across property lines marked by settled peoples and occasionally trampling their crop fields. In the fight between the Biblical and Quranic figures of Cain and Abel, the first two sons of Adam and Eve, we seem to find the archetype for this fundamental human conflict. The Book of Genesis says that 'Abel became a herder of flocks and Cain a tiller of the soil' (4:2). Cain killed his brother, committing the first murder.

There have been innumerable conflicts between sedentary and nomadic peoples in history: for example, the Indo-European migrants into South Asia pushed southwards the Dravidians who had built an advanced civilisation in the Indus River valley 4,500 years ago; the Huns overran most of Europe in the 4th century; Arab bedouins defeated the mighty forces of the Byzantine and Sassanid empires following the death of the prophet Muhammad; the Mongols destroyed the cities of Muslim civilisations in the 13th century; the governments of the United States and Canada marked out borders in the path of the buffalo hunts of the plains Indians, eventually destroying their way of life; the history of Texas is marked by conflict between ranchers and farmers; the cattle-herding Masai in Kenya were driven out of the fertile Laikipia plateau by the politically dominant Kikuyu in the early 20th century.

Governments strive to maintain control over human movement within and across their borders. It is more difficult to extract taxes from people who are constantly on the move. Prior to the emergence of the nation-state, frontiers were frequently shifting and were rarely the hard markers between territories that they are in the present. Human migration is now much more controlled with passports, visas and border checks. Traditional nomadic life is an anomaly in the global sedentary civilisation. There remain pockets of nomadism among tribal groups that continue to move with their herds from mountains to valleys and back with the change of seasons, but they are coming under increasing pressure to settle down. The Roma (i.e. 'Gypsies') in Europe have faced enormous opposition for centuries to their tendencies to keep moving from place to place.

Governmental systems have resisted the accommodation of people without fixed addresses, denying them the assistance available to other citizens. Our societies have often not been kind to the homeless; even travelling salesmen and other itinerants have long been the objects of jokes. Although their lives may be romanticised from time to time, they are usually marginalised from the mainstream of contemporary society and viewed as deviants. The state is structured primarily to meet the needs of settled people and looks upon the nomadic life with suspicion, at best. At worst, the Roma and Jews – also viewed as wanderers – faced mass execution under the Third Reich.

However, not all travellers are treated in the same manner. Pilgrimage has long been a much-revered activity. Tourism is encouraged, as it is conceived as being important to the health of national economies. Cultural and educational travel is also seen as beneficial. Migrant labour, however, tends to be treated more ambiguously. Whereas workers from abroad have been invited for centuries to perform tasks for which there is a short supply of domestic labour, the host society's reception to them has not been uniformly hospitable. Whether they travel as temporary workers or as immigrants, there are myriad social and legal obstacles to their integration.

There are usually better receptions for migrant workers with skills in occupations currently considered vital to the economy. Holders of passports from western countries tend to move easily around the world. The mobility of people with darker skin and non-European features is often challenged. Petra Weyland (1997) illustrates the differential global spaces occupied respectively by the mostly Euro-origin male managerial class, their dependent wives who travel with them to various postings around the world, and the migrant Filipina domestic maids who serve them. The interest of powerful countries and major corporations in globalisation resides more in the elimination of national barriers to goods and services rather than to facilitate the free movement of all people.

Diasporic cultures and global structures

The diasporic migrations of the last few centuries were largely influenced by colonisation and trading connections as well as by the steady improvements in transportation and communications. There also appears to have been a connection between the economic involvement of northern countries in southern ones and the more recent human flows from the latter to the former. Saskia Sassen (1996) indicates that economic links ranging from 'off-shoring' of production, foreign investment into export-oriented agriculture, and the power of multinationals in the consumer markets of developing countries has often resulted in the mass movement of people.

The mass migrations of the 1700s and 1800s led to new economic growth in the countries of the 'New World' (while simultaneously displacing indigenous economies). These included movements of slaves from Africa, indentured labourers from Asia, and settlers from Europe. Following the lifting of restrictions on race-based immigration in the 1950s and 1960s, Asians and Africans began to emigrate in larger numbers to North America, Australasia and Europe. There has also been substantial migration from Latin America into the United States. These movements of people of various origins to different parts of the world have created diasporas that are layered by periods of immigration, the extent of integration into receiving societies, and the maintenance of links with the land of origin as well as with other parts of the transnational group. This layering has resulted in the wide variations of connections and attachments that such worldwide communities have to each other. Retention of ancestral customs, language and religion, marriage patterns, and particularly the ease of communication between various parts of a diaspora help determine its characteristics.

Complex historical, social and cultural dynamics within specific groups and in their relationships with others help shape identities within diasporas. Mandaville views these communities as being continually 'constructed, debated and reimagined' (2003, p.135). The routes followed within transnations are often non-linear; they include life-histories that involve frequent back-tracking and returning to specific locations around the world in sequences that vary between families and individuals. Not only are there multiple types of linkages between the homeland and the diaspora, settlements of transnational communities residing in various parts of the world develop intricate networks among themselves.

The identities that emerge from these variant circumstances are therefore polyvalent. In an essay on the Chicano diaspora, Angie Chabram-Dernersesian notes that:

> these identities will be encountered from particular social and historical loca-
> tions, from situated knowledges, from ethnographic experiences of rupture and
> continuity, and from a complex web of political negotiations with which people
> inscribe their social and historical experiences and deliver their self-styled
> counter narratives. (1994, p.286)

Unlike the citizens of nation-states, members of diasporas do not usually carry identity documentation attesting to their adherence to one group or another. Diasporics have strong or weak identifications with various global ethnicities; these allegiances may grow or diminish according to the passage of time or the unfolding of events in one's individual or communal life. Some may relate to a religious diaspora that is ethnically diverse more than an ethnocultural group; others may feel comfortable engaging with several diasporas or with a conglomeration of people from places such as Latin America, South Asia or Africa.

Diasporas are often viewed as forming alternatives to the structures of worldwide capitalism; but in many instances they are participants in transnational economic activity. From the banking network of the Rothschilds, originating in 18th-century Europe, to the more recent global businesses like the Hinduja Group, diasporic families have been leading players in global transactions. At $450 billion, the annual economic output in the early 1990s of the 55 million overseas Chinese was estimated to be roughly equal to that of the 1.2 billion people in China itself (Seagrave 1995). According to Kotkin, 'global tribes' will 'increasingly shape the economic destiny of mankind' (1992, p.4). Sowell (1996) asserts that similar patterns of economic achievement of some ethnic groups in Australia, the United States, Asia and South America points to the importance of the cultural capital that they bring to these lands. However, studies that focus primarily on the capitalist character-istics of certain diasporas tend to de-emphasise the vast disparities in wealth, education and social status within these communities. Ray (2003) addresses some of the social disjunctures between the multi-generational, lower-caste Fiji Indian immigrants to Australia and upper-caste Hindus who arrive directly from India.

Commentators writing from cultural studies and postcolonial perspectives have tended to view diasporas as ranged against global and national structures of dominance – of the empire striking back. Jon Stratton and Ien Ang suggest that for the postcolonial immigrant to Britain 'what the diasporic position opens up is the possibility of developing a post-imperial British identity, one based explicitly on an acknowledgement and vindication of the "coming home" of the colonized Other' (1996, pp.383–4). The diasporic site becomes the cultural border between the country of origin and the country of residence – Homi Bhabha's 'third space' (1994). This is the zone of intense, cutting-edge creativity born out of the existential angst of the migrant who is neither here nor there. She is Abdul JanMoham-med's 'specular border intellectual' who, 'caught between two cultures . . . subjects the cultures to analytic scrutiny rather than combining them' (1992, p.97). Guillermo Gómez-Peña seeks to oppose 'the sinister cartography of the New World Order with the conceptual map of the New World Border – a great trans- and intercontinental border zone, a place in which no centers remain' (1996).

While the globally dominant Eurocentric cultural structures, particularly media con-glomerates, are being vastly strengthened, there has emerged over the last few decades a variety of voices from the South and from diasporas that attempt to present other world-views. Ella Shohat and Robert Stam have explored a 'constellation of oppositional strategies, which taken together have the potential of revolutionising audio-visual production and pedagogy' (1994, p.10). They refer to the aesthetics of resistance in the New Cinemas of Cuba, Brazil, Senegal and India as well as to diasporic films made in Canada, the United States and England. Just within the South Asian diaspora, one finds a list of accomplished authors that includes Hanif Kureishi (England), Salman Rushdie (India/England), Monica Ali (Bangladesh/England), V.S. Naipaul (Trinidad/England), Bharati Mukerjee (India/Canada/United States), Jhumpa Lahiri (England/United States), Michael Ondaatje (Sri Lanka/Canada), Shyam Selvadurai (Sri Lanka/Canada), Moez Vassanji (Kenya/Tanzania/Canada), Rohinton Mistry (India/Canada), Anita Desai (India/Canada), Anita Rau Badami (India/Canada) and Cyril Dabydeen (Guyana/Canada). Such diasporic artists appear to be at the cutting edge of modernity and cultural life in their countries of settlement. But whereas they do provide other ways of viewing the world, they do not all present a stance that actively resists dominant global discourses.

Diasporic media

The role of ethnic media in global communication flows is steadily growing in importance; the transnational ethnic-based commercial broadcasting infrastructure is integral to the increasingly global ethnic economy. Advertising on ethnic radio and television is viewed by niche marketers as a way to reach growing minority populations in a time of fragmenting audiences. The largest Spanish-language US network, Univisión, 'owns 11 stations and has 19 affiliates, [it] is also carried on 740 cable systems and is seen by 92 percent of Hispanic households in 162 markets across the United States' (Collins 1996, p.C6; also see Dávila 2001). With the availability of new communication technologies, diasporas are able to obtain cultural materials with growing ease from other parts of the world. Governments, on their part, are finding it increasingly difficult to compel them to assimilate minorities into the dominant national culture.

The relatively small and widely scattered nature of communities they serve have encouraged diasporic media to seek out the most efficient and cost-effective means of communication. Technologies that allow for narrowcasting to target specific audiences rather than those that provide the means for mass communication have generally been favoured. Ethnic media have frequently been at the leading edge of technology adoption due to the particular challenges they face in reaching their audiences. Marie Gillespie notes about the Indian community in Southall, England, that many families obtained VCRs as early as 1978 'well before most households in Britain' (1995, p.79).

Whereas governments in developing and developed countries have expressed fears that DBS would erode their sovereignty by transmitting foreign programming to their populations in unregulated manners, this technology is providing remarkable opportunities for diasporic communities. Ethnic broadcasters, previously having limited access to space on the electromagnetic spectrum in northern countries, are finding much greater options opening up for them through DBS. For example, France's main broadcast authority, the Conseil Supérieur de l'Audiovisuel, was actively encouraged by a centre-right government to exclude Arabic stations from licensed cable networks. The response of a significant number of Maghrebi immigrant families was to subscribe to DBS services which provide them programming from Arab countries from across the Mediterranean Sea:

> In the autumn of 1995, a survey conducted for the European satellite company Eutelsat indicated that 21 percent of Arabic-speaking households in France had invested in satellite receivers, compared with 4 percent of the general population. A year later, the number of Arabic-speaking households with satellite dishes was believed to have doubled. (Hargreaves & Mahdjoub 1997, p.461)

Diasporic programming using this technology has grown exponentially in the last few years, well ahead of many mainstream broadcasters. Even as mainstream networks in Europe were making plans to introduce digital broadcasting, the Arab-owned and operated Orbit TV in Rome had begun by 1994 to provide extensive programming via DBS to Arab communities both in Europe and the Middle East. One of the most fascinating uses of DBS technology in the Middle Eastern context is MED-TV, a Kurdish satellite television station (Hassanpour 2003). This is a case of a diaspora within and without the divided homeland attempting to sustain itself and to counter forceful suppression with the use of communications technology. MED-TV faces resistance not only from governments of various states straddling Kurdistan, but also from antiterrorist police forces in the UK, Belgium and Germany.

There have emerged several diasporic DBS-based networks serving Asian diasporas. The Chinese Television Network, headquartered in Hong Kong, has been broadcasting to East Asia, Australia, the Pacific Islands and the United States since 1994. Hong Kong's Television Broadcasts International 'reaches into several Asian markets and to Chinese communities just about everywhere' (Berfield 1997, p.31). The London-based Chinese Channel's programs are received in the UK and in continental Europe. India's state-run network Doordarshan has taken its International Channel to over 40 countries, and Zee TV has emerged as a very popular global Indian network in recent years (Thussu 2000, pp.197–99). Satellite networks in northern countries have realised the viability of ethnic channels and are making them an integral part of their services.

Either Univisión or Telemundo, the two largest Spanish-language networks in the US, is available on almost every cable system in Latin America. 'And in smaller, poorer countries, local television stations often simply tape stories from Univisión or Telemundo's nightly newscasts for their own use, which gives these American networks a degree of credibility and visibility unusual in the region' (Rohter 1996, p.4). The picture that Latin Americans see of American society in these North-South news flows is very different from that presented by mainstream US television and global TV news agencies. Univisión and Telemundo adhere to Latin American news values that favour greater analysis than that offered by mainstream American television.

Transnational communities are also making extensive use of online services. The Internet seems especially suited to the needs of diasporic communities. The global electronic network is allowing for relatively easy connections for members of communities residing in various continents. As opposed to the broadcast model of communication which, apart from offering limited access to minority groups, is linear, hierarchical and capital intensive, online media allow relatively easier access and are non-linear, largely non-hierarchical and relatively cheap. The ability to exchange messages with individuals on the other side of the planet and to have access to community information almost instantaneously changes the dynamics of diaspora, allowing for qualitatively and quantitatively enhanced linkages. As the number of language scripts and translation capabilities of online software grows, an increasing number of non-English speakers are drawn to the medium.

Post-colonial groups as well as older diasporas such as Jews and the Roma are communicating inter-continentally through online networks. The content of their websites largely consists of cultural, heritage, genealogical and religious information. Availability of the technology in developing countries is lagging far behind industrialised ones. Consequently, members of diasporic groups in the North are the most active in producing cultural resources on the Web. A primary motivation on the part of immigrant communities seems to be survival in the face of the overwhelming output of the dominant culture and the limitations of their own access to the cultural industries in countries of settlement.

There appears to be an attempt by diasporic participants in cyberspace to create a virtual community that supposedly eliminates the distances that separate them in the real world. The global dispersion from the home country over a period of several generations is also seemingly reversed by bringing together disparate members of the ethnic group to interact in an electronic 'chat room'. Time and space are erased in this scenario to reconstitute the community and to exchange cultural knowledge held in the diaspora. News groups such as soc.culture.sierraleone, soc.culture.jewish and alt.religion.zoroastrianism allow for subscribers, most of whom tend to be of the particular ethnic, cultural or religious backgrounds, to communicate from any place where they have access to the Internet. Discussions range on topics that include culture, literature, entertainment, politics and current events in the countries of origin and settlement.

One is tempted to view the virtual reassembling of global diasporas within electronic chat rooms; but this conceit belies the reality of the vastly differing levels of access enjoyed by members of communities as well as the inability of the individual newsgroups to support the coherence of more than a handful of discussions and discussants. Ackah and Newman (2003) draw our attention to the continued importance of travel and first-hand human contact in the lives of diasporas, criticising the tendency to eliminate space completely and to locate transnational communities exclusively within cyberspace. Despite the availability of transnational satellite TV services available to various diasporic groups, Sun (2002) and Cunningham and Nguyen (2003) indicate that significant numbers of potential viewers are not subscribing to them. The primary barriers seem to be the accessibility to the services and subscription costs.

Globalisation from below

Richard Falk has distinguished between 'globalisation-from-above' and 'globalisation-from-below'. He identifies the former as reflecting 'the collaboration between leading states and the main agents of capital formation' (1993, p.39). At the inter-governmental tier, international policy and legislation that governs other forms of transnational communication is shaped and policed. Bodies such as the UN, WTO, ITU and WIPO operate at this level. Transnational corporations are also major participants in the globalisation of communication. They include international communications players such as global news agencies, giant advertising companies and media and telecommunications corporations, as well as non-communications global firms that are engaged in massive cross-border information flows.

'Globalisation-from-below' is carried out mainly by organisations that do not have strong links with governments or large corporations. Examples include transnational civil society bodies like Amnesty International and Greenpeace and relief agencies such as the International Committee for the Red Cross and Médecins Sans Frontières. Academic and professional associations, religious organisations, diasporic groups, etc, also participate in globalisation-from-below by developing lateral communication links between members in various parts of the world. They may not directly oppose international governmental activities or transnational corporations, but they are nevertheless distinct from them.[3]

Instead of dwelling on physically reversing historical migrations, much of the cultural production of diasporas involves the creation of imaginative space alongside existing mappings. In the face of the homogenising forces of globalisation, diasporas, as deterritorialised nations, are seeking ways of 'reterritorialising' and 're-embedding' their identities in other imaginings of space (Lull 1995, p.159). Displaced from their homelands, they find that 'Ethnicity is the necessary place or space' (Hall 1997, p.184) from which they can speak to counteract dominant discourses. Hall views this process as operating 'on the terrain of "the global postmodern" ' (p.184), which 'is an extremely contradictory space' (p.187): whereas he acknowledges the danger of extreme nationalism in ethnic assertion he also identifies the immense opportunities for the empowerment of the local, in contrast to the polarised scenario of Benjamin Barber's 'jihad vs. McWorld' (1995).

Notwithstanding the predictions of the declining influence of borders under pressures of globalisation, the spaces of nation-states largely continue to remain exclusive. But diasporas present a significant challenge to this territoriality by seeking to produce their own interstitial spaces that link national and transnational milieus. They make connections between the local and the global, between the colonial and the post-colonial.

The cultural power of British imperialism has been such that African and Asian children being educated in many former colonies tend to know more about the fauna and flora of England than that of their own countries. They are steeped in the details of British history. The old colonial capital of London remains central and the rest peripheral in many minds around the Commonwealth. But this imaginative geography is being increasingly challenged in the contemporary cultural production of diasporas. Claudia Egerer gives the example of the writing of Hanif Kureishi, who was born in England and has Pakistani ancestry:

> Kureishi's London is a city in which the geography of the colonial past is superimposed on the modern English capital, producing its postcolonial present. This London is a hybrid city where the local and the global co-exist uneasily, a locality saturated with contradictory meanings that escape easy appropriation and which as such may well serve to 'produce new forms of knowledge, new modes of differentiation, new sites of power'.[4] This London – no longer the metropolis of imperial England and not yet a postnational, global city – may serve as a metaphor for the power of transformation engendered by the population movements ultimately set in motion by colonialism. (Egerer 2001, p.16)

Whether diasporic cultural workers are involved in the complete rearrangement of dominant cultural mappings is debateable, since Eurocentric worldviews still remain globally hegemonic. But whereas diasporas' imaginings of space do not necessarily displace the dominant geography, what emerges is the coexistence of a multiplicity of cultural cartographies supported by vibrant bodies of literature as well as other intellectual and artistic forms.

The contemporary 'New World' is also the site of diasporic reimaginings. Stuart Hall presents another way in which colonial space is transformed in the 'territory' of Caribbean 'Third (New World) cinema':

> The Third, 'New World' presence, is not so much power, as ground, place, territory. It is the juncture-point where the many cultural tributaries meet, the 'empty' land (the European colonisers emptied it) where strangers from every other part of the globe collided. None of the people who now occupy the islands – black, brown, white, African, European, American, Spanish, French, East Indian, Chinese, Portuguese, Jew, Dutch – originally 'belonged' there. It is the space where creolisations and assimilations and syncreticisms were negotiated. (Hall 2000, p.30)

Caribbean film, reflecting and itself being a site of hybridity, becomes a cultural engine that re-maps the spaces previously marked by imperialism. Hall emphasises that the heterogeneity expressed here speaks not only against colonialism's hierarchical and essentialist human geography but also stands in contrast to that notion of diaspora which necessarily includes a return to the 'original' homeland, a dream that usually involves the displacement of other peoples (p.31).

Migrant communities endeavour to make homes (even if 'temporarily') in milieus that are away from the home(land). John Wise (2000) asserts that the marking out of a space as one's home involves the infusion of that place with one's own rhythms. (Re)territorialisation occurs through sounds and movement – cadencies and action. The languages, accents and rituals spoken and performed in a space establish its cultural connections to its occupants and give it an identity. Diasporas (re)create home by instilling such resonance into the spaces they find themselves in: they do it with their languages, customs, art forms, arrangement of objects, and ideas. Their media, especially electronic media, reterritorialise the diaspora through the resonance of electromagnetic frequencies. However, the milieus that diasporas seek to create are not bounded by the borders of nation-states – their rhythms resonate transnationally to mark out non-terrestrial spaces that stretch out inter-continentally.

Such 'supraterritoriality' (Scholte 1996) of diaspora is created and sustained by imaginatively transforming a milieu: it is not a physical place but an existential location dependent continually on the resonance of cultural practices. Diasporas account for space as an existential location as they seek to redefine and transform their existence from under the historical conditions of colonialism and/or the current exigencies of globalisation-from-above. These dynamics of spatialisation are imaginative; they usually do not involve the appropriation of territory but they necessarily engage in the rethinking of dominant cartographies. The diaspora exists virtually in the relationships maintained in a transnational milieu, held together by and in the intercontinental ' "space of flows" – in mass media, telecommunications, computer connections and the like – [which] is a realm where religions, nations, classes, genders, races, sexualities, generations and so on continuously overlap and interrelate to produce complex and shifting identities and affiliations' (Scholte 1996, p.597).

But diasporic space is not monologic. Watching live television from the homeland does not automatically suspend time and space, as Asu Aksoy and Kevin Robins (2003) demonstrate about the viewers of Turkish satellite television in England. Diasporic media networks hardly negate the day-to-day existence in a location where one also interacts with other cultures and consumes local media content. Santianni (2003) explores how diasporic Tibetan Buddhist media deliberately seek to create solidarity outside the ethnic community. Hybridity, in its multifarious forms, constantly challenges the notions of essentialism and exclusivity that often tend to accompany the traditional conceptualisation of diaspora. We also need to recognise that the mere existence of diasporic media also does not mean that all of a group's members, or even a majority of them, have access to them or are interested in using them (Ackah & Newman 2003).

Diaspora in international communication frameworks

Hamid Mowlana's publication in 1986 of *Global Information and World Communication* reflected an effort to provide a comprehensive examination of international communication – its manifestation and its study. It posited three classes of actors in international communication in a table describing relationships between sources and recipients of information; they were 'Governmental', 'Transnational' (corporations), and 'Individual' (p.16). 'Ethnics and minorities' were listed among the objects of the impact of information flow, not their subjects or initiators. The expanded second edition of the book reproduced the same schema (1997, p.37), but also provided a number of 'Research Questions for the Twenty-First Century' which included the following one:

> Has communication research a role to play in understanding the dynamics of modern world systems in terms of studying the transnational actors, international division of labor, immigrants, refugees, and individual economic, political, cultural, and military elites whose actions and reactions bypass national boundaries and in themselves formally and informally constitute new leases of power, bargaining, and negotiations? (p.231)

Mowlana also asked: 'how will the modern nation-state systems with their secular-oriented national sovereign signifier cope with emerging religious political ideologies such as Islam which is based on universal community or *ummah*?' (p.230). This is a query that he has continued to pursue in his subsequent work, including that published in the current issue of this journal.

Mention of 'the great diaspora of the labor market' had also appeared, albeit all too briefly, in Armand Mattelart's *Mapping World Communication* (1994, p.232) in the context of news reporting of cultural conflict in northern countries. Diasporic communication has not yet become a mainstay in international communication texts, with the exception of occasional sections of chapters (Thussu 1998, 2000). Nevertheless, there has been emerging since the 1990s a corpus of monographs and edited collections dealing with the use of media by transnational communities (Naficy 1993, 2001; Gillespie 1995; Kolar-Panov 1997; Eickleman & Anderson 1999; Cunningham & Sinclair 2000; Bunt 2000, 2003; Sun 2002; Karim 2003). Naren Chitty's article in this issue [of the original publication] gives an integral place to 'ethno-historical collectivities' in his matrix framework of international communication.

Mattelart had encouraged reflection on an 'international third space' – 'a place between intermarket logics and interstate logics that mediate respectively the pragmatism of the merchant and the *Realpolitik* of the prince fettered by the reason of state' (1994, p.234). He referred in this to a dimension in global relations that is distinct from that occupied by activities of nation-states or international bodies as well as those of commercial interests. It is conceivably occupied by transnational civil society organisations as well as diasporas. However, Mattelart seems naïve in implying that *all* commercial relations, not only those of large corporations, would be absent from the global third space. As we have seen above, diasporas use media and communications technologies developed and largely controlled by big and small business. Furthermore, diasporas that may have been part of labour migrations often produce commercial concerns, some of transnational scope.

Some states are working to nurture the cohesiveness of transnational diasporas for economic and foreign policy reasons. Governments such as those of India and Israel have developed elaborate policies to engage with their respective global diasporas and have designated cabinet ministers to oversee their implementation. Sun shows how Beijing uses national symbolism and overseas broadcasts to engender a 'transnational China' (2002, pp.183–216). Hassanpour (2003) has demonstrated how the Kurdish nation exists transnationally via satellite despite the absence of a state's territorial space. 'White Rhodesians' who live in Zimbabwe and in diaspora continue to hold together a common conversation through Internet chat groups (King 2003), long after the disappearance of their state.

The study of international communication cannot disregard the growing strength of diasporic information flows and their impact on the system of nation-states. Even though the latter is far from fading away, it is undergoing significant transformation. Contemporary technologies of travel and communication have vastly enhanced the agency of diasporic actors in international communications. Their liminal placements in the interstices within and among nation-states is engendering innovativeness and creativity that is urging them to be at the leading edge of technology adoption and content production. The transnational spaces they have created are leading to a self-reassessment on the part of the nation-state.

No contemporary analytical framework of international communication that seeks to be comprehensive can legitimately exclude diasporas (or transnational civil society actors). Diasporas share with nations the constitutive (albeit imaginary) characteristic of ethnicity, and as transnations have augmented the cast of players in international relations. They do not replace nation-states but locate themselves within and across them – they intersect without necessarily splitting. Diasporic communication challenges other forms of global communication without seeking to overturn them; indeed, it is dependent on their infrastructures. The theory of diaspora is still under formulation. Its study offers an exciting interdisciplinary area for scholars of global flows of information since transnationalism is playing an important role in the contemporary evolution of the ways in which people interact with each other across countries and continents.

Notes

1   Of course, the more powerful states have greater abilities to maintain national control vis-à-vis international organisations than the weaker ones.

2   Asu Aksoy and Kevin Robins critique the tendency of the concept of 'imaginary community' to essentialise diasporas (2003, pp.92–94, 101–104).

3   Falk tends to limit his conception of 'globalisation-from-below' to groups actively involved in countering the influence of governments and large corporations, but I would like to extend this category also to those who do not necessarily do so.

4   Quotation from Homi Bhabha (1994, p.120).

References

Ackah, W. & Newman, J. (2003) 'Ghanaian Seventh Day Adventists on and offline: Problematising the virtual communities discourse', in K.H. Karim (ed) *The Media of Diaspora*, London: Routledge, pp.203–14.

Aksoy, A. & Robins, K. (2003) 'Banal transnationalism: The difference that television makes', in K.H. Karim (ed) *The Media of Diaspora*, London: Routledge, pp.89–104.

Alia, V. (2003) 'Scattered voices, global vision: Indigenous peoples and the new media nation', in K.H. Karim (ed) *The Media of Diaspora*, London: Routledge, pp.36–50.

Anderson, B. (1983) *Imagined Communities: Reflections on the Origin and Spread of Nationalism*, London: Verso.

Appadurai, A. (1996) *Modernity at Large: Cultural Dimensions of Globalization*, Minneapolis: University of Minnesota.

Barber, B. (1995) *Jihad vs. McWorld*, New York: Times Books/Random House.

Berfield, S. (1997) 'Global TV: Still local, after all', *World Press Review*, February, 31.

Bhabha, H. (1990) 'DissemiNation: Time, narrative, and the margins of the modern nation', in H. Bhabha (ed) *Nation and Narration*, London: Routledge, pp.291–322.

Bhabha, H. (1994) *The Location of Culture*, London: Routledge.

Blaut, J.M. (1993) *The Colonizer's Model of the World: Geographical Diffusionism and Eurocentric History*, New York: Guilford.

Bunt, G. (2000) *Virtually Islamic: Computer-mediated Communication and Cyber-Islamic Environments*, Cardiff: University of Wales Press.

Bunt, G. (2003) *Islam in the Digital Age: E-jihad, Online Fatwas and Cyber Islamic Environments*, London: Pluto Press.

Chabram-Dernersesian, A. (1994) 'Chicana! Rican? No, Chicana-Riqueña!: Refashioning the trans-national connection', in D. Goldberg (ed) *Multiculturalism: A Critical Reader*, Cambridge, MA: Basil Blackwell, pp.269–95.

Clifford, J. (1997) *Routes: Travel and Translation in the Late Twentieth Century*, Cambridge, MA: Harvard University Press.

Cohen, R. (1997) *Global Diasporas: An Introduction*, London: UCL Press/Routledge.

Collins, G. (1996) 'Advertising: Information resources takes aim at the ethnic market, and Nielsen', *New York Times*, 14 May, Section 3, p.3.

Cunningham, S. & Nguyen, T. (2003) 'Actually existing hybridity: Vietnamese diasporic music video', in K.H. Karim (ed) *The Media of Diaspora*, London: Routledge, pp. 119–32.

Cunningham, S. & Sinclair, J. (eds) (2000) *Floating Lives: The Media and Asian Diasporas*, St Lucia, Queensland: University of Queensland.

Dávila, A. (2001) *Latinos Inc.: The Marketing and Making of a People*, Berkeley: University of California Press.

De Santis, Heather (2003). 'Mi Programa es Su Programa: Tele/visions of a Spanish-language Diaspora in North America', in Karim H. Karim (ed.), *The Media of Diaspora* (London: Routledge), pp. 63–75.

Egerer, C. (2001) 'Ambivalent geographies: The exotic as domesticated Other', *Third Text*, 55, pp.15–28.

Eickleman, D. & Anderson, J. (eds) (1999) *New Media in the Muslim World: The Emergence of Public Sphere*, Bloomington & Indianapolis: Indiana University Press.

Falk, R. (1993) 'The making of global citizenship', in J. Brecher, J. Childs & J. Cutler (eds) *Global Visions: Beyond the New World Order*, Boston: South End Press, pp.39–50.

Gillespie, M. (1995) *Television, Ethnicity and Cultural Change*, London & New York: Routledge.

Gilroy, P. (1993) *The Black Atlantic: Modernity and Double Consciousness*, Cambridge, MA and London: Harvard University Press/Verso.

Gómez-Peña, G. (1996) *The New World Border*, New York: City Lights.

Hall, S. (1997) 'The local and the global: Globalization and ethnicity', in A. McClintock, A. Mufti & E. Shohat (eds) *Dangerous Liaisons: Gender, Nation, and Postcolonial Perspectives*, Minneapolis: University of Minnesota, pp.173–87.

Hall, S. (2000) 'Cultural identity and diaspora', in N. Mirzoeff (ed) *Diaspora and Visual Culture: Representing Africans and Jews*, London: Routledge, pp.21–33.

Hamelink, C. (1994) *The Politics of World Communication*, Thousand Oaks, CA: Sage.

Hargreaves, A.G. & Mahdjoub, D. (1997) 'Satellite television viewing among ethnic minorities in France', *European Journal of Communication*, 12:4, pp.459–77.

Hassanpour, A. (2003) 'Diaspora, homeland, and communication technologies', in K.H. Karim (ed) *The Media of Diaspora*, London: Routledge, pp.76–88.

Hobsbawm, E. (1990) *Nations and Nationalism since 1780*, Cambridge: Cambridge University Press.

JanMohamed, A.R. (1992) 'Wordliness-without-World, Homelessness-as-Home: Toward a definition of the specular border intellectual', in M. Sprinkler (ed) *Edward Said: A Critical Reader*, Oxford: Basil Blackwell, pp.96–120.

King, T. (2003) 'Rhodesians in hyperspace: The maintenance of a national and cultural identity', in K.H. Karim (ed) *The Media of Diaspora*, London: Routledge, pp.177–88.

Kolar-Panov, D. (1997) *Video, War and the Diasporic Imagination*, London and New York: Routledge.

Kolar-Panov, D. (2003) 'Video and Macedonians in Australia', in K.H. Karim (ed) *The Media of Diaspora*, London: Routledge, pp.105–18.

Kotkin, J. (1992) *Tribes: How Race, Religion, and Identity Determine Success in the New Global Economy*, New York: Random House.

Lull, J. (1995) *Media, Communication, Culture: A Global Approach*, New York: Columbia.

Mandaville, P. (2003) 'Communication and diasporic Islam: A virtual Ummah?' in K.H. Karim (ed) *The Media of Diaspora*, London: Routledge, pp.135–47.

Mattelart, A. (1994) *Mapping World Communication: War, Progress, Culture*, Minneapolis: University of Minnesota.

Mowlana, H. (1986) *Global Information and World Communication: New Frontiers in International Relations*, New York: Longman.

Mowlana, H. (1997) *Global Information and World Communication*, 2nd edition, Thousand Oaks, CA: Sage.

Naficy, H. (1993) *The Making of Exile Cultures: Iranian Television in Los Angeles*, Minneapolis: University of Minnesota.

Naficy, H. (2001) *An Accented Cinema: Exilic and Diasporic Filmmaking*, Princeton: Princeton University Press.

Ray, M. (2003) 'Nation, nostalgia and Bollywood: In the tracks of a twice-displaced community', in K.H. Karim (ed) *The Media of Diaspora*, London: Routledge, pp.21–35.

Renan, E. (1990) 'What is nation?' in H. Bhabha (ed) *Nation and Narration*, London: Routledge, pp.8–22.

Rohter, L. (1996) 'Broadcast news: In Spanish, it's another story', *New York Times*, 15 December, Section 4, pp.1, 6.

Safran, W. (1991) 'Diasporas in modern societies: Myths of homeland and return', *Diaspora*, 1:1, pp.83–99.

Said, E. (1978) *Orientalism*, New York: Vintage.

Santianni, M. (2003) 'The movement for a free Tibet: Cyberspace and the ambivalence of cultural translation', in K.H. Karim (ed) *The Media of Diaspora*, London: Routledge, pp.189–202.

Sassen, S. (1996) *Losing Control? Sovereignty in an Age of Globalization*, New York: Columbia University Press.

Scholte, J.A. (1996) 'The geography of collective identities in a globalizing world', *Review of International Political Economy*, 3:4, pp.565–607.

Seagrave, S. (1995) *Lords of the Rim*, New York: G.P. Putnam.

Shohat, E. & Stam, R. (1994) *Unthinking Eurocentrism: Multiculturalism and the Media*, London: Routledge.

Sowell, T. (1996) *Migrations and Cultures: A World View*, New York: Basic Books.

Smith, A.D. (1989) 'The origins of nations', *Ethnic and Racial Studies*, 12:3, pp.340–67.

Stratton, J. & Ang, I. (1996) 'On the impossibility of a global cultural studies: British cultural studies in an international frame', in D. Morley and K-H. Chen (eds) *Stuart Hall: Critical Dialogues in Cultural Studies*, London: Routledge, pp.361–91.

Sun, W. (2002) *Leaving China: Media, Migration and Transnational Imagination*, Oxford: Rowman and Littlefield.

Thussu, D.K. (ed.) (1998) *Electronic Empires: Global Media and Local Resistance*, London: Arnold.

Thussu, D.K. (2000) *International Communication – Continuity and Change*, London: Arnold.

Tölöyan, K. (1996) 'Rethinking diaspora(s): Stateless power in the transnational moment', *Diaspora*, 5:1, pp.3–86.

Tsaliki, L. (2003) 'Globalisation and hybridity: The construction of Greekness on the Internet', in K.H. Karim (ed) *The Media of Diaspora*, London: Routledge, pp.162–76.

Weyland, P. (1997) 'Gendered lives in global spaces', in A. Öncü & P. Weyland (eds) *Space, Culture and Power: New Identities in Globalizing Cities*, London: Zed, pp.82–97.

Wise, J.M. (2000) 'Home: Territory and identity', *Cultural Studies*, 14:2, pp.295–310.

Chapter 25

Koichi Iwabuchi

TAKING "JAPANIZATION" SERIOUSLY: CULTURAL GLOBALIZATION RECONSIDERED

N O ONE WOULD DENY Japan's status as a major economic power. While its power has been relatively undermined by a prolonged economic and financial slump since the early 1990s, this only serves to highlight Japan's tremendous economic influence in the world, particularly in Asia. As Japan has become the second biggest economic power in the world, its external influence has come to be discussed in terms of the export of Japanese management and industrial relations techniques and Japanese organizational cultures (e.g., Bratton 1992; Oliver and Wilkinson 1992; Thome and McAuley 1992; Elger and Smith 1994). Such discourses started in the 1970s, when many Western scholars advocated that the West should learn lessons from the Japanese economic success (e.g., Dore 1973; Vogel 1979). Although not exclusively representing post-Fordism, "Japanization" of industrial relations and organizational cultures was discussed specifically in the search for post-Fordist industrial models, whereby "Toyotism" for example, attracted much attention as a more flexible production system than Fordism (Lash and Urry 1994; Dohse, Jurgens, and Malsch 1985; Waters 1995, 82–85).

However, it was not until the late 1980s that the significance of Japan in the global culture market began attracting wider international academic and media attention. It was a time when Sony and Matsushita were buying out Hollywood film studios and the animation film *Akira* was a hit in the Western markets. In the English-language world, many books and articles have been published on Japanese animation, computer games, and the Japanese advance on Hollywood since that time (e.g., *Mediamatic* 1991; Wark 1991, 1994; Morley and Robins 1995; Schodt 1983, 1996; Levi 1996). The Sony Walkman has even been chosen for analysis, as the most appropriate example of a global cultural product, by a British Open University cultural studies textbook, itself prepared for global distribution (du Gay et al. 1997).

Certainly, the emergence of such discourses on the spread of Japanese cultural products in the world reflects the fact that Japanese media industries and cultural forms are playing a substantial role in global cultural flows. It seems that Japanese cultural power may finally match its economic dominance. Yet crucial questions remain unanswered: what kind of cultural power (if any) is conferred on Japan? and how similar or different is it from American cultural hegemony? In this chapter, I will present a theoretical consideration of the recent rise in Japanese cultural exports and will explore how that rise might be situated within the study of cultural globalization. Rather than seeing an easy comparison between Japanese cultural exports and "Americanization," or dismissing this phenomenon as merely frivolous, I will instead suggest that it offers some new and significant insights into understanding the decentered nature of transnational cultural power.

Culturally "odorless" commodities

Even if the cultural dimensions of Japan's global influence have not been widely discussed until recently, this does not mean that Japan did not have any cultural impact before then. Rather, the hitherto assumption of Japan's lack of cultural impact testifies to a discrepancy between actual cultural influence and perceived cultural presence. The cultural impact of a particular commodity is not necessarily experienced in terms of the cultural image of the exporting nation. For example, in the realm of audiovisual commodities, there is no doubt that Japan has been a dominant exporter of consumer technologies as well as animation and computer games. From VCRs, computer games, karaoke machines, and the Walkman, to the more recent appearance of digital video cameras, the prevalence of Japanese consumer electronics in the global marketplace is overwhelming. This development has been based upon the adage "First for consumers" expressed by Ibuka Masaru, founder of the Sony Corporation (quoted in Lardner 1987, 38). After the Second World War, freed from the obligation to devote its research and development energy to military purposes, and with the support of the Japanese government, the Japanese electronics industry successfully inverted the idea of "scientific or military research first." Instead, technological development would henceforth be propelled by consumer electronics (Forester 1993, 4).

Japanese consumer technologies certainly have had a tremendous impact on our everyday life, an impact which is, in a sense, more profound than that of Hollywood films. To use Jody Berland's (1992) term, these are "cultural technologies" that mediate between texts, spaces, and audiences. New cultural technologies open new possibilities for the consumption of media texts by audiences. In turn, by promoting the market-driven privatization of consumer needs and desires, new cultural technologies open up new ways for capital to accommodate itself to the emergent communication space in the service of individual consumer sovereignty. For example, VCRs have facilitated the transnational flow of videotape-recorded programs through both legal channels and illegal piracy. This has given consumers, especially those in developing countries whose appetites for information and entertainment have not been satisfied, access to diverse programs which have been officially banned. In response, governments have changed their policies from rigid restrictions on the flow of information and entertainment to more open, market-oriented controls—for example, the privatization of TV channels (Ganley and Ganley 1987; Boyd, Straubhaar, and Lent 1989; O'Regan 1991). On the whole, this development has consequently encouraged global centralization of the distribution and production of software, as well as facilitating the further spread of American software. Despite the fear of profits being skimmed off by piracy, VCRs have helped Hollywood open up new markets and find ways of exploiting new technologies through video rental and export of TV programs to newly privatized channels (see Gomery 1988; O'Regan 1992).

At the level of the consumer, Japanese electronic technologies have promoted strongly what Raymond Williams (1990, 26) has called "mobile privatization." These consumer technologies give people greater choice and mobility in their media consumption activities in domestic, private spaces. For example, while TV and radio made it possible for individuals in their own living rooms to experience and connect with what was happening in remote places, the Sony Walkman conversely promoted the intrusion of private media into public spaces. vcrs allowed people to "time shift"—to record tv programs and watch them at a later, more suitable time. It is an interesting question why such individualistic, private technologies have been developed and have flourished in a supposedly group-oriented society such as Japan. Kogawa (1984, 1988) coined the term "electronic individualism" to characterize Japanese social relations and argued that Japanese collectivity is increasingly based upon electronic communication and therefore becoming more precarious. Although Kogawa views the contemporary Japanese situation somewhat pessimistically, he points out that it offers the dual possibilities of the emancipation of individuals via technologies and, alternatively, the sophisticated control of individuals. Indeed, as Chambers argues, the consumption of one of the most successful Japanese cultural technologies of the past decades—the Sony Walkman—is an ambivalent "cultural activity" that sways between "autonomy and autism" (1990, 2). Such an activity can be seen as a form of escapism that makes individuals feel a sense of atomized freedom from the constraints of a rigidly controlled society. It also has the possibility of substituting a privatized "micro-narrative" for collective "grand-narratives" (3). Speaking of the Chinese, Chow (1993, 398) argues that listening to a Walkman is "a 'silent' sabotage of the technology of collectivization" (for a more thorough analysis of the Walkman, see du Gay et al. 1997).

Despite the profound influence of Japanese consumer technologies on the cultural activities of our everyday life, they have tended not to be talked about in terms of a Japanese cultural presence. Hoskins and Mirus (1988) employ the notion of "cultural discount" to explain the fact that even though certain Japanese films and literature have had a Western following, the outflow of Japanese popular cultural products (particularly to Western countries) has been disproportionately small. Hoskins and Mirus describe "cultural discount" as occurring when "a particular program rooted in one culture and thus attractive in that environment will have a diminished appeal elsewhere as viewers find it difficult to identify with the style, values, beliefs, institutions and behavioral patterns of the material in question" (500). Cultural prestige, Western hegemony, the universal appeal of American popular culture, and the prevalence of the English language are no doubt advantageous to Hollywood. By contrast, Japanese language is not widely spoken outside Japan and Japan is supposedly obsessed with its own cultural uniqueness. Given the high cultural discount of Japanese films and tv programs, Hoskins and Mirus argue, Japanese cultural export tends to be limited to "culturally neutral" consumer technologies, whose country of origin has nothing to do with "the way [that they work] and the satisfaction [that a consumer] obtains from usage" (503).

Apparently, the notion of "cultural discount" does not satisfactorily explain a consumer's cultural preference for audiovisual media texts such as tv programs. Foreign programs, for example, can be seen as more attractive because they are "exotic," "different," or less "boring." The cultural difference embodied in foreign products can also be seen as less of a threat to local culture precisely because the imported products are conceived as "foreign," while those originating from culturally proximate countries might be perceived as more threatening (O'Regan 1992). The legacy of Japanese imperialism in Asia is a case in point. More importantly, Hoskins and Mirus's argument is highly West-centric. They are not aware that Japanese tv programs and popular music have been exported to East and Southeat Asia, if rarely to Europe or North America, though we also should be cautious not to mechanically explain this trend by employing "cultural discount" or "cultural proximity" in an essentialist manner (see Straubhaar 1991). I will return to this question in later chapters. For the moment, though, I will elaborate more on Hoskins and Mirus's discussion of the nature of Japan's major cultural export to the world (including Western markets).

Notwithstanding the argument about Japanese cultural export outlined above, the term "culturally neutral" seems misleading, too. The influence of cultural products on everyday life, as we have seen, cannot be culturally neutral. Any product has the cultural imprint of the producing country, even if it is not recognized as such. I would suggest that the major audiovisual products Japan exports could be better characterized as the "culturally odorless" three C's: consumer technologies (such as VCRs, karaoke, and the Walkman); comics and cartoons (animation); and computer/video games. I use the term *cultural odor* to focus on the way in which cultural features of a country of origin and images or ideas of its national, in most cases stereotyped, way of life are associated *positively* with a particular product in the consumption process. Any product may have various kinds of cultural association with the country of its invention. Such images are often related to exoticism, such as the image of the Japanese samurai or the geisha girl. Here, however, I am interested in the moment when the image of the contemporary lifestyle of the country of origin is strongly and affirmatively called to mind as the very appeal of the product, when the "cultural odor" of cultural commodities is evolved. The way in which the cultural odor of a particular product becomes a "fragrance"—a socially and culturally acceptable smell—is not determined simply by the consumer's perception that something is "made in Japan." Neither is it necessarily related to the material influence or quality of the product. It has more to do with widely disseminated symbolic images of the country of origin. The influence of McDonald's throughout the world, for example, can be discerned in terms of the bureaucratization and standardization of food; and the principles governing the operation of McDonald's can also be extended to other everyday life activities such as education and shopping (Ritzer 1993). However, no less important to the international success of McDonald's is its association with an attractive image of "the American way of life" (e.g., Frith 1982, 46; Featherstone 1995, 8). McDonald's, of course, does not inherently represent "America." It is a discursive construction of what is "America" that confers on McDonald's its powerful association with "Americanness."

Sony's Walkman is an important cultural commodity that has influenced everyday life in various ways. For this reason, du Gay et al. (1997) chose it as the cultural artifact most appropriate for a case study using the multilayered analyses of cultural studies. While taking note of the social constructedness of any national image, Sony's Walkman, they argue, may signify "Japaneseness" because of its miniaturization, technical sophistication, and high quality. Yet, I suggest, although such signs of "Japaneseness" are analytically important, they are not especially relevant to the appeal of the Walkman at a consumption level. The use of the Walkman does not evoke images or ideas of a Japanese lifestyle, even if consumers know it is made in Japan and appreciate "Japaneseness" in terms of its sophisticated technology. Unlike American commodities, "Japanese consumer goods do not seek to sell on the back of a Japanese way of life" (Featherstone 1995, 9), and they lack any influential "idea of Japan" (Wee 1997).

The cultural odor of a product is also closely associated with racial and bodily images of a country of origin. The three C's I mentioned earlier are cultural artifacts in which a country's bodily, racial, and ethnic characteristics are erased or softened. The characters of Japanese animation and computer games for the most part do not look "Japanese." Such non-Japaneseness is called *mukokuseki*, literally meaning "something or someone lacking any nationality," but also implying the erasure of racial or ethnic characteristics or a context, which does not imprint a particular culture or country with these features.[1] Internationally acclaimed Japanese animation director Oshii Mamoru suggests that Japanese animators and cartoonists unconsciously choose not to draw "realistic" Japanese characters if they wish to draw attractive characters (Oshii, Itō, and Ueno 1996). In Oshii's case, the characters tend to be modeled on Caucasian types. Consumers of and audiences for Japanese animation and games, it can be argued, may be aware of the Japanese origin of these commodities, but those texts barely feature "Japanese bodily odor" identified as such.

Japan goes global: Sony and animation

While the propensity of Japanese animators to make their products non-Japanese points to how a Western-dominated cultural hierarchy governs transnational cultural flows in the world,[2] Japan's hitherto invisible and odorless cultural presence in the world has become more and more conspicuous since the late 1980s. On the one hand, Japan has become one of the main players in the development of media globalization, by virtue of the fact that its manufacturers of consumer technologies have extended their reach into the software production business during the 1990s. It was Sony's purchase of Columbia in 1989, and Matsushita's purchase of MCA (Universal) in 1990, which dramatized the ascent of Japanese global media conglomerates through the merger of hardware and software. There was considerable reaction from within the United States against these buyouts, including claims that the Japanese were "buying into America's soul" (Morley and Robins 1995, 150). In the film *Black Rain*, Japanese costar Takakura Ken replies to Michael Douglas's antagonistic remark about Japanese economic expansion into the United States: "Music and movies are all your culture is good for. . . . We make the machines" (quoted in Morley and Robins 1995, 159). This comment apparently displays a generalized disdain by American media industries for the Japanese fascination with technology: Creative software production should not be controlled by mindless hardware manufacturers.

However, this kind of expression of the creative supremacy of American popular culture has gradually proved to be an American fantasy rather than a reflection of what is really happening. Although Matsushita retreated from Hollywood and Sony at first struggled to make a profit (see Negus 1997), Sony demonstrates that Japanese transnational corporations can make it in Hollywood, as Columbia finally achieved phenomenal box-office sales in 1997. Moreover, apart from the takeover of Hollywood by Japanese companies (as well as by European companies), there is good evidence to confirm that the era in which "the media are American" (Tunstall 1977) has ended. Japanese consumer technologies have become so sophisticated that we can talk about a "technoculture" in which "cultural information and the technical artifact seem to merge" (Wark 1991, 45). More significantly, Japan is not only increasing its capital and market share in the audiovisual global market but also its cultural presence on the global scene through the export of culturally odorless products other than consumer technologies. Japanese animation and computer games have attained a certain degree of popularity and become recognized as very "Japanese" in a positive and affirmative sense in Western countries as well as in non-Western countries. They embody a new aesthetic, emanating in large part from Japanese cultural inventiveness, and capture the new popular imagination (Wark 1994; Schodt 1983, 1996).

Since the release of Ōtomo Katsuhiro's hugely popular animation film *Akira* (1988), the quality and attraction of "Japanimation" has been acknowledged by the American market. In November 1995 the animated film *The Ghost in the Shell* was shown simultaneously in Japan, America, and Great Britain. Its video sales, according to *Billboard* (24 August 1996), reached No.1 on the video charts in the United States. According to a *Los Angeles Times* report, the export value of Japanese animation and comics to the American market amounted to $75 million in 1996 (Manabe 1997). Furthermore, three Japanese manufacturers, Nintendo, Sega and Sony, dominate the market for computer games. The popularity of Japanese game software is exemplified by the popularity of such games as Super Mario Brothers, Sonic, and Pokémon. As a director of Nintendo pointed out, according to one survey, Mario is a better-known character among American children than Mickey Mouse (Akurosu Henshūshitsu 1995, 41–42). The huge success of Pokémon in the global market since 1998 further persuades us to make a serious scholarly investigation into Japanese cultural export. Pokémon's penetration into global markets even exceeds that of Mario.

As of June 2000 Pokémon game software had sold about 65 million copies (22 million outside Japan) and trading-cards about 4.2 billion (2.4 billion outside Japan); the animation series had been broadcast in fifty-one countries; the first feature film had been shown in thirty-three countries, and its overseas box-office record had amounted to $176 million; and there had also been about 12,000 purchases of character merchandise (8,000 outside Japan) (Hatakeyama and Kubo 2000). These figures unambiguously show that Pokémon has become truly a "made-in-Japan" global cultural artifact.

These examples certainly illustrate the rise of Japanese cultural products in world markets, particularly within the domain of animated software. Accordingly, we have observed an increasingly narcissistic interest in articulating the distinctive "Japaneseness" of cultural products in 1990s Japan. As early as 1992, for example, the popular monthly magazine *DENiM* ran a feature article on made-in-Japan global commodities that began "Who said that Japan only imports superior foreign culture and commodities and has nothing originally Japanese which has a universal appeal? Now Japanese customs, products and systems are conquering the world!" (Sekai ga maneshita Nipponryū 1992, 143). In the article, global Japanese exports included food, fashion, service industry offerings, animation, and computer games (see also Noda 1990). This concern was further advanced in a book on Japanese global commodities entitled *Sekai shōhin no tsukurikata: Nihon media ga sekai o seishita hi* (The making of global commodities: The day Japanese media conquered the world). The main purpose of the book was to reconsider Japanese culture in terms of its influence in the world: "It is a historical rule that an economically powerful nation produces in its heyday global popular culture whose influences match its economic power. Such was the case with the British Empire, Imperial France, Weimar Germany and the United States of the 1950s and 1960s. What, then, has Japan of the 1980s produced for the world? Has Japan produced anything that is consumed globally and influences the lifestyle of world consumers?" (Akurosu Henshūshitsu 1995, 6). Consumer technologies, particularly the Walkman, have long been regarded as representative of Japanese global cultural commodities. The editors of the above volume remark that they originally coined the term *global commodities* in 1988 in order to articulate the phenomenal global popularity of the Walkman, but that there has been a proliferation of Japanese global commodities since then (Akurosu Henshūshitsu 1995, 6–8). Made-in-Japan global commodities discussed in the book include not only Japanese hardware commodities such as the Walkman, instant cameras, or VCRs, but also "software" cultural products such as animation and computer games, and that even the system of producing pop idols, a process that has been predominantly exported to Asia, has come more into the foreground.[3]

Euphoria concerning the global dissemination of animation and computer games prompted Japanese commentators to confer a specific Japanese "fragrance" on these cultural products. The emergence of obsessively devoted fans of Japanese animation in both Europe and the United States whose craze for Japanese animation makes them wish they had been born in Japan has been often covered by the Japanese media. Many images of Western fans playing at being would-be Japanese animation characters, wearing the same costumes and make-up, have been presented in popular Japanese magazines as evidence of the "Japanization" of the West (e.g., Nihonbunka kosupure Amerika yushutsu 1996; Amerika nimo otaku ga daihassei 1996; Furansu de kosupure kontesuto 1997; Otaku no sekai kara mejā e 1997).[4] Okada Toshio, the most eloquent spokesperson for the global popularity of Japanese animation and computer games, further argues that Japanese animated culture and imagery has come to evoke, to a certain degree, a sense of Western yearning for "Japan" (1996, 52–56; see also Eikoku ga mitometa Nihonbunka 1996, 30–31). Comparing the passionate Western consumption of Japanese animation to Japan's and his own yearning, via the consumption of American popular culture, for "America,"—the nation of freedom, science, and democracy—Okada (1995, 43) proudly argues that to those Western fans, Japan "looks a more cool country" than the United States. More recently, the Pokémon phenomenon has provoked an increasing Japanese interest in associating its global appeal with Japanese symbolic power. Japanese scholars have observed that, increasingly, American children who love Pokémon believe Japan must be a cool nation if it is capable of producing such wonderful characters, imaginaries, and commodities (Kamo 2000; Sakurai 2000).

Is the world being "Japanized"?

It remains a contentious issue, however, what power status (image of power) the global spread of Japanese animations and computer games may have granted to Japan. How do these products evoke a distinctively Japanese way of life to consumers and audiences? The cultural presence of a foreign country is often interpreted as a threat to national identity and/or to the national interest, or as a sign of the foreign country's status as an object of yearning in the recipient country. In either case, it marks the foreign country's cultural power. Here, the notion of Americanization and cultural imperialism has long informed discussion of the cultural imposition of a dominant country over others. As Said (1994, 387) argues, "Rarely before in human history has there been so massive an intervention of force and ideas from one culture to another as there is today from America to the rest of the world." The unprecedented global reach of American power is all-inclusive, a complex of political, economic, military, and cultural hegemony. In the Cold War era, it is well known that the United States strategically disseminated an American model of a modern, affluent, open, and democratic society to win the ideological battle against the Communist bloc. Mass media and consumer culture were the major vehicles of "Americanization."

American political scientist Joseph Nye (1990, 188) argues that a significant factor that confers on the United States a global hegemony is its "soft co-optic power," that is, the power of "getting others to want what you want" through symbolic power resources such as media and consumer culture: "If [a dominant country's] culture and ideology are attractive, others will more willingly follow" (32). In contrast, Nye contends that Japan is a one-dimensional economic power and its consumer commodities, no matter how globally disseminated, still lack an associated "appeal to a broader set of values" (194)—and thus are culturally odorless.

This is not simply due to the fact that since the end of World War II, Japan has had no manifest policy of political, military, or ideological/cultural exertion of its transnational power. More importantly, what is implied here is that there is an inherent difficulty in comparing the advent of Japanese animations or computer games to an "Americanization" paradigm as suggested earlier. This is not to say that Japanese animation does not embody any specific cultural characteristics that originate in what we call "Japanese culture." American fans of Japanese animations are inescapably "dependent upon Japanese culture itself" (Newitz 1995, 12; Kamo 2000).[5] But to interpret the global success of Pokémon and other Japanese cultural products as the mirror image of the global process of "Americanization" is fallacious. Looking beneath the surface of these celebratory views of Western perceptions of the coolness of Japanese culture, we find a basic contradiction: the international spread of mukokuseki popular culture from Japan simultaneously articulates the universal appeal of Japanese cultural products and the disappearance of any perceptible "Japaneseness," which, as will be discussed later, is subtly incorporated into the "localization" strategies of the media industries. The cultural influence of Japanese animation and computer games in many parts of the world might be tremendous, but it tends to be an "invisible colonization" (Bosche 1997).[6]

One cultural critic, Ōtsuka Eiji (1993), thus warns against any euphoria concerning the global popularity of Japanese animation, arguing that it is simply the mukokuseki (the unembedded expression of race, ethnicity, and culture), the "odorless" nature of animation, that is responsible for its popularity in the world. Likewise, Ueno (1996b, 186) argues that "the 'Japaneseness' of Japanimation can only be recognized in its being actively a mukokuseki visual culture." If it is indeed the case that the Japaneseness of Japanese animation derives, consciously or unconsciously, from its erasure of physical signs of Japaneseness, is not the Japan that Western audiences are at long last coming to appreciate, and even yearn for, an animated, race-less and culture-less, virtual version of "Japan"?

It is one thing to observe that Pokémon texts, for example, are influencing children's play and behavior in many parts of the world and that these children perceive Japan as a cool nation because it creates cool cultural products such as Pokémon. However, it is quite another to say that this cultural influence and this perception of coolness is closely associated with a tangible, realistic appreciation of "Japanese" lifestyles or ideas. It can be argued that the yearning for another culture that is evoked through the consumption of cultural commodities is inevitably a monological illusion. This yearning tends to lack concern for and understanding of the socio-cultural complexity of that in which popular cultural artifacts are produced. This point is even more lucidly highlighted by the mukokuseki nature of Japanese animation and computer games.

As mentioned earlier, Japanese exports to other parts of Asia are not restricted to culturally odorless products but include popular music, TV dramas, and fashion magazines, in all of which textual appeal has much to do with visible "Japaneseness." Though Japan's cultural presence is thus differently but more clearly manifested in the region, the comparison of Japanese transnational cultural power in Asia to its American counterpart nevertheless raises serious doubts. In interpreting the popularity of Japanese popular culture in Asian regions, some Japanese conservative intellectuals argue that Japan has replaced the United States as an object of yearning (e.g., Morita and Ishihara 1989). However, this is refuted by the fact that it matters not that Japanese animations and TV programs are eagerly consumed. It is argued that a sense of yearning for Japan is still not aroused in Asia, because what is appreciated, unlike American popular culture, is still not an image or idea of Japan but simply a materialistic consumer commodity. A critical Japanese scholar of Asian Studies, for example, is unequivocal in his dismissal of the spread of Japanese consumer culture as a mere extension of the Japanese economy. He argues that "Japanese culture is not received in other Asian countries with the same sense of respect and yearning as American culture was received in postwar Japan" (Murai 1993, 26). Though the Asian popularity of Japanese animation, such as *Doraemon*, according to Murai, symbolizes a convenient and enjoyable Japanese consumer culture, Japanese cultural influence is nevertheless much weaker than Japanese economic influence.

Similarly, in his introduction to an edited volume on the Japanization of Asia, Igarashi Akio gives a concise overview of the "Japanization" phenomenon and then wonders whether the Japanese attention to the spread of Japan's popular culture in Asia merely reflects "a simplistic nationalism among the Japanese, a surplus of self-consciousness," as there might actually be no distinctive Japanese cultural influence to be found in the "Japanization" phenomenon (Igarashi 1997, 15). While the notion of "Americanization" includes broad cultural and ideological influences, such as ideas of American democracy and the American way of life based upon affluent, middle-class material cultures, Igarashi argues that "Japanization" only embodies consumer culture and thus represents "more materialistic cultural dissemination" (6). A similar observation is made by a Singaporean scholar, Wee Wan-ling (1997). He warns us not to confuse the presence of Japanese consumer commodities, animation, and popular music in Singapore with a "Japanization" signifying a substantial influence on ideas. Congruent with the view regarding Japanese imperialism's cultural power over other Asians as derivative, this argument expresses a difficulty in seeing specifically "Japanese" influence in the spread of Japanese popular and consumer culture in other parts of Asia. What is experienced through Japanese popular culture is actually a highly materialistic Japanese version of the American "original."

Global cultural power reconsidered: decentered transnational alliances

Certainly, any attempt to interpret the increase in the export of Japanese popular culture in terms of an "Americanization" paradigm would misjudge the nature of Japanese cultural power in the world. There is apparently a different logic of global cultural influence operating here. However, I would argue, it is possible and perhaps productive to take the awkwardness denoted by the notion of "Japanization" as an opportunity to reconsider the meaning of transnational cultural power which has long been understood in terms of "Americanization," and to appreciate the precarious nature of transnational cultural consumption (Appadurai 1996; Howes 1996), rather than to dismiss the pervasiveness of Japanese influence. The rise of Japanese cultural export can, I suggest, be read as a symptom of the shifting nature of transnational cultural power in a context in which intensified global cultural flows have decentered the power structure *and* vitalized local practices of appropriation and consumption of foreign cultural products and meanings. In this sense, it does not seem entirely contingent that the manifestation of Japanese cultural power has occurred in the last decade. This is a period during which the historical process of globalization, as defined by Hall (1995), has been accelerated by several interconnected factors. These include the global integration of markets and capital by powerful transnational corporations; the development of communication technologies which easily and simultaneously connect all over the globe; the emergence of an affluent middle class in non-Western countries, especially in Asia; and the increasing number of people moving from one place to another by migration and tourism. Theoretical reformulation has become imperative in order to cope with these globalizing forces that make transnational cultural flow much more disjunctive, non-isomorphic, and complex than what the center-periphery paradigm allows us to understand (Appadurai 1990).

The expansive force of globalization, the transmission of cultural forms from the dominant to the rest via communication technologies and transportation systems, has brought about a "time-space compression" (Harvey 1989), or the shrinking of the distance between one place and another. As the merger and cooperation of transnational corporations of different countries of origin intensifies, various markets are increasingly integrated and interrelated. This, together with the development of communication technologies, leads to an increasing simultaneity in the cultural flow of information, images, and commodities emanating from a handful of powerful nations, including Japan, to urban spaces across the globe. The speed and quantity of the global distribution of cultural commodities has been rapidly accelerating. The recent simultaneous popularity, and quick decline, of Spice Girls and Tamagotchi (a tiny digital pet) in many parts of the world testify to this trend. Under these developments, discourse on globalization has tended to facilitate myths of global coherence (Ferguson 1992) by its evocation of global synchronization or a utopian view of world unity, in the same way that McLuhan's famous term *global village* connotes a sense of bonding, togetherness, and immediacy.

However, media globalization does not simply promote the global reach of Western media and commodities. It also facilitates "the de-centering of capitalism from the West" (Tomlinson 1997, 140–43) through increasing integration, networking, and cooperation

among worldwide transnational media industries, including non-Western ones. For transnational corporations to enter simultaneously those global, supranational, regional, national,
and local markets, the imperatives are the establishment of a business tie-up with others at
each level—whether in the form of a buyout or collaboration—along with the selection of
new cultural products that will have an international appeal.

It is thus important to place the significance of Japanese inroads into Hollywood, as well
as the international popularity of Japanese animation and computer games, within a wider
picture of transnational media and market interconnections as well. The rise of Japanese
media industries articulates a new phase of global cultural flow dominated by a small
number of transnational corporations (Aksoy and Robins 1992). These moves testify to the
increasing trend of global media mergers which aim to offer a "total cultural package" of
various media products under a single media conglomerate (Schiller 1991).[7] After all, the
reason Sony and Matsushita bought into Hollywood was not to dominate American minds,
but rather to centralize product distribution. The purpose was to construct a total entertainment conglomerate through the acquisition of control over both audiovisual hardware
and software. It was based upon the sober economic judgment that "it is cultural distribution, not cultural production, that is the key locus of power and profit" (Garnham 1990,
161–62). The incursion can be seen as a confirmation of the supremacy of American
software creativity and therefore of Japan's second-rate ability as a software producer.
Japanese trading companies such as Sumitomo and Itochu also invested in American media
giants (e.g., Sumitomo–TCI or Itochu–Time Warner). This suggests that Japanese cultural
influence and presence in the world is still overshadowed by its economic power (Herman
and McChesney 1998, 104). Seen this way, the purpose of the Japanese takeover was
not to kill the American soul; on the contrary, it was to make Hollywood omnipresent.
Japanese ingenuity in hardware production and American genius in software go hand in hand
because (Japanese) consumer technologies work as "distribution systems" for (American)
entertainment products (Berland 1992, 46). These Japanese companies strengthen American
cultural hegemony by investing in the production of Hollywood films and by facilitating their
distribution all over the globe.

Conversely, finding a local partner is particularly important in facilitating the entry of
non-Western media industries and cultural products into Western markets. Morley and
Robins (1995, 13) point out three strategic patterns of activities for global media corporations: producing cultural products; distributing products; and owning hardware that
delivers products. Penetration of transnational media industries into multiple markets needs
the combination of at least two of the above three, particularly production and distribution,
both of which are dominated by American industries. If Sony's encroachment on Hollywood
articulates Japanese exploitation of American software products in order to become a global
media player, media globalization also promotes the incorporation of Japanese, and other
non-Western, media products into the Western-dominated global distribution network.
Japanese media industries and cultural products cannot successfully become transnational
players without partners. The most serious shortcoming of the Japanese animation industry,
despite mature production capabilities and techniques, is its lack of international distribution
channels. Western (American) global distribution power is thus indispensable to
make Japanese animation a part of global popular culture. The process can be called an
"Americanization of Japanization." For example, it was the investment and the distribution
channels of a British and American company, Manga Entertainment (established in 1991 and
part of the Polygram conglomerate) that made *The Ghost in the Shell* a hit in Western
countries. Similarly, in 1995, Disney decided to globally distribute Miyazaki Hayao's animated films. Miyazaki gained prestige from Disney's decision, which helped turn his animated *Mononokehime* into a phenomenal hit in Japan in 1997. As the producer of the film

acknowledged, the fact that Hayao's animations are highly appreciated by the global animation giant, Disney, worked well as the publicity for giving the film an international prominence (Mononokehime, datsu Miyazaki anime de 100 okuen 1998).[8]

The global success of Pokémon also has much to do with America's intervening
partnership. Most manifestly, Warner Bros., one of the major Hollywood studios, handled
the global distribution of *Pokémon: The First Movie*, as well as televising Pokémon on its
own U.S.-wide channel. No less significant is how Pokémon has been localized, or
Americanized, "to hide its 'Japaneseness' " (Invasion of the Pocket Monsters 1999, 68–69)
as part of a global promotion strategy. Significantly, it is the remade-in-the-U.S. version of
Pokémon that has been exported to other parts of the world (except Asia). Thus, the
successful marketing of Pokémon as a global character owes much to American intervention
(handled by Nintendo of America), which testifies to another "Americanization of Japanization." Japanese animation's inroads into the global market articulate the ever-growing global
integration of markets and media. The examples discussed above clearly show that the
Japanese animation industry is becoming a global player only by relying on the power of
Western media.[9]

Global–local complexity: from cultural imperialism to globalization

Decentered processes of cultural globalization have also accompanied a significant theoretical shift—the questioning of the "cultural imperialism" thesis—in studies of asymmetrical
transnational cultural flows in the last decade. The cultural imperialism thesis emphasizes the
unidirectional flow of culture from the dominant (in most cases equated with the United
States) to the dominated. It argues that American popular culture, combined with economic
and political hegemony, is disseminated all over the globe, instilling American consumerist
values and ideologies. The cultural imperialism thesis, as mentioned earlier, tends to
describe the relationship between the West (America) and the Rest as one of unambiguous
cultural domination and exploitation (e.g., Hamelink 1983; Mattelart, Delcourt, and
Mattelart 1984; Schiller 1969, 1976, 1991). But the thesis neglects analysis of empirical
evidence of audience reception in subordinate cultures, and that is particularly problematic.
In considering the global cultural flow and foreign cultural influence in a particular region,
"cultural domination" is in many cases a discursive construct rather than the reflection of
the subordinate people's actual experience. This is what Tomlinson (1991) convincingly
discusses in his book on cultural imperialism and what other excellent studies on the
discourse of "Americanization" also demonstrate (e.g., Kuisel 1993). The cultural imperialism thesis bases its argument of domination on a political economy approach and does not
pay adequate attention to whether, and how, audiences are culturally dominated through the
act of consuming media texts from the center. The thesis explicitly or implicitly sees
audiences as passive "cultural dupes" who, apparently without a critical cultural lens, automatically absorb any messages and ideologies from the dominant center. However, such a
simplifying view of cultural exchange has been refuted by many ethnographic studies which
show that audiences actively and creatively consume media texts and cultural products
(e.g., Morley 1980, 1992; Radway 1984; Ang 1985).

Perspectives of globalization, in reconsidering the nature of transnational cultural
unevenness highlighted by cultural imperialism discourses, instead stress that what is occurring is not simply homogenization through the global distribution of the same commodities,
images, and capital from the Western (and Japanese to a lesser extent) metropolitan centers.
Such dissemination also produces new cultural diversity (e.g., Hall 1991; Robins 1997).
The term *transculturation* refers to this process of globalization, in which the asymmetrical

encounter of various cultures results in the transformation of an existing cultural artifact and the creation of a new style. Mary Louise Pratt (1992, 6) states this succinctly when she writes, "While subjugated peoples cannot readily control what emanates from the dominant culture, they do determine to varying extents what they absorb into their own and what they use it for."

Although Pratt uses this concept to analyze colonial encounters in a "contact zone" through the reading of Western imperial travel writings, the concept of transculturation is helpful for us to understand that it is through engagement with West-dominated global cultural power that non-Western modernities articulate their specificity (Hall 1995). In contrast to the homogenization thesis, this view is concerned more with sites of local negotiation. It suggests that foreign goods and texts are creatively misused, recontexualized in local sites, differently interpreted according to local cultural meaning. Something new is produced in the unequal cultural encounter by mixing the foreign and the local (e.g., Hannerz 1992; Lull 1995; Ang 1996). The ascent of Japanese transnational cultural power should be considered in the context of this wider vista of theoretical paradigm shifts, which attempt to attend simultaneously to the homogenizing forces of globalization and to transformative local practices in the formation of non-Western indigenized modernity, so as to understand the question of transnational cultural power.

The shift from an emphasis on center–periphery relations to a diffusion of cultural power marks the relative decline of the main actor, the United States. It is often pointed out that, contrary to the logic of cultural imperialism, U.S. TV programs are not as popular as "local," or domestically produced, programs in many countries (e.g., Siji 1988; Lee 1991; Straubhaar 1991; Tomlinson 1991). The unambiguous American domination of global culture is also put into question by the rise of other global players such as Brazil (e.g., Sinclair 1992; Tomlinson 1997). Tunstall (1995, 16), the author of *The Media Are American* (1977), argues that American media are still influential but no longer dominant: "The United States is the only media superpower, but it is a media superpower in gradual decline against the world as a whole." Tunstall argues that American TV programs are becoming less popular in the world not because their quality is degrading but, rather, because there exists a process of local indigenization of original American TV formats, a point I will return to later.

This does not mean that the United States has lost its cultural hegemony. Even if the global popularity of American TV programs has declined, American cultural power is still articulated in the recognition that media and cultural forms which originate in America have been fully globalized (Morley and Robins 1995, 223–24). As Bell and Bell (1995, 131) argue, " 'America' has rather come to symbolize the very processes of social and cultural modernization themselves." Likewise, Yoshimi (1997), in his studies of the "Americaniza-tion" of Japan, argues, with a particular emphasis on Tokyo Disneyland, that "America" shifted from a symbol to an invisible system in the 1980s. While the American way of life has lost its manifest appeal in Japan, according to Yoshimi, the Japanese cultural scene has been saturated with the logic of American consumer capitalism. Baudrillard also declares that "America is the original version of modernity and Europe is the dubbed or subtitled version" (1988, 76). Although admitting that American hegemonic power is in decline, Baudrillard argues that the decline merely shows the changing nature of power: "It [America] has become the orbit of an imaginary power to which everyone now refers. From the point of view of competition, hegemony, and 'imperialism,' it has certainly lost ground, but from the exponential point of view, it has gained some" (107). According to Baudrillard, American power has entered a new stage of "hysteresis," which is "the process whereby something continues to develop by inertia, whereby an effect persists even when its cause has disap-peared" (115). America is now ubiquitous as the unmarked model for (post)modern culture.

It is an open question if this transformation of the nature of America's global cultural influence is the pinnacle of Americanization or the demise of Americanization. Smart (1993) criticizes Baudrillard by arguing that an exclusive comparison between Europe and America leads to a failure to realize the limits and decline of all-powerful Western/American modernity. Baudrillard is, deliberately or not, "indifferent to the possibility that America may no longer be the model for business, performance, and international style, no longer the 'uncontested and uncontestable' model of modernity" (Smart 1993, 66). While Smart emphatically refers to Japan as an emerging model of postmodernity, the critical issue here is not the substitution or addition of new cultural centers but overcoming a nation-centric view of global cultural power. At the high point in the development of modernization theories, discussions of non-Western modernization either stressed divergence or convergence with the Western model. Or conversely, Western countries were thought to follow the Japanese modernization model as a process of reverse-convergence (Dore 1973; see also Mouer and Sugimoto 1986). However, the late twentieth century is marked by the fact that there is no absolute societal model to follow (Scott 1997).

The disappearance of an absolute center of global power is often interpreted as evidence that Americanization has not melted into air but into global capitalism. Spark (1996, 96–97) makes the point astutely, referring to the British context: "Americanization might better be considered as only the evidential characteristic of modern consumer capitalism, with the appellation 'American' referring only to the prime, originating characteristics of the model. In this sense, America is not acting to subordinate foreign cultures: the process is one of globalized modernization, and as the experience of the British with America reveals, it is reciprocal." Sklair (1995, 153) extends Spark's point further when he criticizes the view that media and cultural imperialism tend to be equated with "Americanization": "It implies that if American influence could be excluded, then cultural and media imperialism would end. This could only be true in a purely definitional sense. Americanization itself is a contingent form of a process that is necessary to global capitalism, the culture-ideology of consumerism."

Sklair's argument captures the fundamental force of globalization, that generated by the logic of the ever-expanding reach of capital, and few would disagree with this point (Tomlinson 1997, 139–40). However, this argument seems too sweeping a generalization of transnational cultural flows to capture the contradiction and ambivalence articulated in local practices. Hall is more sensitive to the decentralizing feature of global capitalism. He coins the term *global mass culture* to characterize the emerging global diffusion of media images. While acknowledging American and Western hegemony in this process, Hall points out that this is a "peculiar form of homogenization" which does not destroy but rather respects cultural differences in the globe: "[Global mass culture] is wanting to recognize and absorb those differences within the larger, overarching framework of what is essentially an American conception of the world." Capital does not try to obliterate differences but to "operate through them" (1991, 28). Unprecedented concentration of capital in transnational corporations has generated another feature of decentralization, where the recognition of cultural diversity and difference is increasingly exploited by transnational corporations.

Globalization as structuring differences

The theoretical shift from cultural imperialism to globalization thus goes together with a turn from the notion of a straightforward globally homogenizing cultural dominant toward the idea of an orchestrated heterogenization under the sign of globalizing forces; from an emphasis on content to an emphasis on the form of cultural products, which structure diversity and difference in the ever-increasing interconnection of the world (e.g., Wilk 1995; Hannerz 1996; Robins 1997). Globalization brings about, as Hannerz (1996, 102) put it, "an organization of diversity rather than a replication of uniformity," or a "repatriation of difference," which is produced by the local absorption and indigenization of homogenizing forces.

A dichotomous view of global–local would fail to acknowledge the complex, juxtaposed and fractured nature of cultural globalization. We should consider, instead, what Morley and Robins (1995, 116) call the "global–local nexus": "Whilst globalization may be the prevailing force of our times, this does not mean that localism is without significance. . . . Globalization is, in fact, also associated with new dynamics of *re*-localization. It is about the achievement of a new global–local nexus, about new and intricate relations between global space and local space" (emphasis in original). The conception of globalization as an organizing force of new diversity and particularity is also argued by Robertson (1992, 1995). He refers to globalization in terms of the form in which global interconnection is structured and a new kind of particularism is globally institutionalized (1995, 38). Robertson is cautious to distance his view from the "naive functionalist mode" of integration. He emphasizes that homogenization and heterogenization, like globalization and localization, are "complementary and interpenetrative" phenomena (40).

Newly articulated particularism or localism in the local negotiation with globalizing forces testifies to the spread of common forms in which difference and diversity can be claimed. In this sense, while the concept of "hybridity" that tries to deconstruct the essentialization of "original" has gained intellectual currency, it should not simply be read as a celebration of the creative practices of the dominated. It indicates that global homogenizing power is a constitutive and generative part of any local cultural practice (e.g., Hall 1991, 1992; García Canclini 1995; Lull 1995). Arguing that the hybridization perspective should shift our conception of culture from a territorial/static mode to one of a translocal/fluid movement, Pieterse (1995) defines globalization as an ongoing production of a "global mélange" through hybridization processes. He distinguishes structural hybridization, where the production of various hybrid forms is facilitated by "the increase in the available modes of organization" (50), and cultural hybridization, where such hybrid forms represent "new translocal cultural expressions" (64). The ever-increasing hybridization in these two processes actually testifies to "transcultural convergence," as Pieterse argues that "the very process of hybridization shows the difference to be relative and, with a slight shift of perspective, the relationship can also be described in terms of an affirmation of *similarity*" (60, emphasis in original).

Likewise, in discussing the discourse of Japanese cultural uniqueness in the wider context of globalization, Morris-Suzuki (1998b, 164) emphasizes the "formatting of difference," by which she means "the creation of a single underlying common framework or set of rules which is used to coordinate local subregimes" as a significant structuring force of globalization. Difference can be convincingly and successfully advocated precisely because of the diffusion of a common format. As I will discuss in detail in chapter 4, if it can be argued that the hegemony of the global cultural system is articulated in globally shared "forms" (Wilk 1995), the latter also promote the production of multiple, distinct indigenized modernities in the world. In sum, a convincing analysis of the unevenness of global interconnectedness should go beyond a global–local binary opposition. The operation of global cultural power can only be found in local practice, whereas cultural reworking and appropriation at the local level necessarily takes place within the matrix of global homogenizing forces.

The Japanese cultural presence under a global gaze

The decentralizing forces of globalization open the way for Japanese transnational cultural power to be seen in a different light from that of "Americanization." The increasing emphasis on the decentralization of global cultural power does not mean there are no longer dominant centers. The suppliers of transnational cultural products and "forms"—which make creative local hybridization possible—are still limited to a small number of centers. Cultural commodities and images are predominantly produced by a small number of wealthy countries, including Japan, and many parts of the world still cannot even afford to enjoy global cultural consumption (Sreberny-Mohammadi 1991). From an American point of view, the globalization process might testify to the decentralization and decline of American/Western power. From a Japanese point of view, however, it represents a recentralization by means of which new globally powerful nations such as Japan have successfully repositioned themselves.

Nevertheless, it should be reiterated that this reconfiguration of transnational cultural power is occurring in the context in which uneven distribution and circulation of such cultural products are becoming more difficult to trace and the origins of images and commodities become increasingly insignificant and irrelevant. Ang (1996, 13) argues that there has been a significant shift in audience reception of TV texts in the postmodern age, in that audiences are expected to be active, not simply in theory but in their real-life situations, producing meaning out of multifarious media texts. Likewise, it can be argued that the local needs to be creative in articulating difference by indigenizing the global. With the proliferation and accelerated speed of globally circulated images and commodities, the local transculturation process has come to be a quotidian site where the local negotiates and appropriates the global rather than that of the unambiguous cultural domination by the center of the periphery (see Hannerz 1991; Miller 1992).

Although we cannot be too cautious in generalizing this picture on a global scale, gradually disappearing in this process is the perception, not the fact, of derivative modernity, the sense that "our" modernity is borrowed from a modernity that happened elsewhere (see Chatterjee 1986; Chakrabarty 1992). Ubiquitous modernity, in contrast, is based on a sense that "our" modernity is the one that is simultaneously happening everywhere. To put it differently, the Western gaze, which has long dominated the material and discursive construction of non-Western modernity, is now melting into a decentered global gaze. To use Lash and Urry's (1994, 29) words about the nature of current cultural power emanating from the core to the rest, "It is there, it is pervasive, but it is not the object of judgement—one does not assent to it or reject it." This might sound exaggerated. Needless to say, there are still clear-cut protests against American global cultural hegemony and strong anti-America sentiments in many parts of the world. Indeed, "America" still stands as a significant (hated) center. Nevertheless, at the least, the age of "Americanization," in which cross-cultural consumption was predominantly discussed in terms of the production of a sense of "yearning" for a way of life and ideas of a dominant country, seems to be over. Global cultural power does not disappear but is now highly dispersed.

It is the shift from a Western gaze to a decentered global gaze, manifested in the process of indigenizing modernity, that the new meaning of "Japanization" thrives on. Japanese cultural power has paradoxically become visible and conspicuous, as the absolute symbolic center no longer belongs to a particular country or region and transnational cultural power is deeply intermingled with local indigenizing processes. Transnationally circulated images and commodities, I would argue, tend to become culturally odorless in the sense that origins are subsumed by the local transculturation process. By appropriating, hybridizing, indigenizing, and consuming images and commodities of "foreign" origin in multiple unforeseeable ways, even American culture is conceived as "ours" in many places. McDonald's is so much a part of their own world that it no longer represents an American way of life to Japanese or Taiwanese young consumers (Watson 1997).

The multiplicity of indigenized modernities brought about by local creative practices has, for one thing, spotlighted the Japanese experience of transculturation as an exemplar to be followed by other non-Western countries. As mimesis has become associated less with second-hand cheapness and superficiality than with creativity and originality (Taussig 1993), the borrowed nature of Japanese cultural power has come to be seen as not totally ground- less. Tunstall (1995) suggests, in arguing the relative decline of American media power in the world, that the Japanese mode of indigenization of American original media products can be seen as a pattern in the development of non-Western TV industries, which, he predicts, other non-Western countries such as China or India will follow. Local indigen- ization and consumption is, moreover, consciously incorporated into the global marketing strategy of Japanese transnational corporations, as is the case with Sony's articulate strategy of "global localization" (see Aksoy and Robins 1992; Barnet and Cavanagh 1994; du Gay et al. 1997). The Japanese capacity for indigenizing the foreign is reevaluated in globalization theories, and Toyotism has been replaced by Sonyism (Wark 1991). Sony's strategy of globalization has come to signify a new meaning of "Japanization." As Featherstone (1995, 9) argues, "If the term Japanization of the world means anything it is in terms of a market strategy built around the notion of *dochaku*, or 'glocalism.' The term refers to a global strategy which does not seek to impose a standard product or image, but instead is tailored to the demands of the local market. This has become a popular strategy for multinationals in other parts of the world who seek to join the rhetoric of localism."

I will argue in later chapters that the exclusive association of Japanization with glocalism looks tenuous and essentialist (see chapters 2 and 3 [of original publication]). Suffice it to say here that Featherstone's observation is derived from the fact that the Japan-originated market- ing strategy of "global localization"—or "glocalization"—has come to be credited as a leading formula for global corporations in the 1990s in place of "global standardization" (Robertson 1995). Profits brought about by cultural power are becoming articulated less in association with the symbolic and ideological domination by the powerful nation-state and more with local camouflaging which smoothes the economic expansion of transnational corporations.

Power reconfigured in the intraregional cultural flow

As suggested earlier, the ascent of Japanese transnational cultural power is most conspicu- ously illustrated in the specific cultural geography of East and Southeast Asia, as the export of Japanese popular culture to Asia includes a wide range of products such as Japanese TV dramas, pop idols, character goods, and fashion magazines, most of which have rarely found receptive consumers in the West. Although the wide range of Sony's transnational activity can be called "global" and the strategy of "global localization" is deployed in multiple locales in the world, the application of the strategy to the production of popular music and TV programs is clearly limited to the Asian region. Even animations, which are well received in the West, are more eagerly consumed in Asia, and some animations and comics are only exported to Asia (e.g., Ono 1992, 1998; Kawatake 1995). East and Southeast Asian markets were at the receiving end of almost half of the total number of Japanese TV program exports in 1995 (Japanese Ministry 1997). These facts suggest that a Japanese mode of indigenized cultural modernity embodied in popular cultural production is not simply the model for a localizing strategy. Japanese cultural products themselves have come to hold a certain symbolic appeal to other Asian nations—which can be conceived neither as merely "odorless," nor as nonderivative of American cultural power, nor as comparable to the

Americanization paradigm—in the context of the proliferation of non-Western indigenized modernities, which we need to examine with a different analytical tool.

The specificity of the spread and consumption of Japanese popular and consumer culture in Asia reminds us of one important caveat: unsubstantiated use of the two-relational concepts "global" and "local" as empty categories would risk overexaggerating the reach and the impact of transnational cultural flows (Ferguson 1992; Chua 1998). It would underestimate "the historical and cultural situatedness of spaces traversed by [disjunctive cultural] flows" (Ang and Stratton 1996, 28). Even if it has become a common view that globalization processes are too chaotic, decentralizing, and disjunctive to be explained by a center–periphery model (e.g., Lash and Urry 1994; Appadurai 1996), as Ang and Stratton (1996) argue, we should not assume that such flows totally replace the old power relations, as the current cultural flows are always already overdetermined by the power relations and geopolitics embedded in the history of imperialism and colonialism. While, together with the dissolution of the cultural and economic imperialism perspective, fifty years would seem long enough for former colonies, South Korea and Taiwan, to become more tolerant toward, if not to forget, the legacy of Japanese imperialism,[10] this does not mean that Japanese cultural power has altogether vanished. Focusing on supra-national regional flows presents a productive way to analyze how globalization reinscribes Japanese transnational cultural power in a new configuration of more complex, multiple and intersecting power relations in Asia.

The concentration of Japanese cultural export in East and Southeast Asian regions testifies to another facet of the decentralizing globalization process, in which local practices increasingly acquire another importance: the relative decline of American cultural power has brought about the capitalization of intraregional cultural flows, with the emergence of regional media and cultural centers such as Brazil, Egypt, Hong Kong, and Japan (e.g., Straubhaar 1991; Sinclair, Jacka, and Cunningham 1996b; Lii 1998). Given the limited reverse cultural flow from these non-Western semicenters to Western metropoles, the rise of non-Western economic power and its transnational corporations in the global arena has not seriously challenged the Western-dominated "power geometry" (Massey 1991). Nevertheless, the analysis of intraregional cultural flows would highlight alternative patterns of transnationalization of media and popular culture, compared to the sweeping view which equates globalization with Americanization, by turning our attention to another significant facet of "locality"—the transnational appeal of a non-Western mode of indigenized modernity for culturally and/or geographically contiguous nations.

Of particular concern for this book is the question of how transnational cultural power is embedded in the perception of cultural distance, which is in a state of flux under globalization processes. Complexity articulated in the intensification of intraregional cultural flows is closely related with the ambiguity of the meaning of cultural intimacy and distance associated with "locality," in which audiences are thought to find pleasure through the consumption of cultural products from supposedly culturally similar nations (Straubhaar 1991; Sinclair, Jacka, and Cunningham 1996a). The reservation about claims for Japanese cultural power in Asia occurs not simply because Japanese cultural products are supposed to lack the signification of substantially Japanese ideas and lifestyles or because of a lingering, unambiguous, Western cultural hegemony. Japanese cultural power in Asia, I suggest, also tends to slip into a seemingly power-free perception of cultural similarity and local intimacy which is derived from the narrower temporal and spatial distance perceived among East and Southeast Asian countries than is the case with the latter's relation to the West.

However, it should be stressed that the sense of "cultural proximity" (Straubhaar 1991) is never a given attribute equally embodied in cultural products in a specific region and experienced by various strata of people. Rather, the production of locality (see Appadurai

1996, 178–99) itself is to be considered as a site at which a regional cultural power is articulated. The perception of cultural distance among non-Western nations has tended to be swayed by their relative temporal proximity to Western modernity, the standard by which the developmental ranking of the non-West has been determined (see Fabian 1983). As an apt illustration, such a developmental yardstick was earlier exploited by Japanese imperialist ideology to confirm Japan's superiority to other racially and culturally "similar" Asian nations and justify the Japanese mission to civilize Asia (e.g., Duus 1995; Oguma 1995).

The recent spread of Japanese popular culture in other Asian nations in turn suggests a possibility that the diminishing temporal lag between them (re)activates the sense of spatial affiliation in the region. A certain degree of economic growth might have brought about commonalities underlying the formation of modern Asian cultures. However, as the increase in Japanese export of media and cultural products shows, it also produces the asymmetry in which the Japanese mode of indigenized cultural modernity embodied in popular cultural forms becomes more appealing in other parts of Asia. As I will show in chapters 4 and 5, the different ways in which Taiwanese and Japanese perceive cultural and temporal distance in consuming other Asian cultural products—one marked by a sense of coevality, the other by a sense of nostalgia—demonstrate that unequal cultural power relations are deeply inscribed in one's spatial-temporal experience of "familiar difference" in the popular cultural products of cultural neighbors. While the consumption of Japanese popular culture in other Asian nations might not produce the same kind of a sense of yearning for Japan as does (or did) its American counterpart, Japan's relatively dominant position in intra-Asian cultural flows is noted in the fact that Asian consumption of Japanese popular culture generates a positive sense of cultural immediacy.

Although offering stimulating new insights into the investigation of decentered global cultural power relations, intraregional cultural interaction is an underexplored area in the study of cultural globalization. In recent years, theories of modernity and modernization have been criticized for their Eurocentric perspective. Now that many non-Western countries have achieved a certain degree of modernization, it has been fully, though belatedly, recognized that spatial differences were unjustifiably subsumed by the developmental temporality of Western modernity and that equal emphasis should be placed on space so that academics engage seriously with plural modernities (e.g., Featherstone, Lash, and Robertson 1995). Although globalization perspectives surely complicate the straightforward argument for the homogenization of the world based on Western modernity, the arguments for transculturation, heterogenization, hybridization, and creolization still tend not to transcend the West–Rest paradigm. Global–local interactions are predominantly studied in terms of how the Rest resists, imitates, or appropriates the West. There have been fascinating analyses of (non-Western) local consumption of Western media texts (e.g., see Miller 1992, 1995), which go beyond a dichotomized perspective of the global and the local and explore how non-Western countries "rework modernities" (Ong 1996, 64). Nevertheless, even in these examples, "global" still tends to be associated exclusively with the West.

Likewise, the rise of non-Western cultural centers of power such as Japan and Brazil often has been pointed out to refute a straightforward view of Western cultural domination and to support an argument for decentralized Western cultural hegemony (e.g., Morley and Robins 1995; Barker 1997; Tomlinson 1997). However, how such emerging non-Western semicenters exert cultural power through their dynamic interaction with other non-Western modernities has been seriously under-explored. The following chapters aim to take a further step in the analysis of decentered global cultural power relations by exploring from a Japanese perspective the dynamic and asymmetrical relations between Asian modernities.

Notes

1   The term *mukokuseki* was first used in the early 1960s by a Japanese newspaper film critic to describe a new film genre (Koi 1989, 290). Parodying Hollywood Western films such as *Shane*, the Japanese film production house Nikkatsu produced a series of action films which featured a (Japanese) guitar-toting, wandering gunman.

2   As Classen, Howes, and Synnott (1994) show, while "odor," or "smell," seems to be a natural phenomenon, the perceived attraction of any particular odor is, in fact, closely associated with the historical and social construction of various kinds of hierarchies such as class, ethnicity, and gender.

3   In the book, such a shift in Japanese cultural exports toward software is addressed, symbolically, by the designer of the Walkman, Kuroki Yasuo. While Kuroki (1995) stresses the necessity for Japanese manufacturers to change their corporate culture in order to develop the creativity of Japanese designers, he also laments Japan's inability to produce the software that people consume with the Walkman. Yet, he sees hope, in the success of animation and computer games, that Japan is shifting from being a hardware superpower to a software superpower (Kuroki 1995, 14).

4   Japanese animation and comics have been more popular in Asia than in the West, but their popularity in Asia has not been enough to affirm the emerging hegemony of Japanese animation or comics (see, for example, *Nihonjin wa yunīku ka* 1990). In this sense, it can be argued that Japan's nationalistic view of the global spread of animation is still deeply dependent on and collusive with Western Orientalism. Japanese hyper-real culture, in which comics, animation, and computer games feature, has simply replaced Western Orientalist icons such as the geisha or the samurai in the complicit exoticization of Japan (Ueno 1996a; Mōri 1996).

5   With respect to the Japanese romantic comedy animation, *Kimagure Orenjirōdo*, in which the hero and heroine never confess their love for each other and their relationship is full of misunderstanding to the end, Okada observed that American fans wish to experience this Japanese way of love (Eikoku ga mitometa Nihonbunka 1996, 30–31). An American researcher similarly observed about American fans' fascination with the Japanese mode of romance represented in *Kimagure Orenjirōdo* that it was "a form of heterosexual masculinity which is not rooted in sexual prowess, but romantic feelings" (Newitz 1995: 6). Nevertheless, Newitz's analysis shows that this ardent American consumption is articulated in the form of a nostalgia for "gender roles Americans associate with the 1950s and 60s." (13). It can be argued that this nostalgic longing displays an Americans' refusal to acknowledge that they inhabit the same temporality as Japan (see Fabian 1983). Here, as in the Japanese consumption of Asian popular culture which I will discuss in chapter 5, it might be the case that Japan is marked by temporal lag and consumed in terms of a sense of loss; hence the articulation of America's dominant position.

6   See Mitsui and Hosokawa (1998) for this line of discussion concerning the global diffusion of karaoke.

7   Clearly, animation and computer game characters play a significant role in the packaged multimedia business. The comic book characters are intertextual and can be used in a variety of media such as computer games, movies, TV series, CD-ROMs, and toys. Kinder (1991) describes the multiple possibilities of transmedia intertextuality as representing a "supersystem of entertainment" which has come to be a dominant force in the global entertainment business (see especially ch. 4). The worldwide success of Pokémon clearly testifies to the efficacy of such a supersystem. The popularity of Pokémon depends on the multimedia strategy, in which the game, comics, animation, and playing cards interlink with each other.

8   Its Japanese box office revenue exceeded 10 billion yen, surpassing the until-then record amount earned by *E. T.* This record was easily broken by *Titanic* in June 1998, but Myazaki's latest film, *Sen to Chihiro no Kamikakushi* (2001) established a new record. Actually Miyazaki's relationship with Disney has never been peaceful. His stories tend to be long and complicated, defying a simplified distinction between good and evil, as is commonly seen in Hollywood films. He refused Disney's request to shorten the three-hour long *Mononokehime*, and its box-office results in the U.S. market were not successful. However, as evinced by the fact that *Sen to Chihiro no Kamikakushi* won the Best Film prize at the 2002 Berlin Film Festival, the international appreciation of Miyazaki's animated films has been enhanced (Jiburi no mahō 2002).

9   In this regard, Japanese animation is often compared by the Japanese media to Ukiyoe—premodern Japanese color prints depicting ordinary people's everyday lives. Their beauty and value were appreciated as Japanesque by the West, and they had a significant impact on Western artists. It is often suggested that animation faces the same dilemma as Ukiyoe, many of which were taken out of

Japan and exhibited in Western art galleries from the mid-nineteenth century onward. The West (America) may again deprive Japan of animation if Japan fails to recognize its (commercial) value (e.g., Hariwuddo ni nerawareru sofuto taikoku Nippon 1994; Nihon anime no sekai seiha 1996; Nihonhatsu no otaku bunka ga sekken 1996). Precisely because they have come to be universally consumed, they are destined to be copied, studied, and indigenized outside Japan. Thus, Hollywood is trying to develop a new global genre by making use of Japanese animation. American film producers and directors are recruiting Japanese animators to develop American animation and computer graphics (Nihon anime ni sekai ga netsushisen 1996; 2020nen kara no keishō 1997). American production companies, with the help of Japanese animators, have begun producing Japanimation in the United States (Ōhata 1996; Nihonhatsu no otaku bunka ga sekken 1996). Also, the South Korean government has begun to support the promotion of the local animation industry for the sake of the future development of the national economy. A Korean conglomerate has entered the animation business by investing in domestic as well as Japanese animation industries (Nihon anime ni tōshi 1996; Nihon anime ni sekai ga netsushisen 1996). In the face of the increasing number of competitors, the Japanese government has been criticized for its failure to promote Japan's most lucrative cultural software industry (*Kaigai bunka ikusei seisaku* 1997). Responding to such criticism, the Agency for Cultural Affairs belatedly decided to support multimedia software content in 1997 and began a media arts festival in Tokyo in February 1998. Its purpose was to encourage the domestic production of animation, comics, computer graphics, and computer game software. However, there is strong doubt among the industries as to the scale and efficacy of such governmental support to enhance the international competitiveness of Japanese animation.

10   Taiwan removed its ban on broadcasting Japanese-language TV programs and music in late 1993, and in 1998 South Korea also began a step-by-step process that will eventually abolish all restrictions on importing Japanese cultural products.

References

2020nen kara no keishō: Nihon ga kieru 4. 1997. *Nihon Keizai Shinbun*, 5 January.

Aksoy, Asu, and Kevin Robins. 1992. Hollywood for the twenty-first century: Global competition for critical mass in image markets. *Cambridge Journal of Economics* 16: 1–22.

Akurosu Henshūshitsu, eds. 1995. *Sekai Shōhin no Tsukurikata: Nihon media ga sekai o seishita hi*. Tokyo: Parco Shuppan.

Amerika nimo otaku ga daihassei. 1996. *Shūkan Bunshun*, 5 September, 190–91.

Ang, Ien. 1985. *Watching Dallas: Soap opera and the melodramatic imagination*. London: Methuen.

——— . 1996. *Living room wars: Rethinking media audiences for a postmodern world*. London: Routledge.

Ang, Ien, and Jon Stratton. 1996. Asianizing Australia: Notes toward a critical transnationalism in cultural studies. *Cultural Studies* 10 (1): 16–36.

Appadurai, Arjun. 1990. Disjuncture and difference in the global cultural economy. *Public Culture* 2 (2): 1–24.

——— . 1996. *Modernity at large: Cultural dimensions of globalization*. Minneapolis: University of Minnesota Press.

Barker, Chris. 1997. *Global television: An introduction*. Oxford: Blackwell Publishers.

Barnet, Richard, and John Cavanagh. 1994. *Global dreams: Imperial corporations and the new world order*. New York: Simon and Schuster.

Baudrillard, Jean. 1988. *America*. London: Verso.

Bell, Philip, and Roger Bell. 1995. The "Americanization" of Australia. *Journal of International Communication* 2 (1): 120–33.

Berland, Jody. 1992. Angels dancing: Cultural technologies and the production of space. In *Cultural Studies*, edited by L. Grossberg et al., 38–55. New York: Routledge.

Bosche, Marc. 1997. Nihon ni yoru hisokana shokuminchika. Translated by M. Shimazaki. *Sekai*, February, 231–35.

Boyd, Douglas A., Joseph D. Straubhaar, and John A. Lent. 1989. *Videocassette recorders in the Third World*. New York: Longman.

Bratton, John. 1992. *Japanization at work: Managerial studies for the 1990s*. London: Macmillan Press.

Chakrabarty, Dipesh. 1992. Postcoloniality and the artifice of history: Who speaks for the "Indian" past? *Representation* 37: 1–26.

Chambers, Iain. 1990. A miniature history of the Walkman. *New Formations* 11: 1–4.

Chatterjee, Partha. 1986. *Nationalist thought and the colonial world: A derivative discourse?* London: Zed Books.

Chow, Rey. 1993. Listening otherwise, music miniaturized: A different type of question about revolution. In *The cultural studies reader*, edited by S. During, 382–99. London: Routledge.

Chua, Beng-Huat. 1998. Globalization: Finding the appropriate words and levels. *Communal/Plural* 6
(1): 117–24.

Classen, Constance, David Howes, and Anthony Synnott. 1994. *Aroma: The cultural history of smell.*
London: Routledge.

Dohse, Knuth, Ulrich Jurgens, and Thomas Malsch. 1985. From "Fordism" to "Toyotism"? The social
organization of the labor process in the Japanese automobile industry. *Politics and Society* 14 (2):
115–46.

Dore, Ronald P. 1973. *British factory—Japanese factory: The origins of diversity in industrial relations.*
Berkeley: University of California Press.

du Gay, Paul, et al. 1997. *Doing cultural studies: The story of the Sony Walkman.* London: Sage.

Duus, Peter. 1995. *The abacus and the sword: The Japanese penetration of Korea, 1895–1910.* Berkeley:
University of California Press.

Eikoku ga mitometa Nihonbunka wa manga to terebi gēmu. 1996. *Shūkan Yomiuri*, 2 June, 29–31.

Elger, Tony, and Chris Smith. 1994. *Global Japanization: The transnational transformation of the labor process.*
London: Routledge.

Fabian, Johannes. 1983. *Time and the other: How anthropology makes its object.* New York: Columbia
University Press.

Featherstone, Mike. 1995. *Undoing culture: Globalization, postmodernism, and identity.* London: Sage.

Featherstone, Mike, Scot Lash, and Roland Robertson, eds. 1995. *Global modernities.* London: Sage

Ferguson, Majorine. 1992. The mythology about globalization. *European Journal of Communication* 7:
69–93.

Forester, Tom. 1993. Consuming electronics: Japan's strategy for control. *Media Information Australia*
67: 4–16.

Frith, Simon. 1982. *Sound effect: Youth: Leisure and the politics of rock 'n' roll.* New York: Panthenon.

Furansu de kosupure kontesuto nekkyō. 1997. *Asahi Shinbun*, 23 October, evening edition.

Ganley, Gladys D., and Oswald H. Ganley. 1987. *Global political fallout: The VCR's first decade.* Cambridge,
Mass.: Program on Information Resources Policy, Harvard University, Center for Information
Policy Research.

García Canclini, Néstor. 1995. *Hybrid cultures: Strategies for entering and leaving modernity*, translated by
C. L. Chiappari and S. L. López. Minneapolis: University of Minnesota Press.

Garnham, Nicholas. 1990. *Capitalism and communication: Global culture and the economics of information.*
London: Sage.

Gomery, Douglas. 1988. Hollywood's hold on the new television technologies. *Screen* 29 (2): 82–88.

Hall, Stuart. 1991. The local and the global: Globalization and ethnicity. In *Culture, globalization, and the
world-system*, edited by A. King, 19–39. London: Macmillan.

———. 1992. The question of cultural identity. In *Modernity and its futures*, edited by S. Hall et al.
London: Polity Press.

———. 1995. New cultures for old. In *A place in the world? Places, cultures, and globalization*, edited by
D. Massey and P. Jess, 175–214. Oxford: Oxford University Press:

Hamelink, Cees. 1983. *Cultural autonomy in global communications.* New York: Longman.

Hannerz, Ulf. 1991. Scenarios for peripheral cultures. In *Culture, globalization, and the world-system*,
edited by A. King, 107–28. London: Macmillan.

———. 1992. *Cultural complexity.* New York: Columbia University Press.

———. 1996. *Transnational connections: Culture, people, places.* London: Routledge.

Hariwuddo ni nerawareru sofuto taikoku Nippon. 1994. *Dime*, 6 October, 21–25.

Harvey, David. 1989. *The condition of postmodernity.* Oxford: Basil Blackwell.

Hatakeyama Kenji, and Kubo Masaichi. 2000. *Pokemon story.* Tokyo: Nikkei BP.

Herman, Edward, and Robert McChesney. 1998. *The global media: The new missionaries of global capitalism.* London: Cassell.

Hoskins, Colin, and Rolf Mirus. 1988. Reasons for the U.S. dominance of the international trade in
television programs. *Media, Culture, and Society* 10: 499–515.

Howes, David. 1996. Introduction: Commodities and cultural borders. In *Cross-cultural consumption:
Global markets, local realities*, edited by D. Howes, 1–16. London: Routledge.

Igarashi Akio. 1997. From Americanization to "Japanization" in East Asia? *Journal of Pacific Asia* 4: 3–20.

Invasion of the pocket monsters. 1999. *Time*, 22 November, 62–69.

Japanese Ministry of Posts and Telecommunications. 1997. Heisei 9 nendoban Tsūshin Hakusho. Tokyo: Japanese Ministry of Posts and Telecommunications.

Jiburi no mahō. 2002. *Newsweek Japan*, 3 April, 52–62.

Kaigai bunka ikusei seisaku. 1997. Dime, 3 June, 105–7.

Kamo Yoshinori. 2000. Pokemon ga yushutsu shita "kūru" na Nihon to Nihonjin. *Asahi Shinbun*, 20 January, evening edition.

Kawatake Kazuo. 1995. Ajia kyōtsū no terebi bunka kōchiku ni mukete. *Kōkoku*, May–June, 20–24.

Kinder, Marsha. 1991. *Playing with power in movies, television, and video games*. Berkeley: University of California Press.

Kogawa Tetsuo. 1984. Beyond electronic individualism. *Canadian Journal of Political and Social Theory* 8 (3): 15–19.

———. 1988. New trends in Japanese popular culture. In *Modernization and beyond: The Japanese trajectory*, edited by G. McCormack and Y. Sugimoto, 54–66. Cambridge: Cambridge University Press.

Koi Eisei. 1989. *Den Nihon eiga no ōgonjidai*. Tokyo: Bungei Shunjū.

Kuisel, Richard. 1993. *Seducing French: The dilemma of Americanization*. Berkeley: University of California Press.

Kuroki Yasuo. 1995. Nihon no monozukuri wa sekai ni eikyō o ataete iruka. In *Sekai Shōhin no tsukuri-kata*, edited by Akurosu Henshūshitsu, 10–17. Tokyo: Parco Shuppan.

Lardner, James. 1987. *Fast forward: Hollywood, the Japanese, and the onslaught of the VCR*. New York: W. W. Norton.

Lash, Scott, and John Urry. 1994. *Economies of signs and space*. London: Sage.

Lee, Paul S.-N. 1991. The absorption and indigenization of foreign media cultures: A study on a cultural meeting points of East and West: Hong Kong. *Asian Journal of Communication* 1 (2): 52–72.

Levi, Antonia, 1996. *Samurai from outer space: Understanding Japanese animation*. Chicago: Open Court.

Lii, Ding-Tzann. 1998. A colonized empire: Reflections on the expansion of Hong Kong films in Asian countries. In *Trajectories: Inter-Asian cultural studies*, edited by K.-H. Chen, 122–41. London: Routledge.

Lull, James. 1995. *Media, communication, culture: A global approach*. Cambridge: Polity Press.

Manabe Masami. 1997. The wonderful world of *anime*. *Look Japan* (May): 17.

Massey, Doreen. 1991. A global sense of place. *Marxism Today*, June.

Mattelart, Armand, Xavier Delcourt, and Michelle Mattelart. 1984. *International image markets: In search of an alternative perspective*, translated by D. Buxton. London: Comedia.

Mediamatic. 1991. Special issue: *Otaku* radical boredom, 5 (4).

Miller, Daniel. 1992. The young and restless in Trinidad: A case of the local and global in mass consumption. In *Consuming technologies: Media and information in domestic spaces*, edited by R. Silverstone and E. Hirsch, 163–82. London: Routledge.

———, ed. 1995. *Worlds apart: Modernity through the prism of the local*. London: Routledge.

Mitsui, Toru, and Shuhei Hosokawa, eds. 1998. *Karaoke around the world: Global technology, local singing*. London: Routledge.

Mononokehime, datsu Miyazaki anime de 100 okuen. 1998. *Nikkei Entertainment*, January, 42–43.

Mōri Yoshitaka. 1996. Japaniméshon to Japanaizēshon. *Yuriika*, August, 150–57.

Morita Akio, and Ishihara Shintarō. 1989. *"No" to ieru nihon*. Tokyo: Kōbunsha.

Morley, David. 1980. *The nationwide audience: Structure and decoding*. British Film Institute Television Monograph no. 11. London: British Film Institute.

———. 1992. *Television, audiences, and cultural studies*. London: Routledge.

Morley, David, and Kevin Robins. 1995. *Spaces of identities: Global media, electronic landscapes, and cultural boundaries*. London: Routledge.

Morris-Suzuki, Tessa. 1998b. *Re-inventing Japan: Time, space, nation*. New York: M. E. Sharpe.

Mouer, Ross, and Yoshio Sugimoto. 1986. *Images of Japanese society: A study in the structure of social reality*. London: Routledge and Kegan Paul.

Murai Yoshinori. 1993. Oshin, Doraemon wa kakehashi to nareruka. *Views*, 10 March, 26–27.

Negus, Keith. 1997. The production of culture. In *Production of culture/ Cultures of production*, edited by P. du Gay, 67–104. London: Sage.

Newitz, Annalee. 1995. Magical girls and atomic bomb sperm: Japanese animation in America. *Film Quarterly* 49 (1): 2–15.

Nihon anime ni sekai ga netsushisen. 1996. *Aera*, 29 July, 6–9.

Nihon anime ni tōshi. 1996. *Nihon Keizai Shinbun*, 3 September.

Nihon anime no sekai seiha. 1996. *Bart*, 22 January, 20–29.

Nihonbunka kosupure Amerika yushutsu. 1996. *Shūkan Shinchō*, 24 July, 171–75.

Nihonhatsu no otaku bunka ga sekken: Beikoku saishin anime jijō. 1996. *Nikkei Trendy*, October, 86–91.

Nihonjin wa yunīku ka. Vol. 4, Manga. 1990. *Aera*, 12 June, 29–67.

Noda Masaaki. 1990. Mō hitotsu no Nihonbunka ga sekai o kaeru. *Voice*, July, 56–57.

Nye, Joseph S. Jr. 1990. *Bound to lead: The changing nature of American power*. New York: Basic Books.

Oguma Eiji. 1995. *Tan'itsu minzoku shinwa no kigen*. Tokyo: Shinyōsha.

Ōhata Kōichi. 1996. Animerika e no shōtai. *Yuriika*, August, 88–94.

Okada Toshio. 1995. Anime bunka wa chō kakkoii. *Aera*, 2 October, 43–44.

——. 1996. *Otakugaku nyūmon*. Tokyo: Ōta Shuppan.

Oliver, Nick, and Barry Wilkinson. 1992. *The Japanization of British industry: New developments in the 1990s*. Oxford: Blackwell.

Ong, Aihwa. 1996. Anthropology, China, and modernities: The geopolitics of cultural knowledge. In *The future of anthropological knowledge*, edited by H. L. Moore, 60–92. London: Routledge.

Ono Kōsei. 1992. Sekai de shōhi sareru Nihon no terebi anime. *Chōsa Jōhō* 404: 16–20.

——. 1998. Nihon manga no shintō ga umidasu sekai. In *Nihon manga ga sekai de sugoi!*, edited by I. Ogawa, 76–91. Tokyo: Tachibana Shuppan.

O'Regan, Tom. 1991. From piracy to sovereignty: International video cassette recorders trends. *Continuum* 4 (2): 112–35.

——. 1992. Too popular by far: On Hollywood's international popularity. *Continuum* 5 (2): 302–51.

Oshii Mamoru, Itō Kazunori, and Ueno Toshiya. 1996. Eiga to wa jitsu wa animēshon datta. *Yuriika*, August, 50–81.

Otaku no sekai kara mejā e. 1997. *Newsweek Japan*, 30 July, 42–49.

Ōtsuka Eiji. 1994. Komikku sekai seiha. *Sapio*, 8 July, 10–11.

Pieterse, Jan Nederveen. 1995. Globalization as hybridization. In *Global modernities*, edited by M. Featherstone et al., 45–68. London: Sage.

Pratt, Mary Louise. 1992. *Imperial eyes: Travel writing and transculturation*. London: Routledge.

Radway, Janice. 1984. *Reading the romance: Women, patriarchy, and popular literature*. Chapel Hill: University of North Carolina Press.

Ritzer, George. 1993. *The McDonaldization of society*. London: Sage.

Robertson, Roland. 1992. *Globalization: Social theory and global culture*. London: Sage.

——. 1995. Globalization: Time-space and homogeneity-heterogeneity. In *Global Modernities*, edited by M. Featherstone et al., 25–44. London: Sage.

Robins, Kevin. 1997. What in the world's going on? In *Production of culture / Cultures of production*, edited by P. du Gay, 11–47. London: Sage.

Said, Edward. 1994. *Culture and imperialism*. New York: Vintage.

Sakurai Tetsuo. 2000. Sokudo no nakano bunka. *Daikōkai* 35: 52–59.

Schiller, Herbert. 1969. *Mass communication and American empire*. New York: Beacon Press.

——. 1976. *Communication and cultural domination*. New York: M.E. Sharpe.

——. 1991. Not yet the post-imperialist era. *Critical Studies in Mass Communication* 8: 13–28.

Schodt, Frederik L. 1983. *Manga! Manga!: The world of Japanese comics*. Tokyo: Kōdansha International.

——. 1996. *Dreamland Japan: Writings on modern manga*. Berkeley, Calif.: Stone Bridge Press.

Scott, Alan. 1997. Globalization: Social process or political rhetoric? Introduction to *The limits of globalization: Cases and arguments*, edited by A. Scott, 1–22. London: Routledge.

Sekai ga maneshita Nipponryū, Nippon wa erai! 1992. *DENiM*, September, 143–49.

Siji, Alessandro. 1988. *East of "Dallas": The European challenge to American television*. London: British Film Institute.

Sinclair, John. 1992. The de-centering of cultural imperialism: Televisa-tion and Globo-ization in the Latin world. In *Continental shift: Globalization and culture*, edited by E. Jacka. Double Bay, New South Wales: Local Consumption Publications, 99–116.

Sinclair, John, Elizabeth Jacka, and Stuart Cunningham. 1996a. Peripheral vision. In *New patterns in global television: Peripheral vision*, edited by John Sinclair, Elizabeth Jacka, and Stuart Cunningham, 1–32. Oxford: Oxford University Press.

——, eds. 1996b. *New patterns in global television: Peripheral vision*. Oxford: Oxford University Press.

Sklair, Leslie. 1995. *Sociology of the global system*. 2d ed. London: Prentice Hall / Harvester Wheatsheaf.

Smart, Barry. 1993. Europe/America: Baudrillard's fatal comparison. In *Forget Baudrillard?*, edited by C. Rojek and B.S. Turner, 47–69. London: Routledge.

Spark, Alasdair. 1996. Wrestling with America: Media, national images, and the global village. *Journal of Popular Culture* 29 (4): 83–97.

Sreberny-Mohammadi, Annabelle. 1991. The global and the local in international communications. In *Mass media and society*, edited by J. Curran and M. Gurevitch, 118–38. London: Edward Arnold.

Straubhaar, Joseph. 1991. Beyond media imperialism: Asymmetrical interdependence and cultural proximity. *Critical Studies in Mass Communication* 8 (1): 39–59.

Taussig, Michael. 1993. *Mimesis and alterity: A particular history of the senses*. London: Routledge.

Thome, Katarina, and Ian A. McAuley. 1992. *Crusaders of the rising sun: A study of Japanese management in Asia*. Singapore: Longman.

Tomlinson, John. 1991. *Cultural imperialism: A critical introduction*. London: Pinter Publishers.

——— . 1997. Cultural globalization and cultural imperialism. In *International communication and globalization: A critical introduction*, edited by A. Mohammadi, 170–90. London: Sage.

Tunstall, Jeremy. 1977. *The media are American: Anglo-American media in the world*. London: Constable.

——— . 1995. Are the media still American? *Media Studies Journal* (fall): 7–16.

Ueno Toshiya. 1996a. Ragutaimu: Diasupora to "roji." *Gendai Shisō* 24 (3): 238–59.

——— . 1996b. Japanoido ōtoman. *Yuriika*, August, 178–97.

Vogel, Ezra. 1979. *Japan as number one*. Cambridge, Mass.: Harvard University Press.

Wark, Mackenzie. 1991. From Fordism to Sonyism: Perverse reading of the new world order. *New Formations* 15: 43–54.

——— . 1994. The video game as an emergent media form. *Media Information Australia* 71: 21–30.

Waters, Malcolm. 1995. *Globalization*. London: Routledge.

Watson, James L., ed. 1997. *Golden Arches East: McDonalds in East Asia*. Stanford, Calif.: Stanford University Press.

Wee, C.J. W.-L. 1997. Buying Japan: Singapore, Japan, and an "East Asian" modernity. *Journal of Pacific Asia* 4: 21–46.

Wilk, Richard. 1995. Learning to be local in Belize: Global systems of common difference. In *Worlds apart: Modernity through the prism of the local*, edited by D. Miller, 110–33. London: Routledge.

Williams, Raymond. 1990. *Television: Technology and cultural form*. London: Routledge.

Yoshimi Shunya. 1997. Amerikanaizēshon to bunka no seijigaku. In *Gendaishakai no shakaigaku*, edited by S. Inoue et al., 157–231. Tokyo: Iwanami Shoten.

Chapter 26

Marwan M. Kraidy

HYBRIDITY IN CULTURAL GLOBALIZATION

A S "ONE OF THE most widely employed and disputed terms in postcolonial theory" (Ashcroft, Griffiths, & Tiffin, 1998, p. 118), hybridity has become a master trope across many spheres of cultural research, theory, and criticism. While some see hybridity as a site of democratic struggle and resistance against empire, others have attacked it as a neo-colonial discourse complicit with transnational capitalism, cloaked in the hip garb of cultural theory. Hybridity has also been the target of attacks alleging that the concept reflects the life of its theorists more than the sites and communities these theorists write about. The intense controversy swirling around hybridity is symptomatic of the no less heated debate over the political potential and epistemological usefulness of postcolonial theory at large. This lingering dispute has pitted proponents of postcolonial theory's emancipatory claims against those who believe, as Spivak (1999) succinctly puts it, that discussions of postcolonial theory "often dissimulate the implicit collaboration of the post-colonial in the service of neocolonialism" (p. 361). There is an abundant literature on both the contestation and the affirmation of postcolonial theory, as well as on the ambiguity of the term "postcolonialism" itself (see Ahmad, 1992, 1995; Appiah, 1991; Bahri, 1995; Dirlik, 1994; Hall, 1996; Mclintock, 1992; Mishra & Hodge, 1991; Miyoshi, 1993; Shohat, 1992; Spivak, 1999). In communication studies, see the exchange between Shome (1998) and Kavoori (1998) in *Critical Studies in Mass Communication*.

It is only recently that hybridity has gained visibility in international media and communication studies. Several studies have employed hybridity to describe mixed genres and identities (Kolar-Panov, 1996; Tufte, 1995), however, sustained treatments that theorize cultural hybridity as a communicative space or practice (Kraidy, 1999; Naficy, 1994) and thus place hybridity at the heart of communication theory as a field, remain rare. To some extent, this rarity mirrors the paucity of communication scholarship directly engaging postcolonial theory (Hegde, 1998; Kavoori, 1998; Shome, 1996, 1998), although one can find a few articles based on postcolonial thought (Parameswaran, 1997, 1999). Nevertheless, regular discussions of hybridity at recent conventions of the International Association of Media and Communication Research (IAMCR), the International Communication Association (ICA), and the National Communication Association (NCA), point to an emerging saliency of hybridity in communication scholarship.

This trend underscores the need for a critical theorizing of hybridity in the context of communication theory. As a widely used concept, the recent importation of hybridity to areas such as intercultural and international communication, risks using the concept as a merely descriptive device, i.e. describing the local reception of global media texts as a site of cultural mixture. A merely descriptive use of hybridity creates two quandaries, one ontological and the other political. Ontologically, whereas a descriptive approach sees hybridity as a clear product of, say, global and local interactions, I believe that hybridity needs to be understood as a communicative practice constitutive of, and constituted by, sociopolitical and economic arrangements. Understanding hybridity as a practice marks the recognition that transcultural relations are complex, processual, and dynamic. In addition to failing to grasp the ontological complexity of cultural interactions, a merely descriptive use of hybridity also poses the risk of undermining the political potential that hybridity might or might not have. Politically, a critical hybridity theory considers hybridity as a space where intercultural and international communication practices are continuously negotiated in interactions of differential power. References to cultural mixture as resistance to domination have appeared in writings critical of cultural imperialism as an international communication paradigm. However, some scholars have warned that hybridity and domination are not mutually exclusive.[1] Concomitantly, if hybridity consists merely of observing, cataloguing, and celebrating multicultural mixture, the inequality that often characterizes these mixtures is glossed over. Ontological and political requisites thus require a critical theorizing of hybridity in articulation with communication theory.

In this article, I am interested in the theoretical strands of international communication and culture that have moved beyond the paradigm of cultural imperialism. Some of the criticisms against cultural imperialism—conceptual ambiguity, epistemological uncertainty (see Fejes, 1981; Sreberny-Mohammadi, 1997; Straubhaar, 1991)—have some validity. However, the dismissal of cultural imperialism did not serve as an opportunity to build a new critical theory of transnational communication and culture. As a result, research on cultural globalization oftentimes appears to be at best descriptive, at worst a noncritical celebration of transnational culture as global multiculturalism. Since stories on cultural globalization (mainly the global impact of U.S. popular culture) appear on a regular basis in mainstream media in the United States, constructions of cultural globalization in the elite press invite analytical engagement. To that end, this article revisits cultural globalization in the context of a series entitled, "American Popular Culture Abroad," published in the *Washington Post* in October 1998. This article will attempt to address a gap in recent postcolonial theory and criticism. This gap is the paucity of postcolonial analysis of contemporary Western media representation of the non-West, in spite of "the disproportionate influence of the West as a cultural forum" (Bhabha, 1994, p. 21). The *Washington Post* articles take the architecture of representation a step beyond the usual concerns of postcolonial criticism: not only are they Western representations of non-Western sites, but they are representations of how non-Western contexts encode Western representations.

The article opens with a review of the interdisciplinary literature on hybridity and a summary of the critiques leveled at the concept of hybridity. A deconstruction of the discourse of hybridity in the *Washington Post* articles follows. My objective is to answer the following questions: How does the production of hybridity in the *Washington Post* series frame cultural globalization? Do the stories account for the ways in which the global political and economic power structures influence hybrid formations? Or does the *Washington Post*'s production of hybridity justify imbalanced cultural relations, consisting of what Spivak (1999) called "hybridist postnational talk, celebrating globalization as Americanization"

(p. 361)? The analysis concludes with an exploration of hybridity's ability to adequately describe and understand global cultural relations without being reified as corporate multiculturalism.

Hybridity in theory, culture, and communication

Early debates on hybridity emerged in the 18th century in the context of interracial contact resulting from overseas conquest and population displacement in Britain, France, and the United States. Grounded in comparative anatomy and craniometry, these early speculations on the hybrid were chiefly concerned with the perceived contamination of White Europeans by the races they colonized. There were differences of opinion on the vitality of hybrids, oscillating between "hybrid vigor" and "hybrid sterility," but all commonly invoked biology to justify ideologies of White racial superiority and to warn of the danger of interracial breeding described as "miscegenation" and "amalgamation." A typical argument in that debate can be found in Knox (1850) who argued that hybridity was "a degradation of humanity and . . . was rejected by nature" (p. 497, quoted in Young, 1995, p. 15). This early hybridity discourse was symptomatic of the Enlightenment's failure to come to terms with its racist underside (see Young, 1995).

Hybridity took on new meaning in the wake of the decolonization movements that emerged in the non-West beginning in the 19th century, and saw their heyday in the post-World War II decades. In Latin America, for instance, after protracted struggles over nationhood in which some elites attempted to impose a white European national identity, nation-states adopted *mestizaje* as their official ideology in their bids to forge national identities distinct from mere provincial status in the Spanish Empire. The ideology of *mestizaje* was an attempt to mitigate tensions between the indigenous populations and the descendents of Spanish colonists, by positing the new nations as hybrids of both worlds (see, for instance, Archetti, 1999; Hale, 1999; Martín-Barbero, 1993; Mignolo, 2000). However, *mestizaje*, as formulated in the Latin American context, is a deeply racialized concept, which concealed residual imperial relations to the same extent as it celebrated the racial diversity of the new nations.

Hybridity later emerged as an important dimension of postcolonial cultures in Africa, Latin America, Asia, and the diaspora in the West. In *The Black Atlantic* (1993), Paul Gilroy examines the transatlantic flows of people, ideas, and culture that began with the slave trade, arguing that "the invigorating flux of . . . mongrel cultural forms" (p. 3) has been significant for cultural renewal in Europe, Africa, the Caribbean, and America. Similarly, Bhabha (1994) displaces hybridity from its racialized connotation to the semiotic field of culture. He explores hybridity in the context of the postcolonial novel, celebrating it as the resilience of the subaltern and as the contamination of imperial ideology, aesthetics, and identity, by natives who are striking back at imperial domination. He emphasizes hybridity's ability to subvert and reappropriate dominant discourses. Thus, Bhabha affirms that, "The social articulation of difference, from the minority perspective, is a complex, ongoing negotiation that seeks to authorize cultural hybridities that emerge in moments of historical transformation" (1994, p. 2). Bhabha proceeds to argue that what he refers to as "cultures of *postcolonial contra-modernity*" are in fact "resistant to . . . oppressive assimilationist technologies . . . but they also deploy the cultural hybridity of their borderline conditions to 'translate,' and therefore reinscribe, the social imaginary of both metropolis and modernity" (p. 6). One of the chief manifestations of this reinscription is found in Bhabha's analysis of mimicry as a hybridizing process. In his landmark essay, "Of Mimicry and Man," (1994), Bhabha argues that "the ambivalence of mimicry—almost but not quite—suggests that the fetishized colonial culture is potentially and strategically an insurgent counter-appeal" (p. 91). Bhabha's version of hybridity, imbued with political potential, has attracted virulent attacks from materialist critics. Bhabha's work has been equally influential and contested. Moore-Gilbert (1997) devotes a full chapter to Bhabha, arguing that one of Bhabha's most original contributions is to have emphasized "the mutualities and negotiations across the colonial divide" (p. 116), as opposed to Said's focus on the colonizer and Fanon's emphasis on the colonized. On the other hand, Bhabha's Lacanian grounding and his focus on the semiotic domain has made him the favorite target of materialist critics such as Aijaz Ahmad (1992, 1995). Moore-Gilbert offers a solid counter-critique of Ahmad while acknowledging weaknesses in Bhabha's theoretical edifice.

The trope of hybridity has also influenced attempts to address theoretical formulations of globalization as a large scale and yet fragmented process (Appadurai, 1996; García-Canclini, 1989; Hannerz, 1987; Martín-Barbero, 1993; Pieterse, 1994). Most of these studies have approached hybridity as a by-product of the transcultural dynamics between tradition and modernity sometimes conceptualized as the local and the global (i.e. Appadurai's, 1996, notion of "disjuncture," Martín-Barbero's, 1993, reformulation of the concept of "mediations," and García-Canclini's, 1990, "cultural reconversion"). García-Canclini's *Culturas Híbridas* (1989), probably the most systematic treatment of hybridity, is grounded in the political and cultural struggles in contemporary Latin America, where "impure genres" are shaped by "oblique" vectors of power. García-Canclini (1989) adopts a dialectical framework focusing on symbolic vectors and material forces as mutually constitutive. He writes "cultural heterogeneity" is "one of the means to explain the oblique powers that intermingle liberal institutions and authoritarian habits, social democratic movements with paternalistic regimes, and the transactions of some with others" (1989, p. 3).

García-Canclini's formulation of cultural hybridity as a realm that crosses from the aesthetico-symbolic to the cultural politics of citizenship is echoed in performance studies. Leading works in this group include Werbner and Modood's *Debating Hybridity* (1997), Joseph and Fink's *Performing Hybridity* (1999), and Guillermo Gómez-Peña's *The New World Border* (1996). In a statement representative of that formation, Joseph (1999) argues that "the modern move to deploy hybridity as a disruptive democratic discourse of cultural citizenship is a distinctly anti-imperial and antiauthoritarian development" (p. 1). The volume edited by Joseph converges on the idea of "new hybrid identities," understood as a political gesture, as opposed to "the historical conditions of plurality, travel, miscegenation, nomadism, displacement, conquest, and exile that have informed ideas of hybridization globally" (p. 2). According to Joseph, hybridity is "a democratic expression of multiple affiliations of cultural citizenship in the United States" (p. 2), which is always in a state of tension with transnational and national political economy.

Likewise, Werbner propounds an understanding of hybridity as "a theoretical metaconstruction of social order" (1997, p. 1), which in Europe is linked to xenophobia. Hybridity's political potential, according to Werbner, lies in "the transgressive power of symbolic hybrids to subvert categorical oppositions and hence to create the conditions for cultural reflexivity and change" (1997, p. 1). Finally, Werbner advocates a theory of hybridity which "must differentiate, in the first instance, between a politics that proceeds from the legitimacy of difference, in and despite the need for unity, and a politics that rests on a coercive unity, ideologically grounded in a single monolithic truth" (1997, p. 21). Hale (1999), Kapchan and Strong (1999), and Stross (1999) have also grappled with the potential and pitfalls of hybridity.

Critiques of theories of hybridity

Having been enlisted for various political and scholarly agendas, hybridity has emerged as a privileged site for conceptualizing global/local articulations. Even the venerable *Journal of American Folklore* recently devoted an entire issue to "theorizing the hybrid" (Kapchan & Strong, 1999). This widespread use of hybridity has attracted critiques whose tone ranges from cautionary to scathing. These critiques are partly the result of hybridity's conceptual ambiguity, but are mainly caused by strong divergences on the meaning and implications of hybridity. In effect, hybridity is mired in two paradoxes. The first is that hybridity is understood as subversive and pervasive, exceptional and ordinary, marginal yet mainstream. For instance, Werbner (1997) writes that "The current fascination with cultural hybridity masks an elusive paradox. Hybridity is celebrated as powerfully interruptive and yet theorized as commonplace and pervasive" (p. 1). The second paradox is that hybridity's foggy conceptual circumference, in other words its extreme openness, allows for unpredictable, arbitrary, and exclusionary closure. This is illustrated by Gómez-Peña (1996), who proposes the metaphor New World Border as a substitute to that of the New World Order. Proclaiming hybridity as the dominant characteristic of contemporary culture, Gómez-Peña acknowledges the concept's limitations, writing that "precisely because of its elasticity and open nature, the hybrid model can be appropriated by anyone to mean practically anything. Since the essence of its borders is oscillation, these boundaries can be conveniently repositioned to include and exclude different peoples and communities" (1996, pp. 12–13). These paradoxes have become wedges through which critics have attacked hybridity as poststructuralist license, and accused its proponents of reactionary politics wrapped in theoretical jargon.

One form of criticism argues that because of its pervasiveness, hybridity is theoretically useless. Werbner (1997) summarizes this point of view when she writes that "All cultures are always hybrid. . . . Hybridity is meaningless as a description of 'culture,' because this 'museumizes' culture as a 'thing.' . . . Culture as an analytic concept is always hybrid . . . since it can be understood properly only as the historically negotiated creation of more or less coherent symbolic and social worlds" (Werbner, 1997, p. 15). Since all culture is always hybrid, this argument goes, then hybridity is conceptually disposable. Gilroy (1993) offers a slightly nuanced rendition of this argument when he states that "creolisation, *métissage*, *mestizaje*, and hybridity" are "rather unsatisfactory ways of naming the processes of cultural mutation and restless (dis)continuity that exceed racial discourse and avoid capture by its agents" (p. 2).

A second objection to the use of hybridity is that it is a form of self-indulgence by diasporic intellectuals who have the cultural and economic resources that allow them to spend time and effort theorizing. This argument is maintained by several contributors to the Werbner and Modood volume (1997), such as Friedman (1997), who in Werbner's words, finds hybridity discourse to be a form of "moral self-congratulation" (Werbner, 1997, p. 22), or Hutnyk (1997) who sees hybridity as a political deadend that trivializes ethnic politics. In communication scholarship, this argument is taken up against postcolonial theory at large by Kavoori (1998) who argues that the term postcolonial *"is a term less about the world it seeks to describe and more about the world its users occupy"* (p. 201, emphasis in original).

The third argument against hybridity is related to the second. Werbner (1997) writes that "Too much hybridity . . . leaves all the old problems of class exploitation and racist oppression unresolved" (p. 20). Van der Veer (1997) puts it this way, "the hybridity celebrated in Cultural Studies has little revolutionary potential since it is part of the very discourse of bourgeois capitalism and modernity which it claims to displace" (p. 104). The use of hybridity has thus been criticized as politically suspicious because it allegedly lends legitimacy to a corporate rhetoric that frames cultural mixture as a market to be taken by capital, and at the same time elides accusations of economic domination and assorted forms of imperialism. Ahmad (1995) delivered one of the most scathing condemnations of hybridity, arguing that within the current context of global market neoliberalism, "speaking with virtually mindless pleasure of transnational cultural hybridity, and of politics of contingency, amounts, in effect, to endorsing the cultural claims of transnational capital itself" (p. 12).

A fourth criticism of the use of hybridity is found in the discussion of the meanings and implications of multiculturalism. Here, hybridity is seen as a strategy of cooptation used by the power holders to neutralize difference. Chow (1993) encapsulates this view, when she writes: "What Bhabha's word 'hybridity' [revives], in the masquerade of deconstructing anti-imperialism, and 'difficult' theory, is an old functionalist notion of what a dominant culture permits in the interest of maintaining its own equilibrium" (p. 35). Chow (1993) and others (see García-Canclini, 1989), point out that hybridity is hegemonically constructed in the interest of dominant sectors in society.

The insights offered by critics of hybridity underscore the ambiguous and disputed meanings of the concept. However, they merely describe hybridity's controversial status, and stop short of engaging it as a problematic. After all, if hybridity is pervasive, as most scholars of culture seem to agree, then we do need to name hybridity and develop contextual tools to tackle its vexing ambiguity. Hybridity becomes a floating signifier ripe for appropriation, precisely because we use the concept without rigorous theoretical grounding. I am not insinuating that there should be a singular perspective on hybridity that scholars ought to adhere to. Rather, I am contending that a nongrounded use of hybridity is detrimental to theorizing in international and intercultural communication because it encourages superficial uses of the concept. Such uses will tend to be descriptive rather than analytical, utilitarian rather than critical. Since instances of cultural mixture abound in intercultural relations, a merely descriptive use of hybridity is especially threatening because it leads to uncritical claims that "all cultures are hybrid" and evacuates hybridity of any heuristic value. This underscores the importance of grounding hybridity contextually and theoretically, utilizing it tactically in individual projects and strategically in communication theory at large. The following analysis will use the 1998 *Washington Post* series on "American Popular Culture Abroad" as an opportunity to address, first, the implications of the use of hybridity in representations of cultural globalization. Second, the analysis will serve as the initial step in theorizing a strategic vision of hybridity within intercultural and international communication.

Cultural globalization and hybridity in the *Washington Post*

In October 1998, the *Washington Post* published a series of articles on "American Popular Culture Abroad." The first article appeared on October 25, with the headline "American Pop Penetrates Worldwide" (Farhi & Rosenfeld, 1998). Exhibiting its global credentials, the paper credits numerous contributors to the story corresponding from Tehran, Nairobi, Hong Kong, Beijing, New Delhi, Mexico City, London, Paris, Jerusalem, Bogota, Warsaw, Moscow, Berlin, Tokyo, and Toronto. Two articles followed on October 26. One was submitted from Los Angeles with the headline "Hollywood Tailors its Movies to Sell in Foreign Markets," its subheadline claiming "Studios Say 'Ethnic' Films Are Not Popular Overseas" (Waxman, 1998). The other was sent from Kuala Lumpur, Malaysia, and was titled "Malaysians Create Hybrid Culture with American Imports," with the subheadline "Despite Government Censorship, Young People Enthusiastically Embrace Western Music,

Fashions" (Rosenfeld, 1998). On October 27, the *Washington Post* carried the last two articles in the series. "Barbie, 'Titanic' Show Good Side of U.S." was filed from the Iranian capital, Tehran (Lancaster, 1998), while the other, "With Popularity Comes Pitfalls" (Trueheart, 1998), was sent from Paris.

As the newspaper of record in the capital city of the world's sole remaining super-power, the *Washington Post* is highly influential. It is read by the U.S. political elite, whose opinions and policies have global implications. As a significant site of representation, the capital's leading newspaper carries discourses that warrant attention and scrutiny. Due to this status, the *Washington Post*'s discourse of hybridity as the primary characteristic of international cultural relations between the United States and developing nations merits a close reading. An examination of the five articles on "American Popular Culture Abroad" first reveals that in some instances, hybridity is deployed directly, such as in the headline on Malaysia ("Malaysians Create Hybrid Culture with American Imports," Rosenfeld, 1998). In most cases, however, hybridity is generally evoked as a characteristic feature of transcultural dynamics. Due to hybridity's conceptual ambiguity and the controversy over its meanings and implications, the *Washington Post*'s adoption of the concept calls for a critical deconstruction of the articles. In that undertaking, I attempt to answer the following questions: How is hybridity deployed in the articles? Is it embedded in a progressive discourse of cultural globalization that takes into account global inequalities? Or is hybridity used as a shroud for cultural disparity, justifying the cultural, and by extension politico-economic, global order?

As a reading strategy, deconstruction exposes the "discrepancy between a text's explicit 'statement' [hybridity as enlightened diversity] and its implicit 'gesture' [hybridity as a progressive discourse of cultural difference, or hybridity as cultural hegemony]" (Derrida, 1976, p. 162). It proceeds in two phases. The first stage is *renversement*, which means inversing, or overturning, where the critic knocks down the "violent hierarchy" (Derrida, 1972, p. 56) characteristic of discursive formations. This shakes up positions of discursive privilege and privation since "to deconstruct is first of all, at a given moment, to knock down the hierarchy" (Derrida, 1972, p. 57). However, this inversion does not change the systemic rules of the discursive formation, therefore, deconstruction needs to proceed with its second phase, "the irruptive emergence of a new 'concept'," (Derrida, 1972, p. 57) which "never let itself become understandable in the previous regime" (1972, p. 57). It is in the interval between *renversement* and *irruption* that deconstruction occurs, and continues unfolding as an *analyse interminable* (Derrida, 1972, p. 57). Chang (1996) has warned against a popular misreading of Derridean deconstruction, reminding the reader that deconstruction "does not license uncurbed textual freedom, nor does it in any way lead to interpretive anarchy or moral relativism" (p. xii). In this article, deconstruction will serve to disentangle the implicit gesture from the explicit statement on hybridity presented by the *Washington Post*.

Hybridity and the lure of the West

The five articles in the *Washington Post* series "American Popular Culture Abroad" focus on two dimensions of the transnational reception of U.S. mass-mediated culture: Western technology and non-Western desire. Western technology is depicted as an instrument that undermines censorship in non-Western countries, and also as a fetish of Western slickness, modernity, and creativity to which foreign audiences aspire. In the article "Barbie, 'Titanic' Show Good Side of U.S." (Lancaster, 1998), the reader is treated to a detailed report of the impotence of governments worldwide against the cultural tide unleashed onto their countries by Western technology. Focusing on the reception of American popular culture in Iran, which is perceived as the ideological and cultural arch-nemesis of the United States, the article quotes an Iranian journalist saying that "part of the fascination with American movies" is due to "Hollywood special-effects wizardry" (p. A1). The other articles describe a variety of ways by which the United States can project its culture around the world because of its highly developed media technologies. One article quotes an American film marketing executive explaining the popularity of American popular culture abroad: "This is a huge, huge pace, and it's being fueled by the various platforms for American product, whether it's the newest one, DVD, or basic cable, or pay-per-view" (Waxman, 1998, p. A1). Another article claims that,

> There is less to Iranian censorship than meets the eye. Despite stiff fines, satellite dishes are widely if discreetly used, and customs authorities are helpless against the flood of tapes, videocassettes and other illicit materials smuggled from abroad; one diplomat described an Iranian friend who boasted recently of having passed through the airport here with 35 CDs hidden in his clothing and bags. (Lancaster, 1998, p. A1)

This excerpt articulates Western technology with non-Western desire for U.S. popular culture. Technology and desire constitute a potent articulation undermining allegedly authoritarian protectionist tendencies. The frustrated desire that non-Western audiences have for U.S. popular culture is depicted as an irresistible attraction. Accounts of the relationship between U.S. popular culture and foreign audiences are peppered with varying degrees of sexual connotation, casting U.S. popular culture as a dominant male who commands submissive desire from global audiences. The first article's headline sets the tone, proclaiming "American Pop *Penetrates* [italics added] Worldwide" (Farhi & Rosenfeld, 1998, p. A1). In the same article, the authors write about "the *desire* [italics added] to appear more American" (Farhi & Rosenfeld, 1998, p. A1) which motivate Indian youth as they adopt one fad after another from U.S. cultural imports. Another article describes how Malaysia, "like much of the developing world . . . *embraces* [italics added] American popular culture" (Rosenfeld, 1998, p. A23). The article proceeds by claiming that in Malaysia "as elsewhere, *the love affair is fraught with turbulence and passion* [italics added], ambivalence and confusion" (Rosenfeld, 1998, A23). Direct quotes from artists and intellectuals about sexual content in U.S. popular culture are highlighted. For example, a nationally renowned Malaysian cartoonist is quoted saying that people in his native village are no more "*innocent* [italics added]" (Rosenfeld, 1998, p. A23) as a result of being exposed to U.S. popular culture through television. Likewise, a Malaysian advertising executive is quoted claiming that to Malaysian censors "Armpits are a no-no. No bare shoulders or backs. The *American influence they want to keep out is almost always sex* [italics added]" (Rosenfeld, 1998, p. A23). Still another article describes a McDonald's restaurant in a non-U.S. location as a "*pleasure zone* [italics added]" (Trueheart, 1998, p. A19), while another article writes about "*the lure of the forbidden fruit* [italics added]" which has "grabbed younger Iranians by the lapels" (Lancaster, 1998, p. A1). While it is true that U.S. material culture enjoys global popularity, research has consistently shown that audiences prefer locally produced fare because of cultural proximity (see Chadha and Kavoori, 2000; Sinclair, Jacka, & Cunningham, 1996; Straubhaar, 1991; Tracey, 1985). The articles do not contextualize reception by introducing other media texts—national and regional—enjoyed by the international audiences spellbound by U.S. popular culture.

American technology and non-Western audience desire are the discursive axes upon which the transnational reception of U.S. popular culture is aligned. They form the basis of a hybridity discourse paternalistically grounded in a binary between an aspiring non-West and

U.S. popular culture, the latter setting global standards of taste to be emulated by the former. It is ironic that one of the articles quotes no less than the head of the Malaysian Research Centre, supposedly one of the most enlightened members of his society, saying that "we don't know what we want" (Rosenfeld, 1998, p. A23). In the same article, a Malaysian rock star, dubbed "The Bob Dylan of Malaysia," similarly says: "Our own people are very insecure about their music" (Rosenfeld, 1998, p. A23). A condescending tone is also manifest when Hollywood is described as a source of learning, elevating the level of sophistication of worldwide viewers—foreign audiences are claimed to have developed a more refined artistic taste as a result of their exposure to American movies. In support of this claim, Sony Pictures Entertainment President John Calley is quoted saying, "foreign moviegoers want to see anything that's good. They're like us. We have in some way Americanized much of the world; they've assimilated a lot of stuff" (Waxman, 1998, p. A1). The flip side of this equation, according to at least one of the articles, is that U.S. popular culture and public culture suffer as a result. This is expressed by Gitlin, who states that, "Insofar as American-based studios are making stuff for the global market, the stuff is dumbed down" perhaps leading to "the cheapening of social discourse" in the United States (see Waxman, 1998, A1). This view ignores the alternative perspective that the adoption of U.S. commercial broadcasting and its programming formats, largely dependent on sensational talk and game shows, might have "cheapened" social discourse globally. Nevertheless, the articles posit American popular culture as a benchmark, an opportunity for developing countries to shed their allegedly unsophisticated tastes as they attempt to emulate the cultural sensibilities of American audiences. Again, this position ignores numerous landmark reception studies where audiences are seen as actively capable of alternative interpretation (Ang, 1985; Liebes & Katz, 1990; Morley, 1980, 1994). The articles thus contend that foreign audiences *create* hybrid cultures while succumbing to the seduction of U.S. popular culture. The contradiction between granting global audiences agency in creating hybridity, while denying them agency in receiving U.S. popular culture, is complicated further by the articles' concomitant claim that reception is the site where hybrid cultures are created.

Hybridity as corporate multiculturalism

This contradictorily simultaneous granting and denial of agency continues as the *Washington Post* articles establish hybridity as a discursive context in which the American movie industry is largely motivated by customer expectations of overseas audiences, again imbuing these audiences with a sort of consumer agency. Thus one article (Waxman, 1998) begins:

> Most Americans know that our popular culture exerts a powerful influence across the globe, shaping attitudes, trends and styles. But the inverse—a more subtle effect—is also true: The worldwide hunger for U.S.-made entertainment helps steer our own culture, by encouraging projects that will sell overseas and discouraging those that foreign audiences are thought to spurn. (p. A1)

Consequently, according to these articles, the global marketplace dictates studio practices. Hence the headline "Hollywood Tailors its Movies to Sell in Foreign Markets" (Waxman, 1998, p. A1). The article then claims that "The global market is the engine behind Hollywood's assembly-line," thus justifying the high number of violent action films churned out by Hollywood. Some ingredients for global box-office success are added at the last minute:

> Two months before the opening of *Armageddon*, the story of an asteroid hurtling toward Earth, Disney decided to add not only $3 million more in explosions, but also reaction-to-the-asteroid shots from Morocco and Paris. Said Disney Studios Chairman Joe Roth, "It was to make sure the movie had more of an international feel to it." (Waxman, 1998, p. A1)

This cosmetic internationalization of the movie's textual surface in fact begs an alternative explication. What those so-called international scenes do is to cast the United States as the sole protector of the world, since no other country participated in the attempt to destroy the asteroid. In effect, then, the cosmopolitan textual surface asserts the position of the United States as the sole remaining superpower.

Based on a "customer-as-king" cliché arguing in favor of the alleged benefits of transnational capitalism to the world population, hybridity is enlisted as a natural dimension of global strategic marketing, predicated on conquering diverse niche markets. Thus transnational capitalism is painted as a progressive force spearheading the global expansion of democracy. As demonstrated in the preceding pages, this corporate discourse evokes the interrelated themes of customer desire and satisfaction, the retreat or weakness of the state, and the conflation of capitalism with democracy. These are the principal tenets of economic neo-liberalism, a philosophy of governance that has been ascendant for several decades and has become the dominant policy mode in leading political and economic circles. This vision of hybridity is thus grounded in the neo-liberal ideology driving the current stage of globalization, with its relentless push towards opening new markets, dismantling state barriers to market expansion, and widespread consumerism. At the surface of the *Washington Post*'s version of hybridity, foreign audiences are elevated from their initial status as immature viewers to that of an active and sophisticated market audience. In turn, this discourse sets up foreign audiences as a culpable Other in the context of racial tensions in the United States. The articles quote U.S. movie executives defending their propensity not to cast minority actors in major movies, imputing their exclusionary casting decisions to foreign audiences. In "Studios Say 'Ethnic' Films Are Not Popular Overseas" (Waxman, 1998, p. A1), the reporter writes:

> Foreign distributors, according to [Hollywood] executives and producers, are less interested in investing in films that focus on women (*Fried Green Tomatoes* was not a big hit overseas) and have almost no interest in movies that have African Americans or other minority casts and themes. (p. A1)

Insinuated in this statement is the assumption that foreign audiences are racist and misogynist. The article then refers to the lawsuit by Lawrence Fishburne against producer Andrew Vajna, who dropped the actor from the cast after securing the less costly and relatively unknown Samuel L. Jackson for the role in *Die Hard With a Vengeance*. The article describes the objections by minority actors in Hollywood to what they see as institutionalized racism, but the reporter perfunctorily uses the euphemism "racial bias" instead of racism. Similarly, the article does mention that independent movies with foreign funding do not face the same casting restrictions. However, the general tone is the one manifest in this quote by a Sony executive:

> We're cognizant of what does not work internationally . . . Black baseball movies, period dramas about football, rap, inner-city films—most countries can't relate to that. Americana seems to be desired by international markets, but there comes a point when even they will resist and say, "We don't get it,"

and it's generally in that ethnic, inner-city, sports-driven region. He paused.
We can't give 'em what they don't want. (p. A1)

The commercialism of this last passage speaks for itself. To be fair, the reporter attempts to provide some nuance to this theme, describing how Whoopi Goldberg's *Sister Act* was very popular abroad. However, the issue of race is surreptitiously discarded when the reporter concludes, "It's a question, largely, of mathematics. In Hollywood, cold calculations are made based on the projected international box office revenues" (Waxman, 1998, p. A1). This is not to accuse the reporters or newspaper of racism but to underscore that the article's general orientation preempted an adequate treatment of the issue of race. The article goes on to describe the "Star Power" list that Hollywood goes by, with Tom Cruise scoring a perfect 100, followed by Harrison Ford at 99, Mel Gibson at 98, etc. The top 20 list only contains 2 women, with Jodie Foster rating 94 and Julia Roberts 92. The list makes no mention of minorities. According to the articles, the reason Hollywood does not cast African-American, Hispanic, and Asian-American actors in major blockbusters is because minority actors are not popular with foreign audiences. The same case, to a lesser degree, is applied to women actors. Domestic U.S. issues are thus given a global amplification pitting U.S. minorities against foreign audiences.

The newspaper stories offer no critical evaluation of Hollywood's modus operandi, contributing to the erasure of ideological issues in favor of strictly economic explanations of movie industry practices. These practices embody what the Chicago Cultural Studies Group (1992) coined "corporate multiculturalism," and illustrates the "great danger [that] lies in thinking that multiculturalism could be exported multiculturally" (p. 550). In effect, the hybridity enlisted in the pages of the *Washington Post* indirectly enacts a backlash on diversity by claiming that the bottom line determines the color line. The articles thus articulate economic neo-liberalism with socio-political conservatism, foregrounding hybridity to conceal a corporate-justified "racial bias" that operates both within the United States and globally. Hybridity is thus professed as an important element of transnational corporate multiculturalism.

Articulating hybridity and hegemony in cultural globalization: towards an intercontextual theory of hybridity

In light of the deconstruction of the *Washington Post*'s version of hybridity, it is beneficial to reformulate the questions raised in the first pages of this essay: How does the appropriation of hybridity in the *Washington Post* frame cultural globalization? More specifically, does the deployment of hybridity justify, or question, uneven transnational and transcultural relations? This tactical endeavor focusing on one text (the "American Popular Culture Abroad" series) echoes the larger strategic concerns of the postcolonial project, which, according to Shome (1996), are summed up in two questions:

> How do Western discursive practices, in their representations of the world and
> of themselves, legitimize the contemporary global power structures? To what
> extent do the cultural texts of nations such as the United States and England
> reinforce the neo-imperial political practices of these nations? (p. 42)

The *Washington Post* series constructs a monolithic hybridity in which cultures as different as Poland, Iran, Malaysia, Nigeria, and Brazil are lumped together as unabashedly welcoming United States popular culture since it is more appealing than local fare. As stated earlier, research has shown that audiences usually prefer local to imported popular culture products, an issue completely neglected in the articles. Hybridity is thus seen as a capitulation to the seduction of otherness, and not as a mutation and renewal of identity. This point is made clear in the way the *Washington Post* articles construct hybridity as a defeat of local governments in the non-West, depicted as underdeveloped, corrupt, and authoritarian. Finally, the articles do not scrutinize Hollywood's claim that global market demands lead to casting decisions that exclude minority actors. The *Washington Post* "American Popular Culture Abroad" series thus provides a textually seductive but politically unfruitful deployment of hybridity. This recognition gives credence to materialist critics who accuse proponents of hybridity of complicity with the claims and goals of transnational capitalism.

Actually, the articles' characterization of hybridity offers a heuristic exemplar of the vulnerability of the postcolonial project to appropriation. In this case, hybridity is appropriated in an attempt to fix the meanings constructed by global audiences in their reception of U.S. popular culture. This transnational cultural flow occurs in a context where American-based media conglomerates have become increasingly active in the global arena. These transnational corporations control both production structures and program content. To a large extent, they also control the worldwide distribution of their products. However, as nearly two decades of scholarship on active audience formation in media and cultural studies demonstrates, it is the reception of products that is not fully controllable by transnational media corporations. The articles' portrayal of reception as a space of hybrid creation results in the eviction of power imbalances in transnational cultural exchanges, and the concomitant celebration of a nonthreatening hybridity. The hybridity in question here operates to discursively foreclose the reception process, putting the entire chain of signification under the control of transnational capital. In their embrace of a power-free notion of hybridity, the *Washington Post* articles validate Western cultural preeminence.

Exposing this hybridity's explicit statement of enlightened diversity and unmasking its implicit gesture of cultural hegemony clears the scene for an alternative, and critical, theory of hybridity to emerge. This is important because, as stated earlier in this article, the demise of the cultural imperialism model has left a major theoretical void in international communication, culture theory, and research. Moreover, theoretical construction is a necessity because mere criticism offers no exit from the political and conceptual paradoxes of hybridity. These are (a) hybridity's concurrent subversiveness and pervasiveness, and (b) hybridity's extreme polysemy and instability, in that it is always in the process of occurring, unfolding, and undoing the fixity of binary opposites. As such, hybridity is always subject to discursive preemption, like the one performed in the *Washington Post*'s articles. Therefore, a critical theory of hybridity in the context of intercultural and international communication must address hybridity's propensity for conceptual and political slippage.

In this endeavor, it is helpful to theorize hybridity as an undecidable (*indécidable*; Derrida, 1972, p. 58), defined as "that which no longer allows itself to be understood within . . . (binary) opposition, but which . . . inhabits it, resists it and disorganizes it, but *without ever* constituting a third term, without ever leaving room for a solution" (Derrida, 1972, p. 58, emphasis in original). Conceptualizations of hybridity are arduous to the extent that they attempt to constitute a third term, to fix the meaning of the hybrid. In spite of the potential for antiprogressive appropriation and conceptual ambiguity, hybridity is undeniable as a global existential cultural condition (Hall, 1991a, 1991b; Joseph, 1999; Kraidy, 1999; Rosaldo, 1995; Said, 1994; Werbner, 1997). Therefore, despite theorists' discomfort and reluctance vis-à-vis the concept of hybridity, I do not see any credible substitute to characterize the dual forces of globalization and localization, cohesion and dispersal, disjuncture and mixture, that capture transnational and transcultural dialectics. A critical theorizing is crucial precisely because hybridity's openness makes it particularly vulnerable to appropriation by transnational capitalism. Hybridity is such a slippery concept because it is simultaneously an undecidable and a conceptual inevitability.

The theoretical challenge to intercultural and international communication theory thus resides in the following conundrum: Under what conditions does hybridity, as a global pervasive condition, fulfill, or not fulfill, its progressive potential in a local context? In what context do social agents revert to a hegemonic deployment of hybridity? Finally, what attributes should a critical theory of hybridity require for it to be a meaningful heuristic within intercultural and international communication? In other words, what theory will allow us to render hybridity as a mode of lived experience and aesthetic sensibility, while at the same time map up the working of power shaping enactments of hybridity? More specifically, how can we theorize hybridity as a communicative practice of meaning and power, or, how can we articulate hybridity and hegemony in communication theory? These questions have been the driving force behind this article, and the discussion and conclusion that follow attempt to address them.

The articulation of hybridity and power is perhaps best captured by the term "intercontextuality," coined by Appadurai (1996), which allows us to understand text and context to be mutually constitutive in a field of not necessarily correspondent power/signification. I propose an intercontextual theory of hybridity that explicates transnational cultural dynamics by articulating hybridity and hegemony in a global context. By context I do not merely mean an environment or a setting where practices unfold and texts find their grounding. Rather, I use context as a constitutive and constituting force, in the sense elaborated by Jennifer Daryl Slack (1996) when she wrote: "The context is not something *out there, within which practices occur or which influence the development of practices*. Rather, *identities, practices, and effects generally, constitute the very context with which they are practices, identities, or effects*" (p. 125, emphasis in original). An intercontextual theory of hybridity emphasizes how processes of creating consent and coordinating interests in a moving equilibrium underscore manifestations and deployments of hybridity. In the context of international and intercultural communication, an intercontextual theory of hybridity focuses on the mutually constitutive interplay and overlap of cultural, economic, and political forces in international communication processes. Perhaps more importantly, an intercontextual theory of hybridity would examine the relationship between structure and agency as a dialectical articulation whose results are not preordained. In this respect, García-Canclini (1989) writes that:

> The increase in processes of hybridization makes it evident that we understand very little about power if we only examine confrontations and vertical actions. Power would not function if it were exercised only by bourgeoisie over proletarians, whites over indigenous people, parents over children, the media over receivers. Since all these relations are *interwoven* with each other, each one achieves an effectiveness that it would never be able to by itself. (p. 259)

This echoes Hall's proposition: "A theory of articulation is both a way of understanding how ideological elements come, under certain conditions, to cohere together in a discourse, and a way of asking how they do or do not become articulated, at specific conjunctures, to certain political subjects" (1986, p. 53). An intercontextul theory of hybridity, to paraphrase García-Canclini and Hall, will allow us to comprehend how under certain conditions, in certain contexts, ideological elements coalesce in a certain discourse of hybridity. An intercontextual theory of hybridity thus becomes a map of the diffuse workings of power. It recognizes that hybridity is not a posthegemonic state. To go back to international communication theory as an example, an intercontextual theory of hybridity moves us beyond cultural imperialism's economic determinism, and at the same time provides a needed amendment to "postimperialist" work that ignores power and inequality. Applied to transnational cultural dynamics, intercontextuality maintains that hybridity is always articulated with hegemonic power. Our attention, then, needs to be redirected from debating the political and theoretical usefulness of hybridity, to analyzing how hegemonic structures operate in a variety of contexts to construct different hybridities.

The *Washington Post* articles are illustrative of the hybridity/hegemony articulation, because hybridity is summoned up to justify a transnational cultural hegemony made possible by power asymmetries. It is consequently an act of discursive naturalization of unequal relations by those at the privileged end of these relations. This underscores Laclau's argument that "A class is hegemonic not so much to the extent that it is able to impose a uniform conception of the world on the rest of society, but to the extent that it can articulate different visions of the world in such a way that their potential antagonism is neutralized" (1977, p. 161). By articulating a hybrid vision of global culture characterized by nonconflictual relations and a longing for Western culture, the articles on "American Popular Culture Abroad" obscure the vast economic, political and technological inequities between nations. These issues are given marginal treatment, where they are neutralized by a utilitarian deployment of the hybrid.

In order to have a critical edge, hybridity should be understood as a communicative practice. A practice, in Stuart Hall's terms, is "how a structure is actively reproduced" (1985, p. 103). This stands in stark contrast with hybridity as conceptualized in the *Washington Post* articles, which is posited as a result, a product of transnational mediations. Therefore, hybridity should be conceptualized as one modality in which hegemony is practiced, reproducing and maintaining the new world order. In the *Washington Post*, hybridity emerges as a privileged characterization of cultural globalization, one of a few theories advanced to understand intercivilizational interactions in the post-Cold War era (Fukuyama, 1992; Huntington, 1996).

Although hybridity may well be what Derrida (1972) would call an undecidable, we must find arbitrary entry points from which to tackle the practice of hegemony in hybridity. Whereas Derrida's post-Marxist tendency (which Hall, 1985, refers to as "no necessary correspondence") makes tackling the hybrid arduous, Hall's neo-Marxist interpretation allows the critic to narrow down on those conjunctures when correspondence is sutured. To that effect, Hall writes that, "The principal theoretical reversal accomplished by 'no necessary correspondence' is that determinacy is transferred from the genetic origins of class or other social forces in a structure to the effects or results of a practice" (1985, p. 95).

The foundations of an intercontextual theory of hybridity have in fact been under construction, because the burgeoning studies have not led to a unified hybridity paradigm. It is clear that the concept of hybridity has been appropriated to serve a variety of theoretical explorations and political agendas. This undermines any claims to a universalistic theory of hybridity, which would obfuscate the contingent, contextual, and processual imbrication of the hegemonic and the hybrid. If, as Slack (1996) has argued, "the analysis of any concrete situation or phenomenon entails the exploration of complex, multiple, and theoretically abstract non-necessary links" (p. 119), then a theory of hybridity is both useful and necessary to understand global cultural complexity. Critics of hybridity in particular, and postcolonial theory more generally, should heed Butler's (1998) warning against "the resurgence of a theoretical anachronism . . . which seeks to identify the new social movements with the merely cultural, and the cultural with the derivative and secondary" (p. 36).

An intercontextual theory of hybridity provides an initial conceptual platform for a critical cultural transnationalism that helps us understand neocolonial discourses and actions in transnational cultural dynamics. I propose this theoretical development in the hope that future scholarship would take up the challenge to address hybridity in international communication theory and research. For more than a decade, a growing consensus has emerged to discard cultural imperialism, for reasons outlined earlier in this article. Still, cultural imperialism has been a *critical* paradigm whose proponents have exposed power imbalances between the industrialized West and the developing world. Most available alternatives to cultural imperialism tend to implicitly or explicitly espouse neoliberal ideology, without a critical scrutiny of its implications. Grounded in an intercontextual theory of hybridity, critical cultural transnationalism emphasizes *hybridities as practices of hegemony*. Such a theory is useful to the extent that it helps us illuminate the slippery and interstitial workings of power in transnational contexts that ostensibly declare themselves nonpower zones of cultural mixture. An intercontextual theory of hybridity belongs in the arsenal of the critical cultural scholar, because it illuminates issues of context, process, and representation central to intercultural and international communication. We need to continue theorizing hybridity as a condition that is not merely cultural. For, after all, in Hall's words, "The only theory worth having is that which you have to fight off, not that which you speak with profound fluency" (1992, p. 280).

Note

1   Oliveira (1995) argues that *telenovelas* in Latin America (a dramatic genre similar to soap operas) do not constitute "a reaction against an imported worldview," but rather "amplif[y] the creolization of U.S. cultural products" (p. 119). He concludes that the success of locally produced telenovelas in Brazil "enhance[s] not diversity, but domination" (p. 129). In support of his argument Oliveira cites Sinclair (1990) and Beltran and Cardona (1982), in addition to six other Brazilian studies. It is important to note that scholars like Rogers and Antola (1985) and Straubhaar (1991) have reached the opposite conclusion. Rogers and Antola even referred to a "reverse cultural imperialism" (1985, p. 33) from Latin America into the United States. The most recent reappraisal of this debate (Biltereyst & Meers, 2000), based on an "empirical comparative enquiry" (p. 408) of telenovela-flows from Latin America to Europe, recommends that "the telenovela phenomenon should not be treated as a case in the traditional North-South dialogue, but should be firmly located in the debate around globalization strategies of late-capitalist cultural industries" (p. 410).

References

Ahmad, A. (1992). *In theory: Classes, nations, literatures*. London: Verso

Ahmad, A. (1995). The politics of literary postcoloniality. *Race and Class, 36*, 1–20.

Ang, I. (1985). *Watching Dallas*. London: Routledge.

Appadurai, A. (1996). *Modernity at large: Cultural dimensions of globalization*. Minneapolis: University of Minnesota Press.

Appiah, K. A. (1991). Is the post- in postmodernism the post- in postcolonial? *Critical Inquiry, 17*, 336–357.

Archetti, E. P. (1999). *Masculinities: Football, polo and the tango in Argentina*. Oxford, UK: Berg.

Ashcroft, B., Griffiths, G., & Tiffin, H. (1998). *Key concepts in post-colonial studies*. New York: Routledge.

Bahri, D. (1995). One more time with feeling: What is postcolonialism? *Ariel, 26*, 51–82.

Beltrán, L. R., & Cardona, E. F. (1982). Comunicação dominada. Rio de Janeiro, Brazil: Paz & Terra.

Bhabba, H. (1994). *The location of culture*. New York: Routledge.

Biltereyst, D., & Meers, P. (2000). The international telenovela debate and the contra-flow argument: A reappraisal. *Media, Culture and Society, 22*, 393–413.

Boyd-Barrett, O. (1998). Media imperialism reformulated. In D. K. Thussu (Ed.), *Electronic empires: Global media and local resistance* (pp. 157–176). London: Arnold.

Butler, J. (1998, January/February). Merely cultural. *The New Left Review, 227*, 33–44.

Chadha, K., & Kavoori, A. (2000). Media imperialism revisited: Some findings from the Asian case. *Media, Culture and Society*, *22*, 415–432.

Chang, B. G. (1996). *Deconstructing communication: Representation, subject, and economies of exchange*. Minneapolis: University of Minnesota Press.

Chicago Cultural Studies Group. (1992). Critical multiculturalism. *Critical Inquiry*, *18*, 530–555.

Chow, R. (1993). *Writing diaspora: Tactics of intervention in contemporary cultural studies*. Indianapolis: Indiana University Press.

Derrida, J. (1972). *Positions*. Paris: Les Éditions de Minuit.

Derrida, J. (1976). *Of grammatology* (G. C. Spivak, Trans.). Baltimore: Johns Hopkins University Press.

Dirlik, A. (1994). The postcolonial aura: Third world criticism in the age of global capitalism. *Critical Inquiry*, *20*, 328–356.

Farhi, P., & Rosenfeld, M. (1998, October 25). American pop penetrates worldwide. *The Washington Post*, p. A1.

Fejes, F. (1981). Media imperialism: An assessment. *Media, Culture and Society*, *3*, 281–289.

Friedman, J. (1997). Global crises, the struggle for cultural identity and intellectual porkbarrelling: Cosmopolitan versus locals, ethnics and nationals in an era of de-hegemonisation. In P. Werbner & T. Moddod (Eds.), *Debating cultural hybridity: Multi-cultural identities and the politics of anti-racism* (pp. 70–89). London: Zed Books.

Fukuyama, F. (1992). *The end of history and the last man*. New York: Avon.

García-Canclini, N. (1989). *Culturas híbridas: Estratgegias para entrar y salir de la modernidad* [Hybrid cultures: Strategies for entering and leaving modernity]. Mexico City, Mexico: Grijalbo.

García-Canclini, N. (1990). Cultural reconversion (H. Staver, Trans.). In G. Yúdice, J. Franco, & J. Flores (Eds.), *On edge: The crisis of Latin American culture* (pp. 29–44). Minneapolis: University of Minnesota Press.

Gilroy, P. (1993). *The Black Atlantic: Modernity and double consciousness*. Cambridge, MA: Harvard University Press.

Gómez-Peña, G. (1996). *The new world border: Prophecies, poems and loqueras for the end of the century*. San Francisco: City Lights.

Hale, C. (1999). Travel warning: Elite appropriations of hybridity, mestizaje, antiracism, equality, and other progressive-sounding discourses in highland Guatemala. *Journal of American Folklore*, *112*, 297–315.

Hall, S. (1985). Signification, representation, ideology: Althusser and the post-structuralist debates. *Critical Studies in Mass Communication*, *2*, 91–114.

Hall, S. (1986). On postmodernism and articulation: An interview with Stuart Hall, edited by Lawrence Grossberg. *Journal of Communication Inquiry*, *10*, 45–60.

Hall, S. (1991a). The local and the global: Globalization and ethnicity. In A. D. King (Ed.), *Culture, globalization and the world-system: Contemporary conditions for the representation of identity* (pp. 19–40). London: Macmillan.

Hall, S. (1991b). Old and new identities, old and new ethnicities. In A. D. King (Ed.), *Culture, globalization and the world-system: Contemporary conditions for the representation of identity* (pp. 41–68). London: Macmillan.

Hall, S. (1992). Cultural studies and its theoretical legacies. In L. Grossberg, C. Nelson, and P. Treichler (Eds.), *Cultural studies* (pp. 277–294). New York: Routledge.

Hall S. (1996). When was the post-colonial? Thinking at the limit. In L. Curti & I. Chambers (Eds.), *The postcolonial question* (pp. 242–260). New York: Routledge.

Hannerz, U. (1987). The world in creolization. *Africa*, *54*, 546–59.

Hegde, R. S. (1998). A view from elsewhere: Locating difference and the politics of representation from a transnational feminist perspective. *Communication Theory*, *8*, 271–297.

Huntington, S. (1996). *The clash of civilizations and the remaking of world order*. New York: Touchstone.

Hutnyk, J. (1997). Adorno at Womad: South Asia crossovers and the limits of hybridity-talk. In P. Werbner & T. Moddod (Eds.), *Debating cultural hybridity: Multi-cultural identities and the politics of anti-racism* (pp. 106–138). London: Zed Books.

Joseph, M. (1999). Introduction: New hybrid identities and performance. In M. Joseph & J. N. Fink (Eds.), *Performing hybridity* (pp. 1–24). Minneapolis: University of Minnesota Press.

Joseph, M., & Fink, J. N. (Eds.). (1999). *Performing hybridity*. Minneapolis: University of Minnesota Press.

Kapchan, D. A., & Strong, P. T. (1999). Theorizing the hybrid. *Journal of American Folklore, 112*, 239–253.

Kavoori, A. P. (1998). Getting past the latest "post": Assessing the term "post-colonial." *Critical Studies in Mass Communication, 15*, 195–202.

Knox, R. (1850). *The races of men: A fragment*. London: Renshaw.

Kolar-Panov, D. (1996). Video and the diasporic imagination of selfhood: A case-study of the Croatians in Australia. *Cultural Studies, 10*, 288–314.

Kraidy, M. M. (1999). The global, the local, and the hybrid: A native ethnography of glocalization. *Critical Studies in Mass Communication, 16*, 456–476.

Laclau, E. (1977). *Politics and ideology in Marxist theory*. London: New Left Books.

Lancaster, J. (1998, October 27). Barbie, 'Titanic' show good side of the U.S. *The Washington Post*, p. A1.

Liebes, T., & Katz, E. (1990). *The export of meaning: Cross-cultural readings of* Dallas. London: Oxford University Press.

Martín-Barbero, J. (1993). *Communication, culture and hegemony: From the media to mediations*. London: Sage.

Mattelart, A. (1994). *Mapping world communication: War, progress, culture*. Minneapolis: University of Minnesota Press.

Mattelart, A. (1998). Généalogie des nouveaux scénarios de la communication. In J. Berdot, F. Calvez, & I. Ramonet (Eds.), *L'Après-Télévision: Multimédia, virtuel, Internet. Actes du Colloque '25 images/seconde'*. Valence, France: CRAC. Retrieved December 31, 1998, from http://www.monde-diplomatique.fr/livre/crac/21.html

McClintock, A. (1992). The angel of progress: Pitfalls of the term "post-colonialism." *Social Text, 31/32*, 1–15.

Mignolo, W. D. (2000). *Local histories/global designs: Coloniality, subaltern knowledges, and border thinking*. Princeton, NJ: Princeton University Press.

Mishra, V., & Hodge, B. (1991). What is post(-)colonialism? *Textual Practice, 5*, 399–414.

Miyoshi, M. (1993). A borderless world? From colonialism to transnationalism and the decline of the nation-state. *Critical Inquiry, 19*, 726–750.

Moore-Gilbert, B. (1997). *Postcolonial theory: Contexts, practices, politics*. London: Verso.

Morley, D. (1980). *The "nationwide" audience*. London: British Film Institute.

Morley, D. (1994). Active audience theory: Pendulums and pitfalls. *Journal of Communication, 43*(4), 13–19.

Morley, D., & Chen, K. H. (Eds.). (1996). *Stuart Hall: Critical dialogues in cultural studies*. New York: Routledge.

Naficy, H. (1994). *The making of exile cultures: Iranian television in Los Angeles*. Minneapolis: University of Minnesota Press.

Oliveira, O. S. (1995). Brazilian soaps outshine Hollywood: Is cultural imperialism fading out? In K. Nordenstreng & H. Schiller (Eds.), *Beyond national sovereignty: International communication in the 1990s* (pp. 116–131). Norwood, NJ: Ablex.

Parameswaran, R. (1997). Colonial interventions and the postcolonial situation in India. *Gazette, 59*, 21–42.

Parameswaran, R. (1999). Western romance fiction as English-language media in postcolonial India. *Journal of Communication, 49*(3), 84–105.

Pieterse, J. N. (1994). Globalisation as hybridisation. *International Sociology, 9*, 161–184.

Rogers, E., & Antola, L. (1985). Telenovelas: A Latin American success story. *Journal of Communication, 35*(4), 24–35.

Rosaldo, R. (1995). *Hybrid cultures: Strategies for entering and leaving modernity* [Foreword]. (S. López & E. Schiappari, Trans.). Minneapolis: University of Minnesota Press.

Rosenfeld, M. (1998, October 26). Malaysians create hybrid culture with American imports. *The Washington Post*, p. A23.

Said, E. (1994). *Culture and imperialism*. New York: Vintage Books.

Shohat, E. (1992). Notes on the "post-colonial." *Social Text, 31/32*, 99–113.

Shome, R. (1996). Postcolonial interventions in the rhetorical canon: An "other" view. *Communication Theory, 6*, 40–59.

Shome, R. (1998). Caught in the term "post-colonial": Why the "post-colonial" still matters. *Critical Studies in Mass Communication, 15*, 203–212.

Sinclair, J. (1990). Neither West nor Third World: The Mexican television industry within the NWICO debate. *Media, Culture and Society, 12*, 343–360.

Sinclair, J., Jacka, E., & Cunningham, S. (Eds.). (1996). *Peripheral Vision: New patterns in global television*. London: Oxford University Press.

Slack, J. D. (1996). The theory and method of articulation in cultural studies. In D. Morley & K. H. Chen (Eds.), *Stuart Hall: Critical dialogues in cultural studies* (pp. 112–127). New York: Routledge.

Spivak, G. C. (1999). *A critique of postcolonial reason: Toward a history of the vanishing present*. Cambridge, MA: Harvard University Press.

Sreberny-Mohammadi, A. (1997). The many faces of imperialism. In P. Golding & P. Harris (Eds.), *Beyond cultural imperialism: Globalization, communication, and the new international order* (pp. 49–68). London: Sage.

Straubhaar, J. (1991). Beyond media imperialism: Asymmetrical interdependence and cultural proximity. *Critical Studies in Mass Communication, 8*, 29–38.

Stross, B. (1999). The hybrid metaphor: From biology to culture. *Journal of American Folklore, 112*, 254–257.

Tracey, M. (1985). The poisoned chalice? International television and the idea of dominance. *Daedalus, 114*, 17–56.

Truehart, C. (1998, October 27). With popularity come pitfalls. *The Washington Post*, p. A19.

Tufte, T. (1995). How do telenovelas serve to articulate hybrid cultures in contemporary Brazil? *The Nordicom Review, 2*, 29–35.

Van der Veer, P. (1997). The enigma of arrival: Hybridity and authenticity in the global space. In P. Werbner & T. Moddod (Eds.), *Debating cultural hybridity: Multi-cultural identities and the politics of anti-racism* (pp. 90–105). London: Zed Books.

Waxman, S. (1998, October 26). Hollywood tailors its movies to sell in foreign markets: Studios say 'ethnic' films are not popular overseas. *The Washington Post*, p. A1.

Werbner, P. (1997). Introduction: The dialectics of cultural hybridity. In P. Werbner & T. Moddod (Eds.), *Debating cultural hybridity: Multi-cultural identities and the politics of anti-racism* (pp. 1–26). London: Zed Books.

Werbner, P., & Moddod, T. (Eds.). (1997). *Debating cultural hybridity: Multi-cultural identities and the politics of anti-racism*. London: Zed Books.

Young, R. (1995). *Colonial desire: Hybridity in theory, culture and race*. New York: Routledge.

Chapter 27

Mark Deuze

CONVERGENCE CULTURE IN THE CREATIVE INDUSTRIES

> I am struck by the ending of *The Truman Show* [. . .] All the film can offer us is a vision of media exploitation, and all its protagonist can imagine is walking away from the media and slamming the door. It never occurs to anyone that Truman might stay on the air, generating his own content and delivering his own message, exploiting the media for his own purposes. (Jenkins, 2004: 36–7)

INDEED, WHAT WOULD HAPPEN if Truman Burbank decided to stay? Measured by current trends in ways people use media he most likely would have turned *The Truman Show* into a 24/7 videoblog (or audio-only pod-cast), offering a running commentary on the global status quo. Truman would most likely have invited viewers to contribute their views and opinions, perhaps even allowing users to upload or submit media materials themselves. Over time, Truman Burbank and a rather select fan community of 'lead users' would be running the show just like the hundreds of media professionals in Atlanta run the 24/7 television channel *CNN Headline News*, or how a team of producers, writers, managers, assistants and contestants run 24/7 reality television shows like *Survivor* or *Big Brother*. The choices of Truman and his more or less informal editorial collective would be based on trial and error, casuistry, routinization, and other similar ways of determining what kind of messages would be welcomed most. It is this difference, yet at the same time similarity, between amateur and professional media production and consumption that is the main concern of this essay.

Journalism, media and communication studies scholars tend to keep certain domains of inquiry apart. Media consumption is predominantly investigated by focusing on the way audiences receive and give meaning to media content. On the other hand, media production tends to be analyzed in terms of the political economy or sociology of the industry (Jenkins, 2004; Schudson, 2003). Such studies tend to generate answers that reinforce people's social identities either as producers or consumers of media content, and frame their responses either as acts of resisting or enforcing power relationships. If we are to consider Jenkins' suggestion for an alternate ending of *The Truman Show* (1998), what happens when the enforcing and resisting of power occurs simultaneously through media participation (Bucy and Gregson, 2001: 358)? It is in this context where one can observe the consumer of media content also becoming a producer. The key question then becomes, how we can adequately explain the process, content and consequences of media consumption and production when our contemporary media praxis seems to include both at the same time? Furthermore – and more pertinent to the topic of this article – the blurring of real or perceived boundaries between makers and users in an increasingly participatory media culture challenges consensual notions of what it means to work in the cultural industries. In this essay I consider possible strategies to understand and explain these issues, considering media work from the perspective of the individual reflective practitioner. The different forces of change impacting on what it is like to work in today's media are mapped in terms of the ways in which the media professional gives meaning to the affordances offered by the convergence of the cultures of production and consumption of media. This convergence must be seen as recombinantly driven by an industry desperate for strong customer relationships, technologies that are increasingly cheap and easy to use, and a media culture that privileges an active audience.

In this article I first identify and model (see Figure 27.1) the different and sometimes paradoxical trends attributed to the changing ways in which people professionally make media. Second, I discuss four cases of media work that exemplify these trends: *Bluffton Today* (journalism), Amazon (marketing), *Counter-Strike* (computer games) and the CPB Group (advertising). These sites of media work can be considered to be concrete examples of an emerging convergence culture in the mediamaking process (Jenkins, 2004), where media work takes place within a context of creative industries – signifying the convergence of mass media production and individual-level creativity (Hartley, 2005). These trends develop within the context of an increasingly participatory media culture as shaping the way media work gets done in, for instance, journalism (Deuze, 2003), advertising (Leckenby and Li, 2000), game development (Jeppesen and Molin, 2003), television and even film. Third, I will discuss these developments and cases in terms of their potential impact on widely shared notions about the nature of media work. My analysis is thus based on acknowledging and observing the emergence of a global participatory media culture, the gradual convergence of the cultures of production and consumption, and the integration of individual creativity and (mass) production in the cultural industries. I start by outlining these three interlocking premises.

Media participation

People who make media have collaborated with those who use media in the past. Much of the great works of art came into being because rich patrons commissioned painters and sculptors to make specific portraits, decorations and other representations signifying status and prestige in society. Such works were not just created by single art 'producers', but often came into being through intense collaboration and exchange by dedicated teams of artists, their apprentices, sponsors and visitors. Participation as a value and expectation in journalism was first established through letters to the editor sections in newspapers, and later expanded to include functions like newspaper ombudsmen and reader representatives that became an accepted part of news organizations worldwide (Van Dalen and Deuze, 2006). In television, news participation gets established through opinion polls, viewer tip hotlines and more recently by soliciting citizens to submit their own eyewitness photos and videos. Online, media participation can be seen as the defining characteristic of the internet in terms of its hyperlinked, interactive and networked infrastructure and digital culture (Deuze, 2005).

None of this is essentially new, nor is it necessarily tied to the internet. Yet it must be argued that continuous blurring of the real or perceived boundaries between making and using media by professionals as well as amateurs ('proams') has been supercharged in recent years – particularly in terms of its omnipresence and visibility online. Bucy and Gregson (2001), for example, suggest how a growing frustration and skepticism among the public regarding the highly staged, professionalized and exclusionary nature of mediated reality in fact has pushed people towards pursuing alternative – include their own – media formats.

The mass media (broadcast) system is gradually giving way to a more interactive, narrowcast or multicast media ecology, dominated by a fascinating blend of large multinational corporations and grassroots initiatives as exemplified by NewsCorp's acquisition (in 2005) of *MySpace*, a company offering its registered users a chance to build a virtual society similar to the successful South Korean network *Cyworld*. Indeed, media participation is a phenomenon at once top-down and bottom-up, involving both elites – such as Dutch politicians operating their own profile pages on social networking site *Hyves* or ubiquitous corporate weblogs operated by ghostwriters – and the masses. In this process of amplified interaction the process of media production and dissemination also becomes more transparent and open to external intervention, giving users increasing powers of access both outside and within corporate industrial contexts.

Convergence culture

Jenkins typifies the emerging media ecology in terms of a convergence culture, defining the trend as:

> [. . .] both a top-down corporate-driven process and a bottomup consumer-driven process. Media companies are learning how to accelerate the flow of media content across delivery channels to expand revenue opportunities, broaden markets and reinforce viewer commitments. Consumers are learning how to use these different media technologies to bring the flow of media more fully under their control and to interact with other users. (2004: 37)

Jenkins' approach aims to build a bridge between two different but equally important strands of thought regarding the way we respond and give meaning to the role that ubiquitous and pervasive media play in our everyday life. The first approach suggests how (new) media enable or even force us to retreat in a personal information space, where we exercise an unparalleled degree of control over what we watch and what we hear, what we keep, discard or forward (Krishnan and Jones, 2005). Indeed, the emerging new media ecology does give users increasing control over the flow of media – using devices like the remote control, the joystick and the computer mouse, or software like internet portal sites, filtering agents, searchbots and user recommendation systems. In journalism studies Singer (1998) has correspondingly signaled the possible end of the 'gatekeeper' as an appropriate metaphor to coin the professional identity of journalists online – an identity that, according to Bruns (2005), is better described as a 'gatewatcher': monitoring rather than reporting news, managing rather than filtering information. The second perspective describes the current media environment as one where people are increasingly engaged in the collaborative production of 'we media' (Bowman and Willis, 2003), such as Wikipedia, JanJan or Ohmynews, seemingly for no other motives than peer recognition and reputation.

Participatory media production and individualized media consumption are two different yet co-constituent trends typifying an emerging media ecology – an environment where consuming media increasingly includes some kind of producing media, and where our media behavior always seems to involve some level of participation, co-creation and collaboration, depending on the degree of openness or closedness of the media involved. The concepts of 'open' and 'closed' media in this context refer to the extent to which a given media company shares some or all of its modes of operation with its target audiences. A media organization can, for example, increase the level of transparency of how it works, or can opt to give its customers more control over their user experience. Yet, as McChesney and Schiller (2003) remind us, the same communication technologies that enable interactivity and participation are wielded to foster the entrenchment and growth of a global corporate media system that can be said to be anything but transparent, interactive or participatory. Bagdikian (2000) argues that five corporations – Time Warner, Disney, NewsCorp, Bertelsmann and Viacom – control most of the media industry in the US and, indeed, across the globe. This control must not be exaggerated, however, and Compaine (2005), among others, presents evidence that worldwide media consolidation and increased diversity of choice or genuine competition in the production and distribution of content are not anathema. In the context of the model presented here these trends must be seen as co-existing and symbiotic. Evidence collected for the media industries by Jenkins (2006), the service industries by Flew (2004) and the manufacturing industries by Von Hippel (2005) suggests that much of this consumer co-creation is in fact instigated in corporations. Indeed, such multinational organizations can best be seen as 'inhabited institutions' (Hallett and Ventresca, 2006), where people do things together and in doing so struggle for symbolic power in their respective fields of work. Convergence culture thus serves both as a mechanism to increase revenue and further the agenda of industry, while at the same time enabling people – in terms of their identities as producers and consumers, professionals as well as amateurs – to enact some kind of agency regarding the omnipresent messages and commodities of this industry.

The model in Figure 27.1 maps these trends in making and using media production on horizontal and vertical axes, within which contemporary media phenomena can be plotted in two-dimensional space. A third dimension to this model would reflect a temporal trajectory, representing shifts and changes among and between different phenomena under investigation.

The work of authors in various fields defines media content in this context interchangeably as: consumer-generated (Jeppesen, 2005: 351), customer-controlled (Shih, 2001) and user-directed (Pryor, 2002). Researchers in different disciplines signal an industry-wide turn towards the consumer as co-creator of the corporate product, particularly where the industry's core commodity is (mediated) information (Benkler, 2006; Hartley, 2005; Jenkins, 2006). As part of the explanation for this one could consider the creative impulse intrinsic to individuals (as suggested by Amabile et al., 1996), amplified by a proliferation of easy-to-use content creation tools. Among creatives and brand managers in advertising the contemporary focus, for example, centers heavily on interactive advertising, defined as 'the paid and unpaid presentation and promotion of products, services and ideas by an identified sponsor through mediated means involving mutual action between consumers and producers' (Leckenby and Li, 2000). Marketers brainstorm about the potential of upstream marketing, which refers to the strategic process of identifying and fulfilling consumer needs early in product development, up to and including end-users in the product innovation cycle. Executives in computer game companies also consider their consumers as co-developers, where 'innovation and product development [. . .] depend upon external online consumer communities' (Jeppesen and Molin, 2003: 363). Editors of news publications are increasingly expected to develop 'citizen journalism' initiatives in order to reconnect to disappearing audiences, following the advice of researchers at institutions such as the American Press Institute, who conclude that 'to stay afloat, media companies must

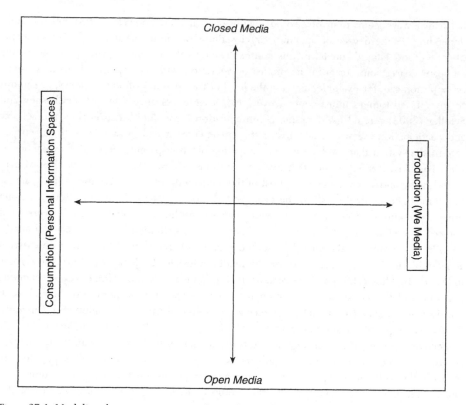

Figure 27.1 Modeling the emerging new media ecology.

reimagine storytelling forms to vie for consumer attention [. . .] and they must react to the consumer's creation of content with awe and respect' (2005: 3). Balnaves, Mayrhofer and Shoesmith (2004) consider this shift towards a more engaged, emancipatory and participatory relationship between media professionals and their publics an example of a 'new humanism' in the domains of public relations, journalism and advertising, constituting 'an antidote to narrow corporate-centric ways of representing interests in modern society' (2004:192). It is important to note here how convergence culture signifies increased as well as diminished corporate control over the creative mediamaking process at the same time.

Creative industries

Media companies operating in fields as diverse and interconnected as public relations, marketing, advertising and journalism traditionally have been considered as cultural industries, representing those companies and professions primarily responsible for the industrial production and circulation of culture (Hesmondhalgh, 2002). In the ongoing academic debate on the definition of culture (or cultural) industries, media production tends to be emphasized as exclusive or particular to the field of action of the companies and corporations involved. In recent years policymakers, industry observers and scholars alike reconceptualized media work as taking place within a broad context of 'creative industries'. The term was introduced by the British Department of Culture, Media and Sport in 1998, defining 'creative industries' as:

those industries which have their origin in individual creativity, skill and talent and which have a potential for wealth and job creation through the generation and exploitation of intellectual property. This includes advertising, architecture, the art and antiques market, crafts, design, designer fashion, film and video, interactive leisure software, music, the performing arts, publishing, software and computer games, television and radio.

The concept of creative industries aims to reconcile the emergence of increasingly individual and small-scale, project-based or collaborative notions of commercial and non-commercial media production with institutionalized notions of cultural production as it exclusively takes place within the cultural industries. Hartley (2005) explicitly defines creative industries as an idea that: 'seeks to describe the conceptual and practical convergence of the creative arts (individual talent) with cultural industries (mass scale), in the context of new media technologies (ICTs) within a new knowledge economy, for the use of newly interactive citizen-consumers' (2005: 5). Although Hartley's definition suggests an optimistic outcome of the merger between individual creativity and mass cultural production, Neilson and Rossiter (2005) warn against uncritical acceptance of the concept, arguing it consists of

> an oxymoronic disingenuousness that wants to suggest that innovation can coexist with or become subordinated to the status quo. In this context, innovation becomes nothing other than a code word for more of the same – the reduction of creativity to the formal indifference of the market. (2005: 8)

A critical perspective is particularly warranted given the emphasis in this article on the increasing precarious nature of media work. The professional identity of media workers has traditionally included some kind of protection of editorial autonomy, which is much more contested in a situation where every savvy internet user can contribute to the creative process, and where each and every contribution is supposed to generate revenue for the industry. It must be noted that the average consumer-turned-producer tends not to enjoy such protections.

Scholars in fields as varied as cultural policy, management and cultural studies have deployed creative industries to challenge established ways of thinking about the role of the individual in the context of mass media organizations.[1] What sets these approaches apart is how creative industries open up ways of thinking about (commercial and non-commercial) cultural production in the media without assuming that the exclusivity of the story-telling experience rests solely in the hands of the professionals involved: journalists, advertising creatives, public relations officers, game developers and so on (Banks, 2002; Deuze, 2003; Jones, 2002; Kent and Taylor, 2002). If the process of telling stories, making meaning and sharing mediated experiences becomes more participatory and collaborative – be it within a multiplayer game, on a newspaper discussion forum, or at a viral marketing site – it becomes crucial to understand the roles of the producer and the consumer as (to some extent) interchangeable and (at the very least) interdependent. The creative industries' approach to sites of cultural production also focuses our attention on the seminal role (the management and organization of) that *creativity* plays in any consideration of media work. This pragmatic use of the creative industries' approach thus opens up a fertile area for considering a future of media work, where professional identity is increasingly influenced and shaped by the various ways in which professionals interact with and give meaning to their publics as consumers *and* co-creators (Deuze, 2005).

Case studies

Using the parameters established in the model (see Figure 27.1), the four particular case studies of media work can be described and mapped: Bluffton Today (journalism), Amazon (marketing), Counter-Strike (games), and the Crispin Porter + Bogusky Group (advertising). In each case I map issues related to the intersections of media participation, convergence culture and creative industries in terms of how the media company involved can be considered to be 'open' or 'closed', and how its mode of production interpellates publics as either (individual) consumers or (co-)creators of content. On a personal note, I have to admit that my observation of these cases is rather optimistic. This is not because there is no reason to assume that commercial media organizations like the Morris Publishing Group or Valve Software are not using consumer-producer collaborative practices to generate additional revenue streams, thus co-opting the creative impetus of convergence culture. Yet there is also no reason to assume that user-generated content should necessarily be read as acts of audience resistance to the prefabricated messages of the corporate media. In all honesty, I find (with Jenkins) both of these traditional approaches in media studies uninspiring and inadequate when trying to understand the implications of the trends in today's new media ecology, where, for example, according to a November 2005 survey report by the Pew Internet & American Life Project, almost two-thirds of online teens create content for the internet – as in creating or contributing to a blog or personal webpage, sharing and remixing original content such as artwork, photos, stories, music or video (Lenhart and Madden, 2005). Considering the exploding global popularity of social networks, weblogs, podcasts and other similarly culturally convergent applications, my assumption is that this content creation trend is not particular to teens, nor to US citizens – it can be seen as part and parcel of an emerging global digital culture (Deuze, 2006). Considering the professional identity of culture creators working in the media industry these trends cannot solely be read as putting new pressures to come up with more compelling yet commercially viable cross-media content. Media workers must also be seen as storytellers increasingly having to share the creative spotlight with 'the people formerly known as the audience', giving meaning to what they do through an ongoing dialogue and exchange with the users of their services, all within the context of a fiercely competitive industry.

The following case studies were selected from the professional and trade literature in journalism, games, marketing and advertising, and were selected based on references by critics and practitioners to 'best practices' in these industries. The case studies can thus be seen as symptomatic rather than representative, and I describe their characteristics in terms of how these may contribute to operationalizing the model of a new media ecology introduced in this article.

Bluffton today

Bluffton Today is a combination of a free daily newspaper (launched 4 April 2005) and a community news website (which went online on 1 April 2005), both published by the Morris Publishing Group (MPG). MPG was founded in 2001 and publishes 27 daily, 12 non-daily and numerous free community newspapers in the United States. The tabloid-size newspaper had an initial circulation of 16,500 and is distributed free to every home in the greater Bluffton, South Carolina area in the United States. Bluffton is a fast-growing affluent community with over 10,000 households on the Atlantic coast of South Carolina. What makes the paper and site a much-lauded example of convergence culture is its choice to have user-generated content as its primary source of news and information. According to

Morris analyst Steve Yelvington (2005), Bluffton Today.com is an 'experiment in citizen journalism, a complete inversion of the typical online newspaper model', as staffers as well as registered community members get a blog, a photo gallery, read/write access to a shared public community calendar, a community cookbook, and access to an application that supports podcasting. Regarding the paper, readers' online comments on stories that appear in the print edition are edited and printed in the hard copy of next day's newspaper. Discussing his company's choices, Ken Rickard, manager of product strategy for Morris DigitalWorks, explicitly notes how Bluffton Today is an example of cultural rather than technological convergence:

> The goals of Bluffton Today are quite simple: to become a part of the daily conversation in Bluffton. The paper needs to build trust, solicit feedback and help develop a sense of shared community. The motto of the Web site, then, is 'It's what people are talking about.' And that's where the convergence comes from. The Web site is entirely created by the residents of Bluffton; those who work for the newspaper and those who do not. (2005)

Rickard ties convergence to the cultural phenomenon of blurring the boundaries between 'producers' and 'users' of content. Writing one month after the launch of the site and paper, he explains the lessons learned by ongoing testing and tweaking of the Bluffton Today publishing model: 'the early results have been very promising. The most notable result has been largely unintended: There exists a level of transparency and dialogue about the creation of the newspaper that engenders a real sense of trust in the community.' For the purposes of this case study, it is important to note here how cultural convergence indeed instills increased levels of transparency in the media system, where producers and consumers of content can 'see' each other at work, as they both play each other's roles. In this context, Yelvington was quoted in an interview at the Online Journalism Review (of 7 September 2005) as saying how he believes people are 'living in this cable TV world of the outside observer instead of acting as participants. We're trying to make people come out of their gates and become players. We want a participative culture to evolve.' Participation seems to be key for understanding the success of both the industry initiative and the community's response – following the creative industries' approach of connecting individual creativity with commercial production.

Counter-strike

The computer game *Counter-Strike* was released on 19 June 1999 as a modification ('mod') for the popular game *Half-Life*. It pits a Counter-Terrorist team and a Terrorist team against each other in a variety of environments and game modes: planting or defusing bombs, rescuing or taking hostages, protecting or assassinating VIPs. *Counter-Strike* is still one of the most popular online action games, claimed to have popularized teamplay in online games. *Counter-Strike* is currently the official game of the Cyberathlete Professional League (CPL), a company that houses two or more US-based LAN competitions for teams (or clans) a year.

What makes *Counter-Strike* an excellent case study for this article is the fact that technically it is not a game on its own – it was developed and released (for free) by two friends who were frustrated with the gameplay and character options offered in *Half-Life*. After downloading the Software Developers' Kit (SDK) for *Half-Life* (providing access to game-building tools is a common practice in the game software developing world), Minh Le (nickname: Gooseman) and Jess Cliff worked together to modify the game. Downloading the mod was free, but it originally required a copy of *Half-Life* to play. The core content of a computer game – like news for a newspaper – is the various maps and scenarios within which players can roam free. In *Counter-Strike*, Minh Le did all of the modeling, animating and coding for the game, but gamers interested in the mod handled the maps, not a dedicated mapping team (as in a game developers' company). Interest in the mod was built up by prepublications and discussions on *Counter-Strike*'s website. The history of the game – leading up until its adoption by Half-Life's corporate headquarters Valve Software, part of erstwhile conglomerate Vivendi Universal, and the release for Microsoft's Xbox game console in March 2004 – is one of ongoing beta-versions. Each new installment or upgrade of the game was developed by Minh Le and Jess Cliff, later on adding the professional producers at Valve and including additions and new mods coming out of the gaming fan communities online. Indeed, the game has been in a constantly evolving state. In an interview commenting on the pending release of *Counter-Strike* for Xbox, developer Cliff remarked:

> I do think [*Counter-Strike*] has reached its maturity level, where we've been tweaking and experimenting and testing things out for years. We have the core gameplay down that we know we want. What we can do now is just add layers of content, with maps, models, weapons, etc. It's a great balance, I think. (quoted in *CS Nation*, 8 November 2003)

The core appeal of the game has been attributed to many factors, of which two are key to the considerations of this article: the emphasis on collaborative authorship over the game – involving fans, software developers, producers and consumers in constantly evolving and shifting roles – and the credited element of (online) team play, influencing game developers and 'modders' worldwide to increasingly focus on the participatory aspect of (online) gaming, both in playing the game and co-creating the game. Interestingly, in an 'about' section on the *Counter-Strike* fan community website *csnation.net*, the author remarks: 'It's anyone's guess as to who is actually "in charge",' suggesting a distinct flattening of producer/consumer hierarchies more readily apparent in 'traditional' media systems.

Amazon

Jeff Bezos started the self-proclaimed largest e-commerce site on the web, Amazon.com, in 1994. Amazon started out as an online bookstore, later on adding CDs, videos, DVDs and games to the catalogue. It continued to add new lines of business, including toys, consumer electronics, software, power tools, home improvement products and online auctions, thus competing directly with eBay. Through acquisitions of online stores in the UK, Germany, Japan, France and Canada, Amazon expanded its reach across the globe with country- or region-specific shopping sites. It later on added the option for site users to sell and purchase used goods, taking a share of every item sold while contributing to shipping costs and buying guarantees (for a company history, see Spector, 2000). As of June 2005, the company has more than 9,000 employees and generates billions of dollars in revenues (after losing money for many years).

Amazon.com's website launched in July 1995. Website visitors could sign up for personalized email notifications and access the status of their orders, browse items recommended to them generated by the previous purchases of other customers, as well as browse contextual content such as lists and reviews submitted by loyal site users. Customers and site users have been influential in determining the look and feel of Amazon; for example, by protesting the news in 1999 that Amazon offered promotional packages to publishers who wanted their books to appear on prime spots on certain pages. The company responded by saying that in the future it would indicate what featured promotions had been paid for and offered customers the chance to return any book that Amazon.com had recommended in the past. According to Massanari, this is but one example that shows how customers believe that Amazon.com is not a 'typical' retailer: 'Clearly, consumers had been won over by Bezos' "customers first" attitude and expected Amazon.com to be more forthright about its marketing tactics and the type of information it was collecting and sharing about them' (2003: 42). As from the very beginnings of the site, Amazon adopted traditional advertising and marketing approaches next to a deliberate orientation on the web's interactive, hierarchy-flattening characteristics.

At the heart of Amazon's success and its relevance to the concepts outlined in this article is the way in which the online retailer combines a fairly straightforward 'industrial' model of commerce with harvesting the individual creativity of its customers (for example, by allowing site users to upload their own pictures of products next to the images supplied by the manufacturers). One should also note its utilization of participatory media culture by combining straightforward sales techniques with auctions of new and used goods, user reviews and customer-community recommendations.

The CPB group

Crispin Porter + Bogusky (CPB) is an advertising agency based in Miami, Florida and Los Angeles, California. The agency started out in the 1960s as a tourism shop, moving into advertising only in the mid-1990s. It is currently considered one of the most talked-about innovative ad agencies to create 'buzz' among its competitors, clients and audiences – as exemplified by winning all the major prizes in the advertising industry, including several Cannes Lions and Clio Awards. In 2002, creative director Alex Bogusky was inducted into the American Advertising Federation's Hall of Achievement.

The agency started in 1997 with nation-wide promotion of TheTruth.com anti-smoking advertisements for the American Legacy Foundation. The web-based campaign contains interactive games, spoofs of television shows, downloadable ringtones for mobile phones, and a question and answer forum – all linked to factual information about the dangers of smoking. A famous example of this agency's work is the 'SubservientChicken.com' campaign for client Burger King: a website featuring someone in a chicken suit you can order around, leading to communities online compiling their own 'subservient chicken request lists'.[2] The agency cultivates a reputation for applying viral marketing techniques to create 'buzz' for a product through email, online user groups and discussion lists. In an interview with *Time*, Alex Bogusky was quoted as arguing that.

> this kind of buzz, or viral, marketing is advertising's future [. . .] In the future, Bogusky predicts, viral ads will offer even more participation. The more stuff people can do themselves with these ads, the better, he says. It's more fun, but they also feel like they own it. They feel more empowered as consumers. (Padgett, 2004)

The key to the approach of CPB is its tactic of including the consumer in the production and pay-off of the advertising campaign. For the specific purposes of this article, the work of CPB is relevant in the way the agency for example developed their campaign for the BMW Mini Cooper, starting in 2002. The website of the Mini, Mini.com, allows users to build their own version of the car, play all kinds of games, participate in discussions, and find information (on their own) about all things 'Mini'. CPB also created a second website where it claimed that counterfeit Minis were being made and sold illegally (counterfeitmini.org), including a series of counterfeit Mini television commercials. The creatives at the agency additionally came up with another elaborate hoax called the 'Mini Cooper Autonomous Robot' (at URL: www.r50rd.co.uk), suggesting a robot, made from the body of a Mini Cooper r50, was spotted in London and Oxford popping up randomly to stop cars from crashing. These sites created a lot of word-of-mouth marketing through discussion forums, mailing lists, chat rooms and instant messaging networks online – especially when people started to debate the truthfulness of the different campaigns. Regarding his company's willingness to veer away from what can been called 'one-way show-and-tell' advertising (Auletta, 2005), Bogusky argues: 'The future of advertising is that it doesn't exist. The party is coming to an end for everybody' (quoted in Padgett, 2005).

Discussion

Considering the implications of convergence culture for media work in the creative industries when analyzing these cases, several observations stand out. First, all of these cases are distinctly commercial in character – and hugely successful at that. This is particularly interesting if one considers the fact that the 'product' in these cases is collaboratively constituted out of the interactions between producers and consumers and within consumer communities online. Second, the engagement of consumers and producers occurs in what Castells (2001) calls networked individualism, similar to the communicational bonds signaled by Lash (2002): in a digital culture people interact, collaborate and engage, but tend to do so strictly individually, enacting their own interests – whether it is in a certain type of news, a certain aspect of a game or a certain product for sale online. Through these activities the simultaneous enactment of community and individualization can be observed – although Bauman objects: 'in my view, both Castells and Scott [Lash, MD] fall victims of internet fetishism fallacy. Network is not community and communication not integration – both safely equipped as they are with "disconnection on demand" devices.'[3]

Third, the relationship between media industry and consumer has traditionally been established on the basis of hierarchy, as in 'show-and-tell' advertising or 'telling people what they need to know' journalism. In these case studies a flattening of such hierarchies takes place, which process manifests itself on different levels: at Amazon, user reviews are organized hierarchically through the ratings of other reviewers; at the various websites of the Mini campaign the advertising agency only offers the building blocks of a commercial narrative – the user is autonomous in the decision what to do with the materials on offer; for Bluffton Today, the reporter in effect competes with people in the community to get her news noticed; the gamer can modify the game any which way she chooses within the parameters set by the software development kit (SDK) offered by the game publisher. Fourth, within this context of more or less sharing control over the production of culture, it is striking to see how the roles of the 'consumer' and 'producer' are constantly shifting. The journalist at Bluffton Today is as much a consumer as a co-creator of the community news agenda, the advertising creative produces all kinds of content, yet can only watch as a consumer to see how the message and payoff are negotiated and constructed by users. It is exactly this element of role ambiguity that may prompt media professionals to respond with doubt and criticism regarding the shift towards more interactive, participatory and collaborative types of mediamaking. Finally one must note the emphasis the professionals involved in all four enterprises put on a replacement media theory to legitimate their praxis: whatever came or was done before will come to an end.

What the four cases as documented in this article suggest, then, is that even among these 'poster-children' for convergence culture in the creative industries multiple models for open or closed media and content versus connectivity are possible. Most importantly the old and new roles for media producers and users are increasingly interchangeable for these companies. Sure, *Counter-Strike* started out as a fun private project, but quickly turned into a commercial enterprise. Consumer empowerment thus goes hand in hand with the quest for profit – and the sharing of control over the media experience sometimes gets curtailed by the practices of closed media: limiting the range of options in an SDK or in the virtual garage where the user builds her own car, filtering the best user-generated content for possible inclusion in the print newspaper, managing a critical user community to protect it against cheating and 'illegal' hacks in the computer game.

Uricchio (2004: 86) describes the key to understanding the new media ecosystem as based on networked technologies that are P2P ('peer-to-peer') in organization and collaborative in principle. Benkler (2006: 60) coins this emerging decentralized, co-creative and nonproprietary media ecology as grounded in commons-based peer production. Considering this argument in the context of a typical media profession like journalism, it seems that the traditional framing and validation of media workers' professional identity in terms of maintaining the false producer–consumer dichotomy has not allowed much breathing room for peer exchange or collaborative authorship (Zelizer, 2004). Such an operational closure of everyday work has indeed been a key element in the self-organization of complex social systems such as media professions (Luhmann, 1990). Following Luhmann's autopoetic social theory, as for example applied to journalism by Weischenberg and Scholl (1998), any previous challenges or penetrations of the producer–consumer model were managed by the system of professions to evolve without having to (radically) change. In other words: any kind of flattening of the hierarchies between producers and consumers in the media until recently primarily served the function of keeping the professional system's boundaries intact. New media work in general, and the practices of the media companies as profiled in this article in particular, show how heterarchy is gaining ground as an alternative for hierarchy in the dominant mode of operations in the business world – and particularly in the media industries. It is in this context where Twitchell notes that the new ironical 'I'm your pal' persona of advertising since the early 1990s 'collapses the usual voice of advertising, which is the strict "I'm your doctor, I know what's best for you" ' (1996: 231). Balnaves, Mayrhofer and Shoesmith similarly signal 'the end of the persuader-as-manipulator in the media professions' (2004: 194). It is therefore perhaps safe to say that the professional identity of media work may be moving towards a more clearly articulated responsive and interactive position vis-à-vis publics.

It must be explicitly noted that this is not a linear, unproblematic or necessarily successful process – as what also comes to mind when considering the histories of the four case studies in the context of an emerging body of literature on new media work (see, for example, Christopherson and Van Jaarsveld, 2005) are elements of distinct disorganization (Leung, 2005) and disequilibrium (Lovink, 2003) embedded in the praxis of the new media ecosystem. Jenkins acknowledges this as well, shrugging off similar concerns by accepting it as a permanent condition: 'For the foreseeable future, convergence will be a kind of kludge – a jerry-rigged relationship between different media technologies – rather than a fully integrated system' (2004: 34). However the literature shows how an increasing emphasis on flexibility, creativity, and innovation in new media work creates a precarious paradox. On the one hand, convergence culture makes room for new forms of creative organization, product development and consumer relationships that have the potential to be more diverse and compelling than ever before. On the other hand, the same trends allow for increasing exploitation of media workers and consumers of media under conditions that Sennett (2006) describes as flexible productivity advocated by corporations operating in an increasingly fickle global market. Indeed, the nature of media work has become rather 'kludgy', whether seen through the lens of industrial and economical change, or from a perspective of emergent behavior by producers (Bruns, 2005) in an increasingly participatory media culture.

Conclusion

In conclusion I would like to attempt to answer the question why this convergence is considered so crucially important at this particular point in time, and how the case studies and model presented in this article may contribute to a research agenda on new media work occurring within the context of creative industries. Even to consider building a new program in media production research based on the interchangeability of mediamaking and using requires partly letting go of some well-established, deep-rooted and arguably valid assumptions about the impact that a mass media-centric culture has had on us. To some extent a political economy of media should still emphasize the powerful hold that multinational corporations have over multiple public spheres, shaping popular reality with a deliberate focus to sell audiences as target demographics to advertisers. On the other hand, this one-dimensional view of media power has changed, as the agricultural metaphor of production and consumption is increasingly becoming an untenable assumption on which to base our understandings of media content, effects and particularly media work. Beyond corporate co-optation and audience resistance lies a new model for understanding the changing nature of media in everyday life. Further research could focus on how professionals and amateurs collaborate, how their roles converge, and what the results of these practices are in the emerging new media ecology, on the level of economy (new and improved returns on investment), technology (development of new hardware and software enabling open media), politics and legislation (creative commons copyright laws, audience encoding rights and open source) and global culture.

Works cited in this article have charted the nature of this new media work as unpredictable, uncertain and constantly changing, which trend can be signified by – paraphrasing Zygmunt Bauman (2000) – a 'liquid' media work. The liquidity of contemporary media work is exemplified by the patchwork career (Lutz, 2000) of a portfolio worklife (Handy, 1998 [1989]) or rather work-style (Deuze, 2007), signaling a continuous blurring between the boundaries of work, life and play, as well as between production and consumption. The case studies as mapped on to the model used in this article suggest that media work is something that is increasingly shared with those who one used to work *for*: audiences. The culture of industry therefore can be seen as spilling over on to the creative process of consumption. A product reviewer on Amazon, a modder on *csnation.net* or a blogger on Bluffton Today now also wields the power of the industry's privileged position of authorship. Further research should shed light on how these 'liquid' media professionals give meaning to working in an industry that expects them to treat their publics as consumers as well as co-creators of content, an industry that is struggling to define its ambiguous role as partner as well as profiteer in a participatory media culture, and as the traditional authoritative voice in public discourses (thus excluding any meaningful role for users of its services other than as audiences). I would like to argue that this kind of research agenda serves two specific purposes. First, it makes us aware what it means exactly when we say that the 'brave new world' of work (Beck, 2000) is so much different or similar to the past, and thus it will help us to articulate much more precisely how 'the' media are what they are – integrating journalism, advertising, marketing, public relations and all other media professions into a critical analysis of media work. Second, it will assist us in preparing students in media and (tele-) communications departments all over the world to enter a world where what they have learned enables them to become 'prosumers' (Toffler, 1980).

In other words, we have to train people to stay inside *The Truman Show*. And make the best of it.

Notes

1   Journals featuring special issues on the creative industries: *Studies in Cultures, Organisations and Societies* (2000); the *International Journal of Cultural Studies* (2004), *Capital & Class* (2004), and on related issues regarding creative organization and the cultural industries: *Media International Australia* (2004), *Fibre Culture* (2005) and *International Journal of Cultural Policy* (2005).

2   One such request list is at URL: dev.magicosm.net/cgi-bin/public/corvi-daewiki/bin/view/Game/SubservientChickenRequestList. On an interesting sidenote, this site is based on the 'wiki' concept, which means anyone can edit, modify and add information to the list.

3   Personal email from Zygmunt Bauman to the author, Monday 5 June 2006.

References

Amabile, Teresa M., Mary Ann Collins, Regina Conti and Elise Phillips (1996) *Creativity in Context: Update to the Social Psychology of Creativity*. Boulder, CO: Westview Press.

American Press Institute (2005) *Synapse: The Future of News*. Briefing on Media, Technology & Society by the Mediacenter at the American Press Institute, April 2005. http://www.mediacenter.org/content/6470.cfm (accessed 2 May 2005).

Auletta, Ken (2005) 'The New Pitch: Do Ads Still Work?', *The New Yorker*, 21 March. http://www.newyorker.com/fact/content/articles/050328fa_fact (accessed 20 October 2006).

Bagdikian, Ben H. (2000) *The New Media Monopoly*. Boston, MA: Beacon Press.

Balnaves, Mark, Debra Mayrhofer and Brian Shoesmith (2004) 'Media Professions and the New Humanism', *Continuum: Journal of Media & Cultural Studies* 18(2): 191–203.

Banks, J. (2002) 'Gamers as Co-creators: Enlisting the Virtual Audience – a Report from the Net Face', in Mark Balnaves, Tim O'Regan and J. Sternberg (eds) *Mobilising the Audience*, pp. 188–213. St Lucia: University of Queensland Press.

Bauman, Zygmunt (2000) *Liquid Modernity*. Cambridge: Polity.

Beck, Ulrich (2000) *The Brave New World of Work*. Cambridge: Polity.

Benkler, Yochai (2006) *The Wealth of Networks*. New Haven, CT: Yale University Press.

Bowman, Shaun and Chris Willis (2003) *We Media*. API Media Center paper. http://www.hypergene.net/wemedia/download/we_media.pdf (accessed 19 August 2004).

Bruns, Axel (2005) *Gatewatching*. New York: Peter Lang.

Bucy, Eric and Kim Gregson (2001) 'Media Participation: A Legitimizing Mechanism of Mass Democracy', *New Media & Society* 3(3): 357–80.

Castells, Manuel (2001) *The Internet Galaxy*. Oxford: Oxford University Press.

Christopherson, Susan and Danielle Van Jaarsveld (2005) 'New Media After the Dot.com Bust', *International Journal of Cultural Policy* 11(1): 77–93.

Compaine, Ben (2005) *The Media Monopoly Myth: How New Competition is Expanding our Sources of Information and Entertainment*. New Millennium Research Council. http://www.thenmrc.org/archive/Final_Compaine_Paper_050205.pdf (accessed 27 October 2005).

CS Nation (2003, 8 November) *Interview Jess Cliff: The Future of Counter-Strike*. http://www.csnation.net/articles.php/interview_173/ (accessed 25 October 2005).

Deuze, Mark (2003) 'The Web and its Journalisms: Considering the Consequences of Different Types of News Media Online', *New Media & Society* 5(2): 203–30.

Deuze, Mark (2005) 'Towards Professional Participatory Storytelling in Journalism and Advertising' [online]. *First Monday* 10(7). http://www.firstmonday.dk/issues/issue10_7/deuze/index.html.

Deuze, Mark (2006) 'Participation, Remediation, Bricolage: Considering Principal Components of a Digital Culture', *The Information Society* 22(2): 63–75.

Deuze, Mark (2007) *Media Work*. Cambridge: Polity Press.

Flew, Terry (2004) 'Creativity, Cultural Studies, and Services Industries', *Communication and Critical/Cultural Studies* 1(2): 176–93.

Hallett, Tim and Mark Ventresca (2006) 'Inhabited Institutions: Social Interactions and Organizational Forms in Gouldner's Patterns of Industrial Bureaucracy', *Theory and Society* 35(2): 213–36.

Handy, Charles (1998 [1989]) *The Age of Unreason*. Boston, MA: Harvard Business School Press.

Hartley, John, ed. (2005) *Creative Industries*. Malden: Blackwell.

Hesmondhalgh, David (2002) *The Cultural Industries*. London: Sage.

Jenkins, Henry (2004) 'The Cultural Logic of Media Convergence', *International Journal of Cultural Studies* 7(1): 33–43.

Jenkins, Henry (2006) *Convergence Culture*. New York: NYU Press.

Jeppesen, Lars Bo (2005) 'User Toolkits for Innovation: Consumers Support Each Other', *The Journal of Product Innovation Management* 22: 347–62.

Jeppesen, Lars Bo and Mans Molin (2003) 'Consumers as Co-developers: Learning and Innovation Outside the Firm', *Technology Analysis & Strategic Management* 15(3): 363–83.

Jones, Richard (2002) 'Challenges to the Notion of Publics in Public Relations: Implications of the Risk Society for the Discipline', *Public Relations Review* 28: 49–62.

Kent, Michael and Maureen Taylor (2002) 'Toward a Dialogic Theory of Public Relations', *Public Relations Review* 28: 21–37.

Krishnan, Aparna and Steve Jones (2005) 'TimeSpace: Activity-based Temporal Visualization of Personal Information Spaces', *Personal Ubiquitous Computing* 9: 46–65.

Lash, Scott (2002) *Critique of Information*. London: Sage.

Leckenby, John, and Hairong Li (2000) 'Why We Need the *Journal of Interactive Advertising*', *Journal of Interactive Advertising* 1(1). http://www.jiad.org/vol1/no1/editors/index.htm (accessed 25 October 2005).

Lenhart, Amanda and Mary Madden (2005) *Teen Content Creators and Consumers*. Pew Internet & American Life Project report. http://www.pewinternet.org/pdfs/PIP_Teens_Content_Creation.pdf (accessed 2 December 2005).

Leung, Linda (2005) 'Postcard from the Edge: Autobiographical Musings on the Dis/organizations of the Multimedia Industry', *Fibre Culture* 5. http://journal.fibreculture.org/issue5/ (accessed 19 October 2005).

Lovink, Geert (2003) *My First Recession: Critical Internet Culture in Transition*. Rotterdam: V2_/Nai Publishers.

Luhmann, Niklas (1990) 'The Autopoiesis of Social Systems', in Niklas Luhmann *Essays on Self-reference*, pp. 1–20. New York: Columbia University Press.

Lutz, Michel (2000) 'Patchwork-Karrieren. Jobchancen und Qualifikationsanforderungen in der Multimedia-Branche', in K. Altmeppen, H. Bucher and M. Löffelholz (eds) *Online Journalismus: Perspektiven für Wissenschaft und Praxis*, pp. 259–81. Wiesbaden: Westdeutscher Verlag.

Massanari, Adrienne (2003) Work Hard. Have Fun. Make History. [Make Money.]: Narratives of Amazon.com. University of Washington Graduate School MA Thesis. http://students.washington.edu/alm2/thesis.pdf (accessed 12 September 2005).

McChesney, Robert and Dan Schiller (2003) *The Political Economy of International Communications: Foundations for the Emerging Global Debate about Media Ownership and Regulation*. Technology, Business and Society Programme Paper Number 11, October 2003. United Nations Research Institute for Social Development.

Neilson, Brett and Ned Rossiter (2005) 'From Precarity to Precariousness and Back Again: Labour, Life and Unstable Networks. *Fibre Culture* 5. http://journal.fibreculture.org/issue5/ (accessed 19 October 2005).

Padgett, Tim (2004, 3 October) 'What's Next After that Odd Chicken?', *Time* Special Report: Marketing. http://www.time.com/time/covers/1101041011/nextmarketing.html (accessed 25 October 2005).

Pryor, Larry (2002) 'Immersive News Technology: Beyond Convergence', *Online Journalism Review*, posted 10–11–2000, modified 04–04–2002. http://www.ojr.org/ojr/technology/1017962893.php (accessed 19 October 2005).

Rickard, Ken (2005) 'A Community in Convergence', *The Convergence Newsletter* from Newsplex at the University of South Carolina 2(10), 4 May. http://www.jour.sc.edu/news/convergence/issue21.html (accessed 12 July 2004).

Schudson, Michael (2003) *The Sociology of News*. New York: W.W. Norton & Company.

Sennett, Richard (2006) *The Culture of the New Capitalism*. New Haven, CT: Yale University Press.

Shih, Ming-Yi (2001) *The Future of Interactive Advertising on the World Wide Web*. http://www.ciadvertising.org/student_account?spring_01/adv391k/ (accessed 3 May 2005).

Singer, J. (1998) 'Online Journalists: Foundation for Research into their Changing Roles' [online], *Journal of Computer-mediated Communication* 4(1). http://jcmc.indiana.edu/vol4/issue1/singer.html (accessed 5 February 2007).

Spector, Robert (2000) *Amazon.com: Get Big Fast*. New York: HarperBusiness Books.

Toffler, Alvin (1980) *The Third Wave*. London: Pan Books.

Twitchell, James (1996) *Adcult USA*. New York: Columbia University Press.

Uricchio, William (2004) 'Beyond the Great Divide: Collaborative Networks and the Challenge to Dominant Conceptions of Creative Industries', *International Journal of Cultural Studies* 7(1): 79–90.

Van Dalen, Arjen and Mark Deuze (2006) 'Readers' Advocates or Newspapers' Ambassadors?', *European Journal of Communication* 21(4): 457–75.

Von Hippel, Eric (2005) *Democratizing Innovations*. Boston, MA: MIT Press.

Weischenberg, Siegfried and Armin Scholl (1998) *Journalismus in der Gesellschaft: Theorie, Methodologie und Empirie*. Opladen: Westdeutscher Verlag.

Yelvington, Steve (2005) '*No Fooling! We Flip the Newspaper Site Model Upside Down*. yealvington.com/media, 1 April. http://www.yelvington.com/item.php?id=988 (accessed 24 October 2005).

Zelizer, Barbie (2004) 'When Facts, Truth and Reality are God-terms: On Journalism's Uneasy Place in Cultural Studies', *Communication and Critical/Cultural Studies* 1(1): 100–19.

Key documents and reports

UNESCO 21st GENERAL CONFERENCE RESOLUTION ON NWICO

21st General Conference of UNESCO (Belgrade, Yugoslavia, from 23 September to 20 October 1980)

The conference adopted the "Resolution 4/19" which, inter alia, says:

The General Conference,

. . .

Noting the increasing attention devoted to communication problems and needs by other intergovernmental organizations both regional and international, notably the Movement of Non-Aligned Countries which, in the Declaration of the Colombo Summit (1976), stated that "a new international order in the fields of information and mass communications is as vital as a new international economic order" and in the Declaration of the Havana Summit (1979), noting progress in the development of national information media, stressed that "co-operation in the field of information is an integral part of the struggle for the creation of new international relations in general and a new international information order in particular",

Invites the Director-General to take the necessary measures to follow up the suggestions presented in his report on the findings of the International Commission for the Study of Communication Problems, and in particular:

. . .

(h) to undertake or sponsor, in particular, the studies and analyses necessary for the formulation of specific and practical proposals for the establishment of a new world information and communication order, and to convene an international meeting of experts for that purpose;
VI
(14) Considers that:

a)   this new world information and communication order could be based, among other considerations, on:

    i)   elimination of the imbalances and inequalities which characterize the present situation;

ii)   elimination of the negative effects of certain monopolies, public or private, and excessive concentrations;

iii)   removal of the internal and external obstacles to a free flow and wider and better balanced dissemination of information and ideas;

iv)   plurality of sources and channels of information;

v)   freedom of the press and information;

vi)   the freedom of journalists and all professionals in the communication media, a freedom inseparable from responsibility;

vii)   the capacity of developing countries to achieve improvement of their own situations, notably by providing their own equipment, by training their personnel, by improving their infrastructures and by making their information and communication media suitable to their needs and aspirations;

viii)   the sincere will of developed countries to help them attain these objectives;

ix)   respect for each people's cultural identity and for the right of each nation to inform the world public about its interests, its aspirations and its social and cultural values;

x)   respect for the right of all peoples to participate in international exchanges of information on the basis of equality, justice and mutual benefit;

xi)   respect for the right of the public, of ethnic and social groups and of individuals to have access to information sources and to participate actively in the communication process:

b)   this new world information and communication order should be based on the fundamental principles of international law, as laid down in the Charter of the United Nations;

c)   diverse solutions to information and communication problems are required because social, political, cultural and economic problems differ from one country to another and within a given country from one group to another,

(15) Expresses the wish that UNESCO demonstrate its willingness in its short-term and medium-term activities to contribute to the clarification, elaboration and application of the concept of a new world information and communication order . . .

2

RECOMMENDATIONS FROM THE
MACBRIDE REPORT 1980

Many voices, one world: towards a new, more just, and more efficient world information and communication order

Conclusions and recommendations

1. Our review of communication the world over reveals a variety of solutions adopted in different countries – in accordance with diverse traditions, patterns of social, economic and cultural life, needs and possibilities. This diversity is valuable and should be respected; there is no place for the universal application of preconceived models. Yet it should be possible to establish, in broad outline, common aims and common values in the sphere of communication, based on common interests in a world of interdependence. The whole human race is threatened by the arms race and by the persistence of unacceptable global inequalities, both of which generate tensions and which jeopardize its future and even its survival. The contemporary situation demands A BETTER MORE JUST AND MORE DEMOCRATIC SOCIAL ORDER, AND THE REALIZATION OF FUNDAMENTAL HUMAN RIGHTS. These goals can be achieved only through understanding and tolerance, gained in large part by free, open and balanced communications.

2. The review has also shown that the utmost importance should be given to eliminating imbalances and disparities in communication and its structures, and particularly in information flows. Developing countries need to reduce their dependence, and claim a new more just and more equitable order in the field of communication. This issue has been fully debated in various settings; the time has now come to move from principles to substantive reforms and concrete action.

3. Our conclusions are founded on the firm conviction that communication is a basic individual right, as well as a collective one required by all communities and nations. Freedom of information – and, more specifically the right to seek, receive and impart information – is a fundamental human right; indeed, a prerequisite for many others. The inherent nature of communication means that its fullest possible exercise and potential depend on the surrounding political, social and economic conditions, the most vital of these being democracy within countries and equal, democratic relations between them. It is in this

context that the democratization of communication at national and international levels, as well as the larger role of communication in democratizing society, acquires utmost importance.

4. For these purposes, it is essential to develop comprehensive national communication policies linked to overall social, cultural and economic development objectives. Such policies should evolve from broad consultations with all sectors concerned and adequate mechanisms for wide participation of organized social groups in their definition and implementation. National governments as much as the international community should recognize the urgency of according communications higher priority in planning and funding. Every country should develop its communication patterns in accordance with its own conditions, needs and traditions, thus strengthening its integrity, independence and self-reliance.

5. The basic considerations which are developed at length in the body of our Report are intended to provide a framework for the development of a new information and communication order. We see its implementation as an ongoing process of change in the nature of relations between and within nations in the field of communication. Imbalances in national information and communication systems are as disturbing and unacceptable as social, economic, cultural and technological (both national and international) disparities. Indeed, rectification of the latter is inconceivable in any true or lasting sense without elimination of the former. Crucial decisions concerning communication development need to be taken urgently at both national and international levels. These decisions are not merely the concern of professionals, researchers, or scholars, nor can they be the sole prerogative of those holding political or economic power. The decision-making process has to involve social participation at all levels. This calls for new attitudes for overcoming stereotyped thinking and to promote more understanding of diversity and plurality, with full respect for the dignity and equality of peoples living in different ways.

Thus our call for reflection and action is addressed broadly to governments and international organizations, to policy makers and planners, to the media and professional organizations, to researchers, communication practitioners, to organized social groups and the public at large.

1. Strengthening independence and self reliance

Communication policies
All individuals and people collectively have an inalienable right to a better life which, howsoever conceived, must ensure a social minimum nationally and globally. This calls for the strengthening of capacities and the elimination of gross inequalities; such defects may threaten social harmony and even international peace. There must be a measured movement from disadvantage and dependence to self-reliance and the creation of more equal opportunities. Since communication is interwoven with every aspect of life, it is clearly of the utmost importance that the existing 'communication gap' be rapidly narrowed and eventually eliminated.

We recommend:
6. Communication be no longer regarded merely as an incidental service and its development left to chance. Recognition of its potential warrants the formulation by all nations, and particularly developing countries, of comprehensive communication policies linked to overall social, cultural, economic and political goals. Such policies should be based on interministerial and interdisciplinary consultations with broad public participation. The object must be to utilize the unique capacities of each form of communication, from interpersonal and traditional to the most modern, to make people and societies aware of their rights, harmon-

ize unity in diversity, and foster the growth of individuals and communities within the wider frame of national development in an interdependent world.

7. As language embodies the cultural experience of people all languages should be adequately developed to serve the complex and diverse requirements of modern communication. Developing nations and multilingual societies need to evolve language policies that promote all national languages even while selecting some, where necessary, for more widespread use in communication, higher education and administration. There is also need in certain situations for the adaptation, simplification, and standardization of scripts and development of keyboards, preparation of dictionaries and modernized systems of language learning, transcription of literature in widely-spoken national languages. The provision of simultaneous interpretation and automated translation facilities now under experimentation for cross-cultural communication to bridge linguistic divides should also be envisaged.

8. A primary policy objective should be to make elementary education available to all and to wipe out illiteracy, supplementing formal schooling systems with non-formal education and enrichment within appropriate structures of continuing and distance learning (through radio, television and correspondence).

9. Within the framework of national development policies, each country will have to work out its own set of priorities, bearing in mind that it will not be possible to move in all directions at the same time. But, as far as resources allow, communication policies should aim at stimulating and encouraging all means of communication.

Strengthening capacities

Communication policies should offer a guide to the determination of information and media priorities and to the selection of appropriate technologies. This is required to plan the installation and development of adequate infrastructures to provide self-reliant communications capacity.

We recommend:

10. Developing countries take specific measures to establish or develop essential elements of their communication systems: print media, broadcasting and telecommunications along with the related training and production facilities.

11. Strong national news agencies are vital for improving each country's national and international reporting. Where viable, regional networks should be set up to increase news flows and serve all the major language groups in the area. Nationally, the agencies should buttress the growth of both urban and rural newspapers to serve as the core of a country's news collection and distribution system.

12. National book production should be encouraged and accompanied by the establishment of a distribution network for books, newspapers and periodicals. The stimulation of works by national authors in various languages should be promoted.

13. The development of comprehensive national radio networks, capable of reaching remote areas should take priority over the development of television, which, however, should be encouraged where appropriate. Special attention should be given to areas where illiteracy is prevalent.

14. National capacity for producing broadcast materials is necessary to obviate dependence on external sources over and beyond desirable program exchange. This capacity should include national or regional broadcasting, film and documentary production centers with a basic distribution network.

15. Adequate educational and training facilities are required to supply personnel for the media and production organizations, as well as managers, technicians and maintenance personnel. In this regard, co-operation between neighboring countries and within regions should be encouraged.

Basic needs

All nations have to make choices in investment priorities. In choosing between possible alternatives and often conflicting interests, developing countries, in particular, must give priority to satisfying their people's essential needs. Communication is not only a system of public information, but also an integral part of education and development.

We recommend:

16. The communication component in all development projects should receive adequate financing. So-called "development support communications" are essential for mobilizing initiatives and providing information required for action in all fields of development – agriculture, health and family planning, education, religion, industry and so on.

17. Essential communication needs to be met include the extension of basic postal services and telecommunication networks through small rural electronic exchanges.

18. The development of a community press in rural areas and small towns would not only provide print support for economic and social extension activities. This would also facilitate the production of functional literature for neo-literates as well.

19. Utilization of local radio, low-cost small format television and video systems and other appropriate technologies would facilitate production of programs relevant to community development efforts, stimulate participation and provide opportunity for diversified cultural expression.

20. The educational and informational use of communication should be given equal priority with entertainment. At the same time, education systems should prepare young people for communication activities. Introduction of pupils at primary and secondary levels to the forms and uses of the means of communication (how to read newspapers, evaluate radio and television programs, use elementary audio-visual techniques and apparatus) should permit the young to understand reality better and enrich their knowledge of current affairs and problems.

21. Organization of community listening and viewing groups could in certain circum-stances widen both entertainment and educational opportunities. Education and information activities should be supported by different facilities ranging from mobile book, tape and film libraries to programmed instruction through "schools of the air".

22. Such activities should be aggregated wherever possible in order to create vibrant local communication resource centers for entertainment, education, information dissemination and cultural exchange. They should be supported by decentralized media production cen-ters; educational and extension services should be location specific if they are to be credible and accepted.

23. It is not sufficient to urge that communication be given a high priority in national development; possible sources of investment finance must be identified. Among these could be differential communication pricing policies that would place large burdens on more prosperous urban and elite groups; the taxing of commercial advertising may also be envisaged for this purpose.

Particular challenges

We have focused on national efforts which must be made to lead to greater independence and self-reliance. But there are three major challenges to this goal that require concerted international action. Simply put, these are paper, tariff structures and the electro-magnetic spectrum.

We recommend:

24. A major international research and development effort to increase the supply of paper. The worldwide shortage of paper, including newsprint, and its escalating cost impose crush-

ing burdens upon struggling newspapers, periodicals and the publication industry, above all in the developing countries. Certain ecological constraints have also emerged. Unesco, in collaboration with FAO, should take urgent measures to identify and encourage production of paper and newsprint either by recycling paper or from new sources of feedstock in addition to the wood pulp presently produced largely by certain northern countries. Kenaf, bagasse, tropical woods and grasses could possibly provide alternative sources. Initial experiments are encouraging and need to be supported and multiplied.

25. Tariffs for new transmission, telecommunication rates and air mail charges for the dissemination of news, transport of newspapers, periodicals, books and audio-visual materials are one of the main obstacles to a free and balanced flow of information. This situation must be corrected, especially in the case of developing countries, through a variety of national an international initiatives. Governments should in particular examine the policies and practices of their post and telegraph authorities. Profits or Revenues should not be the primary aim of such agencies. They are instruments for policy-making and planned development in the field of information culture. Their tariffs should be in line with larger national goals. International action is also necessary to alter telecommunication tariffs that militate heavily against small and peripheral users. Current international consultations on this question may be brought to early fruition, possibly at the October 1980 session of the 154 nation International Telegraph and Telephone Consultative Committee, which should have before it specific proposals made by a Unesco-sponsored working group on "Low Telecommunication Rates" (November 1979). Unesco might, in cooperation with ITU, also sponsor an overall study on international telecommunications services by means of satellite transmission in collaboration with Intelsat, Intersputnik and user country representatives to make proposals for international and regional co-ordination or geostationary satellite development. The study should also include investigation of the possibility and practicalities of discounts for transmission of news and preferential rates for certain types of transmission to and from developing countries. Finally, developing countries should investigate the possibility of negotiating preferential tariffs on bilateral or regional basis.

26. The electro-magnetic spectrum and geostationary orbit, both finite natural resources, should be more equitably shared as the common property of mankind. For that purpose, we welcome the decisions taken by the World Administrative Radio Conference (WARC), Geneva, September–November 1979, to convene a series of special conferences over the next few years on certain specific topics related to the utilization of these resources.

3

GATS: ANNEX ON TELECOMMUNICATIONS

1. *Objectives*

Recognizing the specificities of the telecommunications services sector and, in particular, its dual role as a distinct sector of economic activity and as the underlying transport means for other economic activities, the Members have agreed to the following Annex with the objective of elaborating upon the provisions of the Agreement with respect to measures affecting access to and use of public telecommunications transport networks and services. Accordingly, this Annex provides notes and supplementary provisions to the Agreement.

2. *Scope*

(a) This Annex shall apply to all measures of a Member that affect access to and use of public telecommunications transport networks and services. [1]

(b) This Annex shall not apply to measures affecting the cable or broadcast distribution of radio or television programming.

(c) Nothing in this Annex shall be construed:

    (i) to require a Member to authorize a service supplier of any other Member to establish, construct, acquire, lease, operate, or supply telecommunications transport networks or services, other than as provided for in its Schedule;

or

    (ii) to require a Member (or to require a Member to oblige service suppliers under its jurisdiction) to establish, construct, acquire, lease, operate or supply telecommunications transport networks or services not offered to the public generally.

3. *Definitions*

For the purposes of this Annex:

(a)   "Telecommunications" means the transmission and reception of signals by any electromagnetic means.

(b)   "Public telecommunications transport service" means any telecommunications transport service required, explicitly or in effect, by a Member to be offered to the public generally. Such services may include, *inter alia*, telegraph, telephone, telex, and data transmission typically involving the real-time transmission of customer-supplied information between two or more points without any end-to-end change in the form or content of the customer's information.

(c)   "Public telecommunications transport network" means the public telecommunications infrastructure which permits telecommunications between and among defined network termination points.

(d)   "Intra-corporate communications" means telecommunications through which a company communicates within the company or with or among its subsidiaries, branches and, subject to a Member's domestic laws and regulations, affiliates. For these purposes, "subsidiaries", "branches" and, where applicable, "affiliates" shall be as defined by each Member. "Intra-corporate communications" in this Annex excludes commercial or non-commercial services that are supplied to companies that are not related subsidiaries, branches or affiliates, or that are offered to customers or potential customers.

(e)   Any reference to a paragraph or subparagraph of this Annex includes all subdivisions thereof.

4. *Transparency*

In the application of Article III of the Agreement, each Member shall ensure that relevant information on conditions affecting access to and use of public telecommunications transport networks and services is publicly available, including: tariffs and other terms and conditions of service; specifications of technical interfaces with such networks and services; information on bodies responsible for the preparation and adoption of standards affecting such access and use; conditions applying to attachment of terminal or other equipment; and notifications, registration or licensing requirements, if any.

5. *Access to and use of public telecommunications transport networks and services*

(a)   Each Member shall ensure that any service supplier of any other Member is accorded access to and use of public telecommunications transport networks and services on reasonable and non-discriminatory terms and conditions, for the supply of a service included in its Schedule. This obligation shall be applied, *inter alia*, through paragraphs (b) through (f).[2]

(b)   Each Member shall ensure that service suppliers of any other Member have access to and use of any public telecommunications transport network or service offered within or across the border of that Member, including private leased circuits, and to this end shall ensure, subject to paragraphs (e) and (f), that such suppliers are permitted:

(i)   to purchase or lease and attach terminal or other equipment which interfaces with the network and which is necessary to supply a supplier's services;

(ii)   to interconnect private leased or owned circuits with public telecommunications transport networks and services or with circuits leased or owned by another service supplier; and

(iii) to use operating protocols of the service supplier's choice in the supply of any service, other than as necessary to ensure the availability of telecommunications transport networks and services to the public generally.

(c)   Each Member shall ensure that service suppliers of any other Member may use public telecommunications transport networks and services for the movement of information within and across borders, including for intra-corporate communications of such service suppliers, and for access to information contained in data bases or otherwise stored in machine-readable form in the territory of any Member. Any new or amended measures of a Member significantly affecting such use shall be notified and shall be subject to consultation, in accordance with relevant provisions of the Agreement.

(d)   Notwithstanding the preceding paragraph, a Member may take such measures as are necessary to ensure the security and confidentiality of messages, subject to the requirement that such measures are not applied in a manner which would constitute a means of arbitrary or unjustifiable discrimination or a disguised restriction on trade in services.

(e)   Each Member shall ensure that no condition is imposed on access to and use of public telecommunications transport networks and services other than as necessary:

(i)   to safeguard the public service responsibilities of suppliers of public telecommunications transport networks and services, in particular their ability to make their networks or services available to the public generally;

(ii)   to protect the technical integrity of public telecommunications transport networks or services; or

(iii) to ensure that service suppliers of any other Member do not supply services unless permitted pursuant to commitments in the Member's Schedule.

(f)   Provided that they satisfy the criteria set out in paragraph (e), conditions for access to and use of public telecommunications transport networks and services may include:

(i)   restrictions on resale or shared use of such services;

(ii)   a requirement to use specified technical interfaces, including interface protocols, for inter-connection with such networks and services;

(iii) requirements, where necessary, for the inter-operability of such services and to encourage the achievement of the goals set out in paragraph 7(a);

(iv)   type approval of terminal or other equipment which interfaces with the network and technical requirements relating to the attachment of such equipment to such networks;

(v)   restrictions on inter-connection of private leased or owned circuits with such networks or services or with circuits leased or owned by another service supplier; or

(vi)   notification, registration and licensing.

(g)   Notwithstanding the preceding paragraphs of this section, a developing country Member may, consistent with its level of development, place reasonable conditions on access to and use of public telecommunications transport networks and services necessary to strengthen its domestic telecommunications infrastructure and service capacity and to increase its participation in international trade in telecommunications services. Such conditions shall be specified in the Member's Schedule.

6. *Technical cooperation*

(a)   Members recognize that an efficient, advanced telecommunications infrastructure in countries, particularly developing countries, is essential to the expansion of their trade in services. To this end, Members endorse and encourage the participation, to the fullest extent practicable, of developed and developing countries and their suppliers of public telecommunications transport networks and services and other entities in the development programmes of international and regional organizations, including the International Telecommunication Union, the United Nations Development Programme, and the International Bank for Reconstruction and Development.

(b)   Members shall encourage and support telecommunications cooperation among developing countries at the international, regional and sub-regional levels.

(c)   In cooperation with relevant international organizations, Members shall make available, where practicable, to developing countries information with respect to telecommunications services and developments in telecommunications and information technology to assist in strengthening their domestic telecommunications services sector.

(d)   Members shall give special consideration to opportunities for the least-developed countries to encourage foreign suppliers of telecommunications services to assist in the transfer of technology, training and other activities that support the development of their telecommunications infrastructure and expansion of their telecommunications services trade.

7. *Relation to international organizations and agreements*

(a)   Members recognize the importance of international standards for global compatibility and inter-operability of telecommunication networks and services and undertake to promote such standards through the work of relevant international bodies, including the International Telecommunication Union and the International Organization for Standardization.

(b)   Members recognize the role played by intergovernmental and non-governmental organizations and agreements in ensuring the efficient operation of domestic and global telecommunications services, in particular the International Telecommunication Union. Members shall make appropriate arrangements, where relevant, for consultation with such organizations on matters arising from the implementation of this Annex.

Annex on negotiations on basic telecommunications

1. Article II and the Annex on Article II Exemptions, including the requirement to list in the Annex any measure inconsistent with most-favoured-nation treatment that a Member will maintain, shall enter into force for basic telecommunications only on:

(a)   the implementation date to be determined under paragraph 5 of the Ministerial Decision on Negotiations on Basic Telecommunications; or,

(b)   should the negotiations not succeed, the date of the final report of the Negotiating Group on Basic Telecommunications provided for in that Decision.

2. Paragraph 1 shall not apply to any specific commitment on basic telecommunications which is inscribed in a Member's Schedule.

Notes

1   This paragraph is understood to mean that each Member shall ensure that the obligations of this Annex are applied with respect to suppliers of public telecommunications transport networks and services by whatever measures are necessary.

2   The term "non-discriminatory" is understood to refer to most-favoured-nation and national treatment as defined in the Agreement, as well as to reflect sector-specific usage of the term to mean "terms and conditions no less favourable than those accorded to any other user of like public telecommunications transport networks or services under like circumstances".

4

SUMMARY OF THE WIPO PERFORMANCES AND PHONOGRAMS TREATY (WPPT) 1996

The Treaty deals with intellectual property rights of two kinds of beneficiaries:

(i)   performers (actors, singers, musicians, etc.), and
(ii)   producers of phonograms (the persons or legal entities who or which take the initiative and have the responsibility for the fixation of the sounds).

They are dealt with in the same instrument because most of the rights granted by the Treaty to performers are rights connected with their fixed, purely aural performances (which are the subject matter of phonograms).

As far as performers are concerned, the Treaty grants performers four kinds of economic rights in their performances fixed in phonograms (not in audiovisual fixations, such as motion pictures):

(i)   the right of reproduction,
(ii)   the right of distribution,
(iii) the right of rental, and
(iv)   the right of making available.

Each of them is an exclusive right, subject to certain limitations and exceptions. Not all of those limitations and exceptions are mentioned in the following:

> the right of reproduction is the right to authorize direct or indirect reproduction of the phonogram in any manner or form,
> the right of distribution is the right to authorize the making available to the public of the original and copies of the phonogram through sale or other transfer of ownership,
> the right of rental is the right to authorize the commercial rental to the public of the original and copies of the phonogram as determined in the national law of the Contracting Parties (except for countries that since April 15, 1994, have in force a system of equitable remuneration for such rental),

the right of making available is the right to authorize the making available to the public, by wire or wireless means, of any performance fixed in a phonogram, in such a way that members of the public may access the fixed performance from a place and at a time individually chosen by them. This right covers, in particular, on-demand, interactive making available through the Internet.

The Treaty grants three kinds of economic rights to performers in respect of their unfixed (live) performances:

(i)   the right of broadcasting (except in the case of rebroadcasting),
(ii)   the right of communication to the public (except where the performance is a broadcast performance), and
(iii)   the right of fixation.

The Treaty also grants performers moral rights: the right to claim to be identified as the performer and the right to object to any distortion, mutilation or other modification that would be prejudicial to the performer's reputation.

As far as producers of phonograms are concerned, the Treaty grants them four kinds of rights (all economic) in their phonograms:

(i)   the right of reproduction,
(ii)   the right of distribution,
(iii)   the right of rental, and
(iv)   the right of making available.

Each of them is an exclusive right, subject to certain limitations and exceptions. Not all of those limitations and exceptions are mentioned in the following:

the right of reproduction is the right to authorize direct or indirect reproduction of the phonogram in any manner or form,
the right of distribution is the right to authorize the making available to the public of the original and copies of the phonogram through sale or other transfer of ownership,
the right of rental is the right to authorize the commercial rental to the public of the original and copies of the phonogram as determined in the national law of the Contracting Parties (except for countries that since April 15, 1994, have in force a system of equitable remuneration for such rental),
the right of making available is the right to authorize making available to the public the phonogram, by wire or wireless means, in such a way that members of the public may access the phonogram from a place and at a time individually chosen by them. This right covers, in particular, on-demand, interactive making available through the Internet.

As far as both performers and phonogram producers are concerned, the Treaty obliges— subject to various exceptions and limitations not mentioned here—each Contracting Party to accord to nationals of the other Contracting Parties with regard to the rights specifically granted in the Treaty the treatment it accords to its own nationals ("national treatment").

Furthermore, the Treaty provides that performers and producers of phonograms enjoy the right to a single equitable remuneration for the direct or indirect use of phonograms, published for commercial purposes, for broadcasting or for communication to the public. However, any Contracting Party may restrict or—provided that it makes a reservation to the Treaty—deny this right. In the case and to the extent of a reservation by a Contracting Party, the other Contracting Parties are permitted to deny, *vis-à-vis* the reserving Contracting Party, national treatment ("reciprocity").

The term of protection must be at least 50 years.

The enjoyment and exercise of the rights provided in the Treaty cannot be subject to any formality.

The Treaty obliges the Contracting Parties to provide legal remedies against the circumvention of technological measures (e.g., encryption) used by performers or phonogram producers in connection with the exercise of their rights and against the removal or altering of information, such as the indication of certain data that identify the performer, the performance, the producer of the phonogram and the phonogram, necessary for the management (e.g., licensing, collecting and distribution of royalties) of the said rights ("rights management information").

The Treaty obliges each Contracting Party to adopt, in accordance with its legal system, the measures necessary to ensure the application of the Treaty. In particular, the Contracting Party must ensure that enforcement procedures are available under its law so as to permit effective action against any act of infringement of rights covered by the Treaty. Such action must include expeditious remedies to prevent infringement and remedies which constitute a deterrent to further infringements.

The Treaty establishes an Assembly of the Contracting Parties whose main task is to deal with matters concerning the maintenance and development of the Treaty, and it entrusts to the Secretariat of WIPO the administrative tasks concerning the Treaty.

The Treaty entered into force on May 20, 2002. The Director General of WIPO is the depositary of the Treaty.

The Treaty is open to States members of WIPO and to the European Community. The Assembly constituted by the Treaty may decide to admit other intergovernmental organizations to become party to the Treaty.

Agreed statements concerning WIPO Performances and Phonograms Treaty, adopted by the Diplomatic Conference on December 20, 1996

Concerning Article 1

It is understood that Article 1(2) clarifies the relationship between rights in phonograms under this Treaty and copyright in works embodied in the phonograms. In cases where authorization is needed from both the author of a work embodied in the phonogram and a performer or producer owning rights in the phonogram, the need for the authorization of the author does not cease to exist because the authorization of the performer or producer is also required, and vice versa.

It is further understood that nothing in Article 1(2) precludes a Contracting Party from providing exclusive rights to a performer or producer of phonograms beyond those required to be provided under this Treaty.

Concerning Article 2(b)

It is understood that the definition of phonogram provided in Article 2(b) does not suggest that rights in the phonogram are in any way affected through their incorporation into a cinematographic or other audiovisual work.

Concerning Articles 2(e), 8, 9, 12, and 13

As used in these Articles, the expressions "copies" and "original and copies," being subject to the right of distribution and the right of rental under the said Articles, refer exclusively to fixed copies that can be put into circulation as tangible objects.

Concerning Article 3

It is understood that the reference in Articles 5(a) and 16(a)(iv) of the Rome Convention to "national of another Contracting State" will, when applied to this Treaty, mean, in regard to an intergovernmental organization that is a Contracting Party to this Treaty, a national of one of the countries that is a member of that organization.

Concerning Article 3(2)

For the application of Article 3(2), it is understood that fixation means the finalization of the master tape ("bande-mère").

Concerning Articles 7, 11 and 16

The reproduction right, as set out in Articles 7 and 11, and the exceptions permitted thereunder through Article 16, fully apply in the digital environment, in particular to the use of performances and phonograms in digital form. It is understood that the storage of a protected performance or phonogram in digital form in an electronic medium constitutes a reproduction within the meaning of these Articles.

Concerning Article 15

It is understood that Article 15 does not represent a complete resolution of the level of rights of broadcasting and communication to the public that should be enjoyed by performers and phonogram producers in the digital age. Delegations were unable to achieve consensus on differing proposals for aspects of exclusivity to be provided in certain circumstances or for rights to be provided without the possibility of reservations, and have therefore left the issue to future resolution.

Concerning Article 15

It is understood that Article 15 does not prevent the granting of the right conferred by this Article to performers of folklore and producers of phonograms recording folklore where such phonograms have not been published for commercial gain.

Concerning Article 16

The agreed statement concerning Article 10 (on Limitations and Exceptions) of the WIPO Copyright Treaty is applicable *mutatis mutandis* also to Article 16 (on Limitations and Exceptions) of the WIPO Performances and Phonograms Treaty.

Concerning Article 19

The agreed statement concerning Article 12 (on Obligations concerning Rights Management Information) of the WIPO Copyright Treaty is applicable *mutatis mutandis* also to Article 19 (on Obligations concerning Rights Management Information) of the WIPO Performances and Phonograms Treaty.

5

SUMMARY OF THE WIPO COPYRIGHT TREATY (WCT) 1996

The WCT is a special agreement under the Berne Convention. Any Contracting Party (even if it is not bound by the Berne Convention) must comply with the substantive provisions of the 1971 (Paris) Act of the Berne Convention for the Protection of Literary and Artistic Works (1886).

Furthermore, the Treaty mentions two subject matters to be protected by copyright,

(i)   computer programs, whatever may be the mode or form of their expression, and
(ii) compilations of data or other material ("databases"), in any form, which by reason of the selection or arrangement of their contents constitute intellectual creations. (Where a database does not constitute such a creation, it is outside the scope of this Treaty.)

As to the rights of authors, the Treaty deals with three:

(i)   the right of distribution,
(ii)   the right of rental, and
(iii) the right of communication to the public.

Each of them is an exclusive right, subject to certain limitations and exceptions. Not all of the limitations or exceptions are mentioned in the following:

the right of distribution is the right to authorize the making available to the public of the original and copies of a work through sale or other transfer of ownership,
the right of rental is the right to authorize commercial rental to the public of the original and copies of three kinds of works:

(i)   computer programs (except where the computer program itself is not the essential object of the rental),
(ii) cinematographic works (but only in cases where commercial rental has led to widespread copying of such works materially impairing the exclusive right of reproduction), and

(iii)   works embodied in phonograms as determined in the national law of the Contracting
         Parties (except for countries that since April 15, 1994, have in force a system of
         equitable remuneration for such rental),

         the right of communication to the public is the right to authorize any communication
         to the public, by wire or wireless means, including "the making available to the public
         of works in a way that the members of the public may access the work from a
         place and at a time individually chosen by them." The quoted expression covers in
         particular on-demand, interactive communication through the Internet.

The Treaty obliges the Contracting Parties to provide legal remedies against the circumvention of technological measures (e.g., encryption) used by authors in connection with
the exercise of their rights and against the removal or altering of information, such as certain
data that identify works or their authors, necessary for the management (e.g., licensing,
collecting and distribution of royalties) of their rights ("rights management information").
The Treaty obliges each Contracting Party to adopt, in accordance with its legal system, the
measures necessary to ensure the application of the Treaty. In particular, the Contracting
Party must ensure that enforcement procedures are available under its law so as to permit
effective action against any act of infringement of rights covered by the Treaty. Such action
must include expeditious remedies to prevent infringement and remedies which constitute a
deterrent to further infringements.

The Treaty establishes an Assembly of the Contracting Parties whose main task is to
deal with matters concerning the maintenance and development of the Treaty, and it
entrusts to the Secretariat of WIPO the administrative tasks concerning the Treaty.

The Treaty entered into force on March 6, 2002. The Director General of WIPO is the
depositary of the Treaty. This Treaty is open to States members of WIPO and to the
European Community. The Assembly constituted by the Treaty may decide to admit other
intergovernmental organizations to become party to the Treaty.

Agreed statements concerning the WIPO Copyright Treaty adopted by the Diplomatic Conference on December 20, 1996

Concerning Article 1(4)

The reproduction right, as set out in Article 9 of the Berne Convention, and the exceptions
permitted thereunder, fully apply in the digital environment, in particular to the use of
works in digital form. It is understood that the storage of a protected work in digital form in
an electronic medium constitutes a reproduction within the meaning of Article 9 of the
Berne Convention.

Concerning Article 3

It is understood that in applying Article 3 of this Treaty, the expression "country of the
Union" in Articles 2 to 6 of the Berne Convention will be read as if it were a reference
to a Contracting Party to this Treaty, in the application of those Berne Articles in respect
of protection provided for in this Treaty. It is also understood that the expression
"country outside the Union" in those Articles in the Berne Convention will, in the same
circumstances, be read as if it were a reference to a country that is not a Contracting
Party to this Treaty, and that "this Convention" in Articles 2(8), 2bis(2), 3, 4 and 5 of the

Berne Convention will be read as if it were a reference to the Berne Convention and this Treaty. Finally, it is understood that a reference in Articles 3 to 6 of the Berne Convention to a "national of one of the countries of the Union" will, when these Articles are applied to this Treaty, mean, in regard to an intergovernmental organization that is a Contracting Party to this Treaty, a national of one of the countries that is member of that organization.

Concerning Article 4

The scope of protection for computer programs under Article 4 of this Treaty, read with Article 2, is consistent with Article 2 of the Berne Convention and on a par with the relevant provisions of the TRIPS Agreement.

Concerning Article 5

The scope of protection for compilations of data (databases) under Article 5 of this Treaty, read with Article 2, is consistent with Article 2 of the Berne Convention and on a par with the relevant provisions of the TRIPS Agreement.

Concerning Articles 6 and 7

As used in these Articles, the expressions "copies" and "original and copies," being subject to the right of distribution and the right of rental under the said Articles, refer exclusively to fixed copies that can be put into circulation as tangible objects.

Concerning Article 7

It is understood that the obligation under Article 7(1) does not require a Contracting Party to provide an exclusive right of commercial rental to authors who, under that Contracting Party's law, are not granted rights in respect of phonograms. It is understood that this obligation is consistent with Article 14(4) of the TRIPS Agreement.

Concerning Article 8

It is understood that the mere provision of physical facilities for enabling or making a communication does not in itself amount to communication within the meaning of this Treaty or the Berne Convention. It is further understood that nothing in Article 8 precludes a Contracting Party from applying Article 11*bis*(2).

Concerning Article 10

It is understood that the provisions of Article 10 permit Contracting Parties to carry forward and appropriately extend into the digital environment limitations and exceptions in their national laws which have been considered acceptable under the Berne Convention. Similarly, these provisions should be understood to permit Contracting Parties to devise new exceptions and limitations that are appropriate in the digital network environment.

It is also understood that Article 10(2) neither reduces nor extends the scope of applicability of the limitations and exceptions permitted by the Berne Convention.

Concerning Article 12

It is understood that the reference to "infringement of any right covered by this Treaty or the Berne Convention" includes both exclusive rights and rights of remuneration.

It is further understood that Contracting Parties will not rely on this Article to devise or implement rights management systems that would have the effect of imposing formalities which are not permitted under the Berne Convention or this Treaty, prohibiting the free movement of goods or impeding the enjoyment of rights under this Treaty.

6

UNIVERSAL DECLARATION ON CULTURAL DIVERSITY (UNESCO)

Adopted by the 31st Session of UNESCO's General Conference, Paris, 2 November 2001

The General Conference,

Committed to the full implementation of the human rights and fundamental freedoms proclaimed in the Universal Declaration of Human Rights and other universally recognized legal instruments, such as the two International Covenants of 1966 relating respectively to civil and political rights and to economic, social and cultural rights,

Recalling that the Preamble to the Constitution of UNESCO affirms "that the wide diffusion of culture, and the education of humanity for justice and liberty and peace are indispensable to the dignity of man and constitute a sacred duty which all the nations must fulfil in a spirit of mutual assistance and concern",

Further recalling Article I of the Constitution, which assigns to UNESCO among other purposes that of recommending "such international agreements as may be necessary to promote the free flow of ideas by word and image",

Referring to the provisions relating to cultural diversity and the exercise of cultural rights in the international instruments enacted by UNESCO,[1]

Reaffirming that culture should be regarded as the set of distinctive spiritual, material, intellectual and emotional features of society or a social group, and that it encompasses, in addition to art and literature, lifestyles, ways of living together, value systems, traditions and beliefs,[2]

Noting that culture is at the heart of contemporary debates about identity, social cohesion, and the development of a knowledge-based economy,

Affirming that respect for the diversity of cultures, tolerance, dialogue and cooperation, in a climate of mutual trust and understanding are among the best guarantees of international peace and security,

Aspiring to greater solidarity on the basis of recognition of cultural diversity, of awareness of the unity of humankind, and of the development of intercultural exchanges,

Considering that the process of globalization, facilitated by the rapid development of new information and communication technologies, though representing a challenge for cultural diversity, creates the conditions for renewed dialogue among cultures and civilizations,

Aware of the specific mandate which has been entrusted to UNESCO, within the United Nations system, to ensure the preservation and promotion of the fruitful diversity of cultures,

Proclaims the following principles and adopts the present Declaration:

Identity, diversity and pluralism

Article 1 – Cultural diversity: the common heritage of humanity

Culture takes diverse forms across time and space. This diversity is embodied in the uniqueness and plurality of the identities of the groups and societies making up humankind. As a source of exchange, innovation and creativity, cultural diversity is as necessary for humankind as biodiversity is for nature. In this sense, it is the common heritage of humanity and should be recognized and affirmed for the benefit of present and future generations.

Article 2 – From cultural diversity to cultural pluralism

In our increasingly diverse societies, it is essential to ensure harmonious interaction among people and groups with plural, varied and dynamic cultural identities as well as their willingness to live together. Policies for the inclusion and participation of all citizens are guarantees of social cohesion, the vitality of civil society and peace. Thus defined, cultural pluralism gives policy expression to the reality of cultural diversity. Indissociable from a democratic framework, cultural pluralism is conducive to cultural exchange and to the flourishing of creative capacities that sustain public life.

Article 3 – Cultural diversity as a factor in development

Cultural diversity widens the range of options open to everyone; it is one of the roots of development, understood not simply in terms of economic growth, but also as a means to achieve a more satisfactory intellectual, emotional, moral and spiritual existence.

Cultural diversity and human rights

Article 4 – Human rights as guarantees of cultural diversity

The defence of cultural diversity is an ethical imperative, inseparable from respect for human dignity. It implies a commitment to human rights and fundamental freedoms, in particular the rights of persons belonging to minorities and those of indigenous peoples. No one may invoke cultural diversity to infringe upon human rights guaranteed by international law, nor to limit their scope.

Article 5 – Cultural rights as an enabling environment for cultural diversity

Cultural rights are an integral part of human rights, which are universal, indivisible and interdependent. The flourishing of creative diversity requires the full implementation of cultural rights as defined in Article 27 of the Universal Declaration of Human Rights and in Articles 13 and 15 of the International Covenant on Economic, Social and Cultural Rights. All persons have therefore the right to express themselves and to create and disseminate their work in the language of their choice, and particularly in their mother tongue; all persons are entitled to quality education and training that fully respect their cultural identity; and all persons have the right to participate in the cultural life of their choice and conduct their own cultural practices, subject to respect for human rights and fundamental freedoms.

Article 6 – Towards access for all to cultural diversity

While ensuring the free flow of ideas by word and image care should be exercised that all cultures can express themselves and make themselves known. Freedom of expression, media pluralism, multilingualism, equal access to art and to scientific and technological knowledge, including in digital form, and the possibility for all cultures to have access to the means of expression and dissemination are the guarantees of cultural diversity.

Cultural diversity and creativity

Article 7 – Cultural heritage as the wellspring of creativity

Creation draws on the roots of cultural tradition, but flourishes in contact with other cultures. For this reason, heritage in all its forms must be preserved, enhanced and handed on to future generations as a record of human experience and aspirations, so as to foster creativity in all its diversity and to inspire genuine dialogue among cultures.

Article 8 – Cultural goods and services: commodities of a unique kind

In the face of present-day economic and technological change, opening up vast prospects for creation and innovation, particular attention must be paid to the diversity of the supply of creative work, to due recognition of the rights of authors and artists and to the specificity of cultural goods and services which, as vectors of identity, values and meaning, must not be treated as mere commodities or consumer goods.

Article 9 – Cultural policies as catalysts of creativity

While ensuring the free circulation of ideas and works, cultural policies must create conditions conducive to the production and dissemination of diversified cultural goods through cultural industries that have the means to assert themselves at the local and global level. It is for each State, with due regard to its international obligations, to define its cultural policy and to implement it through the means it considers fit, whether by operational support or appropriate regulations.

Cultural diversity and international solidarity

Article 10 – Strengthening capacities for creation and dissemination worldwide

In the face of current imbalances in flows and exchanges of cultural goods and services at the global level, it is necessary to reinforce international cooperation and solidarity aimed at enabling all countries, especially developing countries and countries in transition, to establish cultural industries that are viable and competitive at national and international level.

Article 11 – Building partnerships between the public sector,
the private sector and civil society

Market forces alone cannot guarantee the preservation and promotion of cultural diversity, which is the key to sustainable human development. From this perspective, the pre-eminence of public policy, in partnership with the private sector and civil society, must be reaffirmed.

Article 12 – The role of UNESCO

UNESCO, by virtue of its mandate and functions, has the responsibility to:

(a)   Promote the incorporation of the principles set out in the present Declaration into the development strategies drawn up within the various intergovernmental bodies;

(b)   Serve as a reference point and a forum where States, international governmental and non-governmental organizations, civil society and the private sector may join together in elaborating concepts, objectives and policies in favour of cultural diversity;

(c)   Pursue its activities in standard-setting, awareness-raising and capacity-building in the areas related to the present Declaration within its fields of competence;

(d)   Facilitate the implementation of the Action Plan, the main lines of which are appended to the present Declaration.

Main lines of an action plan for the implementation of the UNESCO Universal Declaration on Cultural Diversity

The Member States commit themselves to taking appropriate steps to disseminate widely the "UNESCO Universal Declaration on Cultural Diversity" and to encourage its effective application, in particular by cooperating with a view to achieving the following objectives:

1.   Deepening the international debate on questions relating to cultural diversity, particularly in respect of its links with development and its impact on policy-making, at both national and international level; taking forward notably consideration of the opportunity of an international legal instrument on cultural diversity.

2.   Advancing in the definition of principles, standards and practices, on both the national and the international levels, as well as of awareness-raising modalities and patterns of cooperation, that are most conducive to the safeguarding and promotion of cultural diversity.

3.   Fostering the exchange of knowledge and best practices in regard to cultural pluralism with a view to facilitating, in diversified societies, the inclusion and participation of persons and groups from varied cultural backgrounds.

4.   Making further headway in understanding and clarifying the content of cultural rights as an integral part of human rights.

5.   Safeguarding the linguistic heritage of humanity and giving support to expression, creation and dissemination in the greatest possible number of languages.

6.   Encouraging linguistic diversity – while respecting the mother tongue – at all levels of education, wherever possible, and fostering the learning of several languages from the youngest age.

7.   Promoting through education an awareness of the positive value of cultural diversity and improving to this end both curriculum design and teacher education.

8. Incorporating, where appropriate, traditional pedagogies into the education process with a view to preserving and making full use of culturally appropriate methods of communication and transmission of knowledge.

9. Encouraging "digital literacy" and ensuring greater mastery of the new information and communication technologies, which should be seen both as educational discipline and as pedagogical tools capable of enhancing the effectiveness of educational services.

10. Promoting linguistic diversity in cyberspace and encouraging universal access through the global network to all information in the public domain.

11. Countering the digital divide, in close cooperation in relevant United Nations system organizations, by fostering access by the developing countries to the new technologies, by helping them to master information technologies and by facilitating the digital dissemination of endogenous cultural products and access by those countries to the educational, cultural and scientific digital resources available worldwide.

12. Encouraging the production, safeguarding and dissemination of diversified contents in the media and global information networks and, to that end, promoting the role of public radio and television services in the development of audiovisual productions of good quality, in particular by fostering the establishment of cooperative mechanisms to facilitate their distribution.

13. Formulating policies and strategies for the preservation and enhancement of the cultural and natural heritage, notably the oral and intangible cultural heritage, and combating illicit traffic in cultural goods and services.

14. Respecting and protecting traditional knowledge, in particular that of indigenous peoples; recognizing the contribution of traditional knowledge, particularly with regard to environmental protection and the management of natural resources, and fostering synergies between modern science and local knowledge.

15. Fostering the mobility of creators, artists, researchers, scientists and intellectuals and the development of international research programmes and partnerships, while striving to preserve and enhance the creative capacity of developing countries and countries in transition.

16. Ensuring protection of copyright and related rights in the interest of the development of contemporary creativity and fair remuneration for creative work, while at the same time upholding a public right of access to culture, in accordance with Article 27 of the Universal Declaration of Human Rights.

17. Assisting in the emergence or consolidation of cultural industries in the developing countries and countries in transition and, to this end, cooperating in the development of the necessary infrastructures and skills, fostering the emergence of viable local markets, and facilitating access for the cultural products of those countries to the global market and international distribution networks.

18. Developing cultural policies, including operational support arrangements and/or appropriate regulatory frameworks, designed to promote the principles enshrined in this Declaration, in accordance with the international obligations incumbent upon each State.

19. Involving all sectors of civil society closely in framing of public policies aimed at safeguarding and promoting cultural diversity.

20. Recognizing and encouraging the contribution that the private sector can make to enhancing cultural diversity and facilitating to that end the establishment of forums for dialogue between the public sector and the private sector.

The Member States recommend that the Director-General take the objectives set forth in this Action Plan into account in the implementation of UNESCO's programmes and communicate the latter to institutions of the United Nations system and to other intergovernmental and non-governmental organizations concerned with a view to enhancing the synergy of actions in favour of cultural diversity.

Notes

1   Among which, in particular, the Florence Agreement of 1950 and its Nairobi Protocol of 1976, the Universal Copyright Convention of 1952, the Declaration of Principles on International Cultural Cooperation of 1966, the Convention on the Means of Prohibiting and Preventing the Illicit Import, Export and Transfer of Ownership of Cultural Property (1970), the Convention for the Protection of World Cultural and Natural Heritage of 1972, the UNESCO Declaration on Race and Racial Prejudice of 1978, the Recommendation concerning the Status of the Artist of 1980, and the Recommendation on Safeguarding Traditional and Popular Culture of 1989.

2   This definition is in line with the conclusions of the World Conference on Cultural Policies (MONDIACULT, Mexico City, 1982), of the World Commission on Culture and Development (*Our Creative Diversity*, 1995), and of the Intergovernmental Conference on Cultural Policies for Development (Stockholm, 1998).

7

SOFTWARE PRINCIPLES (GOOGLE)

At Google, we put a lot of thought into improving your online experience. We're alarmed by what we believe is a growing disregard for your rights as computer users. We've seen increasing reports of spyware and other applications that trick you in order to serve you pop-up ads, connect your modem to expensive toll numbers or hijack your browser from the site you're trying to visit.

We do not see this trend reversing itself. In fact, it is getting worse. As a provider of services and monetization for users, advertisers and publishers on the Internet, we feel a responsibility to be proactive about these issues. So, we have decided to take action. As a first step, we have outlined a set of principles we believe our industry should adopt and we're sharing them to foster discussion and help solve the problem. We intend to follow these guidelines ourselves with the applications we distribute (such as the Google Toolbar and Google Deskbar). And because we strongly believe these principles are good for the industry and users worldwide, we will encourage our current and prospective business partners to adopt them as well.

These guidelines are, by necessity, broad. Software creation and distribution are complex and the technology is continuously evolving. As a result, some useful applications may not comply entirely with these principles and some deceptive practices may not be addressed here. This document is only a start, and focuses on the areas of Internet software and advertising. These guidelines need to be continually updated to keep pace with ever-changing technology.

We look forward to an ongoing discussion with you and with our partners. We would like to hear your suggestions to improve and update these principles. Please send your comments to software-principles@google.com.

Proposed principles

Installation

We believe software should not trick you into installing it. It should be clear to you when you are installing or enabling software on your computer and you should have the ability to say no.

An application shouldn't install itself onto your computer secretly or by hiding within another programme you're installing or updating. You should be conspicuously notified of the functions of all the applications in a bundle.

Upfront disclosure

When an application is installed or enabled, it should inform you of its principal and significant functions. And if the application makes money by showing you advertising, it should clearly and conspicuously explain this. This information should be presented in a way that a typical user will see and understand – not buried in small print that requires you to scroll. For example, if the application is paid for by serving pop-up ads or sending your personal data to a third party, that should be made clear to you.

Simple removal

It should be easy for you to figure out how to disable or delete an application. The process should try to remove sufficient components to disable all functions of the application, visible or not, without messing up your computer. Once an application is disabled or deleted, it should not remain active or be automatically enabled later by itself or another application.

Clear behavior

Applications that affect or change your user experience should make clear they are the reason for those changes. For example, if an application opens a window, that window should identify the application responsible for it. Applications should not intentionally obscure themselves under multiple or confusing names. You should be given means to control the application in a straightforward manner, such as by clicking on visible elements generated by the application. If an application shows you ads, it should clearly mark them as advertising and inform you that they originate from that application. If an application makes a change designed to affect the user experience of other applications (such as setting your home page) then those changes should be made clear to you.

Snooping

If an application collects or transmits your personal information such as your address, you should know. We believe you should be asked explicitly for your permission in a manner that is obvious and clearly states what information will be collected or transmitted. For more detail, it should be easy to find a privacy policy that discloses how the information will be used and whether it will be shared with third parties.

Keeping good company

Application providers should not allow their products to be bundled with applications that do not meet these guidelines.

Many internet users find that over time their computers become loaded with unwanted software – be it adware, spyware or just plain junk. This is because a few applications they installed came bundled with junk, and that junk generated more junk piled higher and deeper. We believe any situation where multiple applications are being installed should be made very clear to users, so that if you were to ask them several months later – "What's this?" – most will know where it came from and why it is there.

Usually there are complex business relationships among the companies participating in a bundle. This can result in well-intentioned companies benefiting from the distribution or revenue generated by software that does not benefit you. *Getting paid to distribute, or paying money to be distributed with undesirable software enables more undesirable software.* Responsible software makers and advertisers can work to prevent such distribution by avoiding these types of business relationships, even if they are through intermediaries.

We are alarmed by the size of this problem, which we estimate to be causing hundreds of millions of dollars to be changing hands annually. Because of this magnitude and user impact, strong action by the industry is imperative.

We believe that it is in our users' and the industry's interest to work to eliminate this problem. For this reason, we will strive to distribute our software only in bundles where all applications meet the above guidelines, and we think users will benefit if others in our industry do the same.

Note: If you think you have a deceptive application on your computer, or just want to check to be certain, there are a number of programs that can help you. *Spybot Search and Destroy, LavaSoft's Ad-aware*, and *CWShredder* are commonly used. These programs can remove the most common malicious applications, though our users report that you may need to try more than one and having the latest versions is important.

posted: May 18, 2004

CONVENTION ON THE PROTECTION AND PROMOTION OF THE DIVERSITY OF CULTURAL EXPRESSIONS (UNESCO)

The General Conference of the United Nations Educational, Scientific and Cultural Organization, meeting in Paris from 3 to 21 October 2005 at its 33rd session,

Affirming that cultural diversity is a defining characteristic of humanity,

Conscious that cultural diversity forms a common heritage of humanity and should be cherished and preserved for the benefit of all,

Being aware that cultural diversity creates a rich and varied world, which increases the range of choices and nurtures human capacities and values, and therefore is a mainspring for sustainable development for communities, peoples and nations,

Recalling that cultural diversity, flourishing within a framework of democracy, tolerance, social justice and mutual respect between peoples and cultures, is indispensable for peace and security at the local, national and international levels,

Celebrating the importance of cultural diversity for the full realization of human rights and fundamental freedoms proclaimed in the Universal Declaration of Human Rights and other universally recognized instruments,

Emphasizing the need to incorporate culture as a strategic element in national and international development policies, as well as in international development cooperation, taking into account also the United Nations Millennium Declaration (2000) with its special emphasis on poverty eradication,

Taking into account that culture takes diverse forms across time and space and that this diversity is embodied in the uniqueness and plurality of the identities and cultural expressions of the peoples and societies making up humanity,

Recognizing the importance of traditional knowledge as a source of intangible and material wealth, and in particular the knowledge systems of indigenous peoples, and its positive contribution to sustainable development, as well as the need for its adequate protection and promotion,

Recognizing the need to take measures to protect the diversity of cultural expressions, including their contents, especially in situations where cultural expressions may be threatened by the possibility of extinction or serious impairment,

Emphasizing the importance of culture for social cohesion in general, and in particular its potential for the enhancement of the status and role of women in society,

Being aware that cultural diversity is strengthened by the free flow of ideas, and that it is nurtured by constant exchanges and interaction between cultures,

Reaffirming that freedom of thought, expression and information, as well as diversity of the media, enable cultural expressions to flourish within societies,

Recognizing that the diversity of cultural expressions, including traditional cultural expressions, is an important factor that allows individuals and peoples to express and to share with others their ideas and values,

Recalling that linguistic diversity is a fundamental element of cultural diversity, and *reaffirming* the fundamental role that education plays in the protection and promotion of cultural expressions,

Taking into account the importance of the vitality of cultures, including for persons belonging to minorities and indigenous peoples, as manifested in their freedom to create, disseminate and distribute their traditional cultural expressions and to have access thereto, so as to benefit them for their own development,

Emphasizing the vital role of cultural interaction and creativity, which nurture and renew cultural expressions and enhance the role played by those involved in the development of culture for the progress of society at large,

Recognizing the importance of intellectual property rights in sustaining those involved in cultural creativity,

Being convinced that cultural activities, goods and services have both an economic and a cultural nature, because they convey identities, values and meanings, and must therefore not be treated as solely having commercial value,

Noting that while the processes of globalization, which have been facilitated by the rapid development of information and communication technologies, afford unprecedented conditions for enhanced interaction between cultures, they also represent a challenge for cultural diversity, namely in view of risks of imbalances between rich and poor countries,

Being aware of UNESCO's specific mandate to ensure respect for the diversity of cultures and to recommend such international agreements as may be necessary to promote the free flow of ideas by word and image,

Referring to the provisions of the international instruments adopted by UNESCO relating to cultural diversity and the exercise of cultural rights, and in particular the Universal Declaration on Cultural Diversity of 2001,

Adopts this Convention on 20 October 2005.

I. Objectives and guiding principles

Article 1 – Objectives

The objectives of this Convention are:

(a)   to protect and promote the diversity of cultural expressions;

(b)   to create the conditions for cultures to flourish and to freely interact in a mutually beneficial manner;

(c)   to encourage dialogue among cultures with a view to ensuring wider and balanced cultural exchanges in the world in favour of intercultural respect and a culture of peace;

(d)   to foster interculturality in order to develop cultural interaction in the spirit of building bridges among peoples;

(e)   to promote respect for the diversity of cultural expressions and raise awareness of its value at the local, national and international levels;

(f)   to reaffirm the importance of the link between culture and development for all
countries, particularly for developing countries, and to support actions undertaken
nationally and internationally to secure recognition of the true value of this link;

(g)   to give recognition to the distinctive nature of cultural activities, goods and services as
vehicles of identity, values and meaning;

(h)   to reaffirm the sovereign rights of States to maintain, adopt and implement policies
and measures that they deem appropriate for the protection and promotion of the
diversity of cultural expressions on their territory;

(i)   to strengthen international cooperation and solidarity in a spirit of partnership with
a view, in particular, to enhancing the capacities of developing countries in order to
protect and promote the diversity of cultural expressions.

Article 2 – Guiding principles

1. Principle of respect for human rights and fundamental freedoms

Cultural diversity can be protected and promoted only if human rights and fundamental
freedoms, such as freedom of expression, information and communication, as well as the
ability of individuals to choose cultural expressions, are guaranteed. No one may invoke the
provisions of this Convention in order to infringe human rights and fundamental freedoms
as enshrined in the Universal Declaration of Human Rights or guaranteed by international
law, or to limit the scope thereof.

2. Principle of sovereignty

States have, in accordance with the Charter of the United Nations and the principles of
international law, the sovereign right to adopt measures and policies to protect and promote
the diversity of cultural expressions within their territory.

3. Principle of equal dignity of and respect for all cultures

The protection and promotion of the diversity of cultural expressions presuppose the
recognition of equal dignity of and respect for all cultures, including the cultures of persons
belonging to minorities and indigenous peoples.

4. Principle of international solidarity and cooperation

International cooperation and solidarity should be aimed at enabling countries, especially
developing countries, to create and strengthen their means of cultural expression, including
their cultural industries, whether nascent or established, at the local, national and international levels.

5. Principle of the complementarity of economic and cultural aspects of development

Since culture is one of the mainsprings of development, the cultural aspects of development
are as important as its economic aspects, which individuals and peoples have the fundamental right to participate in and enjoy.

6. Principle of sustainable development

Cultural diversity is a rich asset for individuals and societies. The protection, promotion and maintenance of cultural diversity are an essential requirement for sustainable development for the benefit of present and future generations.

7. Principle of equitable access

Equitable access to a rich and diversified range of cultural expressions from all over the world and access of cultures to the means of expressions and dissemination constitute important elements for enhancing cultural diversity and encouraging mutual understanding.

8. Principle of openness and balance

When States adopt measures to support the diversity of cultural expressions, they should seek to promote, in an appropriate manner, openness to other cultures of the world and to ensure that these measures are geared to the objectives pursued under the present Convention.

II. Scope of application

Article 3 – Scope of application

This Convention shall apply to the policies and measures adopted by the Parties related to the protection and promotion of the diversity of cultural expressions.

III. Definitions

Article 4 – Definitions

For the purposes of this Convention, it is understood that:

1. Cultural diversity

"Cultural diversity" refers to the manifold ways in which the cultures of groups and societies find expression. These expressions are passed on within and among groups and societies.

   Cultural diversity is made manifest not only through the varied ways in which the cultural heritage of humanity is expressed, augmented and transmitted through the variety of cultural expressions, but also through diverse modes of artistic creation, production, dissemination, distribution and enjoyment, whatever the means and technologies used.

2. Cultural content

"Cultural content" refers to the symbolic meaning, artistic dimension and cultural values that originate from or express cultural identities.

3. Cultural expressions

"Cultural expressions" are those expressions that result from the creativity of individuals, groups and societies, and that have cultural content.

4. Cultural activities, goods and services

"Cultural activities, goods and services" refers to those activities, goods and services, which at the time they are considered as a specific attribute, use or purpose, embody or convey cultural expressions, irrespective of the commercial value they may have. Cultural activities may be an end in themselves, or they may contribute to the production of cultural goods and services.

5. Cultural industries

"Cultural industries" refers to industries producing and distributing cultural goods or services as defined in paragraph 4 above.

6. Cultural policies and measures

"Cultural policies and measures" refers to those policies and measures relating to culture, whether at the local, national, regional or international level that are either focused on culture as such or are designed to have a direct effect on cultural expressions of individuals, groups or societies, including on the creation, production, dissemination, distribution of and access to cultural activities, goods and services.

7. Protection

"Protection" means the adoption of measures aimed at the preservation, safeguarding and enhancement of the diversity of cultural expressions.
    "Protect" means to adopt such measures.

8. Interculturality

"Interculturality" refers to the existence and equitable interaction of diverse cultures and the possibility of generating shared cultural expressions through dialogue and mutual respect.

IV. Rights and obligations of Parties

Article 5 – General rule regarding rights and obligations

1.   The Parties, in conformity with the Charter of the United Nations, the principles of international law and universally recognized human rights instruments, reaffirm their sovereign right to formulate and implement their cultural policies and to adopt measures to protect and promote the diversity of cultural expressions and to strengthen international cooperation to achieve the purposes of this Convention.
2.   When a Party implements policies and takes measures to protect and promote the diversity of cultural expressions within its territory, its policies and measures shall be consistent with the provisions of this Convention.

Article 6 – Rights of parties at the national level

1.   Within the framework of its cultural policies and measures as defined in Article 4.6 and taking into account its own particular circumstances and needs, each Party may

adopt measures aimed at protecting and promoting the diversity of cultural expressions within its territory.

2.   Such measures may include the following:

  (a)   regulatory measures aimed at protecting and promoting diversity of cultural expressions;

  (b)   measures that, in an appropriate manner, provide opportunities for domestic cultural activities, goods and services among all those available within the national territory for the creation, production, dissemination, distribution and enjoyment of such domestic cultural activities, goods and services, including provisions relating to the language used for such activities, goods and services;

  (c)   measures aimed at providing domestic independent cultural industries and activities in the informal sector effective access to the means of production, dissemination and distribution of cultural activities, goods and services;

  (d)   measures aimed at providing public financial assistance;

  (e)   measures aimed at encouraging non-profit organizations, as well as public and private institutions and artists and other cultural professionals, to develop and promote the free exchange and circulation of ideas, cultural expressions and cultural activities, goods and services, and to stimulate both the creative and entrepreneurial spirit in their activities;

  (f)   measures aimed at establishing and supporting public institutions, as appropriate;

  (g)   measures aimed at nurturing and supporting artists and others involved in the creation of cultural expressions;

  (h)   measures aimed at enhancing diversity of the media, including through public service broadcasting.

Article 7 – Measures to promote cultural expressions

1.   Parties shall endeavour to create in their territory an environment which encourages individuals and social groups:

  (a)   to create, produce, disseminate, distribute and have access to their own cultural expressions, paying due attention to the special circumstances and needs of women as well as various social groups, including persons belonging to minorities and indigenous peoples;

  (b)   to have access to diverse cultural expressions from within their territory as well as from other countries of the world.

2.   Parties shall also endeavour to recognize the important contribution of artists, others involved in the creative process, cultural communities, and organizations that support their work, and their central role in nurturing the diversity of cultural expressions.

Article 8 – Measures to protect cultural expressions

1.   Without prejudice to the provisions of Articles 5 and 6, a Party may determine the existence of special situations where cultural expressions on its territory are at risk of extinction, under serious threat, or otherwise in need of urgent safeguarding.

2.   Parties may take all appropriate measures to protect and preserve cultural expressions in situations referred to in paragraph 1 in a manner consistent with the provisions of this Convention.

3.   Parties shall report to the Intergovernmental Committee referred to in Article 23

all measures taken to meet the exigencies of the situation, and the Committee may make appropriate recommendations.

Article 9 – Information sharing and transparency

Parties shall:

(a)   provide appropriate information in their reports to UNESCO every four years on measures taken to protect and promote the diversity of cultural expressions within their territory and at the international level;

(b)   designate a point of contact responsible for information sharing in relation to this Convention;

(c)   share and exchange information relating to the protection and promotion of the diversity of cultural expressions.

Article 10 – Education and public awareness

Parties shall:

(a)   encourage and promote understanding of the importance of the protection and promotion of the diversity of cultural expressions, *inter alia*, through educational and greater public awareness programmes;

(b)   cooperate with other Parties and international and regional organizations in achieving the purpose of this article;

(c)   endeavour to encourage creativity and strengthen production capacities by setting up educational, training and exchange programmes in the field of cultural industries. These measures should be implemented in a manner which does not have a negative impact on traditional forms of production.

Article 11 – Participation of civil society

Parties acknowledge the fundamental role of civil society in protecting and promoting the diversity of cultural expressions. Parties shall encourage the active participation of civil society in their efforts to achieve the objectives of this Convention.

Article 12 – Promotion of international cooperation

Parties shall endeavour to strengthen their bilateral, regional and international cooperation for the creation of conditions conducive to the promotion of the diversity of cultural expressions, taking particular account of the situations referred to in Articles 8 and 17, notably in order to:

(a)   facilitate dialogue among Parties on cultural policy;

(b)   enhance public sector strategic and management capacities in cultural public sector institutions, through professional and international cultural exchanges and sharing of best practices;

(c)   reinforce partnerships with and among civil society, non-governmental organizations and the private sector in fostering and promoting the diversity of cultural expressions;

(d)   promote the use of new technologies, encourage partnerships to enhance information sharing and cultural understanding, and foster the diversity of cultural expressions;

(e)   encourage the conclusion of co-production and co-distribution agreements.

Article 13 – Integration of culture in sustainable development

Parties shall endeavour to integrate culture in their development policies at all levels for the creation of conditions conducive to sustainable development and, within this framework, foster aspects relating to the protection and promotion of the diversity of cultural expressions.

Article 14 – Cooperation for development

Parties shall endeavour to support cooperation for sustainable development and poverty reduction, especially in relation to the specific needs of developing countries, in order to foster the emergence of a dynamic cultural sector by, *inter alia*, the following means:

(a)   the strengthening of the cultural industries in developing countries through:

  (i)   creating and strengthening cultural production and distribution capacities in developing countries;

  (ii)   facilitating wider access to the global market and international distribution networks for their cultural activities, goods and services;

  (iii) enabling the emergence of viable local and regional markets;

  (iv)   adopting, where possible, appropriate measures in developed countries with a view to facilitating access to their territory for the cultural activities, goods and services of developing countries;

  (v)   providing support for creative work and facilitating the mobility, to the extent possible, of artists from the developing world;

  (vi)   encouraging appropriate collaboration between developed and developing countries in the areas, *inter alia*, of music and film;

(b)   capacity-building through the exchange of information, experience and expertise, as well as the training of human resources in developing countries, in the public and private sector relating to, *inter alia*, strategic and management capacities, policy development and implementation, promotion and distribution of cultural expressions, small-, medium- and micro-enterprise development, the use of technology, and skills development and transfer;

(c)   technology transfer through the introduction of appropriate incentive measures for the transfer of technology and know-how, especially in the areas of cultural industries and enterprises;

(d)   financial support through:

  (i)   the establishment of an International Fund for Cultural Diversity as provided in Article 18;

  (ii)   the provision of official development assistance, as appropriate, including technical assistance, to stimulate and support creativity;

  (iii) other forms of financial assistance such as low interest loans, grants and other funding mechanisms.

Article 15 – Collaborative arrangements

Parties shall encourage the development of partnerships, between and within the public and private sectors and non-profit organizations, in order to cooperate with developing countries in the enhancement of their capacities in the protection and promotion of the diversity of cultural expressions. These innovative partnerships shall, according to the practical needs of developing countries, emphasize the further development of infrastructure, human resources and policies, as well as the exchange of cultural activities, goods and services.

Article 16 – Preferential treatment for developing countries

Developed countries shall facilitate cultural exchanges with developing countries by granting, through the appropriate institutional and legal framework, preferential treatment to artists and other cultural professionals and practitioners, as well as cultural goods and services from developing countries.

Article 17 – International cooperation in situations of serious threat to cultural expressions

Parties shall cooperate in providing assistance to each other, and, in particular to developing countries, in situations referred to under Article 8.

Article 18 – International Fund for Cultural Diversity

1.   An International Fund for Cultural Diversity, hereinafter referred to as "the Fund", is hereby established.
2.   The Fund shall consist of funds-in-trust established in accordance with the Financial Regulations of UNESCO.
3.   The resources of the Fund shall consist of:
     (a)   voluntary contributions made by Parties;
     (b)   funds appropriated for this purpose by the General Conference of UNESCO;
     (c)   contributions, gifts or bequests by other States; organizations and programmes of the United Nations system, other regional or international organizations; and public or private bodies or individuals;
     (d)   any interest due on resources of the Fund;
     (e)   funds raised through collections and receipts from events organized for the benefit of the Fund;
     (f)   any other resources authorized by the Fund's regulations.
4.   The use of resources of the Fund shall be decided by the Intergovernmental Committee on the basis of guidelines determined by the Conference of Parties referred to in Article 22.
5.   The Intergovernmental Committee may accept contributions and other forms of assistance for general and specific purposes relating to specific projects, provided that those projects have been approved by it.
6.   No political, economic or other conditions that are incompatible with the objectives of this Convention may be attached to contributions made to the Fund.
7.   Parties shall endeavour to provide voluntary contributions on a regular basis towards the implementation of this Convention.

Article 19 – Exchange, analysis and dissemination of information

1.   Parties agree to exchange information and share expertise concerning data collection and statistics on the diversity of cultural expressions as well as on best practices for its protection and promotion.

2. UNESCO shall facilitate, through the use of existing mechanisms within the Secretariat, the collection, analysis and dissemination of all relevant information, statistics and best practices.

3. UNESCO shall also establish and update a data bank on different sectors and governmental, private and non-profit organizations involved in the area of cultural expressions.

4. To facilitate the collection of data, UNESCO shall pay particular attention to capacity-building and the strengthening of expertise for Parties that submit a request for such assistance.

5. The collection of information identified in this Article shall complement the information collected under the provisions of Article 9.

V. Relationship to other instruments

Article 20 – Relationship to other treaties: mutual supportiveness, complementarity and non-subordination

1. Parties recognize that they shall perform in good faith their obligations under this Convention and all other treaties to which they are parties. Accordingly, without subordinating this Convention to any other treaty,
    (a) they shall foster mutual supportiveness between this Convention and the other treaties to which they are parties; and
    (b) when interpreting and applying the other treaties to which they are parties or when entering into other international obligations, Parties shall take into account the relevant provisions of this Convention.

2. Nothing in this Convention shall be interpreted as modifying rights and obligations of the Parties under any other treaties to which they are parties.

Article 21 – International consultation and coordination

Parties undertake to promote the objectives and principles of this Convention in other international forums. For this purpose, Parties shall consult each other, as appropriate, bearing in mind these objectives and principles.

VI. Organs of the Convention

Article 22 – Conference of Parties

1. A Conference of Parties shall be established. The Conference of Parties shall be the plenary and supreme body of this Convention.

2. The Conference of Parties shall meet in ordinary session every two years, as far as possible, in conjunction with the General Conference of UNESCO. It may meet in extraordinary session if it so decides or if the Intergovernmental Committee receives a request to that effect from at least one-third of the Parties.

3. The Conference of Parties shall adopt its own rules of procedure.

4. The functions of the Conference of Parties shall be, inter alia:
    (a) to elect the Members of the Intergovernmental Committee;
    (b) to receive and examine reports of the Parties to this Convention transmitted by the Intergovernmental Committee;

(c)   to approve the operational guidelines prepared upon its request by the Inter-governmental Committee;

(d)   to take whatever other measures it may consider necessary to further the objectives of this Convention.

Article 23 – Intergovernmental Committee

1.   An Intergovernmental Committee for the Protection and Promotion of the Diversity of Cultural Expressions, hereinafter referred to as "the Intergovernmental Committee", shall be established within UNESCO. It shall be composed of representatives of 18 States Parties to the Convention, elected for a term of four years by the Conference of Parties upon entry into force of this Convention pursuant to Article 29.

2.   The Intergovernmental Committee shall meet annually.

3.   The Intergovernmental Committee shall function under the authority and guidance of and be accountable to the Conference of Parties.

4.   The Members of the Intergovernmental Committee shall be increased to 24 once the number of Parties to the Convention reaches 50.

5.   The election of Members of the Intergovernmental Committee shall be based on the principles of equitable geographical representation as well as rotation.

6.   Without prejudice to the other responsibilities conferred upon it by this Convention, the functions of the Intergovernmental Committee shall be:

(a)   to promote the objectives of this Convention and to encourage and monitor the implementation thereof;

(b)   to prepare and submit for approval by the Conference of Parties, upon its request, the operational guidelines for the implementation and application of the provisions of the Convention;

(c)   to transmit to the Conference of Parties reports from Parties to the Convention, together with its comments and a summary of their contents;

(d)   to make appropriate recommendations to be taken in situations brought to its attention by Parties to the Convention in accordance with relevant provisions of the Convention, in particular Article 8;

(e)   to establish procedures and other mechanisms for consultation aimed at promoting the objectives and principles of this Convention in other international forums;

(f)   to perform any other tasks as may be requested by the Conference of Parties.

7.   The Intergovernmental Committee, in accordance with its Rules of Procedure, may invite at any time public or private organizations or individuals to participate in its meetings for consultation on specific issues.

8.   The Intergovernmental Committee shall prepare and submit to the Conference of Parties, for approval, its own Rules of Procedure.

Article 24 – UNESCO Secretariat

1.   The organs of the Convention shall be assisted by the UNESCO Secretariat.

2.   The Secretariat shall prepare the documentation of the Conference of Parties and the Intergovernmental Committee as well as the agenda of their meetings and shall assist in and report on the implementation of their decisions.

VII. Final clauses

Article 25 – Settlement of disputes

1. In the event of a dispute between Parties to this Convention concerning the interpretation or the application of the Convention, the Parties shall seek a solution by negotiation.
2. If the Parties concerned cannot reach agreement by negotiation, they may jointly seek the good offices of, or request mediation by, a third party.
3. If good offices or mediation are not undertaken or if there is no settlement by negotiation, good offices or mediation, a Party may have recourse to conciliation in accordance with the procedure laid down in the Annex of this Convention. The Parties shall consider in good faith the proposal made by the Conciliation Commission for the resolution of the dispute.
4. Each Party may, at the time of ratification, acceptance, approval or accession, declare that it does not recognize the conciliation procedure provided for above. Any Party having made such a declaration may, at any time, withdraw this declaration by notification to the Director-General of UNESCO.

Article 26 – Ratification, acceptance, approval or accession by Member States

1. This Convention shall be subject to ratification, acceptance, approval or accession by Member States of UNESCO in accordance with their respective constitutional procedures.
2. The instruments of ratification, acceptance, approval or accession shall be deposited with the Director-General of UNESCO.

Article 27 – Accession

1. This Convention shall be open to accession by all States not Members of UNESCO but members of the United Nations, or of any of its specialized agencies, that are invited by the General Conference of UNESCO to accede to it.
2. This Convention shall also be open to accession by territories which enjoy full internal self-government recognized as such by the United Nations, but which have not attained full independence in accordance with General Assembly resolution 1514 (XV), and which have competence over the matters governed by this Convention, including the competence to enter into treaties in respect of such matters.
3. The following provisions apply to regional economic integration organizations:
   (a) This Convention shall also be open to accession by any regional economic integration organization, which shall, except as provided below, be fully bound by the provisions of the Convention in the same manner as States Parties;
   (b) In the event that one or more Member States of such an organization is also Party to this Convention, the organization and such Member State or States shall decide on their responsibility for the performance of their obligations under this Convention. Such distribution of responsibility shall take effect following completion of the notification procedure described in subparagraph (c). The organization and the Member States shall not be entitled to exercise rights under this Convention concurrently. In addition, regional economic integration organizations, in matters within their competence, shall exercise their rights to

vote with a number of votes equal to the number of their Member States that are Parties to this Convention. Such an organization shall not exercise its right to vote if any of its Member States exercises its right, and vice-versa;

(c)   A regional economic integration organization and its Member State or States which have agreed on a distribution of responsibilities as provided in sub-paragraph (b) shall inform the Parties of any such proposed distribution of responsibilities in the following manner:

(i)   in their instrument of accession, such organization shall declare with specificity, the distribution of their responsibilities with respect to matters governed by the Convention;

(ii)   in the event of any later modification of their respective responsibilities, the regional economic integration organization shall inform the depositary of any such proposed modification of their respective responsibilities; the depositary shall in turn inform the Parties of such modification;

(d)   Member States of a regional economic integration organization which become Parties to this Convention shall be presumed to retain competence over all matters in respect of which transfers of competence to the organization have not been specifically declared or informed to the depositary;

(e)   "Regional economic integration organization" means an organization constituted by sovereign States, members of the United Nations or of any of its specialized agencies, to which those States have transferred competence in respect of matters governed by this Convention and which has been duly authorized, in accordance with its internal procedures, to become a Party to it.

4.   The instrument of accession shall be deposited with the Director-General of UNESCO.

Article 28 – Point of contact

Upon becoming Parties to this Convention, each Party shall designate a point of contact as referred to in Article 9.

Article 29 – Entry into force

1.   This Convention shall enter into force three months after the date of deposit of the thirtieth instrument of ratification, acceptance, approval or accession, but only with respect to those States or regional economic integration organizations that have deposited their respective instruments of ratification, acceptance, approval, or accession on or before that date. It shall enter into force with respect to any other Party three months after the deposit of its instrument of ratification, acceptance, approval or accession.

2.   For the purposes of this Article, any instrument deposited by a regional economic integration organization shall not be counted as additional to those deposited by Member States of the organization.

Article 30 – Federal or non-unitary constitutional systems

Recognizing that international agreements are equally binding on Parties regardless of their constitutional systems, the following provisions shall apply to Parties which have a federal or non-unitary constitutional system:

(a)   with regard to the provisions of this Convention, the implementation of which comes under the legal jurisdiction of the federal or central legislative power, the obligations of the federal or central government shall be the same as for those Parties which are not federal States;

(b)   with regard to the provisions of the Convention, the implementation of which comes under the jurisdiction of individual constituent units such as States, counties, provinces, or cantons which are not obliged by the constitutional system of the federation to take legislative measures, the federal government shall inform, as necessary, the competent authorities of constituent units such as States, counties, provinces or cantons of the said provisions, with its recommendation for their adoption.

Article 31 – Denunciation

1.   Any Party to this Convention may denounce this Convention.

2.   The denunciation shall be notified by an instrument in writing deposited with the Director-General of UNESCO.

3.   The denunciation shall take effect 12 months after the receipt of the instrument of denunciation. It shall in no way affect the financial obligations of the Party denouncing the Convention until the date on which the withdrawal takes effect.

Article 32 – Depositary functions

The Director-General of UNESCO, as the depositary of this Convention, shall inform the Member States of the Organization, the States not members of the Organization and regional economic integration organizations referred to in Article 27, as well as the United Nations, of the deposit of all the instruments of ratification, acceptance, approval or accession provided for in Articles 26 and 27, and of the denunciations provided for in Article 31.

Article 33 – Amendments

1.   A Party to this Convention may, by written communication addressed to the Director-General, propose amendments to this Convention. The Director-General shall circulate such communication to all Parties. If, within six months from the date of dispatch of the communication, no less than one half of the Parties reply favourably to the request, the Director-General shall present such proposal to the next session of the Conference of Parties for discussion and possible adoption.

2.   Amendments shall be adopted by a two-thirds majority of Parties present and voting.

3.   Once adopted, amendments to this Convention shall be submitted to the Parties for ratification, acceptance, approval or accession.

4.   For Parties which have ratified, accepted, approved or acceded to them, amendments to this Convention shall enter into force three months after the deposit of the instruments referred to in paragraph 3 of this Article by two-thirds of the Parties. Thereafter, for each Party that ratifies, accepts, approves or accedes to an amendment, the said amendment shall enter into force three months after the date of deposit by that Party of its instrument of ratification, acceptance, approval or accession.

5.   The procedure set out in paragraphs 3 and 4 shall not apply to amendments to Article 23 concerning the number of Members of the Intergovernmental Committee. These amendments shall enter into force at the time they are adopted.

6.   A State or a regional economic integration organization referred to in Article 27 which becomes a Party to this Convention after the entry into force of amendments in conformity with paragraph 4 of this Article shall, failing an expression of different intention, be considered to be:

(a)   Party to this Convention as so amended; and

(b)   a Party to the unamended Convention in relation to any Party not bound by the amendments.

Article 34 – Authoritative texts

This Convention has been drawn up in Arabic, Chinese, English, French, Russian and Spanish, all six texts being equally authoritative.

Article 35 – Registration

In conformity with Article 102 of the Charter of the United Nations, this Convention shall be registered with the Secretariat of the United Nations at the request of the Director-General of UNESCO.

Annex

Conciliation procedure

Article 1 – Conciliation Commission

A Conciliation Commission shall be created upon the request of one of the Parties to the dispute. The Commission shall, unless the Parties otherwise agree, be composed of five members, two appointed by each Party concerned and a President chosen jointly by those members.

Article 2 – Members of the Commission

In disputes between more than two Parties, Parties in the same interest shall appoint their members of the Commission jointly by agreement. Where two or more Parties have separate interests or there is a disagreement as to whether they are of the same interest, they shall appoint their members separately.

Article 3 – Appointments

If any appointments by the Parties are not made within two months of the date of the request to create a Conciliation Commission, the Director-General of UNESCO shall, if asked to do so by the Party that made the request, make those appointments within a further two-month period.

Article 4 – President of the Commission

If a President of the Conciliation Commission has not been chosen within two months of the last of the members of the Commission being appointed, the Director-General of UNESCO shall, if asked to do so by a Party, designate a President within a further two-month period.

Article 5 – Decisions

The Conciliation Commission shall take its decisions by majority vote of its members. It shall, unless the Parties to the dispute otherwise agree, determine its own procedure. It shall render a proposal for resolution of the dispute, which the Parties shall consider in good faith.

Article 6 – Disagreement

A disagreement as to whether the Conciliation Commission has competence shall be decided by the Commission.

9

TUNIS AGENDA FOR THE INFORMATION SOCIETY (WSIS)

World Summit on the Information Society

Geneva 2003, Tunis 2005

Implementation and follow-up

83. Building an inclusive development-oriented Information Society will require unremitting multi-stakeholder effort. **We thus commit ourselves** to remain fully engaged—nationally, regionally and internationally—to ensure sustainable implementation and follow-up of the outcomes and commitments reached during the WSIS process and its Geneva and Tunis phases of the Summit. Taking into account the multifaceted nature of building the Information Society, effective cooperation among governments, private sector, civil society and the United Nations and other international organizations, according to their different roles and responsibilities and leveraging on their expertise, is essential.

84. Governments and other stakeholders should identify those areas where further effort and resources are required, and jointly identify, and where appropriate develop, implementation strategies, mechanisms and processes for WSIS outcomes at international, regional, national and local levels, paying particular attention to people and groups that are still marginalized in their access to, and utilization of, ICTs.

85. Taking into consideration the leading role of governments in partnership with other stakeholders in implementing the WSIS outcomes, including the Geneva Plan of Action, at the national level, **we encourage** those governments that have not yet done so to elaborate, as appropriate, comprehensive, forward-looking and sustainable national e-strategies, including ICT strategies and sectoral e-strategies as appropriate[1], as an integral part of national development plans and poverty reduction strategies, as soon as possible and before 2010.

86. We support regional and international integration efforts aimed at building a people-centred, inclusive and development-oriented Information Society, and **we reiterate** that strong cooperation within and among regions is indispensable to support knowledge-sharing.

Regional cooperation should contribute to national capacity building and to the development of regional implementation strategies.

87. We affirm that the exchange of views and sharing of effective practices and resources is essential to implementing the outcomes of WSIS at the regional and international levels. To this end, efforts should be made to provide and share, among all stakeholders, knowledge and know-how, related to the design, implementation, monitoring and evaluation of e-strategies and policies, as appropriate. **We recognize** as fundamental elements to bridge the digital divide in developing countries, in a sustainable way, poverty reduction, enhanced national capacity building and the promotion of national technological development.

88. We reaffirm that through the international cooperation of governments and the partnership of all stakeholders, it will be possible to succeed in our challenge of harnessing the potential of ICTs as a tool, at the service of development, to promote the use of information and knowledge to achieve the internationally agreed development goals and objectives, including the Millennium Development Goals, as well as to address the national and local development priorities, thereby further improving the socio-economic development of all human beings.

89. We are determined to improve international, regional and national connectivity and affordable access to ICTs and information through an enhanced international cooperation of all stakeholders that promotes technology exchange and technology transfer, human resource development and training, thus increasing the capacity of developing countries to innovate and to participate fully in, and contribute to, the Information Society.

90. We reaffirm our commitment to providing equitable access to information and knowledge for all, recognizing the role of ICTs for economic growth and development. **We are committed** to working towards achieving the indicative targets, set out in the Geneva Plan of Action, that serve as global references for improving connectivity and universal, ubiquitous, equitable, non-discriminatory and affordable access to, and use of, ICTs, considering different national circumstances, to be achieved by 2015, and to using ICTs, as a tool to achieve the internationally agreed development goals and objectives, including the Millennium Development Goals, by:

a) *mainstreaming and aligning national e-strategies*, across local, national, and regional action plans, as appropriate and in accordance with local and national development priorities, with in-built time-bound measures.

b) *developing and implementing enabling policies* that reflect national realities and that promote a supportive international environment, foreign direct investment as well as the mobilization of domestic resources, in order to promote and foster entrepreneurship, particularly Small, Medium and Micro Enterprises (SMMEs), taking into account the relevant market and cultural contexts. These policies should be reflected in a transparent, equitable regulatory framework to create a competitive environment to support these goals and strengthen economic growth.

c) *building ICT capacity* for all and confidence in the use of ICTs by all – including youth, older persons, women, indigenous peoples, people with disabilities, and remote and rural communities – through the improvement and delivery of relevant education and training programmes and systems including lifelong and distance learning.

d) *implementing effective training and education*, particularly in ICT science and technology, that motivates and promotes participation and active involvement of girls and women in the decision-making process of building the Information Society.

e) *paying special attention to the formulation of universal design concepts and the use of assistive technologies* that promote access for all persons, including those with disabilities.

f) *promoting public policies aimed at providing affordable access* at all levels, including community-level, to hardware as well as software and connectivity through an increasingly converging technological environment, capacity building and local content.

g) *improving access to the world's health knowledge and telemedicine services*, in particular in areas such as global cooperation in emergency response, access to and networking among health professionals to help improve quality of life and environmental conditions.

h) *building ICT capacities* to improve access and use of postal networks and services.

i) *using ICTs to improve access to agricultural knowledge*, combat poverty, and support production of and access to locally relevant agriculture-related content.

j) *developing and implementing e-government applications* based on open standards in order to enhance the growth and interoperability of e-government systems, at all levels, thereby furthering access to government information and services, and contributing to building ICT networks and developing services that are available anywhere and anytime, to anyone and on any device.

k) *supporting educational, scientific, and cultural institutions*, including libraries, archives and museums, in their role of developing, providing equitable, open and affordable access to, and preserving diverse and varied content, including in digital form, to support informal and formal education, research and innovation; and in particular supporting libraries in their public-service role of providing free and equitable access to information and of improving ICT literacy and community connectivity, particularly in underserved communities.

l) *enhancing the capacity of communities* in all regions to develop content in local and/or indigenous languages.

m) *strengthening the creation of quality e-content*, on national, regional and international levels.

n) *promoting the use of traditional and new media* in order to foster universal access to information, culture and knowledge for all people, especially vulnerable populations and populations in developing countries and using, *inter alia*, radio and television as educational and learning tools.

o) *reaffirming the independence, pluralism and diversity of media, and freedom of information* including through, as appropriate, the development of domestic legislation, **we reiterate** our call for the responsible use and treatment of information by the media in accordance with the highest ethical and professional standards. **We reaffirm** the necessity of reducing international imbalances affecting the media, particularly as regards infrastructure, technical resources and the development of human skills. These reaffirmations are made with reference to Geneva Declaration of Principles paragraphs 55 to 59.

p) *strongly encouraging ICT enterprises and entrepreneurs to develop and use environment-friendly production processes* in order to minimize the negative impacts of the use and manufacture of ICTs and disposal of ICT waste on people and the environment. In this context, it is important to give particular attention to the specific needs of the developing countries.

q) *incorporating regulatory, self-regulatory, and other effective policies and frameworks to protect children and young people* from abuse and exploitation through ICTs into national plans of action and e-strategies.

r) *promoting the development of advanced research networks*, at national, regional and international levels, in order to improve collaboration in science, technology and higher education.

s) *promoting voluntary service*, at the community level, to help maximize the developmental impact of ICTs.

t)   *promoting the use of ICTs to enhance flexible ways of working*, including teleworking, leading to greater productivity and job creation.

91. We recognize the intrinsic relationship between disaster reduction, sustainable development and the eradication of poverty and that disasters seriously undermine investment in a very short time and remain a major impediment to sustainable development and poverty eradication. **We are clear** as to the important enabling role of ICTs at the national, regional and international levels including:

a)   Promoting technical cooperation and enhancing the capacity of countries, particularly developing countries, in utilizing ICT tools for disaster early-warning, management and emergency communications, including dissemination of understandable warnings to those at risk.

b)   Promoting regional and international cooperation for easy access to and sharing of information for disaster management, and exploring modalities for the easier participation of developing countries.

c)   Working expeditiously towards the establishment of standards-based monitoring and worldwide early-warning systems linked to national and regional networks and facilitating emergency disaster response all over the world, particularly in high-risk regions.

92. We encourage countries, and all other interested parties, to make available child helplines, taking into account the need for mobilization of appropriate resources. For this purpose, easy-to-remember numbers, accessible from all phones and free of charge, should be made available.

93. We seek to digitize our historical data and cultural heritage for the benefit of future generations. **We encourage** effective information management policies in the public and private sectors, including the use of standards-based digital archiving and innovative solutions to overcome technological obsolescence, as a means to ensure the long-term preservation of, and continued access to, information.

94. We acknowledge that everyone should benefit from the potential that the Information Society offers. Therefore, **we invite** governments to assist, on a voluntary basis, those countries affected by any unilateral measure not in accordance with international law and the Charter of the United Nations that impedes the full achievement of economic and social development by the population of the affected countries, and that hinders the well-being of their population.

95. We call upon international and intergovernmental organizations to develop, within approved resources, their policy analysis and capacity-building programmes, based on practical and replicable experiences of ICT matters, policies and actions that have led to economic growth and poverty alleviation, including through the improved competitiveness of enterprises.

96. We recall the importance of creating a trustworthy, transparent and non-discriminatory legal, regulatory and policy environment. To that end, **we reiterate** that ITU and other regional organizations should take steps to ensure rational, efficient and economic use of, and equitable access to, the radio-frequency spectrum by all countries, based on relevant international agreements.

97. We acknowledge that multi-stakeholder participation is essential to the successful building of a people-centred, inclusive and development-oriented Information Society and that governments could play an important role in this process. **We underline** that the participation of all stakeholders in implementing WSIS outcomes, and following them up on national, regional and international levels with the overarching goal of helping countries to achieve internationally agreed development goals and objectives, including the Millennium Development Goals, is key to that success.

98. We encourage strengthened and continuing cooperation between and among stakeholders to ensure effective implementation of the Geneva and Tunis outcomes, for instance through the promotion of national, regional and international multi-stakeholder partnerships including Public Private Partnerships (PPPs), and the promotion of national and regional multi-stakeholder thematic platforms, in a joint effort and dialogue with developing and less developed countries, development partners and actors in the ICT sector. In that respect, **we welcome** partnerships such as the ITU-led "Connect the World" initiative.

99. We agree to ensure the sustainability of progress towards the goals of WSIS after the completion of its Tunis phase and **we decide**, therefore, to establish a mechanism for implementation and follow-up at national, regional and international levels.

100. At the national level, based on the WSIS outcomes, **we encourage** governments, with the participation of all stakeholders and bearing in mind the importance of an enabling environment, to set up a national *implementation* mechanism, in which:

a)   National e-strategies, where appropriate, should be an integral part of national development plans, including Poverty Reduction Strategies, aiming to contribute to the achievement of internationally agreed development goals and objectives, including the Millennium Development Goals.

b)   ICTs should be fully mainstreamed into strategies for Official Development Assistance (ODA) through more effective information-sharing and coordination among development partners, and through analysis and sharing of best practices and lessons learned from experience with ICT for development programmes.

c)   Existing bilateral and multilateral technical assistance programmes, including those under the UN Development Assistance Framework, should be used whenever appropriate to assist governments in their implementation efforts at the national level.

d)   Common Country Assessment reports should contain a component on ICT for development.

101. At the regional level:

a)   Upon request from governments, regional intergovernmental organizations in collaboration with other stakeholders should carry out WSIS implementation activities, exchanging information and best practices at the regional level, as well as facilitating policy debate on the use of ICT for development, with a focus on attaining the internationally agreed development goals and objectives, including the Millennium Development Goals.

b)   UN Regional Commissions, based on request of Member States and within approved budgetary resources, may organize regional WSIS follow-up activities in collaboration with regional and sub-regional organizations, with appropriate frequency, as well as assisting Member States with technical and relevant information for the development of regional strategies and the implementation of the outcomes of regional conferences.

c)   **We consider** a multi-stakeholder approach and the participation in regional WSIS implementation activities by the private sector, civil society, and the United Nations and other international organizations to be essential.

102. At the international level, bearing in mind the importance of the enabling environment:

a)   *Implementation and follow-up* of the outcomes of the Geneva and Tunis phases of the Summit should take into account the main themes and action lines in the Summit documents.

b)   Each UN agency should act according to its mandate and competencies, and pursuant to decisions of their respective governing bodies, and within existing approved resources.

c)   Implementation and follow-up should include intergovernmental and multi-stakeholder components.

103. We invite UN agencies and other intergovernmental organizations, in line with UNGA Resolution 57/270 B, to facilitate activities among different stakeholders, including civil society and the business sector, to help national governments in their implementation efforts. **We request** the UN Secretary-General, in consultation with members of the UN system Chief Executives Board for coordination (CEB), to establish, within the CEB, a UN Group on the Information Society consisting of the relevant UN bodies and organizations, with the mandate to facilitate the implementation of WSIS outcomes, and to suggest to CEB that, in considering lead agency(ies) of this Group, it takes into consideration the experience of, and activities in the WSIS process undertaken by, ITU, UNESCO and UNDP.

104. We further request the UN Secretary-General to report to the UNGA through ECOSOC by June 2006, on the modalities of the inter-agency coordination of the implementation of WSIS outcomes including recommendations on the follow-up process.

105. We request that ECOSOC oversees the system-wide follow-up of the Geneva and Tunis outcomes of WSIS. To this end, **we request** that ECOSOC, at its substantive session of 2006, reviews the mandate, agenda and composition of the Commission on Science and Technology for Development (CSTD), including considering the strengthening of the Commission, taking into account the multi-stakeholder approach.

106. WSIS implementation and follow-up should be an integral part of the UN integrated follow-up to major UN conferences and should contribute to the achievement of internationally agreed development goals and objectives, including the Millennium Development Goals. It should not require the creation of any new operational bodies.

107. International and regional organizations should assess and report regularly on universal accessibility of nations to ICTs, with the aim of creating equitable opportunities for the growth of ICT sectors of developing countries.

108. We attach great importance to multi-stakeholder implementation at the international level, which should be organized taking into account the themes and action lines in the Geneva Plan of Action, and moderated or facilitated by UN agencies when appropriate. An Annex to this document offers an indicative and non-exhaustive list of facilitators/moderators for the action lines of the Geneva Plan of Action.

109. The experience of, and the activities undertaken by, UN agencies in the WSIS process—notably ITU, UNESCO and UNDP—should continue to be used to their fullest extent. These three agencies should play leading facilitating roles in the implementation of the Geneva Plan of Action and organize a meeting of moderators/facilitators of action lines, as mentioned in the Annex.

110. The coordination of multi-stakeholder implementation activities would help to avoid duplication of activities. This should include, *inter alia*, information exchange, creation of knowledge, sharing of best practices, and assistance in developing multi-stakeholder and public-private partnerships.

111. We request the United Nations General Assembly (UNGA) to make an overall review of the implementation of WSIS outcomes in 2015.

112. We call for periodic evaluation, using an agreed methodology, such as described in paragraphs 113–120.

113. Appropriate indicators and benchmarking, including community connectivity indicators, should clarify the magnitude of the digital divide, in both its domestic and international dimensions, and keep it under regular assessment, and track global progress in the use of ICTs to achieve internationally agreed development goals and objectives, including the Millennium Development Goals.

114. The development of ICT indicators is important for measuring the digital divide. **We note** the launch, in June 2004, of the *Partnership on Measuring ICT for Development*, and its efforts:

a)   to develop a common set of core ICT indicators; to increase the availability of internationally comparable ICT statistics as well as to establish a mutually agreed framework for their elaboration, for further consideration and decision by the UN Statistical Commission.

b)   to promote capacity building in developing countries for monitoring the Information Society.

c)   to assess the current and potential impact of ICTs on development and poverty reduction.

d)   to develop specific gender-disaggregated indicators to measure the digital divide in its various dimensions.

115. We also note the launch of the *ICT Opportunity Index* and the *Digital Opportunity Index*, which will build upon the common set of core ICT indicators as they were defined within the *Partnership on Measuring ICT for Development*.

116. We stress that all indices and indicators must take into account different levels of development and national circumstances.

117. The further development of these indicators should be undertaken in a collaborative, cost-effective and non-duplicative fashion.

118. We invite the international community to strengthen the statistical capacity of developing countries by giving appropriate support at national and regional levels.

119. We commit ourselves to review and follow up progress in bridging the digital divide, taking into account the different levels of development among nations, so as to achieve the internationally agreed development goals and objectives, including the Millennium Development Goals, assessing the effectiveness of investment and international cooperation efforts in building the Information Society, identifying gaps as well as deficits in investment and devising strategies to address them.

120. The sharing of information related to the implementation of WSIS outcomes is an important element of evaluation. **We note with appreciation** the *Report on the Stocktaking of WSIS-related activities*, which will serve as one of the valuable tools for assisting with the follow-up, beyond the conclusion of the Tunis phase of the Summit, as well as the "*Golden Book*" of initiatives launched during the Tunis phase. **We encourage** all WSIS stakeholders to continue to contribute information on their activities to the public WSIS stocktaking database maintained by ITU. In this regard, **we invite** all countries to gather information at the national level with the involvement of all stakeholders, to contribute to the stocktaking.

121. There is a need to build more awareness of the Internet in order to make it a global facility which is truly available to the public. **We call upon the UNGA** to declare 17 May as World Information Society Day to help to raise awareness, on an annual basis, of the importance of this global facility, on the issues dealt with in the Summit, especially the possibilities that the use of ICT can bring for societies and economies, as well as of ways to bridge the digital divide.

122. We request the Secretary-General of the Summit to report to the General Assembly of the United Nations on its outcome, as requested in UNGA Resolution 59/220.

Note

1   Throughout this text, further references to "e-strategies" are interpreted as including also ICT strategies and sectoral e-strategies, as appropriate

10

TUNIS COMMITMENT FOR THE INFORMATION SOCIETY (WSIS)

World Summit on the Information Society

Geneva 2003, Tunis 2005

1. We, the representatives of the peoples of the world, have gathered in Tunis from 16–18 November 2005 for this second phase of the World Summit on the Information Society (WSIS) to reiterate our unequivocal support for the Geneva Declaration of Principles and Plan of Action adopted at the first phase of the World Summit on the Information Society in Geneva in December 2003.

2. We reaffirm our desire and commitment to build a people-centred, inclusive and development-oriented Information Society, premised on the purposes and principles of the Charter of the United Nations, international law and multilateralism, and respecting fully and upholding the Universal Declaration of Human Rights, so that people everywhere can create, access, utilize and share information and knowledge, to achieve their full potential and to attain the internationally agreed development goals and objectives, including the Millennium Development Goals.

3. We reaffirm the universality, indivisibility, interdependence and interrelation of all human rights and fundamental freedoms, including the right to development, as enshrined in the Vienna Declaration. **We also reaffirm** that democracy, sustainable development, and respect for human rights and fundamental freedoms as well as good governance at all levels are interdependent and mutually reinforcing. **We further resolve** to strengthen respect for the rule of law in international as in national affairs.

4. We reaffirm paragraphs 4, 5 and 55 of the Geneva Declaration of Principles. **We recognize** that freedom of expression and the free flow of information, ideas, and knowledge, are essential for the Information Society and beneficial to development.

5. The Tunis Summit represents a unique opportunity to raise awareness of the benefits that Information and Communication Technologies (ICTs) can bring to humanity and the manner in which they can transform people's activities, interaction and lives, and thus increase confidence in the future.

6. This Summit is an important stepping-stone in the world's efforts to eradicate poverty and to attain the internationally agreed development goals and objectives, including the

Millennium Development Goals. By the Geneva decisions, we established a coherent long-term link between the WSIS process, and other relevant major United Nations conferences and summits. **We call upon** governments, private sector, civil society and international organizations to join together to implement the commitments set forth in the Geneva Declaration of Principles and Plan of Action. In this context, the outcomes of the recently concluded *2005 World Summit on the review of the implementation of the Millennium Declaration* are of special relevance.

7. We reaffirm the commitments made in Geneva and build on them in Tunis by focusing on financial mechanisms for bridging the digital divide, on Internet governance and related issues, as well as on follow-up and implementation of the Geneva and Tunis decisions, as referenced in the Tunis Agenda for the Information Society.

8. While reaffirming the important roles and responsibilities of all stakeholders as outlined in paragraph 3 of the Geneva Plan of Action, **we acknowledge** the key role and responsibilities of governments in the WSIS process.

9. We reaffirm our resolution in the quest to ensure that everyone can benefit from the opportunities that ICTs can offer, by recalling that governments, as well as private sector, civil society and the United Nations and other international organizations, should work together to: improve access to information and communication infrastructure and technologies as well as to information and knowledge; build capacity; increase confidence and security in the use of ICTs; create an enabling environment at all levels; develop and widen ICT applications; foster and respect cultural diversity; recognize the role of the media; address the ethical dimensions of the Information Society; and encourage international and regional cooperation. **We confirm** that these are the key principles for building an inclusive Information Society, the elaboration of which is found in the Geneva Declaration of Principles.

10. We recognize that access to information and sharing and creation of knowledge contributes significantly to strengthening economic, social and cultural development, thus helping all countries to reach the internationally agreed development goals and objectives, including the Millennium Development Goals. This process can be enhanced by removing barriers to universal, ubiquitous, equitable and affordable access to information. **We underline** the importance of removing barriers to bridging the digital divide, particularly those that hinder the full achievement of the economic, social and cultural development of countries and the welfare of their people, in particular, in developing countries.

11. Furthermore, ICTs are making it possible for a vastly larger population than at any time in the past to join in sharing and expanding the base of human knowledge, and contributing to its further growth in all spheres of human endeavour as well as its application to education, health and science. ICTs have enormous potential to expand access to quality education, to boost literacy and universal primary education, and to facilitate the learning process itself, thus laying the groundwork for the establishment of a fully inclusive and development-oriented Information Society and knowledge economy which respects cultural and linguistic diversity.

12. We emphasize that the adoption of ICTs by enterprises plays a fundamental role in economic growth. The growth and productivity enhancing effects of well-implemented investments in ICTs can lead to increased trade and to more and better employment. For this reason, both enterprise development and labour market policies play a fundamental role in the adoption of ICTs. **We invite** governments and the private sector to enhance the capacity of Small, Medium and Micro Enterprises (SMMEs), since they furnish the greatest number of jobs in most economies. **We shall work together**, with all stakeholders, to put in place the necessary policy, legal and regulatory frameworks that foster entrepreneurship, particularly for SMMEs.

13. We also recognize that the ICT revolution can have a tremendous positive impact as an instrument of sustainable development. In addition, an appropriate enabling environment at national and international levels could prevent increasing social and economic divisions, and the widening of the gap between rich and poor countries, regions, and individuals—including between men and women.

14. We also recognize that in addition to building ICT infrastructure, there should be adequate emphasis on developing human capacity and creating ICT applications and digital content in local language, where appropriate, so as to ensure a comprehensive approach to building a global Information Society.

15. Recognizing the principles of universal and non-discriminatory access to ICTs for all nations, the need to take into account the level of social and economic development of each country, and respecting the development-oriented aspects of the Information Society, **we underscore** that ICTs are effective tools to promote peace, security and stability, to enhance democracy, social cohesion, good governance and the rule of law, at national, regional and international levels. ICTs can be used to promote economic growth and enterprise development. Infrastructure development, human capacity building, information security and network security are critical to achieve these goals. **We further recognize** the need to effectively confront challenges and threats resulting from use of ICTs for purposes that are inconsistent with objectives of maintaining international stability and security and may adversely affect the integrity of the infrastructure within States, to the detriment of their security. It is necessary to prevent the abuse of information resources and technologies for criminal and terrorist purposes, while respecting human rights.

16. We further commit ourselves to evaluate and follow up progress in bridging the digital divide, taking into account different levels of development, so as to reach internationally agreed development goals and objectives, including the Millennium Development Goals, and to assess the effectiveness of investment and international cooperation efforts in building the Information Society.

17. We urge governments, using the potential of ICTs, to create public systems of information on laws and regulations, envisaging a wider development of public access points and supporting the broad availability of this information.

18. We shall strive unremittingly, therefore, to promote universal, ubiquitous, equitable and affordable access to ICTs, including universal design and assistive technologies, for all people, especially those with disabilities, everywhere, to ensure that the benefits are more evenly distributed between and within societies, and to bridge the digital divide in order to create digital opportunities for all and benefit from the potential offered by ICTs for development.

19. The international community should take necessary measures to ensure that all countries of the world have equitable and affordable access to ICTs, so that their benefits in the fields of socio-economic development and bridging the digital divide are truly inclusive.

20. To that end, **we shall pay particular attention** to the special needs of marginalized and vulnerable groups of society including migrants, internally displaced persons and refugees, unemployed and underprivileged people, minorities and nomadic people, older persons and persons with disabilities.

21. To that end, **we shall pay special attention** to the particular needs of people of developing countries, countries with economies in transition, Least Developed Countries, Small Island Developing States, Landlocked Developing Countries, Highly Indebted Poor Countries, countries and territories under occupation, and countries recovering from conflict or natural disasters.

22. In the evolution of the Information Society, particular attention must be given to the special situation of indigenous peoples, as well as to the preservation of their heritage and their cultural legacy.

23. We recognize that a gender divide exists as part of the digital divide in society and **we reaffirm our commitment** to women's empowerment and to a gender equality perspective, so that we can overcome this divide. **We further acknowledge** that the full participation of women in the Information Society is necessary to ensure the inclusiveness and respect for human rights within the Information Society. **We encourage** all stakeholders to support women's participation in decision-making processes and to contribute to shaping all spheres of the Information Society at international, regional and national levels.

24. We recognize the role of ICTs in the protection of children and in enhancing the development of children. **We will strengthen action** to protect children from abuse and defend their rights in the context of ICTs. In that context, **we emphasize** that the best interests of the child are a primary consideration.

25. We reaffirm our commitment to empowering young people as key contributors to building an inclusive Information Society. **We will actively engage** youth in innovative ICT-based development programmes and widen opportunities for youth to be involved in e-strategy processes.

26. We recognize the importance of creative content and applications to overcome the digital divide and to contribute to the achievement of the internationally agreed development goals and objectives, including the Millennium Development Goals.

27. We recognize that equitable and sustainable access to information requires the implementation of strategies for the long-term preservation of the digital information that is being created.

28. We reaffirm our desire to build ICT networks and develop applications, in partnership with the private sector, based on open or interoperable standards that are affordable and accessible to all, available anywhere and anytime, to anyone and on any device, leading to a ubiquitous network.

29. Our conviction is that governments, the private sector, civil society, the scientific and academic community, and users can utilize various technologies and licensing models, including those developed under proprietary schemes and those developed under open-source and free modalities, in accordance with their interests and with the need to have reliable services and implement effective programmes for their people. Taking into account the importance of proprietary software in the markets of the countries, **we reiterate** the need to encourage and foster collaborative development, interoperative platforms and free and open-source software, in ways that reflect the possibilities of different software models, notably for education, science and digital inclusion programmes.

30. Recognizing that disaster mitigation can significantly support efforts to bring about sustainable development and help in poverty reduction, **we reaffirm our commitment** to leveraging ICT capabilities and potential through fostering and strengthening cooperation at the national, regional, and international levels.

31. We commit ourselves to work together towards the implementation of the Digital Solidarity Agenda, as agreed in paragraph 27 of the Geneva Plan of Action. The full and quick implementation of that agenda, observing good governance at all levels, requires in particular a timely, effective, comprehensive and durable solution to the debt problems of developing countries where appropriate, a universal, rule-based, open, non-discriminatory and equitable multilateral trading system, that can also stimulate development worldwide, benefiting countries at all stages of development, as well as, to seek and effectively implement concrete international approaches and mechanisms to increase international cooperation and assistance to bridge the digital divide.

32. We further commit ourselves to promote the inclusion of all peoples in the

Information Society through the development and use of local and/or indigenous languages in ICTs. **We will continue** our efforts to protect and promote cultural diversity, as well as cultural identities, within the Information Society.

33. We acknowledge that, while technical cooperation can help, capacity building at all levels is needed to ensure that the required institutional and individual expertise is available.

34. We recognize the need for, and strive to mobilize resources, both human and financial, in accordance with chapter two of the Tunis Agenda for the Information Society, to enable us to increase the use of ICT for development and realize the short-, medium- and long-term plans dedicated to building the Information Society as follow-up and implementation of the outcomes of WSIS.

35. We recognize the central role of public policy in setting the framework in which resource mobilization can take place.

36. We value the potential of ICTs to promote peace and to prevent conflict which, *inter alia*, negatively affects achieving development goals. ICTs can be used for identifying conflict situations through early-warning systems preventing conflicts, promoting their peaceful resolution, supporting humanitarian action, including protection of civilians in armed conflicts, facilitating peacekeeping missions, and assisting post conflict peace-building and reconstruction.

37. We are convinced that our goals can be accomplished through the involvement, cooperation and partnership of governments and other stakeholders, i.e. the private sector, civil society and international organizations, and that international cooperation and solidarity at all levels are indispensable if the fruits of the Information Society are to benefit all.

38. Our efforts should not stop with the conclusion of the Summit. The emergence of the global Information Society to which we all contribute provides increasing opportunities for all our peoples and for an inclusive global community that were unimaginable only a few years ago. **We must harness** these opportunities today and support their further development and progress.

39. We reaffirm our strong resolve to develop and implement an effective and sustainable response to the challenges and opportunities of building a truly global Information Society that benefits all our peoples.

40. We strongly believe in the full and timely implementation of the decisions we took in Geneva and Tunis, as outlined in the Tunis Agenda for the Information Society.

11

TRANSFORMATIONAL DIPLOMACY (US GOVERNMENT)

Office of the Spokesman, Washington, DC

January 18, 2006

I would define the objective of transformational diplomacy this way: To work with our many partners around the world to build and sustain democratic, well-governed states that will respond to the needs of their people — and conduct themselves responsibly in the international system . . . Transformational diplomacy is rooted in partnership, not paternalism — in doing things <u>with</u> other people, not <u>for</u> them. We seek to use America's diplomatic power to help foreign citizens to better their <u>own</u> lives, and to build their <u>own</u> nations, and to transform their <u>own</u> futures . . . Now, to advance transformational diplomacy all around the world, we in the State Department must rise to answer a new historic calling. We must begin to lay new diplomatic foundations to secure a future of freedom for all people. Like the great changes of the past, the new efforts we undertake today will not be completed tomorrow. Transforming the State Department is the work of a generation. But it is urgent work that cannot be deferred.

— <u>Secretary Rice, January 18, 2006</u>

Today, Secretary of State Condoleezza Rice announced her plans for global repositioning to restructure both our overseas and domestic staffing, and her vision for the future of the Department of State.

Global repositioning

At present, the allocation of American diplomatic resources still has vestiges of our Cold War posture. We have nearly the same number of State Department personnel in Germany, a country of 82 million people, as we do in India, a country of over one billion people. Diplomats are generally located in embassies in Europe, and centralized within capital cities.

To meet current diplomatic challenges, the Secretary will begin a major repositioning of U.S. diplomatic personnel across the world. In a multiyear process, hundreds of positions will be moved to critical emerging areas in Africa, South Asia, East Asia, the Middle East and elsewhere.

Immediate Action. Beginning this year, 100 current positions largely from Europe and Washington will be moved. To accomplish this goal, existing State Department resources will be readjusted to fit new priorities.

Long Term Commitment. In the coming years hundreds will move across borders and into the front lines of diplomacy where they are needed most.

Regional focus

Many of today's challenges are not limited by country boundaries, but are transnational and regional in nature, and require new thinking and more targeted responses. There are nearly 200 cities worldwide with over one million people in which America has no formal diplomatic presence. Building on regional collaborations and regional forward-deployment of diplomats will facilitate a more effective approach to building democracy and prosperity, fighting terrorism, disease and human trafficking.

Regional public diplomacy centers

Regional public diplomacy platforms are being established in Europe and the Middle East. These centers will take America's story directly to the people and the regional television media in real time and in the appropriate language.

Effective forward deployment

Diplomats are traveling to their area of responsibility more regularly than ever, using their expertise and experience more effectively abroad.

Regional Centers. Information technology will allow work to be done anywhere in the world. Regional Centers of Excellence such as in Frankfurt, Ft. Lauderdale, and Charleston, South Carolina, will perform management support activities such as human resources or financial management.

Localization

To reach beyond the borders of the traditional diplomatic structures and beyond foreign capitals, diplomats will move out from behind their desks into the field, from reporting on outcomes to shaping them. In addition, 21st century technology will be used to engage foreign publics more directly via the media and Internet, and to better connect diplomats in real time.

American Presence Posts (APPs) are currently located in Egypt, Indonesia and elsewhere. APPs are operated by one diplomat who lives and works outside of the embassy, representing America in other key regional population centers.

Virtual Presence Posts (VPPs) are the newest and most cost effective way to expand the American posture locally in a country. Created and managed by one or more diplomats, VPPs provide an internet site enabling millions of local citizens, particularly young people across Europe, and Asia and Latin America, to interact with personnel in embassies.

IT Centralization. Communications capabilities and IT functions will be centralized to ensure that information is dispersed smoothly, accurately and securely. The goal is to provide the State Department workforce with quick access to the knowledge and real-time information they need whether at their desktops or on travel. Cutting-edge information technology will enable sharing information across regions and between agencies.

Creative Use of the Internet. Programs are being developed to enhance America's presence through a medium that young people worldwide increasingly rely upon for their information. Café USA/Seoul and other programs being developed will reach young people through interactive, online discussions.

Meeting new challenges with new skills

To meet the challenges of transformational diplomacy, diplomats must be diverse, well-rounded, agile, and able to carry out multiple tasks. Transformational diplomacy requires that the right people have the right skills in the right place at the right time. Continued training and career development programs will better prepare diplomats and advance their expertise.

Enhanced Training. Building on the training curriculum at the Foreign Service Institute, the training center of gravity will be repositioned from a centralized domestic focus to overseas posts and to each desktop, utilizing technology to promote long distance learning. Localized training and immersion language training will further balance the classroom experience. Training will continued to be offered in Washington, but increasingly more of the coursework will be taken directly to diplomats overseas.

Multi-region Expertise. Diplomats will be required to be expert in at least two regions and fluent in two languages in order to be promoted to senior ranks. Currently, record numbers of diplomats are being trained in critical languages like Chinese, Urdu, Arabic and Farsi.

Post Assignments. Essential to diplomats' career advancement will be service in one of the more challenging posts. These are dangerous but essential jobs often in states that are poorly governed and that are struggling to become secure, developed, and increasingly democratic.

Hands-On Practice. Diplomats will not only be analyzing policy and shaping outcomes, but also running programs. They will be helping foreign citizens to promote democracy building, fight corruption, start businesses, improve healthcare, and reform education.

Public Diplomacy. As always, public diplomacy is an important part of every diplomat's job description. It is crucial to provide a common vision of hope and prosperity while engaging foreign publics and media to promote U. S. interests abroad.

Empower diplomats to work jointly with other federal agencies

Success in transformational diplomacy requires collaborations that result in the more effective dispersion of people and programs to share information on common platforms. Vital to this vision is continued collaboration between civilians and the military. Diplomats must be able to work effectively at the critical intersections of diplomatic affairs, economic reconstruction, and military operations. Ways to enhance this effort include:

Expanding Stabilization Capabilities Created by the President in 2004, the Office of Reconstruction and Stabilization responds to the nation's need for a standing capability that could integrate planning with the military and civilian agencies, and deploy civilians quickly to a post-conflict environment to undertake a mission successfully. Secretary Rice is committed to expanding the capabilities of State's Office of Reconstruction and Stabilization

(CRS). CRS has now received broadened authority and mandate under a new National Security Presidential Directive. Recently enacted legislation allows a transfer of up to $100 million of Defense Department funds for post-conflict operations, funds available to empower CRS in a critical situation. CRS will work to develop a civilian reserve corps in which police officers, judges, electricians and engineers, bankers and economists will be available as needed in post conflict situations.

Political Advisors to the Military Forces serve as the diplomatic and policy advisors to military commanders, deploying with them and giving them the benefit of their diplomatic and regional experience. The presence of the political advisors will be expanded throughout all levels of the military to fully utilize diplomats' regional expertise and political advice.

2006/54 Released on January 18, 2006

12

JOINT PROJECT AGREEMENT BETWEEN THE US DEPARTMENT OF COMMERCE AND THE INTERNET CORPORATION FOR ASSIGNED NAMES AND NUMBERS

Preamble

The U.S. Department of Commerce (Department) has an agreement (the Joint Project Agreement) with the Internet Corporation for Assigned Names and Numbers (ICANN) for the purpose of the joint development of the mechanisms, methods, and procedures necessary to effect the transition of Internet domain name and addressing system (DNS) to the private sector.

The Department continues to support private sector leadership in the innovation and investment that has characterized the development and expansion of the Internet around the globe. Furthermore, the Department continues to support the work of ICANN as the coordinator for the technical functions related to the management of the Internet DNS. Both Parties agree that preserving the security and stability of the Internet DNS is a priority, with ICANN's focus on DNS security matters being critical to this effort.

Agreement between the Parties

In recognition of the Parties' desire to institutionalize the private sector technical coordination and management of the Internet DNS to the private sector, the Parties hereby agree as follows:

I. To strike Section V.B. from the Joint Project Agreement in its entirety and to substitute the following:

B. Department. The Department reaffirms its policy goal of transitioning the technical coordination of the DNS to the private sector in a manner that promotes stability and security, competition, bottom-up coordination, and representation. Consistent with this objective, the Department agrees to perform the following activities:

1. *Transparency and Accountability*: Continue to provide expertise and advice on methods

and administrative procedures to encourage greater transparency, accountability, and openness in the consideration and adoption of policies related to the technical coordination of the Internet DNS;

2.   *Root Server Security*: Continue to consult with the managers of root name servers operated by the U.S. Government and with other responsible U.S. Government agencies with respect to operational and security matters, both physical and network, of such root name servers and recommendations for improvements in those matters;

3.   *Governmental Advisory Committee*: Participate in the Governmental Advisory Committee so as to facilitate effective consideration by ICANN of GAC advice on the public policy aspects of the technical coordination of the Internet DNS; and

4.   *Monitoring*: Continue to monitor the performance of the activities conducted pursuant to this Agreement.

II. To strike Section V.C. from the Joint Project Agreement in its entirety and to substitute the following:

C. ICANN. ICANN reaffirms its commitment to maintaining security and stability in the coordination of the technical functions related to the management of the DNS and to perform as an organization founded on the principles of stability and security, competition, bottom-up coordination, and representation. In conformity with the ICANN Board-approved mission and core values, ICANN agrees to perform the following activities:

1.   *Accountability*: To take action on the Responsibilities set out in the Affirmation of Responsibilities established by the ICANN Board in ICANN Board Resolution 06.71, dated September 25, 2006, (Responsibilities) and attached hereto as Annex A; and

2.   *Reporting*: To publish, on or before December 31st of each year, an ICANN Annual Report that sets out ICANN's progress against the following:
       a.   ICANN Bylaws;
       b.   ICANN's Responsibilities; and
       c.   ICANN's Strategic and Operating Plans.

III. Strike Section VII from the Joint Project Agreement in its entirety and to replace it with:

A. This Agreement will become effective upon signature of ICANN and the Department. This Agreement will terminate on September 30, 2009.

B. In furtherance of the objective of this Agreement, and to support the completion of the transition of DNS management to the private sector, the Department will hold regular meetings with ICANN senior management and leadership to assess progress. In addition, the Department will conduct a midterm review of progress achieved on each activity and Responsibility that will include consultation with interested stakeholders.

C. This Agreement may not be amended except upon the mutual written agreement of the Parties. Either Party may terminate this Agreement by providing one hundred twenty (120) days written notice to the other Party. If this Agreement is terminated, each Party shall be solely responsible for the payment of any expenses it has incurred. This Agreement is subject to the availability of funds.

IV. Except as specifically modified by this document, the terms and conditions of the Joint Project Agreement remain unchanged.

FOR THE NATIONAL CORPORATION
TELECOMMUNICATIONS AND
INFORMATION ADMINISTRATION:
_/s/_____

Name: John M.R. Kneuer

Title: Acting Assistant Secretary for
Communications and Information

Date: September 29, 2006

FOR THE INTERNET
FOR ASSIGNED NAMES AND
NUMBERS:
____/s/_____

Name: Dr. Paul Twomey

Title: President and CEO

Date: September 29, 2006

Annex A Affirmation of Responsibilities for ICANN's Private Sector Management Approved by the ICANN Board of Directors 25 September 2006

ICANN's shall continue in its commitment to the private sector management of the Internet DNS, by promoting the security and stability of the global Internet, while maintaining, and promoting competition through its multi-stakeholder model.

ICANN hereby affirms and agrees to be guided by the following responsibilities:

1) Security and Stability: ICANN shall coordinate, at the overall level, the global Internet's systems of unique identifiers, and in particular to ensure the stable and secure operation of the Internet's unique identifier systems.

2) Transparency: ICANN shall continue to develop, test and improve processes and procedures to encourage improved transparency, accessibility, efficiency, and timeliness in the consideration and adoption of policies related to technical coordination of the Internet DNS, and funding for ICANN operations. ICANN will innovate and aspire to be a leader in the area of transparency for organizations involved in private sector management.

3) Accountability: ICANN shall continue to develop, test, maintain, and improve on accountability mechanisms to be responsive to global Internet stakeholders in the consideration and adoption of policies related to the technical coordination of the Internet DNS, including continuing to improve openness and accessibility for enhanced participation in ICANN's bottom-up participatory policy development processes.

4) Root Server Security and Relationships: ICANN shall continue to coordinate with the operators of root name servers and other appropriate experts with respect to the operational and security matters, both physical and network, relating to the secure and stable coordination of the root zone; ensure appropriate contingency planning; maintain clear processes in root zone changes. ICANN will work to formalize relationships with root name server operators.

5) TLD Management: ICANN shall maintain and build on processes to ensure that competition, consumer interests, and Internet DNS stability and security issues are identified and considered in TLD management decisions, including the consideration and implementation of new TLDs and the introduction of IDNs. ICANN will continue to develop its policy development processes, and will further develop processes for taking into account recommendations from ICANN's advisory committees and

supporting organizations and other relevant expert advisory panels and organizations. ICANN shall continue to enforce existing policy relating to WHOIS, such existing policy requires that ICANN implement measures to maintain timely, unrestricted and public access to accurate and complete WHOIS information, including registrant, technical, billing and administrative contact information. ICANN shall continue its efforts to achieve stable agreements with country-code top-level domain (ccTLD) operators.

6) Multi-stakeholder Model: ICANN shall maintain and improve multi-stakeholder model and the global participation of all stakeholders, including conducting reviews of its existing advisory committees and supporting organizations, and will continue to further the effectiveness of the bottom-up policy development processes. ICANN will strive to increase engagement with the Private Sector by developing additional mechanisms for involvement of those affected by the ICANN policies.

7) Role of Governments: ICANN shall work with the Government Advisory Committee Members to review the GAC's role within ICANN so as to facilitate effective consideration of GAC advice on the public policy aspects of the technical coordination of the Internet.

8) IP Addressing: ICANN shall continue to work collaboratively on a global and regional level so as to incorporate Regional Internet Registries' policy-making activities into the ICANN processes while allowing them to continue their technical work. ICANN shall continue to maintain legal agreements with the RIRs (and such other appropriate organizations) reflecting this work.

9) Corporate Responsibility: ICANN shall maintain excellence and efficiency in operations, including good governance, organizational measures to maintain stable, international private sector organization, and shall maintain relevant technical and business experience for members of the Board of Directors, executive management, and staff. ICANN will implement appropriate mechanisms that foster participation in ICANN by global Internet stakeholders, such as providing educational services and fostering information sharing for constituents and promoting best practices among industry segments.

10) Corporate Administrative Structure: ICANN shall conduct a review of, and shall make necessary changes in, corporate administrative structure to ensure stability, including devoting adequate resources to contract enforcement, taking into account organizational and corporate governance "best practices."

13

BRIDGING THE STANDARDIZATION GAP (INTERNATIONAL TELECOMMUNICATION UNION)

Resolution 123 (Rev. Antalya, 2006)
Bridging the standardization gap between developing and developed countries

The Plenipotentiary Conference of the International Telecommunication Union (Antalya, 2006),

considering

a)   that "the Union shall in particular facilitate the worldwide standardization of telecommunications, with a satisfactory quality of service" (Article 1 of the ITU Constitution);

b)   that, in connection with the functions and structure of the Telecommunication Standardization Sector (ITU-T), in Article 17, the Constitution indicates that those functions shall be ". . ., bearing in mind the particular concerns of the developing countries, to fulfill the purposes of the Union . . .";

c)   that, under the Strategic Plan for the Union 2008–2011, ITU-T is to work to provide support and assistance to the membership, mainly to developing countries, in relation to standardization matters, information and communication network infrastructure and applications, and in particular with respect to (a) bridging the digital divide; and (b) providing training and producing relevant training materials for capacity building,

considering further

a)   that the World Telecommunication Standardization Assembly adopted Resolutions 44 (Florianópolis, 2004), 53 (Florianópolis, 2004) and 54 (Florianópolis, 2004) as well as Resolution 17 (Rev. Florianópolis, 2004) to assist in bridging the standardization gap between developing and developed countries;

b)   that the World Telecommunication Development Conference adopted Resolution 47 (Doha, 2006), which calls for activities to enhance knowledge and effective application of Recommendations of ITU-T and of the ITU Radiocommunication Sector

(ITU-R) in developing countries, and Resolution 37 (Rev. Doha, 2006) which recognizes the need to create digital opportunities in developing countries,

recalling
that the Geneva Plan of Action and Tunis Agenda for the Information Society of the World Summit on Information Society (WSIS) emphasize efforts to overcome the digital divide and development divides,

noting
the following goals in the Strategic Plan for the Union for 2008–2011, adopted in Resolution 71 (Rev. Antalya, 2006) of this conference:
    Goal 1: Maintaining and extending international cooperation among all Member States and with relevant regional organizations for the improvement and rational use of information and communication infrastructure of all kinds, taking the appropriate leading role in United Nations system initiatives on ICTs, as called for by the relevant WSIS outcomes;
    Goal 2: Assisting in bridging the national and international digital divides in ICTs, by facilitating interoperability, interconnection and global connectivity of networks and services, and by playing a leading role, within its mandate, in the multistakeholder process for the follow-up and implementation of the relevant WSIS goals and objectives;
    Goal 6: Disseminating information and know-how to provide the membership and the wider community, particularly developing countries, with capabilities to leverage the benefits of, *inter alia*, private-sector participation, competition, globalization, network security and efficiency and technological change in their ICT sector, and enhancing the capacity of ITU Member States, in particular developing countries, for innovation in ICTs,

recognizing

a)   the continued shortage of human resources in the standardization field in developing countries, resulting in a low level of developing-country participation in meetings of ITU-T and of ITU-R and, consequently, in the standards-making process, leading to difficulties when interpreting ITU-T and ITU-R Recommendations;
b)   ongoing challenges relating to capacity building, in particular for developing countries, in the light of rapid technological innovation and increased convergence,

taking into account

a)   that developing countries could benefit from improved capability in the application and development of standards;
b)   that ITU-T and ITU-R activities and the telecommunication/ICT market could also benefit from better involvement of developing countries in standard-making and standards application;
c)   that initiatives to assist in bridging the standardization gap are intrinsic to, and are a high priority task of, the Union,

resolves to instruct the Secretary-General and the Directors of the three Bureaux
1   to work closely with each other on the follow-up and implementation of this resolution, as well as the operative paragraphs of Resolutions 44 (Florianópolis, 2004), 54 (Florianópolis, 2004) and 17 (Rev. Florianópolis, 2004) and Resolution 47 (Doha, 2006) that assist in bridging the standardization gap between developing and developed countries;
2   to maintain, to the extent practicable, a close coordination mechanism among the

three Sectors at the regional level through ITU regional offices;

3   to further collaborate with the relevant regional organizations and support their work in this area,

invites Member States and Sector Members

to make voluntary contributions to the fund for bridging the standardization gap, as well as to undertake concrete actions to support the actions and initiatives of ITU in this matter.

14

DIGITAL FREEDOM INITIATIVE

A joint program of the US Department of Commerce, US Agency for International Development, US Department of State, Peace Corps, US Small Business Administration, and USA Freedom Corps

One third of the world could be left behind if more is not done to provide developing countries with the skills, knowledge, and access to markets necessary to compete. In globalizing developing countries, per capita income increased 5 percent a year in the 1990s. In other developing countries, per capita income decreased by 1 percent over the past decade. Appropriately designed information and communication technology (ICT) in developing countries can provide inexpensive and critical access to domestic and global markets, allowing the invisible hand of the market to be a helping hand to the poor.

The Digital Freedom Initiative (DFI) helps meet the challenge by promoting free market based regulatory and legal structures and placing volunteers in businesses and community centers to provide small businesses and entrepreneurs with the information and communications technology skills and knowledge to operate more efficiently while competing in the global economy. These objectives are achieved in partnership with U.S. business entities whose voluntary, innovative and entrepreneurial participation in the DFI provides access to new markets and competitive opportunities for developing products and services in emerging economies. Over 90 U.S. business, non-governmental organizations and academic institutions now comprise the DFI Business Roundtable.

The DFI was initiated in Senegal on March 4, 2003. In October 2003 President Bush announced that Peru and Indonesia had agreed to join the DFI program. On June 9, 2004 Jordan became the fourth DFI partner country. More countries are anticipated to join the program in the next four years to increase business activity, develop more efficient markets, create more jobs in the U.S. and DFI beneficiary countries, and help establish a business friendly regulatory framework conducive to U.S. investment and partnerships.

On March 4, 2003, at the White House, Commerce Secretary Evans, USAID Administrator Natsios, USA Freedom Corps Director Bridgeland and Peace Corps Director Vasquez launched the Digital Freedom Initiative (DFI). The DFI is part of the Volunteers for Prosperity initiative (www.vfp.gov). The goal of the DFI is to promote economic growth by transferring the benefits of information and communication technology (ICT) to entrepreneurs and small businesses in the developing world. The approach is bold and innovative; leveraging the leadership of the US government, the creativity and resources of America's leading companies, and the vision and energy of entrepreneurs throughout the developing world. The DFI was piloted in Senegal in 2003. Peru, Indonesia and Jordan are the newest DFI partner countries.

Key elements

Placing volunteers in small businesses to share business knowledge and technology expertise;

Promoting pro-growth regulatory and legal structures to enhance business competitiveness; and

Leveraging existing technology and communications infrastructure in new ways to help entrepreneurs and small businesses better compete in both the regional and global market place.

Supporting the developing world

One third of the world could be left behind if more is not done to provide developing countries with the skills, knowledge, and access to markets necessary to compete.

In globalizing developing countries, per capita income increased 5 percent a year in the 1990s.

In other developing countries, per capita income decreased by 1 percent over the past decade.

Appropriately designed ICT in developing countries can provide inexpensive and critical access to domestic and global markets, allowing the invisible hand of the market to be a helping hand to the poor.

Objectives

Enable innovation through volunteer-led business and entrepreneur assistance

The DFI will place volunteers from the private sector and NGOs with small businesses and entrepreneurs to assist in growing their businesses through the application of technology and the transfer of business expertise.

Drive pro-growth legal and regulatory reform

The State Department, Commerce, USAID, the Federal Communications Commission (FCC), and other public and private sector organizations will assist DFI countries in developing pro-growth regulatory and legal structures to enhance business competitiveness

Leverage existing information and communications infrastructure to promote economic growth

The DFI will identify opportunities to leverage existing infrastructure (e.g., in-country cyber cafés and telecenters) to generate information and services (e.g. financial services, commodity price information, etc.) to help entrepreneurs and small businesses better compete in both the regional and global market place.

Measuring results

At regular intervals, DFI projects will be evaluated based on performance benchmarks that measure small business growth, market efficiency gains, business integration with international partners and markets, and job growth.

EUROPEAN UNION AMENDMENT TO THE 'TELEVISION WITHOUT FRONTIERS' DIRECTIVE, 2007

Directive 2007/65/EC of the European Parliament and of the Council 11 December 2007

[A]mending Council Directive 89/552/EEC on the coordination of certain provisions laid down by law, regulation or administrative action in Member States concerning the pursuit of television broadcasting activities
THE EUROPEAN PARLIAMENT AND THE COUNCIL OF THE EUROPEAN UNION,
Having regard to the Treaty establishing the European Community, and in particular Articles 47(2) and 55 thereof,
Having regard to the proposal from the Commission,
Having regard to the opinion of the European Economic and Social Committee,
Having regard to the opinion of the Committee of the Regions,
Acting in accordance with the procedure laid down in Article 251 of the Treaty,
Whereas:

(1) Council Directive 89/552/EEC coordinates certain provisions laid down by law, regulation or administrative action in Member States concerning the pursuit of broadcasting activities. However, new technologies in the transmission of audiovisual media services call for adaptation of the regulatory framework to take account of the impact of structural change, the spread of information and communication technologies (ICT) and technological developments on business models, especially the financing of commercial broadcasting, and to ensure optimal conditions of competitiveness and legal certainty for Europe's information technologies and its media industries and services, as well as respect for cultural and linguistic diversity.

(2) The laws, regulations and administrative measures in Member States concerning the pursuit of television broadcasting activities are already coordinated by Directive 89/552/EEC, whereas the rules applicable to activities such as on-demand audiovisual media services contain disparities, some of which may impede the free movement of those services within the European Community and may distort competition within the internal market.

(3) Audiovisual media services are as much cultural services as they are economic services. Their growing importance for societies, democracy — in particular by ensuring freedom of information, diversity of opinion and media pluralism — education and culture justifies the application of specific rules to these services.

(4) Article 151(4) of the Treaty requires the Community to take cultural aspects into account in its action under other provisions of the Treaty, in particular in order to respect and to promote the diversity of its cultures.

(5) In its resolutions of 1 December 2005 and 4 April 2006 on the Doha Round and on the WTO Ministerial Conferences, the European Parliament called for basic public services, such as audiovisual services, to be excluded from liberalisation under the GATS negotiations. In its resolution of 27 April 2006, the European Parliament supported the Unesco Convention on the Protection and Promotion of the Diversity of Cultural Expressions, which states in particular that 'cultural activities, goods and services have both an economic and a cultural nature, because they convey identities, values and meanings, and must therefore not be treated as solely having commercial value'. The Council Decision 2006/515/EC of 18 May 2006 on the conclusion of the Convention on the Protection and Promotion of the Diversity of Cultural Expressions approved the Unesco Convention on behalf of the Community. The Convention entered into force on 18 March 2007. This Directive respects the principles of that Convention.

(6) Traditional audiovisual media services — such as television — and emerging on-demand audiovisual media services offer significant employment opportunities in the Community, particularly in small and medium-sized enterprises, and stimulate economic growth and investment. Bearing in mind the importance of a level playing-field and a true European market for audiovisual media services, the basic principles of the internal market, such as free competition and equal treatment, should be respected in order to ensure transparency and predictability in markets for audiovisual media services and to achieve low barriers to entry.

(7) Legal uncertainty and a non-level playing-field exist for European companies delivering audiovisual media services as regards the legal regime governing emerging on-demand audiovisual media services. It is therefore necessary, in order to avoid distortions of competition, to improve legal certainty, to help complete the internal market and to facilitate the emergence of a single information area, that at least a basic tier of coordinated rules apply to all audiovisual media services, both television broadcasting (i.e. linear audiovisual media services) and on-demand audiovisual media services (i.e. non-linear audiovisual media services). The basic principles of Directive 89/552/EEC, namely the country of origin principle and common minimum standards, have proved their worth and should therefore be retained.

(8) On 15 December 2003, the Commission adopted a Communication on the future of European regulatory audiovisual policy, in which it stressed that regulatory policy in that sector has to safeguard certain public interests, such as cultural diversity, the right to information, media pluralism, the protection of minors and consumer protection and to enhance public awareness and media literacy, now and in the future.

(9) The Resolution of the Council and of the Representatives of the Governments of the Member States, meeting within the Council of 25 January 1999 concerning public service broadcasting reaffirmed that the fulfilment of the mission of public service broadcasting requires that it continue to benefit from technological progress. The co-existence of private and public audiovisual media service providers is a feature which distinguishes the European audiovisual media market.

(10) The Commission has adopted the initiative 'i2010: European Information Society' to

foster growth and jobs in the information society and media industries. This is a comprehensive strategy designed to encourage the production of European content, the development of the digital economy and the uptake of ICT, against the background of the convergence of information society services and media services, networks and devices, by modernising and deploying all EU policy instruments: regulatory instruments, research and partnerships with industry. The Commission has committed itself to creating a consistent internal market framework for information society services and media services by modernising the legal framework for audiovisual services, starting with a Commission proposal in 2005 to modernise the Television without Frontiers Directive and transform it into a Directive on Audiovisual Media Services. The goal of the i2010 initiative will in principle be achieved by allowing industries to grow with only the necessary regulation, as well as allowing small start-up businesses, which are the wealth and job creators of the future, to flourish, innovate and create employment in a free market.

(11) The European Parliament adopted on 4 September 2003, 22 April 2004 and 6 September 2005 resolutions which called for the adaptation of Directive 89/552/ EEC to reflect structural changes and technological developments while fully respecting its underlying principles, which remain valid. In addition, it in principle supported the general approach of basic rules for all audiovisual media services and additional rules for television broadcasting.

(12) This Directive enhances compliance with fundamental rights and is fully in line with the principles recognised by the Charter of Fundamental Rights of the European Union, in particular Article 11 thereof. In this regard, this Directive should not in any way prevent Member States from applying their constitutional rules relating to freedom of the press and freedom of expression in the media.

(13) This Directive should not affect the obligations on Member States arising from the application of Directive 98/34/EC of the European Parliament and of the Council of 22 June 1998 laying down a procedure for the provision of information in the field of technical standards and regulations and of rules on Information Society services. Accordingly, draft national measures applicable to on-demand audiovisual media services of a stricter or more detailed nature than those required to simply transpose this Directive should be subject to the procedural obligations established under Article 8 of Directive 98/34/EC.

(14) Directive 2002/21/EC of the European Parliament and of the Council of 7 March 2002 on a common regulatory framework for electronic communications networks and services (Framework Directive) according to its Article 1(3) is without prejudice to measures taken at Community or national level, to pursue general interest objectives, in particular relating to content regulation and audiovisual policy.

(15) No provision of this Directive should require or encourage Member States to impose new systems of licensing or administrative authorisation on any type of audiovisual media service.

(16) For the purposes of this Directive, the definition of an audiovisual media service should cover only audiovisual media services, whether television broadcasting or on-demand, which are mass media, that is, which are intended for reception by, and which could have a clear impact on, a significant proportion of the general public. Its scope should be limited to services as defined by the Treaty and therefore should cover any form of economic activity, including that of public service enterprises, but should not cover activities which are primarily non-economic and which are not in competition with television broadcasting, such as private websites and services consisting of the provision or distribution of audiovisual content generated by

private users for the purposes of sharing and exchange within communities of interest.

(17) It is characteristic of on-demand audiovisual media services that they are 'television-like', i.e. that they compete for the same audience as television broadcasts, and the nature and the means of access to the service would lead the user reasonably to expect regulatory protection within the scope of this Directive. In the light of this and in order to prevent disparities as regards free movement and competition, the notion of 'programme' should be interpreted in a dynamic way taking into account developments in television broadcasting.

(18) For the purposes of this Directive, the definition of an audiovisual media service should cover mass media in their function to inform, entertain and educate the general public, and should include audiovisual commercial communication but should exclude any form of private correspondence, such as e-mails sent to a limited number of recipients. That definition should exclude all services whose principal purpose is not the provision of programmes, i.e. where any audiovisual content is merely incidental to the service and not its principal purpose. Examples include websites that contain audiovisual elements only in an ancillary manner, such as animated graphical elements, short advertising spots or information related to a product or non-audiovisual service. For these reasons, games of chance involving a stake representing a sum of money, including lotteries, betting and other forms of gambling services, as well as on-line games and search engines, but not broadcasts devoted to gambling or games of chance, should also be excluded from the scope of this Directive.

(19) For the purposes of this Directive, the definition of media service provider should exclude natural or legal persons who merely transmit programmes for which the editorial responsibility lies with third parties.

(20) Television broadcasting currently includes, in particular, analogue and digital television, live streaming, webcasting and near-video-on-demand, whereas video-on-demand, for example, is an on-demand audiovisual media service. In general, for television broadcasting or television programmes which are also offered as on-demand audiovisual media services by the same media service provider, the requirements of this Directive should be deemed to be met by the fulfilment of the requirements applicable to the television broadcast i.e. linear transmission. However, where different kinds of services are offered in parallel, but are clearly separate services, this Directive should apply to each of the services concerned.

(21) The scope of this Directive should not cover electronic versions of newspapers and magazines.

(22) For the purpose of this Directive, the term 'audiovisual' should refer to moving images with or without sound, thus including silent films but not covering audio transmission or radio services. While the principal purpose of an audiovisual media service is the provision of programmes, the definition of such a service should also cover text-based content which accompanies programmes, such as subtitling services and electronic programme guides. Stand-alone text-based services should not fall within the scope of this Directive, which should not affect Member States' freedom to regulate such services at national level in accordance with the Treaty.

(23) The notion of editorial responsibility is essential for defining the role of the media service provider and therefore for the definition of audiovisual media services. Member States may further specify aspects of the definition of editorial responsibility, notably the notion of 'effective control', when adopting measures to implement this Directive. This Directive should be without prejudice to the exemptions from liability established in Directive 2000/31/EC of the European Parliament and of the Council

of 8 June 2000 on certain legal aspects of information society services, in particular electronic commerce, in the Internal Market (Directive on electronic commerce).

(24) In the context of television broadcasting, the notion of simultaneous viewing should also cover quasi-simultaneous viewing because of the variations in the short time lag which occurs between the transmission and the reception of the broadcast due to technical reasons inherent in the transmission process.

(25) All the characteristics of an audiovisual media service set out in its definition and explained in Recitals 16 to 23 should be present at the same time.

(26) In addition to television advertising and teleshopping, a wider definition of audiovisual commercial communication should be introduced in this Directive, which however should not include public service announcements and charity appeals broadcast free of charge.

(27) The country of origin principle should remain the core of this Directive, as it is essential for the creation of an internal market. This principle should therefore be applied to all audiovisual media services in order to ensure legal certainty for media service providers as the necessary basis for new business models and the deployment of such services. It is also essential in order to ensure the free flow of information and audiovisual programmes in the internal market.

(28) In order to promote a strong, competitive and integrated European audiovisual industry and enhance media pluralism throughout the European Union, only one Member State should have jurisdiction over an audiovisual media service provider and pluralism of information should be a fundamental principle of the European Union.

(29) Technological developments, especially with regard to digital satellite programmes, mean that subsidiary criteria should be adapted in order to ensure suitable regulation and its effective implementation and to give players genuine power over the content of an audiovisual media service.

(30) As this Directive concerns services offered to the general public in the European Union, it should apply only to audiovisual media services that can be received directly or indirectly by the public in one or more Member States with standard consumer equipment. The definition of 'standard consumer equipment' should be left to the competent national authorities.

(31) Articles 43 to 48 of the Treaty lay down the fundamental right to freedom of establishment. Therefore, media service providers should in general be free to choose the Member States in which they establish themselves. The Court of Justice has also emphasised that 'the Treaty does not prohibit an undertaking from exercising the freedom to provide services if it does not offer services in the Member State in which it is established'.

(32) Member States should be able to apply more detailed or stricter rules in the fields coordinated by this Directive to media service providers under their jurisdiction, while ensuring that those rules are consistent with general principles of Community law. In order to deal with situations where a broadcaster under the jurisdiction of one Member State provides a television broadcast which is wholly or mostly directed towards the territory of another Member State, a requirement for Member States to cooperate with one another and, in cases of circumvention, the codification of the case-law of the Court of Justice, combined with a more efficient procedure, would be an appropriate solution that takes account of Member State concerns without calling into question the proper application of the country of origin principle. The notion of rules of general public interest has been developed by the Court of Justice in its case law in relation to Articles 43 and 49 of the Treaty and includes, *inter alia*, rules on the protection of consumers, the protection of minors and cultural policy. The Member

State requesting cooperation should ensure that the specific national rules in question are objectively necessary, applied in a non-discriminatory manner, and proportionate.

(33) A Member State, when assessing on a case-by-case basis whether a broadcast by a media service provider established in another Member State is wholly or mostly directed towards its territory, may refer to indicators such as the origin of the television advertising and/or subscription revenues, the main language of the service or the existence of programmes or commercial communications targeted specifically at the public in the Member State where they are received.

(34) Under this Directive, notwithstanding the application of the country of origin principle, Member States may still take measures that restrict freedom of movement of television broadcasting, but only under the conditions and following the procedure laid down in this Directive. However, the Court of Justice has consistently held that any restriction on the freedom to provide services, such as any derogation from a fundamental principle of the Treaty, must be interpreted restrictively.

(35) With respect to on-demand audiovisual media services, restrictions on their free provision should only be possible in accordance with conditions and procedures replicating those already established by Articles 3(4), (5) and (6) of Directive 2000/31/EC.

(36) In its Communication to the European Parliament and the Council on Better Regulation for Growth and Jobs in the European Union, the Commission stressed that a careful analysis of the appropriate regulatory approach is necessary, in particular, in order to establish whether legislation is preferable for the relevant sector and problem, or whether alternatives such as co-regulation or self-regulation should be considered. Furthermore, experience has shown that both co- and self-regulation instruments, implemented in accordance with the different legal traditions of the Member States, can play an important role in delivering a high level of consumer protection. Measures aimed at achieving public interest objectives in the emerging audiovisual media services sector are more effective if they are taken with the active support of the service providers themselves.

Thus self-regulation constitutes a type of voluntary initiative which enables economic operators, social partners, non-governmental organisations or associations to adopt common guidelines amongst themselves and for themselves. Member States should, in accordance with their different legal traditions, recognise the role which effective self-regulation can play as a complement to the legislative and judicial and/or administrative mechanisms in place and its useful contribution to the achievement of the objectives of this Directive. However, while self-regulation might be a complementary method of implementing certain provisions of this Directive, it should not constitute a substitute for the obligations of the national legislator.

Co-regulation gives, in its minimal form, a legal link between self-regulation and the national legislator in accordance with the legal traditions of the Member States. Co-regulation should allow for the possibility of State intervention in the event of its objectives not being met. Without prejudice to Member States' formal obligations regarding transposition, this Directive encourages the use of co-regulation and self-regulation. This should neither oblige Member States to set up co- and/or self-regulatory regimes nor disrupt or jeopardise current co- or self-regulatory initiatives which are already in place within Member States and which are working effectively.

(37) 'Media literacy' refers to skills, knowledge and understanding that allow consumers to use media effectively and safely. Media-literate people are able to exercise informed choices, understand the nature of content and services and take advantage of

the full range of opportunities offered by new communications technologies. They are better able to protect themselves and their families from harmful or offensive material. Therefore the development of media literacy in all sections of society should be promoted and its progress followed closely.

The Recommendation of the European Parliament and of the Council of 20 December 2006 on the protection of minors and human dignity and on the right of reply in relation to the competitiveness of the European audiovisual and on-line information services industry already contains a series of possible measures for promoting media literacy such as, for example, continuing education of teachers and trainers, specific Internet training aimed at children from a very early age, including sessions open to parents, or organisation of national campaigns aimed at citizens, involving all communications media, to provide information on using the Internet responsibly.

(38) Television broadcasting rights for events of high interest to the public may be acquired by broadcasters on an exclusive basis. However, it is essential to promote pluralism through the diversity of news production and programming across the European Union and to respect the principles recognised by Article 11 of the Charter of Fundamental Rights of the European Union.

(39) In order to safeguard the fundamental freedom to receive information and to ensure that the interests of viewers in the European Union are fully and properly protected, those exercising exclusive television broadcasting rights to an event of high interest to the public should grant other broadcasters the right to use short extracts for the purposes of general news programmes on fair, reasonable and non-discriminatory terms taking due account of exclusive rights. Such terms should be communicated in a timely manner before the event of high interest to the public takes place to give others sufficient time to exercise such a right. A broadcaster should be able to exercise this right through an intermediary acting specifically on its behalf on a case-by-case basis. Such short extracts may be used for EU-wide broadcasts by any channel including dedicated sports channels and should not exceed 90 seconds.

The right of access to short extracts should apply on a trans-frontier basis only where it is necessary. Therefore a broadcaster should first seek access from a broadcaster established in the same Member State having exclusive rights to the event of high interest to the public.

The notion of general news programmes should not cover the compilation of short extracts into programmes serving entertainment purposes.

The country of origin principle should apply to both the access to, and the transmission of, the short extracts. In a trans-frontier case, this means that the different laws should be applied sequentially. Firstly, for access to the short extracts the law of the Member State where the broadcaster supplying the initial signal (i.e. giving access) is established should apply. This is usually the Member State in which the event concerned takes place. Where a Member State has established an equivalent system of access to the event concerned, the law of that Member State should apply in any case. Secondly, for transmission of the short extracts, the law of the Member State where the broadcaster transmitting the short extracts is established should apply.

(40) The requirements of this Directive regarding access to events of high interest to the public for the purpose of short news reports should be without prejudice to Directive 2001/29/EC of the European Parliament and of the Council of 22 May 2001 on the harmonisation of certain aspects of copyright and related rights in the information society and the relevant international conventions in the field of copyright and neighbouring rights. Member States should facilitate access to events of high interests to the

public by granting access to the broadcaster's signal within the meaning of this Directive. However, they may choose other equivalent means within the meaning of this Directive. Such means include, *inter alia*, granting access to the venue of these events prior to granting access to the signal. Broadcasters should not be prevented from concluding more detailed contracts.

(41) It should be ensured that the practice of media service providers of providing their live television broadcast news programmes in the on-demand mode after live transmission is still possible without having to tailor the individual programme by omitting the short extracts. This possibility should be restricted to the on-demand supply of the identical television broadcast programme by the same media service provider, so it may not be used to create new on-demand business models based on short extracts.

(42) On-demand audiovisual media services are different from television broadcasting with regard to the choice and control the user can exercise, and with regard to the impact they have on society. This justifies imposing lighter regulation on on-demand audiovisual media services, which should comply only with the basic rules provided for in this Directive.

(43) Because of the specific nature of audiovisual media services, especially the impact of these services on the way people form their opinions, it is essential for users to know exactly who is responsible for the content of these services. It is therefore important for Member States to ensure that users have easy and direct access at any time to information about the media service provider. It is for each Member State to decide the practical details as to how this objective can be achieved without prejudice to any other relevant provisions of Community law.

(44) The availability of harmful content in audiovisual media services continues to be a concern for legislators, the media industry and parents. There will also be new challenges, especially in connection with new platforms and new products. It is therefore necessary to introduce rules to protect the physical, mental and moral development of minors as well as human dignity in all audiovisual media services, including audiovisual commercial communications.

(45) Measures taken to protect the physical, mental and moral development of minors and human dignity should be carefully balanced with the fundamental right to freedom of expression as laid down in the Charter on Fundamental Rights of the European Union. The aim of those measures, such as the use of personal identification numbers (PIN codes), filtering systems or labelling, should thus be to ensure an adequate level of protection of the physical, mental and moral development of minors and human dignity, especially with regard to on-demand audiovisual media services.

The Recommendation on the protection of minors and human dignity and on the right of reply already recognised the importance of filtering systems and labelling and included a number of possible measures for the benefit of minors, such as systematically supplying users with an effective, updatable and easy-to-use filtering system when they subscribe to an access provider or equipping the access to services specifically intended for children with automatic filtering systems.

(46) Media service providers under the jurisdiction of the Member States should in any case be subject to a ban on the dissemination of child pornography according to the provisions of Council Framework Decision 2004/68/JHA of 22 December 2003 on combating the sexual exploitation of children and child pornography.

(47) None of the provisions introduced by this Directive that concern the protection of the physical, mental and moral development of minors and human dignity necessarily requires that the measures taken to protect those interests should be implemented through prior verification of audiovisual media services by public bodies.

(48) On-demand audiovisual media services have the potential to partially replace television broadcasting. Accordingly, they should, where practicable, promote the production and distribution of European works and thus contribute actively to the promotion of cultural diversity. Such support for European works might, for example, take the form of financial contributions by such services to the production of and acquisition of rights in European works, a minimum share of European works in video-on-demand catalogues, or the attractive presentation of European works in electronic programme guides. It is important to regularly re-examine the application of the provisions relating to the promotion of European works by audiovisual media services. Within the framework of the reports set out under this Directive, Member States should also take into account notably the financial contribution by such services to the production and rights acquisition of European works, the share of European works in the catalogue of audiovisual media services, and in the actual consumption of European works offered by such services.

(49) When defining 'producers who are independent of broadcasters' as referred to in Article 5 of Directive 89/552/EEC, Member States should take appropriate account notably of criteria such as the ownership of the production company, the amount of programmes supplied to the same broadcaster and the ownership of secondary rights.

(50) When implementing the provisions of Article 4 of Directive 89/552/EEC, Member States should encourage broadcasters to include an adequate share of co-produced European works or of European works of non-domestic origin.

(51) It is important to ensure that cinematographic works are transmitted within periods agreed between right holders and media service providers.

(52) The availability of on-demand audiovisual media services increases the choice of the consumer. Detailed rules governing audiovisual commercial communication for on-demand audiovisual media services thus appear neither to be justified nor to make sense from a technical point of view. Nevertheless, all audiovisual commercial communication should respect not only the identification rules but also a basic tier of qualitative rules in order to meet clear public policy objectives.

(53) The right of reply is an appropriate legal remedy for television broadcasting and could also be applied in the on-line environment. The Recommendation on the protection of minors and human dignity and on the right of reply already includes appropriate guidelines for the implementation of measures in national law or practice so as to ensure sufficiently the right of reply or equivalent remedies in relation to on-line media.

(54) As has been recognised by the Commission in its interpretative communication on certain aspects of the provisions on televised advertising in the 'Television without frontiers' Directive, the development of new advertising techniques and marketing innovations has created new effective opportunities for audiovisual commercial communications in traditional broadcasting services, potentially enabling them better to compete on a level playing-field with on-demand innovations.

(55) Commercial and technological developments give users increased choice and responsibility in their use of audiovisual media services. In order to remain proportionate with the goals of general interest, regulation should allow a certain degree of flexibility with regard to television broadcasting. The principle of separation should be limited to television advertising and teleshopping, product placement should be allowed under certain circumstances, unless a Member State decides otherwise, and some quantitative restrictions should be abolished. However, where product placement is surreptitious, it should be prohibited. The principle of separation should not prevent the use of new advertising techniques.

(56) Apart from the practices that are covered by this Directive, Directive 2005/29/EC of the European Parliament and of the Council of 11 May 2005 concerning unfair business-to-consumer commercial practices in the internal market applies to unfair commercial practices, such as misleading and aggressive practices occurring in audiovisual media services. Moreover, as Directive 2003/33/EC of the European Parliament and of the Council of 26 May 2003 on the approximation of the laws, regulations and administrative provisions of the Member States relating to the advertising and sponsorship of tobacco products, which prohibits advertising and sponsorship for cigarettes and other tobacco products in printed media, information society services and radio broadcasting, is without prejudice to Directive 89/552/EEC, in view of the special characteristics of audiovisual media services, the relation between Directive 2003/33/EC and Directive 89/552/EEC should remain the same after the entry into force of this Directive. Article 88(1) of Directive 2001/83/EC of the European Parliament and of the Council of 6 November 2001 on the Community code relating to medicinal products for human use which prohibits advertising to the general public of certain medicinal products applies, as provided in paragraph 5 of that Article, without prejudice to Article 14 of Directive 89/552/EEC. The relation between Directive 2001/83/EC and Directive 89/552/EEC should remain the same after the entry into force of this Directive. Furthermore, this Directive should be without prejudice to Regulation (EC) No 1924/2006 of the European Parliament and of the Council of 20 December 2006 on nutrition and health claims made on foods.

(57) Given the increased possibilities for viewers to avoid advertising through use of new technologies such as digital personal video recorders and increased choice of channels, detailed regulation with regard to the insertion of spot advertising with the aim of protecting viewers is no longer justified. While this Directive should not increase the hourly amount of admissible advertising, it should give flexibility to broadcasters with regard to its insertion where this does not unduly impair the integrity of programmes.

(58) This Directive is intended to safeguard the specific character of European television, where advertising is preferably inserted between programmes, and therefore limits possible interruptions to cinematographic works and films made for television as well as interruptions to some categories of programmes that still need specific protection.

(59) The limitation that existed on the amount of daily television advertising was largely theoretical. The hourly limit is more important since it also applies during 'prime time'. Therefore the daily limit should be abolished, while the hourly limit should be maintained for television advertising and teleshopping spots. The restrictions on the time allowed for teleshopping or advertising channels seem no longer justified given increased consumer choice. However, the limit of 20% of television advertising spots and teleshopping spots per clock hour remains applicable. The notion of a television advertising spot should be understood as television advertising in the sense of Article 1(i) of Directive 89/552/EEC as amended by this Directive having a duration of not more than 12 minutes.

(60) Surreptitious audiovisual commercial communication is a practice prohibited by this Directive because of its negative effect on consumers. The prohibition of surreptitious audiovisual commercial communication should not cover legitimate product placement within the framework of this Directive, where the viewer is adequately informed of the existence of product placement. This can be done by signalling the fact that product placement is taking place in a given programme, for example by means of a neutral logo.

(61) Product placement is a reality in cinematographic works and in audiovisual works

made for television, but Member States regulate this practice differently. In order to ensure a level playing field, and thus enhance the competitiveness of the European media industry, it is necessary to adopt rules for product placement. The definition of product placement introduced by this Directive should cover any form of audiovisual commercial communication consisting of the inclusion of or reference to a product, a service or the trade mark thereof so that it is featured within a programme, in return for payment or for similar consideration. The provision of goods or services free of charge, such as production props or prizes, should only be considered to be product placement if the goods or services involved are of significant value. Product placement should be subject to the same qualitative rules and restrictions applying to audiovisual commercial communication. The decisive criterion distinguishing sponsorship from product placement is the fact that in product placement the reference to a product is built into the action of a programme, which is why the definition in Article 1(m) of Directive 89/552/EEC as amended by this Directive contains the word 'within'. In contrast, sponsor references may be shown during a programme but are not part of the plot.

(62) Product placement should, in principle, be prohibited. However, derogations are appropriate for some kinds of programme, on the basis of a positive list. A Member State should be able to opt-out of these derogations, totally or partially, for example by permitting product placement only in programmes which have not been produced exclusively in that Member State.

(63) Furthermore, sponsorship and product placement should be prohibited where they influence the content of programmes in such a way as to affect the responsibility and the editorial independence of the media service provider. This is the case with regard to thematic placement.

(64) The right of persons with a disability and of the elderly to participate and be integrated in the social and cultural life of the Community is inextricably linked to the provision of accessible audiovisual media services. The means to achieve accessibility should include, but need not be limited to, sign language, subtitling, audio-description and easily understandable menu navigation.

(65) According to the duties conferred upon Member States by the Treaty, they are responsible for the transposition and effective implementation of this Directive. They are free to choose the appropriate instruments according to their legal traditions and established structures, and notably the form of their competent independent regulatory bodies, in order to be able to carry out their work in implementing this Directive impartially and transparently. More specifically, the instruments chosen by Member States should contribute to the promotion of media pluralism.

(66) Close cooperation between competent Member States' regulatory bodies and the Commission is necessary to ensure the correct application of this Directive. Similarly close cooperation between Member States and between Member States' regulatory bodies is particularly important with regard to the impact which broadcasters established in one Member State might have on another Member State. Where licensing procedures are provided for in national law and if more than one Member State is concerned, it is desirable that contacts between the respective bodies take place before such licences are granted. This cooperation should cover all fields coordinated by Directive 89/552/EEC as amended by this Directive and in particular Articles 2, 2a and 3 hereof.

(67) Since the objectives of this Directive, namely creation of an area without internal frontiers for audiovisual media services whilst ensuring at the same time a high level of protection of objectives of general interest, in particular the protection of minors

and human dignity as well as promoting the rights of persons with disabilities, cannot be sufficiently achieved by the Member States and can therefore, by reason of the scale and effects of this Directive, be better achieved at Community level, the Community may adopt measures in accordance with the principle of subsidiarity as set out in Article 5 of the Treaty. In accordance with the principle of proportionality, as set out in that Article, this Directive does not go beyond what is necessary in order to achieve these objectives.

(68) In accordance with point 34 of the Interinstitutional Agreement on better law-making, Member States are encouraged to draw up, for themselves and in the interests of the Community, their own tables illustrating, as far as possible, the correlation between this Directive and the transposition measures, and to make them public,

Further reading

Abbas, A. and Erni, J. N. (eds.) (2005) *Internationalizing cultural studies: an anthology*. Oxford: Blackwell.

Amin, S. (1997) *Capitalism in the age of globalization*. London: Zed Books.

Appadurai, A. (1996) *Modernity at large: cultural dimensions of globalization*. Minneapolis: University of Minnesota Press.

Appadurai, A. (ed.) (2001) *Globalization*. Durham, NC: Duke University Press.

Arsenault, A. and Castells, M. (2008) The structure and dynamics of global multi-media business networks. *International Journal of Communication*, 2: 707–48.

Atton, C. (2004) *An alternative Internet: radical media, politics and creativity*. Edinburgh: Edinburgh University Press.

Bagdikian, B. (2004) *The new media monopoly*, seventh edition. Boston: Beacon.

Baker, C. Edwin (2007) *Media concentration and democracy: why ownership matters*. Cambridge: Cambridge University Press.

Banerjee, I. and Seneviratne, K. (eds.) (2006) *Public service broadcasting in the age of globalization*. Singapore: Asian Media Information and Communication Centre.

Barker, C. (1997) *Global television*. Oxford: Blackwell.

Beck, U. (2006) *Cosmopolitan vision*. Cambridge: Polity.

Bennett, L. W. (2007) *News: the politics of illusion*, seventh edition. London: Addison Wesley Longman.

Bennett, L. W., Lawrence, R. and Livingston, S. (2007) *When the press fails: political power and the news media from Iraq to Katrina*. Chicago: University of Chicago Press.

Bettig, R. (1996) *Copyrighting culture: the political economy of intellectual property*. Boulder, CO: Westview.

Boyd-Barrett, O. and Thussu, D. K. (1992) *Contraflow in global news*. London: John Libbey/UNESCO.

Boyd-Barrett, O. and Rantanen, T. (eds.) (1998) *The globalization of news*. London: Sage.

Braman, S. (ed.) (2004) *The emergent global information policy regime*. Basingstoke: Palgrave Macmillan.

Braman, S. (2006) *Change of state: information, policy and power*. New Haven: Yale University Press.

Breckenridge, C., Pollock, S., Bhabha, H. and Chakrabarty, D. (2002) *Cosmopolitanism*. Durham, NC: Duke University Press.

Cairncross, F. (1997) *The death of distance: how the communications revolution will change our lives*. London: Orion Business Books.

Castells, M. (2000) *The information age: economy, society and culture*, vol. 1: *The rise of the network society*, second edition. Oxford: Blackwell.

Castells, M. (2000) *The information age: economy, society and culture*, vol. 3: *End of millennium*, second edition. Oxford: Blackwell.

Castells, M. (2004) *The information age: economy, society and culture*, vol. 2: *The power of identity*, second edition. Oxford: Blackwell.

Castells, M., Qiu, J. L., Fernandez-Ardevol, M. and Sey, A. (2006) *Mobile communication and society: a global perspective*. New Haven: Yale University Press.

Caves, R. (2005) *Switching channels: organization and change in TV broadcasting*, Cambridge, MA: Harvard University Press.

Chakravartty, P. and Sarikakis, K. (2006) *Media policy and globalization*. Edinburgh: Edinburgh University Press.

Chakravartty, P. and Zhao, Y. (eds.) (2008) *Global communications: towards a transcultural political economy*. Lanham, MD: Rowman & Littlefield.

Chalaby J. (ed.) (2005) *Transnational television worldwide – towards a new media order*. London: I. B. Tauris.

Chapman, J. (2005) *Comparative media history*. Oxford: Polity.

Corner, J., Schlesinger, P. and Silverstone, R. (eds.) (1997) *International media research: a critical survey*. London: Routledge.

Croteau, D. and Hynes, W. (2005) *The business of media: corporate media and the public interest*, second edition. London: Sage.

Crystal, D. (1997) *English as a global language*. Cambridge: Cambridge University Press.

Curran, J. and Couldry, N. (eds.) (2003) *Contesting media power*, Lanham, MD: Rowman & Littlefield.

Curran, J. and Morley, D. (eds.) (2006) *Media and cultural theory*. London: Routledge.

Curran, J. and Park, J. (2000) *De-Westernizing media studies*. London: Routledge.

Curtin, M. (2007) *Playing to the world's biggest audience: the globalization of Chinese film and TV*. Los Angeles: University of California Press.

Dahlgren, P. (2003) *Media and civic engagement*. Cambridge: Cambridge University Press.

Danet, B. and Herring, S. (eds.) (2007) *The multilingual internet: language, culture, and communication online*. New York: Oxford University Press.

Dayan, D. and Katz, E. (1992) *Media events: the live broadcasting of history*. Cambridge, MA: Harvard University Press.

Downing, J. (1996) *Internationalizing media theory*. London: Sage.

Downing, J. (2001) *Radical media: rebellious communication and social movements*. Thousand Oaks, CA: Sage.

Durham, M.G. and Kellner, D. (eds.) (2006) *Media and cultural studies: key works*, second edition. Oxford: Blackwell.

Eisenstein, E. (1979) *The printing press as an agent of change*, two volumes. Cambridge: Cambridge University Press.

Erni, J. N. and Chau, S. K. (eds.) (2005) *Asian media studies – politics of subjectivities*. Oxford: Blackwell.

Esser, F. and Pfetsch, B. (2004) (eds.) *Comparing political communication: theories, cases and challenges*. Cambridge: Cambridge University Press.

Featherstone, M. (ed.) (1990) *Global culture: nationalism, globalization and modernity*. London: Sage.

Flew, T. (2007) *Understanding global media*. Basingstoke: Palgrave Macmillan.

Frederick, H. (1992) *Global communication and international relations*. Belmont: Wadsworth.

Galtung, J. (1971) A structural theory of imperialism. *Journal of Peace Research*, 8(2): 81–117.

Garcia Canclini, N. (1995) *Hybrid cultures: strategies for entering and leaving modernity*. Minneapolis: University of Minnesota Press.

Garnham, N. (1990) *Capitalism and communication: global culture and the economics of information*. London: Sage.

Garnham, N. (2000) *Emancipation, the media and modernity*. Oxford: Oxford University Press.

Geradin, D. and Luff, D. (eds.) (2004) *The WTO and global convergence in telecommunications and audio-visual services*. Cambridge: Cambridge University Press.

Giddens, A. (1990) *The consequences of modernity*. Cambridge: Polity.

Ginsburg, F., Abu-Lughod, L. and Larkin, B. (eds.) (2002) *Media worlds – anthropology on new terrain*. Los Angeles: University of California Press.

Global Media and Communication (2005) From NWICO to WSIS, special issue of *Global Media and Communication*, 1(3): 264–373.

Golding, P. and Murdoch, G. (eds.) (1997) *The political economy of the media*, two volumes. Cheltenham: Edward Elgar.

Goggin, G. and McLelland, M. (2009) (eds.) *Internationalizing internet studies: beyond anglophone paradigms*. New York: Routledge.

Gunder Frank, A. (1998) *Reorient: global economy in the Asian age*. Los Angeles: University of California Press.

Habermas, J. (1989) *The structural transformation of the public sphere: an inquiry into a category of bourgeois society*. Cambridge: Polity.

Habermas, J. (2001) *The postnational constellation*. Cambridge, MA: MIT Press.

Hachten, W. and Scotton, J. (2006) *The world news prism: global information in a satellite age*, second edition. Oxford: Blackwell.

Hackett, R. A. and Zhao, Y. (eds.) (2005) *Democratizing global media: one world, many struggles*. Lanham, MD: Rowman & Littlefield.

Hamelink, C. (1994) *The politics of world communication: a human rights perspective*. London: Sage.

Hamelink, C. (2000) *The ethics of cyberspace*. London: Sage.

Hamilton, J. (2003) *All the news that's fit to sell: how the market transforms information into news*. Princeton: Princeton University Press.

Hardt, M. and Negri, A. (2004) *Multitude: war and democracy in the age of empire*. London: Penguin.

Harvey, D. (2003) *The new imperialism*. Oxford: Oxford University Press.

Headrick, D. (1991) *The invisible weapon: telecommunications and international politics, 1851–1945*. New York: Oxford University Press.

Held, D. and McGrew, A. (eds.) (2003) *The global transformations reader: An introduction to the globalization debate*, second edition. Cambridge: Polity.

Held, D., McGrew, A., Goldblatt, D. and Perraton, J. (1999) *Global transformations: politics, economics and culture*. Cambridge: Polity.

Herman, E. and Chomsky, N. (1994) *Manufacturing consent: the political economy of the mass media*. London: Vintage.

Herman, E. and McChesney, R. (1997) *The global media: the new missionaries of corporate capitalism*. London: Cassell.

Hesmondhalgh, D. (2007) *The cultural industries*, second edition. London: Sage.

Hills, J. (2002) *The struggle for control of global communication: the formative century*. Champaign: University of Illinois Press.

Hills, J. (2007) *Telecommunications and empire*. Urbana: University of Illinois Press.

Hobson, J. M. (2004) *The eastern origins of Western civilization*. Cambridge: Cambridge University Press.

Hoge, J. and Gideon, R. (2005) *Understanding the war on terror*. New York: Council on Foreign Relations.

Hoskins, C., McFyden, S. and Finn, A. (2004) *Media economics: applying economics to new and traditional media*. London: Sage.

Hughill, P. (1999) *Global communications since 1844: geopolitics and technology*. Baltimore: Johns Hopkins University Press.

Huntington, S. (1993) The clash of civilizations. *Foreign Affairs*, 72(3): 22–49.

Innis, H. (1972) *Empire and communications*, revised edition. Toronto: University of Toronto Press.

Jameson, F. (1991) *Postmodernism, or, the cultural logic of late capitalism*. London: Verso.

Jenkins, H. (2006) *Convergence culture: where old and new media collide*. New York: New York University Press.

Jenkins, H. and Thorburn, D. (eds.) (2003) *Democracy and new media*. New Haven: Yale University Press.

Jensen, K. (ed.) (1998) *News of the world: world cultures look at television news*. London: Routledge.

Kahin, B. and Nesson, C. (eds.) (1997) *Borders in cyberspace: information policy and the global information infrastructure*. Cambridge, MA: MIT Press.

Karim, K. A. (ed.) (2003) *The media of diaspora: mapping the global*. London: Routledge.

Kavoori, A. and Punathambekar, A. (eds.) (2008) *Global Bollywood*. New York: New York University Press.

Keane, J. (1995) *The media and democracy*. Cambridge: Polity.

Kellner, D. (2003) *Media spectacle*. New York: Routledge.

Kraidy, M. (2005) *Hybridity, or, the cultural logic of globalization*. Philadelphia: Temple University Press.

Kurlantzick, J. (2007) *Charm offensive: how China's soft power is transforming the world*. London: Yale University Press.

Lal, V. (2002) *Empire of knowledge: culture and plurality in the global economy*. London: Pluto.

Lash, S. and Lury, C. (2007) *Global culture industry*. Cambridge: Polity.

Latouche, S. (1996) *The Westernization of the world: the significance, scope and limits of the drive toward global uniformity*, translated by R. Morris. Cambridge: Polity.

Lechner, F. and Boli, J. (eds.) (2008) *The globalization reader*, third edition. Oxford: Blackwell.

Lennon, A. (ed.) (2003) *The battle for hearts and minds: using soft power to undermine terrorist networks*. Cambridge, MA: MIT Press.

Lessig, L. (2004) *Free culture: how big media uses technology and the law to lock down culture and control creativity*. London: Penguin.

Löffelholz, M. and Weaver, D. (eds.) (2008) *Global journalism research: theories, methods, findings, future*. Oxford: Blackwell.

Lowe, G. F. and Per, J. (eds.) (2005) *Cultural dilemmas in public service broadcasting*. Göteborg: Nordicom.

Luhmann, N. (2000) *The reality of the mass media*. Cambridge: Polity.

Lull, J. (2000) *Media, communications, culture: a global approach*, second edition. Cambridge: Polity.

Lull, J. (2007) *Culture on demand: communication in a crisis world*. Oxford: Blackwell.

Lynch, M. (2006) *Voices of the new Arab public: Iraq, al-Jazeera, and Middle East politics today*. New York: Columbia University Press.

McChesney, R. (2004) *The problem of the media: U.S. communication politics in the 21st century*. New York: Monthly Review Press.

McDonald, P. and Wasko, J. (2008) *The contemporary Hollywood film Industry*. Oxford: Blackwell.

McKercher, C. and Mosco, V. (eds.) (2007) *Knowledge workers in the information age*. Lanham, MD: Lexington Books.

McMillin, D. (2007) *International media studies*. Oxford: Blackwell.

McNair, B. (2006) *Cultural chaos: journalism, news and power in a globalized world*. London: Routledge.

McPhail, T. (2006) *Global communication: theories, stakeholders, and trends*, second edition. Oxford: Blackwell.

Mansell, R. (ed.) (2002) *Inside the communication revolution*. Oxford: Oxford University Press.

Martin-Barbero, J. (1993) *Communication, culture and hegemony: from media to mediations*. London: Sage.

Mattelart, A. (1994) *Mapping world communication: war, progress, culture*. Minneapolis: University of Minnesota Press.

Mattelart, A. (2003) *The information society*. London: Sage.

Miller, T., Govil, N., Maxwell, R. and McMurria, J. (2005) *Global Hollywood*, second edition. London: BFI.

Mohammadi, A. (ed.) (1997) *International communication and globalization*. London: Sage.

Mooij, M. (2005) *Global marketing and advertising: understanding cultural paradoxes*, second edition. London: Sage.

Moran, A. (1998) *Copycat TV: globalization, program formats and cultural identity*. Luton: University of Luton Press.

Morley, D. and Robins, K. (1995) *Spaces of identity: global media, electronic landscapes and cultural boundaries*. London: Routledge.

Mosco, V. (2004) *The digital sublime: myth, power, and cyberspace*. Cambridge, MA: MIT Press.

Mosco, V. (2009) *The political economy of communication*, second edition. London: Sage.

Mowlana, H. (1997) *Global information and world communication: new frontiers in international relations*, second edition. London: Sage.

Muhlmann, G. (2008) *A political history of journalism*. Cambridge: Polity.

Murphy, P. and Kraidy, M. (eds.) (2003) *Global media studies: ethnographic perspectives*. New York: Routledge.

Nederveen Pieterse, J. (2004) *Globalization or empire?* London: Routledge.

Nelson, M. (1997) *War of the black heavens: the battle of western broadcasting in the Cold War*. Syracuse: Syracuse University Press.

Nightingale, V. and Dwyer T. (eds.) (2007) *New media worlds: challenges for convergence*. New York: Oxford University Press.

Nordenstreng, K. and Schiller, H. (eds.) (1993) *Beyond national sovereignty: international communications in the 1990s*. Norwood, NJ: Ablex Publishing.

Norris, P. (2000) *A virtuous circle: political communications in post-industrial democracies*. Cambridge: Cambridge University Press.

Nye, J. (2004) *Power in the global information age: from realism to globalization*. London: Routledge.

Parks, L. (2004) *Cultures in orbit: satellites and the televisual*. Durham, NC: Duke University Press.

Phillipson, R. (1992) *Linguistic imperialism*. Oxford: Oxford University Press.

Preston, W., Herman, E. and Schiller, H. (1989) *Hope and folly: the United States and UNESCO, 1945–1985*. Minneapolis: University of Minnesota Press.

Price, M. (1999) Satellite broadcasting as trade routes in the sky. *Public Culture*, 11(2): 69–85.

Raboy, M. (ed.) (2002) *Global media policy in the new millennium*. Luton: University of Luton Press.

Rantanen, T. (2005) *The media and globalization*. London: Sage.

Read, D. (1992) *The power of news: the history of Reuters, 1849–1989*. Oxford: Oxford University Press.

Ritzer, G. (ed.) (2002) *McDonaldization – the reader*. London: Sage.

Robinson, P. (2002) *The CNN effect – the myth of news, foreign policy and intervention*. London: Routledge.

Rodriguez, C. (2001) *Fissures in the mediascape: an international study of citizen's media*. Creskill, NJ: Hampton Press.

Rogers, E. (1962) *The diffusion of innovations*. Glencoe, IL: Free Press.

Rosenblum, M. (1993) *Who stole the news*? New York: John Wiley.

Rothkopf, D. (1997) In praise of cultural imperialism? *Foreign Policy*, Summer, 38–53.

Said, E. (1978) *Orientalism*. London: Routledge and Kegan Paul.

Said, E. (1993) *Culture and imperialism*. London: Chatto and Windus.

Said, E. (1997) *Covering Islam: how the media and the experts determine how we see the rest of the world*, second edition. New York: Vintage.

Sakr, N. (2001) *Satellite realms: transnational television, globalization and the Middle East*. London: I. B. Tauris.

Scannell, P. (2007) *Media and communication*. London: Sage.

Seib, P. (2004) *Beyond the front lines: how the news media cover a world shaped by war*. Basingstoke: Palgrave Macmillan.

Servaes, J. and Goonasekera, A. (eds.) (2000) *The new communications landscape: demystifying media globalization*. London: Routledge.

Shoemaker, P. and Cohen, A. (2005) *News around the world: content, practitioners, and the public*. New York: Routledge.

Shohat, E. and Stam, R. (1994) *Unthinking Eurocentrism: multiculturalism and the media*. New York: Routledge.

Silverstone, R. (2007) *Media and morality: on the rise of the mediapolis*. Cambridge: Polity.

Sinclair, J. (1999) *Latin American television: a global view*. Oxford: Oxford University Press.

Sinclair, J., Jacka, E. and Cunningham, S. (eds.) (1996) *New patterns in global television: peripheral vision*. Oxford: Oxford University Press.

Singh, J. P. (2008) *Negotiation and the global information economy*. Cambridge: Cambridge University Press.

Singhal, A., Cody, M., Roger, E. and Sabido, M. (eds.) (2004) *Entertainment-education and social change*. Mahwah, NJ: Lawrence Erlbaum.

Smith, A. (1979) *The newspaper: an international history*. London: Thames and Hudson.

Smith, A. (1980) *The geopolitics of information: how Western culture dominates the world*. London: Faber and Faber.

Smith, A. (ed.) (1998) *Television: an international history*, second edition. Oxford: Oxford University Press.

Sparks, C. (2007) *Globalization, development and the mass media*. London: Sage.

Sparks, C. and Tulloch, J. (eds.) (2000) *Tabloid tales – global debates over media standards*. Lanham, MD: Rowman & Littlefield.

Spigel, L. and Olsson, J. (eds.) (2004) *Television after TV: essays on a medium in transition*. Durham, NC: Duke University Press.

Sreberny-Mohammadi, A. (1991) The global and the local in international communication. In Curran, J. and Gurevitch, M. (eds.) *Mass media and society*. London: Edward Arnold.

Sreberny, A. and Paterson, C. (eds.) (2004) *International news in the twenty-first century*. Luton: University of Luton Press.

Straubhaar, J. (2007) *World television: from global to local*. London: Sage.

Sussman, G. (2005) *Global electioneering: campaign consulting, communications, and corporate financing*. Lanham, MA: Rowman & Littlefield.

Tarrow, S. (2005) *The new transnational activism*. Cambridge: Cambridge University Press.

Taylor, P. (2003) *Munitions of the mind: a history of propaganda from the ancient world to the present era*, third edition. Manchester: Manchester University Press.

Taylor, P. (1997) *Global communications, international affairs and the media since 1945*. London: Routledge.

Tehranian, M. (1999) *Global communication and world politics: domination, development and discourse*. London: Lynne Reiner.

Thompson, J. (1995) *The media and modernity: a social theory of the media*. Cambridge: Polity.

Thussu, D. K. (ed.) (1998) *Electronic empires: global media and local resistance*. London: Arnold.

Thussu, D. K. (2006) *International communication – continuity and change*, second edition. London: Arnold.

Thussu, D. K. (2007) *News as entertainment: the rise of global infotainment*. London: Sage.

Thussu, D. K. (ed.) (2009) *Internationalizing media studies*. London: Routledge.

Thussu, D. K. and Freedman, D. (eds.) (2003) *War and the media: reporting conflict 24/7*. London: Sage.

Tomlinson, J. (1991) *Cultural imperialism: a critical introduction*. London: Pinter.

Tomlinson, J. (1999) *Globalization and culture*. Cambridge: Polity.

Tracey, M. (1998) *The decline and fall of public service broadcasting*. Oxford: Oxford University Press.

Tunstall, J. (1977) *The media are American: Anglo-American media in the world*. London: Constable.

Tunstall, J. and Machin, D. (1999) *The Anglo-American media connection*. Oxford: Oxford University Press.

Vogel, H. (2004) *Entertainment industry economics: a guide for financial analysis*, sixth edition. Cambridge: Cambridge University Press.

Volkmer, I. (1999) *News in the global sphere: a study of CNN and its impact on global communications*. Luton: University of Luton Press.

Waisbord, S. and Morris, N. (eds.) (2001) *Media and globalization: why the state matters*. Lanham, MD: Rowman & Littlefield.

Wallerstein, I. (2004) *World-systems analysis: an introduction*. Durham, NC: Duke University Press.

Wasko, J. (2001) *Understanding Disney – the manufacture of fantasy*. Cambridge: Polity.

Waterman, D. (2005) *Hollywood's road to riches*. Cambridge, MA: Harvard University Press.

Weaver, D. (ed.) (1998) *The global journalist: news people around the world*. Cresskill, NJ: Hampton Press.

Webster, F. (ed.) (2004) *The information society reader*. London: Routledge.

Wessler, H., Peters, B., Brüggemann, M., Kleinen-von Königslöw, K. and Sifft, S. (2008) *The transnationalization of public spheres*. Basingstoke: Palgrave Macmillan.

Wilkin, P. (2001) *The political economy of global communication*. London: Pluto.

Wilson, P. and Stewart, M. (eds.) (2008) *Global indigenous media: cultures, poetics, and politics*. Durham, NC: Duke University Press.

Winseck, D. and Pike, R. (2007) *Communication and empire: media, markets, and globalization, 1860–1930*. Durham, NC: Duke University Press.

Yudice, G. (2004) *The expediency of culture: uses of culture in the global era*. Durham, NC: Duke University Press.

Zhao, Y. (2008) *Communication in China: political economy, power, and conflict*. Lanham, MD: Rowman & Littlefield.

Useful websites

International media

Agence France Presse	www.afp.com
al Hayat (Saudi Arabia)	www.alhayat.com
Al-Jazeera	aljazeera.net/english
All India Radio	http://allindiaradio.org
APTN	www.aptn.com
Associated Press	www.ap.org
BBC World	www.bbcworld.com
BBC World Service	www.bbc.co.uk/worldservice
Bloomberg	www.bloomberg.com
Business Week	www.businessweek.com
CCTV-9	http://english.cctv.com
China Daily	www.chinadaily.com.cn/english
China Radio International	www.chinabroadcast.cn
CNBC	www.cnbc.com
CNN	www.cnn.com
Deutsche Welle	www.dwelle.de
Discovery	www.discovery.com
The Economist	www.economist.com
Euronews	www.euronews.net
The Financial Times	www.ft.com
France 24	www.france24.com/en
Globo (Brazil)	www.redeglobo.com.br

The Guardian	www.guardian.co.uk
International Herald Tribune	www.iht.com
Inter Press Service	www.ipsnews.net
Itar-Tass	www.itar-tass.com
Le monde-diplomatique	www.monde-diplomatique.fr/en
MNet (South Africa)	www.mnet.co.za
Music Television (MTV)	www.mtv.com
NDTV (New Delhi Television)	www.ndtv.com
Newsweek	www.newsweek.com
Phoenix Chinese channel	www.phoenixtv.com
Press TV (Iran)	www.presstv.ir
Radio France International	www.rfi.fr
Radio Free Europe/Radio Liberty	www.rferl.org
Reader's Digest	www.readersdigest.com
Reuters	www.reuters.com
Russia Today	www.russiatoday.com/en
Slate	www.slate.com
STAR TV	www.startv.com/
Telesur	www.telesurtv.net
Televisa (Mexico)	www.televisa.com.mx
Time	www.pathfinder.com/time
United Press International	www.upi.com
Voice of America	www.voa.gov
Voice of Russia	www.vor.ru
Wall Street Journal	www.wsj.com
World Radio Network	www.wrn.org
Xinhua	www.xinhuanet.com/english
Zee TV (India)	www.zeetelevision.com

International organizations

ILO	www.ilo.org
IMF	www.imf.org
ITU	www.itu.int
OECD	www.oecd.org
UN	www.un.org
UNCTAD	www.unctad.org
UNDP	www.undp.org
UNESCO	www.unesco.org
WIPO	www.wipo.org
World Bank	www.worldbank.org
WTO	www.wto.org

Governmental and intergovernmental organizations

Asia-Pacific Broadcasting Union	www.abu.org.my
European Audiovisual Observatory	www.obs.coe.int

European Broadcasting Union	www.ebu.ch
European Union	www.europa.eu.int
Federal Communications Commission	www.fcc.gov
Indian Space Research Organization	www.isro.org
Institut National de l'Audiovisuel	www.ina.fr
NASA	www.nasa.gov

Non-governmental and commercial organizations

AC Nielsen	www.acnielsen.com
Adbusters	www.adbusters.org
AIDCOM	www.aidcom.com
AMIC	www.amic.org.sg
BBC Monitoring Service	www.monitor.bbc.co.uk
Facebook	www.facebook.com
Fairness and Accuracy in Reporting	www.fair.org
Free Speech	www.freespeech.org
ICANN (Internet Corporation for Assigned Names and Numbers)	www.icann.org
Indymedia	www.indymedia.org
Inktomi	www.inktomi.com
International Center for Journalists	www.icfj.org
International Intellectual Property Alliance	www.iipa.com
Internet Society	www.isoc.org
Internet Software Consortium	www.isc.org
Motion Picture Association of America	www.mpaa.org
MySpace	www.myspace.com
NASSCOM (India)	www.nasscom.org
One World.Net	www.oneworld.net
Open Democracy	www.opendemocracy.net
Paper Tiger	www.papertiger.org
Project Censored	www.projectcensored.org
Third World Network	www.twnside.org.sg
TV France International	www.tvfi.com/english
Wikipedia	www.wikipedia.org
World Association of Newspapers	www.wan.org
World Press Freedom Committee	www.wpfc.org
World Wide Web Consortium	www.w3.org
YouTube	www.youtube.com
Zenith Media	www.zenithmedia.com

Media and telecommunication corporations

Apple	www.apple.com
Arabsat	www.arabsat.org
Asiasat	www.asiasat.com
AT&T	www.att.com

Bertelsmann	www.bertelsmann.com
Disney	http://disney.go.com
Ericsson	www.ericsson.com
Eutelsat	www.eutelsat.org
Google	www.google.com
IBM	www.ibm.com
Inmarsat	www.inmarsat.telia.com
Intel	www.intel.com
Intelsat	www.intelsat.com
Microsoft Corporation	www.microsoft.com
News Corporation	www.newscorp.com
Nokia	www.nokia.co.uk
SES-Global	www.ses-global.com
Sony Corporation	www.world.sony.com
Telecommunication Inc	www.tci.com
Time Warner	www.timewarner.com
Viacom	www.viacom.com
Vivendi	www.vivendi.com
Yahoo!	www.yahoo.com

Academic journals

Asian Journal of Communication	www.tandf.co.uk/journals/titles/01292986
Canadian Journal of Communication	www.cjc-online.ca
Chinese Journal of Communication	www.tandf.co.uk/journals/titles/17544750.asp
Columbia Journalism Review	www.cjr.org
Ecquid Novi: African Journalism Studies	www.wisc.edu/wisconsinpress/journals/journals/ajs.html
European Journal of Communication	http://ejc.sagepub.com
Foreign Affairs	www.foreignaffairs.org
Foreign Policy	www.foreignpolicy.com
Global Media and Communication	http://gmc.sagepub.com
Global Media Journal	http://lass.calumet.purdue.edu/cca/gmj
Harvard International Journal of Press/ Politics	http://hij.sagepub.com
International Communication Gazette	http://gaz.sagepub.com
International Journal of Communication	http://ijoc.org
International Journal of Cultural Studies	http://ics.sagepub.com
Javnost (The Public)	www.euricom.si/javnosg
Journal of Communication	www.joc.oupjournals.org
Journal of African Media Studies	www.intellectbooks.co.uk/journals.php?issn=17517974
Journal of Arab & Muslim Media Research	www.intellectbooks.co.uk/journals.appx.php?issn=17519411
Journal of Global Mass Communication	www.marquettejournals.org/globalmass communication
Journal of International Communication	www.internationalcommunicationsjournal.com

Journal of International and Intercultural Communication	www.tandf.co.uk/journals/RJII
Journalism	http://jou.sagepub.com
Media, Culture & Society	http://mcs.sagepub.com
Middle East Journal of Culture and Communication	www.brill.nl/default.aspx?partid=210&pid=28726
New Media & Society	http://nms.sagepub.com
Nordicom Review	www.nordicom.gu.se
Public Culture	www.newschool.edu/gf/publicculture
Television & New Media	http://tvn.sagepub.com
Theory, Culture & Society	http://tcs.sagepub.com

Web addresses current at the time of publication.

Index